OKINAWA
The History of an Island People

OKINAWA

THE HISTORY OF
AN ISLAND PEOPLE

by

GEORGE H. KERR

CHARLES E. TUTTLE COMPANY
Rutland, Vermont   *Tokyo, Japan*

PUBLISHED BY THE
CHARLES E. TUTTLE COMPANY
OF RUTLAND, VERMONT & TOKYO, JAPAN
WITH EDITORIAL OFFICES AT
15 EDOGAWA-CHO, BUNKYO-KU, TOKYO

LIBRARY OF CONGRESS
CATALOG CARD NO. 58-12283

FIRST EDITION, 1958
SECOND PRINTING, 1959

Book design & typography by M. Weatherby
Printed by Kenkyusha, Tokyo
MANUFACTURED IN JAPAN

INSCRIBED TO THE MEMORY OF

HIGA SHUHEI

WHO HAS FOLLOWED MAKISHI PECHIN
INTO THE PAGES OF OKINAWAN HISTORY

TABLE OF CONTENTS

PART ONE
CHUZAN: INDEPENDENT KINGDOM
IN THE EASTERN SEAS

vii

PART TWO
ISOLATION: "LONELY ISLANDS IN A DISTANT SEA"

PART THREE
BETWEEN TWO WORLDS

PART FOUR

OKINAWA-KEN: FRONTIER PROVINCE

LIST OF ILLUSTRATIONS

PLATES

FIGURES

ACKNOWLEDGMENTS

In 1951 the Pacific Science Board of the National Research Council inaugurated a series of scientific investigations of the Ryukyu Islands. These are known as the SIRI series, authorized by the Department of the Army and subsidized by funds appropriated for the relief and rehabilitation of occupied areas, the so-called GARIOA funds. In 1952 the Civil Administrator for the Ryukyu Islands (Brigadier General James M. Lewis) asked the Board for a supplementary study concerning the history of the islands. This, he believed, might throw light upon many problems which the military administration encountered from day to day.

Acting upon suggestions made by Dr. Harold J. Coolidge and Dr. George P. Murdock, of the Pacific Science Board, General Lewis asked me to prepare a historical summary with a view to having it translated into Japanese for distribution in Okinawa. He felt that Okinawan youth, uprooted by war and cut off from Japan, knew very little of its past history and vitually nothing of the circumstances which had drawn the United States to the western Pacific frontier and into Okinawa for a second time within a hundred years. It was apparent, too, that civilian employees of the occupying military organization needed to gain some historical perspective for their tasks.

I undertook a reconnaissance of the historical topography, visiting Okinawa, Iriomote, Ishigaki, Miyako, and Iheya-Izena islands, checking sites of special interest, and listening to local folklore and traditions. I am indebted to Mr. Yonaguni Zenzo for lengthy chronological tables and historical notes to carry into the field. These have since been published by him in Japanese. Messrs. Kakazu Sunao, Nakachi Tetsuo, Kamemura Toshio, Kabira Chosei, and many others proved most helpful guides on these field trips. At Naha and Shuri I was given invaluable assistance by the late Professor Shimabukuro Zempatsu, Mr. Shiroma Chokyo, Mr. Minamoto Takeo, Mr. Kabira Choshin, and the late Mr. Hamada Zenkichi, Curator of the Shuri Museum.

At Tokyo, meanwhile, I inaugurated a search throughout Japan for materials concerning the Ryukyus. An informal committee of prominent Okinawans advised me from time to time on bibliography and on disputed points in history. Among them were Professors Higaonna Kanjun, Nakahara Zenchu, and Takazato Ryokun, and Mr. Yoshida Shien. The principal burdens of research fell on Mr. Higa Shuncho and his most faithful aides, Kuniyoshi Masakane and Kudeken Kenji. Mr. Kudeken continued to serve as research assistant after coming to the United States as a GARIOA scholar.

Many points in Okinawan history are in dispute and many may never be settled conclusively, for the prime resources—the ancient archives of the old kingdom—were destroyed in 1945. Students must now rely upon materials surviving in Japan and upon the works of Japanese scholars who had access to original documents before 1945.

I assume full responsibility for interpretations of fact which may be at variance with traditional views, or may be subjects of irreconcilable dispute among the scholars, and shall be happy if this survey by a foreigner provokes interest among Okinawan students and elicits new appraisals of Okinawan history.

The original study (the Pacific Science Board mimeographed edition) was entitled *Ryukyu: Kingdom and Province before 1945*. It was submitted to General Lewis shortly before his death in 1953. In 1956 a Japanese translation appeared; this was entitled *Ryukyu Rekishi* (*Ryukyuan History*.)

In fairness to my associates in Japan and Okinawa, and to the Pacific Science Board, it should be noted that they may be absolved of all responsibility for the Japanese-language version of the original SIRI report. It was prepared without consultation with them (or with the author) after the original text had passed through the hands of the Director of Civil Information and Education then holding office at Naha, and had been assigned as a project to a committee of eight translators, each undertaking a portion of the work.

On February 10, 1956, the author obtained clearance to publish an

English-language edition based on the SIRI report of 1953. For this I wish to thank Colonel Norman D. King and Mr. Joseph E. Harbison, of the Office of Civil Affairs and Military Government, Department of the Army, Washington.

The original text has been enlarged and recast to bring forward the story of European and American interest n the Ryukyu Islands in the 19th century, and to note (by way of introduction) the manner in which the United States government established a legal basis for the present occupation. These additional materials were developed largely in response to questions raised in 1953–54 at the University of California (Berkeley) by students examining the history of American activity on the western Pacific frontier—the Ryukyus and Formosa—in an attempt to discover the sources of information upon which policymakers at Washington based far-reaching decisions to hold Okinawa after Japan's surrender in 1945. The general bibliography of Western-language references to the Ryukyus available to them has been appended to this summary history.

Neither the Army nor the Pacific Science Board is to be held responsible for the present work.

I am indebted to the Pacific Science Board and to its talented Secretary, Lenore Smith, for support in carrying through the original SIRI project, and to Mary Hawkins Johnson, my secretary at the Hoover Institute, for tireless assistance in preparing the present text. I am likewise under obligation to Dr. Mitsuna Nagamine, Director of Library Research at Tokyo University, and to the librarians at the University of California (Berkeley) and the University of Hawaii for friendly, patient, and painstaking coöperation. So, too, my thanks to Professors E. Wiswell, H. Ikeda, and Y. Uyehara, and to K.M. Thompson for aid in translation and proofreading.

For permission to quote from published materials I am indebted to Professor William G. Beasley and Messrs. Luzac and Company (*Great Britain and the Opening of Japan, 1834–58*); Professor Charles Boxer and the Hakluyt Society of London (*South China in the Sixteenth Century . . .*); Dr. Schuyler Cammann (*China's Dragon Robes*); Dr. John K. Fairbank ("On the Ch'ing Tributary System"); Dr. Earl Swisher ("China's Management of the American Barbarians . . ."); and to

xv

Professors Ryusaku Tsunoda and L. Carrington Goodrich and their publisher Mr. P.D. Perkins (*Japan in the Chinese Dynastic Histories*). The University of California Press has given me permission to quote from the late Professor Yoshi S. Kuno's *Japanese Expansion on the Asiatic Continent*. I am grateful to the authors and publishers of 19th-century materials, no longer under copyright, which I have quoted extensively here.

Plates 1–4, 6–10, and 12 are reproduced from photographs made by Mr. Sakamoto Genshichi in 1937. Figures 9, 11, 13, and 14 are reproduced through the courtesy of the East Asiatic Library, University of California (Berkeley). Portrait photographs reproduced as Plates 26, 27, and 30–35 are used with my thanks to Dr. Yukihide Kohatsu, Mrs. Takahiko Chinen, and Mr. Shuncho Higa. The aerial photograph of the old castle site was supplied through the good offices of Dr. Genshu Asato, President of Ryukyu University. Mr. Clemente Lagundimao, Jr., and the author collaborated on the maps and sketches.

The book is inscribed to my friend the late Higa Shuhei, Chief Executive of the Ryukyu Islands, 1952–56. He was unsparing in his effort to mediate between the Okinawan people and the American administration, attempting always to interpret the needs of the one to the other. His career recalls that of "Ichirazichi," who performed somewhat similar, onerous tasks at Naha more than one hundred years ago.

Honolulu, June, 1958

GEORGE H. KERR

1. *Ryukyu* and *Liu Ch'iu* are the Japanese and Chinese readings, respectively, of the characters 琉球. In preparing this text I have found more than sixty variant readings and transcriptions in Western-language sources, ranging from the common Lewchew and Loo Choo to such oddities as Reoo Keoo, Likiwu, Liquii, Liquea, and Leung-Khieou. In the Okinawan dialect heard at Naha in the 19th century Liu Ch'iu became approximately Doo Choo.

2. Shuri speech—the language of the old royal court—is considered standard or classic. There are many local variant dialects so marked as to render speech mutually unintelligible within a relatively small district or area. A distance of two or three miles brings notable variation. The off-lying islands show the widest diversion from Shuri standards. Standard (Tokyo) Japanese is taught in the primary schools. Japanese texts and European language translations concerning the Ryukyus sometimes record these local variations, sometimes attempt to preserve the classical Shuri readings, and sometimes transliterate into standard Japanese.

3. The Japanese name-order is observed, i.e., the family name precedes the personal name, as in Yoshi Shigeru, in which Yoshi is the surname. Family and personal names precede titles if the title is not translated, e.g., Kudeken Kenji *Oyakata*, in which *Oyakata* is the title.

4. One character may be given variant readings in personal and family names, e.g., the character 城, very commonly found in surnames and place names, may be read *-shiro*, *-gusuku*, *-gushiku*, *-ki*, and *-jo*. Thus Kaneshiro can also be read Kinjo.

5. Names have become fairly standardized in late years, but in the days of the kingdom a man might have a childhood name, an adult name, a posthumous name, and a name derived from court honors or the place from which an honorary stipend was derived.

6. Local usage clearly distinguishes among the inhabitants of Miyako, Yaeyama, Okinawa, and other insular and regional subdivisions within the archipelago. The term "Ryukyuan" is awkward. I have therefore adopted Okinawan as a general term in this text unless closer identification is required, for the political subdivision of the Japanese empire known as *Okinawa-ken* (Okinawa Prefecture) embraces all the subdivisions and peoples of the archipelago south of Amami Oshima, with minor exceptions (Okinoerabu,

xvii

etc.). "The Ryukyus" or "the Ryukyu archipelago," used in a geographical and cultural sense, embraces all of the islands of Okinawa Prefecture plus the Amami Oshima island group and intermediate islets as well.

7. Many chronological problems have yet to be solved. All dates attributed to events in Okinawan history before the 15th century are open to question; many dates thereafter are subject to dispute. The adjustment of the old lunar calendar to the solar calendar and equation with the years of the Christian era has raised many problems not yet wholly resolved. Before 1875 the Okinawans followed Chinese usage in dating official records at Shuri, although there were special practices in dating records at the important trading depot at Ch'uang-chou on the Fukien coast. Old Japanese records relating to the Ryukyus followed the Japanese imperial court usage. Since 1875 the Okinawans have been required to follow standard Japanese usage established at the time of the Meiji Restoration. Nevertheless, the lunar calendar is still referred to in the agricultural communities, and the lunar New Year remains an occasion for annual frolic throughout the countryside. I have adopted dates here upon which there appears to be fairly general agreement, but the reader is warned to allow a margin of error for all dates assigned to events which are not subject to cross-checking from external sources.

8. Japanese units of measurement and value varied considerably before the Meiji era. In modern times the *kin* has been standardized at approximately 13 ounces and the *koku* at 5.11 bushels. The *yen* as a monetary unit was originally based on the value of a *koku* of rice. In early Meiji one yen was worth a little more than one American dollars; in late Meiji the exchange was approximately two yen per dollar; and by 1941 this had fallen to approximately four yen to the dollar.

OKINAWA
The History of an Island People

OKINAWA, THE UNITED STATES, AND CURRENT HISTORY

A "Compact between the United States and the Kingdom of Lewchew" ended the first American occupation of Okinawa in 1854. The second occupation, begun in 1945, was given a legal basis in the treaty with Japan of 1951, but with a masterly lack of precise definition.

America's position in the Ryukyus is unique: the islands are neither a possession, a colony, nor a trust territory. The archipelago shares the fate of many frontier territories too small and too poor to attract attention in times of peace, but doomed to rise to international prominence during crises among the world powers. It lies on the western Pacific rim, between the maritime world and continental Asia. It cannot escape the consequences of wars and revolutions in larger states nearby; the postwar "Okinawa problem" was produced by events set in train long ago by accidents of geography and history.

Commodore Perry's "Lewchew" was a small principality maintained without arms through a period of 450 years, a nation of courteous officials, farmers, fishermen, and traders. It was founded in the 14th century upon a commerce in luxury goods carried from the markets of Southeast Asia and the Indies to the ports of China, Korea, and Japan.

In the early 17th century, Japan felt the pressure of militant Europeans coming overseas from the south—from Portugal, Spain, Holland, and England. Fearing invasion from that quarter (and coveting Okinawa's profitable trade), Japanese from Satsuma invaded the Ryukyus in 1609. The defenseless Okinawans ransomed their king by accepting Japanese control of overseas commerce and by promising to pay heavy annual tribute. Japanese agents in the Ryukyus thereafter kept watch on the southern sea approaches to Japan. In 1816, when the Western powers were again approaching Japan from the south, Napoleon discussed Okinawan history with Captain Basil Hall, R. N. He concluded that no such peace-loving nation could endure. Hall's grandson later wrote that "the most prominent race-characteristic of the Luchuans is not a physical but a moral one . . . their gentleness of spirit and manner, their yielding and submissive disposition, their hospitality and kindness, their aversion to violence and crime."

Submissive mildness brought about the kingdom's downfall. England, France, Russia, and the United States each thought to use Okinawa. In June, 1853, Perry landed a token force from the U.S.S. "Mississippi," marched into the royal castle at Shuri, and asked for Okinawan coöperation in exchange for American friendship. He also demanded permission to establish a military base at Naha. To Washington he proposed, unsuccessfully, that the United States should take Okinawa "under surveillance" pending satisfactory settlement of American claims upon Japan. President Pierce thought conditions did not justify a prolonged occupation. "If, in future, resistance should be offered and threatened, it would also be rather mortifying to surrender the island, if once seized, and rather inconvenient and expensive to maintain a force there to retain it."

With only a fruitless "compact of friendship" in hand, Perry withdrew. England, France, and Holland then asked the bewildered Okinawans to enter into treaty relations. These demonstrations of Western interest in defenseless Okinawa alarmed Japan. Soon after the Meiji Restoration an imperial military force landed at Naha. The Okinawans protested that a garrison would attract Japan's enemies, with whom they had no quarrel. Seven years of stubborn, non-coöperative argument followed. At last exasperated, Japan deposed the king, abolished the royal government, and created Okinawa Prefecture. From 1879 to 1945 Tokyo pursued policies designed to win Okinawan loyalties and to assimilate the island people.

The world heard little of Okinawa until it was wrested from Japan's control in 1945. The invasion began in late March; in June the modern U.S.S. "Mississippi" moved in to train its guns upon the ancient walls of Shuri Castle. Within lay Japan's military headquarters for the raging

Battle of Okinawa, and here Japanese resistance was broken. After eighty-two days of bitter fighting the island was in Allied hands. Some twelve thousand Americans and more than ninety thousand Japanese military men had lost their lives.

Okinawans had no part in formulating Japan's military policies which led to this, and fewer than five thousand trained Okinawan conscripts took part. Nevertheless, the Okinawan people were forced to make a hideous sacrifice on Japan's behalf. More than 62,000 Okinawans perished; the great majority were civilians caught helplessly between opposing armies. The physical heritage of the old kingdom vanished, and more than ninety percent of the population was adrift and homeless when surrender came.

Capitulation at Tokyo in August virtually ended Okinawa's military importance vis-à-vis Japan. The island became an immense, neglected military dump, strewn with the war's debris. Towns and villages were rubble heaps; tens of thousands lived in caves, tombs, and lean-to shacks, or took shelter in relief camps established by the military forces. They were expected to live at subsistence level until a formal peace should restore them to Japanese administration and permit American withdrawal. Farmers became air-base laborers; fishermen became truck-drivers; the old aristocracy disappeared. Cast-off G.I. clothing, American soft drinks, cigarettes, and canned goods supplied a new luxury trade for a totally impoverished people.

Washington virtually lost sight of the Ryukyus, for responsibility lay with the Supreme Commander at Tokyo, who in turn delegated authority through the ranks to distant, obscure Okinawan outposts. For military men the Ryukyus became a place of exile from GHQ and Japan proper, and for ambitious civilians with the army it was "no man's land," "the end of the line," or "the Rock," a veritable Siberia much too far from Tokyo's neon lights. Few men of high caliber and administrative skill were willing to remain on Okinawa. An appalling indifference blanketed the island.

In 1949 the Defense Department suddenly became aware of the neglect of civil affairs; the so-called Vickery Report to the Department of the Army caused anguish at the Supreme Commander's headquarters.

Generals were reprimanded, colonels transferred, civilians dismissed, and new policies formulated which called for progressive rehabilitation of the civil economy.

Then came the Korean War. Okinawa's military importance revived. A vast military base-expansion program inaugurated in 1950 at once overshadowed plans for civil rehabilitation. Funds and energies had to be diverted to meet immediate military needs. Responsible and conscientious officers delegated to manage the civil economy did the best they could, with an inadequate budget. They had no sustained political guidance to relate the social and political consequences of base-expansion problems to political issues affecting United States' prestige throughout Asia—especially in the area of American relations with Japan.

Meanwhile it was proposed that Okinawan bases should be held indefinitely, and in due course this was arranged, as we shall see.

The Korean truce and crises elsewhere diverted public attention; Okinawa was forgotten. Occasional rumors and published stories of Okinawan discontent were condemned out-of-hand as malicious Communist propaganda. Nevertheless, Washington slowly discovered that treaty right to use the island entails heavy obligations. Okinawan restlessness under an alien government, however benign, is inevitably translated into political terms affecting United States relations with Japan.

As President Pierce foresaw, prolonged occupation is costly and embarrassing; some 800,000 Okinawans must be cared for in a wretchedly poor archipelago. More than fifty thousand families have become landless since 1945. Each new facility for American use in Okinawa reduces areas for cultivation; and fields once covered with concrete, macadam, or gravel can never be restored to agricultural use. They become a poor heritage for succeeding generations, and there is relentless population growth. Okinawan demands for some guarantee of future livelihood (and for a clarified national status) inevitably clash with declared military necessities.

While some Okinawan leaders wait for the Congress at Washington to demonstrate sustained and informed interest in Okinawa's long-range economic problems, others translate popular discontent into demands for immediate reversion to Japan. If it is to Japan's political advantage, Tokyo will not hesitate to use the "Okinawa reversion" issue in bargaining with Washington on larger international questions which may have little to do with the Ryukyu Islands.

History throws much light on the dimensions of this American problem vis-à-vis Japan in the Ryukyus, but before we turn to it, we must note events—quite external to Okinawa—which led to the American occupation and provided a legal basis for it.

During negotiations leading to the San Francisco Treaty Conference there was wide public discussion of probable treaty terms. Since Okinawa had been a prefecture of Japan, Okinawans and Japanese alike expected that the islands would revert to Tokyo's control and that the local military bases would come under general provisions governing other foreign bases in Japan. It was expected that the forthcoming document would spell out conditions for reversion, and would name the date terminating U.S. military control of the civil population and economy.

The treaty, signed on September 8, 1951, contained this paragraph:

"ARTICLE 3. Japan will concur in any proposal of the United States to the United Nations to place under its trusteeship system, with the United States as the sole administering authority, Nansei Shoto south of 29° north latitude (including the Ryukyu Islands and the Daito Islands), Nanpo Shoto south of Sofu Gan (including the Bonin Islands, Rosario Island, and the Volcano Islands) and Parece Vela and Marcus Island. Pending the making of such a proposal and affirmative action thereon, the United States will have the right to exercise all and any powers of administration, legislation, and jurisdiction over the territory and inhabitants of these islands, including their territorial waters."

The Chinese invasion of Korea in 1950, with Russian aid, underscored the need for the United States to retain a foothold in the Ryukyus to support the interests of disarmed Japan, the United Nations forces in Korea, and the over-all interests of the United States all along the western Pacific rim. Nevertheless, Article 3 roused deep concern among the Okinawans and provoked sharp political criticism in many quarters. India, for instance, refused to sign the treaty on the representation that it could not thus signify consent to the continued military occupation of an Asian territory by a Western power. Undoubtedly a continued occupation would provide nationalist governments in Asia many propaganda barbs with which to irritate the Western powers. Of more immediate importance, military occupation of a Japanese prefecture continued beyond the effective treaty date would weaken any government at Tokyo desiring to coöperate with Washington. Future premiers and cabinets in Japan would have to explain themselves to a critical electorate if they did not endeavor to recover the "lost" prefecture. As long as the United States maintained jurisdiction in the Ryukyus, parties on the Right and on the Left would find common cause with which to embarrass Japanese-American relations. Of less concern but of latent interest would be the need to maintain a continued occupation in the face of American antipathy to the words "colony" and "colonialism" and of the doctrine that democratic nations must foreswear territorial gain through military conquest.

It must be presumed that Washington weighed all these problems and dangers against the need for Okinawan bases. The hard fact remained that the United States government felt compelled to stay in the Ryukyu Islands.

Some thoughtful Okinawans recognized that in truth the United States was in a better position than postwar Japan to underwrite economic rehabilitation for the Okinawan people, if the occupying authorities cared to undertake the task; Washington could promote emigration (as Japan could not), which must take place to relieve overcrowded Okinawa. Many other Okinawans, however, continued to insist that it would be better to return the civil administration to the Japanese, leaving only military reservations under foreign control. A minority, hearkening to arguments of the left- and right-wing groups at Tokyo, clamored for an immediate end to all American activity in the Ryukyus.

The truce in Korea in 1952 seemed to remove the sense of immediate threat and crisis which had justified the treaty reservations; there was an increased agitation for reversion to Japan. This embarrassed Tokyo and Washington. As a countermeasure, the United States announced that the northern islands of the Ryukyu Archipelago (the Amami Oshima group) would revert to Japanese control as of December 25, 1953. This had something of a soothing effect; soon word spread on

Okinawa that the Amami people had paid a material price in economic hardship in return for the emotional and patriotic satisfaction of reunion with impoverished Japan.

Meanwhile the Secretary of State at Washington, John Foster Dulles, formulated and proclaimed a doctrine of "residual sovereignty," designed to mollify the Japanese and to appease critics everywhere. The United States affirmed that Japan retained legal title to the Ryukyu Islands, although all sovereign rights and obligations were to be in abeyance as provided in Article 3 of the treaty. This new doctrine implied that the United States would not recommend a trusteeship for the islands and that in good time and good faith Okinawa Prefecture would one day return to Japanese control.

Thus, in brief, American interest shifted through three postwar positions, each determined by conditions external to the islands, and each calling for new policies within. Okinawa first had military importance vis-à-vis Japan, which brought about its conquest. Next came the years of indifference, the patrol of a minor area used as a "dumping ground" or place of exile for American personnel unwanted at GHQ or in Japan proper. The third position, assumed in 1949, endowed Okinawa with new importance as a base to be held indefinitely and developed vis-à-vis Russia and rising Communist power in nearby China.

In August, 1956, Secretary Dulles unexpectedly shifted American interest in Okinawa to yet a fourth position. He broadly hinted that if, in its search for formal peace with Russia, Japan were to acquiesce in permanent Russian occupation of certain islands in the southern Kuriles, then the United States might have to reconsider the doctrine of "residual sovereignty" he had put forth in 1953. In other terms, the United States might yet decide to hold the Ryukyus permanently.

For American purposes, Okinawa had assumed important trading value vis-à-vis Russia and Japan in the day-to-day bargaining of power politics. This—on a grander scale—is precisely the use to which Commodore Perry put Okinawa when he proposed to hold the Ryukyus "under surveillance" in 1853 while bargaining for a treaty with Japan. Of more importance, it opened before the American people and the Okinawans a prospect that the United States government might be ready to assume something more than year-to-year responsibility for the Okinawan people and economy.

The present summary of Okinawan history is not concerned with the period of the American occupation, nor with the postwar development of an "Okinawan problem" in international affairs. At the very heart of these two subjects lies the story of Okinawa's traditional relationship with Japan, for it is difficult to believe that the Japanese government would have signed a treaty of peace which permitted unlimited, exclusive alien military occupation of any other prefecture in the country.

Why, then, Okinawa province?

Two things bear on this, which we must examine briefly.

Neither the formal documentation which underlies the postwar occupation nor the treaty anywhere recognizes and defines precisely the traditional or legal relationship of the Ryukyus to Japan. Left thus in a diplomatic twilight zone, uncommitted by the victors or the vanquished, this frontier territory became that diplomat's delight and essential tool, the *quid pro quo*.

Fundamental "Japanese polity" does not hold Okinawa to be a vital part of the nation's body; it is expendable, under duress, if thereby the interests of the home islands can be served advantageously. The mystical Japanese sense of national identity centers in the home provinces, imperial domain (in theory, at least) since the dawn of history. Okinawa, a separate kingdom and a separate people, was annexed only in 1879. Put thus bluntly, the Okinawans reject this thesis, and many Japanese are startled by it, but the record bears out such an interpretation.

First of the formal documents came the Cairo Declaration, issued on December 1, 1943. It smacks of propaganda, designed essentially to mollify Chiang Kai-shek and to keep the Chinese active in the war. Chunking had let it be known that it was dissatisfied with Allied failure to press the war in China and South Asia. Insufficient supplies were reaching the hands of the Nationalist government. The Chinese people were exhausted after many years of civil war and prolonged Japanese invasion. Chinese generals and prominent political figures had a well-known capacity for switching allegiance if there were suitable rewards. It is probable that Chiang himself would not have forsaken the Western alliance—it was his sole source of strength—but he had to prevent further defections among his subordinates. Japan's senior statesman Shigemitsu Mamoru had been in China in 1942 exploring the possibility for arranging terms of peace, and in early 1943 he had become Japan's foreign minister, with increased interest in offering attractive terms to China's vacillating leaders.

Washington and London therefore sought means to hold the Chinese in the conflict as active participants by spelling out the territorial rewards to be made at the war's end. Roosevelt and Churchill met with the Chiangs at Cairo to come to a new understanding. The declaration publicized the schedule of rewards, and concluded with mutual commitments to continue active for the duration of the war. But it also reflected inexact or "slanted" data with which President Roosevelt approached his Asian problems.

After stating that the United States, Britain, and China were fighting to "restrain and punish the aggression of Japan" and that "they covet no gain for themselves and have no thought of territorial expansion," the signatories promised that: "Japan shall be stripped of all islands in the Pacific which she has seized or occupied since the beginning of the First World War in 1914." And that: "All territories Japan has stolen from the Chinese, such as Manchuria, Formosa, and the Pescadores, shall be restored to the Republic of China. Japan will also be expelled from all other territories which she has taken by violence and greed. . . . In due course Korea shall become free and independent."

The declaration was made in the heat of war, when the enemy is always wrong. But in the cold light of retrospection it is fair to note that Japan's position in most of these territories (excluding Manchuria) had been covered by treaties long unchallenged. The use of the word "stolen" here gives the document its propaganda flavor and suggests that sovereign rights which have been transferred by treaty can be recovered without recourse to legal process. It was careless phraseology and held an element of danger for nations which had not yet won the war. Chiang, in his manifesto *China's Destiny* (Chinese edition), had not abandoned China's traditional claims to Hongkong, British Burma, and French Annam. Other Chinese leaders had advanced claims to the Ryukyus. In point of fact, Japan had acquired the Kuriles through peaceful negotiation of a treaty with Russia in 1875, during which the United States played a minor role in an advisory capacity. John Foster, former Secretary of State, had advised the Japanese in negotiating the Shimonoseki Treaty, by which China bargained away Formosa in 1895. Karafuto—the southern half of Sakhalin—had been ceded to Japan by the Portsmouth Treaty, negotiated in New Hampshire, U.S.A., in 1905, under the aegis of the first President Roosevelt. Britain had bargained secretly with Japan during World War I, promising to give her Germany's Pacific islands if, in turn, Japan would enter the war and come to Britain's aid. This bargain was later translated into a permanent League of Nations mandate to Japan. Korea had been made a "protectorate" and then annexed by Tokyo to preclude occupation and control of the peninsula by Chinese or Russian agents. China, in 1943, had no *legal* claim to any of these territories except Manchuria, which the United States, at Yalta, was soon to bargain away to Russia without Chinese consent.

The promises to return "stolen" territories to China were a *quid pro quo;* the Cairo Declaration concluded with the words: "The Three Allies . . . will continue to persevere in the serious and prolonged operations necessary to procure the unconditional surrender of Japan." The fundamental purpose of the declaration was made clear.

Fourteen months later the Yalta Agreement in a similar fashion spelled out rewards to be made to Russia if she would enter the war against Japan. Moscow agreed to break its neutrality pact with Tokyo three months after the war in Europe should come to an end, which was to say, after the other Allies had time to shift the full weight of armament into the Pacific and against Japan, reducing Russia's risk. Russia was to be readmitted to dominant positions throughout Manchuria, from which she had been driven by Japan in 1905. The third condition read: "The Kuril Islands shall be handed over to the Soviet Union."

None of this was known to the few Japanese civilian leaders who were exploring secretly the possibilities of seeking peace through Russian mediation.

On June 8, 1945, the members of an imperial conference at Tokyo reaffirmed, under pressure, the nation's determination to fight to the bitter end, even though Japan, as a nation, might be destroyed forever. But on June 22 the long Okinawan campaign ended in Allied victory.

When it was realized at Tokyo on that day that the "Okinawan barrier" was irrevocably lost, the emperor summoned his highest ministers of state, his admirals and his generals, and let it be known that the army must consider "other means" to bring about an end of war. The "home islands" must not suffer as Okinawa had suffered. The decision to sue for peace and to negotiate surrender had to be made quickly, before a great assault upon Japan proper could get under way. On June 23 the diplomats and imperial councilors redoubled efforts to secure Moscow's aid and a renewed assurance of Russia's continuing neutrality at this supreme crisis in the nation's history.

The Potsdam Declaration, on July 26, spelled out the threat of impending doom and prescribed terms under which the Japanese could escape invasion. Article 7 required Japan's acceptance of an occupation "until such a new [democratic] order is established, and until there is convincing proof that Japan's war-making power is destroyed." According to Article 8, "the terms of the Cairo Declaration shall be carried out and Japanese sovereignty shall be limited to the islands of Honshu, Hokkaido, Kyushu, Shikoku and such minor islands as we determine." The Ryukyus were nowhere named. They were "minor islands."

Then, within a matter of days, came Hiroshima and Nagasaki, and Russia's cynical entry into the war upon the terms arranged at Yalta. Japan surrendered.

World attention focused on Tokyo and on the "big" issues at the capitals, where diplomats and generals sometimes talked in geographic terms and sometimes in terms of political administration. The niggling problems of "fringe areas"—the Kuriles, Ryukyus, and Formosa—received scant attention. Long-range interests were often sacrificed to expediency.

Russia promptly moved into the Kuriles. American ships and planes ferried the Chinese over to Formosa. The Ryukyus were swept into the backwash of the occupation of Japan. Neither the victors nor the vanquished were committed to long-range settlement of the Okinawa question. In effect, Tokyo had "deposited" the Ryukyu Islands with the United States for an indefinite period. From time to time Chinese spokesmen revived old claims to the Ryukyus, but no one paid attention to them nor to a minor Filipino agitation opposing Chinese claims with a proposal that the Philippine Republic should seek U.N. trust responsibility for all the islands lying southward from Japan.

From June, 1945, until April, 1952, Okinawa Prefecture was held as "enemy territory" governed by the rules of land warfare. Under these the occupying power had no obligation to meet damage claims against it or to maintain the Okinawan economy above bare subsistence levels. With the technical advent of peace on April 28, 1952, Okinawa ceased to be "enemy territory"; a new terminology was adopted. The Ryukyus became "friendly territory" under United States Civil Administration; responsibility rested with the Department of Defense, delegated downward through the Department of the Army to the Commanding General, Ryukyus Command, and through him to the Civil Administrator, a brigadier general of the U.S. Army.

Provision was made for consideration of claims made by Okinawans against the occupying power; a representative of the Japanese government was admitted to residence at Naha, to assist in supervising trade and travel between Okinawa and the other prefectures. A local legislature was created, and Okinawan leaders became responsible for the social and economic welfare of the populace, and for its full coöperation with the U.S. forces. A native government of the Ryukyu Islands began to operate under the directives and with the advice of the United States Civil Administration. A Chief Executive—an Okinawan—was appointed by the military governor. Okinawan administration throughout was paralleled by a "watchdog" organization staffed by military men and civilian citizens of the United States. Strong efforts were made to diversify the economy and to increase production. In 1956 the Civil Administrator stated publicly that planning for economic development could now proceed on the basis of a maximum five-year limit at any given time.

Military histories of the Pacific War devote appropriate space to the Okinawa campaign. The record of the occupation will be a new chapter in Okinawan annals—an "American chapter"—which may not be written in full detail until the occupation's end, when the decision will have been made to retain Okinawa as an American possession or to restore it to Japan.

The present text offers a summary review of Okinawa's past, from remote and legendary times until the years of World War II and the surrender. The history of Okinawa is essentially the story of a minor kingdom with few resources, and of an unwarlike people, forever seeking balance between powerful neighboring states. They are of a pliable and easygoing nature, eager to please, responsive to friendly consideration, but with quick recourse to stubborn inaction and evasion, the weapons of the weak who wish to resist unwanted change.

The most noteworthy feature of their social history has been subservience to, and willing acceptance of, two quite different alien standards. The basic structure of society and language indicates that in ages past they were closely akin to the early Japanese. For five hundred years they looked to China for cultural guidance and pridefully counted themselves as tributaries of the Chinese court. But for three hundred of these years they were under heavy obligation to Japan, which they discharged faithfully. An interlude of fifty years, and they have now returned to this old pattern, called upon to divide allegiance, once more obeying one power while aspiring to emulate another. Japan has taken China's old place as the home of spiritual allegiance, while obligations to be discharged in day-by-day economic life and conduct of government are now owed to the United States.

The old Okinawan kingdom produced a culture peculiarly its own, the product of isolation and poverty of human resources. (It is doubtful if there were ever as many as 300,000 people in the islands before 1879.) A multitude of popular heroes are named in folklore, song, and drama, but not a hundred emerge who exercised decisive personal leadership or left strong individual imprint upon the culture and course of history.

There was an even greater poverty of material wealth with which to work. It is extraordinary that, with such meager economic endowments —harsh, thin soil, no metals, and little forest wealth—the Okinawans were able to construct and preserve so long a complex society and government. It was a toy state, with its dignified kings, its sententious and learned prime ministers, its councils and its numerous bureaus, its organization of temples and shrines and its classical school, its grades in court rank and its codes of law, all developed in faithful effort to emulate great China. The whole fragile, minuscule structure survived throughout the centuries at bare subsistence level, suffering a never-ending cycle of storm, drought, famine, and plague. Such was Nature's cruel way of maintaining precarious balance between resources and population. It is noteworthy that the one era of colorful and creative activity in which the Okinawans found a rich expression of their own peculiar culture was that in which the independent kingdom was in full control of its own far-ranging commerce overseas and could supplement, unchecked, the meager resources available to the governing elite. After Satsuma laid hands on Okinawan trade in 1609 the creative genius of the Okinawans began to fade.

Dissolution of this old and curious culture began a hundred years ago with the Western world's intrusion. Soon after Japan annexed the kingdom and introduced a new technology, the population began to increase. The great Japanese sugar corporations moved in; land reforms were imposed which completely altered the traditional economic system. Thousands became landless laborers. Emigration to relieve pressure became imperative at the opening of the present century. By 1944 a total of 331,927 Okinawans and their descendents were living abroad. Of these, more than 180,000 were repatriated perforce after 1946, returning to war-shattered Okinawa without lands and without employment. By 1956 it was estimated that the island of Okinawa had only 61,800 acres of farmland upon which to support 660,000 people.

The area of land left for cultivation has diminished rapidly as the U.S. forces steadily expand installations required for their manifold activities—airfields, rocket-sites, firing ranges, barracks, dependent-housing areas, highways, and recreational areas. By 1955 more than 40,000 acres or 12.7 percent of the total land area of Okinawa had passed into military hands, and there were plans underway to double this. Much of old Okinawa is covered with steel and mortar, cement and stone, and crossed and crossed again with necessary barricades.

Thoughtful Okinawans recall the past with melancholy pride, but few fail to recognize that there can be no return. As their ancestors drifted from the continent in prehistoric times to seek new opportunities on the islands of the sea frontier, so must the Okinawans today move on to other islands nearby, to Japan, and to strange lands beyond the sea.

PART ONE

CHUZAN: INDEPENDENT KINGDOM
IN THE EASTERN SEAS

CHAPTER ONE

THE LEGENDARY PAST

To A. D. 1314

ISLAND PATHWAYS ON ANCIENT SEA FRONTIERS

At some remote time in the past, primitive men and women transported children, meager household gear, and simple weapons from continental Asia to the offshore islands lying on the edge of the great sea. No one now knows what prompted them to venture at great risk from place to place by raft or dugout canoe. Some were undoubtedly driven to the islands by storm. Perhaps some were driven on by enemies; some may have been driven by hunger to seek better hunting or fishing grounds or better land to till. If such was the case, they made a poor choice, for the islands between Japan and Formosa are inhospitable reefs of coral and rugged, rocky mountain peaks thrusting up from the depths of the sea. Nature has never been generous in these islands.

There were three pathways by which continental peoples made their way into the Ryukyus. Wanderers from northern Asia moved southward through the Japanese islands. There are prehistoric sites on Okinawa which contain relics of the ancient Jomon neolithic culture commonly found throughout eastern and northern Japan. Migrants from the tropical Indies or Southeast Asia may have come up through the Philippines or along the China coast, converging on Formosa and passing over the channel waters to Yonaguni, Yaeyama, and Miyako islands. Sites on Ishigaki Island (in the Yaeyama group) have yielded evidence of Malay settlement in the fairly recent past. Adventurous travelers from the heartland of Mongolia or Manchuria may have moved southeastward along the Korean Peninsula, across the narrow straits to the island-dotted coasts of Kyushu. From there some pushed on eastward and northward into the principal Japanese islands, and others went southward along the Ryukyu chain. Many elements in contemporary Okinawan cultural life and legend suggest that here was a well-used pathway into the sea islands. As the migration stream from the continent and the Korean Peninsula spent itself in the islands, it distributed related racial and cultural elements in western Japan, Kyushu, and the Ryukyus.

Thus we may assume that Malay, Mongol, and Caucasoid Ainu stocks mingled in the Ryukyu Islands, but in what proportions we do not know. The migrants who lingered in the Philippines or Formosa or in the islands of Japan proper were fortunate, for there they found fertile lands, rich forest cover, sheltering bays, and deep rocky inlets. Those who for one reason or another pushed on into the smaller and most distant islands found only thin soils and little to protect them from the fierce seasonal storms which sweep through these seas. The process of gradual infiltration and settlement took unnumbered centuries, and even with the dawn of historic times the total population did not exceed a few tens of thousands in the Ryukyu Islands.

The name Okinawa means literally a "rope in the offing" and is an apt enough description for the long, narrow island which dominates our story. On a map the island chain itself suggests a knotted rope tossed carelessly upon the sea. The southernmost island (Yonaguni) lies within sight of Formosa on an exceptionally clear day; the northernmost, seven hundred miles away, lies just off the tip of Kyushu Island in Japan. Between these two points are 140 islands and reefs, but only thirty-six now have permanent habitations on them; the majority will not support human life.

In passing among the islands today, one occasionally sees sunburned fishermen bobbing about in dugout canoes or paddling from place to place with simple gear and a load of silvery fish as ballast on the choppy waters. On clear days and in calm weather it is relatively easy to move from one island to another, for rocky headlands are within sight from any midway point en route. One cannot be many hours afloat offshore without glimpsing the blue line of a distant landfall.

There is one exception to this, an important one, which has some bearing upon the distribution of prehistoric settlements and upon the rate of cultural change (and its direction) within historic times. When traveling northward from Okinawa toward Japan on good days, land is always within sight. When moving south, however, it is necessary to cross a stretch of turbulent sea in which no land may be seen in any direction at the midway point; it is 175 miles from Okinawa to the nearest islands in the Miyako group.

This means that prehistoric migration southward from the larger islands of Japan as far as Okinawa was relatively easy; a day of hard paddling in good weather would bring a man's canoe into safe shelter by nightfall. But to move southward willingly from Okinawa toward the empty horizon, seeking Miyako or the Yaeyama Islands, proposed a greater challenge. This required planning, courage, and a seaworthy craft. It required skillful navigation, as well, to ride out the heavy storms common here throughout the year and to counter the strong, northward-sweeping Black Current. Modern records indicate that a minimum of twelve and a maximum of forty-five typhoons may be experienced in Okinawan waters in the course of any year. At least three pass directly over the main island; others linger nearby. A small storm may be only forty or fifty miles in diameter revolving about the baleful eye; the greater storms sometimes have a two-hundred-mile diameter and a wind velocity in excess of 150 miles per hour. These fearful tempests have been an ever-present element in the changing history of the islands, affecting at once the distribution of human settlement, the physical patterns of Okinawan culture, and the general economic life.

The Black Current too has exercised a constant and pervasive influence, for it runs like a powerful river in the sea, moving up past the Philippines, past Formosa, through the Ryukyus, and on past the islands of Japan.

No one can know how many helpless men and women reached the Ryukyu Islands from the south by riding out the storms, tossed relentlessly before the wind and driven by the ocean currents. Cast upon strange shores with such simple artifacts as they might salvage from a damaged craft, they were forced to make the best of a desperate situation. This was disorganized and involuntary migration. It is fairly safe to suppose that more people entered the archipelago voluntarily from the north in organized groups, bringing with them household goods and personal effects, domesticated animals and tools, weapons and sacred objects, and above all, bringing with them fire.

We have no evidence of large-scale movements of people within the last two thousand years. Chinese colonies and petty kingdoms on the Korean Peninsula effectively blocked off the routes from the inner-Asian regions to the west. Between the 2nd and the 7th centuries of the Christian era the emergence of the Yamato state in Japan blocked off any mass migrations of people from the north.

When the most recently developed techniques of archeology have been brought to bear in the Ryukyus, we may be able to set an outer limit of time upon prehistory of mankind there and to establish the essential details of population movements, throwing light upon racial and cultural developments of nearby Japan as well. Such studies were neglected before 1945. There were no Okinawan scholars trained in archeology in the 19th century, and the Japanese were then preoccupied with problems rising in the home islands. In the 20th century it was Japan's policy to hasten assimilation of the old Ryukyuan kingdom, and thus there was little official enthusiasm for the study of the ancient past. Nationalist policy frowned upon research which might question details of approved mythology, the "Age of the Gods" and the lineage of Japan's first emperor, Jimmu.

Until the 2nd or 1st centuries B.C. there was probably little to distinguish the level of neolithic life throughout the Ryukyus from life in islands to the north and south. About two thousand years ago the accelerated introduction of elements of Chinese civilization via Korea transformed daily habits and language among the Yamato people—the Japanese—who created an active and self-conscious political life centered at the eastern end of the Inland Sea, near present-day Osaka. By the end of the 6th century A.D. Japan had emerged as an organized state prepared to establish formal relations with the Chinese empire on the continent. The Yamato people were conscious of less-developed communities beyond the borders of their authority—the Ainu in eastern and northern Japan, the Kumaso and Hayato people in central and southern Kyushu, and the ancestors of the present-day Okinawans, living in the islands to the south.

The Ryukyu people did not share with the Japanese this early trans-

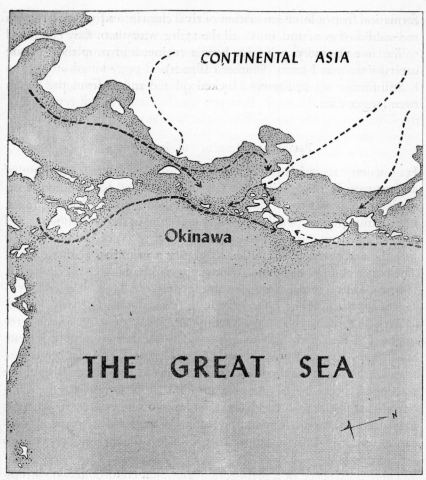

CONTINENTAL ASIA

Okinawa

THE GREAT SEA

N

FIG. 1. MAP: MIGRATION AND SETTLEMENT: ANCIENT PATHWAYS INTO THE SEA ISLANDS.

formation from a loose association of rival clans into a formal state with an established government. Until the 13th century A.D. they continued to live in a shadowy, primitive border region, known at the Japanese capital simply as Nanto (Southern Islands).

Still further south, Formosa lay unexplored and undeveloped for an even longer time.

Prehistoric Life in the Ryukyus[1]

Fragmentary materials found on prehistoric sites tell us something of ancient man in the archipelago. Chipped arrowheads, harpoon points made of wild-boar bone, chipped and polished stone implements (axes, hoes, hammers), and shell ornaments are found in the shell mounds and kitchen middens. Simple decorations applied to crude pottery suggest that the early settlers attempted to gratify a primitive aesthetic sense. The bones of dogs, deer, and swine suggest something of the economy. Human skeletal remains are rare and incomplete. Most perishable articles of wood, fiber, or bone have long since mouldered away.

Archeologists have made a preliminary study of some of these remains. Dr. Kanaseki Takeo suggests that "the last stage of the stone age in Yaeyama . . . was in the early Ming dynasty" or not much before that, i.e., the 14th century. He finds no basis in physical anthropology to support belief in the presence of Ainu elements among the Okinawan people, but on the basis of cultural anthropology he suggests that successive waves of migration from the south worked some modification upon the Jomon culture met with in Okinawa and the islands farther north.

There is evidence of a prehistoric "Yaeyama culture" having strong affinities with the south, with Indonesian and Melanesian cultures; certain forms of agriculture and fisheries and the use of the composite "plank-built" boat have been identified.

On Ishigaki and Taketomi islands in the Yaeyama group such cultural remains are overlaid by strata containing fragments of early Ming pottery. Superimposed on all of this are the complex culture-forms which penetrated these islands from Japan and later, in historic times, from China by way of Okinawa. On Okinawa and the islands north of it the ancient "Yaeyama-type" remains are overlaid and intermingled with the remains of Jomon cultures carried down from Japan proper. Physical characteristics of the Ryukyuans show that they belong to a group which may be called "South Kyushu and Ryukyuan" peoples. Language forms throughout the archipelago show close alliance with the early language of the Japanese islands, and there have been authoritative suggestions that the intonations with which Japanese dialects are used "seem to bear resemblance to that of the Indonesian languages."

In other words, cultural elements penetrated the islands from both the south and the north, overlapping and reacting upon one another. Dr. Kanaseki suggests that the interchange of language and culture was more far-reaching than the interchange or blending of race and physical types, and that "in some features and in some districts the cultural interchange has not been completed yet."

Contemporary Okinawans preserve many visible links with the past —legends, artifacts, and folkways—which have not yet been wholly submerged by importations from the continent (or from the West) in historic times. The so-called "curved jewels" or comma-shaped stones (*magatama*) used by the village priestesses provide a good example. In Korea and Japan they are found in archeological sites associated with the Late Neolithic and Bronze ages, the age of the great burial mounds; they form the sacred jewels of the imperial Japanese regalia, but are never seen in daily use. The curiously shaped "humming-bulb" arrow of early continental origin may be seen in Japan only in a few museums; in Okinawa it still has ceremonial use (in replica) on numerous occasions, such as the dedication of a new house or the festival launching of a canoe, and in village holiday processions. Many legends incorporated in the lively dances of the islands—and the rhythms and patterns of the dances themselves—represent a heritage from prehistoric days.

In historic times the townsmen of Naha and Shuri, Nago and Itoman, and Hirara and Ishigaki have developed an architecture modeled after Chinese and Japanese structures, but in the distant countryside and off-lying islands we may still find farmers and fishermen living in thatched huts whose walls are daubed with clay and whose floor is the beaten earth. More substantial dwellings suggest a tropical origin, for in these

27

a thatched roof covers a mat-covered, raised, wooden platform, with sliding panels or mats which can be raised to throw the structure open on the sides. Communal storehouses survive in many out-of-the-way villages and these seem to be close counterparts of the storehouses which are the most prominent feature in the primitive mountain villages of Formosa. High stone walls enclose individual dwellings and create the most distinctive characteristic of an Okinawan village. These have their counterpart in the massive stone embankments which enclose the individual dwellings of the primitive Yami people on Botel Tobago Island, some two hundred miles south of Yaeyama.

To the layman's eye many current folkways suggest affiliations with other areas and strong surviving links with prehistoric settlement. In well-defined areas of northern Okinawa (and on some of the smaller out-lying islands) the women manage heavy burdens by means of a band which fits across the forehead, passes over the shoulders, and supports weights carried on the back. This is common practice among the

FIG. 2. ANCIENT STOREHOUSES. *These yet remain on northern Okinawa, at Nakijin, Haneji Village, Motobu District.*

tattooed Tayal people of northern Formosa. By contrast, the women of southern Okinawa skillfully balance heavy loads on the top of the head, as the women of Korea do. Until quite recent years the women of Okinawa frequently tattooed the back of the hand and the fingers, and in remote districts one occasionally still sees older women wearing the *katakashira,* a curious off-center topknot into which the hair is drawn in a fashion to be found among the Yami of Botel Tobago, among the Malays on Mindanao in the Philippines, and elsewhere among the islands which served as steppingstones along the sea frontier.

An exploration of the great cave sites, together with a careful mapping of artifacts, religious practices, myths and traditions, and language variations, may someday give us a clearer picture of life in the ancient Ryukyu Islands. There is no ready answer to the question "Where did the early Okinawans come from?" We must turn to early Chinese and Japanese sources for our first written notices of the archipelago.

THE "EASTERN SEA ISLANDS" OF CHINESE TRADITION[2]

Certain ancient knife-shaped coins known as *mei-to-sen* have been found in a shell-heap at Gusuku-dake, near Naha. These indicate a probable contact with the continent as early as the 3rd century B.C. or shortly thereafter. Similar coins were manufactured in North China in the Kingdom of Yen, which fell in 265 B.C. These may have been brought directly into the islands, although it seems more probable that they were traded from settlement to settlement across southern Manchuria, along the Korean Peninsula and southward to Okinawa. Taking a clue from their presence in the refuse heaps of ancient Ryukyu, we may briefly notice the character of legends and historic notices scattered through early Chinese records which concern the "Islands in the Eastern Sea."

According to the *Shan Hai Ching*, the Kingdom of Yen had relations with the Wa (Dwarf) people living in the islands southeast of Korea, i.e., in the neighborhood of present-day Japan. The Kingdom of Yen itself came to an end in a great revolution which overtook Chinese society in the 3rd century B.C. Ch'in Shih Huang Ti, the "first emperor" (221–210 B.C.), destroyed the feudal states, dispersed the ancient hereditary aristocracy, and created an administration which concentrated the physical and human resources of the entire Chinese nation. He was a builder, as well as a destroyer, and conceived his projects in a grand manner. He is famed for his attempt to burn all records of the past (he thus intended to "begin history anew") and for work on the Great Wall of China. We are interested in him because of several expeditions he sent into the Eastern Sea to search for the secret of immortality and for the formula by which base metals could be transmuted into gold. To this end, in 219 B.C. he sent out a mission said to have included three thousand young men and women, numerous artisans, and a cargo of seeds. With these he hoped to win the coöperation of the "Happy Immortals" who dwelt on the islands. His ships never returned, and the legend grew that the expedition had sailed over to Japan or to the Ryukyu Islands and there made settlement.[3]

Ch'in Shih Huang Ti's ambitions and projects set in motion a tremendous revolutionary process in China. Centralization of resources and authority made possible the development of the powerful Han empire which followed (210 B.C. to A.D. 220). Han Chinese armies marched to the borders of India on the west, established outposts in Indo-China, and created important settlements at Lakliang, in northern Korea. Han embassies and trade missions traveled westward to the far-distant Roman frontiers near the Mediterranean and pushed eastward and south through Korea to trade with representatives of the Wa people living in the sea islands. We have no evidence that Han Chinese missions reached the Ryukyu Islands, but we do know that Japanese missions from Kyushu reached the Han capital at Lo-yang; notes concerning an embassy of A.D. 57 refer to a general practice of tattooing among the people of the "hundred kingdoms" in the eastern islands. This is of interest because today tattooing survives only among the primitive Ainu living in Hokkaido, the older generation of Okinawan women, and certain of the mountain communities (notably the Tayal people) of northern Formosa.

The imperial expansion of Han China disturbed and agitated all the "barbarians" living beyond Chinese frontiers. Military expeditions, diplomatic missions, and trading activities created a centrifugal pressure upon weak border peoples.

The Han Chinese court inherited and developed the old Taoist traditions of magic islands in the Eastern Seas. The powerful Han emperor Wu Ti endeavored to send messengers to three fabled islands called P'eng Lai, Fang Chang, and Ying Chou. Among the deities worshipped at the Han court was a "Princess of the Spirits," who spoke through a sorceress. It is said that her cult was introduced at the capital from the North China coastal frontiers. This is consistent with other evidence that in the general area of Korea and the offshore islands women exercised great influence as intermediaries between the spirit world and mankind, and as temporal rulers or chieftains as well.

Han records note that the country of the Wa—i.e., the islands beyond Korea—was divided into more than one hundred independent units, of which thirty-odd had established relations with Chinese settlements in North Korea. Later Chinese records (of the Wei dynasty) note that during a period of intense civil conflict in the 2nd century A.D., an old, unmarried woman referred to as Pimeku became preëminent in the islands through her influence as a sorceress, and that she sent embassies to Chinese settlements in Korea in the period A.D. 238-47 seeking support in local wars. Her death precipitated civil conflict in the sea islands, which subsided only when a girl of thirteen, a relative of Pimeku's, was made ruler. Japanese traditions preserved in the *Kojiki* and *Nihongi* indicate that female rulers were often encountered in western and southern Japan. Chinese writers alluded to the islands as the "queen countries."

These Chinese accounts suggest that until the 2nd century A.D. the inhabitants of western Japan and of Okinawa may have had much in common in their political and social institutions. Elements which were submerged in Japan under the stream of Chinese influence are still visible in the Ryukyu Islands.

A history of the Later Han dynasty (compiled in the 5th century A.D.) says that the Wa people were ruled by women, that they were short and small, that they covered only the upper part of the body, and that they were fond of rearing oxen and swine. Far to the south of the Wa kingdoms lay another "kingdom" inhabited by people said to be only three or four feet tall. This vague record of hearsay contains elements of contemporary interest. Such notes on stature, dress, and swine culture are valid today in describing the primitive Yami people who live on Botel Tobago Island, approximately two hundred miles due south of Yaeyama and Miyako. The *noro* priestesses of Okinawa were closely associated with local government until the 20th century and are still held in awe and esteem in the smaller off-lying islands along the Ryukyu chain. Swine culture was of central importance in the Ryukyuan economy until World War II. Many Okinawans—especially in the older generation—are remarkably small. Politics and religion were closely related. From legendary times until the present day the *noro* priestess has exercised a powerful influence in the Ryukyuan community. Until 1879 a daughter or sister of the king at Shuri usually assumed the role of the chief high priestess as intercessor between the spirit world and the king's household, and was often an important counselor in royal affairs.[4]

It was the *noro*'s duty in most ancient times to preserve the fire on the hearth. It can be imagined with what difficulty fire was transported from island to island in primitive days, and what hardships a community suffered if the precious flames were extinguished by accident. A daughter in each household was assigned the task of conserving and feeding the hearth fire. Fire was a communal treasure, in itself a living thing, handed on from generation to generation. A tabu system grew up about the office of the fire-custodian. She was expected to remain a virgin and was thought to be in close communication with the ancestors from whose care the fire descended. When new households were established, fire was transferred from the family home to the new dwelling or kindled anew with ceremony. In this way the continuity of the fire came to represent blood relationships and family continuity as well. The custodian of the fire upon the oldest hearth in the community assumed an official distinction; her office was hereditary, passing usually to a female child of the *noro*'s brother. A plot of land was set aside for her support. Thank offerings brought by members of the community enlarged her income. Within her house, or near it, three simple hearthstones served as a center of worship, for these formed the locus of the root-deity (*ne-gami*) of the village.

It has been suggested that in ancient days fire was always made by striking stones together and that, through association, the stones themselves became sacred. Another theory suggests that the three stones originally were used to support the earthenware pots over the fire, and so became associated with it. It is noteworthy that the stones are usually brought from the seashore, no matter how far inland the house or village altar may be, and that among the pantomimic seasonal dances performed by Okinawan villagers, there usually is one which tells a legend of the "fire-bringing visitors."

Vestments of white cloth (symbolizing ritual cleanliness) and a string of beads (including the *magatama* or curved jewels) have been symbols of the *noro*'s office since prehistoric times. Her duties require care of the hearth fire, worship of the ancestors through ritual devotion, and divination to settle upon auspicious days for marriage, burial, travel, or the simple tasks of the agricultural community.

The cult is a "living fossil" of a prehistoric age. Although the *noro* has lost prestige and support at Naha and Shuri, she still commands an awed respect as diviner and intercessor for the common man in country villages of Okinawa and in the outlying islands, where she guards the ritual objects on the sacred hearth and attends springs and sacred groves associated with the welfare and protection of the village life.

Here perhaps we glimpse surviving elements of neolithic matriarchal cults once found in many regions of the Eurasian land-mass long before the literate and historic cultures of China, the Middle East, and the Mediterranean areas were evolved. The sacred groves, springs, and wells, the oracular shrines, and the guardian priestesses of pre-Homeric Greek tradition, and of pre-Christian northern Europe and the British Isles, find close counterpart in the 20th-century mysteries of the *noro* cult.

During the period of great agitation among the "queen countries" in southwestern Japan noted by the Chinese annalists, one well-organized military group emerged preëminent in southern Kyushu and gradually pushed on to the fertile plains at the eastern end of the Inland Sea. There it found a permanent base, and there a new state came into being. This was the country of Yamato, the Japan of historic times. Legend ascribes leadership in this important movement to Jimmu, grandson of the Sun Goddess, makes him the first emperor, and names him direct ancestor of the Japanese emperors of modern times.

The succession conflict which rose after Pimeku's death suggests that the ancient matriarchal system was being challenged. Queens who reserved to themselves the exercise of the sacred mysteries, but delegated secular power to the male members of the family, in time found themselves challenged or ignored. They ceased to wield effective temporal authority. Gradually the balance shifted: in Japan the chief high priestess at the Ise Grand Shrine was an imperial princess, living in virginal seclusion. Important political decisions were referred to her with ceremony; oracular decisions were delivered through her on questions of state. As we shall see, traces of this ancient system lingered on in some strength in the Ryukyu kingdom long after they had withered away in Japan proper and the priestesses at Ise had lost all secular power.

We are concerned with these events only as they may throw light on the early history of Japanese-Ryukyu relations. In *Japan: A Short Cultural History*, Sir George Sansom notes the probability that there were large numbers of people in southern Kyushu who had come up into Japan from Southeast Asia or the southern islands along the Ryukyuan chain, and that some of the fighting forces used in the victorious migration eastwards toward Yamato may have been recruited from this southern element in the Kyushu population. There has also been some suggestion that a significant number of defeated people may have fled southward into the Ryukyu Islands during the local warfare which marked the departure of the Yamato migrants from Kyushu.

The study of language throws some light on the distant past. The British scholar Basil Hall Chamberlain, then Professor of Philology at Tokyo Imperial University, made the first modern approach to problems of early linguistic relationship between Japan and the southern islands in his *Essay in Aid of a Grammar and Dictionary of the Luchuan Language* (1895); in the years since, many Japanese and Okinawan scholars have addressed themselves to the subject. They are agreed that the contemporary speech of Japan and of the southern islands springs from a common parent language. The Japanese, however, learned to read and write at least a thousand years before the Okinawans did, and absorbed an overwhelming quantity of Chinese into the older language forms. This enlarged the Japanese vocabulary and accelerated language change reflecting—and reflected in—a host of changing institutions. Nevertheless, it is pointed out that the language of the conservative imperial court of Japan, and of the early literature which records it, preserves archaic

Japanese words and forms upon which Okinawan dialects of the recent past can shed much light.[5]

For this study the Japanese and Okinawan scholars turn to a collection of ancient songs and rituals, the *Omoro Soshi*, which were first recorded in the phonetic *hiragana* script and brought together in written form at Shuri in the 16th century.

The most indefatigable Okinawan student of these early records was undoubtedly Iha Fuyu, who devoted much time to an analysis of language and legend to discover the origins of the Okinawan people and to establish their prehistory. In the story of the two divine progenitors of the Okinawans he detected a fable embodying the meeting and blending of two peoples, possibly on the island of Amami Oshima. The name of the female deity was Amami-kyu, which by process of linguistic analysis he identifies with a fishing people from Kyushu who moved into Oshima and thence, after a long time, pushed on southward into Okinawa. The people of Oshima in turn say that they are descended from Amami-dake, who created Amami Oshima. Some of the *Omoro* songs refer to the Amami-ya ("Dwelling of the Ama-bo" or fishers' community). In the language of the Okinawan country people today the north is referred to as *nishi*, which Iha derives from *inishi* ("the past" or "behind"), whereas the Japanese speak of the west as *nishi*. Iha suggests that in both instances there is preserved an immemorial sense of the direction from which migration took place into the sea islands. In the language of the *Omoro* the verb *noboru* (to go up) is used in referring to travel to Japan from Okinawa, in the sense that country people "go up" to the capital or to the seat of authority.[6]

These are problems which must be left to the philologist and his confreres while we turn here to explore some of the shadowy legends with which the Okinawans seek to explain the remote past.

OKINAWAN ORIGIN MYTHS AND SAFE HAVENS IN THE SEA ISLANDS

Legends of Japan's Sun Goddess, and traditions surrounding the appearance of her grandson Jimmu, concern Hyuga, near the southeast tip of Kyushu Island. Let us note briefly some of the so-called "origin tales" of the Ryukyu Islands nearby.

Two principal origin myths have been handed down. They were not reduced to writing until the 17th century, but one (preserved in the *Ryukyu Shinto-ki*, about 1603) is presumably the older.

According to this account, at the beginning of time two deities were in existence, a male deity named Shineri-kyu and a female named Amami-kyu. In due course they built huts side by side. Although they indulged in no sexual intercourse, the female deity Amami-kyu became pregnant, thanks to the influence of a passing wind. Three children were born to her. The eldest, a son, became the first ruler of the islands; the second, a girl, became the first *noro* or priestess; and the third, a son, became the first of the common people. Fire, which was essential for their well-being, was obtained "from the Dragon Palace," traditionally believed to rest on the bottom of the sea.[7]

With this simple tale the Okinawans provide for the virgin birth of demigods who personify the essential social functions of administration, religious practice, and economic production. The Dragon Palace episode hints at a folk-memory that at sometime in the dim past the fire treasured on every hearth was brought with religious care from somewhere over the open seas.

A more elaborate version of the origin myth was incorporated in the first formal history, the *History of Chuzan*, prepared by Sho Jo-ken (Haneji Choshu) in 1650. Chinese and Japanese elements have crept in, just as the origin myths of Japan, first recorded in simple form in the *Kojiki* (A.D. 712), were enlarged with many Chinese elements in later versions. According to this second account, after the appearance of the male and female deities, generations of mankind lived in caves and fields. At last there emerged a "heavenly grandchild" (*tenteishi*), who had three sons and two daughters. The eldest son became founder of the Tenson dynasty, the first line of Ryukyuan kings; the second was ancestor of the lords (the *anji*); and the third became the first farmer. The elder daughter became the first high priestess (*kikoe-ogimi*) associated with the royal family, and the younger became the first community priestess (*noro*).

In this unsubstantial but interesting realm of tradition and folklore we must note the existence in the Ryukyus of many stories of the Sun Goddess Amaterasu. One of these repeats the tradition of her descent into a great cave and of her return to bring light to the world after fearful darkness. In Japan this legend is associated with a cave near the Ise Grand Shrines on the Shima Peninsula; in Ryukyu it is associated with a deep hillside cavern overlooking the sea on the eastern shores of Iheya Island. This legend of *Ama no Iwa To* may have been introduced from Japan in later years. The cave is still held sacred by the local priestesses, and the Okinawans have not lost pride in repeating local beliefs that the first Japanese emperor, Jimmu, began his great northeastward-moving conquest of Japan from this minor island in the Ryukyus.

The great cave on Iheya Island is also known as the *Kumayaa* (Hiding Place), and about it cluster legends that suggest its early and frequent use as a refuge in times of great storms or of threatening enemies. Hundreds of people could find shelter in its depths. The small entrance is high and safe above the pounding surf; nearby springs seep down through grassy land toward the shoreline; and the outgoing tides each day leave delectable and easily harvested marine food on the mudflats and exposed rocks.

Iheya Island has been held in peculiar reverence in the folklore of Okinawa, as if some dim memory persists of the arrival and shelter there of ancestral people. It is noteworthy, for instance, that until modern times the *noro* priestesses of Okinawa gathered annually at Nakijin, on the Motobu Peninsula, on the tenth day of the eighth month in the old calendar, the month of the most severe typhoons. At a high point in the hills overlooking the channel toward Iheya, they perform a complex ceremony, three times passing around the sacred structure of the hearth gods (*uganju*) with pantomime, and chanted prayers, making the motions of rowing over the waters as they go. Similarly, until the 15th century the lords of Nakijin Castle caused a special place to be constructed from which they could worship facing toward Iheya. It has already been noted that Iheya itself was governed by priestesses until the 19th century, longer than in any other district.

There are other large sheltering caves on the island of Okinawa proper (and on Miyako), each with a legendary or sacred tradition concerning it. All deserve the most careful archeologic investigation for the light they may throw upon successive waves of immigration and periods of settlement. There are sacred caves at Kin and at Futenma, opening to the south and east, which have been associated with Buddhist or (Japanese) Shinto practice in modern times. The Seifa Utaki, on Chinen Peninsula, has been a place of worship since the most remote legendary period. Until the 18th century, all kings of Ryukyu were obliged to visit and worship there, and the site was held in the greatest popular veneration until recent years. The shrine area itself, located on a high promontory over the sea, consists of a number of sheltering caves and overhanging ledges opening to the east and south among towering rock formations. All buildings have been destroyed, but the outer and inner precincts can still be traced.

Nearby and below it to the south, are the twin springs Ukinju-Hainju ("Quiet Water" and "Running Water"), held sacred as the traditional site of the first rice plantation on Okinawa. These two small, clear-running springs supply water to an area of level fields surrounded on three sides by steep, sheltering bluffs. The fourth (eastern) side opens away to extensive flats exposed at low tide. A barrier reef offshore protects lagoon-like fishing areas.

Some distance beyond the reef lies the small island of Kudaka, which has occupied a place of peculiar interest in Okinawan legend and history, for it is here that tradition says the "five fruits and grains" were first introduced by a divine people. It has been suggested that at some prehistoric time strangers put in here from an unknown land bringing with them new fruits or grains and advanced agricultural techniques, and that they made an unforgotten contribution to the barren economy of Okinawa.

Standing among the sheltering rocks at the Seifa Utaki, looking out across the surf-streaked reefs to Kudaka and beyond, one is struck by the persistence and strength of these local traditions which associate the southward coves and promontories and beaches with folk heroes and the age of the gods. It is noteworthy too that the services of worship at these spots embodied ritual prayers of gratitude. We can imagine the joy and relief with which primitive men and women came ashore nearby, to find abundant seafood within the reefs, fresh water and fallow land beyond the beach, and on the hills above a natural shelter from the fearful storms which sweep in across these islands every year.

Research, in time, may lay bare something of the pattern of early settlement. Carbon tests on the camp-sites within the caves may establish some approximate dating for successive waves of immigration.

In a sense "prehistory" ended in the Ryukyus when the Chinese and the Japanese began to record notices of these islands far out on the edge of the world. It is to these notices we turn now to follow the story of Okinawa in historic times.

CHINESE AND JAPANESE NOTICES BEFORE THE 12TH CENTURY

For many years China had been torn by dynastic wars, but in A.D. 581 a powerful general named Yang Chien seized the throne through treachery and declared himself first emperor of the Sui dynasty. He ruled well, and by A.D. 589 China was unified after decades of turmoil.

Chinese influences had long since penetrated the Japanese islands through outlying Chinese colonies and the small kingdoms of the Korean Peninsula. Knowledge of reading, writing, administrative organization, and court ceremonial had slowly transformed many primitive communities in the island of Kyushu and in western and central Honshu. Refugees from the war-torn principalities and colonies of northern China and Korea made their way into the sea islands, welcomed there because of the skills—the arts and crafts—they brought with them. By A.D. 600 Yamato people had been transformed from a loose association of rival, semi-autonomous clans into a nation governed from a settlement established near present-day Osaka. At the time of the incident we are about to relate, the Yamato clans were ruled by the Empress Suiko, who entrusted the secular government to her nephew, Prince Regent Shotoku. This remarkable person desired to reorganize and strengthen the administrative organization of the state and to establish direct communication with China. To this end, in A.D. 605 he ordered the first official embassy to go from the court of Japan to the Emperor of China.

Drawing on wide resources, Yang Chien presided over a brilliant court at Lo-yang. Missions reached the great capital from distant and semi-civilized peoples. Chinese ambassadors and expeditions were sent into the barbarian border states beyond China's frontiers. At the court

Taoist priests and magicians were in high favor. Royal patronage was lavished on the never-ending search for the means of transmuting base metals into gold, and the emperor—like so many of his predecessors—was eager to find the supreme secret, the secret of immortality.

The tradition of an elusive Land of Happy Immortals in the distant Eastern Seas had persisted since the emperors Ch'in Shih Huang Ti and Han Wu Ti had sent out their fruitless expeditions eight centuries earlier. It had not been enough for an emperor to achieve imperial supremacy; temporal success was incomplete without possession of everlasting life.

Ambitious Taoist priests assured the emperor at Lo-yang that the secrets could be found. Thus it was that orders to prepare for an expedition were issued in A.D. 605. The first attempt to reach the Land of Happy Immortals (made in 607) was unsuccessful, but in the next year an expedition reached islands in the Eastern Seas.

They were not peopled by Happy Immortals, and were not composed of gold and silver, as legend had promised. Nevertheless, the Chinese envoy who commanded the expedition advised the primitive islanders to yield to Sui rule and to acknowledge the Chinese emperor as their suzerain. They refused, a battle ensued, and many captives—said to have numbered a thousand persons—were taken back to China. The records note that the invaders were unable to make themselves understood in the islands, for the natives knew no Chinese and the Chinese could not comprehend the language of their captives.

The exact location of these islands has never been determined; the annals are vague, and for centuries the Chinese referred to all the islands lying between Japan proper and the Philippines as Liu Ch'iu, writing the name with characters which the Japanese pronounce Ryukyu.[8] There is a strong presumption that the Sui expeditionary force had indeed reached the island of Okinawa or the islands north of it. While the expedition was abroad, Japan's first ambassador to China (Ono no Imoko) reached Lo-yang accompanied by students and "national leaders" sent abroad for study at the expense of the Japanese government. When the Chinese explorers and their captives returned to the imperial court and laid souvenirs before the emperor, the Japanese envoy exclaimed at once that they must have come from the island of

Yaku, which lies just south of Kyushu. The secret of immortality was not among the souvenirs, but the cloth, the weapons, and the uncouth captives excited the curiosity of the Chinese.

This gives us a clue that the Japanese court at Naniwa was acquainted with the islands south of Japan proper. The heart of Kyushu was not yet fully brought under control, but the waterways of the Inland Sea were open, and the coasts of Kyushu were accessible from the sea.

In A.D. 616 the Japanese annals themselves record notice of a "Southern Islands people" for the first time. Thirty persons were said to have been naturalized and settled within territories controlled by the Empress Suiko's officers. In the next half-century there were occasional notices of barbarians who came into Japanese settlements from the islands of Yaku and Tane and of the dispatch of officers to investigate and make reports concerning the islands lying south of Kyushu. The court maintained a supplemental headquarters in northern Kyushu known as the Dazai-fu, near the present-day cities of Hakata and Fukuoka. It had been established to supervise trade and diplomatic intercourse with the Korean Peninsula and to control administrative outposts in the unconquered mountains of Kyushu.

It may be presumed that the Dazai-fu officials treated border peoples in Kyushu much as the Ainu in eastern and northern Japan were treated in these centuries. Those who were willing to enter into peaceful relations, to receive gifts, and to render tribute were rewarded. Those suffered who refused to accept Yamato rule; military expeditions were sent against them, their settlements were disrupted or pushed back, and their lands placed under officers holding appointments from the distant capital.

Each decade brought some extension of Japanese authority within Kyushu and an increased knowledge of the primitive people settled among the islands in adjacent waters. In the records for A.D. 698 we find clear indication of attempts to establish relations with the Southern Islands (*Nanto*) people, for the *Shoku Nihongi* (Chronicles of Japan) states that in the fourth month of that year a learned courtier named Fumi no Imiko was ordered to claim the islands and was dispatched with a small force for that purpose. Presumably he had authority to enlist the aid of local officials along the way, for this was the custom of the times. Some sixteen months later it was recorded at court: "Men from Tane-jima, Yaku-shima, Amami, Toku-no-shima, and others, accompanied by court officials, came and presented produce from their places. They were given titles and presents, varying in each case. From this time on Toku-no-shima began to obey the central government."[9]

Within the month, these tributes were offered at the Grand Shrine of the Sun Goddess at Ise and at other shrines, in token of a new extension of the imperial authority. Four months later Fumi no Imiko and his aides themselves returned to court, to receive rewards and new ranks. It thus appears that the first Japanese expedition to the Ryukyu Islands known to us had relative success, whereas the Chinese, ninety years earlier, had failed.

This was only part of a general campaign to subjugate restless and defiant communities (the Hayato people) throughout central and southern Kyushu and the small adjacent islands. Ultimately they were forced to submit to superior Japanese arms and organization. A note in the *Chronicles* indicates that the ancient system of female chieftains continued among them, for it is recorded that in A.D. 701: "The female head of Satsuma, Kumehadzu . . . [and other chieftains] . . . followed by Hi people [inhabitants of Hizen and Higo] using arms, threatened the Imperial envoy Osakabe no Maki and his party, who had come to claim their country. Hereupon the viceroy of Tsukushi was given an Imperial order to punish them according to their misdeeds."[10]

In the following year there is a further record: "[Tane-ga-shima] Satsuma, far away from authority, disobeyed orders. [In this predicament] military [forces] were dispatched to bring them to order. After that, census was taken, officials appointed."[11]

Gradually one name and then another appears in the chronicles; Amami and Tokara in 699, Shingaki and Kume in 714. In 720, some 232 persons were received at Nara. They brought tribute and were "given rank," which is to say that they had submitted to Japanese authority and could be assigned a proper place in the elaborate hierarchy of titles and social grades which Japan had adopted from the Chinese court and modified to meet its own needs.

At last, in 753, the name Okinawa itself is recorded, upon the occasion of a shipwreck suffered by a mission sent to China from Nara in the reign of the Empress Koken.

The chronicles in the 7th and 8th centuries tell many stories of border warfare and crude diplomacy on the land frontiers, and of the effect these events had upon policies and government at the capital. It was a struggle which strained further the resources of the imperial court, overburdened as it was with the cost of building and maintaining new capital cities and great temples at Asuka, Fujiwara, and Nara.

A period of early, organized Japanese expansion had run its course by the 9th century, when the natural water barriers north of Honshu and south of Kyushu had been reached. Nevertheless, during these years (and in subsequent centuries) Japanese influences were slowly penetrating communities in the Southern Islands.

We know that from earliest times it was Japanese custom to send into distant exile any noble or official thought dangerous near the court, or in the home provinces. Rugged, isolated peninsulas or small offshore islands served this purpose well. History is full of the exploits of men who, with their faithful retainers, were forced to exchange the luxuries of court life for the hardships of life in exile beyond the frontier. Occasionally criminals, deserting conscripts, vagrants, and others marked for punishment were transported in large numbers to border settlements. Intermarriage with the local inhabitants was common, and it must be presumed that the establishment of each frontier Japanese settlement carried a civilizing and modifying influence into more primitive communities nearby.

We know too that there was a gradual increase in ocean shipping, for the Japanese sought direct intercourse with China, although ships were primitive and the arts of navigation undeveloped. It was customary to avoid the high seas, to hug the coast, and to navigate by sighting promontories and islands along the way. Official missions between Japan and China, inaugurated in 607, continued to pass to and fro at irregular intervals, but in 894 it was recommended that no further official embassies be sent, for the way was long, the rigors of the journey very great, and conditions within China deeply disturbed by revolution and war. The missions were costly; some of them were on a large scale for the times, with five hundred men or more in the ambassador's train, embarked upon several ships. Few if any of these expeditions returned without loss en route. In the earlier years they sailed across the Straits of Tsushima and up the island-studded coast of Korea, then struck across to the Shantung Peninsula. In later years a more southerly route was taken, cruising just west of the Ryukyu Islands while making for the Yangtse River estuary.

There are hints that ships bound for China occasionally touched in the Ryukyus; it is said that the ambassador Kibi no Makibi and his companions went ashore somewhere along the way when he was making his second visit to the Chinese court in 753. One hundred years later a priest-scholar named Chisho was stranded for a time; upon his return to Japan he reported that he had encountered people who were cannibals. Okinawans today are most reluctant to accept this story, and there is no evidence to support it. He may have reached the islands in a time of great famine, which may drive men anywhere to desperate measures. It may be more likely that he heard a confused tale of the ancient ritual burial preparations in Okinawa, which required that the bones of the dead be cleansed in liquor during a time of family ceremonial feasting near the tomb-site.

Be that as it may, it is established that maritime disasters were frequent in these stormy seas, and there are notices of many shipwrecks along the shores of Kyushu. It must be presumed that some of the Japanese castaways remained permanently in the outer islands. The chronicles are dotted with references to priests, ambassadors, scholars, students, and craftsmen who failed to return from the southern waters. We can only guess what influence these castaways may have had upon the less advanced people they encountered under such circumstances. Official missions were suspended in the 9th century, but sea traffic continued, for enterprising merchants, pious priests, and eager scholars made their way across to China and home again throughout these centuries.

Having no record of conditions and events in these years, the Okinawan people in later times invented a legendary history. According to this, one line of paramount local chieftains was singled out and styled a "royal house," called the Tenson dynasty, descended from the gods, who ruled for "seventeen thousand years." We can merely assume that there were many petty local chieftains scattered throughout the islands, often quarreling among themselves, plundering one another's settlements, or joining sometimes in association under outstanding leaders. Japanese adventurers or castaways possessed of superior weapons or cunning in war, or with new technical skills, must have been welcomed into these primitive communities and given honorable place beside the chieftains.

TALES OF TAMETOMO, AN EXILED JAPANESE, AND OF HIS SON SHUNTEN

We are about to consider the tales which surround the first of these outstanding men to emerge with some semblance of historic probability, one who is held to be the founder of the Okinawan kingdom. His name is Shunten, and he is at best a shadowy figure. Thirty-five kings follow him in history, and we should therefore note for a moment some of the ideas of monarchy which have prevailed in Okinawa.

The tradition of the Tenson dynasty, which ruled for seventeen thousand years, illustrates a late effort to find a basis for royal authority in "divine right" and to explain and rationalize the unknown and unrecorded past. It was patterned after Japanese traditions and may have been introduced at a late date. But in fact the Okinawan attitude toward monarchy shows an interesting blend of elements drawn from the continent as well. From China the Okinawans adopted the moral interpretation of kingship as a Heaven-sent mandate to rule through succession in one family, but only as long as the ruler himself is virtuous. A wicked ruler deserves to be overthrown, when the mandate of Heaven is withdrawn and given to a chieftain of another family. Such was the interpretation provided to explain the fall of the Tenson dynasty and of later families in the royal succession. In contrast, the Japanese held that the institution of monarchy can be conserved only within one family, of divine origin, and that the "divine right" continues unbroken, whatever the virtues or shortcomings of individual members may prove to be. As Japanese influence grew stronger in Okinawa, these views were compromised by attributing to the first king, Shunten, a lineage which linked him with Japan's imperial family by a devious route.

Shunten's mother was the daughter of an Okinawan chieftain; his father was a Japanese adventurer of heroic cast. The year of his birth is traditionally said to have been A.D. 1166, but to understand the story as a mirror of those times we must go back a little, for at this point Okinawan legend begins to merge with established history in nearby Japan, China, and Korea. The story itself was not recorded in the Okinawan annals until six centuries after the alleged events took place, and then under circumstances which suggest tampering inspired by political necessity. For our purposes we will strip the account of the many variant details. The Tametomo legend cannot be verified at this time; neither can it be dismissed as pure fiction, for there is nothing in it essentially incompatible with the general conditions of the age. It first takes form at the hands of a Japanese priest named Taichu soon after Satsuma seized the islands (1609), and was written into the formal *History of Chuzan* about 1650 by a regent whose policy centered in the need to reconcile and accommodate Okinawan interests with the demands and interests of the Japanese.

We have already noted that the Japanese (Yamato) center of authority was established at the head of the Inland Sea by the beginning of the 7th century, and that it required some two hundred years to complete the conquest of the Ainu on the northern frontier and the Kumaso and Hayato people in southern Kyushu. The Japanese who went down into these districts were tough and hardy fighting men. Some of the settlements were enlarged by the transfer of outlaws to this frontier. Other Japanese drifted in to take advantage of open lands ready for cultivation. By the 9th century the central government seems to have established preponderant authority; nevertheless, although the garrison forces alloted to the Dazai-fu (Governmental Headquarters) in northern Kyushu were reduced, it appears that no garrison member on the registers was recruited from Satsuma, Hyuga, or Osumi districts, the region which today constitutes Kagoshima and Miyazaki prefectures.

Districts near the imperial capital (Kyoto) were crowded. It was common practice for the court to make grants of land or income-bearing appointments and titles to court favorites and to cousins, nephews, and grandsons of the imperial household. These men, reluctant to leave the capital, often sent resident managers (*jito*) to oversee distant estates. Similarly the title of Provincial Governor was sometimes given to men who remained at the court to enjoy the governor's income, deputizing their duties to acting governors willing to live in the countryside far from the capital city. The growth of the semi-independent domains far from Kyoto is a complex subject, which need not detain us here. Life in the distant provinces was hard. As the work of opening up new lands progressed, the acting governors and the estate managers became less and less willing to respond promptly and obediently to orders sent down from Kyoto. This spirit of independence led in time to the emergence of powerful clans and families who were rivals for power at the court and military rivals in the field.

In the 9th century a grandson of the Emperor Kammu founded the Taira family, which developed important estates and alliances throughout Japan, and in the 10th century a grandson of the Emperor Seiwa founded the Minamoto family, with vast estates in the eastern districts. Minamoto no Tametomo, the traditional link between Okinawa and Japan, was a member of the fifth generation of this Minamoto family.

As the Taira family increased its estates and its power in the outlying border districts, it came to wield growing influence at the Kyoto court. The founding of the immense Satsuma domain (to which the Ryukyu Islands in time became subordinate) is an excellent example of the process. About 1030 a member of the Taira family was acting as viceroy in charge of the government's administrative headquarters in northern Kyushu. He was joined there by a brother who held high office among the powerful police commissioners (*kebiishi-cho*), an organization whose duties included the maintenance of order among landholders and estate managers in the countryside. The brothers, acting in each other's interests, developed huge private estates in southern Kyushu, apparently by using forced labor available to them in their capacity as government officials. These estates in time became part of Shimazu's territory.[12] This was an age of general unrest and turmoil; China was divided and harassed by wars throughout the 12th century, which closed as the Mongols swept out of Central Asia to the sea. Japan was torn by the bitter rivalry of the two powerful families which claimed descent from the imperial house.

The Taira family grew in prestige and authority. In the early 12th century its most bitter enemies were members of Tametomo's family. Tametomo himself was a precocious youth, noted for his great stature, enormous strength, and skill as a bowman. There is a legend that his powerful right arm was several inches longer than his left arm, with which he grasped his bow; hence he could draw his bowstring to much greater advantage than an ordinary man. If the records are to be believed, he was unruly and turbulent as a small boy. His father, Tameyoshi, sent him far away to a distant post in Kyushu. Soon thereafter he associated himself with Ata, the Acting Governor of Kyushu, and secured for himself the grand title of General Superintendent (*Sotsuibushi*). In time he married Ata's daughter, but almost immediately left Kyushu to join in a Minamoto attack upon the Taira-held capital city. He was on the losing side in this affray. The leaders were executed, and young Tametomo was banished after being cruelly punished; the sinews of his bow-arm were cut, and he was sent to the distant islands of the Izu Peninsula in eastern Japan.

This was in 1156; for twenty-nine years thereafter the Taira family were supreme in authority at the court and preëminent throughout many parts of Japan.

To this point the Tametomo traditions agree, but here the story fades. One account says that Tametomo died in Izu and makes no mention of the Ryukyu Islands. A second says that he remained in exile fourteen years and then on a spring day in 1165 attempted to escape by making his way southward through the coastal islands to Oni-ga-shima (Devil's Island), traditionally said to be Okinawa. In this account he is said to have been given aid by his father-in-law, Ata, in Kyushu. A third version of the legend says that he was sailing one day between two of the Izu islands when overtaken by a violent storm. He was blown far out to sea, drifting at last in the storm's wake to Okinawa.

There he and his men were welcomed by a local chieftain, the Lord of Osato, with whose daughter he contracted a marriage. Shunten was born of the union. This was a temporary arrangement; he was eager to get back to the wars in Japan, and after one vain attempt to take his Okinawan wife and child with him, he and his men left Okinawa. They made their way back to the island of Oshima in Sagami Bay and there were destroyed by a military force commanded by the Vice-Governor of Izu. This legend says that when he found himself trapped at last, Tametomo committed suicide with a ceremonial flourish, setting the precedent in Japanese history for *seppuku* (hara-kiri).

Meanwhile, the abandoned wife and infant son settled at the village of Urasoe, on the leeward side of Shuri Hill and just inland from the harbor where farewells had been said. For this reason the shallow inlet has been known until today as Machi-minato (Waiting Harbor).

What reality may underlie this romantic story?

Japan was in a state of political turmoil. The struggle between the Taira and the Minamoto marked in fact the breakup of an old administrative order which had been established in the 7th century. The conflict at the court, hitherto the center of all administrative authority, deeply affected the border regions. Authority itself was shifting to quasi-independent provincial centers. Tametomo's nephew Minamoto Yoritomo at last destroyed the Taira organization in 1186, and removed the center of military government administration from Kyoto to Kamakura, in eastern Japan. The defeated Taira fled into remote mountain retreats or to distant offshore islands to escape ruthless Minamoto vengeance. There is some reason to believe that many Taira adherents fled southward from Kyushu into the Ryukyu Islands. Traditions of such a movement remain strong today.

A shrine dedicated to Taira Kiyomori's second son still stands near Naze on Oshima. Graves on Ishigaki Island (Yaeyama) and on Yonaguni are known locally as *Yamato-haka* or *Yashima-haka*, which links them by tradition to Sanuki Province in Shikoku, the site of a battle lost by the Taira there in 1184. The villagers on Yonaguni who live nearby have always claimed descent from Taira refugees and have kept themselves somewhat aloof from other natives on the island.

It is a reasonable guess—but only a guess—that at some time in the 12th century roving Japanese fighting men and their retainers came into association with petty chieftains on Okinawa and that one of these chieftains, strengthened by the relationship, emerged as a paramount leader in central Okinawa. The Japanese may well have been exiled Taira men, but when the time came centuries later to prepare a history and adorn the legends (that is to say, in the early 17th century) the *de facto* rulers of Japan, the Tokugawa shoguns, were of Minamoto stock. What better man to serve as a link between Okinawa and Japan than the legendary Minamoto Tametomo?

TRADITIONS OF SHUNTEN AND OTHER EARLY "KINGS" ON OKINAWA

Tametomo's son displayed precocious talents, not unexpected in a scion of the Minamoto, who in turn claimed descent from the Japanese imperial house. As a promising lad he won the respect and admiration of the local people within the territory of his maternal grandfather. When he was only fifteen years old he was chosen to succeed as Lord of Urasoe by popular will.

This was a time of great confusion on Okinawa; the local lords and petty chieftains (known as *anji*) were in revolt against the twenty-fourth overlord of the Tenson dynasty. His dissolute behavior brought about his downfall. At last he was assassinated by one of his own retainers, named Riyu, who sought to establish himself as paramount chief. Riyu in turn was destroyed by a popular revolt led by Shunten, the young Lord of Urasoe, who was then twenty-two years old. Shunten was immediately recognized as overlord among the *anji* and ruled thereafter for fifty-one years.

Under Shunten's guidance the people of Okinawa made great progress in developing the political, economic, and social life of the island. Upon his death in 1237 his son Shumba-Junki became king and ruled for eleven years. He too guided his people well. A castle was built on the heights of Shuri, back of Urasoe, one of the most magnificent castle sites to be found anywhere in the world, for it commands the country-side below for miles around and looks toward distant sea horizons on every side. It is related that the art of writing was introduced to Okinawa at this time, when the forty-seven Japanese phonetic *kana* symbols were adopted under Shumba-Junki's patronage. New styles in clothing and headdress were introduced, and annual observances of the New Year were altered significantly.

Shumba-Junki's death brought his eldest son, Gihon, to the throne in 1248, at the age of forty-four. It was a time of disaster; many typhoons swept over the islands; and a drought caused the crops to fail. Then came famine, followed by a year of epidemic sickness when more than half the population succumbed.

Gihon accepted responsibility for conditions within the country, as a king's duty. He therefore called to his side a young lord named Eiso and appointed him Regent (*Sessai*). Six years later Gihon abdicated and " withdrew into the forest alone." The time and place of his death are unknown, although tradition says that he vanished somewhere in the hills at the most remote northern tip of the island, Heda-misaki.

Eiso thus governed as regent from 1235 to 1260 and as king from 1260 until his death in 1299. It is related that this was a half-century of great importance in foreign relations as well as in local development.

Okinawa recovered from the years of famine and epidemic; economic order was restored; the land was divided anew; and a regular taxation system was introduced. Systematic levies upon rice fields and upon household production took the place of earlier haphazard levies, which had been made whenever occasion demanded. Controls were extended from Okinawa to other islands, and in 1264, soon after regular taxation was instituted on Okinawa, the off-lying islands of Kume, Kerama, and Iheya began to send in tribute. In 1266, officials were sent northward into Amami Oshima, halfway between Okinawa and the Japanese island of Kyushu. To accommodate this expanded administrative work a government office was established in Tomari, at the head of an inlet lying immediately below Shuri Castle.

In 1272, King Eiso received a message from the court of the great Mongol overlord, Kublai Khan, who was then preparing to invade Japan by way of Korea. Okinawa was ordered to submit to Mongol authority and to make a contribution toward the proposed expedition. The demand was rejected. Four years later envoys came again from the Mongol court with new demands, and these were again rejected. This time the envoys from China made a show of force, but were driven off, taking some 130 Okinawan captives with them.

Eiso died in his seventy-first year. His son Taisei and his grandson Eiji ruled in succession after him. These were uneventful reigns, but when Eiso's great-grandson Tamagusuku came to the throne in 1314, at the age of nineteen, there began a new time of trouble for Okinawa, and a new era.

The story of Tametomo's amorous adventures in the Southern Islands is frankly romantic and heroic and needs no basis in fact for its appeal to the imagination of latter-day Okinawans. The story of Shunten, on the other hand, has more substance. Shunten may well have been the offspring of a Japanese adventurer and the daughter of an *anji* of some eminence. It was entirely in keeping with custom that some such arrangement would be made for a temporary marriage. The biographical touches suggest a composite picture of the culture hero, based in the first instance on an exceptional leader who made substantial progress in asserting authority over adjacent petty chieftains. It is misleading to attribute full-fledged "kingship" to an Okinawan chief in these early centuries, for it was only by degrees that leadership was institutionalized. That is to say, distinctly individual leadership exercised through force of personality or preëminent skill in arms or political shrewdness was only slowly replaced by formal institutions of government—laws and ceremonies—supported and strengthened by a developing respect for the royal office, regardless of the character or quality of the person holding it.

So it is that tradition assigns to the 13th century an extraordinary number of innovations and developments in the social and political life of the Okinawans. The knowledge and use of writing became known, and it is noteworthy that this was not the use of the complicated Chinese-Japanese characters used at the Japanese court in Kyoto, nor the pure Chinese introduced at a much later date from China. It was the simple phonetic syllabary which had been developed in Japan centuries earlier. It was to become and remain the language form in which the Okinawan court prepared its official documents for use within the island kingdom, and it remained the language of poetic expression among the educated gentry.

Shunten's story involves an interesting point concerning the succession of kings and matters of political virtue. The mandate of Heaven was withdrawn from the last king of the Tenson dynasty; he was wicked and doomed to fall; but tradition does not fasten the crime of regicide upon the heroic Shunten. A wicked and disloyal retainer (Riyu) killed the king and was in turn destroyed by the admirable son of Tametomo.

Meanwhile, what is the meaning of Gihon's strange fate? We are told simply that it was a time of great hardship and that Shunten's heir gave way voluntarily to a regent who claimed descent from the ancient Tenson dynasty and from the gods. Gihon "accepted responsibility," which was in good form according to the Chinese doctrines of royal responsibility for the public welfare. It is possible that Shunten and his adherents were not able to maintain themselves in the face of great disasters and that discontent made it necessary to share authority with a representative chosen from the family of the old paramount chieftains, or that a rival from among the descendants of the Tenson chieftains may have forced Gihon to relinquish power.

Okinawan traditions which preserve memories of great natural disasters—storm, flood, and famine—and attribute them to the 13th century, coincide with the records of a series of calamities suffered by Japan about that time, when earthquakes toppled cities, and typhoons and floods swept the countryside. Crop failures were followed by famines, and famine brought epidemic disease. Across the world medieval Europe likewise suffered great climatic disturbances and exceptional human hardship in the years which embrace reign-periods attributed to Gihon and Eiso.

If for our purpose we accept the stories of Gihon and Eiso as well founded, we may surmise that until Eiso's time the Okinawans were not prepared to cope with the demands of a famine year. Tradition says that more than half the people died of hunger and disease. Stirred by this, Gihon's successors reorganized and regularized land distribution and the collection of taxes in kind (weapons, grain, and cloth). This meant reserves, and reserves meant strength. We have today a very clear idea of the warehouse system which may have been used in Eiso's day. In Okinawan villages untouched by World War II—that is to say, principally in the off-lying islands—there are thatched community storehouses of an ancient type. They are usually associated with village shrines or community common land. In all respects they could have served as models for the line drawings which we find on bronze bells (*dotaku*) unearthed in prehistoric sites in Japan; they are virtually indistinguishable (to the layman's eye) from the thatched and elevated structures of the primitive Yami tribesmen who dwell on an island three hundred miles south of Okinawa, or from the storehouses built in aboriginal Tayal villages of Formosa.

These repositories of grain and of arms enabled the government (under Eiso?) to organize and support levies of men needed in the development of public works—such as construction of the Urasoe Castle near Shuri. It is interesting to note that the extension of Okinawan authority to Amami Oshima at the north and to other nearer islands (Kume, Iheya, and Kerama) is said to have taken place during or shortly after the institution of regular taxation on Okinawa Island itself. This suggests that the government at Urasoe was gaining strength.

The tradition that Eiso was called upon to contribute aid to Kublai Khan at Cambulac (near present-day Peking) is worthy of special note, for it is the first demonstration that a major military contest for possession of the Korean Peninsula nearby brings Okinawa inevitably into temporary prominence. The Great Khan ruled the most powerful empire in the world of that day, a vast area nearly coextensive with the combined Soviet Russian and Chinese Communist empires of the 20th century. Mongol rulers controlled the vast Eurasian continent, from the tip of southern Korea to the borders of Hungary and Poland in Europe, and from the frigid Siberian tundra on the north to the hot jungles of Burma on the south. Mongol rule penetrated the Middle East, covering Persia and the Arabian shores of the Persian Gulf. No continental empire like it had ever risen before, and none has been known since.

The Mongols were preparing to invade Japan by way of the Korean corridor-peninsula, but in 1274 and again in 1281 they were driven from the shores of Kyushu.

Nothing more is said in traditional history concerning relations between Ryukyu and the continent in the 13th entury. Chinese sources must be used with caution because the Chinese referred to all the islands between Japan and the Philippines as Liu-ch'iu, and only later in history make distinction between the Okinawan group of islands ("Great Liu-ch'iu") and Taiwan or Formosa ("Small Liu-ch'iu"), where the name lingers today for an islet just south of the Formosan port of Kaohsiung.

It helps us to set these stories of 13th-century Okinawa in perspective if we recall that during Shunten's long life Marco Polo and his uncles were at the court of Kublai Khan, picking up those persistent tales of gold and silver islands and of happy people who had discovered the elixir of immortality somewhere far out in the Eastern Seas. These tales Polo retold in later years in Italy, at Genoa and Venice. We shall hear more of the legend as our later story of Okinawa and the Western world unfolds.

To the late 13th century and to Eiso's reign tradition ascribes the introduction of Buddhism into Okinawa. A Japanese priest named Zenkan is said to have been shipwrecked and washed ashore sometime between 1265 and 1274. He was given permission to construct a small place of worship, and under the king's patronage a temple was built at Urasoe, named the Gokuraku-ji.

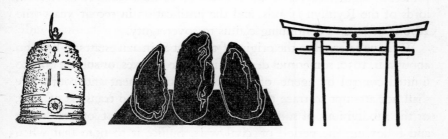

FIG. 3. SYMBOLS OF OKINAWAN RELIGIONS. *A Buddhist bell, sacred hearth-stones of the* noro *cult, and a Shinto torii.*

This story is wholly in keeping with the spirit of the times in Japan; there was a far-reaching missionary activity generated by the growth of evangelical sects throughout the islands. Old temples were rebuilt at Nara and Kyoto, which had suffered heavily in the civil wars. Immense temple organizations sprang up at Kamakura, the seaside town in eastern Japan which Minamoto Yoritomo made the seat of military administration or "camp government." Kamakura was the eastern terminus for shipping between Japan and China, and monks and missionary-priests as well as merchants embarked there for the long and hazardous journey into the Yellow Seas west of Okinawa. It is said that archeological reconnaissance at Urasoe in recent years has revealed fragments of tile and other artifacts which appear to be of Kamakura origin. It is not difficult to believe that a priest, shipwrecked somewhere on Okinawa in those early days, could make his way to the seat of government on the island, and that his missionary efforts to win a hearing would gain support.

Buddhism served thereafter as an important agency for the introduction of arts, crafts, and ceremonial, and to some degree for the promotion of Japanese language and learning.

THE SHIMAZU FAMILY IN KYUSHU: "LORDS OF THE TWELVE SOUTHERN ISLANDS"

We must now go back a few years to trace the rise of the Shimazu princes in southern Kyushu, the foundation of their claim to be rightful lords of the Ryukyu Islands, and the justification in recent years (the 1870's) of Japan's continuing claims to sovereignty.

We have referred to the origin of the vast Shimazu estates in Kyushu about A.D. 1030, sometimes declared immune to taxes, or subject only to limited control by agents of the central government and court. We shall not attempt to trace the agreements, feuds, and transfers of title, or the subdivisions of some estates and the additions of others during and following the period of civil wars. Suffice it to note that when Tametomo's nephew Yoritomo overthrew the Taira and made himself virtual master of Japan, he assumed in succession the offices and titles Superintendent of the Sixty-six Provinces (1190) and "Barbarian-Subduing Generalissimo" or *Sei-i Tai-Shogun* (in 1192). It was within his power to grant titles or to recommend that titles and honors be granted by the imperial court to his own family, retainers, and favorites.

According to accounts which are widely accepted but sometimes challenged, one of his many illegitimate sons, named Tadahisa, was adopted into the Koremune family, and in time received appointment as High Constable (*Shugo*) of Satsuma, in southern Kyushu. Proceeding to his territories in 1196, Tadahisa soon enlarged them by bringing

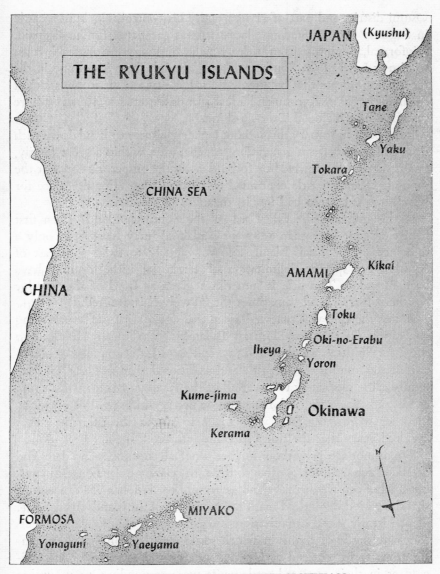

THE RYUKYU ISLANDS

JAPAN (Kyushu)

Tane

Yaku

Tokara

CHINA SEA

CHINA

AMAMI   Kikai

Toku

Oki-no-Erabu

Iheya

Yoron

Kume-jima

Okinawa

Kerama

N

FORMOSA   MIYAKO

Yonaguni   Yaeyama

FIG. 4. MAP: THE ISLANDS OF THE RYUKYU ARCHIPELAGO.

57

Osumi district and part of Hyuga under his control. He built a castle in Satsuma and adopted its place name as the name for his domain. His formal appointments and titles, which were many, included references to him as Lord of the Southern Islands, though there is nothing in the records to indicate that he attempted to govern any territories south of the main island of Kyushu and a few islands scattered nearby in offshore waters. These included Tane-ga-shima.

It has been customary throughout Japanese history to hand down such titles and honors from generation to generation within a great family, unless specifically canceled or forbidden by the emperor's court or the shogun. Often the title continued to be used long after the office for which it was created had lost its meaning or substance.

In this instance, the title Lord of the Southern Islands when first bestowed (not later than 1187 for Tadahisa) may have been only a reference to the small islands known vaguely to exist southeast of Kyushu. No specific delimitation of territorial authority may have been intended. The title is sometimes given as Lord of the Twelve Southern Islands, and sometimes the "Twelve" is omitted.

But as the title was renewed again and again with each succeeding generation (in 1227 for Shimazu Tadatoki, for Shimazu Hisatsune in 1263, for Shimazu Sadahisa in 1325, and so on), the conquest of Ryukyu in 1609 meant that the title and traditional claims of the Shimazu family came ultimately to cover all of the Ryukyu Islands as far south as Miyako, Yaeyama, and Yonaguni, which is within sight of Formosa. In other words, the facts were made to match the title some four hundred years after the title first came into use.[12]

We cannot accept without further proof all the names and dates and details which tradition ascribes to the 13th-century events on Okinawa, but neither can we dismiss them as groundless fictions. We can assume that the period did indeed mark the transition of the islands from a state of prehistoric social organization and primitive political arrangements to a new mode of living in which social, political, and economic institutions were centered at Urasoe, near central Okinawa. The Okinawans in their scattered settlements were responding to mounting pressure from Japan.

Stories of the Shunten and Eiso dynasties cover eight reigns (a span of 160 years) and reflect the increasing penetration of Japanese influence among the Southern Islands. It may be assumed that under this influence the petty chieftains or "kings" in the archipelago were brought together under a paramount chieftain who based his government near present-day Naha and Shuri. Hardships of famine, storm, and epidemic sickness were mitigated as this emerging central administration learned to improve economic organization and administration to meet recurrent crises. This in turn strengthened the Okinawans at Urasoe and made it possible for them to extend their more organized controls and influence to the less-developed outer islands.

We may assume too that with the increase in local revenues made possible by Eiso's economic reorganization, the petty chieftains (anji) enjoyed a rising living standard. For the ruling family and its adherents this may have meant a comparative degree of luxury. Traditional history says that upon the death of Eiji in 1314, his young son Tamagusuku became paramount chief, but that he was dissolute, unfit to rule, and unable to maintain intact the heritage of his ancestors. It is to a consideration of his reign, the breakup of the small kingdom, and the development of foreign intercourse that we must now turn.

CHAPTER TWO

A CENTURY OF CONFLICT

1314–1398

THREE RIVAL CHIEFTAINS BID FOR CHINESE RECOGNITION

Tamagusuku was only nineteen years of age in 1314 when he succeeded his father as paramount chief or king among the territorial
lords on Okinawa. The administration fell into confusion; he could not
command the loyalty and respect of his principal officers. Disputes at
Urasoe soon led to open rebellion.

The Lord of Ozato left Urasoe and retired to his own castle on a
high bluff about ten miles south of Urasoe and a little to the southeast
of the present-day fishing port of Itoman. His retainers and associates
controlled all of southern Okinawa. Each had his own stronghold on
a rocky hilltop, from which the surrounding farms and woodland
could be controlled. Today the broken walls of these enclosures may be
traced at many sites, a number of them scattered over the rolling countryside which became the last battleground of World War II. Ozato
Castle was the largest of these. Little is left of it; a modern primary
school stands within the stone walls of the inner court. Nothing remains
of the ancient residential buildings, and the wellsprings which supplied
it are choked and overgrown. Tradition says that a deep inlet from the
sea at one time reached to the base of the bluff and the walls, bringing
to the very gates of the castle trading ships and fishing craft. The food-
producing farm villages lay to the south and east.

Here the Lord of Ozato now declared himself to be King of Nanzan.
Despite its territorial limitations and the poverty of its resources, his
principality was destined to endure for a century, sustained by the ambitions of seafaring merchants, the boldness and persistence of its chieftains,
and the fortunate location of the castle.

Meanwhile, far to the north of Urasoe, in the mountainous isolation of Motobu Peninsula, the Lord of Nakijin Castle likewise declared himself independent of Tamagusuku. His territories and the territories of the less important *anji* who were associated with him comprised a district far greater in extent than either the lands left to Tamagusuku or the territory controlled by the self-styled King of Nanzan. This northern principality was now called Hokuzan (Northern Mountain), a poor country, embracing many square miles of wild mountainous terrain, with few isolated valley areas and marginal fields between the steep hills and the sea. The farming and fishing settlements of Hokuzan were the most primitive on Okinawa. Land poverty and sparse settlement offset the advantages of extended territory. Even today the people of central Okinawa, who consider themselves more sophisticated, apply the term *yambara* to the people of northern Okinawa, a name which has some of the belittling connotation of the term "hillbilly" in American slang. They continue to be marked off by strong local dialect variations and by a significant number of curious everyday customs, habits, and traditions, enough to suggest the possibility of a strong differentiation in prehistoric times—perhaps even a different geographic and racial origin for the settlers who spread among these northern valleys and seaside coves.

At Nakijin itself a strong castle was erected on an isolated mountain outcropping. Back of it the land falls away steeply for a short distance, then rises toward the central mountain mass of Motobu. On the east there is a precipitous drop into a stream-filled gorge. On the north and northwest the land slopes only a little less steeply toward the shore and a harbor inlet which at one time reached to the mountain foot. Unten Harbor lies approximately five and one-half miles to the east. Enough remains of the old castle-keep and its encircling defensive walls to give evidence of a relatively high degree of engineering in that age. The lord's residence occupied the innermost and highest enclosure. Here was a small, clear spring and a park or garden area. Service buildings and residences for important vassals were at a lower level, but within the principal walls. The remains of three shrines (*uganju*) stand at the crest of this eminence, overlooking the port-inlet below and the channel between Motobu and the Iheya-Izena islands.

Much of the stonework is solid and massive, but it everywhere shows roughness and lack of fine cutting and precision fitting characteristic of castle walls and residential building in central and southern Okinawa of the same period.[1]

Thus three small rival principalities came into being on Okinawa. The territory left to Tamagusuku became known as Chuzan (Central Mountain), which enjoyed the advantages of the most developed castle towns and harbor facilities and a measure of prestige derived from its history as the established source of authority. The lords of Chuzan, Hokuzan, and Nanzan were in fact not "kings" at all, but petty barons, each with his own retainers owing him direct service, and his own estates. Each had the allegiance of *anji* or lesser chieftains whose lands lay nearby. The *anji* in turn were masters of farming and fishing villages and of a body of retainers who bore arms and owed indirect service to the lords who lived in the castles at Urasoe, Nakijin, and Ozato. The lesser *anji* had castles of their own, but these for the most part were stockaded, thatch-roofed dwellings built on defensive hilltop positions from which the nearby agricultural villages could be controlled. We do not now know what feuds and alliances over the centuries had brought into being this division of Okinawa into three units.

The defection of the lords of Hokuzan and Nanzan meant a serious loss of revenue for Tamagusuku's government. Local lords in the outer islands were quick to take advantage of Chuzan's weakened authority and ceased sending tribute to Urasoe.

Tamagusuku died in the third month of 1336, leaving a child of ten years to succeed him. Then followed difficulties which have been experienced in many courts in many parts of the world; the young king's mother meddled in government affairs, abused her privileges and position of authority, and further alienated popular support for her son.

SATTO OF CHUZAN: OKINAWA AND THE CHINESE TRIBUTE SYSTEM

About this time a man named Satto rose to the governorship of Urasoe district, in which the Chuzan court was situated. The king's authority extended very little beyond Urasoe, to embrace only Shuri, Naha, and adjacent villages. When the young king died, in 1349, Satto made himself master of Chuzan. Tradition says that he enjoyed widespread popular support. This may or may not be true; we can assume that he was a vigorous and farsighted man with a talent for effective leadership, for by the time of his death nearly a half-century later, he had brought about fundamental changes in the pattern of Okinawan life.

We now move into consideration of a period of rapid development in the economic and cultural institutions of Ryukyu, for it was in Satto's reign that Chuzan assumed a tributary relationship with China that was to endure for more than five hundred years. Okinawa itself continued to be divided into three small principalities, each competing with the others for recognition by China. The development of formal relations with Korea, China, and Japan, the introduction of Chinese administrative forms modified to meet Ryukyuan needs, and the expansion of trade as far south as the East Indies (Java, Sumatra, and Malacca) are perhaps the three most significant features of the era.

Conditions of formal subordination to China developed which were to become a basic cause of Sino-Japanese disputes in the 19th century, and to give rise to both Chinese Nationalist and Chinese Communist claims to Okinawa in the years following World War II. To understand them we must glance once again at circumstances in nearby Japan, Korea, and China insofar as they influenced the history of Okinawa.

Records of the 14th and 15th centuries suggest evidence of more favorable climatic conditions for development of seaborne trade and exploration. Within Central Asia the organization of the Mongol empire broke up, while under the Ming dynasty, which succeeded it (1368–1644), China's trade dwindled on the long caravan routes though Inner Asia. Transport by sea largely took its place in foreign commerce and was based principally upon the ports of Kwangtung and Fukien provinces. In these years the Japanese and Koreans, sharing the benefits of a milder climate and calmer seas, began to develop far-ranging maritime trade.

A shift in the distribution of power in Japan had important indirect consequence for Ryukyu. Ashikaga Takauji (a Minamoto scion) moved the seat of military government from Kamakura to the Muromachi Ward of Kyoto in the year 1336. The imperial house was divided: for years thereafter two emperors and two imperial courts existed in bitter rivalry in Japan, each supported by a coalition of quarreling feudal barons. Although the Ashikaga shoguns long maintained the fiction of shogunal supremacy at Kyoto, their scattered family estates were steadily diminished. Other great barons felt strong enough to take advantage of the weakened central administration and often defied it with impunity.

We are interested in two effects of this process. The Ashikaga shoguns maintained a show of authority by giving or withholding territorial titles among the barons long after Kyoto lost its power to enter at will upon the territories of these vassals. To create new titles was flattering, but to cancel or withhold an old title provoked hostility and trouble. Thus the Ashikaga shoguns perpetuated the ancient title Lord of the Twelve Southern Islands by conferring it upon successive generations of the Shimazu family. In this way a Shimazu claim to authority in Ryukyu was kept alive, though in fact it was exercised by neither the Ashikaga shoguns nor the lords of Satsuma themselves. The second effect of diminishing territorial authority at Kyoto was to make it impossible for the shoguns to control the activities of Japanese pirates who worked out of local ports in southern and western Japan. Loss of internal revenues which could not be collected from the land by force caused the shogunate to pay more attention to promotion of overseas trade with China.

Turning to 14th-century Korea for a moment, we discover that the peninsula was harassed by Japanese pirates from the south and east, and by raiding continental enemies from north of the Yalu River. An invasion in 1361 marked the beginning of the end for the old Koryo dynasty, and in 1382 Yi T'ae-jo established a new government.

Every nation adjacent to China was deeply disturbed by the collapse of Mongol authority at Peking and the breakup of the vast Mongol empire. Asia was in turmoil. Political refugees, ambitious generals, and dissatisfied princes sought to assert themselves. The established patterns of trade were disrupted, old commercial centers lost importance, and new ones appeared. It was a time of general confusion in Mongolia and Manchuria, Korea and Japan, Annam, Cambodia, and Siam—all the bordering states which had been for a time in the shadow of Mongol power. When the Chinese could tolerate Mongol

rule no longer, country-wide rebellions led at last to the overthrow of
the Great Khan at Peking.

For a score of years China was torn by civil wars. At last a new
central government was established under Hung Wu Ti, first emperor
of the Ming dynasty. He had been born a peasant and had become in
turn a Buddhist monk, a beggar, and a bandit leader. His organized
followers took city after city until, in 1356, he took Nanking. In 1368
he declared himself Emperor of China and began an administration
which lasted thirty years. Order was restored throughout the country.
Internal administrative reorganization made it possible for the central
government to draw on the total resources of the Chinese nation. All
bordering "barbarian states" were called upon to submit to imperial
Chinese authority. Much of Manchuria came under Ming control;
Korea acknowledged Chinese overlords; Nepal and Burma sent tribute
missions to Nanking; Chinese armies and envoys penetrated far into
Central Asia.

Hung Wu Ti sent envoys overseas to Okinawa in 1372. Satto was
called upon to acknowledge Chinese supremacy and to send representatives from Chuzan to Nanking. It is not difficult to imagine what an
impressive show the Chinese mission made. The economic life of the
tiny principality on central Okinawa depended upon uninterrupted
seaborne commerce. Formal submission meant official license to trade
with the largest and most powerful nation in the Far East. Satto seized
the opportunity. In 1374 the king sent his younger brother Taiki over
to Nanking with suitable attendants and a gift of local Okinawan products, a token of readiness to accept Chinese suzerainty in return for the
opportunities to trade. Hung Wu Ti acknowledged the gesture by conferring elaborate gifts upon the Okinawan visitors. All their expenses
were defrayed by the imperial government as long as they were within
the boundaries of the country. Upon his return to Chuzan, Taiki was
accompanied by a high-ranking imperial court official, who carried
gifts of books, textiles, ceramics, and ironware from his imperial master
to the Okinawan king. It was his duty to deliver to Satto a seal, the
symbol of investiture, and documents which in lofty and condescending
terms confirmed the Okinawan king in offices which, in point of fact,
he had assumed quite without Chinese help in 1349. Members of the

Chinese envoy's suite were permitted to carry goods to be disposed of in private trade on Okinawa.

In this way the year 1372 became one of the most important in Okinawa's history, for it marked the beginning of a formal relationship between the court of China and the Ryukyu Islands which was political, cultural, and economic in character and was destined to be maintained without interruption for five hundred years.

Within the next two decades at least nine official missions crossed to the Chinese capital from the Chuzan principality. Prince Taiki led three of them. The tribute goods delivered to China included Okinawan textiles, sulphur (from Tori-jima), and horses, which the Chinese appear to have valued highly. Each mission upon its homeward journey carried costly gifts, but we may assume that reports upon life at the Chinese court and news of Chinese activities throughout Asia were of far greater importance. The process of change which now began to take place among the Okinawans may be compared with the changes which had transformed Japanese court life eight centuries earlier, following the first official missions to China, and were to occur again in the 19th century.

In political terms the Chuzan kingdom on Okinawa took its place in Chinese records on equal basis with many other "barbarian countries" willing to send missions to the Ming court on Chinese terms. With Ryukyu, Korea, Annam, Champa (Vietnam), Cambodia, Siam, and Tibet, China's tribute relations remained formal and constant until the 19th century, but the number of tributary states recorded in Chinese annals changed according to political and economic conditions in the subject countries, or along the routes leading from them into China.

Thus, within the century following Satto's first mission we learn that more than fifty tributary states sent missions to the Chinese court over the southern sea-routes alone. Java, Malacca, Ceylon, and Burma continued with some regularity to comply with Chinese formality as "tribute states," but embassies from Persia, the Coromandel Coast of India, and other distant points were most irregular.

China's traditional claim to the Ryukyu Islands, revived briefly during and after World War II, was no greater and no less than her traditional claims to suzerainty in Korea, Annam, Burma, Cambodia, or Siam, and grew out of a Chinese world-view which admitted no other nation or people to be China's equal. The elaborate tribute system was the formalized expression of this view.

This tribute system must be understood if we are to comprehend the peculiar position into which the Ryukyu Islands now moved. Here lies the key to Okinawa's external relations after 1372. An excellent review of China's traditional attitude toward tributary states—including of course the Ryukyu kingdom—is found in an essay entitled "On the Ch'ing Tributary System" by S.Y. Teng and J.K. Fairbank, published in 1941 in the *Harvard Journal for Asiatic Studies*. Let us summarize some of the important points which affected the Ryukyu Islands after 1372 and baffled Western diplomats throughout the 19th century.[2]

The Chinese had developed a unique and extraordinary culture in the valley of the Yellow River at least thirty centuries before the Ming emperor Hung Wu condescended to recognize the existence of King Satto and his island principality. For centuries China's great state organization and complex ceremonial, her theories of government, her literature and her arts, crafts, and architecture flourished in isolation, ringed about by barbarians. Roving nomads of the steppe country were on the north and west, and the peoples to the south and east (including the coastal provinces of southern China until fairly late in history) lived in primitive simplicity. The Chinese saw gradual change take place among the barbarians as Chinese trade and Chinese armies and colonial settlers penetrated the border regions. This process continued through many centuries. In time the Chinese became aware of the existence of other great cultural centers—Rome, Persia, India—which lay far beyond the encircling barbarian peoples, but the basic attitude of superiority toward all non-Chinese people remained fixed. It was firmly held that all non-Chinese had much to learn from China; China had little or nothing to learn from them.

The Ming (and Ch'ing) dynastic records list Ryukyu among the "unconquered barbarian countries" whose embassies to China were managed by the Reception Department of the Board of Ceremonies rather than by the Department of Colonial Affairs. At one time or another this list included Korea, Japan, Small Ryukyu (i.e., Formosa), Annam, Cambodia, Siam, Champa (Vietnam), Samudra, the Western

Ocean people (Hsi-yang), Java, Pahang, Paihua, Palembang, and Brunei (in Borneo). In point of time Ryukyu was first to establish nominal tributary relations, in 1372, with Korea, Annam, and Champa recorded in the next year. Of all these only Ryukyu and Korea remained constant in the relationship throughout succeeding centuries.*

Although the Chinese emperors could recognize no equals, they were prepared to recognize that even among barbarians there were kings and princes. To them the emperor condescended to grant recognition, usually patents of authority in the form of an engraved seal bestowed upon the barbarian king at his first submission. This seal was to be handed down from generation to generation. The king's heirs were expected to notify the Chinese court of change in the succession and to ask for confirmation and investiture.

Tributary princes and kings were notified of changes in the imperial succession as well, so that envoys might bear expressions of sorrow upon the death of the Chinese ruler and congratulations and good wishes to the new emperor. Official envoys were exchanged upon the birth of an heir or the assumption of office by a crown prince or heir apparent.

It was expected that such official courtesies should also be an occasion for the exchange of gifts, selected with scrupulous regard for the importance of the event and the status of the principals. The Chinese Board of Ceremonies stipulated that gifts which were tokens of submission must be products of the tributary state. In Okinawa's case, as we shall see, an exception was made; since it had no important resources of its own, it was allowed to present rare goods from other lands as well.

Exacting rules governed the size and conduct of official missions. China met the expenses of each mission while it was within Chinese territory. Conversely, the tributary state was expected to defray expenses for Chinese missions sent to them in return. This meant that the value of China's gifts to Chuzan's envoys and the Chuzan court, and the profits from trade conducted by the envoys in their private capacity and by their companions, had to offset the cost of entertaining Chinese missions to Okinawa.

* In later years England, Holland, Spain, Portugal, the Papal States, and France were also classed as "barbarian states" paying tribute to China's emperor.

Each mission was led by a chief envoy. A vice-chief accompanied him to sustain the venture if death or serious accident befell the principal ambassador. These men were met at the point of entry into China by special officers sent from the capital to conduct them to the imperial presence. Regulations rigidly specified the number of persons who could be sent from each tributary state and how many of these could advance beyond the point of entry to the imperial capital itself.

For many years it was stipulated that the Ryukyu kingdom could send no more than three hundred persons to the border station (a port on the Fukien coast) and that of this company no more than twenty persons should proceed to the court. They went overland and by canal, escorted by a large suite of Chinese officials. The route was strictly prescribed and could not be altered.

All this provided a masterly display of imperial power and authority, well calculated to impress barbarian envoys. It is not difficult to imagine the sense of awe with which Satto's envoys first entered the enormous city gates of Nanking, penetrating massive walls which extended for twenty miles or more around glittering new Ming palaces and temples, extensive gardens, and a great complex of streets and avenues. The population of Nanking alone probably exceeded that of the entire Chuzan kingdom in that day. Once within the city, the Okinawan envoys were lodged in a special residence set aside for the entertainment of foreign ambassadors. Before participating in any of the official ceremonies and entertainments—even at the port of entry—the "barbarians" were coached in the minute details of Chinese court etiquette. Of all ceremonies the most important in Chinese eyes was the complicated ritual of the kowtow (k'o-t'ou) required of representatives of tributary rulers and of court ministers of the highest rank. This was prostration of the body nine times in succession and bowing thrice in the direction of the emperor's presence. It was established that this ritual must be performed with minute exactitude at the port of entry upon arrival and departure from the country, and again at the capital. The formula for entertainment required the presentation of gifts (local products of Ryukyu) at the Imperial Audience Hall, at the palace of the empress, and at the residence of the heir apparent. These lofty persons then caused banquets to be given in honor of the Okinawans at the tributary mission residence.

All these immensely complex tributary ceremonies were carefully rehearsed under watchful eyes, and it is recorded that the Okinawan envoys proved so accomplished that the exacting and haughty Chinese officials took special note of it in the court annals.

Not so with the Japanese. For purposes of comparison we may note that the Japanese in that day and in later years took a quite different attitude; they could not bring themselves willingly to make even this formal display of submission to the Chinese emperor and to the haughty Chinese court. In 1368 Wu Ti had sent envoys to call upon the Japanese court to submit and pay tribute, but the Chinese embassy was blocked at Hakata, in northern Kyushu, near the point at which the Mongol invaders had been repelled less than a century earlier. Memories of that continental attempt to subjugate Japan were vivid and fresh. Local barons unfriendly to the Ashikaga shoguns (Japan's nominal military rulers) barred the way and held the Chinese visitors for four years.

When at last their credentials were presented to the Shogun Yoshimitsu, he found them couched in the most condescending terms. Thirty years were allowed to elapse before the Japanese sent a reply to the Chinese message, and this was done even then more in the hope of establishing a profitable luxury trade than in any desire to submit to China. At last a merchant and a priest were ordered to proceed to the Chinese court. They were received, entertained, and then sent back to Kyoto carrying rich presents and a letter for their master, Yoshimitsu, addressed to him as King of Japan. The shogun was willing to accept it, prompted in part by his excessive personal admiration for things Chinese and in part because of his desire and great need for trade. The incident caused intense displeasure among his courtiers and among the Japanese barons. Yoshimitsu's successor, Ashikaga Yoshimochi, broke off all formal relations with the Chinese court, though trade continued intermittently. The diary of a Buddhist priest traveling in China soon thereafter records a serious clash which occurred when certain Japanese refused to be tutored in elaborate ceremonial and demanded instead that the Chinese officials get on directly with the business of trading, for which they had come.

This was rare defiance. The Chinese for the most part succeeded in maintaining observance of their rigid protocol; anyone who wished to

PLATE 1. APPROACH TO THE MAIN GATE OF THE ENKAKU-JI, SHURI. *The principal buildings of this Buddhist foundation were erected under royal patronage in 1492, following the general style and plan of the Enkaku-ji of Kamakura, in Japan. Entirely destroyed in 1945. (See page 109.)*

PLATE 2. INTERIOR COURT OF THE ENKAKU-JI. *Seen here are the main gateway, the bell, and a corner of the Worship Hall (Butsu-den). The temple complex was registered as a National Treasure of Japan.*

PLATE 3. CEREMONIAL SHUREI GATE ON THE MAIN APPROACH TO SHURI CASTLE. *This was originally erected in 1554 to display the tablet inscribed "Land of Propriety," a gift of the Chinese emperor. It was largely reconstructed in 1937 as a monument of national importance, and was totally destroyed in 1945. (See page 133.)*

PLATE 4. SONOHYAN UTAKI GATE, NEAR SHURI CASTLE. *This gate and wall were erected in 1519 to enclose the sacred hearth and grove entrusted to the care of the Chief High Priestess of Okinawa. The gateway reproduced in stone all details of a Chinese prototype of wood. Some fragments survive. (See pages 105–6.)*

PLATE 5. AN OKINAWAN PRINCE. *Fifteenth-century regulations governing court costume remained little changed until the 19th century. The flowing robe and girdle (as interpreted in this 1816 drawing by a British artist) suggest the Japanese kimono and obi, but the stylized turban, colored and patterned according to rank, came originally from the South China coast or from Malaysia. (See page 95.)*

PLATE 6. SOGEN-JI'S MAIN GATE. *Sections of this massive stonework, on the Shuri-Naha highroad near Tomari Village, have been incorporated in a postwar (1952) reconstruction. Within the gate stood a sanctuary containing tablets with the names of all the kings of Ryukyu. As a mark of respect, until 1879 it was customary for all persons, without exception, to dismount and pass on foot before this entrance. (See page 109.)*

trade with them on an official basis was expected to make a show of submission.

When Okinawan envoys withdrew from the Chinese capital they were accompanied through the countryside by high-ranking officials. At the port they rejoined the fellow countrymen who had been detained there, concluded trading affairs, and saw that the cargoes were loaded properly. After a last ceremonial leave-taking (the elaborate kowtow performed while facing in the direction of the distant imperial capital), they embarked for the hazardous homeward voyage.

In time the very life of the small Ryukyu kingdom came to depend upon successful managment of international commerce and the maintenance of a neutral trading position which kept Chinese ports open to Okinawan shipping. The meager resources of the Okinawan countryside could provide only basic foodstuffs and simple building materials. The wealth required to support the king's court and administration had to be found in overseas trading adventures.

The first missions proceeded through Ch'uang-chou, the port of entry, to Nanking, but from 1402 until 1873 they made the long and arduous journey to Peking.

If Satto's successors had observed the Ming trading regulations to the letter of the law, only one mission—three ships—should have been sent across to China every second year, with certain carefully stipulated exceptions. Official records show a fairly close adherence to this rule, but there is evidence of a vastly greater trade carried on in Chinese ports with the connivance of local officials, whose indulgence could be bought. Excuses were found, for instance, to send extra ships to greet Chinese envoys—flattering to the envoys and profitable to the Okinawans, for each ship carried goods for private trade. Sometimes extra ships were dispatched to escort an ambassador upon his return to the Fukien coast.

The recognized official tribute missions carried two kinds of goods with them, "tributary goods" and "supplementary goods." Tributary articles were forwarded to the Chinese court in the name of the King of Chuzan. After suitable presents had been distributed, the goods were offered for sale at prices stipulated by the Chinese court, usually considerably higher than prevailing market prices. On these the Okinawan government could realize a profit, and to this was added the value of the imperial gifts returned to the King of Chuzan and conferred upon the envoys according to their rank.

While all these stiff ambassadorial formalities were taking place there was usually a lively trade in progress. "Supplementary goods" included articles which the envoys and members of their suite were allowed to carry with them for private sale. Theoretically these too were limited in quantity, but in fact both kind and quantity seem to have been determined by Okinawan ability to capitalize the venture and opportunities to arrange successfully for transport to the imperial capital. Goods carried into the port of entry to be disposed of to local Chinese buyers formed the genuine base of the "tributary" system. Upon this foundation was erected the structure of elaborate ceremonial visits to the emperor's court.

Ming regulations—altered from time to time—authorized the reception of one trading mission in each two-year period. Each mission was to consist of not more than three ships and the total number of its members was not to exceed three hundred persons. When envoys went up to Peking—two representatives from the king and eighteen servants and assistants—the large company of sailors, clerks, and traders were expected to linger at the port of entry under close surveillance. There they passed the days in idleness, enjoying such diversion as merchant seamen are wont to find in a port city and its near suburbs. Gradually a permanent Okinawan settlement grew up at Ch'uang-chou. In the 19th century, Europeans noted the ceremonial coming and going of Okinawan envoys, the reception and despatch of tribute missions under the surveillance of the local superintendent of river police, and the presence of many Okinawan tombs in the nearby countryside, which bore silent witness to the age and continuity of this Okinawan community on Chinese soil.

The importance of this settlement cannot be overestimated. Here plebian Okinawans became thoroughly familiar with the daily town life of a Chinese city and with the arts and crafts developed in urban Chinese centers. Returning to Okinawa after a long sojourn abroad, the ordinary seaman, merchant, or clerk carried with him a sampling of the artifacts, the manners, customs, and beliefs of China. Nor of China only; the

Okinawans were not alone among the foreigners trading into the ports of Fukien. Arabs, Indians, Malays, and Siamese entered China for trade and diplomacy at the port of Ch'uang-chou. This was probably the great city of "Zaiton" in which Marco Polo had held an official position at one time. By 1400 the Moslem community at Ch'uang-chou had won the interest and protection of the imperial court. (The ruins of a great mosque stood there late in the 19th century, when the Moslem community continued to number in the thousands.) These were China's "foreign settlements" under the great dynastic governments, usually tolerated, sometimes patronized and protected, but always under restraint and surveillance.

Knowledge of China, which Okinawans carried back to Naha and Shuri, entered at two levels of Okinawan life—affecting the lives of the gentry and officials at the court who were both literate and influential, and the lives and daily habits of the common people living in and near Naha and Shuri. From the waterfront, Chinese influence spread slowly, penetrating in due course to the most distant villages on the outer islands, meeting, modifying, and blending with indigenous cultural elements and the elements of social and political life introduced from Japan.

The benefits of this interchange were enjoyed principally though not exclusively on the Okinawan side. The imperial court took occasion to gather intelligence of political conditions on China's borders; envoys to Chuzan prepared detailed reports and published interesting diaries and travelogues based upon their experiences in the sea islands. The choice of envoys was carefully made. Since Korea took precedence over Ryukyu at the Chinese court, envoys to Korea were chosen among men of the third rank or higher, whereas envoys to Ryukyu (and to Annam) might be of the fifth rank or below, selected from members of the Board of Ceremonies, the Imperial Censorate, or the Hanlin Academy. For the purposes of their journey, however, they enjoyed a temporary "assimilated first rank." That is to say, the Chinese emperor conferred on each envoy the robes and equipment appropriate to men of the first rank, but upon his return to Peking from Ryukyu he turned in his magnificent robes and reverted to his permanent status.

This then was the tribute system into which Satto took his people in 1372. His rival, the Lord of Nanzan, was not to be outdone by Chuzan's success in trade and diplomacy. In 1383 he too sent envoys to China to ask for recognition. This was granted, with the stipulation that Nanzan should send only one ship to China in each tribute period. The Lord of Nakijin sent envoys from Hokuzan as well, and the Chinese, with impartial benevolence toward all these sea-island barbarians, granted seals, investiture, and the right to trade.

Throughout the centuries of tributary relations there was an unresolved conflict of interest; the very proper officials at the Chinese court were never able to prevent the smuggling, bribery, and customs evasion to which the Chinese merchants at the ports, the ships' crews, and the servants in the ambassadorial suites resorted. In 1381 the Chuzan ambassador's interpreter, intercepted at the capital gates, was found to be smuggling a very large quantity of spices. The envoy from Nanzan at about this time was reprimanded for bringing in silver with which he proposed to purchase porcelains.

Okinawa in Maritime Trade Throughout Far Eastern Seas[3]

Okinawa's royal archives were burned during World War II. The oldest documents preserved there were letters exchanged between the King of Chuzan and the King of Siam, dated 1425, in which the text made clear that an extensive trade between Okinawa and Southeast Asia had long since been established. Diplomatic relations followed commercial enterprise.

Official communication with the Korean court is noted for the first time in 1389, when Okinawan envoys bore presents of rare woods, pepper, and other desirable goods from Satto to the King of Korea. These were not products indigenous to Okinawa but came from the East Indies or Indo-China.

In 1390 the local lords of Miyako and Yaeyama began to send tribute and envoys to Satto, for by this time these southerly islands in the Ryukyus had become useful way-stations for the far-ranging merchant ships passing over to the China coast from Naha, en route to ports in Southeast Asia and the Indies. Other off-lying islands such as Kumejima, just west of Okinawa, resumed the subordinate relationship to

Shuri which had been broken off in Tamagusuku's reign fifty years earlier. To the northeast the small island of Tane-ga-shima became a transfer and supply point for Okinawan shipping bound for ports in Japan proper at the head of the Inland Sea.

In 1393 a Chinese immigrant community of clerks and craftsmen was settled on Okinawa at the direction of the imperial government. The records speak of the "Thirty-six Families," but this must not be taken as a literal numeration; it was customary to speak of the "Thirty-six Families of Fukien" or of the "Hundred Names" of China in figures of speech which merely meant a widely representative group.

According to Chinese accounts, the founding of the emigrant community was a gesture of benevolent interest in the welfare of the Okinawans, an extension of imperial grace, through which the Okinawans would learn better methods of shipbuilding and the civilizing arts of Chinese administration.

The Okinawans received the immigrants with genuine and practical expressions of gratitude. The newcomers were given tax-free land upon which to establish homes near the chief anchorage for trading ships. A rice stipend was set aside for the entire community, based on the number of adult males above fourteen years of age. The Chinese were given social privileges at the Shuri court and enjoyed great prestige and special position among the common people.

There is no evidence that they were more than very ordinary folk at home on the China coast from whence they came. On Okinawa, however, they were eagerly looked to, for they were the "modern" people of their day and represented the great nation of which so many Okinawan leaders were eager to learn and from which so many admirable tales had been brought back by envoys and traders.

The immigrants undoubtedly had much to offer the Okinawans. Some of them who were literate taught the Chinese written language and assumed many official and quasi-official clerical duties required in the exchange of communications and trade with China. Some appear to have been shipwrights and navigators. Most of them were specialists in arts or crafts, which were handed down thereafter on Okinawa from father to son until the late 19th century. Papermakers, ink-makers, and writing-brush makers were numbered among them. Of the Chinese

75

customs introduced at this time and taken over into Okinawan life many became so well assimilated to local tradition and custom as to be indistinguishable today, but the origins of others remain traditionally identified with the founding of the village. Among these, for instance, is the *haryu-sen* (dragon-boat racing), a popular festival of South China now held annually in many villages throughout the Ryukyus.

The founding of Kume Village marked a great moment in Okinawan history; thenceforth into modern times the very name *Kume-mura* carried with it connotations of social prestige on the one hand (based on admiration for Chinese literary traditions and etiquette) and, on the other, connotations of alien blood. Association with Kume Village suggested distinction in scholarship and association with matters of foreign trade and diplomacy, just as residence in Shuri suggested association with government and the native Okinawan aristocracy. These distinctions persisted in local social attitudes long after real differences in accomplishment had disappeared and intermarriage had blurred the racial lines. The traditions were strong at the opening of the 20th century and linger today among the older generation. In 1907, for instance, an American visitor took his Chinese interpreter into Kume-mura upon the assurance that he would find there scholarly descendents of the "Thirty-six Families." He did find old men proudly claiming Kume-mura Chinese descent, but otherwise they were indistinguishable from other Okinawans in literary accomplishments, physical characteristics, or social life.[4] In 1954 a young Okinawan was heard to remark, "My cousin is from Kume-mura, but he doesn't look Chinese," indicating that tradition and *expectation* of differences has so long outlived the fact of distinction.

Did the founding of this Chinese settlement on Okinawa reflect a larger policy on the part of the Chinese government? Although Chinese emigrant communities were to be found throughout Southeast Asia and the Indies, the Chinese themselves were not notably active as seafarers. There was a coastal trade in Chinese junks, but adventurous open-ocean voyaging over long distances was not common, and the government had no traditional policy in support of maritime activity. China was essentially a land power, with long-established traditions of overland continental trade. Seaborne trade was brought to China's ports in foreign ships. The Annamese, the Koreans, the Japanese, and the Okinawans were the only neighboring people on the sea frontiers who were conversant with the Chinese language. The collapse of Mongol power in China created turmoil in the vast areas which the khans had ruled to the westward from Karakorum through Samarkand and beyond, and closed the ancient trade routes across Inner Asia. Though Chinese generals pushed westward through the great desert as far as the oasis of Hami, they were unable to carry Ming authority into the non-Chinese regions beyond. Tamurlane was creating a new empire in that quarter and planning the reconquest of China by the Mongol hordes when death ended his career in 1405.

Blocked on the continental west then, the Ming leaders turned to the sea. The timing and the circumstances surrounding the founding of the emigrant community and trading base on offshore Okinawa suggest that this was only a small part of a carefully calculated policy. In the Okinawans the Chinese found excellent middlemen for trade with Japan, Korea, Champa and Khmer, Siam, and Java. However condescending the Chinese showed themselves to be toward these tributary barbarians, it is possible that they recognized in Satto's envoys, and in Satto himself, qualities to exploit in China's interests. Envoys from the Chinese court sent to Okinawa were instructed to report on conditions within the island.

In 1393 the emigrant Chinese community was established at the offshore trading port of Naha, and ten years later the Chinese admirals Ma Pin and Ch'eng Ho began that series of eight extraordinary maritime expeditions which carried Chinese arms and Chinese merchants into the Indian Ocean and the Red Sea. These undertakings involved scores of ships and thousands of men, an immense effort to establish China in maritime trade and to extend Chinese suzerainty throughout South Asia. The ambitious policy continued in effect for a quarter-century. How many years were spent in preparation, and how mercantile interests won the necessary official support at court we do not know. The effort was unique in the long range of Chinese history. We have no evidence to link the establishment of Kume-mura on Okinawa with the policies which flowered in this dramatic undertaking, but it is safe to assume that the interest which approved the sponsorship of one is reflected in the other, and that both were products of a new and short-lived official interest in the promotion of maritime trade.[5]

There can be no doubt that Okinawan sailors, merchants, and diplomats passing back and forth between Naha and Fukien ports were well acquainted with these vast Chinese maritime adventures. It is not impossible that Okinawans were among the crews who manned the expeditions' ships, for they were proved seamen, and many were acquainted with the ports of Southeast Asia, Java, and Sumatra.

These grandiose efforts to establish Chinese trade in the Indies and the Indian Ocean collapsed; the last expedition returned to its home port in 1430, and nothing more is heard of such ventures. By contrast, the little kingdom of Chuzan increased its trade under official direction all along the western sea frontiers. Okinawa maintained its economic life—its very existence—on this far-flung commerce through the succeeding two hundred years.

In accepting formal tributary relationship, Satto brought the principality of Chuzan under direct Chinese cultural influence and laid foundations upon which the Okinawans thereafter were to build a modest but prosperous national life. The Chinese did not need to make a show of arms to secure the relationship; so long as the Okinawans fulfilled ceremonial obligations required to regularize their trade, China made no attempt to interfere in any way with Chuzan's internal administration. It was a highly satisfactory relationship for the island people; it was implied that China would protect them; they received the benefits of a flourishing trade and the gifts of a highly developed civilization. They were (despite all this) free to govern themselves as they wished. Although the quantity and frequency of trade under such a political relationship varied from period to period, and although China failed notably to come to Okinawa's aid in time of crisis, the formal bonds between China and Chuzan endured until 1872.

GROWTH AND CHANGE ON OKINAWA

A few pages back we took note that Satto sent his younger brother Taiki to the Ming court in 1372 and that it became customary thereafter to send promising youths of good family to the Chinese capital to enroll in the school for foreign students (the Kuo Tzu Chien or Kokushi-kan). Through this institution, maintained by the government as a "cultural affairs agency" in the service of foreign policy, the Chinese hoped to influence governments and peoples in the tributary states and to ease the problems of diplomacy. Certainly no single instrument served its purpose so well as this in strengthening ties between the imperial court in China and the small trading kingdom in the Eastern Seas.[6]

Students selected for "national scholarships" came at first from the king's household and the families of his chief ministers and territorial lords. In later years sons of the Kume Village immigrants were eligible for appointment as well, and all were selected on the basis of individual capacity to master the Chinese language. They left Naha with the tribute envoys, making the arduous and hazardous trip to Nanking or Peking as members of the official party. They remained at school in the Chinese capital at the expense of the Chinese government for two or three years, or until such time as they were allowed to return with a subsequent tribute mission.

Students abroad were expected to apply themselves to a study of the classics—history, ethics, poetry—and to cultivate the arts of polite intercourse so highly prized by the Chinese. This they did with such distinction that a Chinese emperor in later years conferred upon the Okinawan king a tablet inscribed to "The Land of Propriety" in recognition of the constancy and perfection of formal relations between the empire and the island kingdom.

To learn the classics and the precedents of Chinese history was to learn the language of diplomacy and of the Chinese bureaucratic system. Certainly there were no courses in "public administration" or in-service training programs comparable to the "national leaders" programs with which we have become familiar since World War II, but the Okinawan student at Nanking or Peking was in a position to observe something of the administrative skills and organization of the Chinese, and to become acquainted with the wide range of interests to which officers of state were expected to address themselves.

It can be presumed that while living on a government stipend in government quarters at the Chinese capital, the Okinawan students, few in number and strangers in the crowded cities, attracted very little attention and were from time to time assailed by all the pangs of homesickness which assault the Okinawan student today who is sent abroad to study in New York, Chicago, and the cities and towns of the American Middle West.

When these young men returned home to Okinawa, however, they formed an elite; high offices in government were open to them; they had prestige gained from foreign travel and firsthand knowledge of the great continental power upon which the Okinawan economy grew steadily to depend. Among themselves there was bound to be developed a strong sense of comradeship and common interest.

Prime importance lay in their role as purveyors of Chinese ideas and Chinese ways of doing things, and as agents who could cultivate trading relations with the Chinese, to Okinawa's great advantage.

In his declining years Satto strengthened the new relationship with China by selecting an Okinawan well known to the Ming court to receive the title of O-sho (King's Assistant). Personal rule was not yet a thing of the past on Okinawa, but this may be said to have fore-shadowed its end and the substitution of a system of king's ministers who could govern in the king's name. Iratu, the man appointed to this important new post, had been five times envoy to the Ming court.

Satto died in 1395 at the ripe age of seventy-five. His eldest son and heir, Bunei, continued the development of commercial ties with China. Envoys and students went to Nanking to announce Satto's death and to seek confirmation of Bunei's accession, and in 1396 the Shuri government built special headquarters at Naha for Chinese diplomatic and commercial missions. Here a suitable residence (the Tenshi-kan) was constructed in which to conduct ceremonial receptions and entertainments for Chinese envoys of high rank. The mansion and its gardens rivaled the king's residence in size and quality. Nearby, a trading center (the oyamise) provided for entertainment and business transactions with the foreign merchants. Special warehouses were established to handle incoming and outgoing trading goods. There is some evidence that about this time a Korean community developed near the anchorage at Tomari and the Chinese immigrant village, and it is probable that merchants and seamen from tropical Asia were seen frequently in the streets and alleyways of Naha. A Japanese priest had long since built a temple on the Nami-no-ue headland, which dominated both Tomari and the Naha harbor-inlet. This was the Gokoku-ji, founded with royal patronage in 1367 and destined to play a curious role in the opening of Okinawa to the Western world nearly five hundred years later. The number of Japanese immigrant settlers on Okinawa was growing.

All three Okinawan principalities sent missions to Korea in 1397, but only Chuzan appears to have established formal relations with the court of the Ashikaga shoguns at Kyoto (1403). In 1409 an official embassy was dispatched to Siam. Traders had long since established relations with Sumatra and Java far to the south. This was a time of great development for the Okinawans, for they were now in a position to draw upon neighbors in periods of great creative cultural activity. A new dynasty in Korea (founded in 1392) was moving into a period of brilliant achievement; while the administration was being organized according to proper Confucian principles, a new capital city (Seoul) was built, a phonetic alphabet was perfected, a movable metal type font was developed, encyclopedias and histories were being written, and ceramic techniques of a high order were perfected. Bunei and his successors sent missions up to Seoul to study as well as to trade, and it is to Korea that Okinawa owed certain developments in Buddhism. Buddhist texts, ceremonies, and ritual furniture were introduced, and possibly some Korean influence was felt in architecture. As a gesture of friendliness, the King of Chuzan ordered that shipwrecked or stranded Koreans should be taken back to Korea, including those who escaped servitude under the Japanese pirates roving in adjacent seas.

It is said that certain (Japanese) Shinto practices were introduced to the Southern Islands about this time and became popular. Certainly Shinto rituals and attitudes toward the worship of natural forces, benevolent and otherwise, had much to recommend them to the common villagers in Okinawa. These were an unphilosophic people, not given naturally to the intellectual effort which a proper study of Buddhist thought demands. Shinto, in its Japanese forms and practices, was closely akin to indigenous Okinawan beliefs, but it offered a more elaborate ritual plus a body of legends and a catalogue of deities which could easily be added to the local pantheon.

With examples of Japan, Korea, and China now so near at hand, with the elaboration of government offices, and with the spread of literacy at the court, it is not surprising to discover that the Ryukyuan leaders ordered the preparation of their own royal annals. The first volume of a *Treasury of the Royal Succession* (*Rekidai Hoan*) was issued in 1403. This series of records, a most important source for the study of Okinawan tradition, was maintained faithfully until 1619.

Meanwhile, political changes were underway that were to alter the succession at Chuzan, unify Okinawa again, and make the Ryukyu Islands known throughout maritime Asia as a profitable trading base.

The last decades of Satto's rule had brought greatly increased prosperity and commercial activity to Naha. This in turn intensified the sense of rivalry felt by the princes at Hokuzan and Nanzan. In 1396 and 1397 all three principalities sent tribute and students to the Ming court, vying with one another for attention and trade.

The old Lord of Hokuzan expired a few months after Satto's death. Haniji, his heir, immediately petitioned China for recognition as lord of all of Okinawa. Envoys were sent to Korea to announce his succession. The situation on Okinawa was tense with rivalry, heightened to the breaking point in 1398 by the death of the Lord of Nanzan, whose brother Yafuso seized power amidst great confusion at the Nanzan court. He too immediately sent envoys to ask for confirmation by the Chinese emperor.

Okinawa was thrown into turmoil. Succession disputes blazed up at all the castle courts. Chuzan's trading relations with China, so carefully nurtured by Satto, were threatened. China in the recent past had recognized one prince on Okinawa; now three were clamoring simultaneously for support and recognition.

To the Okinawan princes this was vital; recognition meant improved trading positions in Chinese ports and elsewhere in southern Asia, where much business was done through the established overseas Chinese communities. The strength of each principality lay in foreign trade, not in local resources. At Nanking decisions were put off. Bunei's petition lay neglected for eleven years, for China itself was torn with succession quarrels and rebellion.

CHAPTER THREE

THE GREAT DAYS OF CHUZAN

1398–1573

HASHI AND THE "FIRST SHO DYNASTY"

China was shaken by succession quarrels on a vast scale. The aged Emperor Hung Wu died in 1398, leaving the throne to a young grandson Hui Ti, who was soon driven from Peking by an uncle. It was believed that he was dead, though no one knew where the boy-emperor had died or by what hand. Thirty-six years later he was discovered living the life of an obscure monk in a Buddhist monastery.

The usurper, known in history as the Emperor Yung Lo, established himself as one of the greatest rulers China has ever known, dedicating himself to the extension of Chinese dominion on all frontiers. He addressed himself at once to the problem of tributary states adjacent to his empire. In the second year of his reign (1406) envoys were sent to Okinawa to confirm Satto's heir Bunei in the title King of Chuzan.

For Bunei this was almost too late. Satto's death had loosened ties which bound the territorial lords, the *anji*, to the prince at Chuzan Castle. One of the younger *anji*, named Hashi, had begun to rise to prominence, first as an able, well-liked administrator within his own estates, and then as leader of a minor rebellion which brought about the downfall of the lord of Azato district, adjacent to Bunei's castle at Urasoe.

This took place in 1402, and thus matters rested for five years. History is discreetly silent concerning intrigues and rivalries about the court, but in 1407—the year following Bunei's recognition as King of Chuzan —Hashi led a wider rebellion within the principality, drove Bunei from Urasoe, and made himself King of Chuzan. The deposed prince vanished, leaving not a trace. Tradition says that no one knew where he died,

83

but it is safe to assume that if he did not escape to some distant island hiding place, he suffered death at the hands of Hashi's partisans. Okinawans in later years may have adapted Hui Ti's story to their need to cover up a case of regicide.

Hashi's career marks one of the high points in Okinawan history. The thorough reorganization of administration on Okinawa and the great expansion of trade under his direction is represented in conventional Japanese histories as a more or less autonomous and logical development of Okinawan affairs. There is ample reason to believe, however, that it reflected in large degree creative forces then stirring in contemporary China. Hashi moved with the times.

Within the next twenty years the Emperor Yung Lo extended Chinese rule into Annam and received tribute and trading missions from Cambodia, Siam, Malacca, Java, Sumatra, Borneo, Luzon, and Ceylon. Ch'eng Ho's expeditions reached Bengal, South India, and ports in Arabia; they may also have touched Africa.

Yung Lo's envoys to Okinawa had just time enough to return to the Chinese capital with a report on Bunei's investiture when Hashi's envoys followed them with news of Bunei's downfall and Hashi's assumption of authority. China's fundamental indifference to the internal affairs of tributary states made it possible for the court at Nanking to accept this swift change without objection. Hashi, on his part, did two things which could be well calculated to please the Chinese sense of propriety and to flatter the top-lofty pride of court officials. He did not assume royal authority for himself, but proclaimed his father King of Chuzan, and he began a wide reorganization of the administration on Chinese patterns.

Envoys went to Peking in 1407 and again in 1408, when at last the coveted patents of investiture were granted. Essentials of Chinese court hierarchy, rank, badges of honor, and boards of administrative supervision were adapted by Hashi on a suitable scale, severely modified, of course, to meet conditions on Okinawa. (The entire area of the Chuzan principality, it must be remembered, was scarcely greater than the area encompassed by Peking's vast city walls and adjacent parks.) The Okinawans adopted Chinese ways quite voluntarily, and by Chinese standards they became "civilized." We must assume that Hashi was able to introduce such changes because he had about him men who had been sent abroad to study after 1372 and had returned from China full of prestige and eager to "modernize" Okinawa.

Under Hashi's direction Shuri Castle was embellished and enlarged as the seat of government for Chuzan. Within the principality distance markers were set out on roads leading from Shuri into the countryside. Naha expanded to accommodate growing trade, and was opened to ships of all nationalities in the Eastern Seas.

Chuzan's rivals were not idle. Although they did not enjoy the natural advantage which the superior Naha and Tomari anchorages could provide, they were eager to trade. Taromai, Lord of Nanzan, won Chinese investiture (in effect a license to trade) in 1415, but his small castle-court was weakened by continuing disputes among his vassals.

The Lord of Hokuzan was harassed by quarrels and defection among his subordinates. Hokuzan offered Chuzan little competition in politics, commerce, or culture, but Nakijin Castle on the Motobu Peninsula was a persistent military threat to Hashi. Surviving records indicate that in the 14th century only nine Hokuzan missions made the long journey to China, whereas nineteen from Nanzan and fifty-two from Chuzan crossed to the continent in the same period. No Hokuzan students ventured over to study at the Chinese capital, and trade was limited to junk traffic in the small inlet below the castle walls.

Hashi shrewdly took advantage of opportunity when three of the northern *anji* came over to his side. Motobu Peninsula was overrun in a short campaign, Nakijin Castle was reduced, and after a fierce defensive action the Lord of Hokuzan and his principal retainers committed suicide.

Today the Hokuzan tradition has faded; the tombs of the Hundred Faithful Retainers (*Momojana*) are pointed out in a cave on the bluffs back of Unten Harbor; and in the countryside a few families cherish heirlooms handed down from the Nakijin period.

The northern principality had been maintained through ninety-one years. Grudgingly, the Hokuzan people submitted to the superior organization of men and resources which Shuri could bring to bear in the rough northern countryside. In 1422 Hashi appointed his younger brother Warden of Hokuzan to ensure order in that quarter, and for many years thereafter special garrisons had to be stationed on Motobu.

Nanzan—almost within sight of Shuri Castle on the southern borders of Chuzan—offered Hashi greater political and commercial competition, but when a bitter succession dispute arose among Taromai's heirs, Hashi moved swiftly to seize control. In 1429 Okinawa was unified; henceforth "Chuzan" meant all of Okinawa, but the old divisions were perpetuated in new administrative names and offices, and the terms "Kunigami," "Nakagami," and "Shimojiri" in the 20th century preserve a lingering memory of the three ancient principalities.

Now at last all of Okinawa's meager resources could be used to support the castle town at Shuri and the settlements below at Naha port and Tomari roadstead. The countryside produced foodstuffs, fuel, and the ordinary artifacts required in daily use. The village people lived at the barest subsistence level. There was no significant accumulation of surpluses in the outlying settlements or within individual households.

Standards of living for the *anji* were very little better than for the poorest peasant and fisherman whose windowless thatched hut stood at a sheltered spot on his lands. The soil was poor, the forest cover thin, and the water supply often insufficient. There was no significant supply of metals. This general poverty of natural resources fostered a readiness—born of dire necessity—to pool community resources in skills and manpower, and to this may be attributed an extraordinary sense of community solidarity, an Okinawan tradition of mutual aid and of mutual obligations which must be met within the family and community.

Local government rested with the *anji*, of whose origin we know little. We can surmise that they descended from chieftains whose prowess and skill in leadership in some prehistoric day had established ownership over tracts of land when the islands were first penetrated and thinly settled. By the time Hashi appeared, local government was in fact merely the personal rule of an *anji* within his estates, while he in turn was responsible to one of the princes at Hokuzan, Nanzan, or Chuzan. The common people farmed and fished, paid over their taxes in kind to the *anji*, and provided the labor and services required of them.

Hashi's success in forcing all the *anji* to look to Shuri, and his skill in

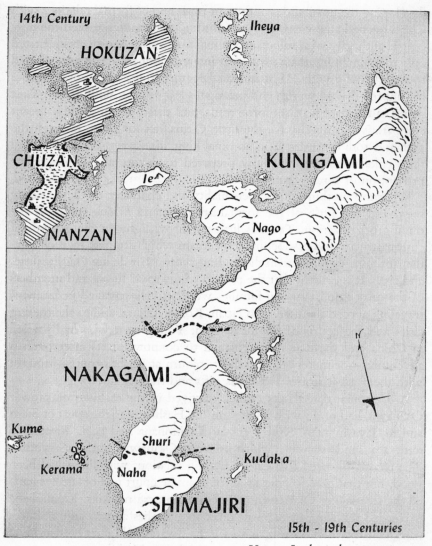

FIG. 5. MAP: BOUNDARIES ON OKINAWA. Upper: *In the 14th century.*
Lower: *In the 15th–19th centuries.*

developing the possibilities of foreign trade and of formal relations with China opened a new era. Some of the *anji* may have accepted the new central authority with reluctance, remaining for the most part interested only in maintaining their own local interests, but for those who elected to work closely with Hashi and his liegemen there were opportunities for unprecedented wealth and prestige. Coöperation with Shuri meant shares in the profits of seaborne trade, and these, accumulating, meant comparative prosperity for the little Okinawan kingdom through the 15th and 16th centuries. The nominal king, his strong son (Hashi), and their chief retainers were now prepared to devote all energies to the promotion of foreign commerce.

We know nothing of the personality and character of these leading men, and too little of the formal arrangements which sustained the trading organization. There is little to throw light on the growth of customary law and of documentary forms which secured to each participant his rightful share in the trading ventures or defined his liabilities and risks. It is evident that the princes of the royal house and members of the most important *anji* families were actively engaged in business, traveling abroad themselves to Japan, Korea, China, and to the trading cities and the courts of Southeast Asia. Young men who had studied in China and the *anji* who returned to country estates after oversea adventures—or merely from a short sojourn at Hashi's court—brought with them great stories as well as gifts and trading goods.

A document dated 1425, which survived in the archives of prewar Okinawa, had to do with a state mission Hashi sent to the court of Siam and to Java in 1419. Shuri's envoy Kakinohana had been directed to settle a misunderstanding which impeded Okinawan trade at Ayuthia. The records showed that earlier trading relations with Siam had been good, but that greedy officials at the Siamese court had of late prevented the free sale of Okinawan cargoes on Siamese markets. Kakinohana persuaded the King of Siam to relax monopolies and to allow Shuri's merchant-mariners once again to sell their wares to highest bidders in an open market. The King of Siam responded to Hashi's respresentations by dispatching a royal mission to exchange courtesies with the Shuri court. The Siamese traveled on Okinawan ships, and we can imagine with what excitement and pleasure the people of Naha and Shuri welcomed the event. On another occasion an Okinawan ship was burned while at anchor in Siamese waters, whereupon the King of Siam dispatched one of his own ships to carry the distressed Okinawans back to the Ryukyu Islands.

Shuri's ties with China were growing stronger, and it is evident that the Chinese court was well aware of the vitality and value of the trading position which the Okinawans were establishing for themselves.

Hashi's father, the nominal king, fell ill and died in 1421. At last Hashi assumed the royal title, which matched the powers he had long held. After a year's mourning he petitioned the Chinese court for recognition and investiture. The writ was delivered at Shuri in due course.

Now followed a test of Okinawan diplomacy measured by the exacting standards of Chinese formality. Hashi's trusted and experienced ambassador Kakinohana was ordered to proceed to Peking to bear thankful acknowledgment of investiture. But this was not all; within the year the great Emperor Yung Lo had died, and so too had his successor Hung Hsi. Kakinohana therefore was required to discharge four obligations, each of which called for complicated and tedious ritual. He had first to convey Hashi's own expression of gratitude, then to express the official distress and sorrow appropriate to the demise of two Chinese emperors, and finally to congratulate the new emperor, the boy Hsuan Tê.

Apparently the mission was a marked success; the pleased Chinese officials raised the rank of Peking's ambassadors who should go thereafter to the court of Chuzan, and upon Hashi the emperor conferred the family name Sho (pronounced Hsiang in Chinese). A new title *Liu Ch'iu Wang* (King of Ryukyu) was recorded in the annals to recognize Hashi's success in bringing the three principalities under one ruler. To underscore these marks of high esteem the Chinese court sent over to Hashi a great lacquered tablet upon which was inscribed the characters for *Chuzan*, together with rich gifts of lacquer and embroidered ceremonial robes.[1]

Hashi proudly caused a handsome gate to be erected at the approach to Shuri Castle, and there, in 1428, the Chuzan Tablet was installed for all to see, and there it remained until the 20th century.

In order to remind his officers and vassals that Chuzan's prosperity rested entirely upon successful management and development of sea-borne trade, the king caused a great bell to be cast and hung in the audience chamber at Shuri Castle. Upon it were inscribed these words: "Ships are means of communication with all nations; the country is full of rare products and precious treasures."

In the next two hundred years Okinawa could be likened to the city-states across the world in Europe which were flourishing then in maritime trade devoted in large part to the import and transshipment of exotic wares from the countries of Asia and Africa—spices, rare woods, jewels, textiles, and the curious substances needed by the alchemist and the pill-maker. The Shuri-Naha urban complex was supported by profitable traffic in luxury goods purchased in the Indies and the markets of Southeast Asia and moved through Naha for distribution to the ports of China, Korea, and Japan. Chuzan did not achieve the wealth of Genoa, the beauty of Venice, or the power of Lisbon, but the essential pattern of economic life was much the same.

It is interesting to recall that for nearly half a century Sho Hashi in Okinawa and the Portuguese Prince Henry the Navigator were con-temporaries, dedicated to the improvement and expansion of ex-ploration and commerce on the high seas as a means to offset poverty and limited territory at home. Prince Henry drew on the sciences of the burgeoning Renaissance, and the Portuguese were fired with quarrelsome missionary zeal, loving a good fight and justifying enor-mities of violence in the name of Christ. Sho Hashi had no such intel-lectual force as the Renaissance behind him (though he may have been stimulated by the short-lived Ming interest in exploration far afield); the Okinawans had no zealots in their midst with burning faith to propagate by fire and sword. They shunned quarrels; they could afford no wars, for they had no strength in manpower and no surpluses to be spent on arms. From this position of weakness they had perforce to learn accommodation, and as we shall see, the first encounter with the Portuguese (at Malacca, 1511) would prove a turning point in Oki-nawan history.

Sho Hashi knew nothing of Europe, but we can assume that he knew vaguely of India and possibly of Arabia, for his officers and men fre-quented ports on the China coast and the markets of Southeast Asia, which had flourishing communities of Arab traders. There is evidence that Okinawan goods passed into Arab hands and on into the ports and markets far to the west. References to the Ryukyu kingdom—or at least to its merchants and their goods—can be found in Arabic texts when Moslem rulers held dominion as far west as Spain and were pushing into India and the Indies, and when there was a flow of trade and of information throughout the Moslem world.[2]

The seas about Okinawa were no longer barriers but highways over which goods were brought to warehouses at Naha, and from there transshipped. Trading vessels usually set out from Naha by twos and threes together, under command of an agent commissioned by the king. This responsibility was an honor accepted by princes and high officers of the court. As many as three hundred persons were sometimes in the company, subject to the king's agent and the ships' captains.

Five months were usually required to make the journey to the Indies; the fleet left in the autumn to cross by way of Miyako and Yaeyama to the China coast, then moved southward from port to port, keeping within sight of distant headlands and offshore islands. With favorable winds the outward voyage to Malacca or Sumatra required about fifty days. After making the first call, the junks put in at other ports and islands in Southeast Asia, picking up and discharging cargo as opportunity warranted until time to turn back and ride the winds toward Naha at the end of spring. The summer months were usually spent at home port during the season of great storms in the China Seas.

Much of the trading and exchange was conducted through expatriate Chinese settled, then as now, in the southern ports of Asia and the Indies. For this reason Chinese interpreters went along on the Okinawan ships. There is some reason to believe that Koreans, too, made these long voyages out of Naha, returning to summer in the Korean settlement near Tomari and Naha.

Okinawa's commerce with the Indies flourished through two centuries, but shifted from port to port with the changing political tides in the kingdoms to the south. Nothing is known in detail of the trade before the 15th century, but between 1432 and 1570 at least forty-four official embassies were dispatched to Annam, Siam, Patani, Malacca, and the small kingdoms on Java. There is scant record of the actual organization and administration of trade from Naha, and no one knows how many unofficial or private trading ventures set out annually for the southern seas.

Some reached Luzon and Borneo, where small Indian and Malayan settlements stood at the water's edge between jungle and sea. Okinawan relations with these islands—never important—had been broken off before the European powers reached their shores.

The Naha archives lost in 1945 held records of at least fifty-eight trading missions to Siam over a period of 146 years, and Japanese scholars who have made careful study of them estimate that at least a hundred other official voyages may have been made for which no records now exist. Formal relations with Java appear to have been established in 1430 and to have continued for approximately one hundred years, first with eastern and then with western Java (Sunda) as political conditions dictated within that war-torn island. Relations with Sumatra did not long persist; a ship which put in at Palembang in 1426 returned to Naha in the next year with a Sumatran envoy aboard. Shuri returned the courtesy with the customary gifts, documents, and trading articles, carried by a mission which lingered at Sumatra for a full ten months. There were later exchanges, but the last for which records survived returned to Naha in 1440.

Trade with Patani on the east coast of Malaya became increasingly important as that port grew large with refugees crowding in from war-torn Java and Malacca. This was the time when the Hindu states of Java were falling before the Moslem conquest. Records of twelve Okinawan missions survived; the last of these touched at Patani in 1541; but it is presumed that many more had taken place. The Naha archives contained documents relating to trade with Malacca in 1463, but these in turn referred to earlier ventures into the straits which were the gateway to the Indian Ocean. Here the Okinawans were at the crossroads of Southeast Asian commerce. Malacca itself had only recently assumed prominence and importance through the influx of refugees from Java and from areas being pressed by the Javan kingdoms. Something is known of twenty Okinawan missions at Malacca, four of which ended in shipwreck.

To the last Okinawan venture at Malacca we will turn our attention on a later page, for the traders found a Portuguese fleet at anchor in the harbor; Malacca was a burned and ravaged settlement; and this encounter with Europeans in 1511 portended disaster of another kind at Shuri.

The Chinese, meanwhile, had recognized in fact the importance of Okinawan trade to them as a source of coveted luxury goods, for despite official attitudes of disdain for foreign commerce and haughty pretense of indifference to mercantile affairs on the part of the literati, Chinese officials did not forego opportunities to enrich themselves and their kinfolk. The elaboration of trading regulations was a supreme art among them. Laws and regulations were put upon the books not so much to be observed as to be circumvented by an appropriate contribution to officials all along the way.

In 1439 a special Ryukyuan trading depot with a permanent staff in residence was established at Ch'uang-chou in Fukien Province, creating a port of entry to which Ryukyuan trade must be confined and through which it was channeled to Peking. These facilities included warehouses, reception halls, and a residential area for Okinawans associated with trade and the diplomatic missions. The depot remained in continuous use for 436 years thereafter, or until 1875, when the last cargo was brought in from Naha. Here Okinawan students came to serve as clerks and to study China's language and its institutions, and it is to this area that we must look for prototypes in artifacts and architecture, agricultural techniques and social patterns which distinguished the old Ryukyu tradition from the Japanese. Okinawa's distinctive tombs and bridges, foodstuffs and textiles, recreations and deportment owe much to the lessons learned here at Ch'uang-chou in Fukien.

Ships putting in at Naha after a voyage to the south, or coming from China or Japan or Korea, provided occasions of holiday interest and excitement in the town. Returning seamen told of adventures on the high seas and in distant ports. Curios and fine objects brought back for the king's court went up to Shuri under the watchful eyes of port officers and the ship's commandant. The chief of mission and the vice-chief, together with the principal officers, made reports, delivered documents, and escorted distinguished visitors to the castle on the hill. Goods for transshipment were off-loaded to be stored near the quay until the next fleet was ready to set out. Objects too damaged for the royal palace or for shipment onward became available for barter and trade among the seamen and their friends.

Who could tell what strange birds, plants, or animals might be brought ashore, what new musical instruments might be among the souvenirs, or what colorful bales and bolts of cloth might be disclosed in the cargo? We read of a shipment of parrots and peacocks sent up to the King of Korea, who in time sent back in exchange a great bronze bell. Monkeys and bright-plumaged chickens were brought in. Earthenware from the south and glazed ceramics from the China coast were imported in quantity, some to be used in Okinawa and some to be sent on to Kyoto, where it was in great vogue among the tea-masters at the shogun's court. Books and ceramics came from Korea; fine screens and lacquerware passed through the Naha warehouses en route to Chinese buyers, and heavy Chinese brocades were imported in exchange. Japanese swords, lacquerware, fans, folding screens, and some textiles were destined for China and the southern ports. From China to Japan by way of Naha went ceramics, fine textiles, medicinal herbs, and minted coins especially prized at Kyoto. To China, Japan, and Korea the ships from Okinawa carried rare woods (such as the dyewood known as *sappan*), pepper and other spices, incense, rhinoceros horn (prized as an aphrodisiac), iron, tin, ivory, sugar, and curious artifacts picked up here and there in the ports of Southeast Asia.

This richness and variety of material things stood in strong contrast with the poverty of native Okinawan goods. It is not surprising therefore to discover that local craftsmen aspired to produce fine wares and that they were encouraged by the Shuri court. The textile industry began to develop high specialization. Weaving and dyeing of fine gauzes of a Chinese type became an important industry in many homes. Using the fibers of a large plantain—a banana plant—an extremely fine textile was produced which is known today as *basa*, peculiarly suited to the needs of a people dwelling in hot and humid climates.

A second fabric, known in Malay as *ikat* and in Japan and Okinawa as *kasuri*, was imported from the Indies. The technique is said to have had its origins in India, and from Okinawa this special craft was transmitted to the Japanese. The threads are dyed appropriately before the weaving begins, and each thread is selected individually and applied to the loom with painstaking care to bring out a desired design and pattern. Okinawan skills brought this to the highest degree of perfection. Tie-and-dye methods and stencil dyeing were likewise introduced from Java and Sumatra, modified to meet local requirements and applied to Okinawan fabrics.

The use of bright colors and large patterns of a distinctive type developed in Okinawa under the influence of imports from the southern islands and from there too came the distinctive turbans or *hachimaki* which the Okinawan gentry used until modern times. (The keen-eyed Captain Broughton, who knew South Asia well, in 1797 noted that the Okinawan coiffure and turbans were "in the Malay style.")

A man's rank was indicated by the quality of the cloth, the color and applied design, and the manner of folding and winding this unique headgear. Something of the sort, of southern origin, may have been in use from early times and was now adapted at the king's command to conform to the Chinese idea of "cap-rank." Headdress thus became the material symbol of status in the court hierarchy, and hence was governed by most rigid rules. For the Okinawans the *hachimaki* was the equivalent of the crowns and coronets of English princes, dukes, earls, and barons.

The *hachimaki* was reserved for the higher officers at court, but almost all males wore their hair drawn up into a small topknot through which they thrust one or more long pins. The style and quality of these pins (called *kanzashi*) proclaimed the status of the wearer. The higher aristocracy wore pins of chased and inlaid gold; silver sufficed for the intermediate ranks; while plain brass or copper or wood were the lot of the lower classes.

The topknot was sometimes worn off-center at a jaunty angle; this can still be seen occasionally among the country women of Okinawa. Tradition ascribes this quaint custom to the late 15th century, alleging that the king of that period (Sho En) had an unsightly wen on the side of his head, which he concealed under his topknot, and that his faithful subjects adopted the mode in consequence. However, the primitive Yami who live south of the Ryukyus on Botel Tobago also wear the hair in this fashion and a similar style may be seen in use in Siam, which suggests that the custom may have had a much earlier origin and a wider use.

Pictures of a somewhat later date than Hashi's reign show that the kings and princes of the royal house wore costumes of Ming Chinese style for high ceremonial occasions. These were made of imported Chinese textiles cut to conform with local Okinawan styles. Straw sandals sufficed for the aristocrats; the common people wore no footgear. There is reason to believe that in Hashi's day the princes, the *anji*, and their chief retainers each wore two swords at the side, in the Japanese manner.

Court ceremonial followed stiffly formal Chinese precedents adapted in scale to Okinawan needs; among the *anji* and the country people, however, there was an easy and natural exchange of courtesies.

The social and emotional life of Okinawans, both in Sho Hashi's time and after, centered in music and poetry, in picnicking and in alfresco dancing. Merchants coming back from the Indies, Malaya, and the China coast brought in stringed instruments and introduced dance forms, which the Okinawans modified and developed to give expression to their own songs and poems. In later centuries (after 1600) much of this passed on northward into Japan.

No occasion was overlooked which might provide an excuse for dancing. Festivals marked each change of seasons; every family gathering, happy or sad, became an occasion for impromptu performance. Arrivals and departures were of special interest among an island people whose very livelihood depended upon the enforced separations and dangers of maritime activity. Traditions of complex refinement clustered about leave-taking and welcome. Dancing and feasting preceded the days of departure. Special emblems were raised on poles before the house from which a traveler was to be absent for some time. As ships left the safety of home anchorage, friends of the crew and family members climbed to open clearings on nearby headlands to watch them go. There they danced and sang about bonfires set to serve as beacons. The voyagers, moving out to sea, looked back, with deep emotion, to the flickering signals of farewell, and the sorrows of parting became preëminent themes in song and story.

In retrospect the reign of Sho Hashi appears to mark the age in which

Okinawan life absorbed many of the exotic elements which thereafter gave it special color and character.

Hashi died in 1439, at the age of sixty-eight. We know little about his personality or his private life; nevertheless, he takes his place as one of the great men of Okinawan history. He had been born in the year in which Satto secured Chinese recognition and took Chuzan into the tributary system. At his death he left Okinawa under a unified administration and in a position of importance and prosperity among the islands along the western Pacific rim. The kingship was still a personal affair; hence his passing meant a new test of loyalties at the court and in the countryside, for each succession required some realignment of officers and disturbed the balance of prestige and wealth associated with offices held by the princes and the *anji*.

The old king left a large family. His second son, Sho Chu, took his place. Ambassadors carried announcement of the change to Peking, with Sho Chu's petition for investiture. Envoys were sent to notify the shogun's court at Kyoto in Japan. One of Hashi's younger sons was appointed Warden of the North and sent to keep watch upon the restless Hokuzan district, which his father had compelled to submit to Chuzan.

Sho Chu lived only five years. The succession passed to his son Shitatsu, but he too ruled only five years. He left no heir. The kingship now reverted to Sho Hashi's fifth son, Kimpuku, whose reign was noted for extensive road-building projects around Shuri and Naha. It was too short to enable him to entrench his own family interests, for within three years he died.

This precipitated succession quarrels and a crisis at Shuri. The heir apparent was Kimpuku's young son Shiro, but his right to the throne was challenged by an uncle, Sho Hashi's sixth son. It is not clear whether this was simple rivalry of factions at court or represented the intrusion of an idea that all royal sons should in turn inherit the royal power. In any case, the consequences were disastrous. Rioting broke out in the castle; both contestants for power were slain; and the palace buildings were burned to the ground. The heavy loss of treasure included the prized silver seals of office which had been conferred by Hung Wu upon the princes of Okinawa as patents of authority and investiture.

Hashi's seventh son, Sho Taikyu, now became king. The Ming court granted his petition for investiture and for new seals of office, but it was easier to acquire these things than it was to win the loyalty and support of the territorial lords, the *anji*, on Okinawa. It is not surprising that this period of conflict gave rise to the tales of romance and loyalty which form the "classic" body of Okinawan song and tradition.

For example, there is the story of Gosamaru, Lord of Nakagusuku Castle, who became suspicious of the conduct of his rival and enemy, Amawari, Lord of Katsuren. Nakagusuku—an immense and impressive ruin today—lies on the heights midway between Katsuren Castle and Shuri. Gosamaru learned that Amawari was maturing plans for rebellion, and so began quietly to mobilize his own men and resources to bar the path from Katsuren to Shuri and the king's court. Before he had completed a muster of forces at Katsuren, however, Amawari learned that Gosamaru was alert to his own treacherous plans. He

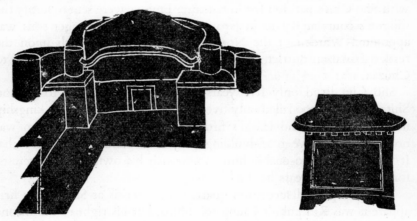

FIG. 6. TOMB AND BURIAL URN. Left: *"Turtleback" tomb.* Right: *Urn from the site of the Unten Harbor Battle of 1609.*

therefore gained the king's ear, disclosed Gosamaru's efforts to mobilize, and persuaded Taikyu that it was Gosamaru and not he who planned rebellion. The king accepted this false accusation and suddenly sent his own forces against Nakagusuku. Gosamaru refused to take up arms against the king and chose suicide, leaving his castle open to the king's men. Too late, the king learned the truth. Orders went out at once to punish the traitor Amawari, who was soon killed in his own stronghold.

Despite such turmoil at the court, by Okinawan standards the island was enjoying unprecedented prosperity, thanks to the accumulation of wealth coming in from overseas. The territorial lords, who shared in this, expanded their castles and elaborated the gardens and dwellings within them. Naha began to take on the appearance of a prosperous town along the waterfront.

It was possible to make extraordinary profits on Naha's seaborne commerce. Japanese scholars estimate that the Okinawan merchants occasionally earned a thousand-percent return on shipments of luxury goods. The maritime risks were terribly high, but they were worth it; the economic alternative was an unremitting and unrewarding struggle to wrest something from the harsh soil of Okinawa itself. As a consequence, the hinterland was neglected, and all the energies of the tiny kingdom were centered on the Naha trade.

It is evident that a considerable import of metals took place at this time. Coins struck in 1458 were modeled after a coin of the Chinese Yuan dynasty (1279–1368), and large bells were cast for temples and shrines constructed under the king's patronage.[3] Upon one of these bells Taikyu caused to be inscribed: "Ryukyu, Beautiful Country of the Southern Ocean." This is an interesting reflection of the pervading sense of cultural orientation at Shuri in Okinawa's days of greatest independence, for here "south of Japan" and not "east of China" hints at the growing influence entering Okinawa from the north.

We will have occasion to review Japan's relations with the Ryukyus in our next chapter. Here it will suffice to note that Sho Taikyu appears to have come increasingly under the influence of Japanese missionary priests and been led into a course of lavish patronage for Buddhist temples and Shinto shrines. At least four new temple foundations were created and endowed—the Kogen-ji, Fumon-ji, Manju-ji, and Tenryu-ji. These temples were not built in response to popular demand nor based on popular support; the king's resources were squandered in building on a scale unwarranted by the position of Buddhism in Okinawa. Undoubtedly such building stimulated the arts and crafts and brought to the Okinawans new concepts of fine workmanship and ceremonial, but there was never the sweeping, popular emotional enthusiasm which so marked the development of evangelical sects in Japan.

The Tenryu-ji at Shuri bore the name of the great Zen temple in Kyoto which at that time had been granted special overseas trading privileges by the Ashikaga shoguns; a Tenryu-ji missionary supervised the construction of the Manju-ji, and (as we shall see) Tenryu-ji monks were moving constantly back and forth as emissaries of Japan to the courts of Korea, China, and Okinawa. There is a hint here that Kyoto was consciously pursuing a policy of cultural penetration in Okinawa coupled with a growing interest in the promotion of Okinawan trade with China and the ports of Southeast Asia.

In 1456 an immigrant Japanese metalworker was commissioned by the king to cast a great bronze bell. This was a votive offering, bearing a long inscription, which reads in part: "May the sound of this bell shatter illusory dreams, perfect the souls of mankind, and enable the King and his subjects to live so virtuously that barbarians will find no occasion to invade the Kingdom."* Unhappily, Taikyu's successors were to discover soon enough that virtue is not a shield and meekness no asset in the struggle for power among great nations.

The pious king died in 1460, leaving to his heirs and court officers the problems of an impoverished treasury. Temple building, metal casting, religious ceremonial, and luxurious entertainment at the palace had consumed the surpluses accumulated by Sho Hashi and his successors. The late king's extravagance now had severe political consequences.

His son Sho Toku was a headstrong youth of twenty-one years when he became king. This was at a time when nearby seas were full of swashbuckling Japanese pirates and privateers, who preyed on shipping along the China coast. It has been suggested that the Okinawans shared largely in these activities, but this is improbable, for the fact remains that the Chinese continued to welcome Okinawan ships and merchants on their coast during periods of fierce dispute and conflict with the Japanese.

Sho Toku decided on an overseas military adventure. In 1465 Oki-

* The bell hangs today (1958) on the grounds of the United States Naval Academy at Annapolis, Maryland, where it rings whenever Navy scores a point in Army-Navy games.

nawan forces embarked for an invasion of Kikai Island, which lay to the north, on the trading route to Japan. The young king himself took command, adopting the banner of Hachiman, Japanese God of War. The emblem of this Shinto deity took the form of a circle within which three comma-shapes lay eye-to-tail. Since Hachiman was generally considered to be the patron of sea adventurers and pirates (the *wako*), it is possible that Sho Toku fancied himself one of these fearless sea barons and proposed to emulate them in making himself a power on the high seas.

The invasion of Kikai Island was not difficult, for it lay nearby, virtually unpopulated and undeveloped. The young king nevertheless treated the expedition as a great success; an officer was appointed to hold the island in the king's interest; the Asato Hachiman Shrine was erected at Naha in token of gratitude; and Hachiman's crest (the three-comma *mitsu-domoe*) was adopted as the crest of the royal house.

This much, and no more, the conventional histories tell us. Future studies may bring evidence that Sho Toku had indeed attempted to link the fortunes of his principality with those of the powerful *wako*, the freebooters and buccaneers who were terrorizing the seaboard provinces of China. Whatever his motivation, it became evident at once that he did not enjoy support among his chief officers at Shuri.

Kikai Island had no economic value. No new resources and no important harbors were acquired by Sho Toku's expedition. The whole adventure proved a drain on the Chuzan treasury without adequate return. Kanemaro, the royal treasurer, and a number of other important figures withdrew from the court and retired to their estates in the countryside. Tradition says that the headstrong young king about this time became enamored of the chief priestess of Kudaka Island, to which he had gone on pilgrimage, and that while he dallied with her, far from the court at Shuri, a conspiracy ripened into open rebellion. This led to the king's death in his twenty-ninth year.

THE "SECOND SHO DYNASTY" AND ITS FOUNDER, SHO EN

Kanemaro, the old treasurer who had served two kings, assumed the royal prerogatives in 1469 and adopted the name Sho En. His family maintained the succession thereafter for more than four hundred years. Official histories—written under the patronage of Sho En's descendents —say that he was prevailed upon to accept the throne because of popular acclaim. Little is said of the mystery which shrouds Sho Toku's death, and the traditional account may be taken to mean simply that Sho En's partisans outnumbered the partisans of the late king among territorial lords and disgruntled officers at court.

Kanemaro ranks with Satto and Hashi as a strong, capable ruler. Sho Toku's family was set aside. His heirs were barred forever from high government office and from marriage into the new royal family, the "Second Sho Dynasty." With Sho En, the government of Okinawa began to be shifted from the personal rule of a gifted individual to an institutional basis. This enabled the dynastic line to survive until the overwhelming pressure of external events swept the tiny kingdom out of existence in the 19th century.

We know little more of Kanemaro's personal life and character than we do of his strong predecessors. In recounting the traditional story of Sho En we must go back a little.

He is said to have been the son of a farmer who lived on Iheya Island, a few miles northwest of Okinawa. When he was about twenty years of age (the story goes) he lost his parents. He undertook to support his uncle and aunt, his elder sister, and a five-year-old brother. A local girl had become his wife when both were in their early youth. He was an exceptionally skilled farmer, and his meager land yielded more than his neighbors could extract from better soil and larger holdings.

This proved disastrous at the time; during a year of drought he was accused of stealing water, a capital crime in communities which depend upon communal resources. His life was in danger; leaving his family, he slipped away from Iheya and crossed the channel to the village of Ginama, near the northern tip of Okinawa. Here he lived for five or six years, but again fell foul of his neighbors. The reasons are not known; we may surmise that he was both ambitious and talented, and he may have been intolerant of the shortcomings and dullness of fishing-village life. From Ginama he went down to Shuri and found employment in the household of Sho Taikyu, who was then the Prince of Goeku.

As the years passed his talents attracted attention: from one position of trust to another he rose steadily in favor. Here in Shuri and Naha he could give play to his skills as a manager. When Taikyu became king, Kanemaro was taken into the royal household organization. Ultimately he became the king's treasurer.

This meant that the excessive expenditures made by Taikyu on behalf of temples, shrines, and ceremonies passed through Kanemaro's hands. None knew better than he the state of the Okinawan economy, the total revenues of foreign trade, and the probable effects of unlimited and injudicious spending. When his patron Taikyu died, Kanemaro was expected to carry on management of the royal finance. We can only guess that he disapproved of Sho Toku's military adventure to Kikai, and that the headstrong young king paid little attention to his treasurer's conservative advice.

Kanemaro by this time had an estate of his own in the countryside, and to this he withdrew after resigning his offices at court. Influential officers nevertheless continued to seek him out for advice and guidance, and it may well be that here in the seclusion of his farmhouse the plot was hatched which led to Sho Toku's downfall.

Sho En applied at once to the Ming court for recognition and investiture and took steps to enhance the prestige and authority of his family among his fellow countrymen. A handsome tomb was constructed on a high promontory at the southern tip of Iheya-Izena Island to hold the bones of his parents. His sister was appointed chief *noro* or high priestess in Iheya, founding a line of *noro* in which the succession continued into the 20th century. Traditional accounts supplied Sho En with "royal" ancestry by asserting that he was in fact descended from the lost King Gihon, who had vanished in the forest nearly two centuries before Kanemaro's birth. This we can dismiss as the fabrication of myth-makers. Sho En worshipped his father's spirit as King of Iheya, a proper gesture of filial piety, but took care that due reverence was shown for all his royal predecessors, including those of the "First Sho Dynasty," which he had displaced.

Kanemaro's first wife, the wife of his youth, had died or had been set aside at an unknown time before he became prominent at Shuri. His second wife, named Yosoidon, gave birth to a son when she was twenty-one years of age, seven years before her husband became king. This lad was only thirteen when the old king his father died in 1477. Again there was tension at court, for once more the succession was in dispute. Sho En's younger brother Seni was made king, but Yosoidon, the queen mother, was not content to see her son set aside in this fashion.

What now followed is obscured in the traditional accounts. It is related that Sho En's eldest daughter occupied the high office of chief *noro* at the royal court. She presently received a "divine message" which advised her uncle Seni to abdicate, and this he did in 1477 after reigning no more than six months. Yosoidon's son, a boy of fourteen years, now became king, inaugurating the longest and most prosperous reign in the history of Okinawa.

Sho Shin's Reign: The "Great Days of Chuzan"

We must surmise that in this instance the struggle for power was confined to members of Sho En's family and that it had a relatively peaceful outcome. Korean court annals preserve a commentary on the Chuzan court at this time, noting that on Okinawa the queen mother was a powerful and ambitious woman who dominated the scene at Shuri for many years after her son had become nominal ruler.

The abdicated king, Seni, took the title Prince of Goeku, and it was arranged that his daughter should marry her cousin, the new king, young Sho Shin. Presently a son was born to the union, and given the title Prince of Urasoe, but he was fated never to reach the throne.

Sho Shin ruled for half a century. These were the great days of Chuzan; Okinawa was indeed an oasis of peace and relative prosperity at a moment in history when most of Asia was torn by war. The militant forces of Islam were moving eastward, crushing successively the old Hindu states of India and of Java and Sumatra, and moving up into Mindanao and Luzon in the Philippines. There were incessant wars among the petty states of Southeast Asia, where Burma, Siam, Cambodia, and Annam struggled among themselves. The coasts of China were harried by pirates, who plundered cities lying well inland from the open sea. Japan was in a state of anarchy, its cities gutted by fire and the countryside laid waste by wars among the barons. Each of these areas was soon to be hard-pressed by the European Christians in search of souls, spices, and gold.

For a century after Sho Shin's accession, Okinawa lay untouched by this turmoil and confusion. We do not know how large the population was, but it is certain that it did not at any time match the population of minor cities in China or Japan in that day, and may not have exceeded one hundred thousand persons. The king and his successors attempted no conquests and entered into no alliances beyond the mild obligations implied in the Chinese tributary system. These, we have seen, were scarcely more than payments for license to trade. It is apparent from the records that Okinawan traders were welcomed in all the ports they sought to enter from Japan and Korea southward to the Indies.

Okinawan farmers and fishermen were no doubt as poor then as they have continued to be in the centuries since, but they were no longer harassed by local feuds among the territorial lords. The townsmen, the merchant-mariners, the *anji*, and the courtiers who lived in and near Shuri and the port of Naha were sharing in benefits which came with the gradual accumulation of wealth based in the first instance upon seaborne trade, and in the second upon the goods and services required to maintain the court and gentry. Under Sho Shin the organization of Okinawa's economy and administration assumed a form which it was to maintain in principle until 1879, though in practice Japanese pressure in time compelled many essential modifications.

To commemorate the thirtieth year of Sho Shin's reign, a monument was erected in the palace grounds, and upon this were inscribed a list of achievements which the king's men believed to be the Eleven Distinctions of the Age. They are a noteworthy reflection of contemporary life, and of the standards by which the court was guided. They can be summarized:

1. Buddhism was patronized by the king.
2. Taxes were lightened and interclass strife abated.
3. Royal control was asserted and confirmed in Yaeyama and Miyako.
4. Private ownership and use of arms were done away with.
5. Law and order were established throughout the country.

6. Shuri was beautified with parks.

7. Places of amusement and pleasure were provided at Shuri.

8. Works of art were introduced at the palace, and music **was** patronized.

9. Relations with China were strengthened.

10. Chinese utensils and books were introduced.

11. A palace in Chinese style was built at Shuri Castle.

Four of these Distinctions of the Age have to do with government. Whereas Sho En had promoted economic development through land reclamation, irrigation works, road-building and foreign trade, Sho Shin's reign was noteworthy for change and improvement in administration. As the court increased in wealth, the independence and power of the *anji* diminished; the days of individual leadership based upon the king's personal capacities were giving way to institutionalized authority, and paradoxically this became possible because of the length and quality of Sho Shin's reign.

Hitherto rank, authority, and wealth rested on divisions of the land, and upon services performed at Shuri and Naha in the king's name. He was in effect merely the most important and powerful among the many *anji* descended from chieftains of the 13th and 14th centuries. Some of these lords lived at Shuri near the king's household, and a few held their lands directly from him, but at the opening of Sho Shin's reign the majority lived at castle-strongholds within their own hereditary estates. Each maintained his own men-at-arms, officers, and servants, and drew his economic support from the labor of hard-working serfs who cultivated his lands or fished in nearby waters. The common people were not free to move about, but were expected to remain on the land unless summoned to work at Naha or Shuri in their lord's interest. There was household work to be done at Shuri if the *anji* was a member of the court, or there might be work to be done near the waterfront, at the warehouses, or on the trading ships in which the *anji* had an interest.

Under these conditions every lord who had large landholdings and many retainers had to be considered potential antagonists to the royal household and court, or possible rivals to the king during recurrent succession crises. Traditional rivalries ran deep among the *anji*, who had from time beyond record formed coalitions in struggles among themselves and had demonstrated their independence under the reign of a dissolute king or the weak reign of a child.

Sho Shin and his advisors proposed to forestall the dangers of insurrection. They were strong enough to compel the *anji* throughout Okinawa to accept a major reorganization which substantially reduced the threat of armed defiance.

It was first ordered that swords were no longer to be worn as personal equipment. Next, the *anji* were ordered to bring all weapons to Shuri, to be stored in a warehouse under supervision of one of the king's officers. Finally the lords themselves were asked to move into Shuri to take up residence near the palace. More than fifty did so at once, each leaving a chief vassal (known as the *anji-okite*) to administer the country estate from which economic support must continue to come and to serve as a link between outlying areas and the castle town. This move loosened the ties of the *anji* with his ancestral holdings and in time led him to identify his interests as much with Shuri as with the land of his fathers. After a few years—a transitional period—the court succeeded in placing in the country districts its own officers and agents, known as *jito-dai*, who carried out administrative orders and kept an eye on the *anji*'s deputies.

Students of Japanese history note these things with interest, for they antedate by one century the so-called "Sword Edicts" issued by Toyotomi Hideyoshi in 1586 and 1587, and by two centuries the edict of 1634 wherewith Tokugawa Iemitsu compelled the feudal lords of Japan to maintain residence at the shogun's capital.

Success in bringing about these radical changes testifies to a firm hand, tact, and foresight in the royal court. To minimize friction among lords whose families perpetuated traditional rivalries, the castle town itself was divided into three wards, one for the *anji* from southern Okinawa (the old Nanzan principality), one for the *anji* of central Okinawa (Chuzan), and one for the men who came down from the north. It is noteworthy that through fear of civil disturbances in the town, or through inability to enforce the order without provoking rebellion, some of the *anji* of the old Hokuzan district were allowed to remain at their homes on Motobu Peninsula and elsewhere in the north, but the king's third son was made Warden of the North to ensure order there.

Carrying the administrative reorganization further, the old divisions of the Three Principalities (the *Sanzan*) were transformed and renamed Shimajiri, Nakagami, and Kunigami, with subdivision according to the estates and territories of the local *anji*. Thus the court officers, whose first allegiance was to the royal house at Shuri, lived side by side with the estate managers responsible to landholders at the court. Gradually the officers of the crown superseded the local representative, but a large degree of autonomy remained with the village communities.

Shuri was transformed. Accommodations had to be found for the lords and for their principal retainers, for their families and for their servants. Masons, carpenters, and metalworkers hastened to construct suitable houses under the shadow of the castle and to surround them with appropriate gardens and high stone walls. Parks, lakes, and pleasant groves were laid out at the king's order. New temples, bridges, pavilions, and monumental gateways were constructed.

Each *anji* drew from the resources of his own country estate to maintain his town establishment. This meant that the countryside economy was stimulated; new areas were opened for cultivation to meet the needs of Shuri and Naha, and the products of forest, farm, and fishing village moved steadily into the administrative center. Skilled craftsmen and artists took on more apprentice-students to meet the demands of the building program. An unprecedented degree of technical specialization became possible. At last the Okinawans themselves began to produce luxury goods of their own design, inspired by imported objects, but bearing the stamp of Okinawan taste and craftsmanship. It is at this period that the use of gold, silver, lacquer, and silk came into fairly common use among the townsmen. New techniques in the cultivation of the silkworm and new weaving implements were imported. Ornamental hairpins of the finest design and workmanship became an essential part of every aristocrat's costume after 1509, for these were regulated anew as important symbols of rank and privilege in the court hierarchy. There was an elaboration of ceremony which required great attention to matters of etiquette and deportment.

In requiring the *anji* to move to Shuri and to break with tradition, Sho Shin's counselors had to compensate in some way for the difficulties which so drastic a change entailed. Intermarriage among the families of the *anji* from different parts of the island was encouraged as a means of blurring lines dividing important regional factions at the court. Royal decrees banned the ancient custom of self-sacrifice and suicide whereby faithful retainers sought to follow their lords in death.

Okinawa was entering upon a century of creative activity. The elaborate new court ceremonies, borrowed from China and modified, required construction of a large new palace in Chinese style. The stone "Dragon Pillars" set before the entrance to the main audience hall reflect cosmopolitan experience. The prototype is not found in Japan or China, but in the temples and palace compounds of Cambodia and Siam. Enkaku Temple, constructed in 1492 under the supervision of an immigrant Japanese priest, was patterned after the great Enkaku-ji which stands in the seaside groves of Kamakura in Japan. In 1496 the Sogen Temple on the highroad to Naha was enlarged and embellished by massive stone gates. Tablets dedicated to the souls of all previous kings were installed within, and all persons—including the king himself—were required to dismount and pass these gates on foot as a sign of respect. Enkaku-ji's great bell was cast in 1496, and a finely-sculptured stone bridge was laid across the pond before the main gate two years later.

Sculptors in stone and wood were engaged in decorating palaces, shrines, and bridges, though they were handicapped by lack of suitable materials native to the island. The palace grounds were surrounded by finely-laid stone embankments and embellished with red-lacquered fencing about the royal park. In 1501, stonemasons completed the austere, pebble-strewn mausoleum enclosure known as the Tama Udon, where eighteen kings, their queens, and royal children of the Second Sho dynasty were to be entombed thereafter.*

Reverence for deceased ancestors was of supreme importance in Okinawan religious life and provided a strong conservative element and continuity in social institutions. It was this, perhaps, which prompted the Queen Mother Yosoidon to lavish so much attention on the rebuilding and enlargement of the royal tombs and the Sogen-ji.

---

* The last crown prince, son of the deposed King Sho Tai, joined his ancestors here on September 26, 1920. The tombs were shattered under bombardment in 1945 and subsequently looted by vandals.

Traditions and forms of ancestor worship offered one of the most serious difficulties which had to be resolved when the *anji* were called into Shuri. Each of the lords as a matter of course expected to continue to worship at his ancestral hearth and tombs, but this created risks; a lord dissatisfied with Shuri life or disgruntled under exacting court controls might find occasion to return to his lands on pretext of worship, and use the opportunity to foment trouble. An ingenious solution was found; it was arranged that each lord would send a representative annually to perform the required ceremonies at the country place while at the capital itself a place for "worship from afar" (*yohai-jo*) was established. One *yohai-jo* was established in each of the city's wards. To this the lord could repair, and there, facing toward his distant home, he could perform the appropriate rituals. In time each of these worship-sites became a major shrine.

Sho Shin sought now for the first time to systematize the indigenous cult and to bring the influential *noro* under the supervision of the Shuri administration. Hitherto they had been autonomous, serving only individual households and interrelated villages; they were not thought to be representative of a *national* cult and had no island-wide organization.[4]

The rites of Chinese ancestor worship were studied and practiced faithfully at the settlement of Kume-mura by the descendents of the immigrants of 1393 and by the Okinawan youths put to school there at the Confucian temple, but there is little evidence that the practice of these imported rituals (so largely of literary content and association) was known beyond the Shuri-Naha complex of settlements. Throughout the countryside and on the adjacent islands the ancient pantheism and rituals of the *noro* priestesses remained predominant.

The chief *noro* of the king's own household was known as the *Kikoe-Ogimi*, who held rank and prestige very nearly equal to that of the king. We have seen, for instance, that Sho Shin himself owed his position to the successful intervention of his sister, the chief *noro*, in 1477. By tradition the *kikoe-ogimi* was always a sister, daughter, aunt, or niece of the reigning monarch. The Chief Noro of Iheya Island (*Iheya no Amaganushi*) ranked second in the kingdom by virtue of her succession to Sho En's elder sister.

Sho Shin removed the residence of the *kikoe-ogimi* from the interior of the palace to a site just outside the palace gates, and in 1519 constructed a high-walled park to enclose the sacred symbolic hearth which she attended. Before it stood a superbly fashioned gate of massive stone, the Sonohyan Utaki, which reproduced in finest detail every feature of a Chinese gateway of timber and thatch.

Concurrently the chief priestess was granted authority to confirm the village *noro* in local office throughout the islands, issuing certificates from Shuri. Thirty-three *noro* held appointment from the king; others were nominated by the district officers (the *jito*) from among the *noro* in the communities under their control. Lands were set aside permanently in each locality to provide income for the village priestesses. Individual households were free to name their own custodians of the hearth fire from among the women of the family. Between the *kikoe-ogimi* at Shuri and the community *noro* stood intermediary priestesses known as *o-amu shirare* or *kimi-bae*.

Although Shuri did not interfere with the choice of hearth-fire custodians within each individual household, it would appear that, in practice, friction developed between the community *noro* holding official appointment and the representatives of individual households. According to Spencer, this encouraged the community *noro* to develop a sense of mutual interest—as a class—and from that time until the present day the village *noro* have drawn together in common meetings and ceremonial occasions.

An indigenous literary tradition began to take form. The Japanese *kana* syllabary had long been in use at court. Since Japanese and Okinawan speech descend from an archaic Japanese parent language, the *kana* provided a more supple means of record than the forbiddingly complex Chinese characters, despite the fact that Ryukyuan possesses several sounds for which no equivalents exist in Japanese and for which there were no *kana* symbols. Under Sho En and Sho Shin the Okinawans became increasingly self-conscious and interested in their own history and traditions. In 1532 the traditional chants, poems, and prayers of the high priestesses of the royal court were recorded under the title *Omoro Soshi*. This collection in its later recensions became the most prized literary treasure of the kingdom, earnestly studied and proudly compared with the poems of the ancient *Manyo* collection and chants preserved in the *Engi-shiki* of Japan.

Sho Shin enriched and enlarged the temples founded by Taikyu. They were the seats of learning at Shuri and the chief agencies through which Okinawa drew upon the arts and crafts of Japan and Korea. The Koreans at this time were masters of ceramic techniques and of the arts of metal-casting. The royal court at Seoul patronized the printing of Buddhist texts which were supreme examples of the art of paper-making, block-printing, and calligraphy.

Both the King of Chuzan and the shogun at Kyoto sent embassies to ask for copies of great works which were being issued from the Korean presses. In 1462 Okinawan representatives returned to Shuri bearing a copy of the Buddhist canon, in an edition probably dating from 1458, which is said to have consisted of no less than seven thousand volumes. This was placed in the Tenkaizen-ji; twice again, in 1479 and 1483, Sho Shin successfully petitioned the Korean king to grant him copies of great texts in fine editions, to be housed in four of the new temples at Shuri.

The development of Shuri Castle and the palace grounds about it deserved well to be numbered among the Eleven Distinctions of the Age. As a royal residence site it was unsurpassed, and into its development the Okinawans poured all the imagination, skill, and wealth at their command. It must not be compared with the massive grandeur of the Forbidden City at Peking, for in total area it would scarcely fill one of the minor parks of that great complex. Nevertheless, in aesthetic fitness for its purpose, it perfectly expressed the character of a mild and generous people who were proud of their tiny island kingdom and looked upon the sea as the life-giving source of commerce.

In Sho Shin's time immense trees clothed the slopes of the rugged hill. Massive walls of cut stone rose one above another to provide terracing among the grey outcroppings of the natural rock. On the level oval which crowned the summit stood the palace Audience Hall of State, flanked by lesser halls constructed for the reception and entertainment of ambassadors. Concentric walls, lacquered fencing, and many gates provided garden settings for subsidiary buildings and the private appartments of the king, his wives, concubines, and courtiers.

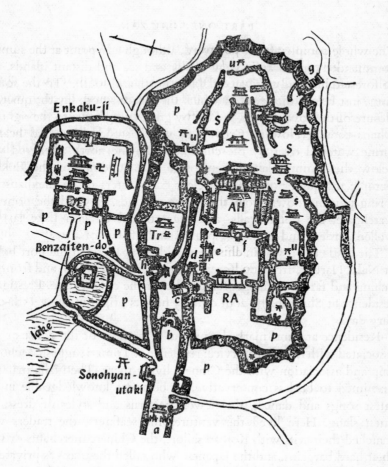

FIG. 7. PLAN OF SHURI CASTLE. *From an 18th-century drawing.* Approaches: a—*ceremonial arch (Shurei-no-mon).* b—*1st gate (Kanki-mon).* c—*2nd gate (Zuisen-mon).* d—*3rd gate (Ryukoku-mon).* e—*4th gate (Kofuku-mon).* f—*5th gate (Hojin-mon).* g, h—*subsidiary outside gates.* Ceremonial and administrative areas: AH—*Audience Hall (Seiden), with flanking reception halls for envoys from China and Satsuma.* RA—*Hall of Royal Ancestors, containing genealogical records, etc.* Tr—*Treasury and subsidiary administrative offices.* Residential areas: ss—*private apartments and pavilions.* pp—*parks, gardens, groves.* uu—*special shrines (uganju) and worship areas (utaki and yohai-jo).* Adjacent national shrines: *The Buddhist foundation* Enkaku-ji *and the indigenous Shinto symbolic hearth-shrine* Sonohyan Utaki *are separated by the artificial Dragon Pool and lie outside, below, and on the northern or protective side of the royal enclosure.*

The whole complex faced westward, although any point at the summit commanded a panoramic view of sky and sea and distant islands, and of forested hills and cultivated fields to north and south.* To the southwest, just below the level on which the palace stood, lay the quiet enclosure of the royal tombs, shaded by great evergreens; to the right lay Ohana-batake (Flowery Grove), in which stood the sacred hearthshrine watched over by the chief *noro*. To the north, sheltered well below the summit, lay the enclosure and buildings of the Enkaku Temple, its quiet pond fed by clear cold waters of an inexhaustible spring pouring down from the palace grounds. Beyond the principal watchgate, the outer walls, and the artificial Dragon Lake lay the walled gardens and homes of princes and officers of state.

The castle town was in effect a world set apart from the port below at Naha Harbor, from the foreign settlements at Tomari, and from the fishing and farming villages scattered over the countryside. Prestige of residence at Shuri in the 20th century had its origin in these 15th-century days.

Residence at Shuri marked a man as a member of the court or one associated with it in daily service; residence at Tomari suggested scholarship and association with the Chinese living there. The Naha man was presumed to be less conservative, to be more knowledgeable in the latest songs and dances, the newest patterns and styles of dress, the latest slang. Here lived the venturesome seafarers, the traders who matched their wits with Korean sailors, the Chinese merchants driving their hard bargains, and the Japanese who sailed these seas as privateers.

Neither China nor Japan exercised significant direct influence upon the common people who lived far from the capital. Foreign contributions were introduced at Shuri and Naha and from there filtered into the rural districts. This process of cultural diffusion was accelerated after the territorial lords came up to live near the court, for each *anji* maintained a household staff recruited from his own estates. After periods of service at Naha or Shuri such young men in service returned to marry and settle in the home village. They took with them new ideas, new

* Within a few hours' time in 1945 these gardens, ancient temples, gates and shrines, great trees, and pleasant parks were utterly destroyed. Today a university is slowly rising on the barren site, high above the desolated countryside.

songs, new dances, as well as material gifts, for these cost nothing to learn and nothing to impart.

The outer islands of the Ryukyu chain began to come more directly under Shuri's control during the long and prosperous reign of Sho Shin. They were of growing importance to the overseas trade, for ships out of Naha began to frequent the anchorage at Miyako and the reef-sheltered coves of Yaeyama. In 1486 a series of disruptive quarrels broke out among the petty lords who held sway on Yaeyama, and at last, in 1500, Sho Shin sent a military force to restore order, to establish a liaison office on Miyako, and to bring Kume Island under firm control. A similar liaison office was set up on Yaeyama in 1524.

Sho Shin's long reign came to an end in 1526. He had governed for fifty years, for so long a time, indeed, that his officers and men had difficulty in finding documents which prescribed the proper rituals with which to celebrate the succession and the forms required by the embassy which must be sent to China to ask for investiture of the new king, Sho Sei.

Okinawa had reached the peak of its prosperity, and had perfected in general terms the institutions and social forms which were to remain intact until the late 19th century. The islands were independent. They were in constant communication and at peace with neighboring states. The Okinawans were in a happy position of freedom to adopt what they wanted, and to remain indifferent—or at best only mildly curious —about foreign artifacts and institutions for which they felt no pressing need. China loomed as the neighbor of unquestioned superiority, and they were in close and constant communication with Japan, but were overwhelmed by neither.

During the three reigns which followed (i.e., from 1526 until 1589), the peak of prosperity was passed. Consumption of wealth at Shuri and Naha far outstripped the development of Okinawa's own meager resources. Maintenance of the high living standards achieved under Sho Shin depended upon the expansion of profitable commerce, but (as we shall see in the next chapter) trade with the south began to be affected adversely by the wars besetting Southeast Asia and the dis- astrous intrusion of European adventurers in Asiatic waters. The shadow of a militant and aggressive Japan began to fall across the little seafaring kingdom. Every excuse had to be found to increase the profit in trade with China and the number of trading missions which could be sent legitimately to the Chinese court. Okinawa was never again to know the halcyon days of Sho Shin's reign.

OKINAWA AND THE OUTER ISANDS: MIYAKO, YAEYAMA, AND AMAMI OSHIMA[5]

It is well here to leave the mainstream of Okinawan history for a few pages to note Shuri's relations with the outer islands of the archipelago. Miyako's principal settlement, Hirara, lies 176 sea miles from Naha; Ishigaki, the one settlement of consequence in Yaeyama, is 262 miles distant; and Naze, the port-town of the Amami group of islands, lies 220 miles away, north from Shuri. It was natural that these should develop as the government grew in strength and prestige on Okinawa, and Shuri moved to gain control of smaller islands along the principal shipping lanes to the China coast and to Japan. These outer islands have presented peculiar administrative, economic, and social problems in the years since World War II, and on these 20th-century problems the early history of the islands throws much light. Since they were relatively undisturbed by direct attack in 1945, there was less physical loss and less displacement of traditional values by a postwar occupation. They hold much promise for the archeologist, the linguist, the folklorist who would record the last faint evidence of archaic life in the Ryukyu island chain.

Certain characteristics of legendary accounts and the early historic period in Miyako and in Yaeyama are shared with the traditions of ancient Okinawa, but they show a time lag of about two centuries in their evolution. That is to say, an analogy can be drawn between the traditions of the first settlement, the introduction and development of artifacts, economic skills, and community organization in Miyako, and the traditions of Okinawa in the 12th, 13th, and 14th centuries. But in Miyako these things are assigned dates corresponding to the 14th and 15th centuries. The Yamato people in Japan passed from a period of intense rivalry among quasi-independent clans to a period of unified central government in the early years of the 7th century. The process becomes apparent in Okinawa after the 12th century, but the inhabitants of Miyako were not brought to a comparable state of organization and economic development until the 14th and 15th centuries. We are sufficiently close to prehistory in Miyako and Yaeyama to discern rather clearly the evolution of institutions which elsewhere in the northern islands are deeply obscured by the passage of time.

The inhabitants of 14th-century Yaeyama and Miyako lived in almost neolithic simplicity; they had few metal tools, knew little of shipbuilding, and eked out a livelihood by the most primitive agricultural methods. It is of considerable interest to note that the legendary figures to whom they attribute the introduction of more sophisticated arts, crafts, and governmental forms appear to have come from China, Japan, and Okinawa quite late, and usually quite by accident. The time lag in development grew less as communication increased among the islands. Major changes took place during the reign of Sho Shin and his successors, but even today, in the 20th century, there is a notable delay in effecting changes decreed at the center of authority on Okinawa.

One consequence of this has been the development at Shuri and Naha, long ago, of a distinct attitude of superiority, of condescension toward the interests and qualities of the inhabitants of the Outer Islands (*Saki-shima*), as the Yaeyama and Miyako groups are called. As the Chinese and Japanese have looked always upon the Okinawans as unsophisticated rustics, so the people of Okinawa have always looked upon the Saki-shima people as socially and intellectually inferior "country cousins." This has had political consequences which continue to be felt. Conversely, a melancholy sense of isolation and a longing for recognition at the capital permeates the songs, dances, and folk tales of Saki-shima.

There is reason to believe that trading vessels made Miyako and Yaeyama points of reference along the coastal sea-routes at least as early as the 13th century. Chinese records say that Miyako sailors en route to Malacca were shipwrecked on the Chekiang coast in 1317, but we may suspect that these were ships from Okinawa which had made their last landfall at Miyako before disaster overtook them. It is said that Yaeyama paid tribute to Shuri as early as 1390.

We have noted that between 1486 and 1500 Sho Shin's officers attempted to intervene in local conflicts. Under the leadership of Oyake Akahachi the people of Yaeyama resisted Shuri, and a chieftain named Untura put up a fight on the neighboring island of Yonaguni. Both were finally overwhelmed by an invasion led from Miyako under a chieftain named Nakasone, and he in turn submitted to Shuri. Order was brought out of confusion; a resident officer from Shuri was placed in charge of Miyako, with a suitable number of aides and interpreters of the dialects to be found in Saki-shima.

Officers were sent down from the capital for three-year tours of duty, during which they acquired local wives and established local families. When they returned to Shuri, however, they were forbidden to bring these families with them to Okinawa. Exceptions were sometimes made. If an officer had no heir at Shuri, he was permitted to take with him one son only; all other members of his Saki-shima family had to remain behind.

Mountainous Yaeyama has relatively few legendary and quasi-historic monuments, but the flat, dry countryside of Miyako is rich in traditional sites, marked now by sacred woods and groves. Here and there in large sheltering caves are ancient wells and springs upon which the community must depend for its survival. Near the caves are ruined enclosures referred to now as "castle" sites, although they appear to represent little more than rough walls thrown up to protect the dwellings of local chieftains. There are many tombs; some resemble the dolmens and sarcophagi of Bronze-age Japan. Others, of quite recent date, resemble the tombs of Okinawa and of the China coast. There are also enclosures within which the dead at one time were exposed to the sun, the wind, and the rain.

Miyako legends reflect late settlement in these remote islands, a period of barbarous lawlessness extending well into the 14th century, with conditions of unrelieved poverty. The early culture heroes are aliens who introduced new tools or weapons and new modes of living from overseas, or natives who traveled far abroad to acquire wealth and strange or precious objects. A third type is represented by the prominent reformers who endeavored to "correct" local folkways by reconciling Miyako practices with the more sophisticated ways of

PLATE 7. BENZAITEN SHRINE, AT SHURI. *Originally constructed on an island in the Dragon Lake to house 15th-century printed Korean editions of the Buddhist scriptures, this was demolished and looted by Satsuma's soldiers in 1609. It was rebuilt in the 17th century and registered as a monument of national importance in the 1930's. Destroyed in 1945. (See page 112.)*

PLATE 8. SHURI CASTLE WALLS AND ENCIRCLING ROAD. *Massive additions were added to the ancient castle in the 16th century. It is said that the work was done under the supervision of a master-mason from Yaeyama, as a form of tribute from the outer islands. Only fragments remained after the 1945 bombardment. (See pages 112 and 114.)*

PLATE 10. SHIKINA-EN, A ROYAL COUNTRY RESIDENCE, MAWASHI DISTRICT. *These gardens and modest residential buildings were developed in the 17th and 18th centuries after Japanese prototypes. Shikina was occupied by members of the Sho family after the king's abdication in 1879. It was totally destroyed in 1945 and the site is now covered by postwar urban settlement.*

PLATE 9. WALLS AND GATE NEAR ENKAKU-JI, SHURI. *Lacking suitable wood in a country subjected to earthquakes and violent storms, the Okinawans carried the stonemason's art to a high degree of perfection, endowing it with a peculiar local style. Most examples at Shuri and Naha were obliterated in the 1945 bombardment, and the remaining fragments have yielded to the bulldozer.*

侍候爵家所藏護得久朝章撮影

PLATE II. SHO EN, FOUNDER OF THE "SECOND SHO DYNASTY." *This stylized portrait allegedly shows Sho En surrounded by his courtiers. Photographed from a painting in the Sho family archives.*

PLATE 12. MADAMA BRIDGE, NEAR NAHA. *Constructed in the early 16th century and totally destroyed in 1945.*

Okinawa. The villain of song and legend is often an intruder from Yaeyama or the traveling merchant-mariner or pirate from Japan or Okinawa, here today and gone tomorrow, leaving behind him broken hearts and many unprotected children.

It is said that in the old days only two general classes of people were recognized on Miyako; the *sima nu pitu* were literally the "island people," to be distinguished from the *yuku-bitu* ("good people"), who were the later, more sophisticated arrivals.

Most of the culture heroes came down from the north. The "Lord of Uputaki Castle" is said to have appeared in Miyako "about 600 years ago" (i.e., sometime in the 14th or 15th centuries) and to have introduced new farming techniques. He dug two good wells, which are still in use, and in general raised standards of living among his own people. After his death the neighboring settlements turned upon his followers, killed them, and took Uputaki Castle. In later years the village was revived by a farmer named Pigitari Yunun-usu, whose successes led to deification and posthumous worship.

The Lord of Takagoshi Castle also is said to have arrived "about 600 years ago" and to have introduced new methods of rice culture and cattle-breeding. In association with two other *anji* (one of them a woman) he attempted to resist the ambitious Lord Yonahabaru of Hirara, who proposed to conquer all the island group. Takagoshi *Anji* was betrayed and committed suicide rather than fall into the hands of his enemy. He was deified and is worshipped today at the sacred grove of Takagoshi. In a similar manner Ungusuku Kanedono is worshipped in nearby Tarama Island in gratitude for his skill in making farming implements and the instruction he gave in their proper use.

One tradition tells of seven Chinese brothers arriving from the west who introduced such noteworthy improvements in daily living that they are worshipped today at seven different sites in Miyako. We may doubt that these were brothers, or we may suspect that one immigrant Chinese is worshipped under slightly different names at seven places, or we may imagine that the crew of a Chinese vessel driven on the island decided to settle there. The fact remains that the people of Miyako were raised from a state of primitive simplicity by late arrivals from the north and west, and that a lively sense of gratitude preserves the memory of individuals who took the lead in promoting community welfare.

Sunakawa *Otono* was deified in recognition of his leadership in introducing Japanese shipbuilding techniques, and two villages which specialize in boat construction are to be found today near the grove in which he is worshipped.

It is not surprising to discover that a number of leading families trace their descent from immigrants from Kume and Okinawa.

Of the latter-day heroes—the men who sought to reconcile Miyako folkways with the more advanced customs of Okinawa proper—we have the story of Nema Ikari, who deplored local attitudes toward ancestors. This worthy made his way up to Naha, studied the proper rites, and returned to introduce new forms of burial and worship and new types of tomb construction on Miyako.

Although expressions of gratitude and appreciation form such admirable themes in Miyako folklore, there were other themes of cruelty, revenge and counter-revenge, attack, and betrayal. Miyako legends are suffused with sadness, and poetic themes and songs are preoccupied with the bitterness of poverty, isolation, disappointment, and hopeless aspiration.

It is noteworthy how many heroes are men who died in overwhelming disaster, and how often the songs and stories tell of tragedy of separation, of the dismal fate which befell the children of seafaring fathers who never returned, and of women abandoned by adventurers who came from overseas, stayed briefly, and moved on to new conquests or returned to official duties on Okinawa.

There is a legend attached to the Kubaka seaside castle ruins which tells of the daughter of the Lord of Kubaka, whose husband, an Okinawan named Tamagushiku, once overheard her address her child as the "son of a wanderer." In anger he declared that he was a man of great importance as a trader to the distant southern islands. Taking the child, he returned to Okinawa. There the boy in time became a great lord, but the disconsolate mother wandered often on the shore below the castle walls, praying for death, which came at last one day to release her when she was swept into the sea by a great tidal wave.

Another tale with a bitter ending concerns the rivalry of two Miyako women for the love of a Japanese; when one produced a handsome son the other brought about the boy's death in a cruel fashion.

Miyako was brought under Shuri's control by conquest, and the theme of subordination and neglect thereafter colors many stories, exemplified best perhaps in the tale of Mahomaru, a beautiful daughter of the rebellious Nakaya Kanemaru. In reprisal upon her father she was forced to go up to Shuri to become one of the concubines of the king (Sho Shin). She became pregnant, but instead of winning protection by the king she was sent back to Miyako, the victim of jealous court ladies who considered her of inferior origin. En route she was shipwrecked and died on Terama Island, where she was enshrined.

The growth of communication with Okinawa in the 15th century sharpened the rivalry of competing chieftains on Miyako and Yaeyama. The contest in Miyako came to a climax in the rivalry of two families. One of them, the Kaneshigawa, were a shipbuilding clan of the Sunakawa area, and were said to have had many ships engaged in profitable trade with Naha. The other was the Nakasone family. Late in the 15th century, Akahachi, the principal chieftain on Yaeyama, proposed to invade Miyako, taking advantage of the division there, but hearing of this, Nakasone *Toyomioya* organized a skillful counterattack, invaded Yaeyama, overwhelmed Akahachi, and crossed over to Yonaguni Island beyond. There he overwhelmed the chieftain Untura and seized Untura's daughter as a prize.

This expedition was the supreme event in Saki-shima history and forms the theme of its principal legends, songs, and dramatic dances retelling Nakasone's exploits and the fate of his captives. Soon after his return to Hirara, Nakasone had to face the formidable expedition sent against Miyako by Sho Shin. Some three thousand men were in the Okinawan force, and there could be no doubt as to the ultimate decision. Nakasone therefore negotiated a surrender on terms which saved the Miyako villagers from disaster. For this he was later deified and worshipped at the principal shrine in the islands.

It required years to develop a satisfactory administrative relationship between Okinawa and Miyako and to bring about unity within the island. In 1500 Nakasone was recognized as Chieftain of Miyako Island (*Miyako-jima Kashira*) and the direct administration was left in his hands. Shuri instituted a system of rewards and punishments. Titles and honors were devised to confirm local chieftains in landholdings they already possessed, and merit awards enabled Shuri's representatives to divide and counter local opposition which could not be put down by direct action.

The Nakasone family were displaced by Meguro Mori *Toyomioya* about 1530, but he had scarcely fought his way to supremacy when he was overthrown by a youth named Yonaha Sedo *Toyomioya*. He proved to be the last of the local rulers, and he too was later deified and shared honors with Nakasone in Miyako Shrine.

In 1532 Shuri established direct control in Miyako by appointing a magistrate from Shuri as governor of the island.

Miyako's opposition to Okinawa gradually subsided, and as the years went by, the meager local resources were made to yield to systematic taxation. Thanks to extreme poverty, the economy assumed a dual character. The men took to the sea as fishermen and as crewmen needed on the far-ranging voyages of the Naha merchantmen. The women stayed at home to farm and to weave. Farming yielded just enough food to sustain the population at a minimum subsistence level. Weaving techniques introduced from Okinawa or by way of Okinawa were gradually perfected.

Late in the 16th century a native of Miyako is said to have been aboard a vessel engaged in the China trade when it was wrecked in a great storm. His skill in assisting in the repair and recovery of the ship was brought to the attention of the Chinese court, which took note of it with high praise in a dispatch to the king at Shuri. The king in turn made a grant of land and a title to this obscure subject in Miyako. As a gesture of gratitude the man's wife devoted immense care and skill to the development of a weaving technique which was known to her. The product of her loom was sent up to the royal court as a thank-offering in 1584. Its perfection attracted attention and patronage, and in time the highly specialized fabric known as *Miyako jofu* became the most valued and most prized export commodity of Miyako, and has so remained until the present day. Its only rival was sugar, said to have been introduced to Miyako from China about 1597, and within a few years thereafter both of these (and certain valued shells) were required by Shuri as tax items, and by Shuri were in turn exported to Satsuma in Kyushu for distribution in Japan.

Under Okinawan direction Miyako thus took its place in the larger economic system. Miyako sailors were considered the most skilled and hardy seafarers, and Miyako's place as a way station on the vital line of communications with China was signified in the Karimata Watch Hill, where a stone direction-marker was erected on a site from which all the nearby islands could be kept under surveillance. From here reports were made to the Shuri officials, giving note of all passing ships and the course each took.

Despite its greater fertility and area, its resources in forest land and sheltered inlets, the Yaeyama Islands never acquired the importance assumed by Miyako in the 16th century and maintained thereafter. Some mystery attends this: in later years it is explained that Yaeyama has had a forbidding record of malarial fevers and snake infestation, but this explanation does not seem to be sufficient, and the question remains shrouded in mystery.

In concluding this comment upon Okinawa's relations with the outer islands, it remains only to notice that while extending controls to the south, Shuri showed comparable interest in the islands to the north, along the sea route to Japan, but there took less action. The frontiers remained on Kikai Island from 1486 until 1537, when an expeditionary force of fifty ships pushed on to Amami Oshima. The occupation was temporary, and a second force had to be dispatched three decades later, in 1571, to reassert Shuri's claims.

It may be that the Okinawans sensed the dangers of close approach to the main islands of Japan or were warned of them, and moved too cautiously to establish a firm footing in these northern islands. Furthermore, the move was made at a time of uncertainty at Shuri. Sho Shin's son ruled from 1526 until 1556, when the throne passed to a prince who was mute. This unfortunate circumstance proved a test of the institutional basis to which Sho Shin had done so much to shift the royal office. A Regency Council of Three (the *Sanshikan*) undertook to act in the king's behalf and at his request. Thenceforth the council grew into the most effective and influential institution within the administrative structure.

The mute king died in 1571. His son, Sho Ei, was the last king of a truly independent Okinawa. His reign ended in 1588. This was a year of ominous portent, for Toyotomi Hideyoshi, master of Japan, in the next season sent down warning to Okinawa that he expected Shuri's coöperation in a projected invasion of China and conquest of Asia. Here indeed was a dilemma for a small kingdom whose commercial life and well-being depended wholly upon the goodwill of its powerful neighbors.

OKINAWAN TRADE WITH THE INDIES AND SOUTHEAST ASIA

Upon the first contact with the marauding Europeans in 1511, the Okinawans began slowly to retreat from ports of Southeast Asia, trading over shorter sea routes and in less varied goods until, in 1611, they found themselves cut off from the south and confined to a narrow range of commerce with China at Ch'uang-chou and with Satsuma in Japan.

Events in the 16th century proved that no prosperous trading port in Asia was secure from the Japanese *wako* or the European conquistadors. Behind the Okinawans, to the north, were the Japanese, watching with deep concern the Portuguese, Spanish, Dutch, and English adventurers in turn come up from India through the Indies, Malaya, the Philippines, Formosa, and the Ryukyu Islands. The white men were willing to trade, but only on their own terms; they gave no quarter to anyone bold enough or foolish enough to refuse their demands. The more prosperous the port, the greater the danger that it would be seized and sacked, or declared a possession newly "discovered" for a Christian king.

It is to Portuguese accounts we must turn, however, for notices of the position, the reputation, and the activities of the Okinawans in Southeast Asia. Our principal sources (reproduced in annotated translations by the Hakluyt Society) are the *Suma Oriental* of Thomé Pires, written about 1512-15; the *Book of Duarte Barbosa*, completed about 1518; and the *Commentaries of the Great Afonso Dalboquerque, Second Viceroy of India*, prepared by his son from dispatches forwarded by the viceroy to the King of Portugal, Dom Emmanuel. In his immense work

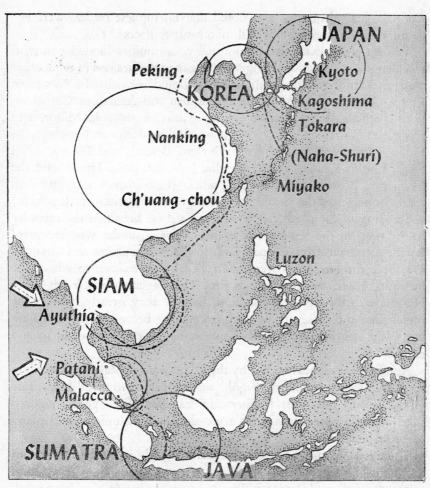

FIG. 8. MAP: OVERSEAS TRADE ROUTES AND INFLUENTIAL CULTURAL AREAS
IN THE 15TH CENTURY.

125

Da Asia, Joaõ de Barros also noted that Portuguese traders were encountering Okinawan ships and merchants at Patani.[6]

Traders at Malacca settled in small communities having common race, language, or national origin. Along the wharves and in the market place the visiting Okinawans brushed shoulders with Moslems from Egypt, Aden, and Mecca, with Abyssinian and Armenian Christians, with Persians, Parsees from India, Turks from Asia Minor, and representatives from many of the small kingdoms and enclaves of India. There were traders from Ceylon, Bengal, and Burma, from Siam, Cochin-China, and Cambodia, Java, Sumatra, Timor, and the Moluccas, Borneo and the Philippines. (Pires names sixty nations, cities. or principalities in addition to the men of *Lequeos*, or Ryukyu.)

Shipping in the roadstead was supervised on behalf of the rajah by an Admiral of the Sea known as the *Lasamane*, under whose control lay the merchants from China, "Lequeos," Cochin-China, and Champa. On shore the foreigners were controlled by *xabandares*, to whom the incoming merchants must make gifts. These agents of the rajah "have become rich through this function, because they greatly overtax the merchants; and these put up with everything because their profits are large and also because it is the custom of the country to do so and endure it."[7]

Among the cargoes handled by the Okinawans at Malacca (according to Portuguese accounts) were gold and copper, arms of all kinds, fine gold-leaf and gold-dust lacquerware, excellent fans, paper, colored silks, damask, porcelains, musk, rock-alum, grains, onions, and many other vegetables.

There is a mention of green porcelains brought in by the Okinawans and transshipped to Bengal. Okinawan goods had a high reputation; they were well made and, says Pires, "just as we in our kingdoms speak of Milan, so do the Chinese and all other races speak of the *Lequjos* [Ryukyus]."

It is evident from these lists that most of the Okinawan cargoes were of goods transshipped from Japan, Korea, and China. The Malacca merchants were aware of this, according to Pires, for: "All that comes from the Lequos is brought by them from Japan. And the *Lequeos* trade with the people of Japan in cloths, fishing-nets and other merchandise." He notes that the Okinawans picked up cargoes not unlike the cargoes bought by Chinese merchants, and that they took "a great deal of Bengal clothing" and were especially fond of a heavy, brandy-like Malacca wine, shipping it out in quantity. Much of their cargo was paid for by them in gold coinage bearing a distinctive stamp.

As for the people themselves and the distant country from which they came, the Portuguese learned that.:

"The Lequeos are called Gores—they are known by either of these names. Lequios is the chief one.

"The king is a heathen, and all the people too, he is a tributary vassal of the king of the Chinese. His island is large and has many people; they have small ships of their own type; they have three or four junks which are continuously buying in China, and they have no more. They trade in China and in Malacca, and sometimes on their own. In China they trade at the port of Foqem [Fukien] which is in the land of China near Canton, a day and a night's sail away. The Malays say to the people of Malacca that there is no difference between Portuguese and *Llequos*, except that the Portuguese buy women, which the Leq̃os do not.

"The *Lequjos* have only wheat in their country, and rice and wines after their fashion, meat and fish in great abundance. They are great draftsmen and armourers. They make gilt coffers, very rich and well-made fans, swords, many arms of all kinds after their fashion. . . .

"They are very truthful men. They do not buy slaves, nor would they sell one of their own men for the whole world, and they would die over this. . . .

"They are white men, well dressed, better than the Chinese, more dignified. They sail to China and take merchandise that goes from Malacca to China, and go to Japan, which is an island seven or eight days' sail distant, and take the gold and copper in the said island in exchange for their merchandise. The *Leqios* are men who sell their merchandise freely for credit, and if they are lied to when they collect payment, they collect it sword in hand. . . .

"The chief [merchandise] is gold, copper, and arms of all kinds, coffers, boxes . . . with gold leaf veneer, fans, wheat, and their things are well made. They bring a great deal of gold. They are truthful men, —more so than the Chinese—and feared. They bring a great store of paper and silk in colours; they bring musk, porcelain, damask; they bring onions and many vegetables. . . . The Lequos bring swords worth thirty *cruzados* each, and many of them."[8]

Pires may have met the last Okinawans who reached Malacca, in 1511, but the presumption must be that he prepared these notes on the basis of inquiry made among residents of Malacca who were well acquainted with Okinawans, who had come hitherto regularly to trade at the port. If allowance is made for the mistake in believing some of the Japanese wares to be products of Okinawa, the account is a fairly accurate one, though at one point Pires relays as hearsay a story that after escape from peril at sea the Okinawans "buy a beautiful maiden to be sacrificed and behead her on the prow of the junk, and other things like these."

Duarte Barbosa (a cousin of the great Magellan), writing about 1518, describes the Okinawans as "certain white folk, who they say are great and rich merchants. . . . The Malacca people say that they are better men, and richer and more eminent merchants than the Chins [Chinese]. Of these folk we as yet know but little, and they have not yet come to Malacca since it has been under the King our Lord [i.e., since 1511]."[9]

In preparing his *Commentaries* upon his father's reports, Dalboquerque the Younger repeats most of the information supplied to Lisbon by Pires, but discusses the location of the Ryukyus at some length, and remarks upon difficulty in securing details:

". . . they are men of very reserved speech, and do not give anyone an account of their native affairs. . . .

"The land of these Gores is called *Lequea;* the men are fair; their dress is like a cloak without a hood; they carry long swords after the fashion of Turkish cimetars, but somewhat more narrow; they also carry daggers of two palms' length; they are daring men and feared in this land [of Malacca]. When they arrive at any port, they do not bring out their merchandize all at once, but little by little; they speak truthfully, and will have the truth spoken to them. If any merchant in Malacca broke his word, they would immediately take him prisoner. They strive to dispatch their business and get away quickly, for they are not the men to like going away from their own land. They set out for Malacca in the month of January, and begin their return journey in August or September. . . ."[10]

In these brief notices the Portuguese accounts return again and again to note the presence of gold bars and gold dust in the Okinawan commerce, and of gold used in the lacquerware brought in from Naha. Their curiosity was roused by this; perhaps these *were* the Rica de Oro and Rica de Plata—the Islands of Gold and of Silver—said to lie far out in the Eastern Seas. Pires finished his great manuscript about 1515; in 1517 he set out as ambassador to the Emperor of China. He was escorted to Canton in a fleet commanded by Fernaõ Peres de Andrade, who ordered a subordinate commander (Jorge Mascarenhas) to proceed with a detachment of vessels up the coast of China to search for the fabled Ryukyu Islands. Mascarenhas got no farther than Fukien Province, where he was trading with profit at Amoy when orders overtook the squadron, directing him to return to Malacca.

The Portuguese were soon trading along the China coast and established themselves as far north as Ningpo, near the mouth of the Yangtse. Gradually they accumulated further data concerning Okinawa. The first book on China printed in Europe was brought out in 1569, the record of the Dominican Father Gaspar da Cruz. In it he noted that there had been misunderstanding concerning the location of the Ryukyus, and has this to say:

"It is an island which standeth in the sea of China, little more or less than thirty leagues from China itself. In this island live this people, which is a well-disposed people, more to the white than brown.

"It is a cleanly and well-attired people; they dress their hair like women, and tie it up on the side of their head, fastened with a silver bodkin. Their land is fresh and fertile, with many and good waters; and it is a people that sail very seldom although they are in the midst of the sea. They use weapons and wear very good short swords. They were in times past subject to the Chinas, with whom they had much communication, and therefore they are very like the Chinas."[11]

Formal Relations with China

We have now to retrace the course of these Okinawan relations with China, the intrusion of Japan upon this relationship, and the events which led to the loss of independence.

The Ming records indicate that the Okinawans showed an embarrassing eagerness to increase the frequency of tribute payments, agreed upon in 1372, and sought every pretext to send official missions to the Chinese capital. Indeed, for precisely five hundred years Okinawan kings were to be the most faithful of all the subject kings, princes, chieftains, and prelates registered as tributaries to the Chinese court. Undoubtedly in part the Okinawans were deeply moved by a sense of moral obligation, for they took Confucian discipline and precepts seriously; China was the "teacher," upon whom they looked with veneration.

But these worthy sentiments were not unsupported by grosser considerations. China was also one of the most populous and powerful countries in the world, and Chinese literature, at least, was full of sententious admonitions that all non-Chinese barbarians must tremble and obey lest they incur the wrath of the emperor and provoke him to expressions of reproval and acts of chastisement. Neither love nor fear were at the heart of the matter; for the Okinawans a profitable and expanding trade with China was vital; China was the best customer for their commercial wares.

For the Chinese, however, the Okinawan trade was unimportant. Peking was in no way dependent upon commerce with the Ryukyus; the official tribute sent over to China was of token value only, and the trade in luxuries was of minor interest in the grand total of Chinese commerce with foreign states and tributaries. In fact, the cost to China in entertainment for Okinawan envoys and gifts to the Shuri court exceeded by far in value the symbolic tribute of sulphur, shells, copper, cloth, and trained horses.

The Ming annals show clearly that the haughty bureaucrats at Peking felt the Okinawans were importunate with their endless requests for additional or larger missions, and that the Chinese ministers of state sought to "regulate" and reduce the number of official exchanges with this overeager tributary.

Had they been allowed to do so, the Okinawans might well have sought to pay tribute annually; in the course of five centuries the periods actually varied from two- to twenty-year intervals. The succession-ritual missions were of unpredictable frequency; upon one occasion at least two royal deaths and two successions were announced simultaneously, but in the case of Sho Shin some fifty years had elapsed between his accession and his death.

It was in the matter of congratulatory missions and condolences that the Chinese felt the Okinawans overdid a good thing; the records suggest that the court officials at Peking often would have been willing to accept the will for the deed. The punctilious Okinawans endeavored to practice what the Chinese had preached in matters of ceremonial politeness and formal duty. They insisted that the birth of an heir to the Chinese throne or the wedding of a crown prince or the death of an emperor required special recognition and a special mission.

Such polite formalities covered additional opportunities for trade. Dry entries in the Ming and Ch'ing records and in the annals of the Shuri court indicate that the Chinese sometimes made the way difficult for the insistent Okinawans. There was "squeeze" to pay to Chinese officials at the port of entry and along the road to Peking. There were presents to be distributed judiciously among the high officers at the court.

There were other troubles; in one instance (about 1477) it was charged that the Okinawan ambassadors had killed some Chinese peasants and burned a village somewhere along the road to Peking, but the Ming records a few years later hint that in fact the disturbances had been caused by Fukien Chinese who were employed in the Okinawan ambassador's suite. This was condemned and the court officials advised the emperor to direct the king at Shuri to employ only Okinawans henceforth in tribute missions. On another occasion (in the reign of Sho Shi-sho) it was reported at Peking that an Okinawan embassy had robbed a Chinese vessel on the high seas; the ambassador was punished at Peking, but his companions—more than sixty in number—were sent back to Shuri to be dealt with by their own king. Shuri at once sent a new embassy to Peking to express regret.

There is considerable evidence that the Okinawans were often accompanied by unwelcome associates on their journeys to the south and to the Chinese court. Japanese freebooters sometimes represented themselves as traders from the Ryukyus, capitalizing on the fair reputation which the peaceable Okinawans enjoyed in foreign ports; sometimes Japanese, Chinese, and Korean *wako* traveled aboard ships from Naha. Chinese dwelling in the foreign settlement at Tomari signed on as crewmen, and local coolies had to be engaged at China's port of entry to transfer baggage overland to Peking. The Ming and Ch'ing annals reflect the trouble which rose from this practice.

Nor were the Chinese always satisfied with the conduct of their own ambassadors sent to Ryukyu; upon one occasion word reached the imperial court that the Chinese envoys had accepted gifts of gold, spices, and Japanese fans in a private capacity, and for this the emperor ordered them to be flogged. There is one mention of eunuchs sent as a gift from Okinawa during the reign of Yung Lo (1403-24). This gift was rejected, and the unfortunate men were sent back to Okinawa with directions that this should not be done again.*

From time to time it was suggested that the Chinese ambassadors need not make the dangerous ocean voyage to Naha, but should instead hand over the documents granting investiture at the port of exit from China, together with customary gifts. This was unorthodox and unacceptable to the Chinese; it may have been prompted by Shuri's desire to avoid the high cost of entertainment which devolved upon the king's treasury while the Chinese ambassadors were in Okinawa. At another time, when piracy was common and the coasts of China were ravaged by freebooters, certain Chinese officials themselves proposed to adopt this device as a means of avoiding travel on the high seas, but this the imperial court would not allow. As a compromise,

* This appears to be the only reference to eunuchs in Okinawa; neither the Japanese nor the Okinawans ever adopted the barbarous Chinese eunuch-system at the royal courts.

instead, a high military officer and a military force were substituted for the usual civil mission. They crossed to Shuri, but the Okinawans in turn made polite objection and petitioned for the resumption of civil missions and the dispatch of scholars rather than soldiers. The petition was granted.

In 1471 an envoy en route to Peking was arrested, charged with wearing robes embroidered with the design of the so-called *mang* dragon, reserved in China for the exclusive use of the highest officials in the empire and for certain ranks of the nobility. The Chuzan ambassador insisted that he had full right to wear the robes, for they had been sent from the Chinese emperor to the king at Shuri, whose representative he was.[12]

To accommodate administration at the busy port of Naha, a town governorship was established in 1528. New buildings were erected to accommodate Chinese envoys and traders who paused there en route to and from Shuri, and a special pavilion in Chinese style was erected within the palace grounds to serve as a reception hall for distinguished visitors from Peking.

The Okinawans were zealous in the study of Chinese etiquette and ritual; the Chinese in turn recognized and admired the fidelity with which the island people met exacting demands made upon them by the stately court at Peking. This reached its highest attestation in 1554 when the emperor deigned to confer upon the king at Shuri a large tablet bearing the inscription *Shurei no Kuni* (Country of Propriety). The king in turn recognized the unparalleled honor which this implied by causing a great gate to be erected on the approach to his castle, in which the tablet was placed for all to see.

Okinawa was of little intrinsic interest to the sophisticated Chinese. Envoys were directed to report on special topics from time to time, and in 1534 the ambassador Chin K'an prepared a history of the Liu Ch'iu kingdom. Occasionally the imperial court made special grants-in-aid to the Confucian school at Tomari, where Okinawan youths applied themselves diligently to the study of the Chinese classics.

In 1908 E. Dennison Ross announced the discovery of a vocabulary of the Liu Ch'iu language prepared at Peking in 1549. This interesting fragment had been compiled for the guidance of interpreters who were associated with the Okinawan missions in China. Similar vocabularies offering comparative data on the Liu Ch'iu, Chinese, and Korean languages are preserved in the Korean annals, and have been described by Frederick Hirth.

For nearly five hundred years there was a community of Okinawan students continuously in residence at Peking. The majority stayed two or three years, but in exceptional cases some stayed much longer. The Chinese government provided clothing, housing, food, and the equivalent of tuition. There they mingled with students from other tributary states and with Chinese youths. We must presume that they applied themselves diligently to their books, did what they could to keep warm

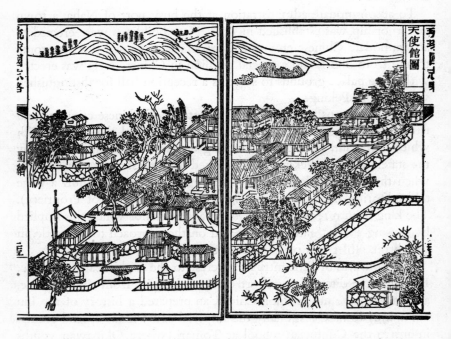

FIG. 9. TENSHI-KAN, A RESIDENCE FOR CHINA'S ENVOYS AT NAHA. *A mansion for China's "heavenly ambassadors" was erected first in 1396. The sketch (and those of Figs. 11, 13, and 14) was drawn by a Chinese artist after the 1756 embassy, published in the 1770's in a Wuying Palace movable-type edition of Chou Huang's* Liu Ch'iu-kuo Chih-lueh, *and reissued in 1830.*

134

during the bitter, dry cold of the Peking winters, and talked politics and government, art and poetry in the immemorial manner of students abroad. We know that they were spirited, forthright, and sometimes disastrously indiscreet, for on one occasion Okinawan students were arrested, charged with improper criticism of an imperial decree, and forthwith executed.

Over the centuries China's purposes were well served by this foreign student training program. Youths selected for it were outstanding among their countrymen both in intellectual accomplishments and in social status; they were assured of high prestige and of lifetime careers in high government office at Shuri and Naha. They were virtually certain to incline to China's interests in questions affecting them; they were the instruments of cultural as well as political diplomacy.

RELATIONS WITH JAPAN: TRADE AND POLITICS

We must now go back a little to review the development of Shuri's relations with Japan.

It will be recalled that in 1369 the Ming Emperor Hung Wu sent envoys into states and territories adjacent to China summoning them in haughty terms to recognize his supremacy and suzerain rights. The princes of Okinawa and the King of Korea had responded promptly, but the envoy sent to Japan had carried this message: "If you are friendly toward the Government, then appear at the Court; otherwise make armed preparations to defend yourselves. In case you attempt raid or robbery, orders will be instantly given to start a war of subjugation. We desire you, O King, to consider well."[13] The imperial message and the Chinese envoys were treated with a marked lack of respect in Japan. Japanese raids along the China coast continued and increased; villages and large cities suffered heavy losses; and normal administration was disrupted in the coastal provinces. For a brief time the Chinese accepted "tribute" from the military governor of Kyushu, one of the barons of western Japan, and in turn addressed him as King, either through ignorance of his true status or (more likely) as a means of saving the imperial face. The great Hung Wu repeatedly summoned Japan to pay homage, and repeatedly the Japanese returned arrogant replies. They were willing to trade, but they held China's threats in open contempt, for nothing came of them; the raids on Chinese territory spread as far south as Kwangtung Province.

Thus matters stood unsatisfactorily for sixty years; China and Japan were not on speaking terms, as it were, but for different reasons. China demanded formal acknowledgment of moral and cultural superiority to clothe all other relationships; Japan wanted trade and acceptance of political equality in any formal exchange.

Meanwhile Okinawa was free to trade with both countries and with Korea. Cargoes brought into Naha from the south and from China were moved on northward, some to Korea direct, but most of them along the Kikai and Amami Oshima route into Kagoshima. There they were again divided; the bulk went into Satsuma's hands, but some remained in the hands of Shuri's agents to be taken by them either to Korea (in company with Satsuma's men) or to Kyoto.

The Daimyo of Satsuma established a trade relationship with the Korean court in 1395. Much of the goods sent over to Seoul had come into Kagoshima in Okinawan ships. In the interests of this highly profitable trade the Shimazu did not hesitate to allow themselves to be called "tributaries" to the Li dynasty. Between 1395 and 1504 no less than 126 missions went over to Korea. Under Satsuma's patronage Okinawan envoys and merchants often traveled with Shimazu's agents.

Okinawan representatives traveled through Satsuma to Kyoto bearing gifts and goods; records survive of seven missions from Shuri to Kyoto between 1403 and 1448. Messages for the Ashikaga shogun were written in the phonetic *kana* system; medicinal herbs, Chinese lacquerware, coins, and other luxury items were among the gifts and trading goods. Taking their cue from the Chinese formula governing these matters, the Japanese recorded Shuri's gifts as "tribute" and in time began to look back on the year 1415 as the first in which the Okinawan kingdom submitted *pro forma* to the shogunate. There was no attempt by Kyoto to interfere with the internal affairs of the distant island kingdom.

As the decades passed, Satsuma became increasingly dependent upon Okinawa as a source of wares to be traded into Japan and Korea. This bred trouble for Shuri.

In 1432 Sho Hashi was called upon to play the delicate role of mediator between great China and recalcitrant Japan. The Ming annals record that: "In the first month of the seventh year of Hsuan Tê [1432]
the Emperor's attention was called to the fact that while all outlying
peoples on every side appeared at the Court, Japan alone had not
brought tribute for some time. The eunuch, Ch'ai Shan, was ordered
to visit Liu Ch'iu in order to have the King of that island admonish
Japan. An Imperial message was given [to the king]."[14]

Sho Hashi was scarcely in a position to "admonish" the hot-tempered
Japanese; nevertheless, his envoys succeeded in bringing about a decided
improvement in official relations between the two quarreling neighbors.

Direct Sino-Japanese intercourse was resumed for a time. Concessions were necessary on both sides; on the one hand the Ashikaga
felt a pressing need for the profits which regular trade with China could
bring, on the other the Chinese had to reduce the terrible losses which
they suffered at the hands of the Japanese sea barons. We have noted
upon an earlier page that bona fide Japanese traders in China were
greatly annoyed by the elaborate formalities demanded of them, and
hinted that piracy would increase if they were not permitted to trade
freely. Relations between the two countries were growing worse; the
situation cried out for remedy, and this could only be found in some
formal arrangement to regularize trade.

A temporary solution was found which saved embarrassment on both
sides. A direct tribute relationship was created between the great Zen
temple Tenryu-ji, at Kyoto, and the Ming court. Peking enjoyed the
privilege of appointing the chief priest for this powerful temple organization, but neither the Shogun nor the Emperor of Japan in these circumstances need consider himself subordinate to the Emperor of China.

No definite date can be fixed to mark the change which now began
to overtake Japanese relations with Okinawa, culminating in established
Japanese suzerainty in the Ryukyu Islands. It can be attributed, however, to the changes in political and economic conditions within Japan
itself, which was entering upon a long period of political anarchy and
economic chaos. The imperial government at Kyoto was powerless
and utterly poverty stricken. The Ashikaga shoguns exercised nominal
government by imperial appointment, but this shadow authority was

challenged successfully in every part of the country. Land revenues needed to sustain a central government were diminished in proportion to the shogun's loss of power to collect taxes.

Because of these internal difficulties the shogunate came more and more to depend upon the profits to be gained in maritime commerce. Out of dire necessity grew the arrangements which granted Tenryu-ji a virtual monopoly of the legitimate China trade. But the priests soon began to subdivide and farm out the privilege (and the revenues) by selling trade licenses to prosperous merchants, territorial barons, and other temples. Thus official trade with China was carried in vessels sailing as "tribute ships." Tenryu-ji missionaries did much to promote intercourse with Okinawa, and among the barons who shared in Ten-ryu-ji trading enterprises was Shimazu, Lord of Satsuma.

The shogun was too weak to curb Japanese pirates whose dangerous enterprises were based on small ports belonging to barons who held the shogunate and the shogun's orders in light regard. From the main islands of Kyushu, Honshu, and Shikoku the marauders expanded their activities until at last they boldly went ashore in China to sack such important cities as Ningpo and Yangchow.

Chinese and Korean adventurers sailed with the *wako*. According to the *Ming Annals:*

"Because in their own country [of China] they were unable to obtain what they wanted, they had made their way over the sea to the islands to become gang leaders. The Wa [i.e., the Japanese] listened to them and were persuaded by them to start raids. Then these buccaneer chiefs, donning Japanese robes with Japanese ornaments and insignia, came in various craft to loot their native land [i.e., China]. As the profit was always enormous, trouble with these pirates became worse day by day"[15]

"Generally only about three-tenths of these [pirates] were real Japanese, while seven-tenths were [others] who followed them. . . . Their discipline was stern and they all fought to the death; but the government forces were effeminate and always gave way and ran."[16]

If the local traditions and folk tales are to be credited, it is probable that many hardy men of Amami Oshima and of Miyako were aboard the pirate ships. Neither the Chinese annals nor the Okinawan records make mention of Naha men as sea rovers.

The Chinese government began to issue passport-certificates known as *kuei-chou* which enabled junks from Naha to pass through the guard-ship cordons stationed at coastal ports and estuaries. To give weight to the certificates and to cover ordinary merchantmen as well as official tribute envoys, the *kuei-chou* stated that the Okinawan bearers were in search of tribute goods for the imperial court. For Japanese traders a similar tally system was devised. Legitimate commerce was possible only if the merchant or envoy could produce documents properly authenticated and dated, which were in effect limited licenses. Ningpo was designated the base for trade with Japan.

It was against this background that the princes of Satsuma assumed a proprietary position between Chuzan, which could trade at Ch'uang-chou, and the government at Kyoto, whose agents could trade legitimately only at Ningpo. Shimazu wanted an ever-larger share in the Naha trade; Shuri was interested in developing its markets in nearby Kagoshima and needed Satsuma's protection in its trade with Korea. It was prepared to accommodate itself to Satsuma's interests.

Shimazu, of course, was unwilling to allow any other covetous Japanese barons to intrude upon this highly profitable arrangement. Many had already sampled the Okinawan trade. In 1450 the powerful Hosokawa Katsumoto, based in Shikoku, plundered an Okinawan vessel bearing cargo into Hyogo for transshipment to Kyoto. Undaunted, the Okinawans continued to risk the dangerous waters of the Inland Sea, for the profits were very great. In the next year they delivered one thousand strings of copper cash to the shogun as "tribute"; nothing could be more welcome at Kyoto, for the extravagant Shogun Ashikaga Yoshimasa stood in special need of Chinese coins with which to maintain his luxurious establishment.

The grant of monopoly interest to Tenryu-ji had failed to meet the shogun's needs. It now appears that Yoshimasa began to give more attention to the importance of the Ryukyuan trade and to see that it was in his interest to coöperate with Satsuma. From fragmentary accounts we sense an increasing disposition on both sides to formalize relations with Shuri and to look to Satsuma for favorable management of shipping interests. In 1458 the shogun deigned to grant a personal interview with the envoys from the king at Shuri, and in 1471 he ordered subordinate daimyo to send their ships to Okinawa to enter upon the lively trade with China and Southeast Asia.

From this it was a short step to direct interference. In 1480 the shogun ordered Lord Shimazu to "supervise" Okinawan shipping and directed the King of Ryukyu to send tribute to Kyoto. As a matter of fact the Ashikaga government at Kyoto was in no position to enforce such orders, but Shimazu was glad enough to have his position legitimatized vis-à-vis the Ryukyus.

Shuri was directed to confiscate all cargoes on Japanese ships at Naha which did not carry trading permits issued by Satsuma. Tribute missions to Kyoto henceforth would pass through Kagoshima and be escorted by Shimazu's agents.

The Okinawans were most reluctant to accept this interference and to lose their full freedom to trade wherever they wished and with all who came peacefully to Okinawa. An embassy proceeded at once to Kagoshima to negotiate in the matter, but little Shuri was powerless; the king could not evade the shogun's orders, issued through Satsuma. Henceforth for a hundred years Shimazu acted (nominally, at least) as the shogun's agent in the Okinawan trade. Shuri tactfully sent congratulatory missions to Kagoshima when new lords succeeded to the headship of the Shimazu family, when new heirs were born, and upon occasions calling for condolence. Each such mission provided an opportunity for enlarged trade, and in turn Satsuma assumed an obligation to protect the Ryukyus and the Okinawan commerce. In a word, Shuri traded on sufferance, and paid tribute to Peking through Ch'uang-chou and to Kyoto through Kagoshima. Satsuma had gained a monopoly on the valuable luxury trade moving from the south to Japan and to Korea.

Other trading barons were jealous. In 1516 the Lord of Bitchu (Miyake Kunihide) decided to challenge Satsuma, and set sail for Naha with an expeditionary force of twelve ships. Word reached Kagoshima in time for Lord Shimazu Tadaharu to assemble forces near Bonotsu Harbor, in Kyushu. In a swift action he fell upon Miyake, killed him, and dispersed his fleet. Satsuma was determined not to be outflanked on the south. A military unit was established in the Tokara Island group, a few miles southeast of the entrance to Kagoshima Bay. From here close watch could be kept upon the sea approaches to the Shimazu domain. Soon a trading depot developed on the offshore island of Tane-ga-shima, and here an Okinawan settlement grew up, providing a permanent staff to handle the reception and transshipment of goods destined for Japan and Korea. All commerce and all travelers entering Satsuma from the south were required to pass through this check-point. The growth of a way station here closely paralleled the development of the Ch'uang-chou trading depot, which had been established on the China coast in 1439.

Satsuma and Shuri, in close correspondence, served as "go-betweens" in diplomacy and trade between Kyoto and Peking throughout the 16th century. It was a painful position for Shuri. Direct legitimate trade between the two powerful neighbors was coming to an end. War threatened, and the king at Shuri had to exercise utmost tact and delicacy in serving as a mediator between the two quarreling governments.

For example, in 1523 the shogun's representative reached the Chinese port of Ningpo bearing valid tallies required for trade. Concurrently, an agent of the powerful, quasi-independent Hosokawa daimyo of western Japan put in his appearance with a considerable body of armed followers. His documents proved to be invalid and outdated; nevertheless, with bluff and arrogance he demanded a share in the goods available for export. The two Japanese factions came to blows. Rioting spread through the city, and before the Chinese could bring the offending foreigners under control, fires had swept through much of Ningpo and ships had been burned in the harbor. The principal troublemaker, Hosokawa's agent, was seized, and died miserably in prison. The outraged Chinese threatened to close Ningpo to all Japanese commerce.

By chance an Okinawan envoy was leaving Peking at this time. Through him the imperial government directed the king at Shuri to forward to the shogun an order, couched in the most haughty terms, demanding the arrest of the Japanese official who had been party to the Ningpo quarrel, and to repatriate a number of Chinese who had been kidnapped during an earlier raid on the China coast. Furthermore, the shogun must explain the misuse of tallies issued as a license for trade. If the shogun did not reply in a satisfactory manner, all Chinese ports would be closed to Japanese commerce and a punitive force would be sent across to chastize Japan.

Shuri dutifully transmitted this unpleasant message. Kyoto did not bother to reply until five years had passed, when in 1530 the shogun asked an Okinawan mission to transmit the answer. This was done as tactfully as possible: "When the officer of the (Chinese) Ministry of Ceremony examined this paper [he found that] it was without a signature. Then he proposed that since the Japanese were too deceitful and treacherous to be trusted, it might be well for the Court to tell the King of Liu-ch'iu to convey instructions to Japan to carry out the previous order."[17]

Thus the Okinawans were repeatedly placed in a most difficult position, for in this age an envoy's life was not secure; it took courage to convey China's haughty messages and threats to the hot-tempered Japanese, although it is just possible that the swaggering barons of Japan were more tempted to laughter than anger by the Chinese attempt to place little Liu-ch'iu between them.

Okinawan ships on the high seas were not often molested by Japanese or Chinese pirates before 1500 but gradually thereafter the dread *wako* began to prey upon vessels entering and leaving Naha, and to make sudden raids upon villages along the shores of Okinawa itself. The most serious of these took place in 1527 and for a time the port of Naha and nearby villages were threatened. Shuri issued weapons from the castle storehouses, villagers were mobilized, and watchmen were established on the headlands north and south of Naha. The threat was so grave that, at last, in 1551 construction began on two forts (Yara and Miei) flanking the entrance to the inner anchorage. These were completed in 1553.

In this year the *wako* carried out their most devastating raids along the China coast. Chinese outlaws in large numbers joined them in terrorizing the countryside far inland. In one great attack the freebooters moved up the Yangtse River to the very walls of Nanking. The Ming court ordered all Chinese ports closed to Japanese ships. Hundreds of thousands of Chinese villagers were compelled to abandon coastal settlements and to move inland. This caused immense hardship; hundreds of Chinese elected to disobey the law, slipping away from Fukien to establish pioneer settlements on Formosa, south of Okinawa and well beyond Ming jurisdiction.

Legitimate trade between Japan and China came to an end. The shogunate, the independent barons, the great trading temples, and private merchants were forced to look about for alternatives. Overseas trade was vital.

Their eyes turned to Okinawa with increasing interest. The peaceful little kingdom was at the height of its prosperity, and at Naha the frustrated Japanese could purchase Chinese goods and share in the commerce in luxury items brought in from Southeast Asia. The number of Japanese ships putting in at Naha increased. With them came priest-missionaries who were ready to teach and preach while acting as agents in trade. Okinawans showed an increased interest in Japanese affairs, and a knowledge of the Japanese language became as important as the knowledge of Chinese hitherto had been. In 1572, Okinawan students began to go to Kyoto to study in the Five Great Temples, which were engaged in maritime trade.

Here began a division of Okinawan sympathies and interests which was to continue in evidence for three hundred years. The student elite who returned from China were naturally inclined to be pro-Chinese in outlook; the students home from Japan (or educated in Japanese at Shuri) tended to support Japan's position in this never-ending conflict of interests. The unwarlike Okinawans numbered then only a few tens of thousands. Of necessity diplomacy was conducted with scrupulous care and politeness. Neither China nor Japan challenged the king's position as long as tribute was paid regularly. But the islands were strategically placed, and prosperous; this state of neutrality could be maintained only if the balance of Chinese and Japanese interests remained undisturbed, and if Okinawa presented no threat, real or fancied, to its powerful neighbors.

THE TURNING POINT

The Okinawans had no desire to be drawn into the Sino-Japanese quarrel, nor to take sides with one or another of Japan's contending barons. When the 16th century opened, Japan was in a state of anarchy;

when it closed, it was united under the military leadership of Hide-yoshi, who proposed to invade China and conquer Asia. At the same time, however, the Japanese were feeling increased European pressure from the south and reacting strongly to it.

A series of events related to each of these issues drew critical Japanese attention to Okinawa's vulnerable frontier position. The Southern Islands, to which Satsuma's daimyo had titular claim, were no longer merely a cluster of unmapped, unrelated islands inhabited by primitive people; Ryukyu was a well-organized kingdom; it had important relations with foreign countries far to the south in Asia; it lay in the quarter from which Europeans began to come with firearms, new methods of warfare, remarkably developed ships, and a new religion which required its converts to look to a foreign prince at Rome for guidance.

Firearms first entered Japan through the Ryukyu trading depot on Tane-ga-shima. The time was about 1542. The details are obscure and disputed, but the general outlines of the event can be accepted, and these associated the European penetration of Japan with the Southern Islands.

In his book *The Grand Perigrination*, Maurice Collis has argued persuasively that Fernaõ Mendez Pinto's great tale of adventure and trade, of physical hardship and spiritual conversion, is a masterly, carefully planned knitting together of truths, semi-truths, and fictions picked up during twenty-years' adventuring in India and the Far East.[18] It is doubtful indeed if Pinto was one of the three Portuguese who reached Tane-ga-shima in 1542 and there acquainted the Japanese with firearms, but there is sufficient substance to his tales of Kyushu, Tane-ga-shima, and Okinawa to suggest that he had listened closely to accounts of others who actually had been there, and wove these into his autobiographical narrative.

Pinto asserts that with two Portuguese companions he took passage aboard a Chinese junk bound from Macao to the Ningpo trading center. A storm blew them far off course. After sighting Okinawa they continued northward until they could put in at Tane-ga-shima, which was, we know, growing in importance as a point of transshipment for the Okinawan trade in Japan. There a Ryukyuan woman conversant in both Japanese and Chinese served as an interpreter. These interviews led to the introduction and first manufacture of firearms in Japan.

The Portuguese discovered that Chinese merchants were able to dispose of their cargoes in Tane-ga-shima at a fabulous profit. After a six-weeks' sojourn there and at the court of Otomo, Lord of Bungo, Pinto relates that he and his companions returned to Ningpo direct, to spread word of the riches which might be had in the market on Tane-ga-shima, trading into Japan.

The Portuguese community at Ningpo was fired with eagerness to get over to Tane-ga-shima, and despite unfavorable weather and ill-conditioned ships, set forth immediately with a fleet of nine. Seven foundered at once on the high seas; two were blown over to Okinawa, where one vanished in a storm and one—Pinto's ship—foundered on the rocky shore. There were only thirty survivors, including five women, but of these four soon died of exposure. The forlorn and miserable castaways sought shelter in the countryside.

Here follows a dramatic story. Collis suggests that it was contrived to present Pinto's view that mercy and compassion can be found among non-Christians as well as among Christians, and that the Portuguese had established for themselves in Asia an unenviable reputation for violence and greed.

Briefly, the story relates that the castaways were found by some kindly villagers, who fed and clothed them and cared for their wounds. The Okinawans were required, however, to arrest all strangers found wandering about. This they did with great reluctance and regret, confining the newcomers in a local temple and sending word to the capital.

Shuri's orders were returned at once, directing that the Portuguese be delivered to the Minister of Justice. This done, they were placed on trial as sea robbers. When they protested that they were merely traders, the Okinawans reminded them that the Portuguese had seized Malacca and had killed many of its inhabitants. This, said the Portuguese, was not trade but war, and therefore was justified.

The king was inclined to release them, and there was every evidence that the public at large entertained their plight with great sympathy. But a Chinese trader present on Okinawa accused them of treacherous intent to raise a rebellion and to seize the Ryukyu kingdom. Upon this, the king condemned the Europeans to death. Through the intervention of villagers, ladies at the court, and the queen mother herself, the king was at last persuaded to grant reprieve and to order their safe return to Ningpo.

Such was Pinto's story. Collis comments that this narrative captures the essential character of the Okinawans—mildness, unlimited kindness, and courtesy. "The little drama of Lu-chu stands for the idyllic aspect of the orient. The East has many faces, and Pinto describes them in turn, giving to each kingdom its most characteristic features."

As an aside we may note two things about this alleged eyewitness account of Okinawa, the first recorded in the literature of the West. Internal evidence suggests that even though he may not have visited Okinawa, Pinto had talked with persons who had been there. Okinawan reluctance to obey official orders in this instance suggests that the Portuguese had been cast ashore in the Hokuzan district of northern Okinawa, which was then held under such strict surveillance by the Shuri court. The allusion to the influence of a queen mother may reflect the wide reputation of Sho Shin's mother, Yosoidon, who had died long before 1542, but about whom many stories were told, some of which survive in the Korean annals. The reference to the sack of Malacca suggests that this act of violence had deeply impressed Okinawans who witnessed it in 1511 and that it was well known and discussed at Shuri and Naha in Pinto's day.

Thus from the south, in one incident, came European religion, trade, and firearms. This was the turning point.

In midsummer, 1549, the Jesuit priest Francis Xavier entered Kagoshima to begin his mission in Japan. He could not have come at a less appropriate time or with less appropriate companions: for he reached Satsuma aboard a Chinese pirate junk, out of Malacca, and his companions in holy orders were three—an ex-soldier, a former merchant, and Yajiro the interpreter. Yajiro (baptized Paul) was in fact a renegade Satsuma man, a fugitive from justice who had left Kagoshima in 1546 and was to abandon the holy faith soon thereafter to take up piracy. Xavier stayed a year in Satsuma with the permission of the daimyo, but he soon so antagonized the Buddhist clergy that he moved on to another feudal territory.

This was in 1550; Japan was aflame with war among the barons, who vied with one another in making and breaking alliances, in acquiring new weapons from the West and adapting them to their own use, and in gaining strength through trade with the Europeans. These were principally Portuguese and Spanish soldier-merchants, and with them always in close association were the priests. Nearly a half-century passed before the Japanese realized that they could have trade and foreign arms without having to accept the trouble-making Christian clerics.

Clerics—Christian and Buddhist alike—were in ill repute in many quarters. It was well known that the Five Great Temples at Kyoto served the shogun as a source for agents and spies. Priests could travel from one fief to another in the guise of devout pilgrims. It was common practice to employ them as secret agents in diplomacy and in military matters. In those days all strangers were objects of suspicion; no baron trusted his neighbor. Each feudatory guarded its frontiers with utmost caution.

So matters stood in Japan when, in 1571, Shuri decided to reassert its claims to the island of Amami Oshima. The reasons for making this move are not clear, but the decision was a poor one under the circumstances. This meant moving a military force—however feeble—close to the borders of Satsuma. It may be that Shuri thought merely to secure its line of communications into Japan, for in the next year (1572) Okinawan priests and students began to travel through Kagoshima to the Five Great Temples at Kyoto, and in 1573 a large diplomatic mission was dispatched to Kagoshima bearing gifts to the Daimyo Shimazu Yoshihisa, an announcement of the accession of a new king at Shuri, and a request for increased trade.

At this moment Satsuma was embroiled in a prolonged and deadly struggle with Otomo Yoshishige, a powerful daimyo of western Japan. Otomo sought to rouse all the allies he could to bring pressure to bear upon Satsuma, from all sides. It may have been this interest which prompted him, in 1577, to send a priest-envoy to Shuri. The embarrassed Okinawans in the following year hastened to send an exceptionally large embassy to Kagoshima bearing elaborate gifts and a message congratulating Shimazu upon his success in conquering three neighboring provinces of Kyushu.

Unfortunately for Satsuma (and for Okinawa) the great General Toyotomi Hideyoshi had sided with Otomo and forced Shimazu to relinquish these hard-won territorial gains. It became evident that Hideyoshi had employed Buddhist priests of the Shin sect to act as spies and diplomatic agents during the campaigns in Kyushu. Shimazu angrily suppressed the sect within his own domains.

The presence of an Otomo mission to Shuri had alerted Shimazu to the dangers of a flanking attack upon Satsuma through the Ryukyu Islands. A company of Satsuma's rough soldiers were dispatched to Okinawa, where they were observed by Chinese envoys attending the investiture ceremony for the young King Sho Ei.

In Japanese eyes the south harbored a growing danger.

It should be remembered that the Japanese were trading with the Spanish in the Philippines and Mexico at this time, and it can be assumed that they sometimes heard of Spanish plans for conquest of all the islands along the western Pacific rim. For example, a letter from Mexico dated January 16, 1570, from Diego de Herrera to Felipe II, of Spain, urged upon that monarch conquest of "China, Lequios, Jabas [Java] and Japan."[19] It was a Spanish mariner's boastful threat (in 1596) which angered Hideyoshi, provoked harsh measures taken against all Christian converts, and prepared the way for the later seclusion edicts. By the close of the 16th century the Japanese were keenly alert to danger coming from the south, and sensitive to the problems of security in the neighboring islands.

PART TWO

ISOLATION: "LONELY ISLANDS IN A DISTANT SEA"

CHAPTER FOUR

CONTINENTAL WAR AND LOSS
OF INDEPENDENCE

1573–1609

WAR IN KOREA SPELLS DISASTER IN OKINAWA

Tradition says that 13th-century Okinawa was ravaged by the Mongols when the Okinawans refused to contribute men and supplies to the Mongol campaign against Japan. Three hundred years later the Japanese prepared to invade and conquer China, traveling over the Korean land-bridge which the Mongols had used. Again the Okinawans were called upon to send supplies and men, this time to Japan. Again the Okinawans refused, with consequences disastrous to themselves and their little country.

After two centuries of anarchy a baron named Oda Nobunaga had made himself *de facto* shogun in 1568 and was moving over bloody fields toward the mastery of all Japan. His principal lieutenant, Toyotomi Hideyoshi, was campaigning in western Japan in 1577 when word reached camp that Nobunaga had been assassinated at Kyoto. Hideyoshi was at that moment engaged in a bitter contest with the powerful Daimyo Mori Terumoto. This was a crisis. Hideyoshi came at once to terms with Mori, abandoned his drive into western Japan, hastened back to Kyoto, destroyed Nobunaga's assassin, and asserted his own supremacy at the expense of Nobunaga's heirs.

This done, he was approached by a minor lord named Kamei Korenori, Daimyo of Shikano (Inaba), who expected a reward for assistance which he had given in the campaign against Mori. Kamei had an interest in foreign trade and shipping as far south as Siam and the Philippines. He thought that he should be given a territory (Izumo) which had a fair harbor on the Japan Sea. To his chagrin he learned that as part of the price of truce with Mori, the latter had been confirmed in possession of Izumo.

Kamei, disappointed, suggested a substitute—the Ryukyu Islands. Hideyoshi was pleased with the idea. He had not the slightest legitimate claim upon the islands, but already grandiose plans to invade China and make himself master of Asia were taking form within his fertile mind. Kamei's proposal meant that Hideyoshi would have a trustworthy vassal stationed advantageously south of Satsuma, and in islands which flanked the sea lanes to China. Picking up his fan, Hideyoshi inscribed upon it the date, his own name, and the legend *Kamei, Ryukyu-no-Kami* (Kamei, Lord of Ryukyu).

In 1591, Kamei set out with an expeditionary force to take control of his "gift," but Shimazu blocked his way and forced him to turn back. In Hideyoshi's view this was a minor quarrel; he was too engrossed with preparations for the invasion of Korea to be concerned with Kamei's discomfiture.

Meanwhile, according to the Ming annals, Hideyoshi proposed to use Koreans in making the advance upon Peking, and to use Chinese in moving upon Chekiang and Fukien along the China coast. Disturbed lest the Okinawans alert Peking to his designs, he ordered them to suspend their official missions to China. This they did not do. Envoys were leaving for Peking on business having to do with the investiture of the new king, Sho Nei. A Chinese at Naha urged them to report Hideyoshi's activities; and this they did, to Japan's annoyance.

The continental conquest was to begin in 1592 with an invasion of Korea, the corridor through which Japanese forces could move upon Peking.

Hideyoshi imagined himself master of an empire which should surpass that of T'ang T'ai-tsung or of Kublai Khan, the greatest the world had ever known. Letters were prepared calling upon the "King of India" to submit; a mission was despatched to Formosa to demand surrender of the island; and a representative of minor rank carried orders to the haughty Spanish governor-general in the Philippines directing him to acknowledge Japan's claims or risk punishment. The letters did not reach India, and no government could be found on Formosa to which the demands might be presented. The Spanish ignored the summons but increased outpost garrisons in northern Luzon and in time constructed two forts and a mission on the northern tip of Formosa.[1]

Satsuma had been called upon to convey a message to the king at Shuri. During the years of confusion preceeding Hideyoshi's rise to supreme power, the Okinawan court had ceased sending official tribute missions to the Ashikaga shogun's court at Kyoto. Shuri was reminded of this neglect, with an order to provide contributions of men and arms for the invasion of Korea.

The perplexed Okinawans demurred; they did not wish to offend China, they had no fighting men, and little goods to spare; and it may well be that they under-rated Hideyoshi's capacity to carry through with his announced campaign. A new king (Sho Nei) had come to the throne at Shuri in 1589. This provided occasion to send an envoy to Kyoto in midsummer, who was given an opportunity to present gifts, apologies, and explanations to Hideyoshi in audience.

Sho Nei's letter to Hideyoshi said this:

"According to our understanding, more than sixty provinces having been completely subjugated, all the people in Japan now pay due reverence to you and pledge their loyalty to the throne. Moreover, we have heard that your authority has been extended to Korea, to the Philippines, and to other islands in the south. Now, under your rule, all the peoples dwelling within the bounds of the four seas are enjoying peace and prosperity. Permit me to congratulate you upon the fact that you have put into actual practice the ancient admonition 'Put aside bows and arrows and protect and bless the barbarians in all four directions.' Our small and humble island kingdom, because of its great distance and because of lack of funds, has not rendered due reverence to you. However, now, in compliance with the instructions that our great lord, Shimazu Yoshihisa, has sent to us by his envoy, Daijiji Seiin-Osho, we have caused Joten Ryotoan-Osho to proceed to your country, carrying with him a humble gift which consists of lacquer ware of the Ming Dynasty, together with some of our local products, as described on a separate sheet. These articles are sent to you with the sole desire to show our sincerity and courtesy, and not because we think them of any great value.

"[Dated] May 17, of the seventeenth year of the Wan-Li era of the Ming Emperor [1589].

"To His Royal Highness the Supreme Imperial Advisor of the Emperor of Japan."

Hideyoshi replied in friendly terms:

"Hideyoshi, the Supreme Imperial Advisor of the Emperor of Japan, hereby addresses His Excellency, the King of Liu Chiu. We have received your letter and have read it repeatedly with an impression that we were in the same hall, and that you were there to address us in person. As you stated in your letter, our nation, which consists of more than sixty provinces, having been subjugated without leaving a single foot of land unconquered, our people are now under a benevolent rule and are enjoying peace and prosperity. Our only regret is that we have not yet established our desired relations with nations of the outside world. We have now received products of your country, and these are of great interest to us. We have therefore become increasingly desirous of extending our observations beyond our boundaries, and thereby increasing our knowledge. In fact, it has long been our cherished desire to place foreign lands under our rule and to have the people therein enjoy our benevolent rule and protection. Of all the nations, yours is the first to send us an envoy, together with rare and unusual things. This has pleased us greatly. It is human nature to be interested in things that come from distant lands, and also to be attracted by things that are rarely seen. For this reason we are particularly impressed with the gifts that you have sent. From this time on, although our countries are separated by thousands of miles, we may nevertheless maintain friendly relations with the feeling that your country, together with the other nations that are within the four seas, constitute but a single family. We are hereby sending you some of the local products of our country, which are described on a separate sheet. Further details will be given you orally by Tenryuki Toan Todo, whom Shimazu Yoshihisa will send to you as his personal representative.

"[Dated] February 28, of the 18th year of the Tensho era [1590].

"The Supreme Imperial Advisor of the Emperor of Japan. To the King of Liu Chiu."[2]

Shimazu Yoshihisa was not anxious to see an armed force raised in Okinawa. He advised Hideyoshi therefore that the Okinawan contribution should be limited to material supplies. Hideyoshi agreed. Yoshihisa notified Sho Nei in October, 1591, that Okinawa must provide enough supplies to sustain seven thousand men through ten months, and that these provisions must be delivered to the harbor of Bonotsu in Satsuma by February, 1592.

The king ignored the order.

In February, Yoshihisa conveyed a warning from Hideyoshi to the king. This time supplies were gathered and forwarded, most reluctantly. The shipment was acknowledged in July, and a new demand made on Okinawa. Again nothing was forthcoming. Yoshihisa was in an awkward position; three envoys went down to Shuri only to be told by the king's ministers that it was impossible to raise military tribute from so poor a country.

When this was reported, Hideyoshi ordered an investigation. Two agents from Satsuma made a survey and reported again to Hideyoshi, but by this time he was too deeply involved in the Korean campaign to give the matter attention. The first of the expeditions into Korea (in 1592) had failed and had been withdrawn. In the course of action the Koreans had captured several wrecked Japanese warships, and aboard one of them was found Kamei Korenori's treasured fan recording Hideyoshi's generous gift of islands which were not in fact his to give.[3]

Sho Nei was greatly embarrassed. He had no quarrel with Korea whatever, and it cannot be doubted that his kingdom had no surplus foodstuffs to send out of the country. Okinawa's limited prosperity was based on a dwindling trade in luxury goods, and not on the produce of the indigenous economy.

When Hideyoshi's demands were received at Shuri the Okinawans immediately notified the Chinese court, but if Sho Nei expected the Chinese to come to his aid, he was doomed to disappointment. China's concept of the tributary relationship placed all the painful obligations, if there were any, upon the side of the subordinate state.

Hideyoshi's death in 1598 ended the Korean campaign and precipitated a fierce struggle for supremacy in Japan. Events leading up to the great battle of Sekigahara in 1600 fully occupied Satsuma's attention;

for a little while pressure upon Okinawa was relaxed. It was a last, brief respite, destined to come to an end in 1609.

Throughout these troubled years the Shuri court continued to maintain the cycle of Confucian state rituals. A new form of evangelical Buddhism was introduced about 1603 and became popular in Shuri and Naha. A Japanese priest named Taichu preached that salvation was possible for all—even the poor and the illiterate—through the simple invocation of Amida Buddha's name. Taichu himself became interested in traditional Okinawan religious practices, preparing the first account of religion in Okinawa, under the title *Ryukyu Shinto-ki*. A number of new temples were established. The Okinawans as a whole continued to be tolerant of all organized religions, if not generally indifferent to them.

In 1606 the cultivation of the sweet potato was introduced from Fukien Province, followed soon thereafter by the introduction of sugarcane culture. These were events of revolutionary importance to the entire Okinawan economy, but a comment on the circumstances which attended these innovations may be left with advantage to a later page.

At Shuri the competition between "pro-Chinese" and "pro-Japanese" factions among the king's councilors became of grave importance, for it found expression in political conflict as well as cultural preferences. Men who had studied abroad formed a substantial element in the government—perhaps a majority in the policy-making levels of administration. Sho Nei's decision to refuse supplies demanded of him by Hideyoshi appears now to have been made largely on the advice of a senior councilor named Jana *Teido Oyakata*, a man of the Kume Village immigrant community who had been educated at Peking. It is recorded that Jana treated one of Satsuma's envoys in a rude and summary manner, and for this he was soon to pay with his life.

SATSUMA INVADES THE RYUKYU ISLANDS, 1609 (KEICHO 14)

Feudal lords and soldiers abroad at the time of Hideyoshi's death in 1598 hastened home to throw themselves into bitter succession disputes. These culminated in the Battle of Sekigahara in 1600; Tokugawa Ieyasu and his adherents emerged victorious. In 1603 he assumed the title and office of Shogun and set about skillfully redistributing feudal territories. The barons who had supported him were styled *fudai daimyo* and were considered eligible for high office in the government seated at Edo (present-day Tokyo) in eastern Japan.

Barons who had opposed Ieyasu at Sekigahara were styled *tozama daimyo* (outside lords). Some were deprived of lands and honors; others were allowed to govern autonomously within their own domains, treated with punctilious respect but excluded from services in the Edo government. Ieyasu took pains to redistribute territory in a manner which separated the *tozama* daimyo from one another and from the capital.

In this manner the Satsuma clan was effectually isolated in southern Kyushu. Shimazu Yoshihiro had ranged himself against Ieyasu at Sekigahara; when the tide of battle turned in favor of the Tokugawa he hastened back to the clan headquarters at Kagoshima to await the effect this misjudgment might have upon Shimazu fortunes.

The Satsuma domain lay at a great distance from Edo. Ieyasu contented himself with ordering Yoshihiro to abdicate as clan chieftain and to assume the tonsure of a priest. His son Tadatsune succeeded him as daimyo in 1602, going up to Edo in the next year to pay his respects to the new shogun and to give thanks for Tokugawa leniency. Ieyasu was pleased by this act of submission. As a mark of honor he conferred one syllable of his own name upon Tadatsune, henceforth to be known as Iehisa, and confirmed him in Shimazu's hereditary titles. These included the title Lord of the Twelve Southern Islands, which had been granted first to a Shimazu in A.D. 1206.

We may assume that Satsuma-Ryukyu relations were discussed at this time, for shortly thereafter Iehisa sent an envoy to Shuri to recommend the king's submission to the new order in Japan and to advise Sho Nei to pay his respects promptly to the new shogun.

This the king declined to do; it is probable that he and his council did not fully appreciate the significance of Ieyasu's victory nor the fundamental changes which had taken place in the Japanese administration. Shuri's reply to Satsuma referred to conditions in Japan as they had been before 1600, not as they were in fact thereafter.

Shimazu appealed for permission to chastise the Okinawans for their rude want of respect. On June 17, 1606, Ieyasu granted this request.

It is probable that the new Tokugawa government was glad to find military diversion for the frustrated men of Satsuma, and at no cost to the shogunate. The Satsuma warriors—a truculent lot by nature—were hemmed in on the north; there could be no expansion on Kyushu, no raids on neighboring feudatories, no entertaining forays across the borders of Satsuma, Osumi, and Hyuga as there had been for centuries past. Shimazu's relations with all other daimyo were under close Tokugawa surveillance.

A Satsuma expedition to the south would relieve discontent; Shimazu was ready to return his samurai to their proper employment after three years of enforced tranquillity, and he was certainly not unmindful of the wealth in trading goods and opportunities which would be his at Okinawa. Ieyasu on his part was at this time deeply concerned with problems of European pressure upon Japan. He mistrusted Spain and feared Spain's activities based upon the Philippines. It would be greatly to Japan's interest to extend garrison forces into these islands through which the Europeans must pass to approach the shogun's port at Nagasaki. With Satsuma's forces, these southern islands could be transformed; steppingstones from the south could become a barrier on the southern sea frontier.

In February, 1609, Satsuma moved against Okinawa. A force three-thousand strong set sail from Yamakawa in Kagoshima Bay under the command of Kabayama Hisataka, whose family thenceforth were to have a close relationship with the southern islands for three hundred years.[4]

A fleet of more than one hundred war-junks moved down through the Amami Islands, past Toku-no-jima and Kikai. There were several fierce skirmishes along the way, and when the samurai landed at Unten Harbor on Motobu Peninsula, they met a brief but stiff resistance, with considerable losses on both sides.

Shuri made a desperate effort to organize a defense, but the Okinawans were untrained and inexperienced. The last occasion for a general rally to arms and widespread fighting had been in the days of Sho Hashi, two centuries earlier; the arms themselves had been called in and put away during Sho Shin's reign; and there had been infrequent need to man the coastal defenses during pirate raids in the century thereafter.

The Okinawans were no match for the hardy Satsuma warriors. They fell away before the Japanese moving down to Naha. On April 5, 1609, the Japanese occupied Shuri Castle. The palace was looted and important treasure taken from the nearby temples and princely houses. Among these were the stores of irreplaceable Buddhist texts which had been sent down from Korea many years before.

These material losses seemed of small importance at the time, for with immense misgiving and alarm the Okinawans saw the king taken prisoner and removed to Kagoshima to answer for his defiant conduct. More than a hundred of his principal officers were made to accompany him.

The administration of the kingdom was put into the hands of a Satsuma samurai named Honda Chikamasa, who acted as deputy for Kabayama Hisataka. Soon fourteen high commissioners (bugyo) arrived from Kagoshima, accompanied by a staff of 168 men under orders to make the first complete survey of the administration and the economic potential of the Ryukyu kingdom, including, of course, the distant islands of Miyako and Yaeyama.

After checking, revising, and adjusting reports brought in from the off-lying islands, they decided that the Ryukyu revenues stood at the equivalent of 94,220 koku of rice (one modern koku is the equivalent of 5.11 bushels) and that upon this basis the Shuri government should be required to pay over to Satsuma an annual tribute of 11,935 koku, or about one-eighth of the total revenues of the kingdom. In addition to this, the king was expected to pay over to Shimazu an annual tribute of approximately 8,000 koku from his private income. The foreign trade was to be monopolized by Satsuma and directed wholly to its interests.

This was a disastrous blow to the economy. In addition, the islands of the Amami group, Yoron, Toku, and Kikai, lying between Okinawa and Kyushu, were removed altogether from Shuri's control and attached to Satsuma, thus bringing the southern border of Shimazu's domain to a point within sight of the northern tip of Okinawa.

The Conditions Laid Down for a King's Ransom

Sho Nei endured exile for three years. Self-possession and dignified conduct won the admiration of his captors, who treated him with ceremonious courtesy. It was a novel and ambiguous position, for he was the first ruler of a foreign country ever seen in Japan.

The king and a number of his attendants were taken to Edo to be presented to the shogun, stopping on the way to pay respect to Tokugawa Ieyasu, in retirement at Sumpu. Shimazu Iehisa savored the political value of the occasion, traveling with great pomp through the Inland Sea and up the Tokaido to the capital with a captive king in his train. Sho Nei was only a "small" king, to be sure, but not even the great *Taiko* Hideyoshi had enjoyed the satisfaction of bringing a foreign monarch in submission to his court.

The king and his high officers served as hostages in Japan while the Satsuma officials made their survey of the economic resources of Ryukyu. This done, it was agreed that Sho Nei could return to Shuri under certain conditions strictly set forth and sworn to within the sacred precincts of a Shinto shrine at Kagoshima. The king himself took an oath and subscribed to three articles which had been drawn up. The document was essentially a bond formalizing relations between the Ryukyu kingdom and Satsuma.

"The King's Oath*

"I. The Islands of Riu Kiu have from ancient times been a feudal dependency of Satsuma; and we have for ages observed the custom of sending thither, at the stated times, junks bearing products of these islands, and we have always sent messengers to carry our congratulations to a new Prince of Satsuma on his accession.

"Such has been custom; but in the time of His Highness Toyotomi Hideyoshi, we, inhabitants of this far-off southern land, had failed

* This stilted English version was the official Japanese translation presented to foreign representatives during the Sino-Japanese sovereignty dispute, 1871–82.[5]

fully to comply with the requisitions made upon us for supplies and services; therein we were remiss in our duty, and were very guilty; thus did we bring trouble to our shore. You, our Lord, Shimazu Iyehisa sent an army against us to chastize us; I was dismayed. I was carried off from my home and became a prisoner in your mighty land; I, like to an unmated bird shut up in a cage, had lost all hope of returning to my home.

"But our merciful Prince has shown his loving kindness; and taking pity on master and servants whose country seemed all lost to them, gave them his leave to return to their homes; not only so, but also allowed them themselves to govern some of their country's islands.

"This is a boon indeed; we know not how to show our thankfulness. So will we forever be the humble servants of Satsuma, and obedient to all commands, and never will be traitors to our Lord.

"II. A writing [i.e., copy] of this Oath I myself will keep and will hand it down to my posterity that they may observe and keep it.

"III. Each and every article of the ordinances already made and of those which shall hereafter be made by Satsuma for our observance shall be faithfully obeyed by us; and herein if we fail, may Heaven visit our sin upon our heads."

The terms of the King's Oath display the highly developed political skills of the Satsuma men who prepared them for the king to sign. Sho Nei is required to state that there is an ancient precedent for Satsuma's claims to an overlordship in the Southern Islands, although the facts of the matter could not substantiate the claim. The king is then made to assume responsibility for the evil days which have befallen his people and himself. Next he enlarges upon the generosity of the Prince of Satsuma, establishing and acknowledging a profound sense of obligation or moral indebtedness which has the most binding ethical force within the Okinawan and Japanese frame of social reference and ethical conduct. Sho Nei acknowledges this obligation and accepts it for his posterity. To make it stronger, he agrees that his court and his heirs will accept any new or further obligations laid upon them by Satsuma.

The king's councilors and associates who were in exile with him were then required to make an oath of three parts and to subscribe to fifteen articles or "admonitions." This was essentially a bond formalizing principles which were to guide them in the internal administration of the kingdom.

"ARTICLES SUBSCRIBED TO BY THE KING'S COUNCILLORS[6]

"I. The islands of Riu Kiu have from ancient times been a feudal dependency of Satsuma; therefore we would have obeyed and carried out an order of any kind whatever given to us upon any matter. Yet now but little time ago, neglecting our duty, [we] fell into the sin of disloyalty. We, master alike and men, were carried away captive and were in despair of returning even with our lives. How great then was our joy when you, Great Lord, had compassion upon us and not only allowed us to return but also granted us unlooked-for emoluments. We know not how to show our thankfulness. Ever hereafter will we remain the loyal subjects of Satsuma.

"II. If, peradventure, any man of Riu Kiu, forgetful of this greathearted deed, ever in times to come, plans a revolt against you, yea, if it were our Chieftain himself who should be drawn to join revolt, yet we nevertheless obedient to the commands of our Great Lord, will never be false to our Oath by abetting a rebel, be he lord or churl.

"III. A writing of this oath [i.e., a copy] we each and all of us will keep [so] that our sons may know forever and observe what we have vowed and therein may never fail."

"THE ORDINANCE OF SHIMAZU IEHISA [PRINCE OF SATSUMA]

"*Art. 1.* No merchandise shall be imported from China without leave first obtained of the Prince of Satsuma.

"*Art. 2.* No emoluments shall be given to any member of any family, however illustrious, on account of distinguished origin alone, but only to those capable of public service.

"*Art. 3.* No emoluments of office shall be given to a mistress of the Chieftain.

"*Art. 4.* No kind of private servitude is allowed.

"*Art. 5.* The number of shrines or temples to be erected shall not be excessive.

"*Art. 6.* No merchants shall be allowed to engage in external trade to or from Riu Kiu without a written permission from Satsuma.

"*Art. 7.* No inhabitant of Riu Kiu shall be sent to the mainlands as a slave.

"*Art. 8.* All taxes or other imposts of a similar kind shall be levied only in accordance with the rules and regulations laid down by the authority from the mainland.

"*Art. 9.* It is prohibited [to the Chieftain] to entrust the conduct of public affairs in the islands to any persons other than San-shi-kuan (Council).

"*Art. 10.* No persons shall be compelled to buy or sell against his will.

"*Art. 11.* Quarrels and personal encounters are prohibited.

"*Art. 12.* Reports shall be made to the authorities in Kagoshima, the castle-town of Satsuma, in case of any official making any claim exceeding the amount of taxes and duties properly to be levied according to law upon merchants and farmers or others.

"*Art. 13.* No merchant ship is allowed to go to any foreign country from Riu Kiu.

"*Art. 14.* No measure of capacity [value] other than the Government standard measure known as the *Kioban* is allowed to be used.

"*Art. 15.* Gambling and all other vicious habits of a like nature are prohibited.

"Strictly observe each one of the foregoing articles! Those who violate the same shall be liable to severe punishment!"

Here again is a skillful use of that powerful device, the sense of moral obligation. The first of the oaths is essentially a duplication of the king's review of past dependency, acknowledgment of default in the discharge of earlier obligation, and recognition of Satsuma's generosity. The second oath, however, was a harsh undertaking; in effect it called upon the lords of Okinawa to promise that upon future demand they would give their obedience and loyalty to the Daimyo of Satsuma rather than to their own king. In the third oath they undertook to bind their posterity to these commitments.

The fifteen articles were essentially concerned with establishing Satsuma's economic controls. Shimazu placed first things first: Article 1 was intended to ensure Satsuma's monopoly of the profitable trade with

China. This was reinforced by Articles 6 and 13, which forbade all foreign trade not approved by Satsuma.

A standard medium of exchange was established by Article 15. The conduct of economic affairs and conditions of labor (taxation, servitude, compulsory sales) are touched upon in Articles 4, 7, 8, 10, and 12. The prohibition upon an excessive temple-building program may have been designed to keep Okinawan assets in a more manageable form, as well as to discourage the elaboration of religious organizations which were not held in high trust. Temptation to exercise undue influence through bribes among the administrative officers or within the king's bedchamber was to be discouraged by Articles 2 and 3. The public peace and morality were given their due in Articles 11 and 15, which prohibited quarrels and forbade gambling and similar vicious habits.

By terms of Article 9 the king could delegate authority only to members of the Sanshikan (the Council of State), but nothing was set forth to define the position or the authority of the Satsuma representatives through whom Shimazu proposed to make his will known to the Sanshikan and the king.

Satsuma ostentatiously proclaimed that it undertook the 1609 punitive expedition because of a fervent desire to punish the king and his councilors for failure to show proper respect for the Tokugawa government and its predecessors. But although the oaths required the king and his councilors to admit to these faults, the articles to which they were forced to put their seals made no mention of ceremonial obligations to the shogun's government. Satsuma was more interested in commercial profit to be wrung from the Okinawans than in costly flattery. Furthermore—as the years would make clear—Shimazu intended to ensure recognition that the Ryukyu kingdom was a dependency of Satsuma and only secondarily, through Shimazu, a dependency of the Tokugawa government. It was to be treated as a private income-bearing property, not as a part of the political fabric of Japan.

All was prepared for the formal signing of these unpleasant documents. The king and his men were brought before the shrine in the presence of the Shimazu clan officers. It was a bitter experience, for which the king could see no alternative. One by one the signatures were set to the papers and sealed. Suddenly tension increased, for one of the king's principal councilors refused to take the prescribed oath or to put his seal to such repugnant articles.

This was Jana *Teido Oyakata*, long the leader of pro-China factions at Shuri and the officer who had urged upon the king the course of action which had led to such disastrous consequences. He would not forswear allegiance to his king nor accept the interpretation placed upon events by the Japanese.

The Satsuma samurai had a simple solution. Jana was taken to one side and beheaded. It was an untidy business, but there was no doubt left in the minds of the Okinawans what the alternatives would be if any others attempted to evade the facts of the situation in which they were placed.

Sadly the king returned to Shuri in the autumn of 1611, to a changed government and a changed national life. Okinawa would never again know independence or prosperity.

It is possible that at heart the Satsuma men admired Jana's bold and fatal decision, for it was in the tradition of their own hotheaded, emotional standards of conduct. Three of Sho Nei's most important officers of state were held at Kagoshima as hostages until the king had resumed his place at Shuri and his government and people had demonstrated acceptance of the new conditions. These men were released in 1612. Two of them returned at once to Okinawa; these were the lords of Ozato and of Katsuren, the latter being concurrently the chief abbot of the great Enkaku-ji temple at Shuri. The third hostage, Kunjan *Anji*, elected to stay at Kagoshima, assumed a Japanese name, and in time joined Shimazu Yoshihisa when he was called up to assist in the Tokugawa attack upon Osaka Castle (1615). His motivation is not clear; perhaps he preferred the soldier's life to the placid life of Okinawa; perhaps he felt disgraced by his share in the subjugation of his people and could not bring himself to face them.

Sho Nei was embittered by memories of exile; subjugation had impoverished the kingdom. Contemplating death, he felt that he had failed to maintain the royal heritage. He was reluctant to enter the presence of his ancestors and for this reason decreed that his body should not lie in the royal tombs at Shuri, but in a hill-cave some miles away, near Urasoe, and that a mask should be placed over his face in death.

SERVING TWO MASTERS: THE PROBLEMS OF DUAL SUBORDINATION[7]

The king lived on for nine years after his return from exile; the kingdom survived, in name, for 268 years.

It was fictitious independence. Shuri became the creature of Satsuma in a bold arrangement designed by Shimazu to circumvent the strict seclusion laws of the Edo government. In theory the Tokugawa shogunate reserved all foreign trade for its own agents, based at the port of Nagasaki, and limited this to Dutch ships and Chinese junks admitted under a most strictly supervised licensing system. Using Okinawa for its purposes, the Satsuma clan boldly flouted the ban on foreign intercourse through any other port, and the Tokugawa were unable to check them.

This placed the Okinawans in a most difficult position. On the one hand they feared reprisals which might be set in motion by Edo or by a change in policy at Kagoshima. On the other hand the Chinese government for many years had sought to regulate all Chinese trade with Japan and for long periods had forbidden the Japanese to enter Chinese ports. What now if Peking should close Ch'uang-chou to Okinawan trade?

Satsuma was determined that there should be no excuse for an embargo on the trade from Naha. The Okinawans were ordered to conceal their true relationship with Japan. Chinese were forbidden to settle in Okinawa, and when Chinese embassies and merchants arrived from time to time, all Japanese resident in Okinawa were required to withdraw from Shuri and Naha, all Japanese objects which might attract attention were concealed, and the Okinawans were ordered to feign ignorance of the Japanese language. For the Okinawan traders and ambassadors to China a special handbook was prepared which contained a variety of probable questions and a list of answers which were designed to evade the issue and conceal the nature of Ryukyuan subordination.

These pretensions and deceptions were practiced faithfully by the

Okinawans through two and a half centuries. They were a matter of form, designed to save Chinese "face"; even the most casual European visitors at Naha and traders writing from Chinese ports and from Nagasaki after 1610 recognized the true state of affairs concerning trade between China and Japan through Naha, but they were puzzled by the arrangement permitting tribute to be paid simultaneously to two neighboring states. The Okinawans explained the anomalous situation by saying that Japan and China were the parents, and that to each respect and deference were due.

The pressures and requirements of "dual subordination" affected the character and the standards of the Okinawan people. Basic elements of race, religious practice, and language formed natural ties with Japan, and the mode of living in the Okinawan countryside was closer in pattern to the life of the ordinary Japanese than it was to the life of the continental Chinese. But life at Naha and Shuri continued strongly under the influence of both China and Japan. Young men continued to be sent to Ch'uang-chou and Peking for training, and Chinese ceremony governed at the court. The Chinese classics studied at the Kume Village center provided the ideal standards of conduct by which the educated elite in Okinawa sought to be guided in its daily life.

Satsuma sought to provide a counterweight to Chinese influence at the Shuri court (and incidently to provide itself with hostages) by requiring that the heir apparent and a number of noble companions spend considerable time at Kagoshima.

As a consequence of this strange life the Okinawans could develop no fixed standards of their own. Each day the governing gentry had to weigh words and actions carefully in every decision of importance, lest they come into conflict with Satsuma or with China; the arts of compromise and evasion were essential to survival. Courtesy and accommodation, hesitancy, delay, and passive resistance were the weapons of the weak which they had perforce to adopt. Acceptance of alien controls became a habit of mind, but the characteristics of initiative, individualism, and self-assertion, which had secured them independence and prosperity, began to fade. Satsuma controlled foreign affairs, overseas trade, and many aspects of the internal administration of the kingdom; it was left to the Okinawans to devise what means they could to eke out a living from the meager resources of the countryside.

In 1611 the king's ministers quietly resumed office at Shuri. Jana's advocacy of a pro-China policy had led them on to disaster, and his execution served warning that Satsuma would tolerate no plots and counterplots. Open rebellion was impossible; survival clearly depended upon coöperation with the Japanese.

A liaison office known as the Ryukyu-kan was established at Kagoshima for Okinawan representatives resident at the Satsuma headquarters, but to cultivate appearances it was arranged for "tribute missions" to proceed to Edo. These were scarcely less fictional than the missions to Peking, for all relations between king and shogun were most strictly supervised.

The importance of such missions must not be underestimated, however, for they proved to be the most important agency through which the governing elite on Okinawa fell under Japanese influence. Eighteen embassies made their solemn way to Edo in the period 1611 to 1850. Leading members of the Shuri government were made ambassadors, who traveled with a large suite. Scholars and craftsmen, administrative officers and merchants went overland to Edo through the Japanese countryside, accompanied by an armed escort from Satsuma. They returned, as we shall see, ladened with ideas as well as with material things of importance to the Ryukyuan economy.

The immediate effect of the Keicho invasion was a sharp break with the past; the Okinawans were cut off from the lively trade which had provided the lifeblood of the island economy. Now they were thrown upon their own resources. General principles of Confucian government interpreted to them anew by the Japanese were perhaps of less importance than the lessons required of them by the hard-driving men of Satsuma who had taken over the administration during the king's exile. The islands of Yoron, Kikai, Amami, and Erabu were lost, but the enforced Japanese survey of the resources in the outer islands led to a strengthened relationship with Kume, Miyako, and Yaeyama. Land measurements and tax reforms meant a more efficient collection of revenues, although the multiplication of administrative offices and agencies involved in this meant increased total costs of government.

In its days of 15th- and 16th-century prosperity the Ryukyu kingdom had become dependent upon a well-managed and far-flung maritime trade. The court, the aristocracy, and the administrative hierarchy were supported by the profits derived from this trade. Now, at the opening of the 17th century, all was changed.

Independent trade with Southeast Asia came to an end. Satsuma took a lion's share in the trade with China, made a remorseless demand for tax tribute, and required the dispatch of embassies to Edo. For these reasons domestic agriculture assumed paramount importance in Okinawa after 1610. Every village was hard pressed to produce enough foodstuffs and textiles to meet the tax levy and to feed the townsmen of Shuri, Naha, Kume, and Tomari. In order to keep the trade with China in motion, Satsuma had to subsidize the tribute missions to Peking, and Kagoshima merchants and samurai provided capital for the commercial ventures at Ch'uang-chou. Living standards at Shuri and Naha steadily declined.

Twice in the course of two succeeding centuries a moderate degree of prosperity was achieved, thanks to the careful direction of state policy, only to have it twice wiped out by natural disasters. The small surpluses of one year were quickly consumed by dearth in another; there could be no significant accumulation of capital resources.

PROTESTANT TRADERS AND CATHOLIC PRIESTS IN 17TH-CENTURY OKINAWA

Okinawa lay in the sea lanes used by Western ships which approached Japan. Portuguese came up through the Indies and Macao after 1542, established outposts on the China coast, and entered Japan. The Spanish came from Mexico and the Philippines about 1580; the Dutch established themselves at Hirado, on Kyushu, in 1611 and soon thereafter established a government on Formosa, which endured for more than thirty years. The British opened a trading post at Hirado in 1613.

Japan's rulers had ample reason to dislike and mistrust the Spanish and Portuguese missionaries, who were trouble-makers, but Tokugawa Ieyasu was eager to encourage trade. He granted a liberal commercial charter to the British and opened all harbors to British ships disabled by storm. By extension through Satsuma, Naha came under these general provisions and was used as a port of refuge and as a way station on the run between Japan, the Philippines, and Siam. Hostile Dutch fleets operating in the seas further south made the long trip to Europe unsafe for the small British vessels. For some years the English voyagers had to content themselves with a carrying trade between ports in East Asia. Already the politics of Europe were penetrating and unsettling the Far East.

In a letter dated December 23, 1614, Richard Wickham, British representative at Naha, reported to his chief at Hirado, Captain Richard Cocks: "The people [of 'Liquea'] much resemble the Chinese, yet speak the Japan tongue, although with difficulty to be understood of the Japans, they wear [their] hair long bound up like the Chinese, with a bodkin thrust through, but it is made up [on the] right side of their heads; they are a very gentle and courteous people."[8]

While this letter was being written, Will Adams, the trusted British friend of Tokugawa Ieyasu, was limping toward Naha port in the damaged junk "Sea Adventure." With a mixed crew of European adventurers and Japanese sailors, he had set out from Japan on November 28 for a voyage to Siam. The ship proved unseaworthy. On December 22 a gale forced the leaking craft inshore at Amami Oshima. Finding no suitable anchorage, Adams took the "Sea Adventure" on down to Naha, putting in on December 27 for repairs.[9]

There were approximately 125 passengers and seamen aboard, a rough lot, numbering among them men of British, Spanish, Portuguese, and Japanese origin. Shuri gave them permission to land their stores and to begin repair work. " We found marvellous great friendship," wrote Adams, but after thirty days the Okinawan officials began to urge the strangers to hasten their departure. Junks were expected to come in from Ch'uang-chou, said the anxious Okinawans, and the Chinese would be angry if they found rival traders at Naha; trade relations with China might be broken off.

In fact, Chinese junks were forbidden to call at Naha. It is probable that the Okinawans were ordered to conceal the presence of Satsuma's agents aboard the Okinawan vessels returning from the China coast. There were other reasons too; the idle crew and passengers were bickering among themselves, making demands upon the hot-tempered Will

Adams, and creating disturbances in the port. A mutinous quarrel broke out between a score of armed men, led by a Japanese named Shobei, and about forty other boisterous seamen. Shuri's chief magistrate was called down to mediate, and by March 15 restored order. Ten days later Shobei treacherously killed his principal opponent.

Despite this first clash between Europeans and Japanese on Okinawan soil, the people of Naha and Shuri treated these uninvited guests with courtesy. Adams was received most cordially; his close friendship with Tokugawa Ieyasu was well known to Satsuma's agents at Naha and to the king's officials, and he himself made a great effort to establish good personal relations; for instance, his diary notes polite words and phrases which he had transcribed for guidance. At the king's invitation he visited Shuri to inspect the castle.

At Naha, Adams dickered for a cargo of grain and ambergris which had been brought up from Miyako, and directed repairs on the "Sea Adventure." It was slow work; the voyage to Siam was given up as an unseasonable venture; and on May 22 Adams sailed for Kawachi in Japan, carrying sweet-potato plants for Cocks' garden at Hirado and such cargo as he had been able to buy at Naha. On June 10 the "Sea Adventure" made port safely.

The record of British expenditures at Naha demonstrates the cheapness of goods and the low value placed upon Okinawan currency. Wheat, "Liquea wyne," a "great Liquea cocke," and "Liquea trenchers" (possibly lacquerware) were among the articles brought in from Naha by the foreign merchants. Cocks' *Diary* notes that on June 2, 1615, his subordinate Wickham took a gift of two pieces of Okinawan cloth and a "dish of pottatos" to the feudal Lord of Bungo. On June 26 he recorded: "Bongo Dono sent to me to have had a jar of Liquea wyne (or *rack*) for that the Emperor hath sent to him to come to Miaco, and therefore he sought for such matters to give in present to great men for a novelitie."[10]

Some traffic in spices still took place by way of the Fukien trading base. Adams notes on June 14, 1615, that " the new botswayn of the junck brought me 2 Liquea brushes and a box of synamon of same place, the best that ever I saw in my life, and Jno. Japan our *jurebasso*, brought me a present of Liquea cloth one peece." Sometimes Adams suspected that his agents at Naha sequestered valuable items which should have been delivered to the English trading depot. He records a quarrel with a subordinate named Damien Marines, who had bought up the local Okinawan supply of ambergris, kept in a "chist" which Adams wanted to inspect. Wickham, too, reports on supplies of this valuable commodity which could be obtained in the Ryukyus. In other entries for 1615 and 1616 Cocks records the desertion of a Japanese employee in Okinawa, and a sum set aside for investment in ambergris at Naha. He also notes that "thirteen barkes laden with souldiers" had left port, ostensibly for Formosa, but he was of the opinion that they were searching throughout the Ryukyu Islands for refugees scattered after the fall of Osaka Castle, where Hideyoshi's heirs and their adherents had been destroyed.[11]

Under date of July 28, 1618, Cocks notes that he had received letters "from Antony the Negro" and two others then stationed at Naha, and in that year Will Adams made his second visit to Okinawa en route to Indo-China.

The English company had no illusions concerning the source of basic authority in the Ryukyus, for Cocks at Hirado was on most friendly terms with "the King of Xaxma [Satsuma] whose vassall the King of Liqueas is. . . ." William Eaton, stationed at Naha, reported to Cocks that he received cordial assistance from the Okinawans because the Lord of Satsuma had ordered them to be helpful to the British. Edmund Sayers, who was often at Kagoshima, noted that "Soyemon Dono told me that the King of Shasma did much esteem our English nation and would suffer us to trade into the Liqueas or any other parts of his dominion."[12]

Six years after these notices of Okinawan friendliness and coöperation were written, all foreigners were forbidden to enter the Ryukyus. Arrest, torture, and execution awaited those who tried to make their way secretly into the islands or through them into Japan. This did not reflect a change in the character of the Okinawans, but a drastic change of policy in Japan, extended and harshly enforced by Satsuma throughout the dependency.

The Okinawans suffered in consequence of events and conflicts of interest in which they had no part. The Portuguese and Spanish missionaries in Japan had become intolerable to the shogun's government; they had on occasion openly preached disobedience to government decrees and sowed mistrust and dissension between Christian converts and the general populace, on the one hand urging their converts to attach their allegiance to the authorities at Rome, and on the other encouraging them to desecrate and sometimes destroy Buddhist temples and Shinto shrines.

When the missionaries refused to give up preaching, some went into hiding, some departed openly aboard European ships only to make their way back secretly into Japan, smuggling themselves aboard European trading ships and Chinese junks. Tokugawa Ieyasu had been tolerant of the Protestant English and Dutch traders, who were indifferent to religious interests. After his death in 1616, however, his successors rigidly restricted European traders to the island of Deshima at Nagasaki and instituted a harsh repression of Christianity. Hidden missionaries were ferreted out, tortured, and executed with great barbarity. Any Japanese known to have sheltered a missionary in any way was subjected to ferocious punishments. Friends and relatives suffered the most brutal treatment.

Persecution reached an extreme degree in the period 1617–36, and in these years Europeans courting martyrdom deliberately began to make their way secretly into the Ryukyus and so into Japan. It is recorded that in 1622 two Christian converts were discovered in Yaeyama and condemned to death at the stake. In 1624 all foreign immigration was most strictly forbidden.

Two years later a Spanish Dominican named Juan de Rueda (or Juan de los Angelos) was discovered in Japan, seized, condemned, and thrown into the sea. It had been disclosed that after a residence in Japan from 1604 until 1619 he had openly departed for Manila. There he had prepared Christian tracts in the Japanese language and with these had made his way successfully through the Ryukyus and slipped into Japan again. It had to be assumed that he received considerable help en route.

In 1631 the daimyo at Kagoshima issued a new prohibition against all Christian activities; shortly thereafter he increased local organization in Yaeyama and opened a special Yaeyama office at Kagoshima. In 1636 two Dominicans, Miguel de Ozaraza, a Spaniard, and William

Courtet, a Frenchman, attempted to slip into Japan through Okinawa. Ozaraza was imprisoned at Okinawa for a year, then taken through Kagoshima to Nagasaki, where, with Courtet, he suffered torture and death.

Threats of another kind strengthened Satsuma's concern; in 1639 a Western ship of unknown nationality put in briefly at Yaeyama and took away a young girl, who was never heard of again. At this, Satsuma sent down a new agent, known as the *Yamato Bugyo* (Japanese Commissioner), who was to report directly and promptly to Kagoshima if new intrusions took place on this most distant frontier.

WAR AND REBELLION IN CHINA AND ITS EFFECT IN OKINAWA

Yonaguni Island now formed the most southerly outpost of Okinawan interest and Japanese concern. Fifty miles away to the west, on a clear day, the cliffs and peaks of northern Formosa lie low on the horizon. In 1623 the Spanish (based on Manila) had built forts and missions at Keelung and Tamsui. The Dutch meanwhile moved in from a temporary base in the Pescadores to the southwest Formosan coast, establishing the first government on Formosa, building a strong military base, and developing an orderly administration and a profitable trade.

In time the Dutch drove out all competitors; the Spanish were evicted from the northern tip of the island in 1628; and the Japanese settlement at Takasago on the west coast of Formosa faded away after the Tokugawa seclusion edicts of 1634 closed Japan itself. It became a capital offense for Japanese to leave Japan or to attempt re-entry from abroad.

Chinese emigrants were moving over to Formosa in growing numbers; some were adventurers willing to leave the crowded villages of China's coastal provinces for the open Formosan frontier, others were political refugees from the mainland. Some willingly took up land under full Dutch administration, but many preferred to settle nearby, clearing ground for cultivation and enjoying the advantages of trade which were created by the presence of the Europeans in and near Fort Zealandia and Anping.

The settlement of Formosa is not properly a part of the Ryukyu narrative, but the conditions on the mainland of China which gave rise to this movement to the sea frontiers south of Okinawa had a very direct bearing on the economic welfare and security of the Ryukyu kingdom. War on the continent generated trouble for the hapless Okinawans.

The Ming government was weakened by corruption in the provinces and the incapacity of eunuch rule at Peking. Taxation grew intolerable as the government tried to meet the demands of a luxurious court and to support an increasing number of military undertakings. Attempts to expel Hideyoshi's forces from Korea had been very costly. From the northeastern borders came a new threat; the Manchus were organizing, soon to invade China through the Great Wall.

China was hard pressed. In 1637 a squadron of five armed British vessels put in at Canton and forced the Chinese there to accept cargoes. This was a demonstration of the European concept of the *right to trade* coming into head-on collision with the Chinese concept of China as the Superior State granting or withholding the *privilege to trade* so persistently sought by the Outer Barbarians.

The affairs and problems of a minor tributary state—Okinawa—were of little importance to Peking under these circumstances, but by 1638, as we have seen, the persistent Okinawans had managed to resume the old biennial tribute-trade arrangement, which had been drastically reduced in 1611.

Now a grave new problem beset the Okinawans. Peking fell to rebels in 1644 and the last Ming emperor hanged himself in the palace. Manchu forces entered the capital and established a new alien government, which they styled the Ch'ing dynasty. Ming loyalists fled southward, maintaining resistance here and there until 1662.

This turn of events posed a problem which Shuri solved with pragmatic simplicity. As long as there were rival claimants to the Chinese throne Shuri's envoys carried credentials which could be used with either Ming or Ch'ing representatives.

In 1646 Shuri sent Uezu *Uekata* to Japan to report on the downfall of the Ming government, and in the next year the death of the king (Sho Ken) provided occasion for a new mission to China and a report to Shuri and Satsuma on the organization of the new Ch'ing (Manchu) government. Questions were raised in Japan concerning Okinawa's relations with Peking under the changed circumstances, but the shogunate left it with Satsuma to decide what adjustments, if any, need be made. The Ch'ing court records preserve the answer: "In 1654 the eldest son of the King of Liu Ch'iu, Shang Chih, handed in the patent and seal of the late Ming period, whereupon an imperial [Ch'ing] command appointed him King of Chung-shan. This country is in the great southeastern sea to the east of Fukien."[13]

During the years of rebellion in China the embassies were often imperiled. Pirates attacked the tribute ships in 1665. In the melee a murder was committed aboard ship and valuable articles were stolen.

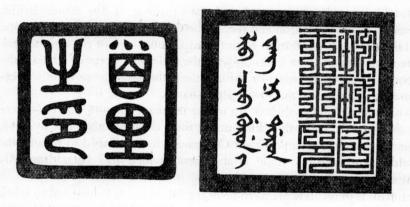

FIG. 10. SEALS OF STATE. Left: *Great seal of the Shuri government.* Right: *Imperial Chinese investiture seal granted to the kings of Okinawa by the Manchu (Ch'ing) court.*

Satsuma held the principal envoy and his deputy responsible, tried them, and sentenced them to death. Seven years later an embassy was waylaid on the road from the port to Peking, but after a fierce encounter the Okinawans got the best of the situation. For this a member of the mission named Hirata Tentsu earned a hero's place in Okinawan traditions.

For a time it was conceivable that Okinawa might become involved in the course of the Manchu struggle to wrest Formosa from the heirs of Cheng Ch'eng-k'ung (Koxinga), who had taken it from the Dutch. Formosa formed one base for a triple revolt against the Manchus.

An Amoy Chinese named Cheng Chih-lung had become master of a great fleet of junks trading and raiding along the China coast from Nagasaki in Japan to Canton and Macao. For a time he sided with the Ming, but in 1628 he went over to the Manchus and used his ships in their behalf to suppress other piratical fleets in coastal waters. Taking advantage of the confusion generated by war on the mainland, he began to assert himself with considerable independence. At last the Manchus persuaded him to place himself and two of his sons under the authority of a Manchu general in Fukien. By a treacherous act he was made prisoner and with his sons and aides was taken to Peking to be executed.

A third son remained independent of Manchu controls and for a decade organized such devastating attacks all along the coast that the Peking government was forced to order the evacuation of eighty-eight coastal townships in Fukien and Kwangtung provinces. In 1662 he turned upon the Dutch in Formosa, basing his forces in the Pescadores. The Dutch surrendered and evacuated their considerable forces and their families to Java. Cheng then declared himself King of Formosa, which he and his heirs held as an independent territory until 1682.

Meanwhile two high-ranking Chinese who had deserted the Ming cause to fight for the Manchus now deserted the Manchus and attempted to carve out similar independent kingdoms for themselves. Wu San-kuei revolted in 1673 and set himself up as King of Chien in Hunan Province; Keng Ching-chung revolted in Chekiang in 1674 and in the course of the struggle sought to establish coöperation with Cheng Ch'eng-k'ung in Formosa.

It was reported at Shuri that the Manchu government might fall as a consequence of these widespread rebellions. To learn the true state of affairs, the Okinawans determined to send a special inspector or commissioner to the continent, bearing letters addressed to Keng Ching-chung as well as to the Manchu emperor. Takara *Uekata* embarked on this delicate mission in 1676, but on November 9 in that year Keng surrendered and went over to the Manchus once again.

Peking was so preoccupied with these affairs that nearly thirteen years elapsed between the accession of Sho Tei to the throne at Shuri (1669) and his ceremonial confirmation as king by the Chinese envoys, who came in 1682. This underscored, if nothing else were needed, the ephemeral quality of any Chinese claims to sovereignty in the Ryukyu Islands.

The natives of Kume Village, near Naha, were faced with a peculiar problem. They were of Chinese and not of Manchu descent. For 250 years (i.e., from 1392) their prestige as representatives of great China and Chinese culture had been sufficient to sustain them as a distinct group in Okinawa. They retained the customs and dress of their ancestral homeland despite the fact that intermarriage had virtually transformed the racial stock of the village residents. Now came orders from the Manchus that all Chinese must adopt the queue and make other signs of loyalty to the new dynasty. This the Kume villagers refused to do. Henceforth they wore Okinawan dress and adopted the distinctive Okinawan style of coiffure. From this time forward, ties of cultural dependency upon China were steadily diminished.

Satsuma took no risks. The Okinawans were allowed to wrestle with their own economic problems as best they could, but Kagoshima reserved for itself all decisions relating to foreigners and foreign trade, nor did the Japanese relax controls upon the king and council.

Under the authoritarian Tokugawa rule, relations between one feudal territory and another within Japan proper were marked by a mean and narrow provincialism. Within each feudal domain the exclusive governing elite regarded the common people with uneasy suspicion. This state of affairs was in part a heritage of centuries of civil war and anarchy and in part a reaction to peasant uprisings bred of economic hardship, which were occurring with disturbing frequency in many scattered fiefs. Under Japanese influence the Shuri government, too, developed an elaborate system of agents, known as *metsuke*, who served as informers and spies, present at all times and everywhere among the common people. If we are to judge from 19th-century accounts written by foreign visitors, there was little effort to conceal their identity and presence in the community. Although they were feared, they were treated with scant respect. Satsuma required them, and they had to be tolerated. No evidence can be found to suggest that the Okinawans at any time contemplated an attempt to throw off Japanese controls; nevertheless, in 1669 Satsuma saw to it that the Shuri government's swordsmithy was abolished, putting an end to the manufacture of swords for ceremonial use, and in 1699 forbade the import of weapons of any kind. A new police inspectorate was created, and a new Japanese garrison post was established in the eastern quarter of Naha.

SATSUMA AND THE OKINAWAN TRADE WITH CHINA

We must retrace our steps briefly to review 17th-century relations with Japan on a wider basis. Satsuma laid a heavy yoke on the Okinawans: this was a form of colonial exploitation, which the "internal autonomy" did little to disguise. A comparison of income suggests the overwhelming weight of resources which Japan could bring to bear upon Okinawa if need be. Satsuma's estimate of the total yearly revenues in Okinawa stood at approximately 90,000 koku, of which the Shimazu clan required a tribute of approximately 12,000 koku from the government and 8,000 from the king's own estates and revenues. The Daimyo of Satsuma at this time enjoyed a total revenue exceeding 700,000 koku per year, and the Tokugawa revenues were calculated at something in excess of 3,000,000 koku.

"The Okinawans must be compared with the cormorants of the Nagara River in Japan; they are made to catch fish which they are not permitted to swallow." Thus the Okinawan scholar Iha Fuyu summed up Okinawa's position in the China-Satsuma trade relationship after 1611. The annual tribute levy paid to Satsuma represented but a small part of the income the Shimazu clan derived from its new dependency. A Shimazu family document dated January 14, 1635, notes that among the clan's major resources was an item of 123,700 koku coming up from Ryukyu. This suggests that more than 100,000 koku represented annual income from the trade conducted through Naha in Okinawan ships.[14] Conversely, it suggests by what a staggering amount the revenues of the Ryukyu kingdom had fallen off since the days of independence. On the basis of these figures, it may be estimated roughly that instead of an income equivalent to more than 200,000 koku, the Okinawans now had less than 80,000 koku, plus a minor and uncertain share of foreign-trading profit allowed to them to meet expenses of each new commercial venture overseas.

Since the trade with China had been the prime object of the Keicho conquest, Satsuma had lost no time in attempting to reëstablish it. A mission was dispatched to China as soon as Sho Nei resumed his residence at Shuri (1611). Shimazu advanced funds to finance the venture.

It has been suggested that the Emperor of China may never have been informed of the Japanese conquest of Ryukyu; by deliberately ignoring the calamity which had befallen one of its most faithful tributaries the Chinese government could evade responsibility for it. Ming officials took the lofty position that the recent unpleasantness must have impoverished the kingdom, and they therefore decreed that Ryukyu need send tribute only once in every ten years. As we have seen, the Ming court itself was beset with internal troubles at this time, and it may have been wary of the changed relationship which now tied Shuri so closely to Japan.

The Chinese decision was not at all to Satsuma's liking; the miserable Okinawan envoys were sent back to China in the following year. They were rebuffed at Peking, the tribute was refused, and they were sent home. Sho Nei's death in 1612 and Sho Ho's succession provided a legitimate excuse for new attempts to increase trade at the end of the ten-year period decreed by Peking. In 1623, investiture missions were exchanged. The Okinawans pressed for the restoration of the old biennial tribute schedule; the Chinese temporized, granting them leave to come up to Peking once in five years. Thenceforth the tribute ships (*shinko-sen*) left Naha with fair regularity. Some were lost in storms at sea; occasionally they were overtaken and looted by pirates. During the Manchu invasion of China there was some uncertainty, as we have seen, and again after 1800 the schedules were affected by Shuri's concern with the Western ships then ranging among the islands.

Satsuma did nothing to disturb the traditional protocol; two tribute ships sailed together from Naha in the spring, passing over to the Fukien coast in about seven days. There the entire ship's company remained at the Ryukyu trading depot until the tenth month, when the envoy and his deputy, with a party of eighteen in attendance and with a numerous train of Chinese coolies and officials, proceeded overland to Peking. There they lodged in the yamen of the Minister of Protocol. Sulphur, copper, tin, and fabrics continued to form the token tribute as of old, although the Manchus ordered Shuri to cease sending along trained horses. Imperial gifts for the King of Ryukyu were received in exchange, together with money and goods sufficient to reimburse the Okinawans for the expenses of the journey. Such Chinese commodities had a very high sales value in Japan, to which they passed ultimately through Kagoshima.

Unlike the tribute missions, the investiture missions were at once more elaborate and much more costly for the Okinawans. Ships bearing the Okinawan and Chinese envoys to and fro on these occasions were known as *kan-sen*. Sometimes the Chinese investiture envoys stayed at Naha as long as nine months, for they were not as ready to venture out on the open seas as often or as fearlessly as the Okinawans were.

It was customary for the principal envoy and his deputy to travel on different ships, for great uncertainty attended the voyages. In 1663, for instance, it required nineteen days to cross over from Fukien to Naha, whereas in 1683 the voyage was made in three days, a record time. The ambassador on that occasion (Wang Chi) remained at Shuri for five months, during which he was called upon to write many inscriptions and autographs for the Okinawans, who admired his literary style and his fine calligraphy. Upon his return to China he prepared two monographs, one having to do with government and history in Ryukyu, the other and longer one a record of Okinawan manners and customs.

The number of Chinese soldiers and servants and minor officials in the ambassador's suite was rarely less than three hundred and at times numbered eight hundred. Since the Shuri government had to bear the expenses of the Chinese mission while it was in residence at Naha, the drain on the treasury was heavy, and the king's officers had to depend upon Satsuma for loans to meet the charge.

The trading ships allowed to accompany tribute ships were known as *sekko-sen*, and it was upon these that Satsuma depended for its great profits in this business. Since it was impossible to increase the frequency with which tribute ships could be dispatched, Satsuma prompted the

Okinawans to obtain permission to increase the number of *sekko-sen*, and to send trading ships along with the *kan-sen* of investiture missions as well.

Both the Satsuma clan government and the merchants of Kagoshima invested capital in the China trade, entrusting it to Naha middlemen in order to preserve the elaborate pretense required to satisfy Chinese sensibilities. At Kagoshima, management of Ryukyuan affairs was largely entrusted to the Ichiki family, and in 1631 one of the Ichiki, in disguise, went along with the Okinawans to keep a close watch on the conduct of business at the trading depot. His success as a "watchdog" for Satsuma's interests was reflected in profits, so great that henceforth agents from Kagoshima concealed themselves among the Okinawan sailors and merchants upon each mission.

Occasionally ships engaged in this trade put in at Kume Island, which lay in the sea lanes west of Naha. Sometimes they needed slight repair, sometimes weather conditions dictated a pause en route. The Japanese soon became aware that the Okinawan sailors were evading Satsuma's agents by off-loading some of the trading goods at Kume to be smuggled later into Okinawa. There were reprisals. In 1667 Shuri was forced to execute one envoy for failure to conduct his mission properly, and a system of fire signals was inaugurated in the islands to warn of the passage of ships, thus rendering it difficult for them to make overlong or clandestine stops along the way.

CHAPTER FIVE

THE YEARS OF ISOLATION

1609–1797

A New Economic Life: Agriculture Takes the
Place of Foreign Trade

By fortunate accident the sweet potato was introduced, in 1606, and by 1620 it was commonly grown everywhere in the islands.[1] This hardy, tuberous plant yielded a cheap but nourishing food for mankind and a substantial fodder for livestock. A heady alcoholic drink could be distilled from it. It could be stored easily. Above all it grew well throughout the islands, even in soil too poor to produce other food crops or too badly situated for irrigation.

Today the Okinawans keep alive the memory of Noguni Sokan, who brought the sweet potato to Naha from China and in so doing substantially altered the course of economic development in the islands. He was a minor official stationed for a time at the Ryukyu trading depot on the Fukien coast. To break the tedium of his assignment there he read Chinese texts on botanical and agricultural subjects and experimented with various plants in his own garden-patch at the trading station. It occurred to him that the sweet potato, only recently brought to the Fukien coast, might be grown in Okinawa and that if this could be done, it might serve to relieve or prevent famine conditions which so often affected country villages in times of crop failure.*

Upon his return to Okinawa, Noguni tried planting seedlings in several places, and the results were promising. Gima Shinjo, an official

---

* The plant is of Central or South American origin; the name *batata* may have come from Haiti. Spaniards took the potato to Europe between 1492 and 1500; it was known in England by 1560; and about 1570 it was taken on to the Philippines by the Spanish. They are said to have forbidden its export from Luzon, but traders took it to the China coast, where Noguni first observed it about 1600.

183

of much higher rank than he, took note of and encouraged Noguni's experiment. Within fifteen years the sweet potato, known as *To-imo* (Chinese potato), was being cultivated throughout Okinawa.

After Noguni Sokan had demonstrated its value in the Okinawan economy, the humble sweet potato was taken to Japan. The diary of Richard Cocks, the English trader at Hirado, has these entries:

"June 19, 1615: I took a garden this day and planted it with potatoes brought from the Liquea [Ryukyu], a thing not yet planted in Japan.

"July 29, 1618: I set 500 small potato roots in a garden. Mr. Eaton sent me them from Liquea. I must pay five shillings per annum for the garden."[2]

According to a *History of Okinawa* prepared by Ijichi Sadaka in 1878, a Japanese named Ryuiemon carried the sweet potato from Ryukyu to Yamakawa Village in Satsuma about 1665 or 1675. After his death in 1705 he was worshipped as the "Master of the Chinese Potato." From Satsuma, sweet-potato cultivation spread throughout Japan.

Meanwhile, a stone altar was built near Noguni's grave in Okinawa in 1700 to honor the spirit of a man whose activities had proved of so great a benefit to his fellows, and in 1937 the Okinawan government created a handsome shrine in a public garden at Naha to recognize Noguni and his patron Gima Shinjo.

Gima's name is associated with the introduction of sugar-cane culture as well. In 1623 an Okinawan envoy to China, named Rin Koku-yo, returned with cane slips, which Gima caused to be planted experimentally. The trial was a success and sugar production was soon established as a basic agricultural industry, providing Okinawa with a luxury item in great demand for the Satsuma trade and Japanese market. Sweet potatoes, by contrast, were established as a basic foodstuff for the local population.

The introduction of these two major crops and their exploitation for home consumption and for the export trade marked an abrupt shift in the basic economy of the Ryukyu Islands from dependency on wide-ranging free commerce to a niggardly share in the China trade and the production of two crops with which to sustain life within the islands. The gentry at Shuri lost much of their independence of action, but the peasants in the hinterland became more important to the government and were stimulated to greater production.

GOVERNMENT AND PEOPLE UNDER SATSUMA'S WATCHFUL EYE

During the first century of Satsuma's domination, the Okinawans evolved a pattern of government and of social relations which was to persist with little change until 1879. The adjustment of relations with Satsuma proceeded smoothly, for the helpless Okinawans were by nature a mild and easygoing people, relatively few in number and without armed forces or a will to fight.

Sho Nei's death in 1621 broke an important link with the past. His successor, Sho Ho, could not merely assume office at the palace and then announce the fact to Japan while awaiting recognition by the Chinese court. Satsuma's approval now came first, enthronement followed, and only then did a mission go off to Peking with Satsuma's blessing and a considerable investment of Satsuma's funds in the cargoes shipped along for trade. Sho Nei was the last king to play an important personal role in government until the 1870's. The kings reigned thereafter through hereditary right and with great prestige, but they were merely ceremonial chiefs of state.

The government's primary functions were reduced to the collection of taxes in kind and supervision of the public peace. The Okinawans had little to do with the conduct of foreign affairs. The nature of some of the offices solemnly established and staffed at Shuri suggests that a secondary function of government was to find ways and means to provide offices, titles, and income for relatives of the royal family, for descendants of the *anji*, and for the gentry. All government organization was held together by an elaborate network of ceremonial relationships prescribed by Confucian standards. As new economic problems rose within the country, or old economic activities developed new importance, new offices were created to supervise them.

By the time Sho Ho reached the throne, Satsuma had returned to the king his powers to organize offices and to administer punishments, though always under the watchful eye of the Japanese resident commissioner. Satsuma reserved the right to approve (or disapprove) appointments to the prime minister's office and to the king's council (the Sanshikan), with whom he shared responsibility.

We may use the English words chancellor or prime minister as an approximate translation for the title *Sessei*. The office was reserved for members of the royal house. Time soon demonstrated that the range of talent in the Sho family was limited; gradually the office faded in importance, though not in prestige, and the Sanshikan (Council of State) emerged as the effective governing body.

Candidates for membership in the Council of State had to be of acceptable lineage, they had to have passed the local literary examinations successfully, and they had to be residents of Shuri. The literary examinations were of course in the Chinese classical tradition, but much less severe than the great examinations held at Peking. They had to be fitted to local needs and local opportunities. The residence qualification reflected the tradition that all aristocrats, descendents of the *anji* and of collateral branches of the royal family, must live at Shuri. Occasionally exceptions were made to this rule when talented men of the Kume scholars' village were allowed to transfer their official residences to the castle town and so become eligible for membership in the Sanshikan.

One organ of government was concerned with legal affairs; a High Court, consisting of a chief judge, fifteen associates of different ranks, a secretariat, and a clerical staff, took care of the ordinary judicial business, and special judicial panels were appointed from time to time to consider unusual cases.

Prime ministers and the Sanshikan were assisted by heads of administrative departments, who were known as the Council of Fifteen when acting together. These men advised on policy and recommended nominations to the Sanshikan when vacancies occurred.

The countryside was divided into districts known as *majiri*, which in the first instance roughly coincided with the old landed estates of the *anji;* the *majiri* were grouped under the three ancient divisions corresponding to the three principalities but now known as Shimojiri, Nakagami, and Kunigami. Shuri sent its representatives to the *majiri* to supervise local affairs, but at that level they dealt with local persons put forward by communal village organizations.

Eligibility for office throughout the government down to the *majiri* level was usually determined by family status plus merit. Members of the gentry who took the qualifying examinations and failed, or those whose performance in office was deemed unsatisfactory, found themselves transferred to offices lying far from the capital, and sometimes they were reduced in rank. Their descendants gradually sank back into the local population as petty village officials. Some became farmers.

The preëminence of Shuri families and the privileges and advantages conferred automatically through residence at the king's capital, created a tradition of prestige which has persisted into the 20th century, for wherever Okinawans assemble for the first time, in Ryukyu, in Japan, or in overseas communities, it is quickly but tactfully established if a man has been born in Shuri, educated in Shuri, or has married a woman of Shuri, in that order of precedence. Members of the royal family who were not rulers or sons of the reigning king traditionally distinguished themselves by writing the character for the surname Sho with two less strokes than the king and his sons were accustomed to use. In the Chinese reading, therefore, Shang became Hsiang. Members of the gentry who can trace a relationship with the royal house of the Second Sho family usually, if not invariably, include a character read *cho* in their personal names, such as Higa Shun*cho*, Kabira *Cho*sei, and so forth.

Gradually the old feudal basis of administrative land divisions began to break up under the pressure of economic need and a shifting, growing population. The watch office in Hokuzan established in 1416 was at last abolished in 1663. New *majiri* were created, and new offices came into being at all levels of the government.

We do not know precisely how many people lived in the Ryukyu Islands in these years; we shall not be far wrong if we assume that the population did not exceed 200,000 of which perhaps 125,000 lived on Okinawa. And of these it has been estimated that more than half lived in the four towns of Shuri, Naha, Tomari, and Kume.*

* Census estimates for Okinawa in the years 1875–90 (before significant economic change under modern Japanese management) provide a rate of increase which forms the basis of this estimate. S. Wells Williams visited Naha in 1837 and hazarded a guess at "less than 200,000"; Captain Basil Hall's staff in 1816 could not agree on an estimate. Extensive studies of Japan's population place estimates at a fairly constant total (about thirty millions) for the 18th and early 19th centuries, under conditions which were somewhat analogous to those on the Ryukyu Islands.

Stimulating new social elements had to be absorbed into the agricultural population in the 17th century. A substantial number of Satsuma men who came down during, or just after, the Keicho invasion decided to settle in Okinawa, took up lands granted to them perforce by the Shuri government, and acquired wives from among the local gentry. These Japanese newcomers shared in the limited privileges of private land ownership, they enjoyed tax benefits, and in some instances they were assigned shares in the revenues of whole villages located on their new properties. Some of these early Japanese landholdings are substantially intact today and remain within the families which were established in the early 17th century. Descendants of the Japanese immigrants have become indistinguishable in dialect, living habits, and customs, for in each generation there was intermarriage with Okinawan families. A tradition of distinction is nevertheless maintained in the 20th century, displayed in recollections of special position and privileges which had been enjoyed by the Japanese squires so long ago.

The social hierarchy may be summarized briefly as, first, the royalty (the Sho family); second, the privileged classes (*shizoku*); and, third, the common men (*heimin*).

The king stood supreme. Next came members of the royal household, brothers and sons of the king. The royal consorts and mothers of princes had to be chosen from among members of a few distinguished noble houses, which were themselves related with the royal house through many generations of intermarriage but were not of the same surname. It has been noted heretofore that grandsons of the king were privileged to retain the Sho family name. Beyond the third generation the king's descendants in collateral branches assumed other princely names.

Among the preëminent noble houses were the O, Ba, and Mo families, all cousins of the royal family in some degree. Next in the hereditary ranks of the *shizoku* were the *anji* descended from territorial lords who had moved into Shuri during and after the reign of Sho Shin. A lesser degree of nobility bore the titles *uekata* or *oyakata*. These families were founded by men who had earned permanent rank and distinction through meritorious service to the state, or by men who were the younger sons of the hereditary *anji* and royal princes.

Below the nobles stood a gentry class divided by a system of titles into three principal grades, each with a junior and a senior rating. These were the *pechin*, *satonushi*, and *chikudun*, descendants of the king's soldiers and retainers, the soldiers and retainers of the *anji*, and scholars, priests, and commoners who earned the gentry status through meritorious service. Within these three ranks a man might rise or fall according to his ability and deserts.

At the downfall of the kingdom (in 1879) there were approximately seventy-two families of noble or royal rank, and this may be taken as a fairly reliable figure for the preceding two and a half centuries with which we are here concerned.

Since the nobility and gentry numbered nearly one-third of the total population—a high proportion—it might be supposed that there was one drone for every pair of active workers in the islands, and that an

FIG. 11. SHO TETSU, KING OF CHUZAN, AND HIS SONS, 1756. *From the same source as Fig. 9. (See page 211.)*

oppressive burden weighed upon a sullen and discontented common people. Such was not the case, for thanks to the policies of Sho Jo-ken, Sai On, and other enlightened leaders, the gentry were the artisans and craftsmen who produced a large proportion of the artifacts required for daily living among all classes, and after the middle of the 18th century an increasing number of townsmen left Shuri and Naha for village and farm life.

The masses (*heimin*) were the common farmers, the fishermen, and the laborers, but in the Ryukyus even a farmer was sometimes given courtesy titles in ordinary usage. A system of indenture permitted children to be sold by impoverished parents. Itinerant players, pig-butchers, beggars, and prostitutes were at the bottom of the social order.

No countrywide leadership or organization existed to give political cohesion to the *heimin;* they were bound and guided by most conservative traditions and concepts of duty. There was little movement to and fro among the villages, and as a consequence strong differences of local dialect developed and persisted through the centuries.

There were no countrywide social organizations, no common schools, and little by way of formal religion. Religion and religious organization offered no common cause or leadership in the Ryukyus. As a precautionary measure Shimazu proscribed and suppressed the evangelical Shin sect of Buddhism, closed its temples, forbade all missionary activity, and dissolved its priesthood in Satsuma and Ryukyu. Henceforth only the Zen and Shingon sects were allowed to maintain organizations; they were of ancient foundation at Shuri. The Shin sect, on the other hand, was of relatively recent introduction; it had little property and scant prestige among the gentry, but it did attempt to appeal to the illiterate common people, and perhaps for this reason it was suspect. Satsuma had not forgotten that in the 16th century Shin priests, representing a powerful temporal organization at Kyoto, had been employed to work against Shimazu's interests.

Relations between the classes seem never to have undergone serious strain despite the barriers of privilege which separated aristocrat from peasant.

The proportion of town-dwelling gentry was very high in relation to the food-producing peasantry in the 17th century. This imbalance had not been serious in the early days of independence, when the farmers produced the basic food requirements, and the luxury trade in the hands of Shuri-Naha men produced surpluses to sustain the gentry. After 1611 this surplus earned in trade was drained off to meet the Satsuma tribute levies.

SHO JO-KEN, PRINCE AND PRIME MINISTER

A prince named Gushikawa Choei led the Chuzan embassy to Edo in 1649, meeting there leading Japanese statesmen and administrators. In 1654 he became *Sessei*, and for twelve years thereafter strove to pattern his administration on Japanese precedent. His successor continued and enlarged these pro-Japanese policies.

Sho Jo-ken, Prince of Haneji, enjoyed high reputation as an essayist and historian, and as such he was keenly sensitive to the position to which the Ryukyu kingdom had been reduced. Since there was no possible alternative—certainly the Chinese had displayed no interest in Okinawa's fate—he wisely pursued a course of conciliation toward Japan.

Unfortunately, perhaps, the Tokugawa leaders whose policies these princes chose to emulate were men who did not fully comprehend the economic character of political and administrative problems. They were first of all Confucian moralists, attempting to apply the inappropriate and bookish precepts of ancient Chinese philosophers to social and economic problems which called for imaginative and experimental contemporary treatment. They were inventive of restrictions rather than of new methods which would lead to increased production and better distribution of wealth. Instead of freeing the economy to enable individual initiative and private enterprise to have free play, social order and economic life alike were subjected to rigid controls.

The Tokugawa government believed that everyone should find his place and keep to it, and that a society well-regulated according to the classics would of itself be free of problems. Consequently, the Japanese leaders often addressed themselves to superficial issues of morals and manners rather than to the fundamental problems of economic change and population growth, which they did not clearly understand.

Okinawan leaders attempted to follow them; the blind were leading the blind. The governing elite sought to freeze the established social order. Restless individual energies were to be taken up in the pursuit of arts and letters, in petty concern with genealogies, dress, and etiquette. These trivia were all time-consuming and precluded any "dangerous thoughts" harmful to the established order.

A proclamation "To Encourage Arts and Learning" was issued in 1667, and there was a steady flow of orders and edicts intended to "correct and regulate" society. The wellborn were encouraged to fritter away their time in meeting the exacting requirements of ceremonial deportment and dress; the common man was told to live frugally, work harder, produce more goods, and observe the decencies of Confucian moral relationships within the home and the community.

At Shuri there was a great concentration of interest on details of court life and of the hierarchical order of things. By royal order, genealogies were reëxamined and corrected. Ceremonial rules were revised and made more complicated, prescribing the days of attendance upon the court, the days upon which summer clothes could be exchanged for winter costume, and the smallest detail of costume itself. The forms and colors of dress were minutely regulated anew for each class of society. The colors and folds of the turban distinguished grades among officers and the quality and style of hairpins gave public indication of a man's basic social status. It had been long established that the higher nobles would wear gold and the lesser ones silver hairpins. Now the system was refined; the second class of nobles could wear silver hairpins bearing a golden flower, the gentry would wear silver, and the common man was allowed brass.

It is significant, perhaps, that the common man was allowed to wear a hairpin at all. The Okinawans never quite brought themselves to believe in the existence of uncrossable social lines and often found occasion to make exception to rules they laid down for themselves after Chinese or Japanese precedents. The paternalistic government issued a multitude of rules to guide the common man, for instance forbidding him to use an umbrella in the hot sun (though he might use one in time of rain), or to use certain patterns of cloth on his dress, or granting him the privilege of wearing wooden clogs.

Peasants lived in utmost poverty, but at the same time there were no extremes of wealth among the gentry. The Dutch scholar Kaempfer, at Nagasaki from 1690 to 1692, wrote: "The inhabitants [of Ryukyu] which are for the most part either husbandmen or fishermen, are a good-natured, merry sort of people, leading an agreeable, contented life, diverting themselves after their work is done, with a glass of rice beer, and playing upon their musical instruments which they for this purpose carry out with them into the fields."[3]

Courtesy ruled all social relationships, and in Okinawa nearly every third man counted himself a member of a privileged class with a formal and polished code of manners by which to live. Another foreign observer (in the 19th century) noted that the rulers ruled "by the flick of a fan" rather than by the blow of a sword or a stick. Basil Hall Chamberlain observed: "In some most important respects the country really deserved the title bestowed upon it by a Chinese Emperor in 1579, and still proudly inscribed on the gate of its capital city, the title of 'The Land of Propriety.' There were no lethal weapons in Luchu, no feudal factions, few if any crimes of violence. . . . Confucius' ideal was carried out—a government purely civil, at once absolute and patriarchal, resting not on any armed force, but on the theory that subjects owe unqualified obedience to their rulers, the monarchy surrounded by a large cultured class of men of birth, and the whole supported by an industrious peasantry."[4]

Prime Minister Sho Jo-ken did not shrink from touching on the most sensitive and conservative areas of community interest. How much he did on his own initiative and how much was done at the direction of Satsuma's agents we cannot tell, but he set about reducing the importance and authority of the *noro* priestesses in the local communities throughout the Ryukyus. In his essay on the *noro* system, Robert Stewart Spencer suggests that the *noro* were the most conservative and antiforeign (i.e., anti-Japanese) element in Okinawan society and that the educated men at court took the rational Confucian scholar's attitude of skepticism toward all religious forms and practices. A court which prided itself on Confucian correctness and believed that human relations should in all things be guided by the Confucian rule book may have encountered resistance among the *noro* when attempts were made to apply Confucian theory to the practice of government in the countryside. In the Japanese agent the *noro* met a rival, and an unbelieving or skeptical rival at that. The *noro* certainly constituted an influential hierarchy, which reached from the chief priestess at the king's court to the meanest village in the most distant countryside and off-lying island, and this Sho Jo-ken proposed to change.

Without preliminary warning, it was announced in 1667 that the rank of the chief priestess would henceforth be considerably reduced, placing her at a level below that of the queen and the prime minister. The office of her assistant, the priestess in charge of divination, was abolished. In 1674 it was announced that the king would no longer make an annual progress to worship at important shrines in Chinen and Tamagusuku and on Kudaka Island; that he would content himself with "worship from afar" and would merely dispatch a master of ceremonies to make offerings as his deputy. This series of ceremonies had been held once in every two years from most ancient times and was one of the most impressive events in the Ryukyuan calendar, for upon these occasions the king customarily traveled with the chief priestess, the highest officials of the court, and a host of attendants. In 1677 it was provided that the office of the chief priestess could be assumed by the queen upon the death of her consort.

While diminishing the importance of the *noro* hierarchy, Sho Jo-ken sought to enhance the importance of Confucian ritual. A Japanese from Satsuma was brought into the palace to instruct the young King Sho Tei in Confucian doctrine. When the handsome new Confucian temple had been completed in Kume Village—a gift of the Chinese Emperor K'ang Hsi—the king himself proceeded to worship there, attended by a concourse of nobles, and it was decided that henceforth the king's son would offer incense before the tablets of Confucius on the second day of each New Year.

Sho Jo-ken's effort to stiffen and formalize life among the gentry at Shuri seems to have had little effect upon the life of the lively people of Naha. They enjoyed tax immunities, and for reasons which are not clear, the sumptuary laws and the regulations governing the size and nature of private dwellings and other properties were not extended to the port city. As in Edo, Osaka, and Nagoya, the great metropolitan centers in Japan proper, the licensed quarters became centers of fashion, good food, the arts, and entertainment. Women of the Tsuji and Naka-shima districts (set aside for them in 1672) earned high reputations for wit and literary accomplishment. As long as Okinawan men were free to travel in Japan and Japanese mariners and merchants came to Naha there was a steady inflow of the latest Japanese forms of popular enter-tainment. Nor did the Japanese remain unaffected; there is considerable evidence that the distinctive Okinawan dances and folk songs, the brightly designed textiles and the lacquerware produced in the Southern Islands were all welcomed by the alert denizens of the Japanese theater world and the craftsmen of Osaka and Edo.

The townsmen of Naha developed a pleasure-loving urban life which was in strong contrast to the poverty and drabness of life in the vil-lages.

Shuri, Naha, and the villages nearby were becoming crowded. Men and women who had been brought in from the countryside for tempo-rary employment preferred not to return to the monotony of life in the farming and fishing hamlets. The towns offered a more varied livelihood and greater opportunities for craft skills. Residents in Shuri or Kume-mura were tax free.

By 1653 serious overcrowding prompted the government to decree that no one would be permitted to transfer his domicile nor bring his family in to be registered at Shuri, Naha, Kume-mura, or Tomari. Sumptuary laws were issued to discourage excessive expenditures by the townsmen, or indulgence which the state councilors deemed to be excessive for common people. The kinds and quantity of offerings which were allowable at funeral ceremonies were prescribed by law, and there was an attempt to establish limiting controls over open-market bartering transactions (1687).

The growth of towns meant an increased use of coinage. Under the new Satsuma monopolies on overseas trade, however, supplies of Chinese coins no longer came into circulation on Okinawa, but were diverted to Kagoshima. The Okinawans could no longer cast great bronze bells or dispatch large sums of copper cash as gifts for the shogun. To meet its needs, the government undertook to recast old coins in lighter, smaller units. The task was entrusted to the Toma family, and the products were known as "dove's-eye coins" (*hatome sen*). As the years passed, these were recast again and again, each time on a smaller scale, until at last they were little more than round flakes of metal, carried on strings, each string representing a certain standard weight and number.

The Okinawans struggled to adjust local economic life to the limitations imposed upon it by Satsuma, but many of the problems were unrecognized in their true dimensions by either Kagoshima or Shuri. The government did little to expand production. Administrative organization was conceived primarily as an agency through which to extract taxes in kind from the farmer and the fisherman.

If the Shuri court economy was to maintain itself at the level of expenditure to which the king, the princes, and the gentry had become accustomed, taxation had to be increased and collected with increased efficiency. Local production on Okinawa (with very little coming in from Miyako and Yaeyama or from Kume Island) had to make up for the loss of revenue from foreign trade.

The village was the tax unit. Each village had an assigned quota to provide through the district chief, who represented Shuri. Certain land areas were set aside to support the licensed community priestess. Other lands were held privately in the name of lords who lived at the capital. The greater part of the cultivated land area was held as common property divided among households throughout the community and assigned to them for cultivation. These land allotments were changed periodically, though the length of time that one household held a specific land area varied from village to village. If a household was unable to produce its full share of the village tax assessment, the other villagers made up the difference. Lack of skill, shiftlessness, poverty of the soil, sickness in the household, or natural calamity could affect the capacity of the individual household to produce its share of the village allotment. The community as a whole accepted the obligation to meet the shortcomings of individual members.

This system of accepted mutual obligations has left its stamp upon the Okinawan character, for it fostered a deep sense of social obligation,

196

of group responsibility in maintaining the welfare of community members who suffered economic hardship. It lies back of the phenomenal record of relief work, and of financial assistance which Okinawan communities overseas have remitted to their friends and relatives throughout the 20th century. The peasant who could not enjoy exclusive ownership of land could develop little pride in doing more than the minimum of work necessary to meet his assessments. He could not hope to acquire land to pass on to his heirs. He was rarely challenged to exert individual initiative or imagination in his work. The system of community rather than individual responsibility among peasants threw a larger burden of responsibility upon the elite or gentry, whose lives

FIG. 12. CENTERS OF COMMUNITY LIFE. Upper: *Home and shrine of a local* noro, *Kudaka Island.* Lower: *A village well, Tobaru-machi, Shuri.*

centered at Naha and Shuri, but whose duties took them on assignment into every village in the islands. This promoted a strong sense of interdependence and coöperation among the gentry at Shuri, the minor officials, and the village headmen in each district.

The Okinawan peasant was obliged and conditioned to work in the community interest. From birth until death his tasks were allotted to him. He developed no large sense of individual rights or "natural privileges." He had few worldly goods; in a mild climate and a static agricultural society he needed few; hard work benefited the community, not the individual.

The 17th-century administrators did not depend exclusively on bookish maxims and Confucian morals in coping with economic problems. Some practical measures were taken as well. The government established a smithy in each district in 1667 with a view to improving agricultural tools, and an improved cane-crushing apparatus was developed by Makiya Jissai two years later. Satsuma approved the opening of new land areas for clearance and cultivation. By this time the farmers had discovered that it was more profitable to produce sugar for export than to cultivate sweet potatoes and grains for domestic food supply. This meant in turn that the reserves of storable food diminished. The government therefore issued orders restricting the area which could be planted to sugar cane (a crop which takes about eighteen months to reach maturity), setting a maximum figure of 1,500 *chobu* or about 1,675 acres (modern measurement) in an effort to return some lands to food production. The restrictive laws were not at once complied with and had to be repeated five years later, in 1698.

A Tea Commissioner's Office had been established in 1676, meanwhile, to supervise production, and Forest Administration officers were sent into central and northern Okinawa. Saltworks, too, were being developed at the Kotabaru seaside.

These developments all meant an increase in the total production of foodstuffs and raw materials, but such gains were more than offset by growth in population and by a series of natural disasters. There was of course an annual loss through storm damage, to which the Okinawans had become inured through the centuries. But a tremendous earthquake, tidal wave, and typhoon struck the island of Tori-shima in 1664, which killed hundreds of people, destroyed homes, and wrecked fishing craft. Famine conditions in the next few years had to be relieved by emergency food shipments out of Naha, which depleted normal stocks held there. There were occasional severe earthquakes felt on Okinawa and

Miyako with loss in property, and in 1694 a great typhoon destroyed or heavily damaged the sea walls, dykes, roads, and bridges in central Okinawa and along the coast. The sweet-potato crop failed in 1706 and famine came. An earthquake killed many people on Miyako, and more than three thousand persons died in 1709 when famine again came in the wake of a great typhoon. The royal palace was destroyed once again by fire in that disastrous year.

The Ryukyu Islands seemed to be engulfed in disaster.

SAI ON'S STATESMANSHIP: THE STRUGGLE FOR ECONOMIC SURVIVAL

In 1711 the Crown Prince Sho Kei was seven years old. The time had come for him to submit to the exacting discipline proper for a future king. When the government looked about for a tutor, the choice fell upon Sai On, a young man of twenty-seven years who had distinguished himself as chief officer of that stronghold of Confucian training, Kume Village. His father, a distinguished Kume scholar, had served several times as ambassador to Peking. The son had spent some years on the Fukien coast as student-interpreter in the trading depot.

Although this background meant that Sai On was steeped in Chinese studies, it is noteworthy that while he was at Ch'uang-chou he is said to have applied himself to the study of certain Chinese texts concerned with economic problems and practical administration, such as the development of irrigation and the management of cropland.

Sai On was called to duty at Shuri Castle in the centennial year of Satsuma's domination. For nearly a decade Okinawa had suffered disastrous fires, famines, earthquakes, and great storms, but no help came from China, and Satsuma did not see fit to remit or reduce the tribute levies. The Okinawans faced a struggle for economic survival; imaginative and firm leadership was needed. Sententious Confucian maxims and state theory were inadequate to meet the demands of a hungry people.

In China and Japan a Confucian scholar's great ambition was to stand at the side of his ruler, giving advice; in practice it was often a thankless task, for the ruler took credit when things went well, the advisor "assumed responsibility" and lost his post (if not his head) when things went badly. Sai On was destined to stand by the side of Sho Kei for more than forty years.

The crown prince became king in his thirteenth year, and in the next performed ceremonies admitting him to adult status. To mark the occasion Sai On was raised in court rank and given a residence at Shuri. This made him eligible for appointment to the state council, the San-shikan. He was not a member of the royal family and hence could not be made prime minister, but the duties of the council members were reassigned and he at once became in effect the most important figure in the Ryukyu Islands. This meant continuity of policy for a half century, a minimum of conflict at the court itself, and of course great prestige for the minister to whom the king in fact entrusted full management of the government.

Sai On was sent to Peking in 1716 to seek the writ of investiture. We can imagine with what pride this descendant of Chinese immigrants went from Shuri to the court of the Manchu emperors to represent his young protégé. Ancestry, scholarly training, and experience meant that he was aware of the extent and power of China. This suggests an interesting contrast with the background, training, and predilection of his distinguished predecessor, Sho Jo-ken, but whatever Sai On's pro-Chinese inclinations may have been, upon his return to Okinawa he had to face the harsh realities of subjection to Japan.

Under Sai On's direction the government entered upon a long period of intensive and often experimental economic-development work. The sententious Confucian edicts and the efforts at moral suasion were not given up, but they were supplemented by constructive and practical action. Within a few years the islands were producing more than ever before.

Sai On did not visit Japan, but he was in a position to open wide the channels of communication with Edo and to bring strong Japanese influence to bear upon many aspects of Okinawan life. How this came about may be better understood if we consider for a moment what was going on at the shogun's court.

Tokugawa Tsunayoshi's death in 1709 brought to a close an era of extravagant spending. The mad shogun's treasury was exhausted and the government was close to bankruptcy. Reform was the order of the day. The answer in Japan was stricter regulation of social life and heavier taxes for the farmer. Nevertheless, some of the Confucian scholars at the shogun's court were practical administrators as well as moralists. Their problems were economic problems on a grand scale, and to these they sought to apply Chinese Confucian state theories as they understood them. This may not have been the most effective approach to the problems of production, distribution, and consumption in 18th-century Japan, but administrative reform was the central topic of discussion among the most prominent officers of the land.

Undoubtedly Sai On was aware of this. In 1710 a mission had gone to Edo numbering 168 persons, the largest ever sent to the Japanese capital. Four years later a mission of 138 men went up through Satsuma and Kyoto to stay at the Shimazu mansion at Edo. The ambassadors and vice-ambassadors on these occasions were princes of the Sho family, who performed arduous ceremonial duties at the shogun's court while their aides met with Japanese scholars, administrators, artists, and craftsmen. Edo was at that time one of the world's largest cities, and held much to interest and stimulate the visitors.

The princes Yonagusuku and Kin led the embassy of 1714, but the most distinguished member was Sai On's elder contemporary Tei Junsoku, a product of the Kume Village community and of the long tradition of Chinese classical scholarship. He was known among his fellow countrymen as the Sage of Nago. Given this superlative opportunity to meet with Japanese leaders, Junsoku sought out scholars and statesmen, among them Arai Hakuseki, the shogun's principal advisor; Ogyu Sorai, a utilitarian moralist; and his outstanding pupil, Dazai Shundai.

They welcomed the Okinawan scholar, and there is evidence that the exchange of ideas was fruitful and of interest to the Japanese. Arai Hakuseki had earlier completed one essay on the Ryukyus and was now stimulated to enlarge his studies, leading to the publication in 1719 of his *Nanto Shi* (History of the Southern Islands). Dazai Shundai subsequently published an essay in economic studies (*Keizai Roku*), in which he observed that the feudal Lord of Tsushima (in the straits between Honshu and Korea) traded profitably with Korea, and that the Lord of Matsumae traded profitably in products from the great northern island of Hokkaido, but that "Satsuma's incomparable wealth is due to its monopolistic sale of goods imported from Ryukyu."

We may assume that Sai On's representatives discussed Shuri's problems with these well-informed men, and that their attention was directed to Japanese government precedents. Many 18th-century economic policies in Okinawa appear to reflect theories and policies then being tried by Edo. The ideal of the merit system and of bureaucratic organization fostered group morality and laid great emphasis upon group responsibility, but the individual faded into the committee or council of which he was a member. Individualism in government office was discouraged; group action became a fine art of compromise and adjustment among the members.

While this important mission drew Edo's attention to the Ryukyu Islands, the shogun's government was stirred by an incident which revived old fears that the Western powers would penetrate Japan through the Southern Islands. On October 10, 1708, a fearless Italian missionary named Giovanni Batista Sidotti, courting martyrdom, had been put ashore, quite alone, on Yaku-shima, in the northern Ryukyus. In December, 1709, he reached Edo under arrest. Arai Hakuseki interviewed him with a mixture of scholarly curiosity and admiration, restrained by official necessity for stern action. The interrogation formed the base for an essay entitled "Notes on the Western World." Sidotti, under house arrest, was strictly forbidden to preach or proselytize; nevertheless, in 1714 he baptized servants who had been assigned to him. For this audacity he was subjected to most cruel punishment, which he endured for a year before his death on December 15, 1715. His action could be interpreted by the Japanese as a demonstration of European determination to penetrate Japan whatever the price might be.

The Sidotti incident prompted the shogunate to order the barons of Kyushu to destroy any European ship which might appear along the coast, and to kill at once any Europeans found attempting to enter the islands as Sidotti had done.

There was other cause for uneasiness. Chinese who reached Nagasaki and Okinawans who returned to Shuri from China between the years

1708 and 1718 reported that Jesuit missionaries—foreign barbarians—were traveling into every part of the Chinese empire, making maps. The great Emperor K'ang Hsi had ordered them to do the work because they were the most accomplished mathematicians at his Peking court, and the most accurate cartographers, but the Japanese could not remain indifferent to the fact that they were also priests of the hated *Kirishitan* religion, traveling to the very borders of Korea and crossing over to the island of Formosa, within sight of territory belonging to the Ryukyu king.

Under these circumstances the Japanese reacted strongly to the presence of large embassies coming up from the vulnerable southern islands. Edo ordered Satsuma to prepare a study of Ryukyuan history, administration, the land system, official ranks and insignia, the clothing of the common people, and other subjects which would help to give the shogunate a better understanding of the Okinawans. Satsuma went further than this; remembering, perhaps, the role which priests had played in Hideyoshi's successful effort to circumscribe the Shimazu domains, orders were now promulgated which forbade Okinawan priests and students to travel beyond Satsuma's borders, as they had hitherto been free to do. Only missions closely supervised by Shimazu agents thenceforth passed along the highroads of Japan to the shogun's capital. This edict in effect narrowed the area of contact between the Okinawans and the Japanese.

Although Sai On was strongly under Chinese influence, he was a realist; his policies consistently attempted to strike a median, to preserve a neutral position between Japan and China. This attitude was embodied in the handbook *Travelers' Advice* (*Ryokonin Kokoroe*), a model for evasiveness, artfully clothed in polite language, intended to guide Okinawans in China in their efforts to conceal Shuri's true relationship with Satsuma and Edo.

A story told of Sai On illustrates the narrow margin of surplus in the Ryukyus as well as his capacity for firmness. A mission from Peking in 1719 objected to the fact that the Okinawans were unable to buy more than one-fourth of the total goods which the Chinese envoys had brought along with an eye to profit for themselves in private trade. Technically, of course, they were not supposed to demean themselves in commerce, and their reports to the throne would show a fine disdain for mercantile activity. The visitors, lodged at Naha, threatened to riot. Sai On attempted to mediate the dispute, and by collecting gold and silver hair ornaments from among the women of Naha and Shuri, he was able to increase the purchasing funds, but only by one-fifth. The Chinese grudgingly accepted this, but went away disgruntled, carrying back to China more than one-half the goods which they had expected to sell at Naha. It is said that one of the envoys, Hsu Pao-kuang, thereafter bore a grudge against Sai On, though his relations with Tei Junsoku remained on a friendly basis and produced a long-continued correspondence between the two scholars.[5]

Junsoku was then magistrate of Kume Village (Sai On's old post) and in an unofficial sense was the "minister of education." At about this time he caused to be reproduced, at his own expense, a volume of Chinese moral maxims, which he presented to the Shogun Yoshimune through the Lord of Satsuma. Yoshimune was impressed; Junsoku's friend Ogyu Sorai was directed to prepare an annotated edition, which in turn was translated into Japanese by Muro Kyuso, one of the shogun's chief advisors. It was reprinted again and again with official patronage and distributed widely throughout Japan, holding its place among Japanese textbooks for nearly three hundred years. Okinawans are fond of boasting that Japan received three great gifts from the Ryukyu Islands —sweet potatoes, sugar cane, and these *Six Courses in Morals*.

For the greater part of his life Sai On's official career ran parallel with that of Tokugawa Yoshimune, who ruled Japan from 1716 to 1751. Under this shogun the Japanese enjoyed the most prosperous era known to them throughout the long Tokugawa period. It may not be too much to say that Sai On's success reflected in part the spirit of inquiry and experiment fostered by Yoshimune. Foreign travel and the Christian religion were proscribed as rigidly as ever, but Yoshimune was curious about the history and scientific progress of the Western world. He eased the ban on Western books and on Chinese works concerning Western science. It may be that reports of scientific work being done then by the Jesuits at Peking reached Edo through the Naha trade. There was some reflection in Okinawa of Jesuit success in correcting the calendar and in revising the astronomical and mathematical work of the Chinese.

The "regulation of the seasons" was of prime importance in Confucian ceremonials developed for an agricultural people both in Japan and China. To this end, Yoshimune prided himself as an amateur astronomer and in 1718 had an observatory built in the castle grounds at Edo. Meanwhile, a band of hard-working Japanese (the *Rangakusha* or "Dutch Scholars") undertook the arduous task of learning Dutch and of translating scientific works from Dutch into Japanese. Their work centered at Nagasaki, and the men of Satsuma nearby kept themselves fairly well informed of it. The Dutch and their Japanese students were concerned with medicine, optics, and the mechanic arts.

Thus the attenuated influence of Western scientific methods indirectly filtered down into Ryukyu. Sai On ordered an Okinawan scholar named Kohatsu Riko and his students to construct a telescope and observatory in 1739, and on the basis of observations in 1740 and 1741 he ordered certain corrections to be made in the local methods of computing time. Okinawans studied medicine at Kagoshima, and in 1742 six doctors were appointed in attendance at Shuri Castle. Others were sent down to Miyako and Yaeyama on three-year tours of duty, with orders to supervise the welfare of the local people and to care for shipwrecked persons. This is not to say that Western medicine was introduced to the Ryukyu Islands at this time, but the interest in medical studies roused in Japan by the *Rangakusha* stimulated Okinawan interest as well.

Promising youths continued to go to Peking for advanced study, but in 1729 the government canceled stipends hitherto granted to residents of Kume Village. These had been available for 350 years; cancellation was actually an economy measure, but it reflected, too, the diminishing prestige of China

Sai On governed through officers dispatched to thirty-five districts. Each district was subdivided into villages and hamlets, which enjoyed autonomous community organization. For the guidance of all, Sai On prepared a *Handbook for Administrative Officers (Yomui-kan)*, which followed precedents set by Sho Jo-ken. It was couched in stilted Confucian phrases, but these do not disguise concern with the need for a realistic adjustment of Okinawan social life to its economic resources.

Sai On attempted to rationalize the productive economy. He limited the craft activities of the farmers, reserving them wherever possible to the townsmen of Shuri, Naha, Tomari, and Kume. Thus the townsmen had something which they could exchange for foodstuffs produced in the countryside, and the farmers and fishermen had reason to carry supplies into the urban center. Concurrently, younger sons of the gentry were encouraged to leave Shuri and settle in other places as artisans, without loss of social status. A mutual-aid fund was established in 1733 to benefit members of the gentry who were in financial difficulty. Men who distinguished themselves by aiding others were given public honors.

Broadly speaking, the government's acts and orders fell into three general categories in this century. The first had to do with restraints and punishments; the second established privileges and offices to support the gentry; and the third concerned problems of economic development.

A short-lived edict attempted to suppress the manufacture of intoxicating liquor. Officers were appointed to extend watch over the people's morals. Orders were issued restricting expenditures for funerals and the elaborate forms of ritual entertainment which were associated with mourning and interment. A ban was placed on feasts for journeying friends. The police administration was enlarged, and in 1752 Okinawa's criminal laws were applied in Yaeyama. The criminal code was revised and its provisions made known to the public through local governors and magistrates.

Acts essentially favorable to the gentry shifted the income basis for the higher lords. They had lived hitherto on income from hereditary lands; annual revenues from their estates were subject to the uncertainties of crop and climate. In 1723 the *anji* were granted a regular rice stipend from the government treasury. They became pensioners of the king, and the revenue from their lands directly entered the public stores. Sai On himself enjoyed a stipend as nominal chief of Gushikawa district though he was in fact the principal minister of state. In 1734 the tax imposed upon town-dwelling artisans was abolished, benefiting the gentry who had been allowed and encouraged to become artisans without suffering loss of rank. Outstanding artists and craftsmen of every class were awarded titles bearing privileges and stipends. Famed dancers, outstanding samisen-players, and the makers of exceptionally fine combs were granted such government recognition. In the king's name new privileges and honors were established for the aged throughout the islands.

All this meant that administrative costs were rising, but it also meant that a moderate prosperity had once again come to Okinawa. Sai On's great personal reputation rests upon the skill and vigor with which he attacked basic problems of rising population, a heavy tribute schedule, and a chronic poverty of resources.

Improved irrigation work and well-conceived conservation programs were the central concern of the government. Noted projects were undertaken along the Yoza River (1726) and the Haneji River (1734), where afforestation and soil conservation were linked with a program of river dyking and the opening of new irrigation canals. The feasibility of digging a canal across the neck of Motobu Peninsula and of removing the seat of government northward to Nago were long debated. Sai On finally decided against the proposals.

Okinawa needed timber for construction purposes and for fuel, but soil and climate did not produce a natural growth rapid enough to replenish depleted forest resources. Sai On made a thorough study of forest growth and forest use and of methods of reforestation and forest control. Ultimately his plans, policies, and observations—fruits of his long experience—were embodied in a series of essays upon the subject. These have had durable interest, and in 1952 were translated, published, and distributed abroad by the Forestry Division of the United States Civil Administration in the Ryukyu Islands.[5] They form remarkable documents in forest-conservation history. Here and there gnarled old pine trees arch the roads and line the crests of mountain ridges in 20th-century Okinawa, thanks to Sai On's policies. A grove planted at Sai On's direction on Tarama in distant Miyako still serves as a model for new windbreaks established to protect the precious topsoil.

Sai On forbade the construction of dugout canoes in order to conserve trees of large girth. Farmers and fishermen were restrained in the indiscriminate cutting of smaller trees needed as watershed cover on steep slopes. Villagers were shown how to plant windbreaks along the shore and on steep mountainsides to check the erosive action of high wind and torrential rain. Housing lots and grave-sites were limited to ensure a maximum use of arable land. Sandy flats lying between Naha and Tomari were reclaimed for building-sites. Irrigation and drainage projects became a major concern of government throughout the kingdom. Sai On's agricultural extension plans, drawn up in 1734, reflect careful observation and constructive long-range consideration.

Prudent planning thus brought about an increase in the total production of wealth. To manage it, the government issued new coinage and opened new public markets to promote local exchange of commodities. In 1729 there was an attempt to standardize weights and measures. Naha harbor was dredged, and port officers were assigned to every important landing place to supervise coastwise traffic between seaside villages. Metal-casting techniques and smithies were improved to increase the efficiency of common tools. Limekilns were established which used coral and shell to produce building material. Agricultural inspectors assigned to each district office encouraged the planting of tea and of banana-like plantains needed as a source of textile fiber. The manufacture of ink-sticks, paper, and objects made of paper, such as lanterns and umbrellas, became important.

There are reasons to believe that nearly half the population on Okinawa was concentrated at Naha and Shuri. To meet some of the problems of increased numbers and of unemployment, farmers were forbidden to move into town, and new villages were created as lands were opened to cultivation. Incomplete records for the 18th century suggest that possibly one new settlement was recognized in each four years. Famine years were anticipated; grain-storage warehouses were established under government direction; and honors were awarded to the farmer who first promoted a new method for planting and harvesting two crops of sweet potatoes annually.

Sai On's authority was challenged only once during his long career. The details are obscured by a cluster of legends. A party formed in opposition to Sai On's policies, charging (whether they believed it or not) that the chief minister was too "pro-Chinese." Heshikiya Chobin and Tomoyose Anjo, the leaders, secretly drew up and delivered a statement of accusations to the resident Satsuma agent in 1734. The affair came to light; Heshikiya and fourteen others were seized and put to death.

A curious, romantic, and oddly incomplete story attaches to this incident.

In the old days of the kingdom the retaining walls and foundations of the castle rose vertically to a great height from the wooded enclosure below, and at the crest of the wall stood one of the royal residential pavilions, set in a garden area. Here dwelt one of the king's daughters. When Heshikiya was condemned to death it was discovered that he and the princess were in love—or at least that the princess was in love with Heshikiya. Despite this, the sentence was carried out and the execution done at Owan Beach, which could be seen at a distance from the castle heights. It was customary, moreover, for a white flag to be run up at the execution ground as a signal to the castle that the king's justice was being done. On the day that Heshikiya and his fourteen companions were put to death the flag appeared at the masthead above the treetops, and at that moment the princess in despair cast herself down from the high parapet. Obviously this was not an ordinary suicide, for when a search was made for the royal body, only one leg could be found; nothing else. After that day in 1734 the garden pavilion in the castle grounds was known as *Kunra Gushiku* (One-Leg Pavilion).

The unhappy princess was the daughter of Sho Kei, who had come to the throne in 1716. His rule was nominal, for throughout this long period the true source of authority lay with Sai On. The king died in 1751, and in the next year his faithful minister retired from his post in the Council of State. He remained an important figure until his death in his seventy-ninth year (1761). Much of Sai On's success was rooted in the unshaken confidence which marked his relations with the king. They had achieved in full the Confucian ideal of Sage and Ruler, working together in complete trust and harmony.

The state ministers who followed Sai On continued his policies for some years, but there was a gradual decline in the fortunes of the kingdom. Okinawa was never again to know the degree of prosperity and well-being which marked the first half of the 18th century. No leader so vigorous and imaginative as Sai On came to the scene; production of wealth fell off. Toward the end of the century there was a marked increase in the number of natural disasters suffered by the economy through fire, flood, storm, and earthquake, but until these calamities began to disturb the kingdom, life for the Shuri gentry (if not for the hard-working peasant) continued in the even tenor established under Sai On's long administration. It is desirable here to review briefly the mild achievements in the arts and crafts and modifications in the social organization which so curiously set Okinawa apart from either of its masters, China or Japan, during the second century of "dual subordination."

CULTURAL AND INTELLECTUAL LIFE IN THE 18TH CENTURY

We have seen that two centuries of enforced seclusion followed three centuries of wide-ranging travel and trade. From a relatively high degree of prosperity and well-being the Okinawans slowly sank to a level of general, grueling poverty surrounded by physical evidence of the great days of Chuzan. In a setting of massive castle walls and gates, mansions and gardens, parks and lakes, shrines and temples, tree-lined racing parks and roads, and fine stone bridges, the aristocrats and gentry of Shuri, Naha, and Kume Village attempted to preserve the standards of ceremony and conduct which they had known in the days of independence. But it was a losing struggle. There were brief periods of moderate prosperity in the 17th and 18th centuries when Nature was kind for a time and administrative skills promoted efficient use of inadequate resources. There is abundant evidence, however, that no matter how hard they tried, the Okinawans could not overcome the problem of slow population growth within an area virtually barren of natural resources, so long as they were forbidden by Japan to trade freely overseas, and were forced to wear the tribute yoke which Satsuma had contrived.

The Okinawans slowly and quite unconsciously blended cultural elements and institutions drawn from China and Japan and from Southeast Asia. There were few innovations, and a gradual simplification of ceremonies and festivals which they could no longer afford to maintain.

We have three interesting accounts of Okinawan cultural life, government, and history as seen through Chinese eyes in 1719, 1757, and 1801.

These are the journals and reports of envoys sent from Peking to convey writs of investiture to the kings at Shuri.

The first of these reports (by Hsu Pao-kuang) relates in great detail the elaboration of ceremonies at the palace and at the mansion built and maintained for the Chinese ambassadors' use.[6] The second (Chou Huang's *Brief History of the Ryukyu Kingdom*) is introduced with a simple map and a review of the traditional history.[7] It describes at length the tribute relationship with China, the nature of the tribute, the ceremonies and edicts concerning investiture. It then proceeds to a description of administration and of the manners and customs of the people. Much of this appears to be a record of things reported to the envoy but not observed by him, and he ventures an opinion that the climate has had much to do with shaping Okinawan characteristics and behavior. Chou Huang's sense of propriety is disturbed by the discovery that Okinawans occasionally practice self-destruction in the Japanese manner —by committing *seppuku* (hara-kiri): this marked the island people as barbarians; nevertheless, he found them courteous and meticulous in the discharge of ceremonial obligations, a subject most dear to the ceremonious Chinese official.

Chou's report touched on temples and temple services and other remarkable buildings, places, and objects. Both architecture and literary monuments he found to be inferior, of course, when judged by China's high standards. The state ritual is described and there is a record of titles, ranks, and offices among the ruling class. In discussing taxes and the tax-gathering system Chou notes that in his opinion the Ryukyu kingdom was the poorest of all countries surrounding China.

A section on military affairs and modes of punishment records that the Ryukyuan government imposed three types of capital punishment and five of less severity. All of these were common in both China and Japan, and all except banishment were cruel and extreme if judged by modern penal standards. Chou noted the civil and social relationships among the Okinawans and made a record of interesting local products. He concluded his report with a catalogue of noteworthy people in Okinawan annals from illustrious kings to notorious vagrants.

The third journal (published in 1803) was made by Li Tung-yen during a sojourn on Okinawa from June 25 until November 28, 1801.[8] The usual record is made of traditional local history and of the investiture rites, notes to be expected in the journal of an envoy sent abroad on a special mission. Li gives an excellent account of the progress of an embassy through the Chinese countryside and of the voyage to Naha, accompanied by certain Okinawan princes who had been at Peking. His comments upon social and economic conditions are of special interest.

There were seven chief families at Shuri, who married only among themselves and with the royal family, and among these were Sai On's descendents, a noteworthy concession to the Kume Village aristocracy of Chinese scholars. Li noted that the Kume students were divided into two groups—those who spoke Chinese and those who read Chinese. They began their studies as small children; at the age of fifteen (after ten years of training) they were received in audience at the palace. Their

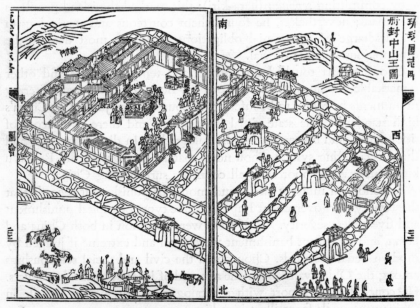

FIG. 13. SHURI CASTLE, 1756. *This and the facing figure are from the same source as Figs. 9 and 11. (See page 211.)*

names were entered upon a special register and they began a career of advancement which could lead them through five grades to a place on the Council of State (Sanshikan), wearing the purple turban and the gold pin of state councilors.

While Li was on Okinawa five noble youths from Shuri took up residence near the Chinese embassy quarters at Naha in order to learn as much as they could through observation and conversation with the visitors. Okinawan scholars cultivated friendships with the Chinese envoys in order to discuss literary matters, but interpreters were needed and much of the exchange took place through written communication. In other words, many could read Chinese texts but few could speak properly in the Peking dialect. Li and his associates were surprised at the style and classical knowledge which the Okinawans could display.

He discussed soldiers and punishments with one of his callers, who observed: "This little country has no knowledge of soldiers. Our punish-

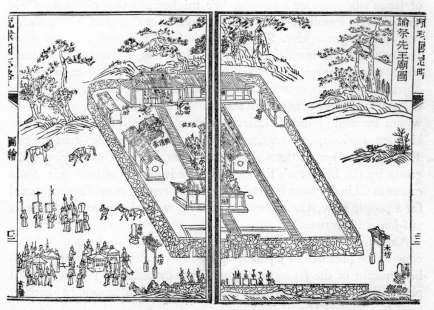

FIG. 14. CHINESE ENVOYS AT SOGEN-JI, 1756. *The envoys are offering sacrifices to the spirits of deceased Okinawan kings.*

ments are only three. A murderer is put to death; one who wounds another grievously is banished; for a lighter crime he is fined, and others are exposed publicly in the hot sun according to their demerit. No one has been executed among us for many years, but when a criminal is to be punished, we usually give him a knife and he performs *hara-kiri*."⁹

Li thought that the absence of crime and the simplicity of punishment betokened an approach to the ideal society set forth in the classics, where all men knew their proper place and none violated the law.

The Chinese visitor saw much of the countryside and wandered about in the port city. He observed the poverty of the market place, wherein only simple artifacts and foodstuffs were bartered; there was none of the noise and variety of the great markets of China. Coins were scarce and of little value.

In discussing this diary before the Royal Asiatic Society in China in 1869, S. Wells Williams noted that there was no mention whatsoever of Japan's position or influence. We might infer that either the Okinawans were inordinately skilled at deception or that the Chinese diarist was most unperceptive. Since neither of these is probable, we must assume that Chinese officials could not admit that the emperor's suzerain claims were compromised by Satsuma's actions. Williams commends Li's objectivity with these words: "No comparisons are made, and he tries to state without disparagement the attainments of the Lewchewans, with whom he could communicate only through interpreters, and whose kindness, curiosity and eagerness to learn about China he often notices. There are no speculations about the desirableness of occupying their group by the Emperor's forces, and the advantages of having its trade center in China's ports; but rather a tone of respect pervades the journal for a people so well and so methodically governed, whom still he ranks as *i-jin* or barbarians."¹⁰

Although at Satsuma's bidding the Okinawans took such pains to conceal the presence of Japanese agents, and under orders pretended to be ignorant of the Japanese language, the evidence of Japan's cultural penetration were everywhere. Attention has been drawn to sketches used to illustrate Hsu Pao-kuang's report, in which the king wears a robe in the Ming style for occasions of high ceremony, and to a late-17th-

214

century Ryukyuan portrait in which "the Prince wears a Liu Ch'iu hat, and his attendants carry Japanese pikes as symbols of power, while a pair of Japanese curtains sets off the picture. In short, the portrait gives an excellent example of the synthesis of cultures in this small island kingdom under the influence of two powerful neighbours."[11]

Once the adjustments had been made to the new order dictated by Satsuma, the Okinawan gentry enjoyed a mild and pleasurable existence, troubled briefly by a series of natural disasters at the end of the 17th century, but resumed once more after Sai On's economic development policies made themselves felt. The easygoing men of Shuri were rarely disturbed by affairs of large importance. The Heshikiya incident suggests that there were divisions and rivalries among the aristocrats, and some of Sai On's edicts and admonitions hint of an undercurrent of discontent with Satsuma's orders and rigorous tax requirements.

It is probable that the energetic, nervous and purposeful samurai from Satsuma often became impatient with the easygoing island people. The art of courteous but successful procrastination was highly developed among the gentry who carried out Satsuma's orders. A foreigner writing of Okinawa in the 19th century observed that if happiness consists of few wants and those easily gratified, then the people of the Ryukyu Islands must indeed have been happy in this era of seclusion.

The days of a gentleman were taken up in long conversations among friends, frequent picnics in the countryside, and the leisurely composition and exchange of poems in Japanese and Chinese styles. Weddings, excursions to noted scenic spots and local shrines, ceremonies at the Buddhist and Confucian temples, and town and village festivals in their proper time filled the day-to-day round of the seasons.

The New Year opened with ceremonious worship of the ancestors on the first, eighth, and fifteenth days of the month. A planting festival was held at court to ensure a good grain harvest for the year, and in the second week lanterns everywhere marked festivities carried on until well into the night. On the sixteenth, ancestral tombs were visited and lanterns were lighted before the burial chambers. On the twentieth the singing girls and prostitutes of Naha enjoyed a special festival, visiting temples and shrines, riding out on horseback, dancing in the open, and playing games peculiar to their social class. The songs, the dances, and the games of Naha displayed many elements imported through the centuries and adapted to the sense and taste of the Okinawans.

Birthday celebrations were held in the first month of the year, with special feasts and dancing to honor those who had reached thirteen, sixty-one, seventy-three, eighty-five, and ninety-seven years. These reflect the sexagenary cycle of years upon which Chinese calendar lore was based.

A festival of grain was held in the second month of the lunar calendar, when men ceased work in the fields and women rested from household chores. On the twentieth day of the month the household well or spring was cleaned ceremoniously. The third month brought a traditional time of picnicking and dancing on the beach, a period of purification, and visits to the ancestral graves again. No one was permitted to cut wood or grass in this month, and prayers were offered to the spirits of the forest to ensure good growth in the woods and groves. Summer clothes could be donned ceremoniously in the fourth month, and horse racing was popular on the *baba* (racing grounds) under the great pine trees. As far as possible everyone refrained from venturing out to sea, for this was a month in which the great storms could be expected, and it was thought not wise to risk provocation of the sea gods while the grain fields were heavy in the head. The fifth day of the fifth month brought exciting tugs-of-war among village teams, who used gigantic ropes woven especially for this occasion. "Dragon-boat" racing took place, in the harbor waters and bays and upon the lake at Shuri. The Harvest Festival came in the sixth month and again there were competitions between villages and village teams. On the seventh day of the seventh month everyone again took picnics into the countryside to make pilgrimage to the family graves, and from the thirteenth to the fifteenth night the Bon dances were held in honor of the dead.

Versifying parties and boating, moon-viewing excursions and picnics, out-of-door plays and dances took place in the eighth and ninth months, when the weather is at its finest. The first day of the tenth month was the official day for winter clothing, and a festival marked the first planting of a new rice crop, followed, in the last month of the year, by ceremonies designed to ward off evil spirits. On the twenty-fourth day the hearth gods took leave and a "godless" interlude continued until the fifth day of the New Year following, when they were welcomed home again with ceremony.[12]

These were the major festivals in the annual cycle. No occasion for singing and dancing together was neglected. Englebert Kaempfer in 1690 noted that workmen carried their musical instruments into the field; Basil Hall's companions observed the same thing in 1816; and the author saw boatmen, policemen, and farmers carrying the samisen about in the off-lying islands in 1952. Musicians were awarded high honors, and the office of Chief Samisen Director was created at Shuri in 1710. Themes for the pantomimic dance-dramas and the songs which accompanied them were drawn from legend and history, treated with a bawdy humor or tinged with melancholy, alternating between rollicking and lusty gaiety and the haunting, sad themes of separation, or poverty, or thwarted love.

No gentleman or lady would venture far abroad without the services of an attendant who carried a lacquered lunch-box. Food and drink were of consequence and represented in variety a blend of Chinese and Japanese tastes. The use of meats—pork and fowl—and rich sauces to appeal to the tongue represented Chinese influence in the cuisine; lavish care in arranging foods to appeal to the eye represented a distinctive Japanese touch. The people of the Ryukyu Islands enjoyed liquors prepared from fermented grains and distilled from the useful sweet potato or sugar cane. Excessive drinking is still common, but quarrelsomeness and outrage seldom mar conviviality.

It is noteworthy that songs, dances, and festival sports incorporated many elements which came from overseas in the high days of Chuzan trade in the Eastern Sea; boxing (*karate*) in which both hands and feet are used had come from Indo-China or Siam; "dragon-boat" racing from South China; the use of teeterboards from Korea; and wrestling from Japan. Precedents for popular horse-racing and bull-baiting may be found in the records of 12th- and 13th-century Japan.

The Okinawans had only a mild interest in religious forms and virtually none at all in religious and philosophic speculation. The majority were content to support the *noro;* they treated the spirits of the groves and hills, sea and sky, wells and springs with suitable respect, but they did not enquire deeply into these mysteries. They were much more exacting in their treatment of the dead, and in respectful display of concern for the welfare of departed parents. Every family felt compelled to spend as much as it possibly could on the family tombs, which were in a sense the focal point of the social unit. Here the influence of Chinese ancestor-worship and rites of interment was most strong. Okinawan tombs for the upper classes were the most prominent man-made feature of the landscape. They were of two forms, a simple rectangular structure (the earlier) and a curvilinear and domed construction said by some to resemble a turtle's back and by others to represent the womb

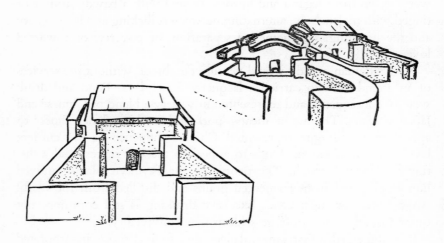

FIG. 15. TYPICAL OKINAWAN TOMBS. *The straight-roofed "house style"* (ie-gata) *is an older type than the "turtleback."*

from which all men must come. Family resources were often exhausted in maintaining an elaborate burial place, usually constructed of coral blocks cemented over with a calceous stucco. In the space before the tomb the family gathered for its feasts and picnics at appropriate times of the year, and when death came to a member of the family he was coffined in a seated position and interred with appropriate ceremony. When next the tomb was opened, his bones were removed, washed, and reinterred in a ceramic pot, which was shelved within the tomb. Thus many generations could be brought together within one chamber. The majority of peasant folk could not afford the luxury of a handsome tomb; interment in the common earth sufficed, but here, too, the family of the dead foregathered on festival occasions.

Scholars in government gave little encouragement to indigenous religious practices, but were prompt to support Confucian rites and ceremonies. The Five Annual Festivals of the Japanese court were adopted by Sho Jo-ken, and most particular attention was devoted to the perfection of rituals appropriate for use before the tombs of kings and princes.

Other rites and practices on a less exalted level had crept in meanwhile. Some Chinese Taoist ceremonies were absorbed into the strict Confucian rule; paper prayers were burned at temples and shrines and in special repositories built at suitable spots along the open way. Fortunetellers known as *yuta* began to rival the *noro* priestesses in the eyes of townsmen, and by 1698 a Taoist "Lord of the Earth" had been enshrined in Omine Village. The *yuta* encouraged gross superstition, drawn from the folklore of the Chinese masses. As they became popular first among Naha townsmen, it is possible that the cult practices were introduced by uneducated sailors passing to and fro from the China coast. The *yuta* were not members of an institutional organization, as were the *noro*, and had no wide support either at the court or in the countryside. In time the government began to frown on their activities, forbidding them to advertise themselves as intermediaries between the dead and the living or to act as exorcists with power to drive out evil spirits. In 1736 they were forbidden to represent themselves as healers of the sick.

Buddhism did not flourish. It is true that the royal house continued to provide modest patronage for the principal temples, but there was no wide base in popular support. The larger foundations held title to land which yielded income; the smaller ones scraped along as best they could, thankful for small private donations. There was a gradual decline of public interest, and restrictive measures imposed upon the

Buddhist clergy after 1611 steadily diminished their prestige until at last the priests were looked upon with something akin to contempt.

In the early days—say from the 12th to the 14th centuries—Buddhist missionaries had played an outstanding part in the transformation of scattered island communities into an organized and literate state. From the 14th to the 17th centuries the temple foundations and organizations had served as centers of learning and of the arts and crafts, when the fine buildings and pageantry of Buddhist ritual had adorned the Shuri court. Now, in the latter days of the kingdom, the Buddhist hierarchy and the temples had become a burden.

The two mystical sects represented on Okinawa—contemplative Zen and esoteric Shingon—were ill-suited to the temperament of the un-speculative Okinawans. Doctrines of the evangelical Shin sect had a wider, warmer popular appeal, but this sect Satsuma rigidly suppressed. Shimazu decrees which forbade priests and students from Okinawa to travel beyond Satsuma's borders accelerated the decline of interest in Buddhism.

The Confucian scholars who formed and controlled the adminis-tration were by training antagonistic to Buddhism. In matters of belief, the Confucian scholar was a sceptic, concerned more with present problems of man's relationship to man than with speculation and con-cern for future lives and afterworlds. In matters of organization and politics the Confucian scholars in Okinawa had before them the histories of Buddhist domination in China and Japan in earlier centuries and the record of frequent discord between the Church as a temporal power in conflict with the State. When the temples on Okinawa ceased to be centers of study and of patronage for the arts and crafts, they ceased to be important.

Architects, stonemasons, and sculptors in wood were employed principally in reconstruction of buildings which had been destroyed by fire or storm. There was little new construction of major importance in the 17th and 18th centuries. Craft skills were brought to their highest development in ceramics, textiles, and lacquerwork created for daily use.

In 1617 three Korean potters reached Okinawa from Satsuma, com-missioned to introduce new ceramic techniques. These were members of a community of Korean craftsmen who had been taken to Satsuma by the Shimazu forces during Hideyoshi's invasions of the peninsula. In time two of these potters returned to Satsuma, but one of them settled permanently at Tsuboya, near Naha, and thenceforth considered himself a subject of the King of Ryukyu. The Okinawans proved apt pupils; soon the wares of Tsuboya's kilns were an important element in the local economy and a craft product of high merit and interest.

The building crafts were stimulated by need to replace structures damaged or destroyed during the brief, bitter conflict in 1611. A great fire swept the Nami-no-ue Shrine at Naha in 1633 and a series of disastrous fires razed the king's palace in 1660, 1690, and 1709. Some construction was undertaken for the Buddhist temple foundations; the Benten-do, a pavilion which had housed the Korean edition of Buddhist texts at Enkaku-ji, was rebuilt at the king's command in 1621, but the priceless volumes themselves had been taken away as booty by the Japanese. A small but architecturally interesting temple known as the Torin-ji was constructed in Ishigaki Village in Yaeyama and another, the Shoun-ji, was built at Hirara in Miyako. These were projected as part of the general development of cultural institutions in the outer islands, and, of all the significant Buddhist architectural and sculptural monuments in Ryukyu, these alone survived World War II.

A new Confucian temple was constructed at Kume Village to accommodate scholars and professors of Chinese. This splendid building, begun in 1671, required four years to complete. It was a gift made to the Okinawans by the young Emperor of China, K'ang Hsi.

A new glazing and firing technique for the manufacture of roof tiles was introduced from Japan at about this time. The government henceforth used tiles on its buildings in an effort to reduce fire hazards. Multicolored glazes were applied to the tiles of the royal palace at Shuri; common red tiles were used elsewhere and were shipped as far as Miyako and Yaeyama to cover the granaries and storehouses maintained there in Shuri's interest.

Okinawan craftsmen were hard pressed for adequate building materials. The forests produced no fine building timber; the moist climate and fierce seasonal storms required special techniques in the use of wood and the dressing of stone to take the place of wood wherever it could be made to do so. We have noted that massive castles were an essential expression of the period of the Three Principalities (14th and 15th centuries) and that much fine stonework was produced in the development of the palaces, residences, temples, walls, and gates at Shuri during the reign of Sho Shin in the 16th century. Now in the 17th and 18th centuries Okinawan masons were set to building superb stone bridges.

Just why the Okinawans became so enamored of bridges remains a mystery: there are few streams worthy to be called rivers and the roads were footpaths. But the finest stone-working skills were lavished on wide causeways and crossings having relatively little importance in the countryside economy. It is also interesting that so much bridge-building should take place in Okinawa at a time when the Japanese government was discouraging the construction of bridges in Japan proper as a matter of internal defense policy. In Okinawa a great body of ceremony and folklore centered about the bridges; offerings were made to propitiate the river spirits before a bridge was thrown across and after the work was completed. Monuments were erected beside these bridges to commemorate construction, and local tales abound which tell of superhuman forces aiding or interfering with the engineers and masons, and of sacrifices required to placate disturbed river-spirits.

There is little reason to doubt that the officers of state who ordered bridges to be built in Okinawa were influenced by the splendid bridges of Fukien Province. Many prominent Okinawans were familiar with the magnificent stone structures for which the Ch'uang-chou area of Fukien was famed throughout China. Some structures dated from the Mongol period. One—built about A.D. 1200 near the mooring basin for junks trading into "Zayton" or Ch'uang-chou from all parts of the East—was 1,500 feet long, constructed of huge blocks of stone magnificently laid. The majority were built in the Ming period, and the tradition established in Fukien was carried over into Okinawa on a modest scale. The Japanese declared the fine bridges of Okinawa to be "monuments of national importance," which were preserved until 1945.[13]

Other crafts began to develop special characteristics which display the taste and ingenuity of Okinawan patrons. The introduction of Chinese techniques for inlaying mother-of-pearl is attributed to the year

1641, and thereafter local lacquer-makers perfected methods in which their successors have remained preëminent. Weavers learned of a Chinese method for producing raised figures in fine fabrics. A man named Taketomi *Uekata* who traveled with the tribute mission of 1664 is credited with the introduction of an extraordinary number of new or improved techniques, ranging from methods of gilding and lacquer-making to improved methods of sugar manufacture.

Painting and sculpture were not neglected but show little creative distinction. The intellectual and artistic life of gentry and commoner alike found its happiest expression in poetry, drama, and music. Dance forms introduced centuries earlier from Southeast Asia and China were blended with the indigenous folk dances inherited from the unrecorded past. Men and women in all classes aspired to proficiency in dancing. No community gathering was neglected as an opportunity for singing, dancing, and storytelling. Farmers and fishermen in the meanest villages delighted to dance on the beach or in any appropriate open spot in the fields—and still do. Poems in the local dialect celebrate the special beauties or noteworthy features of the local district.

FIG. 16. OKINAWAN BRIDGES. Upper: *Madama Bridge, near Naha; seen also in Plate 12.* Lower: *Yomochi Bridge, Shuri; fragments are preserved in the Shuri Museum.*

It is striking that almost without exception foreigners who visited Okinawa before 1850 made special note of the Okinawan mildness and kindliness of character and of a general love and aptitude for singing and dancing. Richard Cocks, in 1614, had noted that "they are a very gentle and courteous people." Englebert Kaempfer noted a universal love of music.

The highest dignitaries of the court were accomplished dancers; three high-ranking officers were invited to dance before the Shogun Iemitsu at Edo in 1629.

Men and women of all classes in Okinawa, Miyako, and Yaeyama distinguished themselves in the composition of brief allusive verses known as *waka*, so highly prized in the literary traditions of Japan. These were written in the Japanese phonetic *hiragana* or cursive syllabary, which lent itself easily to spontaneous expression and imposed no difficulties in recording local dialect. The verse form was governed by strict rules of composition limiting the number of syllables.

Some of the most noted poets were women. A story of romance and pathos attaches to the name of Onna Nabe, a beautiful girl of the countryside and of common origin, whose delicate poems became well known in Naha and at the court. Upon the occasion of a royal progress through the countryside into northern Okinawa, Onna Nabe was notified that she must entertain the king. At once she replied:

Nami nu kwim tumari	Waves, be still!
Kaji nu kwim tumari	And quiet, Wind!
Shu–i tin ga nashi	The king from Shuri comes—
Miun chi ugama.	And we must pay him reverence.[14]

This slight verse is known and quoted throughout 20th-century Okinawa. Perhaps nostalgia for a happier past under the Okinawan kings is reinforced by a romantic tale that Onna Nabe fell hopelessly in love with the king during their brief sojourn together. When he returned to Shuri, the country poet cast herself from a cliff near the beautiful field of Manzanmo, where monuments today commemorate the verse, the romance, and its tragic ending.

If we except the poems recorded in the *kana* script, we may say that the cultural history of Okinawa reflects little creative literary and philosophic activity. The mastery of classical Chinese was a burdensome chore. Sons of the gentry learned to read and write in the Japanese phonetic syllabary before they took up their studies with the Kume

Village tutors. Students who had been sent abroad for years of study at Peking and minor officials stationed for long periods at the Ryukyu trading depot in Fukien became proficient in Chinese, but its use in Okinawa was stilted and artificial. Books introduced from China had limited use and circulation.

Throughout the 17th century there was a gradual increase in the numbers of students and pilgrims who went up to Japan, where publication flourished for a mass reader-audience in the great cities. Literary works brought back into Okinawa circulated fairly widely in manuscript or in book form, but there was no publishing done in the Ryukyu Islands.

Interest in Okinawan history and culture was stimulated by comparison with the institutions and history of Japan. Taichu's study of the indigenous Shinto practices of the Ryukyu Islands, prepared in 1604, was published at Kyoto in 1648. A compilation of Okinawan history (the *Chuzan Seikan*) was undertaken in 1650 by Prime Minister Sho Jo-ken, who prepared it in the Japanese language rather than in literary Chinese. Knowing of Sho Jo-ken's active policy of reconciliation with Japan, we may suspect that this first attempt to produce a formal history of the kingdom was used to strengthen (if not to fabricate) evidence and traditions of ancient close ties with Japan, for here the Tametomo tradition is set forth with abundant detail for the first time.

In 1697 the annals of the royal court (*Rekidai Hoan*) were edited once again. Traditional stories of Miyako were compiled in 1705, and a dictionary of the old Ryukyuan language (the *Konko-ken Shu*) was prepared in 1711.

STUDENTS ABROAD AND RIOTS AT SHURI

Toward the end of the 18th century, two avenues of training led into government office. Kume Village youths of outstanding promise and capacity for Chinese studies periodically stood for two rigorous examinations leading to scholarships at Peking. Four senior and four junior awards were made. The winners normally expected to spend three years abroad pursuing a formal curriculum designed by the Chinese for scholars from tributary states. They were expected to master political philosophy, literature, and medicine or the Chinese almanac, a study concerned with the regulation of human affairs according to the seasons. In exceptional cases individual students were allowed to stay at Peking for as long as eight years. Upon their return to Okinawa these Kume Village youths became government officials or teachers with marked preferment in appointments at certain levels of administration.

The second avenue of approach to government office was open principally to youths from Shuri, sons of princes, nobles, and leading gentry, who were selected to study at Kagoshima at Satsuma's suggestion. The Shimazu family welcomed highborn Okinawan envoys and students and gave them opportunities to see the extent, resources, and strength of the Shimazu principality. Thus, for instance, the young Crown Prince Sho Tetsu and his companions were invited to tour southern Kyushu in 1756.

In 1795 a boy of twelve years named Sho On became king. The question of tutors and of the royal education came again to the fore, and the problems of educational policy for the country at large were widely discussed. Sho On himself appears to have demonstrated most unusual promise; a note of something more than the conventional praise of a king creeps into accounts written of him by his subjects, and Chinese envoys who observed him in his seventeenth year commented on his fine features, his dignity, and his learning. It is apparent that Sho On had a zest for scholarship, and it is therefore not surprising that the time seemed ripe for major changes in the educational system.

The motivation is obscure, but the total effect was to broaden the basis of training for high offices in government, to extend the area of candidacy and choice, and to enlarge the pro-Chinese party (if it can be called such) in the government.

Elementary schools were established in the several wards of Shuri for the children of the gentry and an academy was founded within the palace grounds. Over the principal gate a large tablet was hung for all to read as they entered, and upon this tablet the young king himself inscribed *Kaiho Yoshu* ("Cultivate Men of Ability in the Sea Country").

It was then announced that the number of students sent abroad would be increased and that henceforth young men from Shuri would be eligible to compete for nomination to the Peking scholarships, thus breaking the Kume Village monopoly. This monopoly the Kume Village community had cherished through four centuries. It was not given up without protest, but the order stood. Thereafter the academy at Shuri enjoyed precedence. It is probable that the five noble youths who took up residence near the Chinese embassy headquarters in 1801 were the first Shuri candidates preparing to go to China.

The Kume Village demonstrations were a mild disturbance of the peace and offered no threat whatsoever to the government. Their very mildness illustrates the frailty of this microcosmic society, so delicately balanced in population versus meager resources and limited opportunity, and so precariously placed on political frontiers. The balance of moral obligation felt toward China versus political and economic obligation to Satsuma had been neatly maintained through two centuries, but it could be preserved only under conditions of extreme isolation.

That isolation came to an end in 1797.

The Western Barbarians Reappear: A Second Turning Point

If we are to believe that extraordinary adventurer Count Mauritius de Benyowsky, the first fleeting shadow of modern Europe and the stirring West touched the Ryukyus in 1771. He has a strange story to tell in his *Memoirs*.

According to Benyowsky, he and his companions fled from a Russian prison in Kamchatka. They sailed southward, determined to make their way back to Europe boldly flying the "flag of the Republic of Poland" whenever they encountered Western ships. He described his ship as a corvette, with nearly one hundred persons aboard. It was named the "St. Peter and St. Paul." On Monday, August 15, 1771 (according to his unreliable chronology), the unsound craft and makeshift crew drew inshore and cast anchor at "the island of Usmay Ligon, one of Lequeio." If there is any basis in fact, we may assume that it may have been an island in the Oshima group in the northern Ryukyus.

They were received with reserve and suspicion, generated locally, we must presume, by Satsuma's harsh attitude toward intruding foreigners. But thanks to the natural warmth of Okinawan friendliness, this barrier soon was overcome and cordial relations quickly established. The unmarried girls of the island village were most accommodating, and a bride from the leading family, together with seven attendant maidens, was offered to Benyowsky. When it was discovered that the visitors were Christians, the natives revealed that they possessed the relics of one "Ignatio Salis, Missionary to the Indies, of the Society of Jesus, and of the Portuguese nation" who had reached "Usmay Ligon" on May 24, 1749, with three fugitive companions. One of these spoke a little "bad Portuguese," claimed to be a native of Tonkin, educated in Siam; he made himself known to Benyowsky. Salis had died about 1754 and his tomb was disclosed nearby. Okinawans who were secret Christian converts revealed themselves to the European voyagers. Benyowsky in turn caused a valuable crucifix to be brought ashore from the ship and paraded piously in the village street. (He had stolen it from a church in Kamchatka.)

Overnight, a great warmth of feeling and mutual admiration sprang up, and by Friday, August 19—the day on which they were to sail again—Benyowsky and his companions had agreed to return as soon as possible "with a society of virtuous, good and just men, to dwell upon this island and to adopt the manners, usages and laws of the inhabitants." To make this sure, a compact or contract was drawn up, one copy in Latin and one "in the language of Lequio." In it the Okinawans made certain promises:

"And we, the chiefs and people, call to witness that God who created the heavens and the earth, that we will, at any time hereafter, receive our friend Mauritius, with all those who shall be his friends; that we will share with them our lands, and will assist them in all their labours, until their establishments shall be equal to our own; and, in the meantime, his friends who remain with us, shall be considered as the children of our families, and treated as brothers.

SIGNED: *Mauritius*, in the name of the company of Europeans.
　　　　　Nicholas, for the chiefs and people of Usmay, and the Lequio Islands."[15]

"A prodigious number of islanders followed me" (says Benyowsky) "who by their cries and tears, exhibited an affecting spectacle of goodness of heart and tenderness of disposition. . . ."

What adventure in the Ryukyus this may reflect and what elements of truth it may record we cannot say. It affords a strange link with the politics of eastern Europe in that day, and with the presence of Russia along North Pacific shores. Benyowsky did not return to colonize the Ryukyus, but ended his fantastic career in Madagascar, shot there by the French, in 1786, while under contract to provide slaves to a firm in Baltimore, Maryland.

In the Age of Encyclopedists, the armchair philosophers of London and Paris, Philadelphia and Boston let their imaginations play freely over the world, and demanded to know more and more of the obscure corners of the globe. Men of action undertook to satisfy this dynamic curiosity. Daines Barrington, in the preface to his extraordinary *Miscellanies* (London, 1781), suggested that "the coast of Corea, the northern part of Japan, and Lieuchieux Islands should be explored." Captain King (who took charge of Cook's last expedition in Hawaii) noted that "navigation of the sea between Japan and China afforded the largest field for discovery."

Captain Vancouver was of like opinion. But more than "armchair philosopher's curiosity" lay behind this. Late-18th-century European conflicts were reflected along the China coast and in East Asian waters. Russia was in Alaska and the Aleutians and was pressing down upon China from the continental north. Russian treaties with China were renewed or supplemented in 1768 and 1792, but without important trade provisions. The Dutch were entrenched in the Indies and maintained their monopoly upon Western commerce with Japan through Nagasaki. In 1795 they too sent an embassy to Peking to seek a commercial treaty, but were rudely dismissed, without satisfaction, although they submitted to the formalities required of all "tributary states."

In the 1790's the Industrial Revolution was sharpening the rivalries of all the western European trading nations. Great Britain searched for overseas markets and new sources of raw materials to satisfy the factories of England and to fill her ships. London was eager to break through into the Pacific, probing the coasts of China for admission to trade with Ch'ien Lung's vast empire, and seeking to breach the Dutch monopoly in Japan.

In 1793 Earl Macartney's embassy from the King of England to the Emperor of China traveled in state and was received with honor, but the haughty Chinese took care to advertise the British mission as an embassy bearing tribute from the country of England to the imperial court. Macartney failed to win a treaty or agreement admitting Britain to the commerce which he sought, but his detailed reports drew fresh attention to the possibility of vast markets in China and roused the keenest interest in Europe and America. Withdrawing from Peking, the large company traveled overland to Canton, as the emperor's guests, attracting wide attention all along the way.

"While thus delayed [en route to Canton] the boats were overtaken by two genteel young men who were curious to see the Embassador, and followed him from Han-choo-foo. They were honoured themselves with the same office from the King of the Lequese islands. Their dress was a very fine sort of shawl, manufactured in their own country, dyed of a beautiful brown colour, and lined with the fur of squirrels; the fashion was nearly Chinese. They wore turbans, one of yellow, the other purple, silk, neatly folded round their heads. They had neither linen nor cotton in any part of their dress that could be perceived.

"These young men were well-looking, tho of a dark complexion, well-bred, conversable and communicative. They had just arrived at Han-choo-foo in their way to Peking, where their chief sends delegates regularly every two years, charged to offer a tribute, and pay homage from their master, to the Emperor. They landed at the port of Emouy, in the province of Fo-chen, which alone was open to those strangers. They understood Chinese; but had also a proper language of their own. They said, that no European vessel had, to their recollection, ever touched at any of their islands; but that, should they come, they would be well received; that there was no prohibition against any foreign intercourse; that they had a fine harbour capable of admitting the largest vessels, at a little distance from their capital, which was considerable in extent and population; that they raised a coarse kind of tea, but far inferior to that of the Chinese; and had many mines of copper and iron, but none of gold or silver had been discovered.

"From the geographical position of those islands, they should, if dependent, naturally belong to the Chinese or the Japanese. The latter were indifferent about them, but the former first sent an embassy to them to explore their strength and situation, and afterwards an expedition against them, which reduced them to a tributary state. Upon the decease of the prince, his successor receives a sort of investiture or confirmation from the Emperor of China."[16]

The author (Sir George Staunton, Secretary of Embassy) was quick to note the official rank of the young Okinawans, the quality and character of the textiles of their dress, the possible extent of a market opportunity at the Okinawan capital, its port facilities, and, lastly, the political situation. This confused him, and he may have "corrected" his notes before committing them to text (how else could he explain the presence of tribute bearers in China?), but it is more probable that the young envoys were taking pains to conceal Okinawa's true relationship with Satsuma.

Staunton's record of this brief encounter between envoys of the King of England and the King of Ryukyu was published in 1797. In that year, in May, two British ships bearing one hundred and fifteen men entered Okinawan waters. H.M.S. "Providence" (four hundred tons and bearing sixteen guns) and its tender (a schooner of eighty tons) were en route to survey the northern coasts of Asia, searching meanwhile for the lost explorer La Perouse.

As they entered the treacherous waters surrounding Miyako, the "Providence" suddenly foundered on a hidden reef. Captain William Robert Broughton took off all his men in the tender and the longboats. Anchoring inshore nearby, the ship's company spent a few days attempting to salvage what they could from the disintegrating "Providence." Broughton records in careful detail "the singular humanity of the natives of Typinsan to us, in our distressed situation."

Officers sent ashore to establish relations with villages nearby "were received in a most friendly manner, and the boats returned full of water.

In the afternoon they sent in canoes a much larger quantity, with some wood and large packages of canary seed [sesame seed?], and also some poultry and pigs, without asking anything in return, or seeming to expect it. They strongly expressed a desire for us to proceed to the eastern village, where they could more conveniently supply our wants. . . . After breakfast, on the following day, we paid a visit to our humane friends, who received us with the greatest civility, in a large and convenient house well adapted to the country; the floors were well matted, and everything relating to the furniture extremely neat. . . ."[17]

Some of the ship's officers and men had been sent in longboats to another island nearby to search for salvageable materials cast up on the beach and to recover what they could from the wreck offshore. There, after a time, Broughton joined them. "Before our arrival at the island, the inhabitants had brought them [the salvage party] water and potatoes, and in many other instances, during their absence, did they receive the same kind attentions. These good people were fully acquainted with our misfortune, and naturally conceived our greatest wants were the articles of life which, such as they possessed, they parted with in a most friendly manner. . . . In the morning of the 23rd [of May] we received from our friends the remainder of their presents, which amounted in all to 50 bags of wheat, 20 of rice, and 3 of sweet potatoes; each bag containing 1 cwt; also one bullock of 3 cwt; six large hogs, and plenty of poultry. Indeed, whatever we asked for they immediately sent us; but our small vessel would not admit of anything more, and what was most acceptable, they gave at last all their jars full of water, containing five gallons each, at least as many as we could store upon deck."[18]

Broughton and his men were grateful, and all who could do so contributed some "trifling present"—a drawing of the ship, a telescope, and so forth—to a collection of gifts to be made over to the elders of the community on behalf of the ship's company. After refreshment at the principal house in the village the people crowded to the shore to take leave of their unexpected British guests. To their great delight Broughton turned over to them, fully equipped, the longboat. "They received her with great joy, and directly took possession. Thus did we part most amicably with these humane, civilized people, not unaffected by the favours we had received from them in our distressed situation."[19]

With these emergency supplies, cheerfully given and gratefully received, the crowded schooner left the islands and the wreck on May 26 and made its way to Macao on the South China coast. There the captain arranged to transfer the majority of his companions to other British ships, retaining only thirty-five young men to continue with him on his exploratory voyage in the tender.

Six weeks later Broughton visited the Ryukyus again, putting in at Naha aboard the schooner on July 9. Seeking an excuse to go ashore and become better acquainted with the government and people of these islands, the officers represented themselves to be in need of supplies, but the Okinawans, well aware that they had just come over from the China coast, thought it strange that they needed to be supplied again so soon. "Early in the morning our friends sent us a bullock, hogs, fowls, and potatoes, with abundance of wood and water, and strongly urging our departure. . . . In the forenoon a junk arrived from Typinsan; and a Japanese junk sailed out of the harbour, and proceeded on her voyage towards Niphon. . . ."[20]

Broughton and his companions left Naha on July 12. In proper time full reports were made to the Admiralty at London and to the public.

Textile manufacturers, trading corporations, and the owners of ships were eager for word of new markets; the government, at their prompting, was concerned with the protection of British interests in every quarter of the globe. Broughton spoke with a wide experience, for his voyages had taken him to the northwest coast of North America as well as to the crowded ports China and South Asia. The Okinawan adventure had unique quality, for nowhere else had he encountered quite the same degree of open hospitality. In passing he notes Sir George Staunton's references to Ryukyu and quotes from Gaubil's account of of the Chinese embassy to the islands in 1719. His own account, he said, "will also prove how vessels in distress may really benefit by the humanity and liberality of these islanders, who confer favours, as far as I can judge, without expecting any return for so doing. In every other respect, except for allowing us to land, they were obliging, civil and attentive, bringing off vegetables, and some of their spirits called sakki, and at all times behaving with a degree of politeness, which rendered their company very pleasing. They were also open and unreserved in their manners. We had only to lament our ignorance of their language, which prevented our acquiring any knowledge of their government. . . . The port [of Naha] is convenient for commerce, and seems to be the center of trade between Japan and the Southern Islands. They also trade to China and Formosa."[21]

The Admiralty was impressed. It was proposed to undertake an exploration of the Ryukyu Islands and to survey the currents, reefs, and shoals throughout the archipelago. The China markets were the great target, but British ships would have to move in these waters, if only to counter growing Russian and American activity along the coasts of Asia.

But before plans could be matured and expeditions put in motion, British naval resources were concentrated for the Napoleonic wars in Europe and then drawn into the quarrels with the young American republic.

British ships-of-the-line did not return to Okinawan waters until 1816.

PART THREE

BETWEEN TWO WORLDS

CHAPTER SIX

THE BARRIER ISLANDS

1797–1853

WESTERN RIVALS IN EASTERN WATERS

To understand 19th-century Okinawan relations with Japan and with the Western powers we must consider events which intensified Japan's fear of conquest through the Southern Islands.

From four centers, four great Western powers sent agents into the Ryukyu Islands during the first half of the 19th century. They sought to penetrate Japan, by diplomacy if possible, by force if need be. No other highly organized nation of the world had succeeded in maintaining such close seclusion. Each of the powers—Russia, Great Britain, France, and the United States—had expanding economic, political, and military interests in the Far East which seemed to demand that Japan must be opened to the West and made to declare itself on one side or another in the conflict of Western power interests.

The waters about Japan became a focal point upon which converged Russian interests moving down from the north, British and French interests moving up by sea from southern Asia, and American interests coming from the east.

The Japanese were aware of growing pressure well before the turn of the century. Through the narrow door at Nagasaki they had learned of revolutionary change in the American colonies of the English king, the overthrow of the old monarchy in France, and the onset of Napoleon's wars. The Dutch did all they could to stimulate Japan's fears of other Western powers, Holland's commercial rivals. Of a Russian threat Edo had direct experience.

The czar's agents—explorers and colonists—had moved across Siberia to Pacific shores and Kamchatka, reaching the sea by 1639. Fifty years later they had established a common border with the Chinese empire. By 1711 they were in the northern Kuriles, and for a hundred years thereafter they attempted again and again to enter Japan's ports. Japanese settlers in Sakhalin, Ezo (Hokkaido), and the southern Kuriles often came into conflict with the Russians. By 1796 a Russian settlement was made on the island of Urup, almost within sight of territories under the feudal Lord of Matsumae. The shogun's government in desperation tried to strengthen its defenses along the northern frontier. At last, in 1804, a representative of the Russian-American (Trading) Company—a great colonizing enterprise—reached Nagasaki with Russian naval units, to demand that Japan be opened to Russian trade. They were refused, and in retaliation the Russians raided Japan's outposts on Sakhalin, the Kuriles, and Ezo. It was evident that Akihiro, the Lord of Matsumae, could not secure his fief from attack; he was removed, and the central government at Edo established a direct administration, determined to close the northern borders.

This Russian pressure upon Japan was only part of a much larger pattern of Russian expansion. From Kamchatka the Russians pushed on across the Aleutians and Alaska, and down the coasts of Canada. The founders of the Russian-American Company planned an empire which would embrace the North Pacific. By 1812 they had established a fort near the Spanish mission of San Francisco on the California coast, and five years later another Russian fort appeared on the island of Kauai in the Hawaiian Islands.

From the south came a threat from Britain—the development of a vast colonial empire based on maritime strength and command of the seas from strategic points in the Mediterranean, the Indian Ocean, and Southeast Asia. The British were eager to preclude Russian occupation of Pacific bases and the control of North Pacific waters.

From the east (by way of Cape Horn) a new power was moving swiftly into Far Eastern waters, heightening commercial rivalries all along the western Pacific frontier. In 1797 the first American ship to visit Japan—the "Eliza"—put in at Nagasaki under charter to deliver a cargo for the Dutch merchants stationed there. Holland was losing its preëminent position as a trading nation. War with England, Prussian intervention, French invasion, and the confusion of the Napoleonic era isolated Holland from its Far Eastern stations, and American ships were chartered to carry goods to and from Japan. This drew Yankee attention to the potential of Japanese trade. But the Edo government had to be persuaded—or forced—to abandon its seclusion policies.

For six years the annual Dutch shipments to Nagasaki were made in American vessels willing to fly the Dutch flag while cruising in Japanese waters. In 1800 the alarmed Japanese refused to trade with an American brig which put in at Nagasaki demanding direct exchange under the U.S. flag. Pressure was increasing. There were thirty-four American vessels trading at Canton on the China coast in 1801. Yankee merchants would not long be content in this fashion to leave Japanese trade in the hands of weak Dutch monopolists.

For fifty years the Tokugawa government resisted stoutly.

THE RYUKYUS ON JAPAN'S DEFENSE PERIMETER

Japanese leaders at Edo knew that what had happened on the northern frontier could very well happen in the south; merchants backed by the navies of the West would soon be demanding open ports and the right to trade. The Lord of Satsuma would be subjected to a far greater pressure than the Lord of Matsumae had known.

Shuri's relations with Satsuma at this time were conditioned by mounting economic and political crises within Japan itself. The Tokugawa government did not fully grasp the significance of economic change which made early feudal institutions obsolete. Many daimyo were profoundly dissatisfied with Edo's seclusion policies. The country was seething with discontent. In Sir George Sansom's words, "Every force but conservatism was pressing from within closed doors: so that when a summons came from without they were flung wide open, and all these imprisoned energies were released."

From the Japanese point of view the Ryukyu kingdom formed an outer barrier, a line of first defense before these "closed doors." From the Western point of view Okinawa was a threshhold; if the West could gain a foothold on Okinawa, the penetration of Japan might follow with much greater ease. Broughton's encouraging report of 1798 was supported by all subsequent reports until 1853, when, from an Okinawan base, Perry at last broke in upon the Japanese.

Edo, the shogun's capital, lay about midway between the Kurile Islands to the north and the Ryukyu Islands to the south. These outposts took on new significance. In 1786 a party of Japanese was sent to explore the northern frontier, and maps of the Ryukyu Islands, drafted by Takahara *Pechin*, were sent up to Edo through Satsuma in 1797. Prominent men were deeply concerned with Japan's position and vulnerability; the scholar Hayashi Shihei came from northern Japan, where the menace of Russian encroachment was most keenly felt. During three visits to Nagasaki he learned of European pressures coming along the trading routes from the south. He was convinced that Japan must become better informed of the territories adjacent to it on the west and south. In 1786 —the year in which a Russian man-of-war coasted along the main islands of Japan—he published *A Study of Three Countries* (*San Koku Tsuran Tosetsu*), in which he discussed Ezo, Korea, and the Ryukyu kingdom.[1] In 1789 Matsudaira Sadanobu, the regent at Edo, called Hayashi in for an interview, during which Shihei emphasized his concern for the coastal defenses of Japan, and on this subject he later published *Military Talks Concerning the Coastal Provinces* (*Kaikoku Heidan*).

Pressed from within to look to its defenses, and pressed from without by barbarians who demanded trade, the Tokugawa government was torn with indecision. Circumstances required that it leave problems of the Ryukyu frontier to the judgment of Satsuma. But at Kagoshima, too, there was unsettling indecision. Some leaders felt that the islands should be closed tightly and put in a state of garrisoned defense against all Western demands and attempts to enter. Others advocated opening a trading depot for the Western powers on Okinawa, analogous to the depot maintained at Naha for the China trade. This they believed might satisfy the Western powers and keep them at arm's length, while at the same time Satsuma, circumventing Edo, would be enriched by a monopoly on commerce with the European nations.

The debates at Kagoshima and at Edo were long drawn out; Western merchant ships and men-of-war began to visit the islands with increasing frequency. Naval diplomats, traders, and missionaries began to conceive and write of opportunities at Naha. None clearly understood the ambiguous state of "dual subordination" into which Okinawa had fallen. Gradually it came to be thought that Okinawa offered prime opportunity to bring pressure to bear upon the shogun's government. Missionaries dreamed of introducing Christian tracts to Japan through Naha and Kagoshima. Naval diplomats proposed to use the islands for rendezvous, supply, and repair while cruising in Chinese and Japanese waters. Merchants planned to trade into Japan through the Japanese agency at Naha.

In this unenviable position the impoverished Okinawans were caught between the pressures of the West and the resistance of Japan.

Years of Economic Disaster

Hardship crowded the opening years of the 19th century on Okinawa. The local economy was shattered by a series of storms, tidal waves, and long droughts. The people of Yaeyama had had a foretaste of this: a submarine earthquake shook the island, the seas withdrew, and then swept inland in an enormous tidal wave, destroying most of the principal town of Ishigaki and taking a dreadful toll of lives. Between 1800 and 1854 all the islands suffered again and again. Epidemic disease and repeated famines weakened the kingdom. By the time Commodore Perry reached Naha in mid-century the Ryukyuan people had reached a common state of economic and political exhaustion.

If we remember that the total population may not have exceeded 150,000 persons and certainly did not surpass 200,000, the following bald figures—a partial record—suggests the dire impoverishment of the islands through these calamitous years:

1802–03: Epidemics took 425 lives, including those of the young King Sho On and his infant son and successor, Sho Sei.

1824–25: Two typhoons and famine, during which 3,355 persons died.

1826: A typhoon took 30 lives, destroyed more than 100 fishing craft and ships and thousands of dwellings on Okinawa. More than 2,200 persons died of starvation.

1832: Storms destroyed nearly 100 craft and more than 3,000 houses. There was widespread famine and some deaths.

1835: A drought, typhoon, and epidemic disease took more than 600 lives on Yaeyama.

1839: A great drought and dearth of food.

1842: An earthquake caused widespread damage on Miyako, followed by epidemic disease.

1844: A terrible typhoon swept Miyako, destroying more than 2,000 houses and damaging crops.

1847: Miyako was again swept by fierce storms in midwinter.

1850: A long drought brought the islands to the verge of famine.

1852: A typhoon, a tidal wave, famine, and a typhus epidemic scourged Miyako, leaving more than 3,000 dead.

1853: An epidemic (probably of cholera) swept Yaeyama, killing more than 1,800 persons.

1854: Drought and typhoons on Okinawa, and an epidemic on Miyako which took more than 600 lives.

Western accounts written in the early 19th century note how often the Okinawans describe themselves as an impoverished people, too poor to meet the demands for supply and trade which the foreign visitors put upon them. The Europeans tended to interpret this as a form of deception, practiced at Japan's insistence in order to maintain seclusion. The facts of the case were precisely as the Okinawans represented them. Custom decreed that they should furnish foodstuffs to shipwrecked persons and supplies to others who came in search of them. But custom also decreed that no payment should be taken for such supplies. The succor of shipwrecked persons was accepted as a moral obligation among these seafaring people. As for offering provisions gratis to those who demanded them, this too was in part based in a code of moral obligation to meet the needs of strangers received as guests in the country, and in part it was a means of circumventing Japan's fiercely enforced decrees forbidding unauthorized trade with foreign peoples.

Famine deaths and epidemic sickness undermined the productive strength of the farming communities. Costs of repair and rebuilding after disastrous storms consumed material reserves. Loss of small craft affected villages engaged in fishing and in coastal transport. The government at Shuri became increasingly dependent upon loans from Kagoshima to finance its formal relations with China. Shuri pressed the country villages too hard. By mid-century the exhaustion of the local economy and of the local spirit of faithful subordination to the Shuri government was reflected in incidents of protest; unrest here and there grew into riotous action.

Each natural disaster added to the burden on Shuri's modest budget. The government tried to economize in the administration and to stimulate production. The magistrates attempted to enforce stricter supervision of the forests after 1806. Water conservation tanks were built here and there. Sugar-extraction machinery was improved somewhat. The hardy *sotetsu* palm was planted everywhere so that its unpalatable but nutritious seeds would be available in times of need. A competitive exhibit of farmers' products is said to have been organized as early as 1814 in order to encourage greater production throughout the countryside.

In 1819 Shuri decided to reduce the stipends which had been paid hitherto in the elite community of Kume Village, from which were drawn the clerks who managed trade with Satsuma and China, the routine operations of government, and the education of the gentry. Now at last they began to feel the pinch; they were asked to eat less well and to pay over more to the government in taxes. In 1821 a government order canceled certain types of debts; in this dangerous and trouble-making policy the Okinawans followed administrative policies of Matsudaira Sadanobu, late regent at Edo.

Against this somber background of uncertainty, hardship, and confusion the development of an educational policy for Okinawa stands out in bright relief. The National Academy (*Kokugaku*), founded in 1798, was given appropriate buildings on the castle grounds at Shuri in 1800 and 1801. Elementary schools for the gentry were established in the administrative quarters of Shuri and Naha and new official positions were created to manage them. A new "Hall of Learning" was established at Naha by a private donor, Owan *Pechin*, in 1824, and in 1837 a Confucian shrine was established on the grounds of the National Academy. Schools were opened in Yaeyama (1844) and in Miyako

(1846) and new textbooks in Confucian moral studies were issued on Okinawa.

The troubles of the court and the administration in these decades were intensified by an illness of the king, Sho Ko, whose behavior became strange, unbalanced, and unpredictable. The Council of State was forced to act; an embassy submitted the government's proposals to Satsuma; and in 1827, with Satsuma's approval, Sho Ko was forced to abdicate and to retire into the countryside.

This was only the second abdication in Ryukyu's long history, and such an unusual change in the royal household brought one more burden upon the government treasury. A mission had to be sent to Peking to announce the change and to ask for a writ of investiture for Sho Ko's successor. Accession rituals were costly and Chinese envoys had to be entertained. A second royal household had to be maintained in the countryside in a manner befitting the prestige and dignities of an abdicated king.

FIG. 17. OBJECTS OF VENERATION. Left: *Reverence for kings and royal ancestors was symbolized by the Royal Mausoleum, Shuri.* Right: *Popular superstitions centered about such objects as as this wayside stone figure, Naha.*

Mystery surrounds the name of Sho Ko and the circumstances of his retirement. A "Testament" attributed to him reads now as a veiled criticism of his times, a protest against the role which he and his people were forced to play by Satsuma: "Darkness prevails; nobody awakens, while the bell will soon announce the arrival of dawn. It is hard to rule when both the ruler and the people are hard pressed, and are robbed by those among them whose storehouses are filled with spoils. Any blame will I take on myself. Only relieve the people of their privations; quench their thirst by opening the fountain. After all, men live but once."[2]

Could it be that Sho Ko was indeed rational, but that he toyed with the idea of breaking away from Satsuma and opening his tiny kingdom to unrestricted intercourse with foreign nations?

His abdication contributed to the public uneasiness, already great in the face of natural calamities and the threat of foreign invasion. It was not possible to keep the former king from the public eye; he is said to have wandered erratically about on the public roads, in a strange dress, and to have insisted on sending produce from his private gardens up to the public markets in Shuri.

The royal castle and the person of the king had become the most enduring symbols of Ryukyuan nationhood. They were the outward and visible symbol of national self-esteem and self-respect. The royal house gave Okinawa an identity vis-à-vis Japan and China and the Western world. The fate of the gentry and common people alike was bound up in the king's relations with these external forces. Okinawa's ties with China were founded on the king's formal relationship with the court at Peking, and it had been in the king's name that the country was committed to Satsuma in 1611. It was felt that so long as the court could prevent Western envoys from penetrating to the king's presence at Shuri, the dangers of entanglement or of binding commitments to them might be avoided.

In the eyes of the common man the king's ministers of state derived their authority from him; hence the necessity to remove a king from office implied a weakness in, or question of, delegated authority. Moreover the king's behavior—in theory at least—was expected to fulfill at all times the highest traditional standards of all that was considered right and proper. The abdication challenged fundamental beliefs and standards, and threatened the pattern of subordinate relationships with Satsuma and Edo.

SATSUMA EXPLOITS OKINAWA TO EVADE THE SECLUSION EDICTS

Satsuma clan leaders felt no love for the Edo government and little loyalty to the Tokugawa family. They were irked by the Tokugawa monopoly on foreign trade through Nagasaki, maintained in the name of "national security." There is evidence that the Okinawan trading depot in China was Satsuma's source for large-scale smuggling into Japan. Satsuma maintained about fifteen junks in the Ryukyu trade, each making two round trips to Naha per year. This was an accepted and well-known arrangement; but Shimazu desired to improve on this by attracting Chinese trade directly to Satsuma ports. To this end Chinese language schools and information centers were opened at several small anchorages along the coasts of southern Kyushu. These would provide interpreters and translators, who could compete with the established facilities available to Chinese and Dutch traders under Tokugawa auspices. In 1802 certain articles of European origin were uncovered in a shipment of Satsuma goods at Kyoto. The Kagoshima authorities were called upon to explain the matter, but Edo could do little to check or punish the powerful Satsuma men. At the turn of the century Shimazu Shigehide was in close and friendly association with officers of the Dutch trading station on Deshima. His extravagance had brought him under heavy obligation to Osaka merchants and moneylenders, to whom he pledged the revenues of his Ryukyuan trade in return for a credit of five million *koban*. At about the same time he reached a secret agreement with the Dutchman Hemmij, chief of the Deshima trading depot, in which it was proposed to send secretly one foreign ship each year to Satsuma in direct contravention of the exclusion edicts. Disclosure might have led to a Tokugawa war upon Satsuma had Shigehide not been the shogun's father-in-law. It meant, however, that Satsuma's interest in direct foreign trade was checked for a time.[3]

The illegal use of Okinawa as a trading base through which Satsuma accumulated wealth sharpened Edo's sense of vulnerability on the southern frontier. Tokugawa policies were self-defeating, a form of economic strangulation; within a few decades a coalition of Western clans led by Satsuma were to bring about the downfall of the shogunate, and the revolution was to be financed very largely through Satsuma's profits from the Okinawan trade.

Satsuma began to exploit control of the Ryukyu kingdom for political purposes, using the relationship to enhance Shimazu prestige at the imperial court. Shimazu Nariakira's sister was the shogun's wife, which gave him access to the highest social circles at the Edo court, although, as a *tozama* daimyo, he was barred from high administrative office. Now he coveted high rank at the imperial court as well. As nationalism revived and anti-Tokugawa royalist sentiment increased, old Kyoto titles granted directly by the emperor regained importance which they had lost hundreds of years before.

The successful invasion of Okinawa in 1609 had won for Iehisa the junior third grade of imperial court rank and the nominal office of *Chunagon*. These were not hereditary, however, and so his descendant Nariakira determined to regain them if he could by manipulating his control of the Ryukyu kingdom.

The shogun claimed to receive tribute from the King of Korea, but only Shimazu among all the daimyo could claim to receive tribute from a foreign state. No opportunity was missed to stress this point. Although the Okinawans at home were ordered to go to any length to conceal their true relationship with Japan, whenever Shuri's envoys traveled in Japan—overland from Kagoshima to Kyoto and Edo—there was a great display of Okinawan costume, language, and manners. Satsuma encouraged the publication and wide distribution of woodblock prints illustrating these diplomatic processions, and every effort was made to underscore the "foreignness" of the Okinawans. In other words, while the Okinawans had been trying for so long to adopt Japanese ways and to conform to Japanese wishes, Satsuma's policy was dedicated to emphasizing differences.

Satsuma's efforts to exploit the vassalage of the Ryukyu king met with limited success; in 1836 Shuri was directed again to enforce the edicts banning use of the Japanese language or Japanese artifacts in the presence of foreigners, and forbidding any revelation of the true state of Okinawa's dependency upon Satsuma. In 1841 and 1842 the King of Ryukyu was required to sign a petition to the Lord of Satsuma, ostensibly his own but actually prepared at Kagoshima, which represented to Shimazu that Shuri might experience difficulties if precedents were not obeyed and the Lord of Satsuma did not receive promotions at the imperial court; Shimazu was advanced to ranks unusual for military men, but failed at that time to reach the exalted place for which the clan intrigued.*

All of this left the Okinawans in a state of confused uncertainty, for they were required by Satsuma to take great risks vis-à-vis the shogun's policies. At home they were to deny subordination; in Japan the subordination was ostentatiously emphasized. It is small wonder that foreigners who visited Okinawa were perplexed by the air of mystery which lay over Shuri's relations with Japan, nor is it surprising that Western observers felt that the Okinawans—otherwise so friendly and refreshingly direct—were guilty of duplicity and vacillation, and were wanting in the power of initiative or decision in official undertakings.

On their part the Okinawans were shaken by fear and uncertainty when the Western ships began to call at Naha. Shuri had no firm precedents to govern its behavior. As we shall see, Satsuma's official attitudes veered with changing policies at Kagoshima, sometimes encouraging foreign intercourse for the sake of trade, sometimes frowning on it, and always meting out heavy punishments to those who violated orders. The Europeans who came were unacquainted with the rituals and procedures traditionally associated with the reception and dispatch of embassies and trading missions, and this led to many crises within Shuri Castle walls.

CHINA'S ATTITUDE TOWARD THE WESTERN BARBARIANS

Peking could give no guidance to Shuri, for the Chinese were baffled by Europeans who insisted that they had a right to trade in China and that the Chinese government had an obligation to throw open the country to foreign commerce. Hitherto, successful alien invaders of China—the Mongols and the Manchus—had come overland into China and after military conquest had accepted Chinese civilization and adapted themselves to it. All other barbarians were admitted on sufferance as tributary peoples. The idea of sovereign equality among

---

* After the Tokugawa had been overthrown, the clan was well rewarded, numbering in the Shimazu family alone two princes, one count, and eight barons in the imperial court hierarchy.

nations was incomprehensible to the Chinese. If the rude red-haired barbarians so eagerly desired to trade, let them conform to age-old custom; there seemed to be no reason to alter the tribute and trading regulations.

Shuri was well aware of China's attitude. Lord Macartney's embassy from the British sovereign to the Chinese emperor in 1793 had been proclaimed a tribute mission by the Chinese court. It had been refused trading privileges on the representation that "China had everything it needed within its own borders." A Dutch trading mission had been treated rudely and turned away empty-handed in 1795, even though the merchants were willing to perform the humiliating k'o-t'ou. A Russian envoy refused to perform this act of submission in 1806 and was not allowed to approach Peking. Lord Amherst's embassy in 1816 was dismissed abruptly and turned away without an audience. At last China and Great Britain came to blows; the issue was to be resolved by force.

The Anglo-Chinese War of 1839–42 had repercussions in Okinawa, as we shall see. It underscored Shuri's dilemma for it demonstrated beyond question that Western nations were prepared to use force to gain their ends. Obviously, if Shuri opened Okinawa to foreign intercourse it risked reprisals from both China and Japan; if it refused to accede to Western demands, it might suffer attack and occupation.

BRITISH VISITORS: CAPTAIN HALL'S MOMENTOUS VOYAGE AND NAPOLEON'S INTEREST IN THE RYUKYUS

Typhoons and droughts, epidemics and famines, and even perhaps the abdication of a king were as nothing compared to the dread threat of foreign intrusion. Here indeed the Okinawans were caught between hammer and anvil, between Japan's fierce determination to exclude the foreigner and the foreigner's persistent search for an opportunity to penetrate Japan.

From an economic point of view the unheralded and irregular visits made by foreign ships were costly incidents, hard to be borne by the Okinawan economy. Nothing of equal value was received in return for provisions or for the entertainment offered by this ever-courteous people. Shuri had to meet the costs of increased personnel in all ranks in order to look after the needs of (and to keep close watch upon) the foreign vistors. Missions had to be sent to and fro between Shuri and Kagoshima to report on each intrusion and to explain policy in meeting importunate foreign demands. There was lurking fear that either China or Japan would cut off trade with Okinawa, which would mean starvation, and dread that these foreign visits might provoke Satsuma or Edo to invade and garrison the islands in the name of national defense.

Against these dour considerations must be set the Okinawan's innate curiosity and his fundamental friendliness. This conflict between duty and inclination is reflected again and again in the observations and diary records preserved from the hands of Western visitors.

European and American ships put in more than thirty times in fifty years. Some came singly, some came in squadrons. Merchantmen and men-of-war, driven in by storm, were wrecked or damaged on the reefs and rocks of the archipelago; some came to Naha Harbor with clearly-formulated plans for trade. Official reports, diaries, and published travel accounts brought Okinawa to the attention of the Western world when early-19th-century "armchair travelers" welcomed each new account with gusto, when private commercial interests were eager to explore every potential market and source of raw materials with which to feed an expanding industrial complex in the Western world. Christian revivalism swept Britain and America in the early decades and found expression in fervent missionary interest in all "heathen" people. Politics, commercial rivalry, and military conflict among the European powers prompted governments to encourage exploration and to watch with keen interest the reports brought back from hitherto unknown lands.

It is not possible now to identify all Western ships reported to have reached the Ryukyu Islands in these years, nor is it certain that all arrivals were recorded in the annals of the kingdom or in the logbooks and diaries of the Western voyagers.

Characterizations of the Okinawans vary in detail, but they are virtually unanimous in noting contradictory aspects within Okinawan life. The visitor was invariably struck by the absence of arms or incidents of violence, by the unfailing courtesy and friendliness of all classes, by the intelligence of the gentry, and by the absence of thievery among the common people. These were on the credit side. On the debit side they noted the apparent duplicity of officials in all matters touching upon Okinawa's true relationship with Japan, and they were irked by the system of restraint and close watch under which they were forced to spend their days and nights ashore. They were troubled by the Okinawans' inexplicable insistence that under no circumstance must the local people or the government accept payment for goods and services rendered on behalf of foreign visitors.

In their notes the early Western visitors were virtually unanimous in praising the friendly courtesy, which stood in such contrast to the rude receptions usually experienced on the nearby coasts of China, Korea, and Japan. Nevertheless, the foreigners often grew impatient with Okinawan insistence upon elaborate formality in the conduct of business, and with the presence of "spies."

They were of course as ignorant of Okinawan ceremonial standards as the Okinawans, their hosts, were ignorant of good form and custom governing international intercourse in the Western world. Extreme formality at Naha and Shuri reflected centuries of Okinawan experience with Chinese precedent. In Okinawan eyes ceremonial niceties were the mark of a cultured man.

As for the irritating "spies," these were actually attendants of two sorts. Some were assigned to accompany the visitors because the Okinawans believed that envoys and gentlemen of rank expected to have subordinates always at their side, ready for instant service; it was simple courtesy to provide them. Moreover, in centuries of experience the Okinawans had observed that foreign visitors in China and Japan invariably had a close guard assigned to accompany them through the countryside wherever they went, ostensibly to protect them from the uncultured but curious common people.

The second category of unwanted attendants were indeed the real spies, the prying, common agents (*metsuke*) who served the Japanese representatives stationed at Naha. The *metsuke* were held in low regard, but they were feared. If by chance they were not present, the Okinawans showed an eager interest in all that could be learned of the Western world, and there was a ready exchange of information and of gifts; under the eyes of the *metsuke*, gifts proffered by foreign visitors were rejected and conversation became stiff, cautious, and noncommittal. Since few Europeans penetrated the mystery of hidden Japanese authority, few grasped the significance of the ambivalent Okinawan behavior. The presence of Satsuma's agents was felt but never clearly understood.

On the whole, the early Western diarists—diplomats, naval officers, merchants—were sensitive to the qualities of the Okinawans with whom they met. They noted sometimes with an air of surprise that they had encountered a people who were "almost civilized" though they were not Christians. Even the missionaries sometimes grudgingly admitted an appreciation of good manners and warm friendliness.

Western ships touched at Naha in 1803, 1804, and 1811, but not until 1816 did the British Admiralty act on the plans inspired by Broughton's report. His Majesty's ships the "Alceste" and the "Lyra" were in the Yellow Sea waiting for Lord Amherst to withdraw his embassy from Peking. To use the time profitably it was decided to survey the west coast of Korea and the Ryukyu archipelago.

On September 15, these ships were searching for a suitable anchorage near the northern end of the main island (Okinawa). Several canoes came off to hover about the "Lyra." "No people we have yet met with have been so friendly, for the moment they came alongside, one handed a jar of water up to us, and another a basket of boiled sweet potatoes, without asking or seeming to wish for any recompense. Their manners were gentle and respectful. . . . Another canoe went near the Alceste, and a rope being thrown to them, they tied a fish to it and then paddled away. All this seemed to promise well, and was particularly grateful after the cold repulsive manners of the Coreans."[4]

The English visitors were not disappointed. By the time they left the island on Sunday, October 27, they had established friendships of a quality and character which may have no parallel in the annals of 19th-century voyaging. From the captains (Sir Murray Maxwell and Basil Hall) to the last seaman in the ranks there was a sense of universal appreciation that this was a unique experience.

Captain Hall, of the "Lyra," comments upon the individual character of the Okinawans who became friendly companions during the autumn sojourn. The narrative of Dr. John M'Leod, surgeon on the "Alceste," supplements Hall's account with wide-ranging remarks upon the character of the countryside, the habits and customs observed during long rambles in the wooded hills and fields near Naha. He notes the innate dignity and cultivated manners displayed by the ranking men of Okinawa. Americans who have become acquainted with the ravaged island since 1945 find it difficult to credit M'Leod's description of the landscape:

"[They] seemed to enjoy robust health, for we observed no diseased objects, nor beggars of any description, among them. . . .

"Cultivation is added to the most enchanting beauties of nature. From a commanding height . . . the view is, in all directions, picturesque and delightful. . . . To the south is the city of Napafoo [Naha] . . . and in the intermediate space appear numerous hamlets scattered about on the banks of the rivers, which meander in the valley beneath; the eye being, in every direction, charged by the varied hues of the luxuriant foliage around their habitations. Turning to the east, the houses of Kint-ching [Shuri], the capital city, built in their peculiar style, are observed, opening from among the lofty trees which surround and shade them, rising one above another in a gentle ascent to the summit of a hill, which is crowned by the king's palace; the intervening grounds between Napafoo and Kint-ching, a distance of some miles, being ornamented by a continuation of villas and country houses. To the north, as far as the eye can reach, the higher land is covered with extensive forests.[5]

.   .   .

"This island can also boast its rivers and secure harbors; and last, though not least, a worthy, a friendly, and a happy race of people.

"Many of these islanders displayed a spirit of intelligence and genius, which seemed the more extraordinary, considering the confined circle in which they live; such confinement being almost universally found to be productive of narrowness of mind. Our friends here were an exception to the general rule.—*Maddera* [i.e., Maedera] *Cosyong*, one of our most constant and intimate friends, acquired such proficiency in the English language, in the course of a few weeks as to make himself tolerably understood.

"He was gay or serious, as occasion required, but was always respectable; and of *Maddera* it might be truly said, that he was a gentle-man, not formed upon this model, or according to that rule, but 'stamped as such by the sovereign hand of Nature.'

"They all seemed to be gifted with a sort of politeness which had the fairest claim to be natural; for there was nothing constrained—nothing stiff or studied in it.

"Captain Maxwell having one day invited a party to dine with him, the health of the King of Lewchew was drank in a bumper:—one of them immediately addressing himself with much warmth and feeling to the interpreter, desired him to state how much they felt gratified by such a compliment; that they would take care to tell it to every body when they went on shore; and proposed, at the same time, a bumper to the king of the *Engelees*. A Chinese mandarin, under the like circumstances, would, most probably, have *chin-chinned* (that is, clenched his fists) as usual; he would have snivelled and grinned *the established number* of times, and bowed his head in slavish submission to the bare mention of his tyrant's name; but it would never have occurred to him to have given, in his turn, the health of the sovereign of England.

"This superiority of manner brought to our recollection the boorish-ness of the Chinese near the Pei-ho. Certain mandarins, who were not of sufficient button [rank] to be entertained in the company of the embassador, were invited to dine with the officers; and some of them, after gnawing the leg of a fowl, would without any ceremony thrust the remains of it into any other dish near them. . . ."[6]

M'Leod notes Okinawan readiness to observe British ways and to accommodate themselves to British custom when aboard the "Alceste" or the "Lyra"; he was impressed by the development of good relations between ordinary seamen and Okinawan laborers engaged to assist in the ship's repair. "That proud and haughty feeling of national superiori-ty, so strongly existing among the common class of British seamen, which induces them to hold all foreigners cheap, and to treat them with contempt; often calling them outlandish lubbers *in their own country*, was, at this island, completely subdued and tamed, by the gentle man-ners and kind behaviour of the most pacific people upon earth. Although completely intermixed, and often working together, both on shore and on board, not a single quarrel or complaint took place on either side, during the whole of our stay; on the contrary, the natives were always seen in cheerful association around the sailors' mess tables, and each succeeding day added to friendship and cordiality."[7]

Both M'Leod and Hall also observed that throughout the long sojourn at Naha not one theft was reported. The British visitors were aware that the Okinawans lived perpetually under an unnatural restraint:

"Notwithstanding it was an infringement of their established rules for strangers to land upon their coasts [writes M'Leod], yet they granted in this respect every possible indulgence, and conceded the point as far as they could; for their dispositions seemed evidently at war with the unsocial law. When any of the officers wandered into the country beyond the bounds prescribed, they were never rudely repulsed, as in China or Morocco, but mildly entreated to return, as a favour to those in attendance, lest they should incur blame; and, as this appeal was powerful, it was never disregarded."[8]

"We never saw any punishment inflicted at Loo-choo [writes Hall]; a tap with a fan, or an angry look, was the severest chastisement ever resorted to, as far as we could discover. In giving orders, the chiefs were mild though firm, and the people always obeyed with cheerfulness. There seemed to be great respect and confidence on the one hand, and much consideration and kind feeling on the other. In this particular, more than any other that fell under our notice, Loo-choo differs from China, for in the latter country we saw none of this generous and friendly understanding between the upper and lower classes."[9]

One morning, riding in the countryside, Captain Sir Murray Maxwell fell from his horse. He fractured and dislocated the forefinger of one hand, a painful but not serious injury. When the Okinawans insisted that the best physician amongst them should treat the finger, the British officers decided to let them do so. Under Dr. M'Leod's watchful eye, they were given an opportunity to demonstrate what they knew of medicine. This reflects the high esteem and mutual confidence which had sprung up in a few brief weeks.

Several of the crew suffering minor illnesses were lodged in a pavilion ashore. Many people of Naha and Shuri paid daily calls, and with solicitous concern brought to the patients small offerings of eggs, fruit, and cakes. One young seaman had been mortally ill when the ships arrived. Upon his death a great concourse of Okinawans, many of them dressed in mourning clothes of black and white, attended the funeral and asked permission to erect a monument. An English-language inscription was traced in India ink upon a stone, which they then cut and placed at the grave. It bore these words:

"Here lies buried,
Aged Twenty-One Years, William Hares, Seaman,
Of His Britannic Majesty's ship Alceste
Died Oct. 15, 1816.
This Monument was erected
By the King
And Inhabitants
Of this most hospitable Island"

The conduct of the Okinawans upon this melancholy occasion made a lasting impression upon the British officers and men in all ranks. To commit a fellow countryman to a lonely grave in foreign soil was not an unusual experience but always a poignant one; not infrequently the last Christian rites had to be administered in the presence of hostile, overcurious, or suspicious people. The courteous sympathy of the Okinawans was recorded with profound appreciation. There was a romantic element about it which caught the imagination of all who later read of it, for the story is retold many, many times by Victorian writers.

Another incident, however, was destined to have more profound consequences for the Okinawans themselves. Writing from Dingle, County Kerry, Ireland, on February 9, 1843, Lieutenant Herbert J. Clifford, Royal Navy (ret.), launched a public appeal for funds for a "Loo Choo Mission." After recounting the incidents and hospitality which British mariners had enjoyed in Okinawa, he had this to say: "One

Sabbath day, while we remained amongst them, I was asked by the attendant chiefs who had been dismissed from the *Alceste*, while Divine Service was going on—'What are they doing aboard the *big* ship that we are sent away?' I replied, 'They are *chinchinning Joss* (worshipping God) —just as you do.' My conscience has smitten me ever since for this reply, but I knew not the Lord at this time and sinned ignorantly."[10]

The Okinawans, as we shall see, were destined to pay a heavy price for Clifford's sense of sin and his belated remorse.

Before parting from their friends at Naha, the British staged a great celebration with much pageantry, feasting, and fireworks in honor of the King and Royal Family of Ryukyu, and the foreigners in turn were feted by the Okinawans. As the visit drew to a close, a deputation of high officials waited on the boatswain of the "Alceste" with a proposal that he should leave his wife behind; she had been the only foreign woman ever seen in Okinawa, they said, and had attracted much attention. It was assumed that this proposal came from the king's household, from which a lady of high rank had come upon occasion to meet and inspect the strange-looking Western woman. It was a flattering offer, politely declined.

The ships prepared to weigh anchor. A concourse of Okinawans, dressed in their best robes, performed services at a seaside temple to invoke the gods "to protect the *Englelees*, to avert every danger, and restore them in safety to their native land!" Tears were shed during a lingering farewell, and M'Leod noted that "this happy island . . . will be long remembered by all the officers and men of the *Alceste* and *Lyra;* for the kindness and hospitality of its inhabitants have fixed upon every mind a deep and lasting impression of gratitude and esteem."

M'Leod closes his book with a poem in twenty-five stanzas, entitled "The Farewell," an awkward expression of deeply felt but strangely mixed emotion. These professional mariners had been reared in the Western European Christian tradition that heathens were to be pitied and patronized and, if possible, brought to conversion. Here they had discovered a people who were governed by a code of high refinement in personal relations, whose manners were polished, and whose agreeable conduct and candor with strangers compelled not only admiration but friendship on a basis approaching social equality.

"The following Lines, written by Mr. Gillard, on leaving our hospitable friends at Grand Lew Chew, speak not only his own, but the general, feeling on that occasion.

.   .   .

"While friendship thus was shown to all
Congenial minds attached a few;
And Memory oft will pleased recall
The names of 'Madd'ra' and 'Ge-roo.'

"Farewell, dear Isle!—on thee may ne'er
The breath of civil discord blow!
Far from your shores be every fear,
And far—oh! far—the invading foe!"[11]

Captain Hall describes the leave-taking:

"I took this opportunity of giving each of the chiefs some trinket, as a farewell present, and they in return gave me their pipes, fans and knives, as memorials, accompanied by many friendly expressions. Mutual assurances then passed between us, of long being remembered, and the natives rose to take their last leave of us. Ookooma, who, as well as the others, was much agitated, endeavoured to say something, but his heart was full, and he could not utter a word. The rest did not attempt to speak; and before they reached their boats, they were all in tears. . . .

"While we were heaving up the anchor, the natives assembled, not only in canoes round the ships, but in vast crowds along the neighbouring heights; and as we sailed away for ever from their interesting island, they all stood up, and continued waving their fans and handkerchiefs till they could not longer be distinguished."[12]

On the homeward voyage the "Lyra" put in briefly at St. Helena, where the principal officers were presented to the exiled Napoleon. The "Alceste" had been lost, Lord Amherst's mission at Peking was a failure, and there had been other adventures and misadventures to mark this ambassadorial tour around the world, but it was to the curiously mild and happy experience on Okinawa that the conversation turned. When Napoleon was told that there existed a kingdom in which no

arms were found and (as the visitors believed) the art of war was unknown, a society governed by a code of polite manners and good behavior among all classes, the general who had set Europe aflame refused
to believe that such a kingdom and such a people could exist. Hall felt
that he was fortunate in having something of exceptional conversational
interest, and Napoleon "devoured information" about the Ryukyu
kingdom and the Okinawan people:

"Several circumstances . . . respecting the Loo-Choo people surprised
even him a good deal; and I had the satisfaction of seeing him more
than once completely perplexed, and unable to account for the phenom-
ena which I related. Nothing struck him so much as their having no
arms. 'Point d'armes!' he exclaimed; . . . 'Mais, sans armes, comment
se bat-on?'

"I could only reply, that as far as we had been able to discover, they
had never had any war, but remained in a state of internal and external
peace. 'No wars!' cried he, with a scornful and incredulous expression,
as if the existence of any people under the sun without wars was a mon-
strous anomaly."

Napoleon enquired closely into the economics, religion, customs,
habitations, and dress of the people, and pressed questions concerning
agriculture on Okinawa: "He appeared considerably amused by the
pertinacity with which they kept their women out of our sight; but
repeatedly expressed himself much pleased with Captain Maxwell's
moderation and good sense, in forebearing to urge any point upon the
natives which was disagreeable to them, or contrary to the laws of their
country."[13]

Two principal records, from which we have already quoted, were
later issued; Captain Basil Hall, commanding officer of the "Lyra,"
published an *Account of a Voyage of Discovery to the West Coast of Corea
and the Great Loo-Choo Island*, and John M'Leod, M.D., surgeon aboard
the "Alceste," published a *Voyage of His Majesty's Ship Alceste to China,
Corea, and the Island of Lewchew with an Account of her Shipwreck*. Both
accounts went into several handsomely illustrated editions. Hall wrote
with a fine touch, sensitive to the qualities of this experience. For many
years thereafter he traveled over the world and published exten-

sively, but no experience touched him quite as this one had. He drew a picture of idyllic peace, of a happy people, of an exquisite landscape, and of a quality of human relationships which altogether appealed to the romantic spirit of the early 19th century. For three decades his book was accepted as a standard work, for it combined accurate and pains-taking investigation with a warmly felt appreciation of the high character and quality of the Okinawan people. Anyone who proposed to visit the islands thereafter turned to his volume for information.

This had an odd consequence. The romantic picture of life at Shuri and Naha in 1816 created expectations which were not fulfilled when naval diplomats and missionaries of France, England, and the United States began to frequent Okinawan waters. Political and economic con-ditions within the island had changed considerably; the Japanese had developed and stiffened policies toward Okinawa, and the island people themselves had become further impoverished through a continuing series of natural disasters. There was a sense of disillusionment on both sides. The Okinawans in time became tired of demands made upon their hospitality by foreign ships, not all of which were commanded by men of the high quality of Sir Murray Maxwell and Captain Hall. On the other hand, when receptions were not so cordial the dis-appointed foreigners tended to heap blame on Hall and his colleagues for "misrepresentation." But, on the whole, navy men and merchant seamen usually came away with a happy impression; the missionaries, however, were aggrieved. Hall's glowing account had stirred them to highest expectation of an easy evangelical conquest, a harvest of souls easily gathered. When in fact the Okinawans said "No thank you" the evangelists were offended. Their notes, commentaries, and letters to the press reflected a sense of injury and resentment, toward Captain Hall, who had so badly "misled" them, and toward the Okinawans, who compounded refusal's injury by being, on the whole, polite about it.

MISSIONARIES, MERCHANTS, AND NAVAL DIPLOMATS:
THE ANGLO-CHINESE WARS

Meanwhile, on November 19, 1819, the brig "Brothers," flying the British flag, dropped anchor at Naha to take on supplies and to seek permission to trade. The ship's company were astonished at the "tolerable" English spoken by some of the Okinawans, and inspected with great interest the notebooks and drawings which were brought aboard as proud records of the "Alceste" and "Lyra" visit. William Upton Eddis subsequently published notes on the incident:

"When they took leave, they requested me on no account to go on shore, as it would occasion much trouble. I smiled and said, I would go with them the next day. We shook hands, bowed, &c, and I remained in astonishment at their kind, polite and unexpectedly European manners. They possessed much curiosity, but not for a moment intrusive. When anyone wished to examine anything, his looks were as expressive as any words could be, and touched nothing until permission was first gained. I could not help wishing some of my late Russian friends present to see their manners.

"As it appeared fruitless and nearly impossible to trade, I sailed on the Saturday morning, after a stay of only 44 hours, in which short time it was scarcely practicable to acquire any other knowledge further than sufficient to excite surprise and admiration at these worthy, hospitable, and indeed partly polished people. They appeared by nature to possess the virtues, without the vices of what we called civilized life. I did not observe the appearance of any offensive weapons whatever. They very readily partook of anything offered, wine, &c; of noyeau they highly approved, and I have no doubt, the good interpreter will recollect the name."[14]

Eddis gave the interpreter a copy of Broughton's engraved "Panoramic View of Napachan," which delighted the Okinawans. He offered them a copy of the New Testament in a Chinese translation; this they could read fluently, but they refused it, saying that acceptance meant death. They pretended not to be able to read Japanese and would accept no other books.

For the next quarter-century British policy toward the Ryukyus was one of moderate interest in trading possibilities. The record was marred by one incident—in 1824—which bred difficulties.

A British ship dropped anchor at Tokara-jima, the small island lying between Amami Oshima and Kyushu, used by the Okinawans as a point of transshipment for goods en route to Kagoshima. British sailors seized and killed cattle and took what supplies they wanted wherever they found them. Angry villagers tried to drive them off, and in the melee several persons were killed on each side. This was reported to Edo at once, whereupon the Japanese government in 1825 issued a new expulsion decree, which was expected to apply in the Ryukyus:

"As to the mode of proceeding on the arrival of foreign vessels, many proclamations have formerly been issued, and one was expressly issued in 1806 with respect to Russian ships. Also several years ago an English vessel committed outrages at Nagasaki [the 'Phaeton,' in 1808], and in later years the English have visited the various ports in boats, demanding fire-wood, water and provisions. In the past year they landed forcibly, and seized rice and grain in the junks and cattle on the islands. The continuation of such insolent proceedings, as also the intention of introducing the Christian religion having come to our knowledge, it is impossible to look on with indifference. Not only England, but also the Southern Barbarians and Western Countries are of the Christian religion which is prohibited among us. Therefore, if in future foreign vessels should come near any port whatsoever, the local inhabitants shall conjointly drive them away; but should they go away (peaceably) it is not necessary to pursue them. Should any foreigners land anywhere, they must be arrested or killed, and if the ship approaches the shore it must be destroyed."[15]

This surly rejection of all foreign intercourse had little effect in the Ryukyus. Tokara was within Satsuma's domains; this was a clash between the Japanese and the Western world which they were determined to exclude, but it took place uncomfortably close to Okinawa.

In 1827 H.M.S. "Blossom" put in twice at Naha. In a narrative published later the commanding officer, Captain Beechey, devoted a chapter to the Ryukyus, noting the solicitous care with which the "humane Loochuans" attended the needs of the sick among his ship's company: "These good people had been put to much trouble and anxiety on account of the strangers, and had so ingratiated themselves with them, that as the moment approached, the desire for their departure was proportionately lessened, and when the day arrived, they

PLATE 13. THE PRINCE OF RYUKYU AND HIS SONS, 1816. *A sketch from life, published in 1818 to illustrate Captain Basil Hall's account of his voyage to Korea and Okinawa. (See page 249 et seq.)*

PLATE 14. A PRIEST AND A GENTLEMAN OF RYUKYU, 1816. *The plates illustrating Hall's narrative were prepared at Calcutta by Wm. Havell, after sketches made on Okinawa by C.W. Browne of the Royal Navy.*

PLATE 15. OKINAWANS OF ALL CLASSES BIDDING AFFECTIONATE FAREWELL TO THEIR BRITISH FRIENDS, 1816. *Several 19th-century traveler's journals describe the admirable friendliness with which visitors were greeted in the Ryukyus and the emotional nature of Okinawan farewells. Here the British artists have caught the spirit which pervaded Hall's sojourn in the islands. (See page 258.)*

PLATE 16. A TRIBUTE SHIP BEING PREPARED AT NAHA FOR THE VOYAGE TO CHINA IN
1828. *The despatch and reception of tribute ships and embassies were great occasions in the
lives of the isolated Okinawans. Here a tribute ship ready to sail has been sketched by William
Smyth and engraved by F. Finden to illustrate Captain Beechey's narrative, published at
London in 1831. (See pages 262–63.)*

PLATE 17. A "GENTLEMAN OF LOO CHOO." *Another sketch made during Hall's visit. This illustrates the manner in which the design of a pin (kanzashi) thrust through the topknot indicated the rank of the wearer. The loose, ungirdled cloak is marked by designs of Chinese origin.*

testified their regret in a warm but manly manner, shook Captain Beechy and all the officers heartily by the hand and each gave some little token of regard, which they begged the officers to keep in remembrance of them. As they moved from the anchorage, the inhabitants assembled on the housetops as before, upon the tombs, on the forts, and on every place that would afford them a view of their operations, some waving umbrellas and others fans."[16]

While at sea they had encountered an English whaler, the "Tuscan":

"The master of the 'Tuscan' informed me [writes Beechey] that the preceeding year his ship's company had been so severely afflicted with disease, that he found it necessary to put into Loochoo, where he was well received, and his people treated with the greatest kindness. He was supplied with fresh meat and vegetables daily, without being allowed to make any other payment than that of a chart of the world, which was the only thing the natives would accept.

"The salute which the Alceste and Lyra had fired on the 25th of October [1816] was well remembered by these people, and they had an idea that it was an annual ceremony performed in commemoration of something connected with the King of England. On the return of this day, during the Tuscan's visit, they concluded that the ship would observe the same ceremony, and looked forward with much anxiety and delight to the event, that the Master of the whaler was obliged to rub up his four patereroes, and go through the salute without any intermission, as the Loochooans counted the guns as they were fired."[17]

In August, 1832, the British ship "Lord Amherst" cruised northward along the China coast and crossed over to Naha, exploring commercial prospects in the China Sea and probing Japan's outer line of defense. These were official interests, represented principally in the person of M.H.H. Lindsay, of the Honorable East India Company in China, and Captain Rees, commander and surveyor in the Royal Navy. Lindsay was conversant with the Chinese language, but as an assistant interpreter and surgeon, the "Lord Amherst" carried a medical missionary, the Reverend Dr. Karl Friederich Augustus Gutzlaff.

This was an interesting and significant combination of military, commercial, and religious enterprise; the governments of England,

France, and the United States each in turn tried to promote one or another of these interests on Okinawa as a means to a greater end, the penetration of Japan.

Lindsay's report to the British Parliament illustrates a civilized and tolerant approach: "The principal object which I had in visiting Loo-choo was to make the experiment whether the inhabitants might not willingly engage in commercial intercourse. The description given in Captain Hall's voyage of the hospitality and amiable manners of these people has excited a lively interest concerning them. I therefore could not avoid feeling that it was incumbent upon us to bear in mind that what little connexion has hitherto subsisted between our countrymen and its inhabitants has been marked by the purest benevolence on their part. No British ship has ever touched here without experiencing their hospitality. Their motives for this conduct might appear doubtful, did it only apply to the King's ships which touched at Loo-choo in 1816 and 1827, but exactly similar hospitality and kind feeling was exhibited to our countrymen in distress, when His Majesty's ship Providence was wrecked here in 1797. I determined to deliver a short statement expressive of our wishes, but if it was objected to comply with them, not to press it in any way which might prove disagreeable, or tend to lessen those friendly sentiments which were established by the kind and judicious conduct of Captain Maxwell towards them. I therefore drew up the following paper, to be presented to the chiefs with whom we might first communicate; and if the proposal made was favorably received, it would then be fitting time to write a petition to the King, and accompany it with suitable presents."[18]

Lindsay's paper for the "chiefs" stated briefly the nature of this voyage of commercial exploration, reviewed the history of Ryukyu-British relations, and expressed British appreciation for the hospitality which had invariably been found on Okinawa's shores. It then continued: "These friendly sentiments subsisting between us, we have now come here wishing to establish commercial intercourse, whereby mutual advantages may arise to both parties, and the revenues of your country would be increased, whilst it would contribute towards the prosperity of the people in general. We therefore request the great mandarins to consult together on the subject, and report it to the highest authorities."

Lindsay in due course delivered this, and while waiting for the reply he and his associates (including Gutzlaff) spent some time ashore in pleasant social intercourse with a number of Okinawan officials: "However prominent urbanity and gentleness of disposition may be among the Loo-chooans, it could not blind us, though strongly prepossessed in their favour, to the utter indifference to truth, which they manifest on all occasions. Truth, indeed, appears barely to be considered in the light of a virtue among them, if we may judge from the careless manner in which they saw themselves convicted of the most flagrant self-contradiction in the space of a few minutes."

Gutzlaff's narrative makes clear that these contradictions had to do generally with Okinawa's foreign relations, and most particularly with her relations with Japan.

On August 26 Lindsay received a reply, which quoted back to him the text of his request, omitting all his complimentary references to the Okinawan people, and concluded: "Upon examination, it appears that the wish entertained by your honourable kingdom to establish trade with our mean nation originated in sentiments of cordial friendship, for which we are highly grateful; but our mean country is a mere jungle and by no means extensive; the land is sterile, so that there is scarcely any produce; neither is any gold or silver found in it. Thus we possess nothing to offer in exchange for your cloth, camlets, and calicoes. Moreover, our mean kingdom has never had any law for the regulation of trade with foreign nations. Though this is a trifling concern, yet we can by no means change our laws, which are very strict; therefore it is truly difficult to report to the King. . . . We conclude, we beseech Hoo Hea-me Tajin [Lindsay] to examine thoroughly these reasons, as before assigned, which prevent our trading. This is the reply."[19]

Lindsay conceded the position and gave up further effort to open trade, thanking the government meanwhile for its courtesies. He noted with interest that the local scholars were attempting to build up a dictionary of English terms, begun during Hall's visit and continued with the help of Beechey's men and of Captain Stavers of the ship "Partridge," which had visited Naha in February, 1832.

The Rev. Dr. Gutzlaff lacked Lindsay's delicacy of feeling; he was a zealot unshakably confident that, in any conflict of interests anywhere,

Christians, by definition, were right, heathens were by definition wrong. With the first notation in his journal concerning Okinawa he sets the tone of subsequent Protestant missionary activity for twenty years:

"Some of the mandarins immediately invited us on shore. They spoke the mandarin dialect fluently, and showed us every attention, but objected strongly to our going farther than the jetty. . . . We . . . however, went up to the temple [nearby] without taking any notice of their objections.

"They showed us a card, left by Captain Stevens [Stavers] of the Partridge, who had been here in February. We saw also the commencement of an English and Loo-choo dictionary, written in their own and the Chinese character. In their behaviour, they are friendly and polite, though very inquisitive about the China men we had on board. But when they saw our wish to walk, they were highly displeased. . . . We could perceive a certain distrust, and an extreme reserve about them, which seemed to us unaccountable. . . ."[20]

In Gutzlaff's account, too, we find an early example of attempts to discredit or belittle the highly favorable reports on Okinawa which had reached the public through Broughton, Hall, Maxwell, M'Leod, Eddis, and Beechey. The mariners all had reason to be grateful for the hospitality of the Okinawans; the missionaries, by contrast, expected— indeed, demanded—that the Okinawans show gratitude for opportunities to abandon heathen religions and the superstitious ways of their ancestors.

But even Gutzlaff softened a bit:

"We were conducted, by several mandarins, to the temples which [in 1816] had been converted into a hospital by the humane Loochooans. Though not so picturesque as the description would lead us to suppose, it is indeed a beautiful place. . . .

"Anjah, so often mentioned by Captain Beechy, was introduced to us today. He spoke some phrases in Chinese, but soon recollected a few sentences of English which he repeated very formally. He likewise was very reserved at first; but soon forgot the restrictions laid upon him, and uttered his feelings in unrestrained, and often striking remarks.

They were generally so complimentary, and so excessive in their professions of friendship, that we were at a loss how to answer all their polite observations. . . . I distributed today, some books among them, which they received very gladly. I perceived no reluctance to receive freely what was offered freely; but could plainly see that the principal mandarins by no means wished the people to take them. . . .

"We received [August 24] the first provisions consisting of fruits and other vegetables. The Loochooans have so graceful a manner in making their presents, that the value is quite enhanced by it. . . .

"We found in the Lin-hae Temple a great number of mandarins, anxiously awaiting us where they had prepared a very palatable collation. They showed more good sense in their conversation today than ever we had observed in China. By their questions respecting the trade which several European nations carried on at Canton, they discovered [i.e., disclosed] much geographical knowledge. They were able to converse upon politics with great volubility, and gave us to understand that they preferred the friendship of China to that of England because the former was nearer. We do not doubt that they have received strict orders from China to keep strangers aloof, and to treat them with distance and reserve, yet they are too good natured to confess it. Though they frequently alluded to their intercourse with China, at Fuh-chow, where Anjah had seen us this year, yet they disclaimed all intercourse with Japan, and said that the three junks from Satsuma which lay in the harbor [at Naha] had been driven hither by stress of weather. . . ."[21]

Gutzlaff and his companions were eager to gather information concerning Japan; he therefore took his doctor's kit down to the harbor. Despite opposition strongly expressed by the unhappy Okinawan officials, he insisted upon treating several Japanese sailors who suffered a venereal disease, distributing missionary tracts the while.

"We could never discover the reason of their objections to our distributing books among the people; but we overcame their scruples by giving them freely to all the officers as well as to the people, and after receiving them, they generally came to pay us their thanks. Whenever we gave anything else *privately*, they would gladly accept it, though they have taken books in preference; but everything *openly* offered them, was always declined. For the least thing which we gave them, they offered something in return, but their giving and receiving was all by stealth. . . .

"We tried today to go into the village, and notwithstanding their extreme anxiety to prevent us, succeeded. We entered a house, or rather a temple, around which the tablets of their ancestors were very neatly arranged. We afterwards scrambled over the splendid mausoleums, which were built in magnificent Chinese style. . . . We concluded that they are as profuse in their offerings to the manes of their forefathers, as the Chinese are. I am anxious to know how they will regard the treatise on the immortality of the soul, which I gave them.

"The promise which they yesterday made of sending us the provisions today, they kept punctually. They were liberal also in their gifts. We, on our part, had sent to his majesty the King, or rather the Chee-foo of the islands, a variety of presents, and among them three bibles, which were very well received. O, that the glorious Gospel may enter the hearts of these amiable people, and form them for heaven!"

After a well-served dinner Gutzlaff noted:

"We admired the good order and propriety exhibited in the feast, among a great crowd of spectators. Good manners seem to be natural to the Loochooans.

"After dinner we took a long walk among the hills and groves of this delightful island. We saw several women working very hard in the field; and the peasantry appeared to be poorly clad and in poor condition; yet they were as polite as the most accomplished mandarins. . . .

"We took an affectionate leave of our kind hosts. In reviewing our intercourse with them, I think that their politeness and kindness are very praiseworthy. They are, however, by no means those simple and innocent beings which we might at first suppose them to be. Upon inquiry we found that they had among them the same severe punishments as at Corea; that they possessed arms likewise but are averse to use them. The Chinese *tael* and cash is current among them, but very scarce. The manufactures are few and neat; their houses and clothes are always kept clean. They are certainly a diminutive race, and everything which they possess or build seems proportionately small. While the Japanese regard them with utmost contempt as an effeminate race, we will freely acknowledge that they are the most friendly and hospitable people, which we have met during all our voyage."[22]

Adversity in mission work on the China coast did not sweeten Gutzlaff. He visited Okinawa for the second time, in 1837, aboard the British warship "Raleigh," which was bound for the Bonin Islands to claim them for the British crown. At Naha, Gutzlaff transshipped to the American ship "Morrison," which lay in the harbor. This was a merchantman en route to Japan in a vain effort to return five Japanese castaways who had been for some time at Canton.

Aboard the "Morrison" were the missionary-doctor Peter Parker and the missionary-interpreter Samuel Wells Williams. Both left records of adventures ashore while waiting for the "Raleigh" to come in. The doctor tried forcibly to demonstrate smallpox vaccination. With the interpreter Gutzlaff he pushed into private houses and into temples and shrines with callous indifference to public and private feeling.

The Okinawans were alarmed by this rendezvous in the harbor. Here was no chance accident of adverse winds or shipwreck bringing foreigners to their shores. The "Raleigh" proposed to seize Ogasawara, territory which the Japanese for centuries had believed to be their own; the "Morrison" was attempting to breach the seclusion laws. The two had met, according to plan, at Okinawa. The presence of the two ships was made known at once to Satsuma and Edo.

Williams, Gutzlaff, and Parker, all of whom knew some Chinese, showed unquenchable curiosity about the town of Naha and its suburbs, brushing aside all requests that they stay close to the quay and the waterfront. The Okinawans mistrusted the rude visitors and resented such intrusion. Their attitude annoyed the missionaries.

"To my knowledge [wrote Gutzlaff] no foreign trader committed ever any violence here; yet the natives, always dreaming of conquest, can scarcely imagine that a ship should come to these remote regions without entertaining hopes of subjugating the islands." He likened the country women to ponies, "with whom they seemed to rank on a par. We had at this time better opportunity for observation than our predecessors. The general aspect of things renders the impressions which remained from my last visit less favourable; the Loo Chooans do not improve upon nearer inspection. Several circumstances conspire to keep the great mass of the people in a state of poverty. . . ."[23]

By this time Parker, Williams, and Gutzlaff had discovered the role which Satsuma played in Okinawan affairs, and had recognized the heavy economic disabilities under which the people struggled to satisfy Satsuma's tax and tribute requirements. They had discovered the strength of Okinawan ties with Japan, denied by the Okinawans but no longer possible to conceal. This knowledge suggested the possibility that Japan could be penetrated for God through Okinawa. Converts made among the Okinawans and tracts left there could be expected (they thought) to reach the Japanese through Kagoshima. A grand scheme of doctrinal infiltration now took shape; missionary policy toward the Ryukyus dated from this "Morrison" visit and was maintained with great persistence until Perry opened Japan to direct intercourse.

Both Parker and Gutzlaff gave medical aid freely to persons suffering from diseases of the skin and spent hours explaining Western pharmacology to doctors sent down from Shuri to interview them. "Being recognized by several Loo Choo chiefs with whom I had become acquainted at my previous visit, they heartily welcomed me, and made many inquiries about my former companions. They repeatedly asked how many vessels may still be coming, and evidently were tired of supplying them with provisions. At the fort on the entrance they had stationed seven soldiers with clubs, in order to give something like a military appearance to their harbour. For the provisions furnished to H.M. Ship *Raleigh* they obstinately refused receiving any compensation, lest it might have the appearance of bartering or trading with foreigners."[24]

The British were not satisfied with China's desire to regulate and control foreign trade, nor with Japan's desire to exclude it. Traffic in opium—a trade with which Gutzlaff and other pious men did not hesitate to associate themselves—became a prime issue at Canton in 1839, and late in that year the first Anglo-Chinese War began.

British naval vessels gathered along the China coast, making the

Chusan Islands the point of rendezvous. On August 14 the transport "Indian Oak," with some seventy persons aboard, was thrown up on the northern shores of Okinawa in a heavy storm.

Two Indian seamen managed to get a line ashore, and soon the entire ship's company was safely on the beach. "We were met by the islanders and greeted with great kindness and hospitality. . . . Here they presented us with hot tea, and rice made up in balls. I only regret my inability to do justice to those kind-hearted people. Greater kindness and hospitality could not be shown by any nation than was shown to us by them."[25]

The narrator (J.J.B. Bowman, British agent for transports) spoke Malay; two of the ship's carpenters, Chinese from Malaya, spoke an "indifferent Malay" with Bowman and sufficient Fukien dialect to make themselves understood among some of the Okinawans. Thus awkwardly the castaways began a sojourn of six weeks on Okinawa. Soon, however: "We found one Lewchew gentleman of some rank, and a very intelligent man, that spoke and understood a few words of English, which he said he learned from Captain Beechy of H.M.S. Blossom that had touched at the islands about fourteen years before on a visit."[26]

Having surveyed the wreck and taken measure of the problem, the Okinawans promised to send the strangers to Singapore or Canton on an Okinawan vessel, but requested the forlorn group to stay meanwhile within a village near the beach while all hands set about helping with the salvage work.

"Nothing can exceed the honesty of these good and kind-hearted people; greater temptation could not be offered to any men; articles of gold, silver, clothing, wines, beer and spirit strewed in every direction [from the point of shipwreck] but not one even touched or missing; the greatest anxiety and every means used to render our situation comfortable.

"[We continue] to experience the same kind treatment from these excellent and polite people. As yet have not seen any arms among them; from eighty to one hundred men with ten to twenty canoes assisting our people in saving articles from wreck. . . ."[27]

A house and barracks were built to accommodate the officers and men, and it was determined to build a small craft, using salvaged material plus such other supplies as the Okinawans could provide. With this it was proposed to cross over to the Chusan archipelago, where units of the British fleet were known to be.

Bowman's diary continued: "The kindness and attention of these good people to all our little wants exceeds everything; every convenience, even a bathing house, is attached to our dwelling."

Suddenly this friendly scene was thrown into utmost confusion. On August 30—two weeks after the disaster—the spokesmen for the Okinawans sounded an alarm; a great party of armed Japanese had appeared nearby. It was necessary to call in all the shipwrecked men to confine them close within the barracks. A small craft which had been salvaged from the "Indian Oak" now hastily put out to sea, pursued for some distance by a canoe filled with hostile Japanese.

On shore, meanwhile, Okinawans begged the English officers and men to hide their arms, and to make no show of resistance, but to leave matters of parley with them. These, they said, were men from Tokara, and were wicked and dangerous. We now know that they were a Japanese garrison force dispatched from Tokara by the Satsuma officers. All were in a uniform battle-dress, heavily armed with two swords, matchlocks, and bows and arrows.

It was obvious that the Europeans had been cast up on the reefs against their will and that they were not demanding trade; on the contrary, they were eager to get away from the island. On this point the Okinawan leaders seem to have made a convincing case with the Japanese, who withdrew to camp at a distance, making no further effort to intervene directly in the salvage operation.

Working together, the Okinawans and the crew of the "Indian Oak" in time constructed a rude craft or junk, which they dubbed the "Lewchew." The British were amused to learn that Chinese at Naha had assured the Okinawans that British forces on the China coast had been roundly beaten by the imperial Chinese army and navy.

On September 16 two British ships hove into sight searching for the "Indian Oak." They were the brig "Cruizer" and H.M.S. "Nimrod," under Captain Barlow's command. They had picked up the small boat which had escaped a fortnight earlier. Barlow wished to repay the Okinawans for the labor and materials which were going into the makeshift craft, the "Lewchew," and to requite them in some way for the provisions and shelter which had been so freely made available:

"The Lewchewans positively refused payment, stating all they expected or wished was, that in the event of any of their vessels calling at our ports, or meeting with a similar fate, they might be treated kindly and returned to their country.

"[We] received up to the last moment the same kindness and attention we have ever experienced from the first moment of our landing from the wreck."

As they prepared to depart on September 27 the British officers felt that some gesture of thanks must be made. Accordingly the narrator "accompanied lieut. Williams and the young gentlemen on shore, with the presents from her majesty queen Victoria to his majesty the king of Lewchew, presented by Captain Barlow, viz: a picture of a female reclining on a couch, twelve copies of the Saturday and Penny magazines, a telescope, and one small looking glass."[28]

This gift list reads rather like the inventory of a junior officer's cabin aboard the "Nimrod," but these trivial gifts served their purpose as tokens of respect for hospitality pleasantly given and gladly received.

In his report to the *Nautical Magazine and Naval Chronicle for 1841* (London), Bowman concluded: "Indeed, how much is there which might be copied by civilized nations in the behaviour of the uncivilized people of the Loo Choo islands." And in writing some years later to the founder of the Loo Choo Naval Mission he observed: "I shall ever consider that a heavy debt of gratitude is due by me, and all those who were, by the wreck of the Transport 'Indian Oak,' thrown upon their bounty."[29]

The entire incident—and Shuri's position in the matter—was carefully reported to the shogun's government at Edo by the special envoy, Hamahiga *Pechin*.

During 1842 and 1843 several other British ships touched at Okinawa. Captain Sir Edward Belcher, in H.M.S. "Samarang," spent twenty-one days ashore in Yaeyama and Miyako, charting reefs and shoal waters and making observations needed by the Admiralty in London. He quite accurately assessed the administrative arrangements which bound the outer islands to Shuri. He noted no arms whatsoever among the people and decided that government rested on moral suasion rather than on force. He found the island people living for the most part in utter poverty and in squalor.

He employed local men in the survey work: "Sometimes our coolies and attendants amounted to fifty or more, and being repeatedly changed as we moved from village to village or to other islands, it may be computed that our property passed through the hands of hundreds. Not a solitary case of dishonesty or what could be called theft occurred. . . . In every instance, when parts of our instruments were accidently missing, the utmost grief and uneasiness was exhibited until everything was recovered. These exhibitions of feeling lead one naturally to the conclusion that they are an eminently moral people. Quarrels were not witnessed, and the humble and modest *kowtow* of the . . . Lewchewans was in universal use among the highest classes. . . ."[30]

Britain's victory in China resulted in the Treaty of Nanking, signed August 29, 1842. By its terms five Chinese ports were opened to foreign trade and residence; Britain acquired Hongkong as a crown colony; and Christian missionaries were granted permission to operate anywhere within one day's journey of an open port. A supplementary treaty in 1843 provided for further trade regulations and promised "most favoured nation" treatment, which is to say, China promised to extend to the British any privileges which she might thereafter extend to any other foreign nation. This opened the way for other powers to seek trading privileges and concessions along the China coast: soon the United States, France, Belgium, Sweden, and Norway had similar treaties, and there were new Chinese treaties with Russia.

All this was made known to the Okinawans at Fukien, though not without some inaccuracy. They were alarmed, and so were the Japanese. If China hereafter made formal claim to the Ryukyu Islands, based on the tributary subordination, the terms of these treaties might be construed to apply at Naha. It was becoming evident that the old arrangement of "dual subordination" would soon be challenged, and the old pretenses of suzerainty would have to be given up, either by China or by Japan.

FRENCH PRESSURE AT SHURI AND SATSUMA'S REACTION[31]

In March, 1844, the French warship "Alcmene" put in at Naha, demanding trading privileges, which Shuri steadfastly refused to grant. The French told the Okinawans that the British were planning to invade Japan and would seize Okinawa as a base of attack. They proposed therefore that the Ryukyu kingdom should place itself under French protection. This too the Okinawans refused to consider.

To Shuri's great consternation, however, the French warship insisted on putting ashore a Catholic missionary, named Forcade, and his Chinese assistant, Augustine Ho. These men, the French said, would remain on Okinawa for language study; they would be needed as interpreters when a large French naval force returned to press for formal agreements between the Emperor of France and the Ryukyu kingdom.

The unwelcome strangers were lodged in the Ameku Seigen-ji, a small Buddhist temple used as a hostel for foreign visitors since 1816. Close watch was set on all their movements. Priests and military threats —here was the dread combination again, on Okinawan soil in direct violation of Edo's expulsion decrees.

Edo was well informed of events on the China coast—the British demands, the war, and the concessions wrung from China by the Treaty of Nanking. With an eye to their own interests, Dutch monopolists at Nagasaki warned Japan that both Britain and France were planning to establish bases on Okinawa. These events in 1844 seemed to bear out the story.

There were two schools of thought at Edo. One advocated a moderate policy and possibly some conciliatory enlargement of foreign commerce. The other advocated stern rejection of any further overtures from the Western powers, and for a time these latter views prevailed.

Soon after Hamahiga *Pechin* reported to Edo on the "Indian Oak" affair, an envoy reached Japan from the King of Holland to advise the shogun that it would be in Japan's interest to relax the seclusion laws voluntarily, before the other European powers took matters into their own hands. Months of debate and conflict at Edo produced a reply which said in part: "When the time came for determining with what countries [Japanese] communication should be permitted, intercourse was limited to Korea and Luchu, and trade to your Excellencies' country [Holland] and China. Aside from these countries, all communication was strictly disallowed. . . . Henceforth pray cease correspondence."[32]

This was not an end to the matter. Satsuma saw here a new opportunity. Plans were matured at Kagoshima which would enable Japan to keep persistent foreigners at a distance by granting them a trading base at Naha not unlike the restricted trading station occupied by the Dutch at Nagasaki. If this were done, Satsuma would enjoy the fruits of a monopoly on trade between Naha and Kagoshima which the Edo government had declared legitimate.

Meanwhile, the missionary Forcade and his Chinese aide made no progress whatever at Naha. They reported that Okinawans were a happy people who were quite ready to make friends, but they themselves—the missionaries—were restricted, spied upon, and made uncomfortable in a thousand ways. They became aware of Satsuma's role in this, and of Japanese agents keeping watch on the Okinawans.

The French government had learned nothing from history. It would have been impossible for them to select agents less suited to their needs and to their interests in Okinawa as a steppingstone into Japan. The association of missionary effort with diplomacy and military pressure revived and heightened the issues to which the Japanese government had reacted so violently in the past. Added to this was the blundering use of a Chinese interpreter, who was discovered to be an uncultured refugee, a "rice Christian," once the inmate of a Chinese jail. He could gain no hearing among the educated officials at Shuri and Naha.

On May 2, 1846, the French warship "Sabine" dropped anchor at Naha. To the dismay of the Okinawans, a second priest, named Leturdu, was put ashore. The "Sabine's" commanding officer, Captain Guerin, made an official call upon the chief magistrate of Shuri. In the course of this interview he announced casually that he intended to move his ship to Unten Harbor on the Motobu Peninsula. There he was to rendezvous with Admiral Cecille and the warships "Cléopâtre" and "Victorieuse."

This move was made on June 7 over Shuri's strong objections. Satsuma's agents and the Okinawan authorities wanted to keep the foreigners under closest surveillance, which was difficult to do at such a distance. On June 8 Admiral Cecille received the local magistrate from the Hokuzan district aboard the "Cléopâtre" at Unten. Ten days later the admiral went ashore at Kami-Unten Village with great fanfare of drums and trumpets to meet the king's representatives and to open formal but unsuccessful negotiations for a treaty.

The French were rude and arrogant. If the move to Unten was designed to make it more difficult for the Okinawans to negotiate and to limit opportunities for conference and concert of policy among the highest officials at Shuri, then it was a success. If it was designed to intimidate the Okinawan representatives and shorten the discussions leading to a treaty satisfactory to the French, then it failed. Certainly in Okinawan eyes the insistence upon the remote and shabby fishing village of Unten as a site for official negotiations was incredibly ridiculous.

While all these things were taking place on Okinawa, a series of conferences were held at Kagoshima and at Edo. Shimazu Nariakira (known also as Saihin) was then heir presumptive to the headship of the Satsuma clan. He was interested in developing foreign relations, for he had much more than trade in view.

Saihin was sensitive to the changes which were overtaking Japan's international position and was convinced that seclusion policies soon would have to be changed drastically. In the French proposal to open trade with the Ryukyu kingdom he saw a larger opportunity. He was prepared to put up a large sum—from ten to twenty thousand gold *ryo*—to capitalize a trading venture with the foreigners. An important party of stubborn conservatives at Kagoshima rejected his views and proposals; nevertheless, he took his plans to the highest officers at Edo.[33] Here again he found divided opinion and serious opposition in the most important departments of government. But some prominent men approved—most notable among them Lord Abe Masahiro, Chief of the Great Council of State, who had been recalled to office by news of the French action in Okinawa. At last the shogun summoned the Lord of Satsuma and his heir, Saihin, and in secret conference on May 27, 1846, indirectly sanctioned a trading agreement with the French. He did this by leaving decisions in Saihin's hands, with an admonition that the matter must be concealed from the other feudal lords and that it was to be worked out in a manner which would cause no future trouble for Edo.

Saihin now attempted to exploit the government's policy in a peculiar and devious way. While he publicly declared himself in support of the exclusion policies, and advocated strong coastal defences, he expanded trading operations at the Ryukyu depot in Fukien, with a view gradually to transfer operations to Naha and thence, perhaps, to a port within his own domains in Kyushu. He projected the development of a monopoly on heavy-arms manufacture within his fief. By rousing the fears of the country, the demand for arms would increase steadily. By using Naha as an intermediary base, he expected to profit from the import of weapons. He shrewdly decided that Edo would be unable to resist French or British demands on distant Okinawa if they were backed by force and that concessions acceptable to the foreigners there—especially freedom to trade—might satisfy the Western powers and divert their attention from the ports of Japan proper.

While these long-drawn-out negotiations were concluded favorably at Edo, the Shuri government, unaware of them, delivered a note to Admiral Cecille on July 5, 1846, stating that the King of Ryukyu must decline the offer of a treaty with the King of the French. On July 17 the French squadron left Unten for Japan, taking with them the missionary Forcade, but hinting darkly that French warships would come again to make known the French king's reaction to Shuri's unsatisfactory answer.[34]

Another missionary, Mathieu Adnet, had meanwhile joined Leturdu at Naha in a study of the Okinawan language. They did not prosper. They made no converts, but in 1847 a young Japanese named Iwajiri Eisuke arrived from Kagoshima, sent down by the Satsuma authorities to study French. It was represented to the missionaries that this man was from Tokara Island, the midway trading station. Saihin hoped to have his own well-trained interpreter ready when his plans could be put in motion. This was not to be; young Iwajiri died in 1848 at Naha, and on July 1, in the same year, Mathieu Adnet also died, leaving a discouraged Leturdu and Augustine Ho alone at the mission station. On August 27 a French ship put in, took the two men aboard, and sailed away.

THE MISSIONARY BETTELHEIM APPEARS IN OKINAWA

On May 1, 1846 (the day before the French warship "Sabine" arrived), the British ship "Starling" came in, bringing a missionary named Bernard Jean Bettelheim, his wife, two infants, a spinster "infant-teacher," and a Chinese assistant. The hospitality which the Okinawans had shown to British naval officers and seamen for half a century was now to be repaid in strange coin.

Herbert John Clifford's "Mission to the Loo Choos" was about to begin. The brash and thoughtless young lieutenant of 1816, who lightly talked of "chinchinning Joss," had been swept up and transformed in the zealous missionary movement which so deeply agitated England and the United States in the 1830's and 40's. The memory of the incident in Naha Harbor had preyed heavily upon him. This was his repentent gesture.

He had organized the "Loo-choo Naval Mission" and had become its Honorable Secretary. His Grace the Duke of Manchester, Commander of the Royal Navy, became a patron; vice-patrons were admirals; the trustees and committeemen were captains, commanders, and lieutenants. There were branches in Ireland and Scotland, and a special plea for support went to naval personnel and merchant seamen who had at one time or another visited the Ryukyu Islands. It was in this a remarkable organization. Clifford's publications on behalf of the mission were issued under the title *The Claims of Loochoo on British Liberality*, and Britain's obligation to repay the Okinawans in some measure formed a constant theme in his appeals for funds: "I am not aware that any return has ever been made to the Loochoo people for all their hospitality and kindness to two of her Majesty's ships, and therefore I feel that a debt of gratitude is still due, and would now urge on the British Christian public, that as we have reaped their carnal things, we should repay them in spiritual things by sending them, even at this late hour, after a lapse of a quarter of a century, the Word of Life, in return for all their more than Samaritan benevolence to our people."[35]

Clifford's appeals brought a remarkable response; a substantial fund was raised, and a search was made for suitable men to go into the field. It was planned to send an ordained minister with a medical assistant, but competition for qualified men was keen and candidates were few. The missionary societies of the Established Church and of such dissenting congregations as Clifford approved were unwilling or unable to extend their activities to a new field, where, he feared, "the iron fangs of Popery, or the more smooth, cat-like talons of Puseyism [will] fasten their deadly grasp on my long loved Loochoo."

The choice fell upon Dr. Bettelheim. To understand the events of the next eight years at Naha and the formulation of British and American policy, we must review his remarkable earlier career in Europe, which throws light upon his behavior in Okinawa. We must rely upon his own statements, for what they are worth, in sketching his life before he became a convert to Christianity and reached England.[36]

Bettleheim was born into a noted Jewish family of Pressburg, Hungary, in 1811. His early studies were designed to prepare him to become a rabbi. It is said that he could read and write Hebrew, German, and French before he was ten years of age, but for reasons undisclosed he left home in his twelfth year and began to teach, pursuing his studies meanwhile at five different higher schools. In September, 1836, he took a degree in medicine at Padua, Italy. If we are to credit his biographers, he filed no less than forty-seven "scientific dissertations" with the Imperial Court Library at Vienna within the next three years, for an average of better than one dissertation completed per month.

While engaged in such prolific writing, he traveled from practice to practice, from Padua to Trieste to Unsine, then back to Trieste, to Naples, Sicily, and Greece. In 1840 we find him "chief surgeon" on an Egyptian man-of-war, then shortly thereafter "head surgeon" of a regiment in the town of Magnesia, in Turkey. There he fell in with British missionaries, who gave him "an Italian Bible, a Popish prayer-book and a German Gospel," and with these he began the study of Christianity. This led to his conversion and baptism by a British chaplain at Smyrna. Meanwhile he found time to dispute with local rabbis, summing up his theological arguments in a controversial pamphlet which he published in French.

At this point he resigned his post, wrangled over salary settlements at Constantinople for some months, and at last reached London. He was fired with determination to be "authorized" by the Established Church of England to preach to the Jews of the Mediterranean area. From this time forth he kept voluminous diaries.

At London he was further inspired by an opportunity to stay in lodgings frequented by well-known missionaries, including Dr. Peter Parker and Karl Friederich August Gutzlaff (who had been together on Okinawa in 1837), by David Livingstone and others. He spent some months in a huge controversy with the bishops of the Church of England. According to Bettelheim, these narrow men demanded that he spend at least three years in study at Oxford or Cambridge; they refused to accept his parade of European degrees and they objected to the ordination of one so recently converted from the Jewish faith.

In disgust he left the Church of England and attached himself to an independent home-mission chapel in London. About this time he became a naturalized British subject and married the only daughter of a wealthy thread manufacturer. Ten months later a child was born, whose name, Victoria Rose, embodied that of the queen and of the infant's godfather, Sir George Rose, president of the London Jews' Society, an association of converts from the Jewish faith.

"After much research of scripture" and a quarrel with his sponsors, Bettelheim resigned his pastorate with the independent-church group and rejoined the Church of England. According to Bettelheim, he was now appointed agent or missionary of the London Jews' Society, which promised to send him to the Middle East. According to the society's records, however: "Dr. Bettelheim made two applications for work under our Society, but was never appointed on the OFFICIAL staff. His only connection with the Society was as a probationary missionary, and after a short term his connection with our Society was severed."[37] His departure from this association was abrupt, but he counted it a blessing in disguise, for about this time he was asked by the Loochoo Naval Mission to accept appointment as its medical missionary to Naha.

Lieutenant Clifford (who lived in Ireland) appears to have known little of Bettelheim personally, but wrote that he had "testimonials perhaps unsurpassed by any missionary who has gone forth from this land to the heathen." Bettelheim later asserted that he had been promised ordination by the Church Missionary Society after one year's field service, but this never took place.

In proper naval style, Lieutenant Clifford issued a body of "Instructions Given for the Guidance of Dr. Bettelheim" in the name of the Loochoo Mission Committee. Having heard, perhaps, that Dr. Bettelheim was an unusually forthright individual, Clifford stressed restraint:

"The Committee would suggest that great caution on your part will be necessary . . . from the peculiarly suspicious character of the authorities regarding strangers of every description. . . . The Committee have great confidence in your prudence and talent, that you will blend 'the harmlessness of the Dove with the wisdom of the Serpent' . . . that you may be enabled to meet the stratagems of some of the most wily diplomatists in the world.

"Should you be permitted to take up your abode among the friendly Loochooans, the Committee will not attempt to dictate your mode of operation, as to securing the esteem of the people and the authorities. . . .

"Again, the Committee beg to urge the practice of the '*sauviter in modo*' with the '*fortiter in re*' in all your dealings with the kind and hospitable inhabitants of Loochoo. . . .

"It must be remembered that Loochoo is not one of the free Ports open to British commerce."[38]

With these instructions in hand, the family of three sailed from Portsmouth on September 9, 1845. After one month at sea, a son was born to them and named Bernard James Gutzlaff Bettelheim. Gutzlaff had by this time become important on the China coast, succeeding Robert Morrison as secretary-interpreter to the British legation in China, and acting as an aide to the Superintendent of Trade under the Anglo-Chinese Treaty provisions.

The Bettelheims reached Hongkong in January, 1846. The next four months were spent studying the Chinese language and cultivating friendships among British missionaries and prominent officials. At last passage across to Naha was arranged aboard the ship "Starling," of British registry but owned by a New York merchant named Henry Fessenden.

From Bettelheim's correspondence it appears that he expected to be given a princely welcome, although both he and his wife gave some thought to stratagems which might be used to get them ashore if the Okinawans showed reluctance to receive them. On the eve of departure from the China coast, April 13, 1846, Bettelheim addressed Clifford a letter in which he asked for more funds, and Clifford in turn soon found that the mission was costing just double the sum which he had anticipated would be required.

There are four sets of records which must be reconciled in order to approach the true story of Bettelheim's activities in Okinawa. There are his own voluminous diaries and letters, there are his reports to the mission (and the summaries and interpretation developed from them by Lieutenant Clifford), and there are the journals, letters, and official papers prepared by men who observed Bettelheim in Okinawa. There are, finally, the records and letters of Okinawan officials who had to grapple with the Bettelheim problem.

Bettelheim's reports to Clifford dated September 29 cover the first four months of residence on Okinawa. In these he praised God for having smoothed the way, assuring Lieutenant Clifford and his patrons that they enjoyed great prospects. "... Instead of mountains we had only to level hills to effect our reception here; we had thought to pass at least one month under the naked roof of the sky, and behold we were well-housed, even the first night of our arrival here; at present we are even comfortably lodged here; opportunities of evangelizing the country are not wanting, the authorities do us no harm, and the people wish us well. . . ."[39]

As the "Starling" anchored, a well-dressed, dignified port officer came off to greet the captain and to enquire of his needs. For a moment Bettelheim believed that perhaps the King of Ryukyu himself had come out to welcome him. Captain McCheyne, the ship's master, had made an estimate of his passenger, and was most reluctant to put the missionary family ashore over official protest. Miss James, the "infant-teacher," decided at the last moment that it would be wiser to return to the China coast aboard the "Starling."

Bettelheim circumvented Captain McCheyne and deceived the Okinawans by a simple ruse. Small Okinawan craft had put alongside late in the afternoon. When the boatmen came aboard to bring supplies, to rest, and to look about, the doctor bribed members of the "Starling's" crew to take them below decks and ply them with drink. While they were entertained in this fashion, other members of the ship's company helped Bettelheim get his immense baggage and his family over the side into the Okinawan boats. When all was ready, the tipsy, happy Okinawans were put over the side and persuaded to row in to the harbor quay. They landed late in the evening, too late to be sent back to the "Starling." Taking pity on Mrs. Bettelheim and the children, the Naha officials offered to let them stay overnight in a temple nearby, the ancient Gokoku-ji, which stood on the Nami-no-ue headland overlooking the harbor. The baggage—including a kitchen stove—was removed to shelter there. The priests tactfully moved out for the night, to give Mrs. Bettelheim privacy.

But when they returned next morning, the missionary and his family flatly refused to leave, nor could the officials from the Naha magistrate's office dislodge them. While the argument was prolonged, the "Starling" weighed anchor and sailed away, leaving port just as the French warship "Sabine" came in to put the second French priest, Leturdu, ashore.

The Bettelheims did not surrender Gokoku-ji for seven years. To prevent the rightful occupants from returning each day to worship, the clever doctor accused them of "coming to look at his wife," and thought it a good joke when the priests took him seriously and gave up attempts to repossess their property. He boarded up the sanctuary and threw out "the heathen furniture of idolatry." Although the Shuri government protested many times that this was "a place of prayer for the whole country," Bettelheim counted it an early triumph of Christianity to be able to deny it to public use.

In due time the missionary attempted to strengthen his position. He prepared an address to the government, offering to practice medicine and to teach English, geography, and astronomy. Shuri replied that the Okinawans were satisfied with Chinese medical practices, that the people were too stupid to learn or to require English, and that they were sufficiently familiar with geography and astronomy to take care of their own needs. When Bettelheim asked for instruction in Chinese, this was allowed. Tutors were assigned with the understanding that the Chinese classics were to be the texts. Again and again he attempted to use his tutors in translating Christian tracts and the Gospels into Chinese. This they refused to do, or were withdrawn at once when his activities became known to the government.

The two French priests meanwhile lived under surveillance in strict seclusion on the outskirts of Naha. They too were allowed to study Chinese, and Forcade (who later became an archbishop) is said to have compiled a dictionary list of more than ten thousand Okinawan words. These men behaved themselves with patient restraint and made no overt attempts to win converts to Christianity.

Not so with Bettelheim. At first the little family was treated with courtesy, but as the months dragged on his extravagant and rude behavior first perplexed and then angered the Okinawans. Official attempts to curb him merely provoked blustering, alarming threats. Foreign visitors soon found the doctor and the government officers "living in a state of undisguised hostility."

The growing family was a costly burden for the government. (Lucy Lewchew Bettelheim was born on Okinawa.) Shuri thought it necessary to detail nearly one hundred men to keep watch upon the intruders. A guard station was erected near Gokoku-ji, and men were assigned to accompany Bettelheim at all times when he moved about between Naha and Shuri and in the nearby countryside. Guards and tutors were changed if the magistrate felt that they were becoming too lax or lenient in their surveillance.

The problem of food, too, was a serious one. The populace was forbidden to sell directly to the foreigners, and under the watchful eye of the *metsuke* in the market place the common people usually deserted their stalls when either of the Bettelheims showed interest in their wares. To meet this difficulty the missionaries simply took what they wanted, estimated a value, and threw down whatever they considered to be a fair price. During a time of near-famine in the country the doctor once seized a load of sweet potatoes being carried through an alleyway near his residence. He was driven off by an aroused crowd. In the first few months the innate courtesy of the people and their curiosity gave him some encouragement. They gathered to watch him, and individuals dared to make friendly overtures, but this gradually gave way to tolerant indifference.

He tells with relish in his letters that he made a practice of literally breaking into houses in which he wanted to preach God's word. He records that upon one occasion children were called in from the streets at his approach and the house gates closed, whereupon he simply broke through the outer fence, beat a hole in the mat walls of the house, and forced his way in. "I was little moved with the cries of the women or the frightened screams of the children, but seated myself in the first room I could get access to and began to preach."[40]

He reported to the home mission that on occasion he made his way to Shuri to stand just outside the closed palace gates and shout his sermons in a loud voice, hoping that someone within would take heed. Sometimes he pushed his way into public town meetings, causing them to break up in confusion and despair while he harangued the scattering crowd.

He overreached himself in such zealous pursuit of souls. On January 6, 1850, he was thrown out of a private house. Six or eight guards handled him roughly and he was stoned. He lay in the streets (he claims) for more than two hours before Mrs. Bettelheim found him and put him to bed. Though he suffered from bruises and shock, he relished this hint of possible martyrdom.

He had brought with him a multigraph machine and a stock of ink and paper. With Mrs. Bettelheim's help he prepared tracts, broadsheets, and religious pictures, which he scattered in the streets. These the authorities collected and returned to him, but when they observed that he simply used them again as soon as possible, they were gathered up and handed over to the magistrate, thus gradually exhausting his resources.

His extravagant behavior could not fail to attract large crowds whenever he took up his position in the public way. He was ordered to cease these harangues, but he openly defied authority and dared preach civil disobedience, urging the people to refuse service to the government.

In an excess of zeal, on Sundays he sometimes attempted to knock burdens from the backs of workmen passing through the streets and in other ways sought to interfere with public business "on the Lord's day."

The doctor kept two vicious dogs, and he wore large spectacles which gave him a grotesque appearance in Okinawan eyes. These two features were caricatured in a popular term *In Gan-cho* (Bespectacled Dog-doctor), which passed into local usage as a term of abusive imprecation.

Bettelheim was more than a little mad; his erratic behavior may have preserved his life. The Japanese crucified missionaries and converts, including women and children; the Chinese often resorted to terrifying and deadly mob violence; but the Okinawans set on Bettelheim with sticks and stones only once in the eight long years they had to endure his

FIG. 18. GATEWAYS, SHURI CASTLE. Upper: *Zuisen-mon, the second gate.* Lower: *Kanki-mon, the first gate.*

presence. It is possible that superstitious fear of the mentally deranged restrained them, but it is more likely that the presence of French, British, and American naval forces in nearby waters had something to do with this. Bettelheim did not hesitate to suggest that these military forces would retaliate upon the kingdom if he were molested.

Bettelheim had studied some Chinese on the way out to Okinawa. For the first five years at Naha he studied the phonetic *katakana* and then attempted to learn to write in the local dialect, making what he professed to be a "translation" of the scriptures.[41] He reported to his sponsors in England that he had mastered the Okinawan dialect. This is doubtful, but nevertheless he preached for hours at a time in the open streets and market place, convinced that the Okinawans heard him with understanding. How much theological argument actually took place and how much of what he reported was merely a record of his fantasies must remain an open question. He says that he discussed the problems of heretical beliefs in the Christian church and the fine points of inter-pretation in Old Testament history. To provide a setting for his own theological views and skills in argument he records remarkable questions which (he says) were addressed to him by the Okinawans, a notably unspeculative people. One example will suffice: "If in a spiritual way we eat the body and drink the blood of Christ, what kind of a mouth has the soul?"[42]

In reports such as this he was playing to the British public which financed his activities rather than reporting on the verities of evangelical work on Okinawa, much as his close friend Gutzlaff was doing in his stories of singular travels along the China coast.

It is difficult to imagine what the Okinawans thought of such spiritual nutriment, if indeed Bettelheim's harangues made any sense to them at all. When his audience failed to respond properly, he berated them as liars, deceitful people, full of cunning and the devil's wiles. His ego could not tolerate opposition. Each new difficulty was interpreted as a "testing by the Lord"; each rebuff was a manifestation of the devil at work, spurring him on to new tirades against the Shuri government and explosive annoyance with the common people.

Bettelheim made one avowed convert in seven years. The story of this unhappy man is obscure. When his profession of Christian faith became known, he was arrested and confined. Bettelheim managed secretly to visit the wretched man. This too came to the knowledge of the officials, who forthwith had the prisoner transported to a spot far from Naha. It was reported then that he had died of the rigors of imprisonment. Bettelheim claims that he was beaten to death and was therefore a martyr.

The doctor's letters were accepted in good faith by Lieutenant Clifford and the officers of the Naval Mission. Funds were forwarded regularly to be deposited to the Bettelheim account in Hongkong. A "corresponding committee" in support of the Loochoo Mission was formed on the China coast, and every opportunity was seized upon to ship supplies to Naha. Most of these things were gifts. It became customary for officers and men aboard ships visiting at Naha to make up donations for these isolated, dedicated evangelists.

Among the ships touching briefly at Naha during these years were merchant vessels ladened with tea, textiles, or opium for the China trade, and naval vessels on Far Eastern patrol. Mariners were always glad to discover Caucasians in residence ashore, and the records attest to great generosity. Ship's carpenters made furniture for them; they were given shoes and soap, food and wine. One Welsh seaman volunteered to make trousers for the little James Gutzlaff Bettelheim, another gave Mrs. Bettelheim an accordion with which to sing hymns in the market place. The captain of H.M.S. "Sphynx" ordered a flagstaff to be erected in the Bettelheim's dooryard on the high bluff overlooking Naha Harbor.

Remittances of cash and supplies from Hongkong and Canton were irregular, but while life was monotonous, the Bettelheims suffered no great privation. Occasionally the Okinawan trading ships carried mail and packages between Naha and the Fukien coast. This was a courteous gesture and concession made by the Okinawan officials, but the doctor wrote of it as a service due him.

BETTELHEIM CREATES A PROBLEM FOR THE BRITISH GOVERNMENT

The missionary professed to love the people and to hate the government of Ryukyu. In every difficulty he saw official machination. On one occasion, not finding six hundred dollars which he had secreted at the Gokoku-ji, he instantly sent off a letter to Shuri, angrily charging that a theft had been arranged in an effort to embarrass him. In such ways every personal frustration was translated into new expressions of animosity and brought new threats against the Okinawans.

Whenever foreign ships appeared, Bettelheim pushed forward immediately, vigorously playing the self-assumed role of principal interpreter and translator. European visitors took him at his face value upon first acquaintance, delighted to find a Caucasian resident in the islands through whom they could address the government. The Okinawans soon resigned themselves to this, but they did not hesitate, many times, to call upon Bettelheim to translate and to transmit petitions fervently begging visiting captains to remove the troublesome doctor and his family. Foreigners who received such petitions through Bettelheim's own hands thought this somewhat strange, but the missionary showed no embarrassment.

Frustration prompted the doctor to think of other ways in which he could assert himself importantly. He developed the idea that he was in a key position to force Japan to open its doors, but he persuaded himself that the British government did not appreciate his true worth. He tried repeatedly to bring about an exercise of British pressure upon the Ryukyu kingdom in satisfaction of his personal demands. "I thought it not only allowable, but even my duty, to threaten that I would bring the matter before the English Government." Every foreigner who visited Naha heard his views. His long letters to the press stirred up sympathies along the China coast and in England, and these in time were translated into pressure upon the British Foreign Office to "do something" to improve the position of British subjects so grossly abused as the Bettelheims represented themselves to be at Naha.[43]

The damage he was doing could be concealed from the Loo Choo Mission officers at London, but some of the missionaries and officials on the China coast began to feel uneasy and to question his qualifications to represent the Christian faith and British interests.

Admiral Sir Thomas Cochrane visited Naha in October, 1846, scarcely four months after Bettelheim had reached the island and at the time when the energetic but not always truthful doctor was reporting to

London high prospects of success. Cochrane accused Bettelheim of masquerading as a British official. He recommended that the missionary's naturalization papers be canceled.

Bettelheim's presence had of course been reported to Satsuma. After three years of annoyance, Shuri turned to the Chinese (whether on its own initiative or at Satsuma's direction is not clear) with the request that the imperial authorities in Fukien take up the matter with the British at Canton and Hongkong. This they did, pointing out that the Nanking Treaty opened only five ports to missionary activity and that such activity had to be restricted to an area within one day's journey of the harbors. When he learned of this, Lieutenant Clifford's sense of naval discipline surpassed his missionary ardor: "We therefore trust in the Lord to overcome this difficulty also, as we cannot expect any infringement, ever so trifling, to be made in a treaty made by Britain, even though it be for the furtherance of the Gospel."

By 1849 the "Bettelheim problem" ceased to be a local affair and began to assume an international character of some concern. British authorities, with growing uneasiness, sensed that an untoward incident at Naha might affect larger plans for bringing pressure to bear upon Japan. In February an occasion was found to send H.M.S. "Mariner" to Naha to look into the causes of friction and complaint. Upon landing, March 8, the commanding officer (Captain Matheson) and the vice-consul (Robertson) were invited by Naha's chief magistrate to dine at the official reception hall to work out preliminary arrangements for a conference with the regent. Bettelheim had boarded the ship in harbor before the Naha officials could present themselves, and now, on shore, he persuaded the visitors to leave the official reception hall and remove to his own home at the temple on the hill. This they did. It was an uncalled-for rudeness, which made it necessary for the magistrate to have his feast carried to the Bettelheims' own house. On the next day the regent was entertained aboard the "Mariner." After the usual exchange of courtesies and presents, the regent presented a petition, begging the British captain to remove Bettelheim. Bettelheim, unembarrassed, translated this document and interpreted during the conference which followed. Matheson offered passage to the doctor, who refused to leave. The Okinawans insisted. Matheson informed them that they had not proved Bettelheim guilty of illegal acts and that he was therefore without power to intervene. Shuri then placed in Matheson's hands a formal petition addressed to the British government, which complained of Bettelheim's presence and requested his removal. Bettelheim countered by preparing his own petition to the British Parliament, asking it to direct that British ships be sent to Naha regularly to "protect" him.[44]

In the subsequent long-drawn-out exchange, the "Bettelheim problem" was raised to the highest Cabinet levels at London. British officials on the China coast and in London showed evident distaste for Bettelheim as a person (Hongkong's governor, Bonham, was cautious, fearing that if the doctor were given an inch of official support he would take a mile of advantage), but Matheson and the vice-consul saw in this issue an opportunity to pry open the Ryukyu Islands for trade and further to increase pressure upon Japan. The formal letter from the Okinawan officials addressed to the British government seemed to offer an entering wedge; the Okinawans might accept a plan to establish a neutral trading ground at Naha.

There was an element of international competition in this; in 1848 Commander Glynn, of the U.S.S. "Preble," had put in at Naha, en route to Japan in an unsuccessful attempt to open Japanese ports to American commerce.[45] Bettelheim had represented himself convincingly as an authority on conditions within the kingdom, and he was consulted at length. Into Commander Glynn's ears poured his complaints against the Okinawan government and people, painting them as cunning and full of all duplicity. His views colored Glynn's official report to the Navy Department at Washington. Shuri, as usual, begged Glynn to remove Bettelheim aboard the "Preble." This he declined to do, observing that Bettelheim was a British subject.

On May 22, 1849, the British yacht "Nancy Dawson" put in, commanded by a Captain Shedden. Bettelheim prepared a letter to Shuri on his own behalf, which he then persuaded the captain and his wife to present to the Okinawans as if they were arguing the doctor's case.

Meanwhile Bonham, Britain's principal officer on the China coast, had referred the "Bettelheim problem" and the question of possible trade at Naha to Gutzlaff, godfather to the Bettelheim son and by now

Chinese Secretary in the Superintendency of Trade. Gutzlaff advised support for Bettelheim and was favorably disposed toward Robertson's proposal. The matter was referred to London. There the Foreign Office decided to explore this byroad into Japan. A letter was drafted to the Okinawan government (August, 1849) from the government of Her Majesty Queen Victoria, outlining the advantages of trade and recommending Bettelheim to the authorities at Shuri.

This missive, couched in condescending terms suitable for a backward people, was sent out to Bonham, who entrusted it to Britain's senior naval officer at Hongkong for delivery at Naha, with directions that he was to show Bettelheim such personal attentions as might "raise him in the estimation of the Loochoo authorities."[46] This was precisely what Bettelheim most desired. At the same time Bonham, shrewdly estimating Bettelheim's character, tried to limit the obligations which British warships might have to assume on the doctor's behalf.

The Okinawans replied to Queen Victoria's minister on December 28, 1849, citing their refusal to trade with the French (in 1846) and pleading quite truthfully that they were poor and had no surpluses to offer as a basis of trade with Britain. As for Bettelheim, Shuri cited the severity of Japanese laws prohibiting intercourse with other countries, and again begged the British government to remove the unwanted missionaries.

In reporting on this, Bonham noted that Bettelheim was in no personal danger beyond that which he might provoke through his own indiscretions, that he had had no success as a missionary, and that he knew nothing about trade or the possibilities of trade in the islands. Lord Palmerston at London took the position that Bettelheim was entitled to protection by his government, and in July, 1850, requested the Admiralty at London to have a ship look in now and then at Naha.

In October, 1850, H.M.S. "Reynard" dropped anchor there. Captain Cracroft and the Bishop of Victoria (Hongkong) spent a week with Bettelheim, seeing Okinawa through the doctor's eyes, but with some reservations:

"The regent of this miniature kingdom gave us a public entertainment, and before our departure received a return of British hospitality on board the ship. Everything was done to secure a better position for the missionary. But the same system of passive resistance and baffling his attempts to hold intercourse with the natives was resumed. A *cordon* of native police was drawn around his dwelling. His domestic servants were appointed by the Government and changed every ten days. Fixed rations of food were served to him and his family. His bodily safety was insured, but all intercourse with the people was effectually stopped.[47]

"The principal island is supposed to contain 50,000 people, of whom 20,000 belong to Napa and the same number to Shudi, the capital. . . . The people are sunk in the greatest poverty, and appear to have nothing beyond the simplest necessities of life. If to have few wants, and those easily satisfied, constitute riches, the Loochooans may be considered a contented, cheerful people. During my excursions as I viewed their merry countenances and listened to their lighthearted voices, I could not help reflecting on the universal law of compensation by which a wise and merciful Providence tempers the lots and equalizes the conditions of mankind. . . .

"Both Protestant and Catholic missionaries give an estimate of the moral state of the people greatly at variance with the impressions gathered during the brief stay of Captain Basil Hall. Lying, fraud and petty theft prevail among them."[48]

Bishop Smith and Captain Cracroft were asked to carry away a new petition addressed to the British government by Shuri. When in due course it came to Lord Palmerston's attention, he was incensed; London's letter of 1849 should have settled the matter; the queen's government had recommended a British subject to this petty Okinawan principality, and that should have been the end of it. Another letter was prepared for Shuri, and in it the British Lion growled ever so slightly. Palmerston threatened "less friendly visits" by British warships if Bettelheim did not forthwith receive better treatment.

This letter, like its predecessor, was delivered by warship from Hongkong, but by this time, too, Bonham in charge there was disturbed and cautious; there was evidence that Bettelheim was bursting with self-importance as he found himself to be the cause of so much official correspondence with London, and of movements by the British fleet

in China waters. Mistrusting Bettelheim's services as interpreter-translator of official documents concerning himself, Bonham now dispatched
T.T. Meadows to Shuri to make certain that London's communications
were reaching the Okinawan government in unaltered form. "Meadows
report was hostile to Bettelheim. It described him as imprudent and
dictatorial, and warned that he would undoubtedly obtain 'a virtual
dictatorship in the principality' unless the Foreign Office were particularly cautious as to the manner in which it supported him."[49]

About this time there was a change of government at London;
Palmerston was succeeded by Granville, who continued to recommend
better treatment for Bettelheim. On the China coast, however, official
attitudes stiffened. There was a new Superintendent of Trade (Bowring), who rebuked Bettelheim for trying to use Her Majesty's fleet
and government in a missionary crusade.

Bettelheim was not to be discouraged. His letters and reports began
to indicate that in isolation he had become a little overripe and more
than a little careless of the truth. Although Palmerston had left office,
the missionary in a letter of fulsome praise, virtually proposed to
Palmerston the conquest of Japan—if only the British government and
people would recognize the importance of his (Bettelheim's) position.

This was dated September 19, 1852. Across the world, near Washington, ships were being readied for an American expedition to Japan,
which was to have profound effect upon the Okinawan government
and people. In a sense, Bettelheim had indirectly set the framework in
which Commodore Perry approached Japan through Okinawa, for
Perry drew upon Commander Glynn's recent report in shaping policy,
and what Glynn knew of Okinawa was Bettelheim's interpretation.

On November 24, 1852, the American squadron weighed anchor at
Norfolk, Virginia, outbound for Naha and for Japan.

Meanwhile, an incident took place in Okinawan waters which
threatened to involve the little kingdom in a quarrel with China on the
one hand and with the British and American governments on the other.
In showing their traditional hospitality to stranded mariners, the Okinawan officials on Miyako had unwittingly given aid to pirates.

The ship "Robert Browne," under Captain Lesley Bryson, had sailed
from Amoy on March 21, 1852, carrying 410 indentured coolies to the

California gold fields. As they neared Miyako the Chinese mutinied, overpowered the crew, and took the ship in toward the beach. Hundreds of coolies swarmed shore, taking some of the crew with them. Questioned by local Okinawan officials, the ringleaders declared that the ship had been damaged and hence forced to put in at Miyako for repair.

Suddenly the men ashore saw the "Robert Browne" hoist sail and disappear swiftly toward the China coast and Amoy. Members of the crew who were still aboard had by a stratagem overcome the mutineers left to guard them, and had repossessed the ship.

For two weeks the Okinawans had to feed and shelter hundreds of unruly Chinese. Then suddenly three warships appeared. The U.S.S. "Saratoga" and the British warships "Riley" and "Contest" came to anchor, landed forces, and seized as many of the mutineers as they could find. Scores, however, fled into the countryside. There they concealed themselves until the warships weighed anchor for China with only seventy prisoners aboard.

The incident had at once been reported to Shuri, which in turn notified Chinese officials on the Fukien coast. The Okinawans were ordered to detain the culprits and to send them back to China. In the words of the Chinese official report to Peking: "The prince of the said country [Ryukyu] as the tyranny of the English barbarians was extraordinary, greatly feared that if they were not delivered up immediately the barbarian ships would return, make an exhaustive search, and give rise to trouble."[50]

At last, on November 1, 1853, two ships put out from Miyako with 280 of the Chinese aboard. The burden on impoverished Miyako had been very great, and the Shuri government lived in dread of intervention by the Western barbarians.

It was against this background, at the height of Shuri's uneasiness and fear of foreign reprisals, that Commodore Perry made his first descent upon the Ryukyu Islands.

CHAPTER SEVEN

THE MOUSE AND THE EAGLE:
PERRY IN OKINAWA

1853–1854

AMERICAN PRESSURE ON JAPAN: COMMODORE PERRY'S
PLANS FOR OKINAWA

Perry's official *Narrative of the Expedition of an American Squadron to the China Seas and Japan* was prepared under his close supervision by an admiring friend, the Reverend Francis L. Hawks. The commodore was the most noted and perhaps the most accomplished officer in the United States naval service in his day. He had been born during George Washington's first administration, matured during the exciting years of the second war with England (in which his elder brother became a great naval hero), and distinguished himself in the Mexican Wars. He had much to do with policy guiding the United States Navy in transition from sail to steam, which is to say that he was acutely aware of the technological revolution overtaking mankind, of which he himself was destined to be a most remarkable agent in the Far East.

He was a statesman of high measure in the sense that he explored the meaning of technological change and economic expansion in terms of fundamental, long-range national policies and the continuing military needs of the United States. He foresaw, accurately, that Britain and Russia would become rivals to American interests and influence in the northern Pacific and Far East and, with this in view, shaped his policies in forcing Japan to come to terms.

Perry was humorless, immensely vain, and a hard disciplinarian, but his pomposity and his qualities of command well fitted him for the difficult task to which he was assigned—a diplomatic assault upon Japan, backed by a powerful military striking force.

297

The *Narrative* cannot be taken altogether at its face value. The Reverend Dr. Hawks was not a member of the expedition. At numerous points the *Narrative* glosses over discrepancies between Perry's official orders and his actions. The ultimate success of the expedition was so great that the questionable details were completely overshadowed. Hawks was not discouraged if he sought to present all Perry's actions in the best possible light, and Perry saw to it that it had the widest possible circulation among members of Congress and the administration.*

Perry supposed that he had under firm control all diaries, journals, logbooks, and other reports compiled by members of the expedition, who had been ordered to submit all written materials to the commodore. Ostensibly this was to ensure that all relevant data would be incorporated in the official *Narrative*. In studying the first American occupation of Okinawa, that voluminous document must be supplemented by reference to official correspondence which passed between the commodore and Washington, to the candid, uncensored, and sometimes critical journals of S. Wells Williams, Chief Interpreter; Acting Master Edward Yorke McCauley; Bayard Taylor, journalist; J.W. Spalding, clerk aboard the "Mississippi"; and to Okinawan sources. These did not pass through the commodore's hands.

Hawks asserts that the expedition was proposed by Perry himself and that the commodore conceived the idea of a direct approach to the shogun's capital, avoiding Nagasaki and the Dutch intermediaries. Such was not the case. American shipping had entered the northern Pacific and Asiatic waters at the turn of the 19th century; it has been estimated that by 1846 nearly a thousand American vessels were in Far Eastern waters, and of these two-thirds were whalers, operating in the

* Ten thousand sets of his three-volume official *Narrative* were printed for distribution to appreciative congressmen; one thousand were printed for Perry, who gave five hundred to his collaborator, Hawks. The cost to the American taxpayer was $360,000. In matters of personal vanity, censorship, use of discretionary powers, attitudes toward the civil government at Washington, and preparation of quasi-official reports, comparisons may be made between Perry's career and General MacArthur's, bracketing an era in Japan's history. MacArthur's costly "narrative" was suppressed at Tokyo before publication.

rough seas near Japan, exposed often to the dangers of storm and shipwreck along Japan's rocky coasts. Commercial interests at Canton and Shanghai joined with the merchants and mariners of New England in pressing Congress and the administration to "do something" about Japan. Washington had long shared with London, Paris, and St. Petersburg the belief that Japan must be opened, through negotiation if possible, by force if necessary, in order, first, to ensure the security of whaling ships and, secondly, to penetrate markets hitherto reserved to the Dutch.

In 1835 Edmund Roberts was commissioned to deliver a presidential letter to the Emperor of Japan, with orders which directed him to "enter some other port nearer to the seat of government" than Nagasaki. He died at Canton before this could be attempted. The voyage of the "Morrison" in 1837 had been a private attempt, and the unarmed vessel (with Gutzlaff and Williams aboard) was driven out of Kagoshima Bay by the Satsuma clansmen.

Bills appropriating funds to enable the president to establish commercial relations with China were before Congress in 1843; Washington was ready to take advantage of British success in the Anglo-Chinese wars, and it was certain that commerce would be extended to Japan. In 1846 a congressman from New York (Pratt) recommended that the government make a "vigorous effort" to open Japan.

Official Washington had reacted strongly to the affront which Commodore Biddle suffered in Japan in 1845, and in this incident we must find one source for Perry's subsequent hard policy toward the Okinawans. Biddle was trying to open official conversations aboard ship in Edo Bay, and in transferring from one craft to another he was rudely struck and thrust back by a common Japanese soldier. Since he lacked authority to make a show of force on this occasion, the Americans withdrew. The story that a Japanese commoner could strike a high American officer with impunity spread like wildfire throughout Japan and was carried down to Okinawa.

Commander Glynn's report had this to say: "On my way to Nangasacki in the Preble, I touched at Napa Keang in the Loo-Choo Islands. There foreigners are allowed to mingle with the natives, because there are no means to prevent it. I found a Christian missionary [Bettelheim] there, and from him I learned that very exaggerated reports had reached the islands of the chastisement which had been in-flicted upon an American officer who had visited Yedo Bay in a 'big' ship, and it was the impression of my informant that we were en-countering a want of accommodation [in Okinawa] on the part of the local officers, in consequence of the flag we wore. The indignation ex-cited by this information imparted a character of *brusqueness* to my intercourse with the authorities at Nangasacki that I have not regretted since, under the belief that it had the effect to create in Japan another feeling towards our country."[1]

Glynn had lingered at Naha for three days in April, 1849. He had been successful in securing the release of the shipwrecked Americans so long held in confinement in Japan and had undertaken a long voyage thereafter. His return to the United States aroused wide interest and editorial comment. On January 3, 1851, the *New York Herald* said: "On her way to Japan the Preble touched at the Loo-Choo islands, a kingdom in themselves, yet dependencies of Japan. For gentle dignity of manners, superior advancement in the arts and general intelligence, the inhabitants of this group are by far the most interesting unenlight-ened nation in the Pacific Ocean."[2]

At that moment the American ship "Sarah Boyd," outbound from Mazatlan, Mexico, to Shanghai, was approaching the coasts of southern Okinawa. At a point some four miles off the Mabuni beaches, the ship hove-to, a whaleboat was lowered over the side, and three Japanese wearing Western clothing bade cordial farewell to the ship's master and made for shore. These were Nakahama Manjiro—known widely in the United States as John Mung—and two companions seeking to slip into the Ryukyu Islands and on through Satsuma to their home in Tosa. Exactly ten years earlier (in January, 1841) Nakahama and three other fishermen had been driven out to sea in a violent storm, rescued by an American vessel, the "John Howland," and taken to Hawaii. Nakahama went on to Massachusetts, where he received a welcome home and a fair education. Now he and two friends were making their way back to Japan, determined to return to their families and to report on their marvelous adventure. They knew well that they might be seized and executed for violating the grim seclusion edicts.

On the third day of the Japanese New Year, after a night in hiding near the beach, they made their way to a farmhouse. The Okinawan farmers, astonished by the strange appearance of the three adventurers, called in local officials, who in turn took them on to be interrogated by higher officers and by Satsuma's agents at Naha. Their story was heard with interest, and their books, instruments, and other gear were examined with great care.

For seven months they were detained on Okinawa under surveillance, subjected to constant questioning, but always treated with respectful and friendly consideration. Word of their arrival had gone at once to Satsuma, and at last they were summoned to Kagoshima to the presence of Shimazu Nariakira. With his recommendation they were then sent on to Nagasaki and ultimately reached the shogun's capital. There Nakahama became a chief source of information concerning the United States, its political organization, and its strength and policies, insofar as he understood them.

Meanwhile the merchants of New York and New England were determined to solve the "Japan problem" and to penetrate Japanese markets. An influential businessman (Aaron H. Palmer, of New York) brought pressure to bear in Congress and an expedition was proposed. Commodore John H. Aulick, USN, was selected to head the mission as naval-diplomatist in his capacity as Commander in Chief of the East India Squadron. Problems rose which made it inadvisable for him to take charge. The Navy Department, with the concurrence of the Department of State, then selected Perry.

Perry showed reluctance to accept the assignment; he felt it was not sufficiently important and preferred to be assigned to the Mediterranean Fleet command. Both the Navy and State departments flattered and cozened the commodore, increased the title and area of his authority, permitted him to lay down many of the terms of his orders, and assured him that everything would be done in a manner commensurate with his personal rank and dignity.

Perry's orders became effective in March, 1852. At once he began thoroughly to prepare himself and his staff for the task, reading all that he could find concerning Japan (scarcely half a hundred books) and reviewing all official and unofficial dispatches in the archives. Of these Commander Glynn's was the latest; in it the harshness of Japanese policies toward shipwrecked merchant-seamen and toward high-ranking officers of the navy were points sure to catch the commodore's eye. So too was Glynn's description of treatment accorded Christian missionaries, as represented to him by Bettelheim. It was to this official report that Perry turned in contemplating policy to be adopted toward the Ryukyus and toward Japan.

That policy was one of coercion, calculated to ensure that a suitable reputation for unshakable firmness of decision and action should precede the expedition into Japan. Perry believed that the United States government and the U.S. Navy must never again be exposed to indignities such as Commodore Biddle had endured. As for the Okinawans, Dr. Bettelheim (apparently speaking from years of experience) had reported that they were a mean and pusillanimous people, cunning and deceitful. Perry took the missionary's word for it at its face value; he would not be misled as the British Captain Basil Hall had been. The Okinawans were in need of stern, corrective guidance. Poems and tearful friendships would not enter into his arrangements.

Perry warmed to his assignment during the long voyage to the China coast and during the two years he was engaged upon the expedition. His reflections upon the possible consequences of American expansion into the Pacific and his projection of policies which he felt must be pursued in the national interest might now be called "Perry's Grand Design." He proposed that the United States should occupy the Bonin Islands in order to secure a communications base on the sea lanes from California to China and Japan. Japan should be brought into communication with the Western world under American patronage and guidance. The Ryukyu Islands should be placed under "surveillance" and Naha port opened to the commerce of all nations; Formosa should be placed under a joint Chinese-American administration in which "residual sovereignty" rested with the Chinese but effective authority and economic development with the United States. He proposed a technological aid program for Southeast Asia and the adjacent island areas; improved agriculture and local manufacture would expand or improve markets for American wares. He felt Great Britain to be a serious rival but foresaw a frontal clash with Russia in the northern Pacific.

Perry's final orders were based upon a communication made from the Acting Secretary of State (C.M. Conrad) to the Secretary of the Navy (J.P. Kennedy), dated November 5, 1852. The first concern was to secure from the Japanese government a substantial agreement to render aid to shipwrecked or distressed mariners; the second was to arrange a basis for commerce, if possible. No force was to be used to gain these concessions, but Japan was to understand that any further outrages committed upon stranded Americans would bring reprisals. Perry was given powers to negotiate treaties with other sovereignties if opportunity arose.

This document forms the basis for the first American occupation of the Ryukyu Islands. I have introduced italics to note passages which become of special interest as the narrative proceeds:

"Every nation has undoubtedly the right to determine for itself the extent to which it will hold intercourse with other nations [wrote Conrad]. The same law of nations, however, which protects a nation in the exercise of this right imposes upon her certain duties which she cannot justly disregard. Among these duties none is more imperative than that which requires her to succor and relieve those persons who are cast by the perils of the ocean upon her shores.[3]

       .   .   .

"The objects sought by this government are—
"1. To effect some permanent arrangement for the protection of American seamen and property wrecked on these islands, or driven into their ports by stress of weather.
"2. The permission to American vessels to enter one or more of their ports in order to obtain supplies of provisions, water, fuel, &c., or, in case of disasters, to refit so as to enable them to prosecute their voyage.
    "It is very desirable to have permission to establish a depot for coal, if not on one of the principal islands, at least on some small, uninhabited one, of which, it is said, there are several in their vicinity.
"3. The permission to our vessels to enter one or more of their ports for the purpose of disposing of their cargoes by sale or barter.
    "It is manifest, from past experience, that arguments or persuasion

addressed to this people, unless they be seconded by some imposing manifestation of power, will be utterly unavailing.

"You will, therefore, be pleased to direct the commander of the squadron to proceed, with his whole force, to such point on the coast of Japan as he may deem most advisable, and there endeavor to open a communication with the government, and, if possible, to see the emperor in person, and deliver to him the letter of introduction from the President with which he is charged. . . .[4]

"If, after having exhausted every argument and every means of persuasion, the commodore should fail to obtain from the government any relaxation of their system of exclusion, or even any assurance of humane treatment of our shipwrecked seamen, he will then change his tone, and inform them in the most unequivocal terms that it is the determination of this government to insist, that hereafter all citizens or vessels of the United States . . . be treated with humanity; and that if any acts of cruelty should hereafter be practised upon citizens of this country, whether by the government or by the inhabitants of Japan, they will be severely chastised. . . .

"It is impossible by any instructions, however minute, to provide for every contingency that may arise. . . . For this reason . . . *it is proper that the commodore should be invested with large discretionary powers, and should feel assured that any departure from usage, or any error of judgement he may commit will be viewed with indulgence.*

"If the squadron should be able, without interfering with the main object for which it is sent, to explore the coasts of Japan, and of the adjacent continent and islands, such an exploration would not only add to our stock of geographical knowledge, but might be the means of extending our commercial relations and of securing ports of refuge and supply for our whaling ships in those remote seas. With this in view, he will be provided with powers authorizing him to negotiate treaties of amity and navigation with any and all established and independent sovereignties in those regions."[5]

On December 14, 1852, Perry posted a letter from Madeira to the Secretary of the Navy, outlining his proposed course of action. He saw that he would need a base near Japan from which to work:

". . . It will be desirable in the beginning, and indeed necessary, that the squadron should establish places of rendezvous at one or two of the islands south of Japan, having a good harbor, and possessing facilities for obtaining water and supplies, and by kindness and gentle treatment conciliate the inhabitants so as to bring about their friendly intercourse.

"The islands called the Lew Chew group are said to be dependencies of Japan, as conquered by that power centuries ago, but their actual sovereignty is disputed by the government of China.

"These islands come within the jurisdiction of the prince of Satsuma. . . . He exercises his rights more from the influence of the fear of the simple islanders than from any power to coerce their obedience; disarmed, as they long have been, from motives of policy, they have no means, even if they had the inclination, to rebel against the grinding oppression of their rulers.

"Now, it strikes me, that the occupation of the principal ports of those islands for the accommodation of our ships of war, and for the safe resort of merchant vessels, of whatever nation, would be a measure not only justified by the strictest rules of moral law, but by what is also to be considered by the laws of stern necessity; and the argument may be further strengthened by the certain consequences of the amelioration of the conditions of the natives, although the vices attendant upon civilization may be entailed upon them."[6]

This letter establishes clearly that Perry had a fair knowledge of the relationship existing between the Ryukyus and Japan. He proposes an occupation of the islands, and finds moral justification to support "stern necessity."

Washington's response, prepared by Edward Everett, Secretary of State, was prompt and pointed:

"The President agrees with you in thinking that you are most likely to succeed in this object in the Lew-Chew islands. They are, from their position, well adapted to the purpose; and the friendly and peaceful character of the natives encourages the hope that your visit will be welcomed by them.

"*In establishing yourself* at one or two convenient points in those islands, *with the consent of the natives,* you will yourself pursue the most friendly and conciliatory course, and enjoin the same conduct on all under your command. Take no supplies from them except by fair purchase, for a satisfactory consideration. Forbid, and at all hazards prevent, plunder and acts of violence on the part of your men toward these simple and unwarlike people, for such they are described to be. *Let them from the first see that your coming among them is a benefit, and not an evil to them. Make no use of force, except in the last resort for defence if attacked, and for self-preservation.*"*[7]

Perry traveled to the China coast on the U.S.S. "Mississippi," but the "Susquehanna" was to be his flagship. It had been at Hongkong and had gone on to Shanghai when Perry reached the Macao roadstead on April 6.

The Bettelheims at Naha were unaware of this movement of ships, nor did the Shuri officials tell them of word which had come over to Naha that a foreign fire-vessel was in China waters, en route to Japan. On April 9 Bettelheim noted in his diary that he had been asked most urgently to prepare an explanation of the principle of steam power applied to shipping. How did a steamship work? With Mrs. Bettelheim's help and with reference to his small library, the missionary prepared an illustrated text, which he sent up to Shuri on April 13.[8]

On May 23, 1853, four American vessels—the "Susquehanna," the "Mississippi," the "Supply," and the "Caprice"—left the China coast for Naha. On May 25 all hands were assembled to hear a reading of General Orders 11 and 12; these related to discipline to be observed aboard ship while at Naha, and enjoined upon all the strict necessity to cultivate most friendly relations with the people. The expedition would not "resort to force but from the sternest necessity."

Near Naha anchorage these ships were joined by the U.S.S. "Saratoga," out of Hongkong, bringing a chief interpreter-translator to assist the commodore. This was S. Wells Williams, a lay-missionary who had been twenty years on the China coast as managing editor of the Mission Press for the American Board of Foreign Missions. He did not profess to know either the Okinawan dialects or Japanese, but

* The italics are mine.—G.H.K.

he was a distinguished scholar of the Chinese language, fully competent to supervise diplomatic correspondence in that language. His knowledge of the Ryukyu kingdom was extensive; he had carefully studied the Chinese records of Okinawa's position in the Chinese tributary system; he had visited Naha aboard the "Morrison" in 1837 and had published an important account of that experience. As editor of the *Chinese Repository* at Canton he had seen masses of Bettelheim's correspondence and had published some of the missionary's letters in 1850.

PERRY'S FIRST VISIT, MAY AND JUNE, 1853

As the squadron moved into Naha anchorage on May 26 the British flag was observed rising to the top of a staff on the Nami-no-ue bluff, at the temple-residence of Dr. Bettelheim.

Perry's first act was one of calculated brusqueness. Okinawan officials put out from Naha quay to pay their compliments, discover the purpose of this visit, and arrange to supply the squadron's wants. Williams had not yet come aboard the flagship; the officials' formal cards were therefore examined by one of the commodore's Chinese messboys, and the surprised Okinawans were abruptly told to leave the ship because they were of too low rank to be received—or so Perry thought. He had determined at once to take a "hard" line of approach.

"Scarcely had [the Naha officials] gone before Dr. Bettelheim came on board in a native boat; and such were the relations in which he stood to the islanders that he hailed the arrival of the squadron with delight, and manifested no little excitement of manner. He was conducted to the Commodore's cabin, where he remained for two or three hours; . . . in the course of the interview it appeared . . . that a year and a half had elapsed since any foreign vessel had been at Napha, and that he was almost beside himself with joy. Grog and biscuit were given to his boatmen, and in their exhilaration, when they started for the shore, they contrived to carry the missionary some three miles up the coast."[9]

On the morning of May 27 a small boat was sent to bring the missionary out to breakfast with the commodore, the chaplain, and the chief interpreter, Williams. It was decided to override all objections the Okinawan government or people might offer to thorough exploration of the island and the establishment of a supply base on shore.

Bettelheim's diary implies that at his first interview he had proposed to the commodore that the squadron should promote mission interests in Japan, and that Perry instantly and firmly rejected the suggestion. The missionary accepted this, glad enough that the Japanese were soon to feel the heavy pressure which the squadron could bring to bear upon the government he had grown so to dislike. "I offered to serve him as a son serves a father . . . and to obey him strictly, even when my humble opinion differed from his in all matters pertaining to the propriety and success of the Expedition."[10]

On the same morning the magistrate of Naha sent off gifts customarily offered to ships just in—goats, a bullock, fowls, eggs, and vegetables —usually so welcome aboard ships which had been long at sea. These were rejected at once, and the baffled Okinawans were told to remove their tokens of goodwill from the ship.

On the next day Dr. Williams and Lieutenant Contee went ashore, joined Bettelheim, and went to call on the magistrate, who received them politely but let it be known that he was greatly chagrined by the manner in which his goodwill gifts had been rejected. The lieutenant, a gentleman, did his best to cover up for the commodore, explaining that American custom forbade the acceptance of such gifts aboard naval vessels and that it was embarrassing to have to reject them. He could not foresee that soon enough the commodore would be demanding gifts. The explanation was accepted for what it was worth at the time, and the most amiable relations were established.

Bettelheim knew Williams by reputation and was delighted to know that the editor was with the squadron, but the first meeting left him with a sense that Williams was cold and distant. After this interview with the magistrate of Naha, Bettelheim decided that Williams was not competent to act as official interpreter-translator. He noted in his diary: "May 28. Had a quite sleepless night, the mistakes of yesterday's interpretership giving me no rest till I resolved to write to the Commodore on the subject. . . ."

At the Naha interview, it was arranged for the regent of the kingdom to call upon the commodore, by inference establishing Perry as the superior officer.

On the morning of the reception, writes Williams: "At ten o'clock the Commodore sent a boat for me and my [Chinese] teacher, but on reaching the flagship I was surprised to receive a letter from his hands, written by Bettelheim, couched in the strangest style of entreaty and advice respecting the conduct of the expected visit of the Regent to the flagship, and concluding with the hope that the natives would not come near the ship, which I myself more than thought would be the upshot of it, for no promises could be given by the persons I saw yesterday. It was about the oddest melange I ever read from Bettelheim, whom the Commodore had sent for and who ere long reached the ship. He soon was all in motion, and it was about concluded that if the Regent came off Commodore Perry should not see him. . . .

"The Commodore, after reflection, concluded to receive them in his cabin, and though I had for a little while been swayed by what Bettelheim had said, I was not sorry that he [Perry] saw them, for the party came at his invitation to see him, and why not receive them?"[11]

"One of the most striking features in the visitors was their general imperturbable gravity [records the *Narrative*]. It was indeed plain that they had intense curiosity not unmingled with considerable alarm, but they were careful to preserve the most dignified demeanor. They were conducted to the captain's cabin and thence shown over the ship. They observed everything with great gravity, but when they reached the ponderous engines their assumed indifference was fairly overcome, and it was evident that they were conscious of having encountered in it something very far beyond their comprehension. They were much quicker of perception, however, than the Chinese, as well as more agreeable in features and much more neat and tidy in apparel.

"Up to this time they had not seen the Commodore. He had remained secluded in solitary dignity, in his own cabin. It was not meet that he should be made too common in the eyes of the vulgar."[12]

The "vulgar" in this instance was the aged regent of the kingdom, with his principal aides, being escorted about the flagship by Perry's captains. When at last they were admitted to the commodore's presence, he received them graciously enough and presided over an elaborate dinner.

While at table Perry announced that he would call at the royal palace at Shuri on Monday, June 6. "He further added that he should expect such a reception as became his rank and position as commander of the squadron and diplomatic representative of the United States in those regions." This caused great consternation; every argument was adduced and spun out to persuade Perry to abandon this plan. The king was a mere boy, whose accession had not yet been confirmed by China, and the queen dowager was ill. On these grounds the regent begged the commodore to confine his visit ashore to the official reception hall for ambassadors at Naha or, failing that, to be satisfied with an entertainment at the regent's mansion at Shuri. It was made unmistakably clear that he was neither expected nor welcome at the royal palace on June 6, and that unrestricted visits ashore were not allowable under the laws and customs of the land.

Perry was adamant. He had conveniently forgotten the president's directive that he was to establish himself ashore "with the consent of the natives," but he had, perhaps unwisely, chosen a point of etiquette as his weapon in this battle of wills.

Williams describes the conclusion of this painful confrontation, the first of a series: "The party left after a visit of about two hours; a few of them seemed to enjoy it, but such a melancholy set of faces, fixed, grave and sad, as if going to an execution, was hardly ever before seen on board the 'Susquehanna.'

"Bettelheim talked a good deal, and his way of making signs and motioning with his face was very much disliked and wrongly interpreted. I hardly know what to think of the man, for he whisks about in his opinion like a weathercock, and after the Regent had gone said it was the best thing which could have been done, to see the Commodore, though his letter of four pages was to urge the contrary."[13]

Once the Okinawan officials had taken leave, Perry immediately gave orders permitting the squadron's personnel to go ashore and to go anywhere they pleased, provided they took care to maintain friendly relations with the inhabitants at all times. A well-armed party of four

PLATE 18. COMMODORE PERRY DEMANDING ADMISSION TO SHURI CASTLE. *Yielding to this show of force on June 6, 1853, the Okinawans reluctantly opened the castle gates. (See page 316.)*

PLATE 19. THE ROYAL AUDIENCE HALL. *Making his way through the gates and into the castle itself, Perry discovered the royal family had withdrawn, in silent rebuke to the intruding commodore. He was met instead by the regent. (See pages 316–17.)*

PLATE 20. TOMARI TEMPLE, COMMANDEERED FOR REST AND RECREATION, 1853. *Here the naval expedition's staff artists, Heine and Browne, record the American enlisted man ashore with gun, camera, and pet monkey, accompanied by Chinese messboys from the squadron. (See pages 311–12.)*

PLATE 23. THE AMERICAN FLAG ON OKINAWA. *Here Perry's artist records the raising of the flag in a rural temple courtyard, 1853.*

officers, four enlisted men, and four Chinese coolies set out overland to explore the interior and east coast of the island, brushing aside all objections offered to this by the unarmed Okinawan officials ordered to follow them.

Not unexpectedly, the official *Narrative* minimizes the evidence that Perry's policy in Okinawa was throughout based on coercion. Spalding and Williams (and, to a less degree, McCauley) reflect this in their journals, at times with indignation. Bettelheim reveled in it; at last he saw the Okinawan authorities forced to accept him, and to see him in close association with the powerful commodore.

But by May 29 he began to feel that his services on behalf of the squadron were not being sufficiently rewarded. From his diary we can infer that he let this be known when he was given a few cigars by some of the officers. On the next day the purser from the "Susquehanna" came off with an expression of the commodore's appreciation and with directions that the Bettelheims should be rewarded either with provisions or with money, as the doctor preferred. To this he responded that it was entirely up to the commodore. Twenty-four hours later the purser sent ashore a large and diverse gift, including barrels of pork and beef, bread, and flour, sacks of rice, a box of candles, and ten gallons of whiskey.

Bettelheim kept the candles and the whiskey, but immediately sent the other gifts back to the ship. He complained that he lacked proper storage facilities, that he wanted calico, soap, lamp chimneys, shoes, and butter. Furthermore, he felt that it was awkward to receive gifts of provisions from the ship while he was at the same time pressing the reluctant Okinawans to furnish large quantities of fresh supplies for the squadron.

On May 30 Perry sent two officers ashore to acquire a house. Williams accompanied them. Bettelheim conducted the party through the outskirts of Naha to Tomari, the settlement at the juncture of the shore road and the highway to Shuri. Coming to the large "town hall" or assembly place, they found it locked. One of the party went over the wall and succeeded in breaking open the gates from within. The Americans and Bettelheim took possession. Soon officials came to protest that this was a schoolroom, which indeed it was. According to the *Narrative*, the principal officer to whom they addressed themselves "promptly declared that it would be utterly impossible for the Americans to occupy a house on shore. . . . He was then asked if two or three of the Americans might not sleep in the house for that night, and replied that no American must sleep in a house on shore. Upon being pressed further, he seemed to become somewhat impatient, and rising from his seat, he crossed over to where the officers sat, and dispensing with the aid of an interpreter (through whom all communications had thus far been made) to the surprise of our gentlemen, said: 'Gentlemen, Doo Choo man very small, American man not very small. I have read of America in books of Washington—very good man, very good. Doo Choo good friend American. Doo Choo man give American all provision he wants. American no can have house on shore.'"[14]

The officers continued to insist, but after conferring for some hours with his superiors, the Okinawan (named Ichirazichi) returned and, "with a polite bow and marked emphasis, he replied 'you cannot.'" Thus caught between the commodore and the Okinawan government, the visitors chose to risk the wrath of the Okinawans, and simply stayed at the Tomari public hall for the night.

Williams was disturbed: "It was a struggle between weakness and right, and power and wrong, for a more high handed piece of aggression has not been committed by anyone. I was ashamed at having been a party to such a procedure, and pitied these poor defenseless islanders who could only say no. . . .

"I was glad to get into the fresh air and terminate my first night in Lew Chew, the unwilling agent, in so doing, of violence and wrong."[15]

The commodore sent off a sick officer and a servant to replace the men who had so forthrightly established squatter's rights at the Tomari town hall. The Okinawans made no further attempt to dislodge the unwanted intruders; on the contrary, they showed great concern for the comfort of the invalid who had come ashore, bringing him gifts of fruits and vegetables. This solicitude again demonstrated the conflict between personal inclination to cultivate friendly relations with foreigners, on the one hand, and the pressure of duty to obey the government's instructions (inspired by Satsuma) on the other.

"It is surprising [wrote Williams] what a degree of quiet resistance an organized government like this can offer to violence without any overt act of violence, without giving any excuse for wrong by doing the like themselves. They feel their weakness and have no intention probably of resisting by force; but the complete sway they have over the common people enables them to wield what power they have to the best advantage."[16]

The ships had been in port less than one week and Perry had not yet been ashore when, on June 2, he wrote to the Secretary of the Navy:

"This beautiful island is a dependency of Japan, and is governed by the same laws; the people are industrious and inoffensive, and I have already made considerable progress in calming their fears and conciliating their friendship; and, as I propose to make this a port of rendezvous for the squadron, it may be hoped that, in the course of time, the whole population of this island may become quite friendly.

"I am only waiting here to establish a good understanding with these people before my visit to Japan, that information of our friendly demonstration towards the Lewchewans may precede us, and assure the Japanese that we have no hostile intentions."[17]

On that day the "Caprice" left to transport mail and laundry to Shanghai. Said Williams: "The letter-bag takes Bettelheim's first letters sent off for eleven months, besides $800 sent over to put in the bank there to his credit—his 'own sweat and blood' he says. He says that he has not been able to come to any explicit understanding with the rulers or people as to the price of provisions he consumes; they bring food and he lays down money, and no accounts are drawn out. He eats what they bring, they take away what he lays down."[18] The Loo Choo Mission at London was hard-pressed to meet its budget, as Williams well knew. We are not told from whence came Bettelheim's surplus cash, but we know that he provided souvenirs and other services for officers and men whenever ships put in at Naha.

Perry pushed ahead with plans to make a great progress to the royal palace. The Okinawans tried every argument to alter his decision. A letter was sent off to the commodore inviting him to be the regent's guest at a banquet in Naha; when the hour came, no commodore appeared. Officials were then sent out to the ship to carry some of the special dishes to him there. They were treated with utmost rudeness: no seats were offered to them when they came aboard; the commodore declared that he had received only a verbal invitation and had therefore sent back only a verbal reply, though Williams later found the written invitation aboard ship, and suspected that someone had failed—perhaps deliberately—to deliver it or to explain its significance. On Saturday, June 4, the regent himself made a second trip to the flagship to present a formal written petition asking Perry to give up his projected visit to the royal palace.

"Captain Buchanan offered them some drink so strong that they could not take it; for all I know [wrote Williams] it was clear brandy. He showed in every action his unwilling consent to have them remain long, and this was increased by Bettelheim's appearing, who, it seems, had been invited off by the Regent to facilitate intercourse.

"Dr. Bettelheim wrote a letter to the Commodore in his usual singular fashion (calling him 'father,' and desirous to obey his orders, and talking of 'glorious mission,' and the flagship a 'throne,' and Perry an 'autocrat' whose glance should be law to the natives) yet finding fault with everything which has been done, chiefly, as far as we can learn, because he was not consulted. Yet when he read Adams' reply in Perry's cabin yesterday he called it 'excellent' and approved of it all. The man does not seem to know his own mind for a day, but evidently wishes to be consulted about everything and have his advice followed. He is not at all backward in sending or begging for things, while he, Jew-like, puts his money in the bank. However, this must be added, that he cannot spend much money here for his family, even if he wished, for he is not allowed to buy at will, and this sum may be the surplus from his salary."[19]

"Owing to the fresh breeze, Captain Buchanan sent the Regent ashore in a cutter, and was glad to be rid of him. Bettelheim had a long talk with Perry; he is becoming more than ever disliked by everybody, and took an unlucky step in coming aboard today when he was unwished."[20]

Bettelheim had proposed that he should go to Japan with the squadron: "June 4. . . . Commodore also ordered me during his absence in

Japan to bring to paper whatever I knew by hearing or otherwise of the history of Loochoo, which I of course unhesitatingly promised. I had incidentally the most decisive information of my not accompanying the Squadron to Japan."[21]

Meanwhile, Williams had an opportunity to examine the regent's latest petition, which was in effect a clear declaration that Perry was neither welcome nor expected at the palace. The communication said in part: "Now it is plain to all that the capital and towns of this little country are quite different from the provincial capitals of China; here there is only a palace for the king, and no halls, official residences, markets or shops; and, up to this time, no envoy from a foreign country has ever entered into the Palace. In February, of last year, an English general came here, bearing a public letter, and was strenuous to enter the palace, there to deliver it; the high officers repeatedly requested that it might be given them elsewhere, but he refused, and forced himself into the palace. At that time, from the young prince and the Queen Dowager down to the lowest officers and people, all were alarmed and fearful, hardly keeping soul and body together; and the queen dowager has been dangerously sick even to this day. . . . All the officers in the country are really troubled and grieved on this account and . . . they urgently beg of your excellency . . . that you will take the case of the queen dowager and her severe indisposition into your favorable consideration, and cease from going into the palace to return thanks. If you deem it necessary to make this compliment, please go to the residence of the prince, there to make your respects in person. . . ."[22]

Monday, June 6, was a sparkling day. Nature was prepared to smile on Perry's progress to the palace, though the Okinawans frowned. "It was a matter of policy to make a show of it," says the *Narrative*, "hence some extra pains were taken to offer an imposing spectacle."

The captain of the "Susquehanna," in full-dress uniform, led off, flanked by the two interpreters, Williams and Bettelheim. Behind them were drawn two fieldpieces, each surmounted by an American flag. The band from the "Mississippi" came next, followed by a company of marines in full dress.

Then came the commodore, in the most imposing uniform he could arrange, seated in a sedan chair, which had been knocked together for the occasion by the ship's carpenter, and decked out with paint and curtains of red and blue material. Four Chinese coolies carried it, with four trotting alongside as auxiliary bearers. Two marine bodyguards, a pageboy, and a Chinese valet or steward marched beside the palanquin as Perry's personal attendants.

Following Perry at a respectful distance came a company of marines and a Chinese servant bearing presents for the royal household, each bearer accompanied by a guard. Then followed the officers of the expedition, their personal servants attending them, the band from the "Susquehanna," and at last, a company of marines forming a rear guard. Some two hundred men took part.

Crowds gathered to watch this glittering procession wind along the highroad with bands playing, through Tomari, up the pine-clad hills, and into the stone-walled town of Shuri. The regent and the highest officers of state met the commodore at the great outer gates and begged him to honor them by stopping at the regent's mansion for refreshments. Williams at once suspected a maneuver designed to draw the commodore away from his prime objective. The regent's gesture was ignored. The column marched firmly on to the very gates of the palace.

They were closed.

It was hardly to be expected that the fieldpieces would be used to blast a way into the royal residence, but the Okinawans had no assurance that Perry would stop short of this, so as he waited in his grand sedan chair, messengers were sent around to the inner courts and the gates were at last opened. The Americans marched in, to the tune of "Hail Columbia!"

Technically, Perry had won his point and entered the royal palace, but it was an empty gesture. No signs of entertainment of any sort were in evidence. There was no king, no queen dowager, and not a vestige of preparation.

Places were hastily arranged in one of the palace chambers. The commodore and his officers took positions along one side, the regent and his principal officers faced them across the room. The presents for the royal household were placed on the floor between. These had been brought along as a matter of form, though Perry himself believed (incorrectly) that the dowager queen was a mythical person, a mere excuse to put him off. It may have been hard for him to concede that the Okinawans had in fact won their point; they had indicated that the regent was the highest personage in the state to whom he could address himself, and they held to the issue successfully.

FIG. 19. THE AUDIENCE HALL, SHURI CASTLE.
The main building and the stone dragon-pillars which flanked its approach. (See page 109.)

The regent and his men moved exactly half way across the audience hall and bowed stiffly. "The Commodore and all the officers rose and bowed in return; but without precisely understanding what the homage of the Lew Chewans particularly meant; they were determined, however, not to be outdone in the outward symbols of civility."[23]

After some delay, cups of weak tea and "twists of very tough gingerbread" were produced from within the palace. The regent was invited to take dinner aboard the flagship. According to Williams: "The Lewchewans seemed to have nothing to say, but rather to endure our presence, and Perry did not intend to introduce any topic." At last, after painful silences, the regent renewed the invitation for Perry to dine at his mansion nearby. It was accepted, with relief, for as the humorless *Narrative* records "the interview was becoming rather uninteresting, and it was quite plain that the magnates of Lew Chew were, for some cause or other, not quite at their ease."

The foreigners withdrew from the palace grounds. Perhaps Bettelheim was the only member of the company to draw complete satisfaction from the incident, for he had at last been admitted to the palace.

He was wearing borrowed American plumage, to be sure, and had been allowed to enter only because the well-armed commodore would have it so, but he had had his hour of triumph. The officers with him must have sensed his elation, for he had written and talked much of his persistent efforts to penetrate the royal house, only to be driven away from Shuri as a public nuisance.

Perry went on foot from the castle gates to the regent's mansion nearby, where an elaborate feast had been waiting during the painful hour at the palace. According to the *Narrative*, this was a congenial interlude, during which it was discovered that the regent's interpreter had spent three years at Peking, perfecting his knowledge of Chinese. This was the language in which he conversed with Williams, who in turn interpreted for Perry. Soon it was disclosed that he knew a little English as well and that a number of high officers present had read in Japanese texts of the geography and history of the United States and of George Washington.

The *Narrative* endows the whole day at Shuri with an air of success, and notes that at the end of the eighth course the commodore rose to propose a toast to the prince, the queen dowager, and the people of the Ryukyus, saying: " Prosperity to the Lew Chewans, and may they and the Americans always be friends." According to Williams, this was done only after the regent himself had taken the lead in proposing a toast to the United States and the American guests.

"Novel as was this bill of fare [says Hawks], the gentlemen of the expedition endeavoured with true courtesy, to do honor to the repast, and at the end of the twelfth course respectfully took leave, though they were assured there were twelve more to come. The number of courses indicated the desire to do our countrymen a double share of honor, inasmuch as twelve is the prescribed number for a royal entertainment."[24]

That, at least, was what the commodore had been assured in flattering terms by Bettelheim. The Williams, McCauley, and Spalding reports show that this had been a lugubrious affair; Williams and Spalding were indignant that the commodore, bored with the proceedings, had simply left the feast honoring him before it was fully served: "There was no lighting up of faces of the old men [writes Williams], and they were evidently wishing us away, tho' a good many of the younger people were amused. . . . After two hours we left, the four chiefs accompanying Perry to the door, and then hastening back with joyful steps as tho' relieved."[25]

Perry had gained access to the empty palace, and his men were wandering about wherever they willed. The problems of the coal station and of commercial transactions remained unsettled.

There had been military drills on every ship and on shore each day after the squadron came in. On the day following the Shuri Castle visit, a full-dress review of auxiliary craft was held in the harbor. "Seventeen boats, fully equipped and armed, and five of them carrying twelve and twenty-four pounders" were paraded for the Okinawans to see. Against this display, Perry's officers pressed the Naha officials for an agreement which would govern commercial transactions and provide for the payment for supplies sent off to the ships. They yielded the point, breaking with age-old tradition that ships in need should be serviced without charge. They had no choice. Once having come to this point, the Americans found the Okinawans to be shrewd bargainers and quick to raise prices. It was no longer necessary to try to entrust all the provisioning arrangements to Bettelheim. Said Spalding: "When other mediums than himself were adopted for the procurement of eatables &c, we generally found that we succeeded better."

June 8 brought a minor crisis in Bettelheim's relations with the commodore. Perry had ordered construction of an enclosure within which a number of cattle and sheep could graze. His men selected the grounds around the "upper temple" which the Bettelheims had preempted for their use on Nami-no-ue headland. The doctor objected:

"The Commodore took this quite unfair of me, telling me I had premises spacious enough without the upper temple, and that he saw no reason why to allow me to occupy so much ground. He moreover thought, as I knew he only wished to civilize this nation, I should rather have been glad to see a new breed [of cattle] introduced, etc. I contended the cattle could be reared quite as well and much better in another place, and that we used the upper temple as belonging to our establishment these seven years; that in time of bad weather this was the only place where my wife and children can take a walk . . . and finally, that we have there a flagstaff planted . . . and I could thus not give up so easily possession of a ground thus constituted.

"Commodore Perry told me rather angrily, he did not like it. . . ."[26]

The American establishment on shore now included buildings commandeered for barracks, for a photographer's laboratory, and for a sick bay. Although the Okinawans no longer tried to evict the Bettelheims from the Gokoku-ji, they had not given up claims to the ancient temple. They objected to having its precincts used as a cattle stable. Bettleheim continues: "On our back way, Ichirazichi came to say, the door of the upper temple would be required to be kept open, as they had therein gods which they wished to worship. (It is near seven years that no sort of worship whatever was carried on in either the lower or the upper temple.) The Commodore said they had gods enough to worship in other places. . . ."[27]

On June 9 two ships from the squadron left Naha for the Bonin Islands, which Perry proposed to survey and to claim, if possible, for the United States.

THE AMERICAN BASE ON OKINAWA: JULY, 1853–JULY, 1854

When Perry returned to Naha on June 23 it was discovered that the regent had resigned, been deposed, or committed suicide. This caused general uneasiness among the American officers who assumed that the old man's failure to prevent intrusion upon the palace was the cause of his disgrace. Perry preferred to assume—and perhaps correctly—that the government saw the need of a more vigorous hand in control at a time of unparalleled crisis for the kingdom.

"The report that Shang Ta-mun has ripped himself up is gaining ground [wrote Williams], and excites no little displeasure among some as one of the sad results of our course; but I have grave doubts about it. . . .

"Dr. Bettelheim came aboard after his service was over in the Plymouth, and made himself somewhat dubious by the way he spoke of the succession to the Regency, and the fate of the old one. This same Dr. Bettelheim contrives to heap a deal of ill-will and contempt up against himself by his conduct."[28]

Hawks notes that Bettelheim was pleased to learn that his old antagonist had lost authority: "Dr. Bettelheim (who did not seem to feel any pity for the degraded dignitary) stated that he would probably be banished, with his family, to one of the smaller islands."[29]

It was now Perry's turn to give a formal dinner aboard the flagship for the new regent. There was a heavy rain-squall, the guests were very late in making their appearance, so late that Perry sent Williams and Bettelheim off toward shore to discover the cause for the delay. "We met them all aboard the two cutters and had our row in the rain for nothing; Bettelheim was cross, too, because the Regent was ahead of him, and halloed to the boats in vain, making me wish I was out of his company."[30]

The new regent proved to be a younger man, less poised than the old prince, his predecessor. The dinner was a colorful occasion, for the regent wore a magnificent purple robe, his principal aides wore robes of yellow or pearl white with crimson turbans, richly worked Chinese silk girdles, and massive ornamental golden pins in their hair. Inferior attendants wore blue and yellow.

The *Narrative* notes that the guests "showed but a very sorry appreciation of the virtue of temperance . . . thus almost equalling Christendom in genteel dissipation." Perry ordered the band's soloists to play; perhaps for the first time Okinawans heard the music of the flageolet, clarinet, oboe, and cornet.

There were many courses, washed down with French and German wines, Madeira and sherry, Scotch and American whiskeys, Holland gin, and maraschino. On this occasion the guests of honor made no move to leave the ship before formalities were at an end and the last of the many wines were sampled.

Said Williams:

"While dining, many sorts of spirits were drunk, and Bettelheim evidently acted as if under their influence, getting up and sitting down, talking and gesticulating in a strange way. . . .

"I tried to ascertain from the interpreter whether the old Regent was in Shuri, but had no chance; Bettelheim thought he was imprisoned or banished, and increased the dislike of some to him by the smirk with which he told of the poor man's fate—a fate which I think is doubtful. I don't much wonder at his [Bettelheim's] feelings, however, living here for so many years and deprived of common comforts through this man's [the Regent's] means, it is not surprising he should wish a change of rulers.

"The party of Lewchewans left at sunset, but he remained to try to settle accounts with the purser or caterers, and nearly got a discharge from the ship by accusing the officers of cheating him. It is strange to hear the dislike felt against him by the squadron, yet I can explain it mostly without deeming him to be a scoundrel as others do. . . ."[31]

On June 26 Bettelheim preached aboard the "Plymouth"; he was advised to keep it short, "which induced me the more warmly to pray and preach to them," and with relish he chose the text "Thou hast prepared a table before me in the presence of mine enemies."

The harbor was filled with activity on July 2. Soon after noon the commodore left Naha, turning northward with two steamers and two sloops-of-war to make his first attempt to penetrate Japan. "All seemed very well satisfied to get away from Lew Chew [says the Narrative]. The picturesque interests of the island were, for the time being, thoroughly exhausted, and the dull realities of life began to weigh heavily on the visitors."

Perry's approach to Japan had been reported through Satsuma, as he expected it to be. He did not know, however, that Nakahama Manjiro (John Mung of Fairhaven, Massachusetts) was being used as a consultant at Edo. It is doubtful if Nakahama would have survived if he had attempted to land in Japan itself directly from a foreign ship. The friendly reception in Okinawa had given him six months in which to tell a story which intrigued the Lord of Satsuma, gave him protection, and preserved him in the services of the shogunate. He was not allowed to meet with the American visitors (extreme Exclusionists thought he knew too much English and was too liberal in his views), but he served as consultant on many issues.[32]

President Fillmore's letter was delivered at Uraga on July 14, with a statement that Commodore Perry would return in due course to receive the emperor's reply.

On July 25 the ships returned to Naha. Perry's relative success in Japan and his impatience to proceed to the China coast appear to have toughened his attitude. "The Commodore had no time to spare, as his present visit was intended to be very short, and he was not disposed to be put off for a moment by the usual temporizing policy of the slow-moving Lew Chewans, so he demanded at once an interview with the regent; the demand was immediately granted, and a day appointed for the meeting."

Somewhere along the way the commodore had forgotten the president's instructions to act only with the consent of the natives, and remembered rather the "broad discretionary powers." His aides were given instructions to prepare the regent for his terms:

"Establish rate and pay for rent of house for one year. State that I wish a suitable and convenient building for the storage of coal, say to hold six hundred tons. If they have no such building, I desire to employ native workmen to erect one . . . or if the Lew Chewan government prefers, it can be done under the inspection of the mayor, at government expense, and I will agree to pay an annual rent for it. Either one or the other agreement must be made.

"Speak about the spies, and say that if they continue to follow the officers about, it may lead to serious consequences, and perhaps to bloodshed, which I should deplore, as I wish to continue on the most friendly terms with the authorities. That should any disturbance ensue, it will be the fault of the Lew Chewans, who have no right to set spies upon American citizens who may be pursuing their own lawful business. . . .

"It will be wise therefore, for the Lew Chewans to abrogate those laws and customs which are not suited to the present age, and which they have no power to enforce, and by a persistence in which they will surely involve themselves in trouble.

"Let the mayor clearly understand that this port is to be one of rendezvous, probably for years, and that the authorities had better come to an understanding at once.[33]

A formal communication was then addressed to the regent, stating these demands in firm language:

"It is repugnant to the American character to submit to such a course of inhospitable discourtesy, and though the citizens of the United States, when abroad, are always regardful of, and obedient to, the laws of the countries in which they may happen to be, provided they are founded upon international courtesy, yet they can never admit of the propriety or justice of those of Lew Chew, which bear so injuriously upon the rights and comforts of strangers resorting to the island in the most friendly and peaceful intentions.

"With the highest consideration,

M. C. PERRY

Commander-in-Chief of the United States Naval Forces, in the East India, China, and Japan Seas."[34]

The formal meeting at which the regent's answers were to be presented took place at Naha on July 28. The imperious commodore brushed aside preliminary amenities and directed the regent to proceed with business. The regent indicated that the formal reply would be ready during the course of the dinner, which proceeded stiffly. At the eighth course, the official document, bearing the great seal of Ryukyu, was handed to the regent, who handed it to Perry. Dr. Williams was ordered to read it at once.

"It commenced [says the *Narrative*] by affirming the small size and poverty of the island, stating that Dr. Bettelheim's residence among them had given them much trouble, and that if we should erect a building for coal their difficulties would be greatly increased. Besides, they said, the temple which they had appropriated to our use was thereby rendered useless to them, and their priests were prevented from performing their worship in it. The productions of the island were few, as they derived all of their teas, silks, cloths and many other articles from Japan and China. With regard to the shops and markets, that was a matter that depended upon the people themselves, and if they chose to keep their shops closed, the regent could not interfere. He declared, moreover, that the persons who had followed us whenever we had gone ashore were not spies, but officers appointed to act as guides, and to prevent us from being annoyed by the people. Since we had not found them to be of service, and objected to them, they would be directed not to follow us in future."

This reply was not what the commodore expected. It was instantly returned to the hands of the regent, as something unacceptable. Perry then repeated his demands, upon which, says the *Narrative*, "the Regent attempted to come forward and again present the reply; but the Commodore rose and prepared to leave, declaring that if he did not receive satisfactory answers to all his demands by noon the next day, he would land two hundred men, march to Shuri, and take possession of the palace there, and would hold it till the matter was settled. With this declaration he left . . . the regent attending him to the gateway. . . ."[35]

The threat to occupy Shuri forced the Okinawans to capitulate. They conceded all points.

The official *Narrative* comments here that "the Commodore was not to be balked of his purpose by any of the shams and devices of Lew Chew policy, and went straight to the end proposed, without allowing himself to be diverted from a broad, honest course of fair dealing." Some of the members of his staff, however, privately took a different view of these proceedings.

Williams gave vent to his indignation in the pages of his private journal:

"It was a struggle between weakness and might, and the islanders must go to the wall; it was as well-planned on their part as possible, and they were doubtless disappointed in the result."[36]

"We stopped at Dr. Bettelheim's to bid him goodbye, and found others there on a similar errand, more as a mark of respect than goodwill. While his wife has grown in the good opinion of the squadron, he has contrived to get the suspicion or active dislike of almost everybody. His intrusion into the interview last Thursday [July 28] was little pleasing to the principal actors, and tends to mix us up with him in the minds of the native authorities. His proceedings have been so anomalous that I am really unable to say what and how much good he is doing, though I hope he will come out bright at the last, and his work stand the fire. The counsel and opinion of a fellow-laborer would do him service and enable his patrons to form a better judgement."[37]

On August 1 the commodore sailed from Naha once again, leaving a small staff to supervise the coaling depot and to maintain and cultivate the "cordial relations" which he fondly believed himself to have established among the Okinawans.

The *Narrative* relates that, upon leaving Okinawa this time, Perry began to reflect upon the consequences of his visits, and found them good. Traditional resistance to foreign intercourse was weakening. The blessings of civilization were beginning to be felt.

Unknown to Perry (as we shall see in the next chapter) certain decisions had been made at Kagoshima; Shimazu had conceived a policy which would exploit this Western eagerness to penetrate Japan, while taking advantage of Tokugawa weakness at Edo. To the degree that it deemed safe, Kagoshima had prudently relaxed pressure upon Shuri; the Okinawans now had less reason to fear reprisals by Satsuma.

Perry meanwhile was maturing plans which he felt appropriate and necessary to his success in Japan. He had found that the Okinawans were easily coerced, and he feared that British, Russian, or French naval diplomatists prowling Far Eastern waters might seize the Ryukyus. He therefore argued that the United States should forestall such a possibility. His views were set forth in letters to Washington dated December 24, 1853, and January 25, 1854:

"Considering that I am acting very much upon my own responsibility, I should desire to be instructed as to policy, which I do not hesitate to recommend, of continuing the influence which I have already acquired over the authorities and people of the beautiful island of Lew-Chew. . . .

"The department [of the navy] will be surprised to learn that this royal dependency of Japan . . . is in such a state of political vassalage and thralldom, that it would be a merit to extend over it the vivifying influence and protection of a government like our own.

PLATE 24. MACHIMINATO HARBOR IN 1854. *Scenes such as this (the site of Tametomo's farewell to his wife and infant son in the 12th century—see page 49) were prepared by the staff artists to illustrate the official narrative of Perry's expedition.*

PLATE 25. THE COURT INTERPRETER, 1853–54. *Perry's editors identify this daguerreotype as a portrait of "Shin." A Japanese text says it is Itarashiki (the "Ichirazichi" of the Perry account), who later became Makishi Pechin and paid with his life for negotiating the secret Satsuma treaty with France. (See page 312.)*

PLATE 26. THE REVEREND DOCTOR BERNARD JEAN BETTELHEIM (1811–1870), THE MOST UNWELCOME MISSIONARY. *(See page 280 et seq.)*

PLATE 27. HIS ROYAL HIGHNESS SHO TAI (1841–1901). *This was the last King of the Ryukyu Islands, deposed by the Japanese in 1879. (See page 382.)*

PLATE 28. A NAHA STREET-SCENE, 1854. *From the Perry narrative.*

PLATE 29. THE RUINS OF NAKAGUSUKU CASTLE, NEAR SHURI. *Here Perry's men are seen exploring the remains of this once-famous castle. (See pages 310–11.)*

"It is self-evident that the course of coming events will ere long make it necessary for the United States to extend its territorial jurisdiction beyond the limits of the western continent, and I assume the responsibility of urging the expediency of establishing a foothold in this quarter of the globe, as a measure of positive necessity to the sustainment of our maritime rights in the east.

"I shall continue to maintain the influence over the authorities and people of Lew-Chew which I now command, but it is important that I should have instructions to act promptly, for it is not impossible that some other power, less scrupulous, may slip in and seize upon the advantages which should justly belong to us. . . ."[38]

" . . . It is my intention, should the Japanese government refuse to negotiate [a treaty] or to assign a port of resort for our merchant and whaling ships, to take under *surveillance* of the American flag, upon the *ground of reclamation for insults and injuries committed upon American citizens*, this island of Great Lew-Chew, a dependency of the empire, to be held under such *restraint*, until the decision of my government shall be known, whether to avow or disavow my acts. Until such action is had, the responsibility will rest solely upon me, and I shall assume it as a measure of political precaution, for it is certain that if I do not take preliminary steps before leaving this port [Naha] for Yedo, for adopting such course, the Russians or French, or probably the English, will anticipate the design."*[39]

The Secretary of the Navy promptly rejected the proposals: "Your suggestion about holding one of the Lew-Chew Islands . . . is more embarrassing. The subject has been laid before the President, who, while he appreciates highly the patriotic motive which prompts the suggestion, is disinclined, without the authority of the Congress, to take and retain possession of an island in that distant country, particularly unless more urgent and potent reasons demanded it than now exist. If, in future, resistance should be offered and threatened, it would also be rather mortifying to surrender the island, if once seized, and rather inconvenient and expensive to maintain a force there to retain it. Indulging in the hope that the contingency may not arise to occasion any

* The italics are Perry's.

resort to the expedient suggested . . . it is considered sounder policy not to seize the island as suggested in your dispatch."*[40]

The full squadron did not gather again at Naha until January 24, 1854. Eight ships rode at anchor, waiting for the "Saratoga" to join them. Perry was impatient to get on to Edo Bay.

A pre-emptory notice informed the regent that the commodore intended to call at the palace once more, that he wanted suitable horses and sedan chairs made ready for the "courtesy call," and that he expected a proper reception.

The regent at once demurred, saying that the Ryukyu government preferred to receive and entertain the commodore elsewhere. Perry was angered by this "crooked policy" and evasive behavior and, on February 1, sent a company of marines to Shuri to the palace gates "for exercise." On February 3 he again had himself carried up to the palace with considerable display. The precedents set in June, 1853, were followed closely; he was not received by the young king nor by the queen dowager. Having made the gesture, the commodore and his military aides withdrew from the palace to the regent's mansion for a dinner.

Perry took this occasion to make several new demands upon the Ryukyu government. He wanted a number of Okinawan or Japanese coins to send to the government mint at Washington. The regent declared that he was unable to comply with the request, for Ryukyu had no coinage of its own, and the few coins in the island were in possession of the Japanese residents. Perry was admant; he believed the Okinawans were attempting to deceive him, for had not Bettelheim declared that money was in use? Leaving about fifty dollars' worth of American coins at Shuri, Perry declared with great firmness that he expected to be supplied with an equivalent value in Okinawan or Japanese coins before he left the island.

* This exchange is not quoted in the *Narrative* edited by Hawks for Perry; there, on p. 324, the following appears: "It was not proposed by the Commodore to take Lew Chew, or claim it as a territory conquered by, and belonging to, the United States, nor to molest or interfere in any way with the authorities or people of the island, or to use any force, except in self defence. In fact, there was not likely to be any occasion for violence, as the Americans already possessed all necessary influence in Lew Chew, which had been acquired by kindness and non-interference with the laws and customs of the island."

On the eve of his departure for Japan a number of gifts were sent off from the squadron for the regent, the royal household, and the government. Concurrently, the Shuri government sent off to the ships a gift of Okinawan products. But with it came a communication from the regent, who regretted that it was still true that Okinawa produced no significant coins, that trade in Okinawa was on a barter basis, that the gold and silver used in making hairpins used by the gentry was imported metal, and that the coins which Bettelheim had reported were in fact held and used only by the Japanese. The American coins which had been left at Shuri were returned to the commodore.

Perry was enraged. He immediately ordered all the Okinawan gifts sent ashore and sent word to the regent warning him that the coins must be ready when he returned from Japan. Williams made this comment: "The Commodore . . . on hearing the paper read, ordered all the presents back into the boat, and gave them his own communication to take to the Regent, with the coins he had given him at the Palace. In doing so I think Perry acted like a disappointed child, and was piqued at being unable to effect the exchange of coins he had set his heart on. He bids me tell them that he asks only for what is reasonable, and that the exchange of national coins is a sign of friendship; these islanders are known and allowed to have no mint of their own, but a breach of amity is made to depend upon their furnishing the coins of another land, which they deny to have or be able to get. I think this matter was carried much too far, and, as I will tell no lie for Perry or anyone else, I never told them he asked only what is reasonable. . . . If the coins desired were Lewchewan, the case would be materially altered; as it is I think Perry is in the wrong in pressing the exchange to such a degree."[41]

Before leaving Naha for Japan on his epochal second trip, Perry issued a proclamation saying that until he had secured what he wanted at Edo he would hold the Ryukyu Islands under "limited authority" and that he would therefore assign "two master's mates and about fifteen men to look after the United States Government property and other interests during his absence."

Soon after the American squadron steamed northward, three Russian warships came in—a steamer (the "Vostock"), a frigate (the "Pallas"), and a 24-gun corvette. Perry's men promptly warned the intruders that Okinawa "had been taken under American protection" by the commodore. Vice Admiral Putyatin merely smiled, and sent his men ashore. For ten days the Russians drilled at Tomari, explored Naha, and listened skeptically to Bette heim's denunciations of the amiable Okinawans.

Perry, at Edo Bay, was negotiating with stubborn determination. On March 17 he demanded that five Japanese ports be opened to commerce and navigation. Naha was named. The Japanese commissioners countered with an assertion that "Lew Chew is a very distant country, and the opening of its harbor cannot be discussed by us." The Emperor of Japan was alleged to have very limited authority in the Ryukyu islands. This Perry interpreted as a disclaimer of responsibility sufficiently clear to give the Ryukyu kingdom the status of an independent sovereignty.

The negotiations at Kanagawa, near Yokohama, were concluded on March 31, 1854. After suitable celebrations and a short cruise to Hakodate in northern Japan, the American squadron returned to Naha, anchoring on July 1.

The "Lew Chew Compact" with the United States

The two master's mates left on Okinawa with their small company had been joined in May by the officers and crew of the "Lexington," Lieutenant Glasson commanding. Relations between the Americans and the Okinawans had not continued in that degree of harmony so confidently described to Washington by the commodore. Some Okinawan children had taken to stoning the Americans upon occasion and in early June, during a scuffle in the market place, two Americans had been beaten up, and a third had been done to death by an angry mob. Glasson took up these incidents with the magistrate of Naha, and upon Perry's return the incidents were reviewed and the case of death by violence was reopened.

The commodore's account in the *Narrative* does not agree in all details with the case as set forth in Williams' private notes. Both the Okinawan officers and the Americans agreed that the stoning was a minor "accident." The *Narrative* states that one of the two seamen quarreled with a butcher in the market, and that the butcher had beaten the American with a club. The Naha magistrate asserted that the seaman had taken meat from the butcher without paying for it and that when this was protested, the American had set upon the Okinawan with a knife. Williams tells a third version; three seamen—Scott, Smith, and Board—were on a tipsy spree in Naha. Scott and Smith bought something, paying for it in coin. This illegal transaction was witnessed by a petty officer of Naha, who promptly confiscated the money. This angered the Americans, who sought to drive the Okinawan officer away; he called his friends and in the scuffle Scott was knocked to the ground and beaten severely. Smith made his way to his friends and Board wandered off. Scott lay drunken and bleeding in the street until Lieutenant Glasson found him and had him taken off to his quarters. "The probability is [says the *Narrative*] that the general feeling aboard ships was that the sailor got no more than his deserts." This incident was smoothed over, however.

But after leaving his friends, Board had entered a house in town and committed rape. The victim's screams brought a crowd, which chased Board through the streets, pelting him with stones. He attempted to reach the waterfront and the safety of a small boat, but at the quay's edge he was felled by a stone (or stumbled) and plunged into the water. By the time he could be pulled out he was dead.

"The Commodore, upon enquiry, soon became convinced that the man's death, though unlawfully produced, was probably the result of his own most gross outrage on a female, and, in such case, not undeserved; still he felt that, for the security of others, both Europeans and Americans, who might subsequently visit the island, it was important to impress upon the authorities the necessity for the full investigation and proper punishment, by the local authorities, of acts of violence committed upon strangers who might visit them. He therefore made a peremptory demand upon the regent or superintendent of affairs to cause a judicial trial to be instituted, conformably to the laws of Lew Chew.

"This demand was at once complied with [continues the *Narrative*], the court consisting of six superior judges, and the regent and first treasurer giving their constant personal attendance during the entire proceedings."[42]

Williams, the interpreter, attended some of the sessions; rough methods were used to prod and prompt the memories of men who had been in the crowd which pursued Board, but there was a genuine attempt to discover the leaders. Williams was familiar with Chinese methods in these circumstances—when any jailbird would do, produced as the guilty one, in order to end quickly the responsibility and involvement of officials brought under pressure by the "foreign devils"— and he recorded his reaction to procedures in this Okinawan court: "Mean and simple as this Lewchewan courthouse is, such men as are here convened, to do what they deem (or feel) due to justice, raise one's opinion of the nation, and add new respect for their institutions. And then, too, whatever may be the reality, either as to the provocation offered by Board to this woman, or her disregard of his offer or attempt, we certainly must place external morality at Napa greatly beyond what it is in Simoda, and Lewchewan officers above Japanese for decency and respect."[43]

Having settled upon certain men as the leaders in the incident, the Okinawan officials brought the principal one to Perry aboard the flagship, and there delivered him to the commodore. He was at once returned to the custody of the local officials, under guarantee that the men would be suitably punished. One was to be banished to Yaeyama for life; the others were to be sent to Miyako under sentence for eight years.

While these proceedings were under way, Perry was also pressing Shuri to settle satisfactorily the matter of the exchange of coins, once and for all. As he conversed with the Okinawan officers on the flagship at the close of the trial, "the Commodore also told them [wrote Williams] that he wished a bell to hang at the top of the Monument at Washington, and I really believe he thought more of the procurement of this bell than the settlement of the case of murder and mob."[44]

Perry was anxious to be on his way home; this visit to Okinawa had become an anticlimax. American interest in the Ryukyu Islands in effect came to an end when the Treaty of Kanagawa was signed, opening

Japan to foreign intercourse. He had crossed the frontier islands successfully; signed treaty copies were on their way to Washington. The base
at Naha could be abandoned, and to this end the commodore ordered
that the coal supplies at Tomari were to be taken aboard ship once
more. Nevertheless, he cautioned the Okinawans to hold the depot in
readiness against possible need on another day. Perhaps he felt that the
presence of an American coal depot—even though it was an empty one
—would serve as a technical check upon British, Russian, or French
interests.

He had now only to tidy up his relations with the Shuri government
and the Okinawan people, and to prepare for his own return to
Washington. A number of points required consideration. He must be
careful to arm himself with proof that he had followed the president's
orders and had pursued a course of friendship and justice and had acted
with the "consent of the natives." The files at Washington contained
his early statements maintaining that Ryukyu was an autonomous
principality. There was the practical problem of reserving American
interests at Naha against unforeseeable emergencies in China or Japan,
and there was the ever-present threat of European intrusion.

A treaty with the Shuri government would provide for these things,
establishing a record in black and white that the Ryukyu kingdom and
the United States were in agreement and on friendly terms. It would
create a formal relationship which the other Western powers could not
lightly brush aside. It could be used as precedent for other treaties, if
such were demanded.

On July 8 Perry's representatives presented to the regent the rough
draft of a "Compact" which the commodore desired to have. A pream-
ble stated that the Okinawans were signing the compact voluntarily
and as an independent and sovereign people. To this the king's officers
refused to put their signatures, and instead brought forth a list of things
which they desired the United States government to guarantee. Williams points out that these were a catalogue of the pressures to which
they had been compelled to submit during the period of American
occupation. The Okinawans wanted the text clearly to show that the
document was drawn and signed under compulsion.

Perry's men returned to the ship and consulted with the commodore.

A company of marines landed with orders to stay at the Ameku Temple at Tomari, to which it was proposed to summon the regent if there were any further difficulty about signing. On July 10 the officers appointed to negotiate went ashore again "to hold another interview with the regent, when they soon succeeded in arranging all the terms of the compact satisfactorily to both parties and obtained from the regent a promise that a bazaar should be opened on shore, on the succeeding Wednesday and Thursday, for the officers of the ships. It was also arranged that the Commodore would visit the regent at an appointed hour on the morrow. On the next day, in the morning, the Commodore sent on shore a number of presents for the regent, treasurer and other officers of the island, consisting of revolvers, lorgnettes, a dressing case, and numerous valuable agricultural implements. He was particularly careful to send a handsome present to the poor woman who had been the subject of Board's outrage. At noon he landed himself, and with a small escort of marines, visited the regent at the town hall."[45]

Thus the official *Narrative* describes the evolution of the compact. Spalding (who later became a rear admiral) presents a somewhat different version, ending his account with an explosion of indignation. The "small escort" mentioned by Perry consisted of one large howitzer from the "Mississippi," one large howitzer from the "Powhatan" (each manned by crewmen bearing cutlasses), two bands, and forty-eight marines in parade dress. "Our government should pay a little attention to the fantastic tricks which its commodorial gentry cut up in such countries as Loo Choo—'fixed ammunition,' 'cutlasses' and 'ball-cartridges' taken ashore among a people whose forts are disarmed; among whom not one offensive weapon was noticed after months of intercourse; and whose nation in its present condition, reversing the remark of Chatham, might be driven with a crutch."[46]

At the Naha town hall on July 11 copies of the "Compact with Lew Chew" were signed and exchanged. Spalding dubbed it the "Compact of the Chicken with the Horse in the Stable—I won't tread on your toes if you won't tread on mine."

The text follows:

"COMPACT BETWEEN THE UNITED STATES AND THE KINGDOM
OF LEW CHEW, SIGNED AT NAPHA, GREAT LEW CHEW,
THE 11TH DAY OF JULY, 1854

"Hereafter, whenever citizens of the United States come to Lew Chew, they shall be treated with great courtesy and friendship. Whatever articles these persons ask for, whether from the officers or people, which the country can furnish, shall be sold to them; nor shall the authorities interpose any prohibitory regulations to the people selling; and whatever either party may wish to buy shall be exchanged at reasonable prices.

"Whenever any ships of the United States shall come into any harbor in Lew Chew, they shall be supplied with wood and water at reasonable prices; but if they wish to get other articles they shall be purchaseable only at Napha.

"If ships of the United States are wrecked on Great Lew Chew, or on islands under the jurisdiction of the royal government of Lew Chew, the local authorities shall dispatch persons to assist in saving life and property, and preserve what can be brought ashore till the ships of that nation come to take away all that may have been saved; and the expenses incurred in rescuing these unfortunate persons shall be refunded by the nation they belong to.

"Whenever persons from ships of the United States come ashore in Lew Chew they shall be at liberty to ramble where they please, without hinderance, or having officials sent to follow them, or to spy what they do; but if they violently go into houses, or trifle with women, or force people to sell them things, or do other such like illegal acts, they shall be arrested by the local officers but not maltreated, and shall be reported to the captain of the ship to which they belong, for punishment by him.

"At Tumai [Tomari] is a burial ground for citizens of the United States, where their graves and tombs shall not be molested.

"The government of Lew Chew shall appoint skilful pilots, who shall be on the look-out for ships appearing off the island; and if one is seen coming toward Napha, they shall go out in good boats beyond the reefs to conduct her in to a secure anchorage; for which service

335

the captain shall pay the pilot five dollars, and the same for going out of the harbor beyond the reefs.

"Whenever ships anchor at Napha the local authorities shall furnish them with wood at the rate of three thousand six hundred copper cash per thousand catties; and with water at the rate of six hundred copper cash (43 cents) for one thousand catties, or six barrels full, each containing thirty American gallons.

"Signed in the English and Chinese languages, by Commodore Matthew C. Perry, commander-in-chief of the United States naval forces in the East India, China and Japan Seas, and special envoy to Japan, for the United States; and by Sho Fu Fing, superintendent of affairs (Tsu-li-kwan) in Lew Chew, and Ba Rio-si, treasurer of Lew Chew, at Shui, for the government of Lew Chew; and copies exchanged this 11th day of July, 1854, or the reign Hien Fung, 4th year, 6th moon, 17th day, at the town hall of Napha."[47]

Spalding's comment was that "as a mouse in the talons of the eagle, they promised everything."

The commodore was entertained ashore for the last time. Gifts were exchanged, and according to the *Narrative*, the principals in this small diplomatic drama parted on a note of friendly goodwill. Perry had his way, and the Okinawans had put the best face on it that they could.

As for the gifts which Perry made in the interests of his "technological development program," Spalding noted that they included a cotton gin and butter churn, neither of which was of any conceivable use on Okinawa. An Okinawan was asked to guess what the churn might be; he concluded that it must be a fan used to cool people working at the threshing machine near which it stood. The "handsome present" for the outraged woman consisted of several yards of cotton cloth. No one knows what became of the lorgnettes; and the revolvers for the regent seemed curiously inappropriate to the royal house of the Ryukyu kingdom.

In return for these Perry asked for stones to be placed in the fabric of the Washington Monument, then under construction. Two were provided, but one of them was not to his liking and was broken up aboard ship to be used for scrubbing decks. A bell was sent down from

Shuri to the ship, but upon examination it was found to be imperfect and was rejected. In its stead a second bell was sent out. This was the great Gokoku-ji bell which had been cast for King Sho Taikyu in A.D. 1456. It had been hanging in Bettelheim's temple-residence and the Okinawans were willing to part with it. Bettelheim was delighted to assist in dismantling the Gokoku-ji; he wrote: "I was greatly rejoiced . . . and loudly expressed the comfort I felt at seeing a heathen temple breaking up now in real earnest. . . . 'So let thy enemies perish, O Lord. Let their house be made desolate, and their Bishoprick let another take.' "*

Williams wondered if Perry's plan to hang this bell at the top of the Washington Monument meant that it would be used "to bring tired statesmen together or to ring assembly for Fourth of July orations," and noted that Perry was so delighted to have it that he seemed to forget the irksome subject of the coins.

THE END OF THE BETTELHEIM AFFAIR

Many kindnesses had been showered on the Bettelheims by visiting ships—the casks of wine left by the French admiral, the seven pairs of shoes left by Commander Glynn, an accordion given to Mrs. Bettelheim to use in hymn-singing, cakes and clothes for the children—and these months of the American occupation brought them considerate attention. The children were made much of, and Mrs. Bettelheim enjoyed many small courtesies, of which she had been so long denied. In association with the Americans, the family had been able to move about with unprecedented freedom, but nothing could overcome the animosity with which the Okinawans regarded them. It was transferred to their successors.

Mrs. Bettelheim and the three children sailed for Shanghai on February 8, 1854, aboard the U.S.S. "Supply." Her husband was to join her later on the China coast. A missionary named E. H. Moreton and his family came in to replace the Bettelheims, arriving aboard the

* The stone from Okinawa is embedded in the monument wall on the 220th landing; the bell was rejected by the Washington Monument Committee and was bequeathed by Perry to the Naval Academy.

British ship "Robena," carrying a cargo of coolies for American ports. Spalding described Moreton as "a pleasant-voiced little preacher with a mild face and cockney aspiration of the letter h. He had come with his wife and child from England to dwell at Napa, as spiritual teacher to a people who are about as well-prepared to receive Christianity as they were when his predecessor, six years before, went among them."[48] Williams noted that a great coolness at once developed between Dr. Bettelheim and his unfortunate successor, and that the squadron's officers and men tended to side with the Moretons.

On July 10 the government of Ryukyu addressed a final long petition to Commodore Perry, beseeching him to take away both Bettelheim and the Moretons:

"FROM THE AUTHORITIES OF LEW CHEW TO COMMODORE PERRY:

"A prepared statement. [We] earnestly beg your excellency's kind consideration of some circumstances; and that, to show compassion on our little country, you will take away back to their own land Bettelheim and Moreton, who have remained here long. . . .

"In the years 1844 and 1846 some French officers came, and the Englishman Bettelheim also brought hither his wife and children to reside, and they all required something to be daily given them, to our continual annoyance and trouble. Whenever an English or French ship came in, we earnestly represented these circumstances to them, and besought them to take these people away with them. The Frenchmen, knowing our distresses, went away in the year 1848 to their own country, and have not hitherto returned; but Bettelheim has loitered away years here and not gone, and now, further, has brought Moreton with his family to take his place and live here, greatly to the discomfort of the people, and distress and inconvenience of the country.

"We have learned that your excellency has authority over all the East Indian, China and Japan seas, and not a ship of any western country can go from one of these seas to the other but you know and regulate its movements. Wherefore we lay before you our sad condition in all its particulars, humbly beseeching your kind regard upon it, and requesting that, when your fine ships return, you will take both Bettelheim and Moreton away with you. This will solace and raise us up from our low condition, and oblige us in a way not easy to be expressed. We wish your life may be prolonged to a thousand autumns, in the enjoyment of the highest felicity."[49]

Perry yielded to this entreaty to the degree that he promised to speak informally with the British authorities at Hongkong concerning the position of the mission at Naha.

Officers and men alike felt a kindly interest in this lonely Christian outpost, and the interest was enhanced by the circumstances of its origin and support among naval personnel. They were not unmindful of Bettelheim's personal services as commissary agent to themselves in 1853 and 1854. To record their appreciation they presented him with a metal cup, suitably inscribed. As a gesture of goodwill toward the mission itself, a fund of $275 was collected in individual contributions throughout the squadron. On July 13 Williams and several others went ashore to present this as an American gift to the British Loo Choo Naval Mission: "We found Dr. Bettelheim just going afloat with a boatful of baggage, including chairs, tables and many things which surprised us in one going where such articles of furniture are plenty; and on reaching the house [Gokoku Temple] we saw it was bare enough. Mr. Moreton merely remarked in reply to our observations that he thought Dr. Bettelheim would have taken the house too, if he could have done so. Something must be wrong about Bettelheim to act in such strange ways, and when we heard how he had claimed half the money given to the mission and had gone to Edgarton and some other sailors to ask them to whom they supposed they had given their subscriptions, his mercenary spirit was too plain."[50]

The doctor had enjoyed the prestige of association with the pompous commodore and was capable of indulging in extremes of flattery. This appears to have reached its highest public expression on the last Sunday at Naha, upon an occasion recorded by Spalding: "The next Sunday on board, a sermon, blasphemous in character, was preached by a missionary [Bettelheim] in which the American commander was likened to another Jesus Christ, and a parallel deliberately instituted between our Saviour's mission on earth and Commodore Perry's mission to Japan. That functionary [Perry] sat on the quarterdeck, meanwhile, listening to all this without evincing, so far as one could perceive, the slightest displeasure."[51]

Bettelheim had a busy last week making ready to leave Naha. He had done well financially; he had claimed half the squadron's gift to the mission, he had managed to save and bank money presumably from his missionary stipend, and it appears that as he left the islands the government returned to him in lump sum all that he had "spent" since 1846. The coins left in the market place had been gathered in by watchful officials. With this windfall went bundles of pamphlets and tracts collected and stored over the years. Perhaps the Shuri gentlemen found amused satisfaction in thus at last fulfilling the laws forbidding commerce and the the distribution of Christian propaganda. According to the *Narrative*: "Whatever satisfaction the American departure may have afforded the Lew Chewans was doubtless enhanced by the fact that the ships took away Dr. Bettelheim. . . . The earnestness of application to the Commodore to take Dr. Bettelheim away with him forcibly demonstrates the very little prospect there was of any useful labors, on his part, among the natives. . . ."[52]

In this view Bettelheim's missionary colleagues in other ports were ready to concur. The seamen's chaplain at Honolulu had called for an impartial investigation of "most singular reports . . . respecting the manner in which that mission is now conducted," and a doctor on the China coast noted that "many of the ways and means employed to further Bettelheim's cause seemed only to aggravate and hinder, and were often of such a nature as to demean himself and lose respect for Christianity."[52]

On July 14 the commodore gave a state dinner aboard the flagship to honor the regent and his principal officers. On the next day the "Lexington" sailed for Hongkong. On July 17 the last American ships left the waters of Okinawa, the "Powhatan" bearing Dr. Bettelheim and the "Mississippi" carrying away the redoubtable Perry.

A Chinese returning to the Middle Kingdom aboard one of these ships wrote that in their conduct the men of Okinawa "resemble those of the golden age of high antiquity." This was the highest tribute he could pay. The day closed an exciting chapter in Okinawan history; quiet descended for a brief time on Okinawa's hills and harbors. But the "golden age" did not return.

In the name of the boy-king Sho Tai, the regent submitted a report to the emperor at Peking. This was forwarded by the Fukien officials under date of February 12, 1855. The text reflects Shuri's conformity to China's style of treating with barbarians:

" . . . The Admiral [Perry] stated that on February 3rd he would conduct his officers and soldiers to the palace for a personal interview with the Heir Apparent and his Ministers for New Year's felicitations and other purposes. The officials were repeatedly instructed to request that the meeting be solemnized with the ministers at the T'a-pa (Naha) *yamen*, but the barbarians would not agree.

"On the 3rd he did force his way into the palace at the head of his troops. The barbarians paid their respects and led their troops away in silence. . . .

"As to the said barbarians, the Moretons, they still wilfully loiter about, and for the things of their daily use they employ a great deal of extortion, exhausting the country and embittering the people. And even worse, they insist we must accept Christianity, are a constant annoyance, and there is no telling what kinds of calamities they will induce. Our anxiety is so great we can hardly eat or sleep. Please tell the English chief to send a ship for Moreton and his family and take them so that there may be peace and quiet."[54]

The Lew Chew Compact was submitted to the United States Senate, which advised ratification on March 3, 1855; six days later the President of the United States proclaimed it to be in effect, but other matters rising as a consequence of Perry's success in Japan proved to be more important to Washington than the price of six barrels of water at Naha and the cost of wood sent off to foreign ships.

CHAPTER EIGHT

JAPAN "PROTECTS" THE OKINAWANS

1855–1878

OKINAWA, SATSUMA, AND THE EUROPEAN POWERS:
THE MAKISHI-ONGA AFFAIR

Okinawa and the Lew Chew Compact were quickly forgotten in the United States. Perry's success was overshadowed by recurrent domestic political crises leading on to civil war and harsh years of reconstruction in the rebellious South.

Perry had demonstrated Japan's weakness to European powers, and the importance of Japan's territorial waters was pointed up during the Crimean War. Russia sought to push into the Mediterranean through the Dardanelles, and Britain and France were determined to block Russian expansion into the warm seas. They proposed to check Russian naval activity in the northern Pacific halfway round the world and, if they could, to blockade the Russian bases on Kamchatka. They needed neutral ports for shelter and supply nearby.

Commodore Perry was followed at Edo Bay by Admiral Sir James Stirling, who signed Britain's first treaty with Japan on October 14, 1854. Vice Admiral Poutiatine signed the first Russo-Japanese treaty on February 7, 1855. And thereafter, one by one, the European powers established formal relations with the Tokugawa government.

Treaty texts, revisions, and supplements attempted to prescribe the rights and privileges of foreign nationals in Japan and to define the boundaries within which Japan's sovereignty would be recognized henceforth in international law. Sooner or later the problem of the Ryukyu relationship would have to be defined and settled.

Great Britain made no effort to establish formal treaty relations with the kingdom; Okinawa was not important to British commercial and military interests after the ports and markets of Japan became accessible. Occasionally a British ship dropped anchor at Naha, but there were no significant commercial resources to be developed, and data for the Admiralty's hydrographic charts could be obtained without reference to Shuri. The Moretons quit the island in 1856, unable longer to bear a legacy of public hostility and ostracism. The Loo Choo Mission was abandoned.

A treaty with Holland, dated 1859, had no significant consequence for either the Netherlands government or the Ryukyu kingdom.

A French treaty negotiated in 1855 was never ratified by Paris, but it was a minor landmark, for it became part of Satsuma's intrigue to increase Shimazu's power in Japan vis-à-vis the Tokugawa government.

Shimazu Saihin (or Nariakira) dominated Satsuma clan affairs from 1851 until his sudden death in July, 1858. It will be recalled that as heir apparent he had been consulted at Edo in 1846, when the French made their first overtures through Okinawa, and that he had received the shogun's tacit permission to come to some accommodation or trading arrangement with the French. Having succeeded to the clan headship, he was now in a position to act, alert to every move which Perry made to breach the seclusion walls.

The Edo government had been weakened by the Kanagawa Treaty. Throughout Japan subordinate daimyo were restive; there was no agreement upon coastal-defense policies and the regulation of foreign intercourse.

Saihin was determined that Satsuma should have a large share of foreign trade on terms favorable to the Shimazu clan. Between 1806 and 1859 Okinawan tribute ships had crossed to China at least forty-five times. The profit to Kagoshima was immense. If the Chinese were free to enter Japan's ports, or if Western vessels were at liberty to transport cargoes from China directly to Japan proper, Satsuma stood to lose heavily. Early discussions with the French had come to nothing, but Perry's actions at Edo Bay and at Naha had required keen consideration. Inviting prospects of trade had to be weighed against the military risks of foreign intervention.

A decade of entanglements with the French, the British, and the Americans on Okinawa (1845-55) emboldened Nariakira. Nakahama

Manjiro's stories of the Western world intrigued him. Against bitter opposition within the Satsuma clan itself—not least from his half-brother Hisamitsu—he moved ahead, maturing plans for a monopolistic trade relationship with France, through Okinawa.

Two months after Perry left Naha for the last time, Kagoshima sent a memorandum to Shuri which concerned the treatment of foreigners. Shuri responded with a document of its own stating Okinawan views, based upon unique experience. Concurrently, a series of regulations, prompted by experience with American bluejackets ashore, were issued to govern Okinawan relations with any foreigners who might put into Naha thereafter. Singing, dancing, and samisen playing were to be prohibited while foreign ships were in port, and there was to be no private commerce at open trading booths. In this fashion both morals and monopolies would be preserved.

Satsuma instituted a close inquiry into the religious life of the Okinawan people. Although the American expeditionary force was under most strict orders to demonstrate that the United States government believed in the separation of Church and State and was not seeking to promote the proscribed Christian religion, Satsuma's agents had become aware that some members of the American force had violated orders and had attempted privately to distribute Christian religious tracts among the common people.

Apparently no Christian converts could be found, but in the course of the inquiry some converts to the proscribed evangelical Shin sect of Buddhism were ferreted out. In Shimazu's eyes these were almost as dangerous, politically speaking, as the dread "Kirishitans" might be. Fourteen Okinawans were seized and banished to Yaeyama.

In January, 1855, French ships came again to Naha. They desired to revive the Catholic Mission and to obtain a treaty. In March a house was built ashore for the new missionary, Father Furet, and his Chinese assistant. By October negotiations for a treaty were well under way. On December 17 the French vice-admiral, Nicholas-François Guerin, exchanged validating signatures with the regent.

This time the Okinawans had Satsuma's full consent to treat with foreigners. Nariakira directed each move from behind the scenes.

Okinawan officials were gaining experience which could be of later value to Satsuma. He rewarded Itarashiki *Satonushi* (the "Ichirazichi" of Perry's account) for his skill in handling the unpredictable and stubborn strangers. It was proposed to send Satsuma agents secretly to study the French language at Naha.

By 1856 Nariakira's plans were well advanced; he was one of the most influential men in Japan and one of the most wealthy daimyo. His revenues from Okinawa alone at this period were estimated at the equivalent of $900,000 annually. He enjoyed the confidence of many important feudal lords throughout Japan and of the imperial court at Kyoto. His strongest opponent, however, was his own half-brother Hisamitsu, the heir-presumptive, and between the two there was a bitter enmity.

All went well with his plans for about eighteen months. In February, 1857, the French Mission at Ryukyu presented to young King Sho Tai an artillery fieldpiece with all auxiliary equipment. It was in effect a sample of the "trading goods" in which Shimazu Nariakira was most interested. Itarashiki was ordered to become familiar with the use of this formidable new weapon.

In June, Satsuma relaxed orders restricting "fraternization" between the French visitors and the common people, maintaining only the strict prohibition upon Christian missionary work. In August, a Satsuma representative named Ichiki Shoemon came down from Kagoshima with instructions to conclude a secret agreement with the French.

The problem of a trading agreement was first discussed with the two Okinawan leaders Itarashiki and Onga. Ostensibly the commercial agreement was to be an Okinawan affair, worked out between Shuri and the French officers. The goods were to be delivered to Satsuma through Naha. Details of this first conference were reported to Kagoshima in September. In October, Ichiki and Onga widened the basis for negotiation by giving secret instructions to the Shuri officials. These related to the classes of goods which could be supplied to, and purchased from, the French.

Nariakira was meanwhile kept well informed of the negotiations for a commercial treaty between the shogunate and the United States, then being carried on by Townsend Harris at Shimoda. This treaty, he feared, would strengthen the Tokugawa monopoly on foreign trade, and threatened his carefully nurtured plans for trade with France through Okinawa. In December he ordered three men on Okinawa (Owan, Ichiki, and Iwashita) to study the English language, in anticipation of negotiations for a share of American or British commerce. This arduous task they were expected to undertake while dealing with the French.

In February, 1858, Ichiki and Itarashiki took up direct negotiations with the French. For this purpose Ichiki represented himself to be a Ryukyuan doctor from Tokara Island. Under the treaty of 1855 it was agreed that certain students would go to France for study, that Ryukyu would purchase a small war-vessel and certain arms from France, and that regular commercial traffic would be established.

Extensive French records of this period in Okinawa come principally from the hands of the missionary-priests, who worked closely with the French government.[1] Furet was forbidden by Shuri to preach publicly or to proselytize, but he and his assistant were free to travel about and to study the language. He was not a Bettelheim, but a man of superior intellectual gifts and of a sympathetic, enquiring mind, whose papers reflect an appreciation of Okinawan scholars and scholarly traditions. In letters dated at Naha, June 1, 1858, he described the two academies in which Okinawan leaders were being educated. At Shuri a basic curriculum in Japanese studies prepared the Shuri gentry for lifetime work in the general administration. At Naha (Kume Village) the curriculum was Chinese, still devoted to the Chinese classics and dedicated to the preparation of men for the "China service." (Of all the government's important administrators at this time, only the magistrate for Naha was customarily appointed from among the Kume scholars; all others were prepared at Shuri.) Between the two institutions Furet discovered an intense rivalry; the Shuri men enjoyed authority and relative economic well-being, whereas the men of Kume lived in scholarly but happy indigence, confident in a sense of superior cultivation in the classical Chinese tradition. Furet and his associates had six teachers at Shuri and three at Naha. He found them letter-perfect in the Chinese language, expert calligraphers, but weak in interpretation. They seemed to have little genuine understanding of the intellectual content of texts mastered through repetitious discipline of eye, hand, and memory.

It now briefly appeared that there would develop on Okinawa two additional schools, the one dedicated to the study of English and the other to French, with Okinawan students mingling with Japanese students sent down from Satsuma but representing themselves to be from the northern Ryukyu islands.

In April, 1858, Itarashiki was rewarded handsomely for his services in negotiating with the American commodore and the French vice-admiral; he was made nominal Chief of Makishi District and took thereafter the title Makishi *Pechin*. In May, Ichiki and Onga went up to report at Kagoshima. Plans were drawn for a new "foreign affairs" office, which was established at Shuri in July, the month in which the American Townsend Harris brought to successful conclusion long negotiations for a Treaty of Amity and Commerce at Edo (July 29, 1858).

Shimazu Nariakira died suddenly on August 25, in his forty-ninth year. His successor, Hisamitsu (later known as Saburo), immediately reversed Satsuma's policies in Ryukyu. The boy King Sho Tai and his chief ministers were required to renew the ancient oath of obedience to the Shimazu overlords.[2] The vindictive Hisamitsu was determined to destroy every vestige of his half-brother's program, and with great cruelty persecuted Nariakira's associates.

Within the month Ichiki hastened back to Naha with orders that all commodities ordered from France must be delivered by the French within six months, that is to say, by March, 1859. This was obviously impossible. Ichiki himself did not appear to discuss the problem with the French officers. (It was represented to them that he had been killed in a fall from horseback, and a newly-made tomb was shown to the Frenchmen to support the tale.) This demand for quick delivery was merely a shallow excuse to lay on the French the onus of breaking the contract because they would be unable to meet terms newly introduced into the negotiations. The agreement was forthwith canceled, and the French mission sailed away from Naha.

Ichiki emerged from hiding, returned to Satsuma, and lived for many years, but his Okinawan associates were not so fortunate. Satsuma's agents collected documents relating to the French-Okinawan negotiations, an official named Zakimi was found at Shuri ready to charge his fellow countrymen with acts of treason against the king. The accused were arrested in September, 1859. A number of prominent men were banished from Okinawa. Onga died under the rigors of imprisonment and torture in March, 1860. In June, 1862, Makishi *Pechin* was summoned under close arrest to Kagoshima to answer for his part in Nariakira's schemes. He set sail in July under heavy guard, but when the ship was a few miles north of Motobu Peninsula, the prisoner leaped overboard, choosing suicide rather than further imprisonment and torture at the hands of the relentless Shimazu Hisamitsu.

Satsuma's attitude toward foreign intercourse was stiffening on all points. The slogan "Exalt the Emperor! Expel the Barbarians!" began to be heard throughout Japan, and for the first time there were open cries of "Down with the Tokugawa government!" These anti-Bakufu forces extracted from the emperor at Kyoto a secret agreement to issue an order expelling all foreigners from Japan no matter what the consequences; June 23, 1863, was fixed for this extreme defiance of the Western powers. Every concession to foreigners or foreign intercourse was treasonable and all who advocated compromise with the West were under deep suspicion. Shimazu and his advisors felt peculiarly vulnerable in the Ryukyu dependency, used so openly as a base for foreign military and commercial operations. The Ryukyu treaties and negotiations with the French were exceptionally embarrassing.

Two months after Makishi *Pechin* killed himself, one of Shimazu's retainers killed a British subject named Richardson in an incident at Namamugi, near Yokohama. Several others in the foreign party were wounded. The British government demanded satisfaction at Edo and at Kagoshima. The shogunate was evasive and the Satsuma clan defiant. Seven British warships entered Kagoshima Bay in August, 1863, to demand reparations. They were fired upon, but the British guns soon silenced Satsuma's shore batteries and disclosed at once the ineffectiveness of Japan's shore defenses. A number of Satsuma's ships and Okinawan junks were sunk in the harbor.

This enlightening incident brought an extraordinary right-about-face at Kagoshima. Hisamitsu's intense hostility toward the Western world was transformed. This bombardment illustrated how little he knew of it. Henceforth his admiration for the British navy knew no

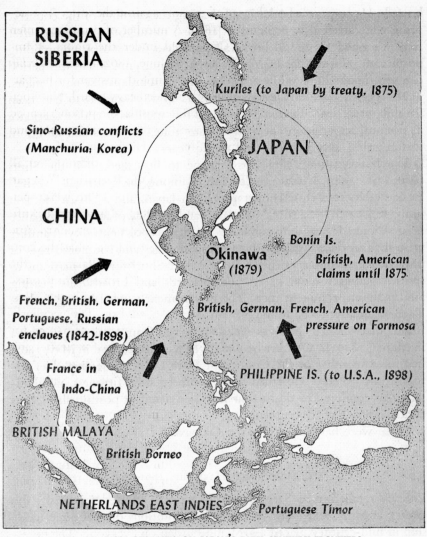

RUSSIAN
SIBERIA

Kuriles (to Japan by treaty, 1875)

Sino-Russian conflicts
(Manchuria; Korea)

JAPAN

CHINA

Bonin Is.

Okinawa
(1879)

British, American
claims until 1875.

French, British, German,
Portuguese, Russian
enclaves (1842-1898)

British, German, French, American
pressure on Formosa

France in
Indo-China

PHILIPPINE IS. (to U.S.A., 1898)

BRITISH MALAYA

British Borneo

NETHERLANDS EAST INDIES   Portuguese Timor

FIG. 20. MAP: OKINAWA ON JAPAN'S 19TH-CENTURY FRONTIERS.

bounds. He became a leader in advocating the opening of the country, promoted the development of a Japanese naval force patterned after Britain's great navy, and broke all precedent in 1866 by entertaining the British minister, Sir Harry Parkes, at Kagoshima. From this period dates the marked preëminence of Satsuma men in Japanese naval affairs.

The persecution of Okinawan leaders in 1858 and 1859 had been fruitless, cruel, and wasteful. Shuri had few men with wide experience in political negotiation and could spare none, for the small kingdom was entering upon difficult and tragic years.

The Makishi-Onga affair, as it came to be called, split the Shuri court leadership. A cleavage developed among the gentry; a "white" faction advocated close coöperation with Japan, and a "black" faction urged resistance to Satsuma's demands and a policy of increased reliance upon China. It was impossible to maintain cool neutrality. Families were torn in their loyalties. There were charges and countercharges of unprecedented bitterness in Okinawan life. Shuri forbade partisans to spread vicious rumors or to post placards and broadsheets bearing attacks upon prominent men. The government needed strong leaders. There were few to be found.

An officer named Ginowan *Uekata* returned from a mission to China in March, 1859. In October he was given a high post and in May, 1862, became a member of the Council of State and the effective chief administrative officer. He ruled with unprecedented firmness, not hesitating to condemn to death four men convicted of posting slanderous attacks upon the government.

These were harsh measures for Okinawa.

CONFUSION AND HARDSHIP, 1861–72

Political retaliation by Satsuma upon Okinawa affected principally the gentry at Shuri and Naha, but general conditions of economic hardship in mid-century placed a growing burden on everyone. The necessity to negotiate with foreigners on one hand and with Satsuma on the other brought into play all the administrative talent Shuri could muster. Taxes were laid on to the limit, for there had been no opportunity to accumulate a margin of surplus in foodstuffs or trading goods upon which the government could draw in meeting crisis needs. In 1855 there had been riots on Tarama Island, and officers had to be dispatched to Kume Island to curb unrest. Typhoons, epidemic sickness, and a long drought brought the people of Miyako to a state of chronic starvation. Here conditions were desperate. Material resources were exhausted; the normal formalities and organization of social life began to distintegrate. The formal ties of marriage, family, and village life and of administrative order began to mean little in the presence of elemental privation. There was rebellious unrest. Officers were sent into the Miyako countryside and nearby islands to investigate and alleviate conditions wherever possible. The criminal laws were read publicly as a warning to all, but taxes were lightened for families which had many children.

As if these disasters were not enough, a tribute ship was lost, but the envoy was rescued and returned to Naha aboard an American whaling ship.

In the midst of political turmoil a serious inflation shook the economy. Four hundred years had passed since the first known Ryukyu coins were issued, and the tiny "pigeon-eye" *sen* manufactured locally during the 17th and 18th centuries had acquired a value of ten per Japanese *mon*. They were meaningless in the new era of potential foreign trade. To offset this, a mint was established at Temposan in Kagoshima to manufacture coins for trading purposes in Ryukyu. These were known as *Ryukyu tsuho* ("current treasure of Ryukyu") and were valued at a hundred Japanese *mon* each at the time of minting. This gave the new Ryukyu coin a value of one thousand of the pigeon-eye *sen*, which by now had become absurdly small flakes of metal which could be handled effectively only in strings bearing a hundred or more.

Within a year the value of the new *tsuho* dropped fifty percent, but the coins were welcomed into wide use. In March, 1863, a Price Control Magistracy was set up, which restored the Ryukyu coin briefly, but again the value declined. The economy was too disorganized to permit an easy transition from barter to currency, and the government too inexperienced to apply its fumbling policies with success.

A blight had fallen upon the leadership resources of Okinawa. The younger men who had done remarkably well in meeting with the

French, the British, and the Americans before 1845 had been driven from the government and silenced. Curiosity and readiness to learn Western languages had meant death and torture, personal abuse and exile. Hisamitsu's sudden and complete reversal of policy at Kagoshima did not bring a revival of interest in foreign affairs at Shuri. While determined young men of the Satsuma clan—Okubo Toshimichi, for instance—defied the Tokugawa edicts and made their way abroad secretly to study the Western world and its institutions, the elders at Shuri shrank from the challenge, and their young contemporaries at Shuri and Naha were given only the dry crumbs of Confucian literary training to prepare them for the revolution which was stirring Asia. On Okinawa the traditional semiannual examinations required exercise in the composition of classical poems in the springtime and of brief formal essays in the autumn. Ryukyu fell far behind, and the Okinawans were left unprepared for the final challenge to its existence as a kingdom.

THE LAST ENTHRONEMENT AT SHURI AND THE MEIJI RESTORATION IN JAPAN

In 1864 Okinawan envoys went over to Peking to seek investiture for the young King Sho Tai. Two years later Chinese ambassadors came to confirm him in his dignities, unaware that they were the last to perform rites which had continued in an unbroken tradition for five hundred years. In November, 1866, they returned to China.[3]

In Japan, three months later (February 13, 1867), Crown Prince Mutsuhito, fifteen years of age, succeeded his father at Kyoto as Emperor of Japan. On October 3, representatives of some forty feudal lords met at Kyoto to consider a memorial which had been submitted to the shogun at Edo, advising him to relinquish his authority to the young emperor and his councilors. Komatsu, representing Shimazu of Satsuma, was the first to signify agreement.

This revolutionary declaration of policy came from a coalition of feudal lords too powerful for the shogun to defy. His resignation was submitted to the emperor on October 14. Formal acceptance on December 15 marked the end of Tokugawa military government, which had endured for 267 years. From January, 1868, the reign-name was changed to Meiji, meaning "Era of Enlightened Government."

Technically, the Tokugawa clan had surrendered control only of those territories over which it exercised direct feudal rule. The new imperial government now had to call on all the other lords individually to surrender their domainal authority as the Tokugawa family had done. The four most powerful clans in the country were Satsuma, Choshu, Tosa, and Hizen. Satsuma took the lead; in August, 1869, the Shimazu family yielded control of Satsuma, Osumi Province, and part of Hyuga to the throne. Within the next two years 272 daimyo followed Shimazu's example.

To ease the problems of administrative transition, the imperial government appointed many of the hereditary lords to be governors in their old fiefs and allowed them a percentage of the fief revenues as salary. For a time the old clan officers carried on as officers of the new central government. Shimazu Hisamitsu (Saburo) was appointed "Governor of Satsuma and Ryukyu."

In August, 1871, an imperial decree ordered the old feudal divisions (han) to be replaced by a new system of prefectures (ken), within which departmental subdivisions were established. Representatives of the central government would take over many of the important posts within the new prefectural administrations.

The old domains of the Shimazu family were split up. Hyuga became a department of Miyazaki Prefecture; Satsuma and Osumi became departments in the new prefecture of Kagoshima; but the Shimazu were still powerful, and in Kagoshima Prefecture alone all offices in the administration were reserved to Satsuma men.

In this division the northern islands of the Ryukyu chain, which had once been part of the Ryukyu kingdom, but had been controlled directly by Satsuma after 1609, were now attached to Osumi Department within Kagoshima Prefecture.

What now to do about Ryukyu? Should the annual tribute exacted from Shuri by Shimazu be sent up to the imperial government at Tokyo? Should it be counted as tax due to the new Kagoshima prefectural government? Should it be shared by Osumi Department, or should it go exclusively to Satsuma? Should it be included in calculations of prorated income for the Shimazu family? Above all else, what attitude toward the Ryukyu kingdom would be adopted by Japan in international affairs?

UNDEFENDED OKINAWA: A FRONTIER PROBLEM FOR JAPAN

The political crises which led to the restoration of imperial authority and to Japan's emergence as a world power were brought about in large degree by threat of foreign aggression and the Tokugawa administration's inability to meet it satisfactorily. The new government, a coalition of strong anti-Tokugawa factions and forces, was acutely sensitive to every pressure on the frontiers. These were vaguely understood and ill-defined in 1853 when Perry came to press his demands. It will be remembered that when he asked for treaty right to trade at the port of Matsumae in Ezo (Hokkaido) and at Naha on Okinawa, he was told that these outposts were too distant to be considered and that the emperor exercised only limited authority there. Perry had promptly concluded a separate compact with the Ryukyuan government. This was a hint that if Japan did not define and assert her claim in the off-lying islands, they would soon be lost and in the hands of aggressive foreign powers.

We can better understand what is about to take place in Okinawa if we draw an imaginary circle about the main islands of Japan, centered at Tokyo, and note the critical boundary disputes which took place in the twenty years following Perry's visit. Both the United States and Russia played a significant part in them.

To the north Japan had to block Russian encroachment in Sakhalin and the Kuriles: Russian designs upon the rich, undeveloped island of Ezo had become unmistakably clear. A treaty in 1855 stipulated territorial division of the Kuriles, but left the problem of Sakhalin unresolved, and there Russian and Japanese colonists were in open conflict. Missions to Russia in 1862 and 1866 were inconclusive. In 1870 the Japanese asked a former Secretary of State of the United States (William Seward) to mediate. He had recently completed the purchase of Russian Alaska for the United States and now proposed to Japan that it purchase the island of Sakhalin. This Tokyo tried to do, but the Russians did not complete the transaction. A final settlement of the threatening northern boundary dispute was not achieved until Admiral Enomoto Buyo signed a treaty at St. Petersburg on May 7, 1875. Tokyo secured clear title to the Kuriles in exchange for a release of all Japanese claims in Sakhalin.

While the boundary quarrel with Russia was in progress at the north, Japan was drawn into a triangular sovereignty dispute in the Bonin Islands, which lay only five hundred miles southeast of the Japanese capital. It was held that these islands had been granted in fief to Ogasawara Sadayori in the late 16th century, but Japanese interest and settlement had been intermittent. In June, 1827, Captain Beechey of H.M.S. "Blossom" had surveyed the archipelago and posted a declaration of possession in the name of the British crown, an inscribed copper plate nailed to a tree on an uninhabited island. Two years later a group of settlers sponsored by the British consul at Honolulu, but under the leadership of an American named Nathaniel Savoury, appeared in the Bonin Islands. During the next twenty years a mixed colony of British, American, Hawaiian, Portuguese, Italian, French, and Spanish adventurers developed, with fluctuating fortune, on these islands.

Perry surveyed the Bonins, bought land there for a coaling depot, and declared his intention to claim that they were under the protection of the United States. Savoury was ordered to run up the American flag. The British at Hongkong protested, courteously but strongly, and Washington repudiated Perry's unauthorized action. The Japanese were alarmed; the shogunate sent officers over to the Bonins in 1864 to reassert Japan's traditional claims, but the sovereignty question remained in dispute until 1875, when the United States and Great Britain agreed to abandon all claims.

On the western segment of Japan's frontiers the government was plunged into a bitter dispute with Korea. For five centuries the Korean court had paid tribute to Peking, as the Okinawans did, and upon special occasions had sent envoys and gifts to the court of Japan. The small island of Tsushima, lying in the straits between the two countries, served as the point of transshipment for trade and the gateway for diplomacy. The local daimyo of Tsushima had enjoyed prosperity out of all proportion to the natural resources or territorial extent of his domain. Immediately after the Restoration of 1868 Japan sought to establish clear boundaries in these waters and to give precise definition to political and economic relations with Korea. The Koreans would have nothing to do with this new order of things, accused the Japanese of betraying their Far Eastern heritage, and charged them with subservience to the Western powers, with which Korea wanted nothing to do. Korea's refusal to recognize the new government at Tokyo was couched in offensive terms. This rancorous dispute prompted a strong faction in Japan to demand war upon Korea, and the crisis was not resolved until the essential points at issue were covered by the Treaty of Kangwha, signed in February, 1876.

In the midst of all these crises, north, west, and east, there occurred an incident far to the south, in Formosa, which brought to world attention the exposed position of the Ryukyu Islands and the uncertain status of the Okinawan kingdom.

THE FORMOSA INCIDENT: JAPAN'S EXCUSE FOR STRONG ACTION[4]

In December, 1871, one of Shuri's tribute ships was blown off course and wrecked on the wild coast of southern Formosa. Aborigines of the Botan tribe fell upon the survivors, murdered fifty-four of them, and plundered the wreck. Seven men escaped into the jungle and made their way to a nearby Formosan Chinese border village.

In time news of the affair reached Shuri and was reported to Kagoshima. From Kagoshima the story went up to Tokyo. Shrewd leaders there saw in this incident several political advantages, which they were quick to exploit. It is noteworthy that upon the consequences of this accident in Formosa Japan erected and defended all subsequent claims to full sovereignty in the Ryukyu Islands, but that from the moment Shuri's report and petition for help reached Kagoshima, the Okinawans themselves had virtually nothing whatever to do with the affair.

In September, 1872, the Japanese minister at Peking asked China to punish the aborigines on Formosa. China disclaimed all responsibility for law and order on the Formosan east coast or in mountainous regions, which constitute two-thirds of the island.

In choosing to make a point of this, Tokyo had skillfully adopted an issue in which the Western maritime powers were deeply interested, but peculiarly frustrated. The wild, unmarked coasts of Formosa and the undisciplined inhabitants had become a major threat to Western shipping in Far Eastern waters. Loss of life and cargo increased each year. Peking was unable to police the island and was indifferent to the problem. Chinese government officials were sometimes accessories to the crimes committed in Formosan waters. (For instance, local Chinese officers had ordered the cold-blooded execution of 187 castaways on one occasion in 1842.) Western governments would look with favor on any action designed to improve conditions in Formosa—or so the Japanese believed.

At this point they engaged the services of an American who had an unmatched knowledge of Formosa, of the Chinese officials there, and of the attitudes and personalities of foreign representatives in China. This was General Charles W. LeGendre. He had been for some years American consul at Amoy, with Formosa under his consular jurisdiction. After years of fruitless effort to persuade either the Chinese or the American governments to take disciplinary action on the island, he had set out for home. As he passed through Tokyo he was asked to confer with the Japanese government on the Formosa problem. He forthwith resigned his consular commission in the U.S. foreign service, dating his resignation at Tokyo, December 19, 1872.

The first exchange of official views at Peking included references to the Okinawan victims of the incident as "subjects of Japan," whose interests the Japanese were entitled to defend. Japan's Minister of Foreign Affairs Soejima Taneomi went to Peking in early 1873 to negotiate on this and other outstanding Sino-Japanese problems, thus raising the question to the highest levels of diplomatic reference. He saw the confusion of China's vacillating government and observed Peking's efforts to win foreign aid in checking Japan's development as a neighboring modern state.

Soejima returned to Tokyo convinced that the time was ripe for a military expedition into Korea, for China was too weak to offer important opposition, and an overseas venture of this sort would serve as a safety valve for discontent among the samurai within Japan.

The Japanese Council of State was split on the Korean issue; Soejima sided with Saigo Takamori and other military men who wanted to bring Korea to terms satisfactory to Japan and so consolidate Japan's position vis-à-vis Russia and China on the peninsula. This "war party" was opposed by the leading statesman Iwakura Tomomi, who had just returned from a tour of America and Europe convinced that Japan's first need was order within her domestic administration and strength in her economy. Moreover, he feared that the Western powers might be drawn into a Korean conflict, to Japan's disadvantage.

A bitter debate was held in the emperor's presence on October 14, 1873. A political crisis of the gravest import had developed. When the decision went against the advocates of war in Korea, they resigned from the State Council. Something had to be done now to concentrate and divert the pent-up emotions of dissatisfied samurai who looked to Saigo for leadership.

The unsatisfied claims upon China for redress in the Formosa incident served the purpose. A decision was taken to send an expeditionary force to Formosa to punish the aborigines for the murder of Japan's Okinawan "subjects."

It is significant that the diplomatic and military questions in this were entrusted to two former samurai of Satsuma. Saigo Takamori's brother, General Saigo Tsugumichi, was given direction of the military campaign, and political management of the affair was entrusted to Okubo Toshimichi. The Okinawans were not consulted. By tradition and training these Satsuma men expected unquestioning acquiescence at Shuri in any program involving them which Satsuma men might choose to dictate.

The Japanese soon discovered that European diplomats at Peking and at Tokyo were not pleased by Soejima's successes at Peking, nor happy to see the rapid increase in Japan's importance as an emergent power in Far Eastern affairs. Settlement of the Formosa question and recognition of claims to sovereignty in the Ryukyus now became an affair of honor with the Japanese.

In early 1874 the Japanese government engaged three Americans to assist in carrying through the proposed Formosa expedition. The first, General LeGendre, was granted the temporary personal rank of a minister in Japan's diplomatic service. Lieutenant James R. Wasson, lately of the U.S. Army Corps of Engineers, was engaged and was given colonel's rank in the Japanese Army. Lieutenant Commander Douglas Cassel of the United States Navy was asked to join the organization with a commodore's rank in Japan's new navy. This he did upon the recommendation of John Bingham, American Minister at Tokyo. The U.S. Navy at Washington released Cassel to inactive duty status, sent out hydrographic charts of Formosan waters, and provided other data. A British and an American ship were engaged for transport services.

Suddenly the Chinese at Peking changed their minds. They now claimed full sovereignty throughout Formosa and claimed the Ryukyu Islands as well. There is evidence that they were encouraged in this bold right-about-face by the British minister at the Chinese court. The Russian chargé d'affaires at Tokyo warned all Russians to abstain from participation, for a diplomatic storm was brewing; faced with this new turn of affairs the American minister (Bingham) reversed himself, withdrew his approval, and ordered Americans and American ships to withdraw from the proposed expedition.

The details of the Formosa expedition are not properly part of a history of the Ryukyu Islands and can be summarized.

Foreign pressure upon the Japanese government was great, and at one point Tokyo ordered the expeditionary forces to wait at Nagasaki until the problem was clarified and all the dangers of foreign intervention were assessed.

General Saigo, however, refused to accept such orders of the civil government. He assumed full responsibility for his actions and ordered the Japanese ships to sail. This was perhaps the first instance in modern times in which the Japanese military high command openly defied the orders of the civil administration. Since Japan won her point in this affair with China, Saigo was deemed successful and was therefore forgiven, but he had set a disastrous precedent for the commanding generals who followed him.

The Chinese put up no serious resistance in the field. General Saigo's forces landed on South Formosa, chastised the aborigines of the Botan tribe to his satisfaction, and settled down to await the outcome of negotiations between the Chinese and Japanese governments. The Chinese commissioner on Formosa (Pan Wi) was represented to have full powers to arrange a settlement with General Saigo, and in conferences on June 24 and 25 the two men reached an agreement. When the terms became known at Peking, the Chinese government repudiated them and demanded that all Japanese forces should be withdrawn from Formosa before a new settlement could be negotiated. This reversal and rebuff angered the Tokyo government and inflamed public opinion; a declaration of war against China seemed imminent. Okubo hastened to Peking. September and October were spent in rancorous debate, during which the foreign diplomats brought all the pressure they could to bear upon Okubo. He held to his point, and at last, on October 31, 1874, a brief, formal document was signed and sealed at Peking to close the incident. By its terms China formally recognized the propriety of Japan's action, promised to pay for the roads, bridges, and buildings Japan had constructed on Formosa, and specified that consolation money would be paid over to the Okinawan survivors of the 1871 massacre and to the families of those who had lost their lives.[5]

The Japanese were not confident that China would fulfill its promises in this; Thomas Wade, Britain's minister at Peking, was called upon to provide a personal guaranty, in the form of a contract appended to the formal agreement.

In this agreement the Okinawans were referred to four times, but only as " subjects of Japan." Tokyo had succeeded in winning China's formal recognition of paramount Japanese interest in the Ryukyus and to this Great Britain's representative had set his signature.

Japan had now to persuade the king and government at Shuri to accept all the consequences of this new relationship, arranged and proclaimed by Tokyo without Okinawan consent.

TOKYO PROCLAIMS PARAMOUNT RESPONSIBILITY FOR THE RYUKYU KINGDOM

Okinawan leaders were told bluntly what they were expected to do. The severity of Japan's attitude in the period 1872–79—from the time the "Formosa incident" was adopted as an issue until the king's forced abdication—may be understood against the background of much larger events in Japan's national life. The need to close the southern frontier was more clearly evident than ever before. The Ryukyu kingdom was too weak to stand alone. China's weakness and the meddling interference by foreign diplomats at Peking and Tokyo made it appear that if Japan did not assert outright control in the Ryukyus, one of the European powers might sometime take them, under cover of a treaty bargain or a reparations claim made upon China.

The proud Japanese statesmen were determined not to yield positions once taken in international diplomacy. It was a matter of national honor, affecting the prestige of the emperor and his principal ministers.

For the prominent men of Satsuma who were concerned with the Ryukyu problem it was intolerable that the insignificant Okinawans continued to embarrass Tokyo from time to time while the imperial government was endeavoring to win recognition of its claim to the Southern Islands.

The adjustment of administrative relations between Shuri and Tokyo had been a matter of concern from the moment Shimazu surrendered his feudal privileges. We must go back a few years to take up the thread of this story. In January, 1872, two prominent Japanese went down to Shuri to open discussions. The chief of the mission was Narahara Kogoro, *hanshi* or chief retainer managing affairs for the former daimyo Shimazu Saburo. (Narahara is reputed to have been the samurai who had cut down the Englishman Richardson at Namamugi in 1862, although another man of less importance had been executed in his place.) Narahara's associate was Ijichi Sadaka, member of the family traditionally charged with the management of Shimazu's interests on Okinawa.

The two Japanese met with the Council of State at Shuri to discuss the servicing of debts, the payment of principal on obligations to the Shimazu family, and the disposition of the tribute hitherto sent to Kagoshima. It was agreed that Shimazu would cancel the obligation (approximately fifty thousand yen) if Shuri would use an equivalent sum for the relief of destitute families among the Shuri gentry. This was a move certain to generate a measure of goodwill for Tokyo at Shuri and to win support for pro-Japanese policies.

A second series of discussions covered the problem of exploitation of coal deposits known to exist on Yaeyama. Japan was determined to industrialize as rapidly as possible; every corner of the empire was to be explored in search of minerals. While the negotiations were in progress at Shuri, a Japanese ship was surveying Yaeyama waters, using modern methods, and plans were being made at Tokyo to develop all known coal resources. The islands of the Oshima group were a third subject for discussion. Sho Nei had surrendered full control to Satsuma in 1609, but "residual sovereignty" rested with the Ryukyu kingdom by terms of the agreement signed at Kagoshima under duress. Japan proposed to annex the northern islands to Kagoshima Prefecture.

In February, Ijichi conferred with the regent concerning over-all administrative policy in the new era. This was a most delicate problem, for at Tokyo there was strong opposition to Satsuma's growing influence in the Restoration government. It was well known that the Kagoshima prefectural government was little more than the old *han* administration continuing in power under a change of office names and titles. Finance Minister Inoue Kaoru, of the Yamaguchi clan, was determined that the obligations of the old Ryukyu kingdom should be transferred from Kagoshima to the central government. The Okinawans found themselves pawns in a bureaucratic conflict at Tokyo and drawn into the factional strife then pushing Japan to the verge of civil war. Shuri was not being asked for advice or consent; it was being told what to do, never sure which of the contending groups would prove ultimately triumphant. Memories of the Makishi-Onga affair haunted them. The impatient Satsuma samurai were pitted here against hesitant, procrastinating Okinawans. Progress was slow.

In June a customs official and a secretarial staff from Tokyo reached Naha to take up the problems of economic adjustment. These included the determination of responsibility for the issue of Okinawan coinage, which was being minted at Kagoshima. The central government was no longer willing to have a separate coinage within a dependency of the empire nor to risk a "customs leak" through Kagoshima.

While discussions were in progress, word reached Shuri of the massacre of the fifty-four shipwrecked Ryukyuans on Formosa. A report was forwarded through Kagoshima to Tokyo, and the Shuri government was prompted to petition Tokyo for redress of wrongs and damage suffered.

The most important issue which Narahara and Ijichi had to raise with the reluctant Okinawans touched on the relations of the Okinawan king to the Japanese emperor. The imperial government "advised" King Sho Tai to pay his respects to the emperor at Tokyo. The king's presence at the capital would provide opportunities to review the whole range of Ryukyuan-Japanese problems. Obviously, too, this would become a public demonstration of Sho Tai's subordination to Mutsu-hito.

The Okinawan king declined to accept the advice. Instead, he sent word to Tokyo that he was ill. His uncle Prince Ie, and the foremost minister of state, Ginowan *Uekata*, made the journey on his behalf, bearing gifts of the finest products of the Ryukyu Islands. The ambassadors were received with many courtesies by the Japanese Foreign Office, and we have descriptions of them "with Ainu Chiefs and other foreign envoys" attending the opening of the first railway in Japan.

On October 14, 1872, the foreign minister summoned the Okinawans to his presence. Without forewarning he read to them a brief imperial decree: "We have here succeeded to the Imperial Throne of a line unbroken for ages eternal, and now reign over all the land. Ryukyu, situated to the south, has the same race, habits and language, and has always been loyal to Satsuma. We appreciate this loyalty, here raise you to the peerage and appoint you King of Ryukyu *Han*. You, Sho Tai, take responsibility in the administration of the *han*, and assist us eternally."[6]

Prince Ie was taken by surprise. He could do nothing but accept the emperor's decree with a formal expression of thanks.

To cover the bluntness of this declaration of control over Ryukyu, the imperial court ordered a residence to be established in Tokyo for the King of Ryukyu *Han*, provided him a grant of thirty thousand yen, and sent a variety of presents to Shuri. Sho Tai found himself in much the same position as the daimyo who had surrendered their *han* after 1868 and had been confirmed as "governors" in their former feudal domains. Ryukyu was no longer to consider itself an autonomous state (*koku*) but a dependent feudal territory (*han*) holding authority from the emperor. Shuri was directed to hand over to the Foreign Office all treaty correspondence with other states and the original copies of compacts made with the United States, Holland, and France. Henceforth Shuri's foreign relations would be managed by Tokyo.

In November, Tokyo formally notified foreign governments that Japan had assumed responsibility for the Ryukyu kingdom. The United States minister (DeLong) immediately reminded Japan that Shuri had treaties with foreign powers, and that such unilateral action by Tokyo might raise difficult questions. He referred the problem to Washington and, while waiting for instructions, began to collect all the information he could find which might bear upon the status and history of the Ryukyu kingdom.

The Japanese Foreign Office meanwhile assured the United States and other interested powers that Tokyo would assume full responsibility for all obligations and rights affected by the treaties in question. This satisfied everyone concerned but the Okinawans. Washington issued instructions to DeLong on December 18, 1872, to accept the Japanese position.

Prince Ie's mission had been essentially of a diplomatic character. A second mission of some thirty members was now sent to Tokyo under the leadership of Yonabaru *Oyakata* to work out the practical details of this changed relationship. It was agreed that the old rice tax would be canceled, together with the tax laid on in lieu of sugar shipments to Satsuma. The tribute traditionally sent up to Satsuma would hereafter go to Tokyo in the form of the money equivalent for 8,500 *koku* of rice, based on average Osaka Rice Exchange prices in the autumn months. This was in effect a considerable tax relief for Okinawa.

On March 3, 1873, the envoys returned to Shuri. Three weeks later a memorial was issued in the king's name which acknowledged the emperor's gifts, the new title *Han-O*, and the court rank of First Class. The king pointedly though politely indicated that these attentions had come upon him as a complete surprise.

Japan, at this time seething with unrest, was moving toward civil war, but was fearful of foreign intervention and the threat of war with China. The samurai, pensioned off and forbidden to wear swords, were frustrated, dissatisfied with the government, and irritated by the need to make a living in open competition with common people. Japanese prisons were overcrowded with political offenders; the government was preoccupied with the Korean crisis, rebellions in Hizen and Saga, and assassination plots directed against powerful ministers of state.

By contrast the Ryukyus had become a backwater of inactivity in the years 1873 and 1874. A festival was held throughout the islands to celebrate the fact that in all the prisons of Ryukyu not one prisoner was to be found. Reporting on this, certain Tokyo journalists jeered at the Okinawans, saying that they lacked spirit. It did not occur to them that the government at Shuri may have taken this means to show that it was making no effort whatever to prosecute Okinawans who refused to obey new regulations and orders imposed upon Ryukyu by the Japanese. Many of Tokyo's requests, instructions, and demands went unheeded.

Nevertheless, there were signs of change. The introduction of the solar calendar of Western origin was of prime significance. From time immemorial calendar-making had been a matter of state concern in China, involving the emperor's supreme position as "Mediator between Heaven and Earth" and "Regulator of the Seasons." To adopt the Chinese calendar and the ceremonies associated with it had been taken to be evidence that a barbarian people were becoming assimilated to Chinese culture. It came as a disagreeable shock to the Peking bureaucrats to discover that the Ryukyu kingdom had made this concession to Japan and to the West.

A doctor trained in modern (i.e., Western) medical techniques was appointed to local government service on Okinawa, and the "Okinawan Dispensary" came into being. Portraits of the Japanese emperor and empress were sent down to Shuri as an official gift, a delicate reminder of the changed status of the king. The Japanese Ministry of Foreign Affairs opened an office at Naha to replace the old Satsuma agency.

SHURI CHALLENGES AND ANGERS THE TOKYO GOVERNMENT

Making the issue of sovereignty in the Ryukyus a point of departure, Japan's leaders took the nation to the brink of war with China. The quarrel in Formosa had been intended as a *divertissement* for the rest-less samurai at home, but the foreign powers were ranging themselves in support of Peking.

In an atmosphere of grave crisis Home Minister Okubo Toshimichi went to the Chinese capital in September, 1874, to bring about a settle-ment. To his astonishment and chagrin (and to the delight of the Chi-nese), he discovered that Okinawan tribute ships had proceeded as usual from Naha to China, and that envoys from Shuri had performed the customary formal acts of submission to the Chinese throne. A mission reached Peking while he was there.[7]

The presence of Okinawan tribute envoys at the Chinese capital obviously challenged the claims upon which Japan based its policies in the Sino-Japanese controversy. The ink was scarcely dry upon the agreement which Okubo had negotiated in settlement of the Formosa incident. Chinese signatures had been secured for the document, and thereby China had, in effect reliquished claims to the Ryukyus. Okubo was angered. Japan was "losing face." He demanded that the envoys be brought before him. This was refused.

Okubo left Peking late in November. On December 15 the Peking *Court Gazette* published notice of the arrival of the Okinawan tribute mission as if it were a routine matter. Japan's chargé d'affaires (Tei Einei) demanded to see the envoys from Shuri, but, as in the earlier instance, this was not arranged.

In January, 1875, Okubo made a report to the Japanese emperor which reviewed the Formosa incident and formally brought to an end the whole affair. This contained only one passing reference to the Ryu-kyus, in a statement that "the position of a subject *han* [Ryukyu] is for the first time cleared up."

In an affair touching directly upon the imperial Japanese court it was intolerable to Okubo that his official statements to the throne were being contradicted by the actions of the Shuri court and by the presence of its envoys at Peking. He now began to bring pressure to bear on Okinawa, and Shuri began to pay heavily for its indiscretions.

The Okinawans were directed to break off all communications with China forthwith and to close the Ryukyu trading depot on the China coast. The regent and the councilors of state would thenceforth be appointed by Tokyo on the recommendation of the Okinawan government. Official ranks in the Ryukyu kingdom were to be reclassified and reduced in relative importance; the king would continue to hold the rare first-class court rank at Tokyo, but the regent's honors would correspond only to the fourth rank in the Japanese hierarchy, and the councilors of state (members of the *Sanshikan*) would hold rank equated only with the sixth rank. This was a blow which damaged the prestige of Okinawan officers at Tokyo who attempted to work with the Japanese; it affected their power to negotiate and restricted official and social intercourse, limiting it to lower ranks in the Japanese bureaucracy.

The gentry at Shuri resented deeply this Japanese intrusion upon Okinawan affairs. Orders to break off relations with China precipitated a crisis. Prince Ie and Ginowan *Oyakata* were held responsible for having accepted the surprising imperial message of 1872 and were subjected to abuse when the consequences began to be apparent. Many Okinawan leaders advocated a formal appeal to China. Such a gesture in 1872 might have had some effect; in 1875 it was too late: China had signed away her rights, if any, as the suzerain state.

Tokyo summoned a mission from Okinawa to hear a formal statement closing the Formosan affair and to receive the indemnity paid by China under terms of the Peking agreement. The envoys could anticipate a reprimand for allowing tribute ships and envoys to proceed to China after 1872.

The mission, numbering some fifty persons led by three officers of state (Ikegusuku *Oyakata*, Yonabaru *Oyakata*, and Kochi *Pechin*), left Naha on February 16 and took up residence at the Ryukyu mansion in Tokyo on March 18. Ten days later they were received in audience by the emperor, to whom they presented the customary tribute gifts.[8]

For political reasons of its own, the Japanese press publicized the presence of these curiously dressed Okinawans in Tokyo. The authoritarian government had recently instituted harshly repressive press laws in an effort to control the restive samurai and to restrain political action directed against itself. Newspapers and journals at the capital found in the Ryukyu problem a new issue with which to harass and embarrass the administration. They called into question the government's right to reprimand the Okinawans and asked the government to produce a treaty or formal agreement by which Shuri was bound to accept To-kyo's demands. The *Hochi Shimbun* advised Japan to abandon the Ryukyus entirely.

While smarting under such journalistic attacks, Okubo summoned the envoys on March 31 to give them some indication of the demands which Japan was about to make upon the Ryukyu kingdom. He urged them to recognize that swift change had overtaken the international situation in the Far East and that it was necessary to adapt ancient institutions to meet modern crises. He pointed out that the internal administration of the Ryukyu *han* must be brought into conformity with the administration of the new *ken* or prefectures of Japan proper. He outlined five requirements:

1. The King of Ryukyu should visit Tokyo to give thanks to the emperor for Japan's effort to protect the interests of Ryukyuans cast away on Formosa.

2. Shuri should abandon the use of Chinese reign-names and should substitute the Meiji era-name throughout the islands. Furthermore, Ryukyu should adopt all Japanese national official festivals according to notification from Tokyo. This would mean island-wide celebration of the emperor's birthday, observance of the traditionally accepted Accession Day of the first emperor, Jimmu, and adoption of the New Year celebration in conformity with Western practices.

3. Shuri should adopt the criminal law codes of Japan developed in the Justice Ministry at Tokyo, and should send three officials to Tokyo for instruction.

4. The administrative organization at Shuri must be revised, and to this end the Home Ministry would send down experts to develop a liaison with Tokyo.

5. Ten youths should be selected by Shuri for education at Tokyo in order that they might come to understand the trend of the times in new Japan.

Okubo dwelt at length on the outcome of the Formosan affair and introduced the subject of the indemnity paid by China, assuring the envoys that relief rice would be paid over to the shipwreck victims and their families. To provide safer inter-island communications, he promised that a steamship would be given to the Ryukyuan government. In order to protect the people, a Japanese garrison force would henceforth be stationed in the Ryukyu Islands.

Okubo had made a skillful approach to a difficult subject. The five specific requirements presented no insuperable demands. The king's visit to Tokyo would be carried out with courteous ceremony, but it would demonstrate publicly the true state of affairs. A change in reign-name usage and the adoption of Japanese and Western holidays might be resented by the gentry in Okinawa, but it would work no hardship on the illiterate masses, and would be a step toward standardization of practice in Japan proper and the dependency. New criminal law codes and procedures would have far-reaching effect, but the significance of this was blunted by the suggestion that only three men were needed for training at Tokyo. The implication that the Home Ministry at Tokyo would wait for Shuri to reorganize administration of its own volition put a mild appearance on the fourth point. There should be no objection to a program for the education of Okinawan youths at Tokyo.

By enlarging upon the prolonged negotiations with China, the risks that Japan had taken on behalf of Ryukyu, the magnanimity of the gesture granting relief rice and a steamship, Okubo plainly expected to play upon the Okinawan's well-developed sense of propriety, obligation, and gratitude. Even the announcement that a garrison force would be established in the Ryukyus was represented as a Japanese sacrifice on behalf of the Okinawan people.

Home Minister Okubo did not treat this conference as a negotiation; it was a polite but forthright statement of orders from Tokyo to Shuri. He had no reason to be pleased therefore when the envoys withdrew to their headquarters for a week of deliberation.

On April 8 they were again received by Okubo, to whom they expressed appreciation for Japan's interest. Going at once to the heart of the matter, however, they represented to Okubo that since Ryukyu was a distant and impoverished kingdom, it had never required a military force to defend it. Thus far it had relied successfully upon friendly negotiations to maintain good relations with other people. It had been successful even in dealing with Western ships and had enjoyed peace for centuries. *A military garrison established now might attract the hostile attention and action of foreign powers with which Ryukyu had no quarrel.* As for the gift of a steamship, Ryukyu had no way in which to maintain or pay for it because of recent great financial losses. In respect to the relief rice which Japan so generously offered, the Shuri government had already long since taken care of the distressed families.

Here Okubo, the proud Satsuma statesman, met with unexpected firmness and frankness. His keen perception could not miss the implied comparison of Okinawan success in treating peacefully with the Western powers and Satsuma's spectacularly unsuccessful clash with the British in 1862. There was a touch of irony in the reference to Shuri's impoverishment, for it had been Japan's action which cut off the normal trade with China. Furthermore, under the well-known terms of the settlement with China, Tokyo was under moral obligation to pay over to the Okinawans a major share of the Chinese indemnity, the equivalent of 500,000 yen (approximately $550,000 in 1874).

Okubo once again reviewed the arguments, stressing Japan's magnanimity, and ended sharply that a refusal to accept imperial gifts was construed to be a grave affront. Nothing daunted, the envoys remained firm; conferences with the Home Ministry officials on April 18 and 28, and again on May 2 and 3, brought only a minor compromise; the envoys agreed that Ryukyu would observe Japan's national holidays and would send law enforcement officials and students to Tokyo.

While these conversations were in progress at Tokyo—if indeed it can be called "progress"—four representatives of the Shuri government, led by Kochi *Oyakata* (Sho Toku-ko), a member of the Sho family, reached Foochow on April 8. They had been sent secretly to ask for China's help. The Chinese legation at Tokyo was at once ordered to raise the question of Ryukyu's status with the Tokyo government.

Okubo, patience exhausted, adopted a more coercive attitude. In a meeting on May 8, he curtly stated that there could be no further argument. A garrison force would be sent to Okinawa, drawn from the Sixth (Kumamoto) Division; the steamship would be delivered to Naha; and 1,740 *koku* of rice would be distributed to the families affected by the shipwreck of 1871.

Yonabaru *Oyakata* and his colleagues, having in mind the experience of Prince Ie and of Ginowan *Uekata*, responded to this with the statement that they could not accept these conditions without reference to the Shuri government.

DIRECT INTERVENTION: THE MATSUDA MISSIONS, 1875 AND 1879

Okubo did not wait for Yonabaru to report to Shuri. The Japanese Council of State published notification that the steamer "Taiyu-maru" was being given to the Ryukyu government, that 1,620 *koku* of rice were being provided for the families of fifty-four men killed by the Formosan aborigines, and that ten *koku* of rice were being granted to each of the twelve survivors, making a grand total of 1,740 *koku*. An unverifiable rumor reached the foreign community in Japan that the Okinawan envoys refused to accept the Chinese indemnity for "patriotic" reasons and were offered the steam vessel instead.

Thus the Okinawans received only a small fraction of the indemnity stipulated in the terms of the Chinese agreement. The " Taiyu-maru" became nominally the property of the Okinawan government but in fact remained in the hands of the Japanese.

Okubo became increasingly firm. He realized, however, that envoys sent to Tokyo without full diplomatic powers could legitimately refuse to commit the Shuri government. This had two disadvantages; long delays were involved in communicating with Okinawa and (more importantly) the recognition of envoys with full diplomatic powers, if they should be sent, implied that Japan was continuing to deal with an autonomous or independent government.

Okubo changed tactics. On June 12, Matsuda Michiyuki, Chief Secretary of the Home Ministry, left Tokyo aboard the "Taiyu-maru" with a suitable number of aides. This second-hand vessel was to be the gift of the Japanese emperor to the King of Ryukyu, but was in fact destined to be used principally in the transport of Japanese officials to and from the Southern Islands.

The Matsuda mission reached Naha on July 10 and proceeded to Shuri Castle four days later. Matsuda was not received by the king, who was said to be ill, but by the king's personal representative, Prince

Nakijin; by the regent, Prince Ie; and by members of the Council of State.

Within these few days the Japanese had moved in a more practical way. A detachment of the Kumamoto Division landed on Okinawa to establish the Okinawa Garrison, and the Foreign Ministry office at Naha was replaced by a branch office of the Home Ministry, responsible directly to Okubo.

With this support Matsuda now revealed a much more comprehensive program for change in Okinawa and made much more serious demands than any hitherto presented to Okinawan envoys at Tokyo. The Japanese were not satisfied with the mere letter of thanks which the Council of State and regent had sent to Tokyo; the king himself must go up to the imperial court to express Ryukyu's gratitude for Japan's benevolence. The local hierarchy of court and government must be revised, with a new distribution of ranks and offices among the Shuri gentry. The king would become a *chokunin* official of the first rank, and he alone would receive direct imperial appointment. Six officials only would enjoy *sonin* rank, appointed with the emperor's approval, and selected from among men of the fourth to the seventh court rank. Junior officials would be drawn from a classification equated with Japanese court ranks eight to fifteen. Appropriate salaries would be paid to these officials out of the local government treasury. This was a severe downgrading of the importance of leading Okinawans within their own country, and a rough intrusion upon the king's prerogatives.

After several days Prince Ie and the councilors called upon Matsuda to ask that the king's visit to Tokyo be postponed until Sho Tai had recovered his health. Only once before had a king left the country, in 1609, to become a hostage in Satsuma; under existing circumstances the Okinawans were most reluctant to agree that the king should go to Tokyo. They proposed that Prince Nakijin should proceed to Tokyo as the king's personal representative. Matsuda agreed, on condition that all other demands were accepted promptly.

Public feeling ran high. This small society concentrated about Shuri and Naha, rich in local traditions which set it apart from both China and Japan, was beginning to break up under irresistible pressure. Comfortable prerogatives were threatened, prerogatives which had been enjoyed for centuries by the unarmed and unmilitary *han-shi* or Okinawan samurai and by the subsidized academic and clerical gentry.

There were riots here and there. Crowds gathered before Matsuda's headquarters. Shuri's officials were abused and interfered with as they passed to and from the conferences. Negotiations were concluded with great difficulty.

Matsuda left for Tokyo in September. Prince Nakijin, six students, and two officials destined for legal training followed soon after. Whether by accident or by design, these numbers were fewer than the figure specified by Okubo in March. On November 22, Prince Nakijin presented to the emperor the king's letter of appreciation for Japanese action on behalf of Okinawa.

At Naha and Shuri orderly administration gave way to chaos. Officials who had accepted the Japanese memorial of 1872 or had negotiated with the Japanese since that time became objects of public attack and abuse. Ginowan *Oyakata* was forced to resign all public office and to withdraw to the countryside in bitterness and ill-health. On the eve of his death in 1876 he is said to have composed a verse which suggests the tumult of conflicting advice and criticism which had driven him from the king's service:

> "There are all kinds of insects
> Chirping in the fields—
> Who can tell one from another?"

Kume Village became a center for anti-Japanese agitation. The villagers of Chinese descent were imbued with traditional views of China as the great "Middle Kingdom," to which all others—including Japan—must look for universal leadership. They continued to believe that China was the world's most powerful state, for Peking's defeats and humiliation after 1840 were represented in the Chinese view as magnanimous concessions to the Western barbarians. The Kume Village scholars shared the Korean view that Japan had betrayed its Asian heritage.

It was not unreasonable, too, that they should fear Chinese displeasure in consequence of their submission to Japan. The Chinese government even then was putting down a great Moslem rebellion in Eastern Turkestan. Peking might decide to chastise the Ryukyu kingdom as well if it failed in its tribute obligations.

The Tokyo press published widely a memorandum prepared by Ikegusuku *Oyakata* in which he attempted to explain the Okinawan position in terms of moral obligation to China. The Okinawans, he said, were prepared to accept Japanese demands and to coöperate with Tokyo upon certain conditions. Tokyo should send an envoy to Peking to arrange for a Chinese ambassador to visit Shuri bearing a memorial releasing the king and his ministers from their formal obligations to the Chinese emperor and directing Sho Tai to accept Japan's exclusive jurisdiction. The Japanese had argued that no woman could serve two husbands at one time and that no country could serve two overlords. Ikegusuku pointed out that "Japan is our Father and China our Mother" and that many sovereigns in Europe received a necessary confirmation of independent sovereignty from the hands of the pope at Rome, who was himself a temporal sovereign. He cited Poland's status under conjoint rule of Russia, Austria, and Prussia.[9] Neither China nor Japan could consider Ikegusuku's quixotic solution, but both were aware that European powers might well begin again to fish in these troubled waters.

The Japanese representatives who remained at Naha made little progress in effecting Tokyo's orders after Matsuda's departure. The gentry tried to return to the old patterns of life. Buffeted by storms of public opinion, the Shuri officials were driven to serious indiscretions.

In the period 1875–78 the Okinawans were aware that the threat of civil war was growing within Japan. Emboldened by this, members of Ikegusuku's mission at Tokyo submitted no less than fourteen petitions to the Tokyo government, asking for restoration of the old forms of dual subordination. Concurrently they appealed to the foreign envoys of the United States, France, the Netherlands, and China to act on their behalf.

The most serious indiscretion was the despatch of Kochi *Oyakata* and Rin Sei-ko to China as secret envoys begging for Chinese support vis-à-vis Japan. Peking blandly announced their arrival at the imperial capital, describing this as a traditional mission come to offer condolences on the death of the late Emperor T'ung Chih. China had no genuine interest in the political fortunes or welfare of the little dependency, which meant nothing to them. Certainly it would take no serious risks on behalf of Okinawa, but in the present incident Peking thought it saw an opportunity to play off Japan against the Western powers and —as we shall see—spent ten years in fruitless effort to involve them in a dispute concerning the Ryukyus.

While the Peking courtiers and bureaucrats debated, the Japanese acted. A barracks was built to accommodate troops at Naha, where a half-battalion was deemed enough to dominate the peaceable Okinawans. In May, 1876, Kinashi Seiichiro was sent from Tokyo to act as resident-in-charge of the Naha branch of the Home Ministry, with powers to control travel overseas, direct the police, and control judicial affairs. Travel regulations applicable in Japan proper were henceforth applicable throughout the Ryukyu Islands. Anyone who desired to cross to China would first apply for permission from the Foreign Office at Tokyo. There applications were referred to the Home Ministry, and from the capital the matter was referred to the branch at Naha for clearance and approval. When a decision was made at Naha, notification went back to the Home Ministry in Tokyo, across to the Foreign Ministry, and back again to the applicant at Naha. The answer, after all of this, would almost certainly be "no." Such a cumbrous bureaucratic device was expected effectually to curb Okinawan interest in travel overseas. Anyone who crossed to China without valid permits risked arrest and punishment.

As the months passed, some Okinawans found Japanese restrictions insupportable. A score of residents from Kume Village slipped out of Okinawa to exile, taking up residence at the old Ryukyu trading depot on the Fukien coast. Others followed from time to time. The Ryukyu trading headquarters and office at Kagoshima was destroyed mysteriously by fire.

Few Japanese were interested in the fate of the Ryukyu kingdom, but the Okinawan problem continued to make an excellent political issue with which to embarrass the Tokyo government, dominated by the Satsuma-Choshu oligarchy. An influential political association known as the Risshisha, led by Itagaki Taisuke, was demanding a broader basis for the administration and called for the creation of an assembly, diet, or parliament for Japan. In a memorial to the throne in June, 1877, these political dissidents charged that the government was failing in its duties and cited the situation in the Ryukyus as part of the evidence: "Loochoo constitutes a Japanese *han*. Our troops are garrisoned there, the post-office and a branch of the Naimusho [Home Ministry] have been established there; but both the King and the people of Loochoo are endeavouring to free themselves from the authority of Japan. China is endeavouring to do the same with Loo-choo as Russia has done with Saghalin. If China succeeds, our territory will gradually decrease, and with it our power."[10]

Itagaki's group was considered the "liberal" party in Japanese political life, and by comparative standards they were; here, however, was no demand that the king and people of Ryukyu should be given freedom to shape their own political destiny, but rather a complaint that the government had not taken a bold enough stand vis-à-vis China.

The Ryukyu question lay dormant throughout most of 1877 and 1878. This was a time of internal crises which challenged the very existence of the Tokyo government. The Satsuma Rebellion was put down after eight months of bitter and costly campaigning in Kyushu, where some forty thousand men had risen against the central government. Okubo Toshimichi, the Satsuma leader who had formulated and directed policy concerning Ryukyu in his capacity as Home Minister, was assassinated in May, 1878.

Late in 1878 Tokyo discovered that the Chinese proposed to raise the question of Ryukyuan sovereignty with General Ulysses S. Grant, former President of the United States. He was to be in Peking on a world tour in the early months of 1879, traveling as a private citizen, but with enormous prestige. It was assumed that anyone who had wielded the powers of the presidency must continue to have a decisive role as an "elder statesman." Both Peking and Tokyo were aware that it might be difficult for Grant to decline a request to act as arbiter in this Sino-Japanese dispute, that the parties to the dispute would be under heavy pressure of public opinion to submit to arbitration, and that a public statement by the former President of the United

States would sway international public opinion, to which the Japanese leaders at the time were peculiarly sensitive.

Tokyo determined to remove the problem from the area of public discussion by presenting the Chinese (and General Grant) with a *fait accompli;* the Ryukyu problem must no longer be a "question."

The subject was debated in the Council of State at Tokyo. Admiral Enomoto (who had so recently negotiated the northern boundary settlement with the Russians) recommended formally that the Ryukyu *han* be abolished and that Okinawa *Ken* (Prefecture) be created in its place. It did not matter what the Okinawans might think of this; the Chinese and General Grant would be faced with a knottier problem if they called upon Japan to surrender an integral part of "home territory." And it would be doubly difficult to intervene if there were no Ryukyu king and quasi-autonomous government in being to serve as a rallying point for Okinawan discontent. Enomoto's recommendation was adopted.

On December 28, 1878, the Japanese Council of State abruptly issued a brief order to the officers of the Ryukyu *han* who were stationed in Tokyo: "It is hereby notified that the notification as to the residence in Tokyo of the representative officers of your *han* having been countermanded, you are ordered to return to your *han* at once."[11]

The Ministry of Home Affairs was ordered to speed the return of the Okinawan envoys. Their presence in Tokyo suggested that the Ryukyu kingdom still enjoyed a quasi-autonomous status. Scarcely ten days later, on Wednesday, January 8, 1879, the three principal commissioners from Shuri embarked at Yokohama with their aides and servants. They were to transfer at Kobe to a special ship ready to speed them to Naha. One Okinawan commissioner was ordered to remain at the Iidabashi residence-office of the Ryukyu *han* in Tokyo. The chief secretary of the Ministry of Home Affairs (Matsuda) left once again for Shuri with secret instructions.[12]

By this time Ito Hirobumi had replaced Okubo as Minister of Home Affairs. The management of the Ryukyu difficulty was in the hands of Japan's most able statesman; nevertheless, there was some public concern when these government actions became known. In general, the

Japanese press supported any move which would clarify the ambiguous status of the *han* within the framework of the empire. A decade had passed since the Restoration. Elsewhere the boundaries were clearly defined; the 272 former *han* had been thoroughly reorganized, and the rebellions in Saga, Hizen, and Satsuma had been put down. The Ryukyu *han* alone remained to be assimilated. There was an underlying uneasiness concerning China. No one was quite sure how far a challenge to China might be pushed, how far Peking would yield, nor what strength China might be able to bring into a military contest with Japan. The Japanese were in no mood to permit the "backward," poverty-stricken and unarmed Okinawans to jeopardize Japan's overall policies and prestige.

Chief Secretary Matsuda reached Naha on January 24. His stay was brief but to the point. The king's ministers were handed a résumé of Japan's complaints concerning neglect and failure in local administration, and a list of issues in which Shuri was at conflict with Tokyo. With pointed reference to Kochi *Oyakata's* mission to Peking, Matsuda reminded Shuri in writing that all travel overseas—whether to Tokyo or elsewhere—required advance notification to the Ministry of Home Affairs and its approval.

This was a final survey of conditions on Okinawa while the government at Tokyo prepared its orders for the dissolution of the *han* government. Matsuda left Naha February 4, reported to Tokyo February 13, conferred with government leaders, and on March 12 left Yokohama again.

This time he was accompanied by a very large staff of civil aides, Second Police Superintendent Sonoda Yasutaka, and at least 160 policemen. Simultaneously, a captain from the General Staff headquarters and a major commanding half a battalion left Kagoshima. The Japanese mission reached Naha on March 25. Its arrival at Okinawa spelled doom for the Chuzan kingdom.

PART FOUR

OKINAWA-KEN: FRONTIER PROVINCE

CHAPTER NINE

THE RYUKYU KINGDOM COMES
TO AN END

1879–1890

Crisis at Shuri: The King's Abdication, March 27, 1879

Proceeding with full display of force to Shuri Castle on March 27, Matsuda handed to Prince Nakijin a communication announcing Tokyo's decision to abolish the *han* and end the monarchy. The principal points were four:

"1. The Ryukyu *Han* is abolished and Okinawa *Ken* is established.

"2. This action is taken as punishment for failure to obey Tokyo's orders of May 29, 1875 and May 17, 1876.

"3. Prince Ie and Prince Nakijin will be granted the status of peers in Japan, as an act of Imperial grace.

"4. The deposed King, Sho Tai, is immediately required to visit Tokyo."[1]

Supplementary provisions related to the king's withdrawal from the ancient castle and established procedures for the transfer of authority and public business to Japanese officers.

The castle gates were closed and put under heavy guard. The Kankei Gate alone was used, and all Okinawans who entered or left the castle grounds were searched until the transfer of important documents was completed.

Shuri and Naha were swept with anxiety and tense foreboding. As he delivered the official communication to Prince Nakijin, Chief Secretary Matsuda caused a public proclamation to be made: "Because the Imperial Decree issued in Meiji 8th year (1875) has not been complied with, the Government was compelled to abolish the feudal clan. The

381

former feudal Lord, his family and kin will be accorded princely treatment, and the persons of citizens, including *samurai*, their hereditary stipends, property and business interests will be dealt with in a manner as close to traditional customs as is possible. Any acts of maladministration, and exhorbitant taxes and dues levied during the regime of the former clan government will probably be righted upon careful consideration. Do not be misled by irresponsible rumors. All are advised to pursue their respective occupations with ease of mind."[2]

On March 3 Tokyo had prepared the way for transfer of administration by appointing Kinashi Seiichiro of the Home Ministry to the post of Acting Governor of Okinawa-ken. This was now made known. He decreed that the new provincial government would operate temporarily in the ministry's branch office at Nishimura, Naha.

At Tokyo a brief notice bearing the prime minister's signature read simply: "It is hereby publicly notified that the Loochoo *Han* has been abolished and Okinawa *ken* established in its place."

A second notice (dated April 8) clarified the status of the northern islands: "It is hereby notified that the islands Oshima, Kikaigashima, Tokunoshima, Okiyerabushima and Yoronshima, under the jurisdiction of the Kagoshima-ken will hereafter be called the Oshima-gori (Oshima Department) and belong to the Province of Osumi."[3] Tokyo expected to complete all transfer formalities by mid-April.

The king's withdrawal from the palace took place on the evening of March 30. This was a most poignant and dramatic moment. Great crowds waited, tense and silent, as Sho Tai and his household passed from the castle grounds through the *Kokugaku-mon* (Gate of National Learning) into exile. This was the symbolic break with the past. For the first time in five hundred years the palace ceased to be the seat of authority and the symbol of nationhood.

It was immediately occupied by Japanese troops from the Kumamoto Garrison.

An imperial court chamberlain (Tomokoji) arrived aboard the "Meiji-maru" at Naha, prepared to hand to the deposed king an expression of imperial appreciation for the king's coöperation and to discuss the protocol of Sho Tai's impending trip to Japan. Tomokoji was to accompany the royal suite to Tokyo. The Japanese were surprised and chagrined to learn that the former king was too ill to make the journey. His heir apparent, aged twelve years, would go with Tomokoji to Tokyo to pay his respects and to petition that his father be permitted to defer the long-awaited courtesy call upon the emperor.

Tokyo found further delay intolerable. General Grant's visit to China was impending. It was imperative that the Ryukyu situation be under full control. The former king's presence on Okinawa contributed an element of uncertainty which must be removed. Suppose he became the center of an anti-Japanese demonstration? Or worse, suppose he should be spirited to China to appear before General Grant as a petitioner for support vis-à-vis Japan?

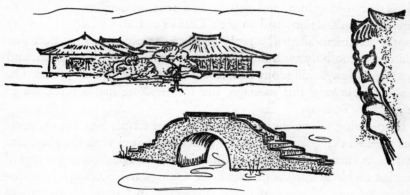

FIG. 21. VIEWS OF THE SHIKINA-EN. *The main buildings of the royal country residence (seen also in Plate 10); the half-moon bridge in its garden; and a wooden demon mask surmounting a pillar.*

On May 18 the "Tokai-maru" reached Naha with the first governor, Nabeshima Naoakira, and his staff. Also aboard ship were an imperial court physician and a major attached to the Imperial Household Ministry. Ignoring Okinawan protests and petitions, Dr. Takashina certified that Sho Tai was physically fit for the journey to Tokyo. Major Sagara was in a position to underline the physician's decision.

On May 27 the last King of Ryukyu, now aged thirty-six years, set sail for exile in Japan, accompanied by a suite of ninety-six courtiers. The sad and reluctant group docked at Yokohama on June 8 and on the following day proceeded to Tokyo by train.

Two days later Sho Tai was presented to the young Emperor Mutsu-hito. The deposed king was unpopular at the imperial court, his posi-tion made delicate and difficult because he had obeyed the summons to Tokyo with such manifest reluctance. The strength of the Restoration government at this time rested in public acceptance of a doctrine of absolute and unchallengeable imperial authority, and this authority Sho Tai had tried to evade.

The Okinawans bowed to the inevitable, but not without a last gesture designed to salve the former king's wounded pride. Presenta-tion at court was accompanied by a public explanation that Sho Tai had been ill for eight years because of deep concern for the welfare of the Ryukyu kingdom, and that he had sent messengers to China to explain Japan's actions and to seek China's aid and advice. On May 20, the statement alleged, a reply had been received to the effect that China was too busy with internal affairs to act on behalf of Shuri, and that the Ryukyu kingdom henceforth must obey Japan's orders. On the day following this message, the former king had determined to proceed to Tokyo.

By phrasing the public explanation in these terms, Sho Tai's councilors implied that the final decision to act had rested with the king, and that he in turn had acted upon China's advice. The Japanese accepted this last feeble gesture with which the Okinawan leaders sought to dis-charge an age-old sense of moral obligation to China. Okinawa and the Okinawans had escaped stronger coercive action after 1875 princi-pally because neither Tokyo nor Shuri had means to gauge China's true capacity to wage war, or its diplomatic strength or weakness. Tokyo was under some restraint: would China risk armed conflict on behalf of the Ryukyu kingdom?

Years were to pass before all threat of war could be removed and the sovereignty issue brought to an end.

THE RYUKYUS AGAIN BECOME AN INTERNATIONAL ISSUE: GENERAL GRANT'S MEDIATION

As the deposed king set sail from Naha on May 27 another ship was in nearby waters, bearing General Grant from Shanghai to Tientsin, en route to a series of meetings with the Chinese Viceroy Li Hung-chang and the regent, Prince Kung. Grant was traveling as a private person, but Viceroy Li was determined to use him, if possible, to embarrass Japan and to estrange Washington and Tokyo. As soon as his distinguished guest arrived, Li made a determined effort to reopen the Ryukyu sovereignty question, ostensibly on behalf of Sho Tai.

To understand the American position we must go back for a decade to pick up the thread of the Okinawan story as one of temporary international significance.

After 1868, Japan endeavored to shift her traditional relations with China, Korea, and the Ryukyu kingdom to a basis in binding and well-defined Western legalistic forms. The Chinese did not understand (or chose to ignore) the significance of the 1874 agreement in which they had admitted Japan's right to act on Formosa in behalf of Sho Tai's subjects. Western diplomatists and writers at the time failed to recognize that the investiture rituals and other ceremonies associated with the tribute system carried with them an implied moral obligation, strongly felt by the Okinawans. From this Shuri sought to be released by a formal declaration by the Chinese court, signifying that the ceremonial relationship had come to an end. To the unaccustomed Western eye, much of this concern for form seemed unnecessary if not indeed absurd.

In 1875 the American minister at Tokyo (John A. Bingham) reported to Washington that the Ryukyu kingdom was appealing to Japan to return to the traditional but anachronistic state of "dual subordination." In July the State Department directed Bingham to prepare a review of the status of the American "Lewchew Compact" negotiated by Perry, whereupon he repeated Japan's assurances that all treaty obligations would be met by Tokyo.

When Japan refused to let the traditional tribute ships clear from Naha for Fukien in 1876, the imperial Chinese treasurer at Foochow asked Shuri for an explanation. The Okinawans undertook to describe their difficult position to Peking, at the same time appealing to the American, French, British, and Dutch envoys at Tokyo to intercede for them.

Washington directed Bingham to make no formal representation to the Japanese government but to hold himself ready to assist in smoothing over the problem if he were asked to use his good offices. Bingham believed the Japanese to be in the wrong here, but the Department of State maintained that so long as the 1854 compact provisions were observed, the United States could not intrude in this affair. But the dispute continued, and in 1878 the American government for the third time directed its minister at Tokyo to review and report on it.

The Chinese hopefully pressed efforts to raise the question to a level of international discussion. Ho Ju-chang, the Chinese minister at Tokyo, had been instructed to reopen the issue, but the Japanese government refused flatly to discuss it. At Peking, Prince Kung made no better progress in broaching the subject to the Japanese envoy, and in exasperation exclaimed that the minister was no more than a "mere post office," without information and without instructions.

Li Hung-chang and the Chinese Foreign Office considered four proposals made to them by Ho Ju-chang in 1878:

1. China might send warships to compel Ryukyu to pay the biennial tribute.

2. China might form an agreement with Ryukyu whereby Ryukyu would start a war with Japan, in which China would then support Ryukyu.

3. China might take up the question with Tokyo through diplomatic channels, with a view to arranging arbitration.

4. China might sell her claims to Ryukyu for a sum of money.[4]

Li Hung-chang conducted a long correspondence with Ho at Tokyo, much of which came to the attention of other foreign envoys there—and to the attention of the Japanese—because of a personal quarrel between the Chinese minister and his principal assistant at the legation.

Ho advised Peking to consider threatening war if the Japanese did not withdraw from the Ryukyu Islands. He predicted that if Tokyo were successful in detaching Ryukyu from the Chinese tributary system, it would not be long before Korea, too, would be removed from China's orbit and dominated by Japan. He furthermore thought that the island-bred people of Ryukyu would provide Tokyo with good conscript material for her growing navy. He asserted that the United

States would not allow Japan to hold Okinawa because America's Far Eastern shipping had to pass through the Ryukyu archipelago.

Li, at Peking, agreed that China should fight to assert her claims upon the Ryukyus, but he knew very well that Peking was in no position to become involved in a war with Japan unless it were made certain that the Western powers would come to China's aid. According to Li, General Grant indicated that he would mediate in the Ryukyu dispute provided China would alter its laws governing Chinese migration to California.

The Okinawan prince Kochi *Oyakata* was still in China. The Chinese discussed the possibility of using him to replace the deposed king, Sho Tai. Japan's representatives at Tientsin demanded that the Okinawans be sent to them. This the Chinese refused, and Viceroy Li gave orders that Kochi and his associates were to be protected and given financial aid.

Viceroy Li hoped to invoke General Grant's interest and sympathetic support, knowing that he would later meet with the Japanese emperor and talk with the principal ministers of state at Tokyo. He planned to associate Grant and the United States with China's claims, by inference if not by technical fact. Li appears to have misunderstood, in some degree, the position of a former president and to have attributed to him a greater influence in political matters than he actually enjoyed.

The viceroy met Grant at Tientsin and there reviewed China's arguments in the Ryukyu case. Grant promised to give the matter thought and asked his staff to gather data for consideration. At Peking, Prince Kung, in charge of foreign affairs, received Grant twice in settings of elaborate and flattering entertainment. The general was assured that China was interested neither in the internal problems of Ryukyu nor in the number of countries to which the Okinawans might desire to send tribute, provided the traditional investiture ceremonies continued to be observed. Peking wanted to see the deposed king return to Shuri, the Japanese garrison withdrawn, and a declaration that Japan abandoned claims of exclusive sovereignty in the Ryukyu Islands.

Grant was not impressed by Prince Kung's protestation of Chinese interest in the welfare of the Ryukyuans nor the claim to a right in continuing tribute payments. As for the military implications, this seasoned old warrior had formed an opinion that "a well-appointed body of ten thousand Japanese troops could make their way through the length and breadth of China, against all odds that could be brought to confront them."

He cautiously promised Prince Kung at Peking that he would inform himself on the subject in dispute. At Tientsin, Viceroy Li resumed his efforts to enlist Grant's sympathetic interest in China's claims. Li noted that the islands were semi-independent and that China had never exercised sovereignty, although she accepted tribute payments. He observed that the king and people of the Ryukyus were not Chinese, although a few people of Chinese descent played an important role in government and education there. China had no officials stationed in the Ryukyus, levied no taxes, and in the event of war neither received nor extended aid. Ryukyu had always benefited through the special trading facilities on the China coast, and the leading men of the kingdom sent their sons to Peking to study. Li assured General Grant that the Ryukyuan people preferred to be associated with China.

From this he turned to a discussion of the strategic importance of the islands, noting that they lay as a screen off the China coast and in the international shipping lanes. He predicted that if Japan were allowed to remain in the Ryukyus, Formosa would some day be taken as well.

The general listened patiently and made no commitments.

On July 3, 1879, Grant reached Tokyo. Here he was strongly impressed by the vigor and progressive character of Japanese leaders, who had undertaken revolutionary modernization of an ancient country. He recognized its internal political weaknesses, however, and feared that it might suffer disastrously if drawn into war with China, for there was a strong probability that the Western powers would intervene. An informal occasion was arranged at Nikko on July 22 during which he could review the Ryukyu problem with Home Minister Ito Hirobumi, War Minister Saigo Tsugumichi, and the Japanese envoy to the United States, Yoshida Kiyonari.

While these conversations were in progress the Chinese had formally requested the United States to exercise its good offices. In a letter dated July 8, the Secretary of State at Washington accepted China's request upon condition that the Japanese government likewise ask for Ameri-

can mediation. Coming at the moment of General Grant's conversations, the Chinese move may have been designed to force the Japanese
to make a similar request, but in view of Tokyo's official position that
no question of sovereignty existed, such a request could not be forthcoming.

The Japanese were prepared to discuss their problems with General
Grant as a friendly private individual, but they refused to permit it to
be raised to the level of official recognition. The former president was
fully aware of this fine distinction, but he foresaw war between China
and Japan if the issue were not settled by negotiation. He therefore
chose to address identical letters to Iwakura Tomomi (Japanese Prime
Minister) and to Prince Kung (Chief of the Chinese Ministry of Foreign
Affairs and of the Imperial Council). He wrote in his private capacity
as an American citizen who had been entertained and honored in both
countries.

The communication, dated August 18, 1879, recommended (a) that
China withdraw certain offensive correspondence which had been addressed officially to the Japanese government on October 7, 1878; (b)
that China and Japan each appoint commissioners to appraise the problem with a view to arranging impartial arbitration; and (c) that no
foreign countries or foreigners be allowed to become parties to the
dispute itself, or to be employed in any way in connection with the
affair, except, perhaps, as interpreters. Japan's friendliness toward China
was mentioned. Grant suggested that China would do well to follow
Japan along the road to modernization and independence of foreign
controls.

There was no public official reaction to the letters at Tokyo.

The Chinese continued to explore ways and means through which
they could force Japan to admit the existence of the question. At
Washington on December 1, 1879, President Rutherford Hayes informed Congress that the American government had indicated willing-
ness to do what it could to promote a peaceful solution of the Ryukyu
dispute. Tokyo continued to maintain silence, but the Japanese leaders
were disturbed. China displayed remarkable capacity to keep the sovereignty issue alive, and continued to seek foreign support for Peking's
claims. Inspired letters were published in Europe and the United States

offering highly colored versions of the historical background to an uninformed public. China was represented abroad as the magnanimous champion of Okinawan interests.

Tokyo decided at last to explore the possibilities of direct negotiation, suggested by General Grant, but while doing so continued to act publicly as if the question were closed. On March 11, 1880, foreign governments were notified that all claims against the former royal government of the Ryukyu kingdom must be presented to the Japanese Ministry of Finance not later than May 30, and that debts which had been contracted after 1843 would be met with government bonds and money; earlier debts would not be liquidated. Concurrently, the Japanese minister at Peking (Shishido Tamaki) was quietly given full powers to work out an agreement with China. The Chinese in turn led Tokyo to believe that Peking's representative (Prince Kung) had similar full powers to represent his government in the discussions.

These commissioners began negotiations on August 15, 1880. In the course of the debate it was suggested that the archipelago should be divided, that China should take Miyako and Yaeyama, that Japan should withdraw to the Amami Islands at the north, and that Kochi *Oyakata* (Sho Toku-ko) should be installed as king on Okinawa. The neutrality of Okinawa would be guaranteed.

Shishido knew that influential Chinese statesmen were becoming apprehensive of Russia on the northern borders and hoped to improve relations with Japan by removing the irritating Ryukyu issue. What could Japan ask as a *quid pro quo?* Tokyo was eager to secure a modification of the Treaty of Tientsin, which excluded her from most-favored-nation treatment in China. After two months of discussion the Chinese on October 21 presented draft proposals which were acceptable to Japan.

A settlement was agreed upon—or so the Japanese thought—which would give China undisputed possession of Miyako and Yaeyama, leaving Japan in dominating control of Okinawa and the islands to the north, and would grant Japan the trading privileges and concessions she so ardently desired. Needless to say, the Okinawans were not consulted.

It was agreed to sign the documents on October 31.

A storm broke within the councils of the Chinese government; those who feared Japan more than they did Russia protested angrily that the concessions to Tokyo were unnecessarily great. Those advocated signature who felt that Japan should be played off against Russia, and that Russia represented a greater threat than Japan. Viceroy Li recommended a compromise which would concede Japan's control throughout the Ryukyu Islands, but would withhold the concessions to be made under the revision of the Tientsin Treaty. This, of course, was simple recognition of the *status quo*.

The Peking government repudiated its negotiating representatives in this as they had repudiated the powers granted to their representatives on Formosa in 1874. The Japanese minister at Peking sent repeated inquiries to the Chinese Foreign Office, and at last on November 23 he accused the Chinese government of bad faith. Delay followed delay. On December 20 an imperial Chinese decree explained that there had been insufficient preparation on China's part and that Peking would not sign the new convention.

Shishido was understandably indignant and on January 5, 1881, notified the Chinese government that he considered the Ryukyu question permanently closed. He left Peking on January 20, and it never again became a matter for formal discussion between the two governments.

This did not put an end to the matter, however.

In the next year (1882) a memorial was addressed to the throne at Peking (by Chang Pei-lun) advising preparation for war with Japan. This was referred to Viceroy Li for comment: "I entirely agree with the views expressed by Chang Pei-lun that we must prepare for war with Japan, and therefore must develop our naval armaments so as to win. . . . Our best case for causing a rupture with Japan is not over the Korean question, but in regard to the Loochoo Islands. We have an indisputable right to these islands, and every foreign Power will have to admit our claim, if we demand the restoration of our rights over them. . . ."[5]

Li asked Washington to exercise its good offices in reopening the Ryukyu issue with Japan, hoping again by this means to associate the United States with China in bringing pressure upon Japan. The Department of State was not interested: Li had reversed himself too many times. He was advised to seek direct negotiations with Tokyo on the basis of the settlement terms which had been set forth in the abortive convention of 1880. Peking did not act and nothing was heard of the Ryukyu question for a decade.

The official *Peking Gazette* continued to publish occasional notices of the Ryukyus as a "tributary state" until 1890. It was painful to admit change; for example, after some fishermen had been driven ashore by storm in Fukien the *Gazette* solemnly noted (November 3, 1889) that these Okinawans had been shipwrecked while "sent on an official mission to Foochow, but had brought no dispatches." After 1891, however, entries concerning the Ryukyus began to appear in notices of "Foreign Affairs."

In 1892, for the last time, Viceroy Li attempted to use the Ryukyu sovereignty issue as a means to embarrass Japan when Peking and Tokyo were engaged in a rancorous dispute concerning Korea. War came soon after, and China's defeat in 1895 removed the Ryukyus from consideration in Sino-Japanese relations for fifty years.

UNDER THE SHADOW OF WAR: PROBLEMS OF POPULATION, EDUCATION, AND SOCIAL CHANGE

Japan had denied Okinawa to the Chinese and had closed the southern frontier. There was some slight gain in political prestige for the government, for it had outmaneuvered Peking, but this was offset by the heightened danger of war, and by the unsympathetic reaction generated among Western diplomats at Tokyo and Peking. Annexation of the Ryukyus brought no economic advantage to Japan. There were no strong sentimental or traditional ties to prompt wide Japanese interest in the welfare of the Okinawan people. On balance the islands were a liability.

Elsewhere in Japan—in all the other prefectures—a feverish "change everything" spirit prevailed, but the government leaders at Tokyo correctly assessed the conservatism of the older generation on Okinawa. The interests of law, order, and garrison security in the Ryukyus came first in the new prefecture. As long as there were prominent Okinawan exiles living in China, supported by the Chinese government, Tokyo had to assume that some danger of strong political reaction continued to exist on Okinawa. Time alone would diminish the importance of pro-Chinese members among the older leaders. They must be replaced by a new generation educated to be obedient and pliant subjects of the emperor.

Thus, while the Tokyo government pushed forward a vigorous modernizing program elsewhere in Japan, Okinawa drifted in the backwaters of national policy for fifteen years. Contrasts between Okinawa and the other prefectures were heightened rather than diminished. More than forty years would pass before the Okinawans were represented in the Diet at Tokyo on a basis of technical and legal equality with other Japanese subjects.

The closing decades of the 19th century were filled with hardship. A cholera epidemic swept the islands in 1879. Some 11,200 persons fell ill and of these more than 6,400 died. The Shuri treasury was empty. Okinawan leadership was paralyzed.

Ota Chofu describes the first tense weeks of the new era, when Okinawan office holders (of whom his father was one) simply ceased to perform their duties as clerks and managers in government affairs. The Japanese police seized a large number of leaders, held them in jail, subjected them to long persuasive lectures, and threatened them with physical violence.

The Okinawan gentry were no longer masters in their own house. Key posts were filled by Japanese from Tokyo. Hundreds of newcomers took precedence over the old aristocracy, forming a new elite. The old pattern of town-bred aristocracy at Naha and Shuri versus country-bred peasant was now changed. Henceforth it was to be a pattern of Okinawans-by-birth versus Japanese from other prefectures in the empire, the latter enjoying greater privileges of income and preferential treatment in government and commerce.

Tokyo's first problem was to make an exact record of the distribution of human resources. Upon this inventory all other economic or administrative planning must rest. No one knew precisely how many people there were in the Ryukyus. The inquiry made by Satsuma's agents in the early 17th century had formed the basis of all subsequent surveys.

In the confusion which attended the transfer of authority in 1879 many records had been destroyed and many had been carried off to Tokyo and Kagoshima.

The first modern Japanese estimates, made in 1875, had placed the population figure at only 165,930, and of these 117,316 were believed to be living on Okinawa itself. Again, more than half of this number lived in the four interrelated towns of Shuri, Naha, Tomari, and Kume.

Each recheck in later years reflected greater accuracy of method in gathering statistics. A census in 1879 indicated a total population of more than 310,000 persons registered in 63,506 households. A recount raised the population figure to 351,374 and the number of households to 74,189. This census was considered fairly accurate for Naha and Shuri, where there was a maximum organization for collecting data. Naha then had 6,000 households and 23,600 people, whereas Shuri had fewer but larger households. As the years passed Naha grew steadily, but Shuri declined in population and importance, for the Japanese immigrants tended to stay at Naha, the administrative center, and Okinawans employed by the government moved down to the new prefectural capital.

In the old days all the outer islands had served Okinawa, and Okinawa had served Shuri. The people of Shuri looked down upon other Okinawans and the Okinawans looked down upon the inhabitants of the outer islands as rustic and unsophisticated country cousins, who were not permitted to move to Okinawa. Now this was changed. Japanese newcomers discriminated equally against natives of Naha and Shuri, Miyako and Yaeyama, Kume and Kerama. In terms of "colonial treatment" they were all "Okinawans."

On Okinawa itself the old distinctions of nobility and gentry were soon blurred under the heavy pressure of this Japanese discrimination and the leveling effects of poverty shared by all classes. At the time of the transition from kingdom to prefecture there had been some 330,000 subjects. Among these, some 22,500 households (approximately 95,000 persons) represented the gentry enjoying privileges denied by custom to the common people.

The old patterns of court life were shattered. Soon after the Japanese garrison occupied the palace grounds, a visiting foreigner found the principal buildings dilapidated, stripped of furniture and decoration, falling to ruin at the mercy of winds and rains. Many Shuri mansions were decaying. Hereditary pensions were reduced or canceled, and income from private lands in the countryside dwindled. Servants were dismissed. Members of aristocratic families sought employment in the village offices, which the Japanese were enlarging or establishing for the first time. Many drifted from Shuri and Naha to the outer islands to seek employment as teachers or town clerks. Men who had a small sum in pension funds or bonds to invest did so at promising village centers, and thus the foundations were laid for the growth of towns of considerable local importance, many miles from Shuri. Retainers who had served in Shuri households scattered to the countryside to become farmers, fishermen, or craftsmen in the village centers.

At Tokyo the former king and his family were treated with respect due one of the lesser nobility and granted an income from the imperial household coffers. Royal grandsons passed into the ranks of the *anji* or nobles. There were on Okinawa at this time only six non-royal princely families (*oji-ke*), each with an annual stipend ranging from three hundred to four hundred *koku* of rice or its equivalent, and from this very limited income each prince had to maintain a considerable establishment. This they had been able to do when there were many other perquisites of rank and office, but after 1879 the commuted stipends to which they were reduced compelled them to give up the old ways of life at Shuri and to find gainful employment as individuals. The Japanese government nominated two of the six princely houses to the peerage, in time granting Prince Nakijin and Prince Ie the titles and status of Japanese barons. By 1895 only these two families—numbering about thirty-five members in all—attempted to maintain the local social position and privileges of princes of the old regime.

The *anji-ke* were the households of the descendents of princes and of the medieval territorial lords. These numbered only thirty-six families in 1879. Each noble had enjoyed a modest hereditary stipend ranging from forty to eighty *koku* of rice or its equivalent, paid from the royal treasury, plus various emoluments and perquisites of offices to which they held nominal title. These sums did not begin to meet the annual costs of a household in the new era.

The government of old Ryukyu had in fact been based in the effective services of some seventy aristocratic families ranking below the princes and the nobles, and it was from this stratum of the old hierarchy that the Japanese drew the administrative officers for the new provincial government. Shuri government stipends had ranged from forty to eighty *koku* of rice. Senior members were classed as *sojito-ke* and were either descendents of *anji* enjoying hereditary status or men from lower ranks whose services were recognized and rewarded by promotion to the highest possible grade open to them. If a member of this group were appointed councilor of state, he was entitled to an income ranging from two hundred to three hundred *koku* of rice for the period of service. Junior houses of the administrative gentry were called *wakijito-ke*, and this classification embraced distant descendents of nobles, men whose houses had held and lost rank as *sojito-ke*, and men who were just beginning their careers in government service.

One other class of dependents upon the king's treasury in 1879 were called *shimamochi*, who were pensioners rewarded for meritorious services by small grants which were continued through one or two generations only.

In April, 1879—at the height of Tokyo's exasperation with the stubborn Okinawans—it was announced at Tokyo that with the exception of the three favored families—Sho, Ie, and Nakijin—all the Okinawan nobles and gentry would become commoners, dependent henceforth on their own resources. The outcry and agitation at Naha and Shuri were enough to force reconsideration; in December the order was rescinded, a commutation of stipends and pensions was scheduled, and the budget for 1880 carried a total appropriation of 189,134 yen, to be paid out semiannually. Grants were to range from a maximum of two thousand yen to a minimum of two hundred, and the pensioners were to include Buddhist and Shinto priests, hitherto subsidized from the Shuri treasury. In all some 380 families were affected.[6]

Following precedents established a decade earlier in Japan, the government soon commuted the semiannual pensions into bonds, using the 1879 rates of exchange between rice and yen at Osaka. This meant that a small number of men receiving pensions in the higher brackets had some capital funds to invest in new business ventures. Superficially it looked as if they were better off than they had been under the old regime, for they had few responsibilities and virtually no personal expenditures on behalf of official duties and ceremonies. In fact, however, inexperience, poor management, and lack of opportunity quickly brought many pensioned families to the verge of bankruptcy. A craft workshop was established at Shuri to give them opportunities for work, and by 1885 this was subsidized by as much as thirteen thousand yen.

This could be only a temporary relief measure. Under pressure of increasing poverty the members of old aristocratic families began to take a more liberal view toward residence elsewhere in the islands and toward intermarriage with families not of their own rank and class in court society.

These were painful changes. The former king's conduct was admirable throughout. Once the decision to abdicate had been forced upon him, he accepted the obligations imposed by its terms and honored them faithfully. In October, 1879, he addressed a message to the former councilors of state on Okinawa directing them to coöperate with the Japanese from other prefectures. Prominent Okinawans continued to slip away secretly to China from time to time and to lend themselves hopefully to the schemes of Li Hung-chang and his associates, but there is no indication that the deposed king lent his name or the influence of his family to these rash undertakings. In 1884 he was permitted to visit Okinawa for one hundred days, during which the prefectural governor treated him with great honor and consideration. In that year he was created a marquis (ko-shaku) in the new peerage of Japan, but he continued to be kept under a polite restraint at Tokyo, maintaining a degree of formality and some of the old court practices of Shuri within his own household until his death in 1902. His household finances were well managed, and his descendents have continued to hold their place among the most prosperous men of Okinawan descent.

THE JAPANESE IN OKINAWA AFTER 1879

The extension of Japanese organization and influence to the old Ryukyu kingdom set a pattern which was followed later in Formosa and Korea, but in Okinawa the Japanese enjoyed certain special advantages; the mild and instinctively friendly nature of the people provided one such advantage, the community of basic language-forms and tradition another. Officials sent from Tokyo to fill the principal administrative posts were often men of high intelligence, well educated, and filled with a sense of responsibility. They had entered public life at a time of revolutionary change and were eager to achieve unification within the empire, so lately emerged from feudal organization. Some, it is true, were arrogant products of the days before the Restoration, when common people were expected to withdraw from the path and grovel before lords and governors as they passed, but they were representatives of a government which was struggling to transform itself and to be recognized in the Western world on a basis of accepted equality in law and in social institutions.

As the lower ranks of government and of commercial management on Okinawa began to be filled, however, the newcomers began to be drawn from less well-educated classes and from the ranks of unemployed and restless men who had not fully adjusted to the new order in Japan proper. For many years Kagoshima men dominated all private and public activities on Okinawa. A high percentage were men who had failed to find permanent employment after the abortive Satsuma Rebellion and now drifted into the police force and lower administrative offices of Okinawa.

The new commercial field seemed promising. Okinawans were entirely inexperienced in the mercantile and manufacturing world which was developing so rapidly in Japan. Migrants from Kagoshima and Osaka assumed a dominant position at Naha, living apart as a group identified as "resident merchants," who coöperated among themselves to block the development of competition by natives of Okinawa Prefecture. Ota Chofu, who had long experience with these "resident merchants," asserts that an Okinawan who sought to break through the monopolies established at Naha or Osaka and Kobe was looked upon as "presumptuous" and suffered discriminatory action and economic retaliation.

Japanese who visited Okinawa on business or in fulfillment of official duties tended to carry back to other prefectures stories of the bizarre and unfamiliar things which they had seen. The government asserted that Okinawa Prefecture was an integral part of the Japanese empire, but to unsophisticated Japanese eyes the strange ways and speech of the Okinawans set them apart as rustic, second-class cousins within the Japanese nation-family.

The easygoing people of the "Land of Propriety" felt that they were being pushed and hurried into the modern mechanized age. However lofty the purposes of the Japanese governors, their agents in the lower echelons of administration were often insensitive and poorly educated policemen ordered to enforce unwelcome rules and regulations. Their harshness and the rude arrogance of the "resident merchants" generated ill will and wounded Okinawan pride. The phrase "looking aside indifferently" summed up the attitude which the helpless island people adopted when they came into conflict with Japanese who had the upper hand in commerce and law enforcement.

A minority group among the old and now powerless elite of Okinawa recognized the trend of the times and advocated speedy accommodation to the demands of reorganization. To strengthen this realistic appraisal of the situation in which they found themselves, a number of influential men formed an association known as the Kai-ka To, which proved to have a moderating influence in a small society undergoing forced reorganization.

Okinawans sometimes wryly observed that Okinawa served as a training ground for administrative talents applied elsewhere in Japan. (For example, Matsuda Michiyuki became mayor of Tokyo, the empire's most important city, after he had managed the abdication of the Okinawan king.) The governorship changed hands no less than eight times in the first thirteen years of provincial administration.

The first two governors (Nabeshima Naoakira, of Saga, and Uesugi Shigenori, of Yonezawa) were members of ancient and distinguished feudal families. Uesugi and his wife won the friendship and admiration of the Okinawans through their liberal conduct and their encouragement of students at Naha and in Tokyo. The lords of Yonezawa had been famed as patrons of scholarship, and long after Uesugi left the governorship of Okinawa he continued to make substantial gifts toward the support of Okinawan students in Japan. His tenure of office was cut short, for Tokyo frowned on the extent and vigor of his reform program at a time when the sovereignty question was still at issue with China. The fourth governor (Nishimura Sutezo) was concurrently Director of the Civil Engineering Bureau in the Home Ministry at Tokyo. Under his guidance harbors and roads were developed as a foundation for strengthening the total economy of the islands, and new buildings sprang up to house the administration at Naha. The sixth governor (retired Major-General Baron Fukuhara Minoru) devoted himself wholeheartedly to the reconciliation of the Okinawan people and the Japanese of other prefectures, maintaining to the end of his life a cordial correspondence with the friends he found at Naha.

The eighth governor (Narahara Kogoro) was appointed in 1892. He was to hold office at Naha for fifteen momentous years, bringing to an end the "Do Nothing" era and inaugurating a period of active development, a new chapter in the history of Okinawan affairs.

TOKYO'S POLICIES: THE "DO NOTHING" ERA AND THE PUBLIC WELFARE

In 1880 the prefecture was subdivided anew for administrative purposes. Shuri and Naha were given the status of cities; Okinawa Island continued to be divided approximately as it had been in the period of the three 14th-century principalities; and the islands of Iheya, Kume, Miyako, and Yaeyama became districts, each with its dependent islets. The business of local government was little changed.

A printing office was established—the first in Okinawa—to facilitate government business, and by 1881 the governor's staff moved into new buildings at Naha. A Cabinet order decreed that customary law would be maintained in civil matters for the time being, but that in criminal affairs the laws of Japan proper would apply uniformly in Okinawa Prefecture. Provisions were made to transport convicts from Okinawa to Yaeyama, where primitive living and working conditions in the countryside made this a rigorous form of exile.

Miyako and Yaeyama presented peculiarly difficult problems, for there was less traditional organization there upon which to base a new administration, and conditions of extreme hardship prevailed. An investigation in late 1881 disclosed a high disease and death rate and a general condition of social disorder. The local people had not been able to recover from the long series of disasters which had overtaken them in the previous century. A continuing feud embittered relations between the natives of Miyako and the victims of typhoon and famine who had been removed to Miyako from the nearby island of Irabu.

To meet these special conditions the police superintendents in Miyako and Yaeyama were charged concurrently with the management of civil affairs, an arrangement which continued in force until 1893.

By 1891 the administrative organization was well established. Iheya and Kume islands were brought under the control of Shimajiri district on Okinawa; distant islets of the Daito group had been explored, declared Japanese territory, and brought under the administration of Naha City. Local and district courts were established under the Nagasaki Court of Appeals. In 1893 a system of village assemblies was created to advise on the local budget and to reflect public opinion on matters of distinctly local interest. This was the first step on the long road to equal representation in the national government.

One thousand yen were granted by the imperial household to inaugurate an Okinawan public health and welfare program in 1880. Such patronage was intended to emphasize the importance which the government attached to health problems, but the sum was inconsequential if measured against the size of the task to be done. Public-health administration was entrusted to the police, but few policemen in that day understood the most elementary principles underlying a modern sanitation program. Nevertheless, prefectural health records show a gradual over-all improvement from 1879 until 1945.

Fifty-six doctors were granted permits to practice in support of the program inaugurated in 1880. They had only the most rudimentary knowledge of medicine, but with their assistance the police launched a general vaccination campaign. An effort was made to clean up the streets, alleyways, and residential areas of Naha and Shuri; it was forbidden to keep swine or dogs within the town limits; public toilets were constructed in the Tsuji quarters; and the excellent Japanese system of periodic city-wide house cleaning ultimately came into effect. Regulations were issued to govern the handling and distribution of foodstuffs and beverages. The police were ordered to supervise the maintenance of community wells and springs, and an inspection system was set up for the public bathhouses and brothels.

In 1884 the primitive practices of the *yuta* were suppressed; they could no longer offer to relieve pain and sickness by incantations and spells. A prefectural hospital was opened in 1885, and a licensing system for midwives was established, but midwifery training courses were not instituted until 1890, when a second hospital (Wakasa Byoin) opened its doors. It became possible about then to institute a standard examination for all medical practitioners.

The organization of an Okinawan branch of the Red Cross Society opened the way for appeals for help from overseas in times of emergency, but taken all in all the public health and welfare measures instituted in the "Do Nothing" period fell far short of the needs to be met in the prefecture.

Food shortages in 1885 weakened many people; epidemic sickness followed in 1886. More than 5,000 persons contracted smallpox and 1,500 fell victim to cholera. Approximately 2,500 persons died.

ECONOMIC CHANGE UNDER THE NEW DISPENSATION

Tokyo's "peace at any price" policy for the new prefecture is most clearly demonstrated in the failure to bring about significant changes in economic life until after the Sino-Japanese War. The government did little to improve the tax basis for the administration and virtually nothing to advance the development of private enterprise beneficial to the individual Okinawan.

Okinawa had no potential wealth to exploit, and Tokyo did not have surplus wealth to invest in a profitless regional economy. Ota Chofu makes an interesting note on the contrast between Japanese policies toward Hokkaido, at the north, and Okinawa at that time. Capital funds and administrative talent were poured into the northern island, where the scattered Ainu aborigines offered no political problem, and the mines, the forests, and the fisheries yielded a rich return. The Ryukyus, in contrast, had no material assets of value, and a large population divided and uncertain in its political and cultural loyalties.

Little was done to develop overland transportation within the islands until after the Sino-Japanese War. A road for wheeled vehicles was constructed across Okinawa in 1885, but little more was accomplished in a decade thereafter. Government and people alike continued to depend upon coastwise transport by small craft and upon the unimproved storage and transfer facilities at seaside villages and anchorages.

Okinawa's economic life henceforth depended upon shipping services between Naha Harbor and the ports of Japan proper. The approach to Naha anchorage was narrow, choked with silt, and obstructed by off-lying reefs. Not more than fifty ocean-going vessels entered and left the port annually at the time the kingdom came to an end. Clearly Naha was inadequate for use as a naval base in time of war; hence the government at Tokyo was reluctant to invest much in waterfront improvements. Adequate marine surveys of the archipelago were not complete until 1888, and the establishment of a regular meteorological reporting service was delayed until 1890.

The Okinawans were at the mercy of Japanese shipping interests. At the time of the Formosa expedition (1874) the Japanese government had given thirteen ships to Iwasaki Yataro, and with these he had developed the powerful Mitsubishi Company, which held a virtual monopoly on Japan's international shipping.

At the time of the king's abdication the Shuri government held nominal title to one steam vessel, the "Taiyu-maru," which had been the emperor's "gift" to the king, paid for by Chinese indemnity funds. Soon after the prefecture was established, Tokyo directed that this vessel be handed over to the Mitsubishi Company to operate between Osaka and Naha, via the anchorage at Naze in Amami Oshima, but soon thereafter (1882) Mitsubishi was ordered to transfer the "Taiyu-maru" to a new sea-transport company which had been founded by an enterprising Kagoshima resident.

The Okinawans themselves did not reënter shipping and gain a small share in the most important economic link with Japan and the outside world until 1887, when Marquis Sho's household founded a shipping line, which continued in operation for about twenty-five years.

Capital investors at Kagoshima, Osaka, Kobe, and Tokyo were not interested in Okinawa; the rapidly expanding economy of Japan proper offered many attractions, the new prefecture offered none. The laggard development of essential community services, poverty of resources and of markets, and underlying political uncertainty all repelled private Japanese investment.

There was virtually no local capital available at Naha. It has been estimated that no more than two or three Okinawans held property valued at more than twenty thousand yen in 1880. Those who possessed capital assets valued at two thousand yen were considered wealthy. Private lands held in the rural areas formed only a small percentage of the total area, for the ratio of public land to private holdings was approximately 76 to 24. Only four or five men owned as much as 12.5 acres (five *cho*), and a man who could command as much as one hundred bags of land-rent rice per year was considered an important landlord.[7] There had been no accumulation of private capital under the old regime, hence there was little to sustain economic life during the crisis of change.

Villagers who had from time immemorial farmed under a variety of communal land holding arrangements continued to do so throughout the "Do Nothing" era, but with ever-increasing hardship and difficulty. Hitherto they had bartered foodstuffs for handicrafts, objects produced in Naha and Shuri, Tomari, and Kume. Now the economy of the townsmen was shifting to a money basis, standards of urban life were slowly rising, and cheap goods of Japanese manufacture were entering the islands. The movement of people from Naha and Shuri to the villages, taking with them urban standards, added to the demands upon the country economy. Farm-dwellers had to produce foodstuffs and textiles for their own needs and enough in addition to pay for the new things which they now believed to be necessities.

Members of the privileged gentry classes—some 95,000 of them— were most severely hurt in this period of transition. They eked out a living as traders or craftsmen on the smallest scale, borrowing very small sums as temporary capital to carry them over in day-to-day operations. Those who had lived hitherto in modest comfort by Okinawan standards were reduced to the barest level of subsistence. Every member of the family had to work, and family heirlooms were sold or bartered.

The *moai* system of mutual-aid financing introduced among the aristocrats by Sai On in 1713 continued to play an important part in Okinawa until about 1907. Men who were comparatively well-off contributed twenty or thirty *koku* of rice to the revolving fund upon which their less fortunate colleagues could draw.

Gradually the dispossessed aristocrats adjusted themselves, found new sources of income, and began to enter employment as minor clerks in the expanding government offices or as employees of Japanese who were opening new commercial establishments. The women went out to work in the fields or took the initiative in setting up shopkeeping enterprises or small roadside market stalls.

The agricultural pattern changed. Restrictions upon the area which could be planted to sugar cane were lifted; the Japanese became interested in sugar production and pushed it vigorously, for the profits were great in the Osaka and Tokyo markets. Much rice-land was quickly converted to cane field. Within twenty-five years the total sugar output rose from 11,500,000 *kin* to nearly 47,000,000 *kin*, but the Okinawans who produced it enjoyed very little gain in this; they were at the mercy of the sugar brokers at Kagoshima and Osaka.

FIG. 22. COLUMN BASES. Left: *Worship Hall, Enkaku-ji (see Plate 2)*. Center: *Entry, Sho family mansion, Shuri*. Right: *Main gate, Sho family mansion*.

The government continued to collect taxes in kind until 1903—long after the practice was abandoned in other prefectures. No private sales of sugar were permitted until the government's assessment had been met through deliveries to the warehouses. The village, not the individual, remained the taxed unit, and the government saw to it that quantitative payments in sugar remained high while monetary credit for it remained low.

An unnatural situation arose wherein energetic and ambitious individuals who brought in good crops in one part of the island could not dispose of their surplus products after taxes until all the villages had met the government's requirements. This made close coöperation among the villages necessary and indeed compulsory. This and the *moai* system of mutual-aid financing were two strong incentives to full participation in mutual-aid programs of all kinds.

Taxes in kind (sugar and textiles) were delivered to the government by the village. The government in turn shipped the yield to Osaka, where officers of the Ministry of Finance supervised its disposal in the public market. Since sugar was the most important item (from Tokyo's point of view), the prefectural government encouraged sugar planting. A loan fund was set up to help the farmer avoid bankruptcy at the hands of the private moneylenders; the Sugar Commission was created to check upon and maintain acceptable standards of production.

The sudden expansion of sugar production to satisfy Japanese interests meant a rapid reduction in the area planted to essential foodstuffs needed on Okinawa. The farming community lost self-sufficiency even at a minimum standard of living. Farm villagers as well as town residents became dependent upon overseas shipping. The entire population was vulnerable to chance market fluctuations at Osaka, where the price of sugar was determined. In 1889 there was a short-lived attempt to found and develop a small textile factory to be operated by a number of the disestablished and impoverished aristocrats.

The so-called "resident merchants" from other prefectures were indifferent to the dangerous insecurity of food supply which now developed in the Ryukyu Islands. Between 1881 and 1903 an Agricultural Experiment Station sponsored the introduction of new grains, fruits, and vegetables, but no market existed in the farming villages for surpluses of bananas, papayas, and citrus fruits, and the farmers themselves preferred to plant sugar, unable to appreciate the danger of dependence upon a one-crop economy subject to the vagaries of an overseas market.

Some government officials were troubled by the problem; an effort was made to promote and control the production of the nutritious but unpalatable seeds of the cycad (*sotetsu*), which Okinawans traditionally considered "famine food," and when drought and typhoon damage brought the threat of starvation to many in 1885 and 1886, the government issued orders requiring licenses for the collection, transport, and sale of the *sotetsu* palm and its products. The palm grows wild on hillsides barren of all other edible growth, and its handsome fronds had begun to be exported in quantity to Europe by way of Osaka to be used for funeral wreaths. Other forest-control regulations were instituted to govern operations of any kind on public and private properties and to promote control of insect pests in the fields and forests. Much of this effort was merely paper work, a statement of government wishes rather than a record of achievement in fact. Nevertheless, agricultural associations began to be formed with a view to helping the government perfect and extend its controls.

The prefectural government's interests were concentrated on Okinawa, although sugar plantations were opened on Miyako, Yaeyama, and Kume. The coal mines of Iriomote on Yaeyama were handed over to the Mitsui Company in 1885. Sho family interests attempted to develop copper mining on Okinawa in 1887, but with no substantial result.

Poverty of resources and productive industry was reflected in the slow development of wholesale and retail trade. Naha had no more than two or three small retail merchant shops on permanent location in 1879. Most barter took place in small temporary stalls in the market place or along the streets. These, by tradition, were usually operated by women.

The newcomers from Japan soon established themselves in virtual monopoly upon the supply of wholesale goods for the Okinawan market, and the women of Naha and Shuri became the middlemen or agents between Japanese importers and the keepers of stalls and small shops throughout the islands. Kagoshima men led the way in developing modern retail trading. In general the "resident merchants" dominated all external trade. Marquis Sho's business managers alone were able to offer some competition, which they did on a moderate scale by organizing a company (the Maruichi Shoten) at Osaka through which Okinawan products could be marketed in other prefectures. Ota Chofu notes that the "resident merchants" group consisted principally of Kagoshima men who imported grain and exported sugar and Osaka traders who handled general merchandise and dry goods, and that long after the Okinawans succeeded in making a place for themselves in overseas commerce, the Osaka-Kagoshima division could be noticed in the orientation of Okinawan economic life.

According to Ota (who was closely associated with Okinawan efforts to achieve an equality of position in Japan's economic life), it required more than three years to effect the transition from the old coinage of the Ryukyu kingdom to a general acceptance and use of standard Japanese yen and sen. Agents were appointed to appraise the worn coins brought into the market places to be called in for re-minting. The conservative Okinawans were reluctant to accept unfamiliar yen and sen, and for a time gave each other supplementary notes promising to pay in the old bronze coins. This annoyed the government, which declared such notes null and void and threatened to punish anyone who attempted to use them.

The first bank established (in 1879) was set up by Kimbara Meizen, of Shizuoka Prefecture, and was commissioned to act as the national treasury's agency in Okinawa. When it closed its doors in 1887, its successor agency, the One Hundred Forty-seventh Bank, of Kagoshima, continued and expanded a moderate land-reclamation and irrigation program which had been undertaken by its predecessor.

A Japanese agent named Kawarada Moriharu had kept port records for the year 1875 as an investigative measure. At that time imports and exports were approximately balanced in value. A review of subsequent import-export figures shows that throughout the "Do Nothing" era imports exceeded exports in value. There was a great increase in the variety of consumer goods in demand for the Okinawan market, and an over-all increase in production figures. This must be taken to reflect a general rise in living standards throughout Japan; though Okinawa Prefecture shared in this advance, it lagged far behind other prefectures in the *rate* of advance. The Okinawans themselves felt that until about 1907 the islands were used as a dumping ground for inferior Japanese products which could not be sold elsewhere. They had also to accept dependence upon an export-crop market over which they had no control whatsoever.

This was a true "colonial period." The Okinawans took what they could get and made the best of it, but the lion's share of profit and the power to make economic policy for the prefecture did not rest with them. They had no effective representation at the national capital, and few Japanese at Tokyo felt much interest—economic, political, or humanitarian—in the welfare of the Okinawans.

Newcomers from other prefectures mistook the extreme poverty of the Okinawans as evidence of indifference and inferior capacity.

FOREIGNERS IN OKINAWA AFTER PERRY'S VISIT

Perry's compact cleared the way for an easier foreign intercourse with Okinawa, but the opening of Japan nearby reduced Naha's importance to the vanishing point. Ships touched occasionally—some were in search of fresh supplies, but usually curiosity alone prompted a short visit. H.M.S. "Dwarf," Captain Bax commanding, put in on September 10, 1871, while passing through the archipelago from South China to make a survey of Siberian coasts. The officials were ready now to accept payment for servicing the ship, and requests for permission to go ashore met with only the slightest show of hesitation. Officers and men rambled about freely, impressed by the civility of the people, the cleanliness of the town of Shuri, and the beauty of the countryside: "The people appeared most polite, everyone we met on the road bowing profoundly; they were curious to see us, but were not at all rude like the Chinese are. . . ."

Bax noted the cleanliness and parklike character of the old capital and compared it favorably with Naha, which, he thought, much more closely resembled a Chinese town in architecture and general untidiness. As they took leave on the quay September 12 they were presented with a gift of vegetables, fowls, and a pig, made to them in the king's name. In return for this and in token of appreciation for Okinawan hospitality, Captain Bax sent off a letter to the king at Shuri with a gift of "blankets, serge, pictures and books." Shopkeepers at Naha, however, refused to trade, hiding themselves whenever an Englishman in search of mementoes approached the premises.[8]

In 1883 members of a scientific expedition aboard the British ship "Marquesa" found the Japanese in full control. As they sat chatting over tea at a police box near the waterfront, a gaunt Caucasian ap-

peared, a veritable apparition of a man, dressed in tattered clothes—
sombrero, boots, and a long tail-coat—who described himself as an
American, one of two who had lived for some time on Okinawa. He
stayed only briefly with the visiting scientists, but before he vanished,
shuffling away in the alleys of Naha, they surmised that he was an
adventurer with a dubious past in the California goldfields, an example
of the human driftwood which was gathering all along the coasts of
Asia in those days.[9]

In July, 1873, the German schooner "R.J. Robertson," en route
from Foochow to Adelaide, was driven by storm upon the coral reefs
of Miyako, near the point upon which Captain Broughton's ship the
"Providence" had been wrecked in 1797. A British ship, the "Curlew,"
aided in the rescue of the crew. For thirty-four days the men of the "Robertson" lived among the people of Miyako, who provided what they
could of traditional hospitality, although the island was suffering severe
privation in these years. This generosity and the character of the local
Okinawan officials deeply impressed the stranded seamen. Reports on
the incident appeared in the European press in February, 1874. Germany
at this time was actively seeking territory in the Far East, and found in
the incident an excuse to dispatch a warship, the "Cyclop," to cruise
in Okinawan waters in 1876. Ostensibly it was there to return thanks
for Okinawan hospitality. A large monument was erected at Hirara
in the kaiser's name, and honors with token monetary rewards were
distributed to the principal Okinawan officials. Since Japan had assumed
responsibility for foreign affairs in the Ryukyu kingdom, the awards
were made through Tokyo, with Japanese approval, and with a reward
or two to the appropriate Japanese officials, who had had nothing
whatever to do with dispensing Okinawan hospitality.[10]

In 1887 an American ventured upon a reconnaissance of Okinawa as
a potential field for Christian missionary activity. Thirty years had
elapsed since Moreton and his family had abandoned the ill-starred
British Loo Choo Naval Mission, but the time was still not ripe. At
last, in 1892, the American Methodist Episcopal Mission at Nagasaki,
the American Baptists, and the Church Missionary Society each sent
Japanese evangelists into the Ryukyus to attempt "gospelizing this
ancient, civilized people." They chose to send Japanese Christians in

the belief that they could more readily approach the Okinawans. The tables were turned indeed; Christianity, so long and so cruelly forbidden, was now urged upon the people of Naha and Shuri by Japanese financed by foreign interests. It soon became evident that the fundamental Japanese attitudes toward the "inferior" Okinawans merely reinforced Okinawan opposition. The evangelists—aided and encouraged by occasional visits made by the American missionaries—found that they could make progress among their fellow Japanese in Okinawa, but the Okinawans remained unmoved and suspicious.

Substituting New Loyalties for Old

With the National Education Act of 1872 the Tokyo government had attacked the immense problem of regional loyalties in conflict with central authority in Japan proper. By the time the Ryukyu kingdom became Okinawa Prefecture, "obedience to the emperor" had replaced traditional standards of loyalty to the local clan or daimyo throughout most of the old feudal territories, but the problem was by no means completely solved. The Satsuma Rebellion of 1877 had brought the threat of general civil war and had betrayed weakness within which invited attack from without.

If Okinawa were to be assimilated, the prejudices of the older generation would have to be overcome, and the loyalties of the younger generation would have to be shifted from Shuri to Tokyo. Traditional and sentimental ties with China would have to be dissolved and the old days of the independent Ryukyu kingdom must be forgotten. Easy-going, casual life in the Okinawan community must give way to a more vigorous, disciplined organization; the individual must learn to snap to attention and to believe that his duty to the Japanese state overrode all other considerations.

The Japanese who addressed themselves to this problem in Okinawa enjoyed certain advantages. In the first instance, they could draw upon a decade of practical experience in other prefectures. In the second, they took up this new task in a community which held scholarship in high regard. Literacy was synonymous with privilege and authority in the eyes of the illiterate peasant.

Families were prepared to make any sacrifice in order to provide education for promising youth, and villages took pride in young men who aspired to take the literary examinations. Conversely, the Confucian ideal of the son's obligation to his parents meant that a youth who accepted these sacrifices on his behalf felt himself to be under heavy moral obligation to the family and to the community. Teacher and student commanded the highest respect in the community. In the Ryukyus an opportunity to study—at least to learn the elements of reading —was part of the birthright of every youth of the upper classes. Approximately thirty schools existed at the time of the king's abdication.

The Education Ministry at Tokyo determined to create a school system in Okinawa which would provide a corps of young men to be used in carrying through a general provincial reorganization. Ultimately the system would be extended into all the islands and would touch every household having school-age children.

The schools of Okinawa had been closed during the months of crisis and uncertainty preceding the king's abdication, and were not reopened until December, 1879. It was at once evident that these schools were not suited to Japan's needs. Children in village schools heard professional storytellers recite traditional tales of propriety and filial piety. Children of the gentry studied Chinese calligraphy and elementary Chinese classical texts. Youths who were allowed to enter the Shuri Academy at the age of seventeen or eighteen years studied the classics in detail, heard formal lecture commentaries upon them, and studied Japanese texts. Youths who entered the Kume Village Academy concentrated on Chinese studies.

Tokyo immediately appropriated funds to support the two academies and to supply salaries for teachers in the lower schools.

Early in 1880, Tanaka Fujimaro, a farsighted and influential vice-minister of education, visited Okinawa to see for himself what the problems were. He had been one of the principal authors of the Education Act of 1872; his presence suggested the importance attached to the problems of education in the new prefecture.

A need for interpreters came first. The Japanese could converse with the educated leaders at Shuri and Naha, but could not make themselves understood in the countryside. Moreover, it was a matter of pride as well as policy that the new authorities should refuse to speak local dialects. The Okinawans must learn to speak and read the standard Japanese used at Tokyo. To this end therefore a "Conversation Training Quarter" was opened in the precincts of the Tempi Shrine in February, 1880, and soon an elementary *Okinawan-Japanese Conversation Book* was prepared in two volumes. It was proposed to develop here a corps of clerks and interpreters who could use standard Japanese in the government service. In June a normal school was established to increase as rapidly as possible the number of teachers competent to spread the new learning in the lower schools. Toward the end of the year the old Shuri Academy was transformed into a middle school, three primary schools were opened at Shuri, ten opened in the Shimajiri district, and one in the northern part of the island. Thenceforth the expansion of educational facilities was rapid. By 1885, primary schools had been opened not only in rural Okinawa, but on the outlying islands as well, bringing the total to fifty-seven.

It was relatively easy for the government to decree the opening of a primary school, but it was not easy to persuade parents to enroll their children and keep them there. It is estimated that there were more than 75,000 children of school age in the province in 1884, but that only 1,854 were actually at school. The peasants were reluctant to send children to school; they were afraid that the costs would be too great, and they did not trust the newcomers who were intruding themselves upon the Okinawan community everywhere. They resisted rapid change.

To overcome these objections the prefectural government provided school supplies and exempted parents from varying degrees of labor service normally expected of them in the community. An element of compulsion was introduced by establishing a "school-attendance quota" for each village, which brought into play the pressure of public opinion and the feeling of mutual responsibility which is such a marked characteristic of Okinawan community life.

The normal school was established in the old official residence of the Satsuma clan representatives at Naha. Five young men graduated from the normal school's short course in May, 1881. These pioneers in the new era were sons of distinguished families at Shuri. The choice they had made was significant; opportunities for a career in government were not promising and business life was unfamiliar and unpopular among the dispossessed gentry. They turned to education as a field in which they could distinguish themselves.

The government was glad to encourage this. In 1882 five young aristocrats were sent to Tokyo to study at public expense. All were destined to become important leaders whose names appear again and again in the annals of Okinawa Prefecture.*

Three girls were permitted to enter the primary classes attached to the normal school in 1885. This marked the beginning of general education for women throughout the prefecture. A private high school for girls opened its doors five years later.

Study of the English language was introduced as a required subject in the curriculum at the Shuri Middle School. Formal gymnastics—setting-up exercises—were introduced to serve the needs of a physical-health program, which later became the basis for military-drill schedules, inaugurated at the Middle School in 1887. The government sought to stimulate public interest through exhibitions and through the organization of educational associations. Students entering the teacher-training courses were given a small subsidy, essential supplies, and living equipment such as charcoal, teapots, and mosquito nets.

Most important of all, the influential Mori Arinori, Minister of Education at Tokyo, found time to tour Okinawa Prefecture, where he found only 4,824 students enrolled. This represented approximately eleven percent of the boys and one percent of the girls of school age.

These students were eager to acquire an education, but assimilation to Japanese ways and manners was slow. More than 1,800 were above fourteen years of age and some were married. They were reluctant to abandon traditional dress and to assume the costume and distinctive student habits then being adopted in other prefectures. Change began in the normal school and spread slowly. In March, 1888, the normal-school students and children in the Shimajiri Higher Primary School had their hair cut; the old topknot and pin denoting social rank gave

* Jahana Noboru, Takamine Chokyo, Nakijin Choban, Kishimoto Gasho, and Ota Chofu. The latter's book *Fifty Years of Administration in Okinawa Prefecture* (*Okinawa-kensei Goju-nen*) forms the principal source of data for Chapters IX and X of this historical summary.

way to the close-cropped hair styling common among Japanese students. Middle-school boys abandoned sash, kimono, and headband in the next year in favor of uniforms, and all teachers were urged henceforth to wear the standard uniform of a government employee.

Ten years after the king's abdication, the Ministry of Education at Tokyo arranged to place portraits of the emperor and empress in every school in Okinawa Prefecture. They were treated as semi-sacred objects by the Japanese teachers, who sought (with slight success) to inculcate among the Okinawans a feeling of awe and reverence in the presence of these symbols of national unity and exaltation of the state.

There was little upon which to graft this artificially created creed of state worship. The seventh governor (Maruoka Kanji) had at one time been chief of the Shrine Bureau at Tokyo. He was an extreme nationalist, fervently determined to revive and promote Shinto as a state religion throughout Japan. During his administration the ancient temple on Nami-no-ue Bluff overlooking Naha Harbor was declared a state shrine of the third class, entitled to annual government subsidies.

With the downfall of the kingdom, the ancient Buddhist temples lost the state support which had carried them through the centuries. Ankoku-ji alone was designated a "public temple" and given some assistance; the majority of Buddhist organizations and buildings fell into decay.

There was still a wide gap to be closed between the governing Japanese and the governed Okinawans. A significant change was heralded when Japanese scholars began to become interested in the natural history, language, and literature of the islands. The bibliography of Japanese studies concerning Okinawa Prefecture reflects the work of ornithologists, botanists, marine biologists, and geologists who were eager to make new contributions in their fields in the late 19th century. They had virgin territory in which to work in the Ryukyu Islands. Tajima Risaburo prepared *Materials for the Study of the Ryukyu Language (Ryukyu-go Kenkyu Shiryo)*, and Basil Hall Chamberlain, then Professor of Japanese Philology at Tokyo Imperial University, visited Okinawa in 1894 to collect materials published in 1896 as *An Essay in Aid of a Grammar and Dictionary of the Luchuan Language*. Chamberlain's grandfather, Captain Basil Hall, had done more, perhaps, than any other

415

individual to bring the old Ryukyuan kingdom to the attention of the Western world at the opening of the 19th century; now at its close the grandson published a number of essays descriptive of conditions within the new prefecture.[11]

A number of prominent Okinawans who had taken part in the transition or had matured during this "Do Nothing" era were quietly preparing notes and essays recording their own experiences and observations. The Japanese, however, did not encourage investigations of historical interest, and pursued a conscious policy of neglect of the old culture, the ancient monuments, and the old buildings. Okinawans who suggested that a study of local history should be introduced into the school curriculum met at once with determined opposition.

The Meiji constitution, promulgated in 1890, promised wide representation in the national Diet; local interests were to be given a larger voice in the management of local affairs. But it was at once made clear that these benefits were not to extend to Okinawa, despite the constitution. Barriers of language and custom had not yet been surmounted, nor had economic institutions there been revised. The prefectural administrative organization was not ready to support local representation in government. Communal land tenure and the system of taxes paid in goods rather than in money continued to set Okinawa apart from all other prefectures.

The most serious problem to be overcome was *prejudice*. Minor Japanese officials who were the effective administrators, far from the national capital and the constitution, were jealous of authority in remote and unrepresented communities. An incident at Hirara in Miyako illustrated the problem. Natives of Miyako were allowed to visit Tokyo in 1893 for the first time—fifteen years after the islands had been declared a prefecture. Miyako had continued to be under an intolerant, inefficient, and oppressive police administration. A land dispute concerning taxes at last precipitated crisis. The police threatened to summon a warship to Hirara for punitive action. Calmer officers at Tokyo restrained police and military hotheads and paved the way for a committee of leading Miyako natives to visit Tokyo. They were sent off with great popular acclaim bearing gifts of local produce for the government leaders at

Tokyo. There they were received courteously by Prince Konoe Atsumaro, member of the House of Peers and leading advocate of Pan-Asian solidarity. They were given opportunity to discuss their problems with Marquis Okuma Shigenobu, Minister of State and founder of Waseda University. After Miyako's grievances had been laid before these prominent men the petitioners were given gifts by the government and dismissed.

Tokyo ordered a petty official of Niigata Prefecture (named Nakamura Jissaku) to accompany the group to Miyako. He was instructed to investigate and report upon the grievances they had laid before the government. The crowds at Hirara greeted the returning travelers with immense acclaim, but Nakamura behaved with such intolerable arrogance that the reception quickly turned into a riot of protest. He acted, it was said, like a bear-keeper returning his charges to their cage after an exhibition.

Nakamura was merely part of an immense bureaucracy which stood between the capital, with its good intentions, and the remote islands, under an indifferent police administration. Representative government provided for in theory by the constitution at Tokyo was not believed to be politically feasible or desirable for the new prefecture. In truth, of course, Okinawa was not ready for it; the new educational system had not yet produced enough leaders to meet the demands of national political life.

There were 101 schools in existence on December 31, 1891, but there were only 11,360 students enrolled. Many students did not attend class regularly. Conditions at the Shuri Middle School and in the normal school reflected the problems of the time. It was to these higher schools that the Japanese government must look for qualified young leaders. Nevertheless, under the unnatural restraints placed upon the prefecture by Tokyo's "colonial" outlook, they were not yet functioning effectively. Ota Chofu noted that many students in the middle school were idlers who would not take their studies seriously; ambition was stunted, for they saw no prospect of significant opportunity either in government or in local economic life. Of a class of forty-one members which had enrolled in 1880, only three finished the course eight years later. By 1895 the middle school had graduated thirty-eight men. Only three or four entered the government service. The normal school had a better record, perhaps because every graduate could anticipate immediate employment and the highest degree of prestige in any community in the Ryukyu Islands. Between 1880 and 1895 a total of 109 young men had finished the teachers' training course.

Ambitious youths in Okinawa began to seek opportunities to go up to Osaka and Tokyo, where the capable individual faced less discrimination as an "Okinawan" and found much wider economic prospects. On Okinawa itself youths who had been educated in the new schools, developing some enthusiasm for Japanese innovations in daily life, were in a minority; their contemporaries and their elders were not yet persuaded that exclusive control by Japan was either honorable or profitable.

In 1890 ten young men volunteered for military training as noncommissioned officers in the Japanese Army. Seventeen others followed them in the next year. This was promising, from the Japanese point of view, but the Tokyo government was by no means ready to extend Japan's conscription laws to the island prefecture. If an Okinawan smarting under Japanese restraints openly criticized this state of affairs, he immediately heard charges that the people of Okinawa Prefecture wished to discriminate against Japanese from other prefectures. If the critic persisted, he was charged with disloyalty.

The situation was not a healthy one; the crisis of Sino-Japanese relations concerning Korea was soon to flare into open war. Tension increased within Okinawa between advocates of pro-Chinese and pro-Japanese points of view. For thirty years the bitterness born of the Makishi-Onga incident had infected life at Naha and Shuri. Families and friends were divided. Members of the "white" faction mistrusted members of the "black." Many older people were filled with the paralyzing fear that China would indeed soon invade Okinawa to punish her disloyal tributary people. On the other hand, students at the normal and middle schools organized "patriotic societies" in support of the Japanese point of view.

Tokyo had sufficient grounds for caution; fear that China would reopen the sovereignty issue were well founded, for the Chinese minister at Tokyo (Li Ching-shu) did not hesitate openly to make an issue of it, and the Japanese could not be certain upon which side of the issue in Korea the foreign powers might choose to align themselves.

China, Japan, and Russia were facing one another in an angry mood on the peninsula nearby and the shadow of this quarrel fell darkly across the Ryukyu Islands.

CHAPTER TEN

ASSIMILATION BY JAPAN

1890–1940

WAR AND POLITICS: THE CHINESE THREAT REMOVED

Three events, external to Okinawa, brought an end to the "Do Nothing" era and powerfully affected the course of Okinawan history after 1890. These were the inauguration of the forms of parliamentary government at Tokyo, the successful prosecution of a war with China, and the acquisition of Formosa.

The clansmen who forced the Tokugawa to relinquish power were divided among themselves. Those who formed the Cabinet or dominated the principal ministries of state defended their privileged positions with bitter determination. Politicians and statesmen who were out of power sought with equal vigor to whittle away the prerogatives of the Cabinet, calling for a constitution, a parliamentary form of government, and a wider distribution of responsibility. In granting a constitution (in the name of the emperor), the oligarchs bowed to public pressure in the matter of forms, but yielded little of the substance of power.

The Meiji constitution, providing for representative government, went into effect in 1890. Throughout the campaigns, elections, and sessions of the first three diets, the national administration was carried on in an atmosphere of unrelieved hostility between Cabinet officers and members of the parliament. Neither trusted the other. "The people's rights" (*minken*) had been a central theme in public political debate for some twenty years, and the issue of "special privileges" was constantly before the public eye.

It cannot be said that there was deep concern or widespread interest in the political welfare of the Okinawan people or of the new prefecture, but it was not possible for one prefecture alone to remain outside the normal administrative framework; every nation-wide measure debated in the Diet chambers required special debate on the exceptional treatment to which Okinawa must be subjected. Regularization of Okinawa's provincial status could not long be postponed.

As for the effect of the Sino-Japanese War, it is doubtful if any government leader at Tokyo in 1890 thought war could be avoided. It was rather a question of choosing the most advantageous time to bring about a decisive change in relations with the giant neighbor on the continent. The question of rivalry in Korea had to be settled, and the ghost of the Ryukyu sovereignty issue had to be laid forever.

Party opposition to the government reached an extraordinary degree of bitterness just after the general election of March, 1894. The government had administered the election with gross abuse of police powers. Cabinet and Diet were at loggerheads. The Diet session lasted only three weeks, during which the premier's foreign policies were subjected to violent attack. Demands for war with Korea and with China had been deflected in 1872 and 1874 by the Formosa expedition; now again attacks upon the government were suddenly deflected, and the country rallied to its support, by a declaration of war.

Hostilities began on July 25, 1894, and war with China was formally declared six days later. Throughout the country, political factions temporarily submerged their differences in tumultuous patriotism. People throughout the provinces clamored for the chastisement of China and hastened to arms.

Only the Okinawans hung back. The excitement at Naha was intense, but there was no unity of support for the government. Many persons fully expected a Chinese fleet to appear in Okinawan waters. Families were sent to the countryside to await this crisis. Hot argument embittered friends and neighbors who were not agreed on the proper course of action if the Chinese should land.

The war continued through seven and a half months. No Chinese appeared in the Ryukyu Islands, and China's decisive defeat appeared to banish the Ryukyu sovereignty question.

Japan's victory was confirmed in the Treaty of Shimonoseki, signed April 17, 1895. For the moment it seemed that Japan had won great prestige; at one stroke she had defeated Asia's most extensive empire and had become a colonial power to boot, for she had acquired the Liaotung Peninsula, Formosa, and the Pescadores.

As far as the majority of thoughtful Okinawans were concerned, Japan's victory was greeted with relief, and Tokyo's prestige soared there as it did throughout the world. China's ancient claims to military and political greatness were dissolved by this revelation of her weakness. Nevertheless, three incidents at this moment alerted the Japanese government to the possibility that some traces of Chinese influence might linger on in the Ryukyus.

On May 5, less than three weeks after the Shimonoseki Treaty was signed, Japan was forced to promise to return the Liaotung Peninsula to China; Russia wanted it for herself and had found a devious way to prevent Japan's intrusion there. This hard blow was brought about by successful Chinese intrigues with Russia, France, and Germany, who joined to bring pressure upon Japan which Tokyo could not resist. This was precisely the kind of intervention which Japan had so long feared in the Ryukyu sovereignty dispute. At about the same time it was discovered that an unscrupulous man from Kagoshima (Yamanojo Hajime, a primary school teacher and a rascal) was swindling pro-Chinese Okinawans by representing himself as a secret agent for China's Viceroy Li Hung-chang, ready to arrange Chinese aid for Okinawans who agreed to oppose Japan. Concurrently it was discovered that Chinese officials at Peking and Nanking were actively supporting a so-called "republic" in Formosa and encouraging local Chinese in Formosa to appeal to foreign powers to prevent Japan from assuming control in the island which had just been ceded by Peking. It was not inconceivable that the same thing might be attempted in the Ryukyus.

In fact, Okinawan interest in China faded rapidly after the war. The sentiment which stirred in the hearts of conservative older people could be ignored, but damage had been done. Official policy stiffened and remained hostile thereafter to all local traditions and folkways which marked off Okinawans from other loyal subjects in the empire and retarded the assimilation of the younger generation.

Victory also brought possession of Formosa, a rich, unruly, and

PLATE 32. MAJIKINA ANKO (1875–1933). *Distinguished author of* A Thousand Years of Okinawan History.

PLATE 33. IHA FUYU (1876–1947). *As a historian, folklorist, and teacher, Iha sought to promote the cultural rehabilitation of the Okinawan people through appeals to pride in past achievements, notably in his study* Old Ryukyu.

PLATE 34. VICE ADMIRAL KANNA KENWA (1877–1950). *As captain of the ship bearing Crown Prince Hirohito to Europe and as aide to the future emperor, Kanna rose to prominence in the 1920's and served as Parliamentary Vice Minister in the Tokyo government. After his retirement, he sought to promote the interests of Okinawan emigrants in South America.*

PLATE 35. THE HONORABLE HIGA SHUHEI (1892–1956). *Higa, a farmer's son of Yutenja, Okinawa, graduated from Waseda University (Tokyo), spent thirty years teaching English in Okinawa and other prefectures of Japan, and distinguished himself as a public leader during the crisis of surrender in 1945 and its aftermath. In 1952 the U.S. Army high command on Okinawa appointed him the first Chief Executive of the Government of the Ryukyu Islands.*

PLATE 36. AERIAL VIEW OF THE SHURI CASTLE SITE IN 1957. *The administrative buildings and classrooms of Ryukyu University cover the old royal enclosure; faculty housing occupies the Enkaku-ji site; and dormitories and playing-fields cover the old park-land of the Sonohyan Shrine.*

undeveloped island southwest of Okinawa and about fifty miles west of the Yaeyama group. When sovereignty in Formosa passed to Japan, Okinawa ceased to be a frontier area. Henceforth the prefecture would be of secondary importance, merely an economically unrewarding territorial link between Japan proper and the new "treasure island."

From the Japanese point of view Okinawa's peculiar customs, dialects, and costumes were thrown into new and perhaps better perspective; they were odd, to be sure, but not so odd and difficult to understand as the speech, dress, and customs of the Formosan Chinese or of the aborigines in the Formosan hills. The similarities of culture in Okinawa and Japan proper could now be seen more clearly; it was readily apparent that these outnumbered the cultural differences which had to be overcome. It was appreciated that the docile Okinawans had yielded to Japanese rule without significant struggle; by sharp contrast it was to require ten years of bloody campaigns and reprisals before the Formosans could be reduced to a sullen acceptance of Japanese rule.

ADMINISTRATIVE CHANGE AND THE BASIC LAND REFORM

The eighth governor of Okinawa was Baron Narahara Kogoro (Shigeru), a haughty samurai from Satsuma, who took office in July, 1892, as the country moved toward war with China. Tokyo knew that he would rule with a firm hand for he had been closely associated with Okinawan affairs during the transition period in the 1870's. He was not popular in Okinawa, but during his long tenure of office great progress was made toward political and economic assimilation with other prefectures. His principal assistant, Hibi Kimei, succeeded him as governor in 1907, carrying forward Narahara's policies until June, 1913. Such a continuity of administration, maintained through twenty-one years, was of great importance, for in the succeeding period of twenty-one years changing ministries at Tokyo sent no fewer than fifteen governors to Okinawa.

Soon after Narahara took office, a newspaper—the *Ryukyu Shimpo* —was founded. This strengthened leadership and promoted the development of informed opinion on matters of public concern.

In the years 1893–96 a number of highly qualified men surveyed the problems of administrative reorganization, of representative local government bodies, and of taxation. The Cabinet was determined to strengthen administrative controls throughout the social and economic life of the islands. This would offset the unavoidable necessity of granting an increasing measure of representation through local assemblies and (ultimately) Okinawan representation in the Diet. As the functions and services of government were enlarged, costs had risen in proportion, and quite naturally Tokyo wanted to shift a maximum share of the cost burden to the local people.

It will be recalled that in 1892 and 1893 representative assemblies had been convoked in each district, and that local leaders were permitted to express their views upon the local budget. In 1896 the districts were realigned, and the assemblies were granted modest power to influence local taxation and budgeting for local expenditures. By 1897 Yaeyama and Miyako—always lagging a little—were brought into harmony with the prefecture-wide system.

Assemblymen were elected by popular choice, subject to the governor's confirmation; all other members of the administration were appointed by him and were paid from the national treasury.

By 1895 it was clearly apparent that there could be no substantial progress in Okinawa until a far-reaching land reform was carried through. A Temporary Land Readjustment Bureau was created in 1898 to begin the formidable task of converting nearly seventy-six percent of the total area—traditional communal land—to private ownership, capable of sustaining private enterprise, individual taxation, and a modern administration. Taken in all its political and economic consequences, this undertaking must be ranked as one of the great turning points in Okinawan history, and the most significant event to take place between the king's abdication in 1879 and the American invasion of 1945.

In the nature of things, such a shift from communal to private ownership was certain to cause a profound disorganization of traditional community life. It had to be imposed from Tokyo, working through the prefectural and district officers, and it provoked bitter opposition. The rancorous "Black and White" dispute was transmuted now into fierce opposition to government policies on the one hand and support for them on the other.

A number of prominent men formed an organization called the Kodo-kai, through which they sought to restore unity to the Okinawan community and to reassert some measure of Okinawan leadership in affairs of vital importance to every native of the old kingdom. Their intentions were excellent, but they did not sufficiently understand the political implications of some of their proposals.

In good faith the Kodo-kai proposed that Governor Narahara be recalled and that Marquis Sho Tai be sent down to take his place. In 1875 the statesman Okubo Toshimichi had proposed a hereditary governorship to be maintained in the family of the former king. It was believed that if the king were granted the nominal title and honors of governorship, the most stubborn anti-Japanese elements in Okinawa would unite with the liberal advocates of modernization.

By implication this recommendation challenged the wisdom of the emperor's appointment of Narahara, and the move could be interpreted abroad as evidence of misrule in Okinawa—or at least of grave dissatisfaction with Japanese administration. It might draw attention once again to the sovereignty issue. Tokyo crushed the Kodo-kai movement at once.

The general land system has been described in an earlier chapter. Three-fourths of the land was subject to periodic reallocation among farm households and villages. Of the remaining one-fourth some comprised private estates held by the nobles, some was set aside for the support of the village *noro*, and some, which had been held by the Shuri court, was now managed by the prefectural government. The length of time during which an individual household was permitted to hold and cultivate a given plot varied from hamlet to hamlet. Usually a family did not hold a piece of land for more than ten years. Only reclaimed land of a certain character could be held, bought, and sold privately.

If a household could not meet its tax assessment, the group of households to which it belonged undertook to make up the difference. Tax assessments laid on the village were determined by a most complicated formula. Every village belonged to one of five classes. The land itself was graded according to its nature as determined in the long-outdated surveys which Satsuma had made in the period 1609–11. A combination of the village class plus the land grade led to a determination of the tax to be levied. This cumbersome and inefficient system could not meet the demands of a modern economy, but it continued in effect until the land reform was completed in 1903.

In that year an officer in the Finance Ministry at Tokyo (Mori Kengo) prepared a report which noted that the farmers of Okinawa bore a disproportionate share of the prefectural tax burden, and that the periodic reallocation of land deprived the individual farmer of incentives inherent in private ownership. The report noted that land was allotted without consideration of the distance at which it might lie from the farmer's house and that this was wasteful of time, labor, and transport. Since the great majority of people owned no land, they had none to use as security on loans. The farmer could borrow only against his crops, which were of uncertain value from season to season, and hence he was required to pay exorbitant rates of interest.

The land reform was pronounced complete in October, 1903. Few villages were left untouched or little modified. Owners of hereditary lands were confirmed in their titles; lands assigned to support village *noro* became the private property of the *noro*'s family. Plots of land were now registered in the name of the individual farmer who qualified as head of a farm household. Henceforth the individual would pay land tax, and it would no longer be paid as tax in kind, but in money.

By 1903 the population numbered 480,000. The reorganization of the tax base produced a severe shortage in prefectural government revenue—income for an area which yielded 460,000 yen under the old village-tax system now yielded only 126,000 yen. It looked as though the prefectural administration of Okinawa would become a permanent burden on the national treasury. The number and variety of local taxes upon goods, services, and licenses was steadily increased, but it became apparent that relief would have to be achieved through two measures: population pressure would have to be reduced through migration from Okinawa, and the total production of goods would have to be increased to meet internal local consumption demands and to provide an exportable surplus.

DEVELOPMENT OF REPRESENTATION IN GOVERNMENT

Repeated changes and adjustments at last brought the structure of local government into line with the general administrative system in other prefectures. In 1908 Itoman was created a town (*cho*), followed soon after by Hirara, Ishigaki, and Nago. Old administrative names were abandoned; the *majiri* became *son* or *mura;* the three ancient principality divisions became *gun* or counties. Salt, camphor, and tobacco monopolies were united under one office, new taxes were laid on local business, and the prefectural treasury began to bear a larger share of the cost of local government.

In 1909 a prefectural assembly was convoked for the first time. The chairman was Takamine Chokyo, one of the five men who had been sent to Tokyo at government expense in 1882. Assemblymen were elected by fellow members of the county, town, and city councils. These men in turn had been elected by residents of Okinawa Prefecture who paid at least ten yen annually in taxes on real property. This was a very narrow base for a system of indirect representation, but it was a step forward. Two local political organizations offered mild competition in seeking votes; one (known as the Doshi-kai) elected sixteen assemblymen, the other (known as the Minyu-kai) placed fourteen nominees. These "parties" or political associations were concerned with local issues and were not affiliated with the national political parties of Japan.

Nevertheless, Tokyo watched the elections and first sessions of the Okinawan prefectural assembly with keen interest. Special observers were sent to Naha to report on the conduct of the meetings.

The principal measures introduced by Chairman Takamine reflected accurately a concern with education, geographical isolation, and public health. Takamine proposed that a second middle school be established at prefectural expense, that a submarine cable be laid to link Miyako with Okinawa, and that an investigation of provincial health problems be pursued in order to develop a system for the free distribution of medicines.

In the next year the way was paved for Okinawan representation in the national Diet, but Yaeyama and Miyako were excluded from the electoral district. The first two men sent to the Lower House at Tokyo (in 1912) were Takamine Chokyo and his associate of early school days in Japan, Kishimoto Gasho. In a sense this was a reward for thirty years of patient, often thankless effort to bring about a true assimilation of Okinawa to the Japanese empire.

Following this advance toward representative government the political parties at Tokyo moved to capture the votes of the Okinawans. But party politicians at the national capital had very little to offer in exchange for only two votes cast by Diet members who were newcomers without significant personal influence or backing in national politics. The Seiyu-kai opened a branch office at Naha in 1912, but abandoned it three years later. For two years Okinawa was ignored by the national political parties. In 1917, however, the Seiyu-kai found itself hardpressed by its rival, the Kensei-kai, and needed every vote it could muster to hold its preëminent position in the Diet. The Naha office was reopened, despite little local interest in national politics and virtually no contributions forthcoming for the party's national treasury.

Marquis Sho, the former crown prince, held a hereditary seat in the House of Peers by virtue of his rank. In 1918 he was joined for the first time by a Japanese resident on Okinawa appointed to represent the highest taxpayers of the prefecture.

Election laws for Okinawa were revised once again during the administration of Hara Kei, the first commoner to hold the highest political office in Japan. Yaeyama and Miyako were brought into the electoral district, Okinawan representation was raised to five members for the Lower House, and on April 1, 1920, the people of the prefecture for the first time enjoyed legal equality of representation with other Japanese in the law-making body of the empire. Forty-one years had passed since the king's abdication.

Much remained to be done to secure equality in social and economic affairs. With only five representatives in a Lower House membership of 381, the Okinawans carried little weight in budgetary matters and virtually none in the crucial matter of appointments to the governorship. The governors, on their part, exercised great and often decisive power in election matters within the prefecture, for they controlled the police, who administered election laws and had the power of veto in certification of candidates for elective offices.

After the "Narahara-Hibi" era (1892–1913) the governor's office was filled by party men. Few showed sympathy or understanding for the basic problems which beset Okinawa. One appointee (Odagiri Bantaro) so disliked the idea of "exile" to a remote province that he resigned the governorship seven days after accepting appointment at Tokyo, without setting foot in the islands. This provoked resentment.

Some of the governors made a conscientious effort to grapple with a problem which had no solution, the problem of achieving a self-sufficient economy.

After 1890 the government encouraged the organization of Young Men's Associations, Young Women's Associations, Ladies' Patriotic Associations, Army Reservists' Associations, Farmers' Associations and the like. In theory, membership was voluntary and the choice of associations by the individual was dictated by social and occupational interests. In fact, these associations were highly developed throughout the empire to serve public finance and policing purposes. The individual gained a considerable return in mutual-aid benefits and coöperative investment of time, effort, and association funds. Membership fees and contributions of time, labor, material, or money formed a substantial supplementary income for the local government, which expected the associations to perform many civic services which otherwise would have to be paid for by the government—or would be left undone. For example, the costs of fire fighting, road repair, maintenance of shrine grounds and parks, work on public buildings, and similar enterprises were in large part defrayed by "volunteer" work.

Ostensibly these associations were spontaneous community organizations which offered a focal point for village social activity, but in fact they were usually proposed and promoted by government officials "acting in their private capacities" and were essentially policing organs. Virtually everyone in a community was expected to belong to one or more of the associations. They served as a check and cross-check upon individual activities. It was not easy to refuse membership; the individualist who hesitated to join was looked upon askance by the police, the joiner won approbation and minor opportunities and privileges.

ECONOMIC CHANGE IN THE 20TH CENTURY

Okinawa was rapidly becoming overcrowded. Plans for land reclamation, colonization in Yaeyama, and emigration to foreign lands were put in motion by the prefectural government.

The Matsuyama land-reclamation project inaugurated in 1894 was expected to bring some 12,250 new acres (5,000 *chobu*) under cultivation. Agricultural schools and vocational-training courses gradually improved the efficiency of the farmer. Research and experiment in government institutions improved the varieties of grain, potatoes, fruits, and vegetables distributed through the farmers' associations. Superior breeds of livestock were introduced. Specialists in sericulture and in fisheries were sent from Japan proper to instruct the Okinawans.

Sugar production offered the greatest profit to brokers and shippers in Japan; hence the government gave this great attention. Limitations on acreage were lifted in 1888, but raw sugar was accepted as tax in kind until 1904. Before land reform and redistribution was effected, the sugar industry was monopolized by men from other prefectures, who controlled marketing and shipping. After 1903 the Okinawans gradually asserted their own interests. There was new incentive to produce. Ota Chofu promoted the establishment of a research office at Osaka through which the Okinawans themselves could discover ways to enter metropolitan markets. A Sugar Dealers' Association was founded. After 1905 Japanese from other prefectures discovered that they were being challenged by Okinawan investors and management.

Inexperience led to the organization of too many small independent sugar companies, and a series of failures occurred. Working conditions and extraction methods were primitive. Standards of quality for the manufactured sugar were not high. In 1907 the Ministry of Agriculture and Commerce at Tokyo organized an Okinawa Prefectural Sugar Improvement Bureau, to which the governor himself gave enthusiastic support. For a time the leading newspaper company—the Ryukyu

Shimpo-sha—led in promoting competition among farmers by holding exhibits, awarding prizes, and stirring the public interest in higher production levels of superior quality. After 1912 all sugar leaving the islands had to meet certain standards set by the bureau. Capitalists at Tokyo and Osaka began to invest in the Okinawan sugar industry, and the government subsidized experimental farms.

As the plantations on nearby Formosa began to be developed on a large scale a curious rivalry grew up in the councils of the government; agricultural experts from the Sapporo Agricultural College (Hokkaido) became leading advocates of expansion in Formosa, whereas experts from the Komaba Agricultural Department of the Tokyo Imperial University were "champions" of the industry in Okinawa. From 1915 onward the influence of the industrial capitalists was in the ascendant at Tokyo. Decisions affecting over-all agricultural policies for the prefecture (and for Formosa) were not being made so much with an eye to the welfare of the local economy as to profits which would accrue to the companies which had greatest influence in the government. This rapid expansion of the Okinawan sugar industry through investment of capital from Osaka and Tokyo was not fundamentally healthy; the major share of profit derived from Okinawan land and labor left the prefecture. Local reinvestment by the holding companies tended to be for the benefit of the sugar industry only. A high percentage of Okinawa's farming population became entirely dependent upon the metropolitan markets, which left them extremely vulnerable to price fluctuations caused by conditions in Formosa or in Japan proper.

In 1915 Governor Omi Kyugoro proposed an elaborate ten-year economic development program, but some of his actions exposed him to charges that he was acting more in the interests of large Japanese business corporations than of the Okinawan economy. At his direction the entire assets of the Okinawa Sugar Improvement Bureau—which had been heavily subsidized and developed with public funds—were suddenly transferred to the Okinawa Sugar Company, and this in turn was absorbed by the powerful Taiwan Sugar Corporation. The Okinawa-Taiwan Colonization and Sugar Company likewise passed to the Taiwan Sugar Corporation, in which the principal shareholders were the Imperial Household, and the Mitsui and Mitsubishi companies. In this fashion, control of Okinawa's basic agricultural industry passed entirely out of Okinawan hands. "Economic colonization" had replaced "political colonization."

Within forty years the area planted to sugar in Okinawa had been increased more than tenfold; production volume had increased in about the same proportion; but after 1919 the value of export-import trade showed increasing export deficits, until by 1928 the islands imported goods valued at 11,200,000 yen more than the value of exported products. This great disparity reflected growth of population and steadily rising standards of living.

A tenfold expansion of the most important agricultural industry and of trade in goods and services could take place only if there were adequate basic communications between Ryukyu and Japan proper. When Basil Hall Chamberlain visited Okinawa in early 1894, one ship, leaving Naha every eighteen days for Kobe by way of Kagoshima, provided the only regular service. The Sino-Japanese War stimulated development of shipping and telegraphic services. A submarine cable linked Kagoshima with Naha and Yaeyama, and a link laid in 1897 tied this in with the international cable services along the China coast by way of Formosa and Amoy. Miyako remained isolated until the prefectural assembly voted funds with which to lay a cable between Naha and Hirara in 1913. The police organization had telegraphic and telephonic services at an early date (Chamberlain speaks of a telephone line between Naha and Shuri in 1894), but these were not open to the public until 1906 and 1910, respectively. As soon as wireless telegraphy became practicable, the Japanese government established services throughout the empire; by 1917 a wireless station was opened even in the remote Daito Islands.

These outlying wireless facilities served the dual purposes of national defense and of weather forecasting, which was especially important to farmers and to mariners in the typhoon season. In 1915 the Ryukyu Newspaper Company arranged for a civilian to demonstrate the new flying machine in Okinawa; although the demonstration was not a success (the contraption would not leave the ground), the Okinawans on that occasion had their first glimpse of an invention which was to revolutionize their lives.

The threat of hostile naval action in the seas near Okinawa during the Sino-Japanese War and again during the war with Russia underscored the vulnerability of the prefectural economy. Gradually the Mitsubishi's Osaka Shosen Kaisha emerged as the dominant shipping line upon which the economic health of Okinawa must depend. The government provided heavy subsidies to keep ships regularly on the Kobe-Naha route, for the import-export trade was not great enough in volume or value to justify commercial services for many years. Technical experts from Japan inaugurated a twenty-year harbor-development program in 1907. Lighthouses were constructed on important headlands and weather-reporting services and facilities extended into the outlying islands.

Coastal shipping continued to be important; hitherto small sailing craft and dugout canoes carried most commercial goods and passenger traffic from beach to beach among the islands. A short vehicular road leading some distance from Naha had been opened in 1885, but significant road work did not begin until 1897. Naha quickly became the center of a transport network. Jinrikishas and other wheeled vehicles were brought from Japan proper for town use and farm service.

A system of town and village projects for building and maintaining roads was introduced in 1907 and 1908, but it was uneconomical and poorly coördinated; the well-kept roads of one village might lead only to the unimproved paths of another. Gradually the prefectural government took over responsibility for all roads. By 1915 a main highway had been constructed between Naha and Nago at the center of the best agricultural district at the north. Subsidies from the national treasury provided for the construction of a light horse-drawn tram system, centering at Naha and reaching across the island to Yonabaru and Awase, north to Kadena, and south to Itoman.

Direct subsidies from the national treasury decreased in number though the size of subsidies for special projects (local railroad building, harbor construction, and the like) grew in proportion to the size and duration of the undertakings. In time Okinawa Prefecture acquired all the physical equipment necessary to support a modern agricultural economy on a very modest scale. Roads, railroads, airfields, postal, telegraph, and radio services, and modern meteorological services had become part of the everyday life of the Okinawan. The records show a steady increase in per capita wealth as it was reflected in savings deposits in banks and in the postal-savings service. These things had come to Okinawa slowly; by almost any standard of measurement Okinawa's physical economy was last and least in comparison with the advances which had been made in other prefectures of Japan.

The Russo-Japanese War stimulated the expansion of basic heavy industries throughout Japan; opportunities for manufacturing and trade presented by World War I were dazzling. While the battles raged in Europe, Japan supplied the Allies, and Japanese shipping was in every ocean and sea. A peak of activity and apparent prosperity was reached in 1918. Okinawa shared these fluctuations of fortune in common with the total empire economy. Only sixty-five years after the day when Perry, with all his guns and ships, could not extract a handful of copper coins from the bartering kingdom, the total value of goods produced exceeded eighty million yen, and bank deposits in Okinawa exceeded ninety-six million yen.

Then came a sharp break. Okinawa shared in the empire-wide post-war depression; having the least reserves upon which to draw in emergency, it suffered heavily. Thousands were without work and without food. In 1925 and again in 1928 the Diet at Tokyo voted millions in relief funds to be used in the rehabilitation of industry and trade in Okinawa Prefecture, the banks were reorganized, and an office was opened in Tokyo to promote the use of Okinawan products at the capital and in other prefectures.

This program had scarcely got under way when the Japanese empire was engulfed in the world-wide economic depression. Okinawa suffered extreme hardship; the prefecture was at the bottom of the list in the distribution of aid on a national scale. Social unrest throughout the islands called forth a maximum effort to organize relief for the farming and fishing communities, which had no reserves in money or goods. A new industrial development plan and a plan for extensive migration was drawn up by Governor Ino Jiro in 1933, but conditions of general misery prevailed throughout Okinawa until the coming of the war in China in 1937.

The invasion of China stimulated production everywhere in the empire; Okinawans found a ready market for foodstuffs and opportunities for employment in other prefectures, but by 1941 the government was compelled to invoke the national mobilization laws, which meant totalitarian control of all aspects of economic and social life in all prefectures and colonies. A National Savings Association branch was opened in Okinawa, detailed regulations controlled all food-producing activities and the rationing system was imposed in every village and outlying island. By this system of rigidly enforced controls Japan was able to prolong its economic life.

War with the Western world was near at hand.

Population Pressure and the Emigration Problem

Physical isolation and social discrimination cut off the Okinawans from the Japanese of other prefectures. Thousands of persons traveled back and forth from the islands to the metropolitan centers each year, but there could never be the easy interplay of economic life which other prefectures enjoyed across common and continuous borders. The other prefectures were overcrowded, too, offering little attraction to the uneducated Okinawan peasant or fisherman. Natural disasters continued to strike as frequently and as severely as they had in centuries gone by, although there were more agencies now to provide relief and a greater understanding of what could be done to anticipate and prepare for calamity. Great storms swept Yaeyama in 1899 and 1901. An eruption of Tori-shima in 1903 forced the transfer of the entire population (690 persons) to Kume-jima in the following year, disrupting the precarious economy of that small island. A great drought in 1904 brought widespread suffering. The Home Ministry at Tokyo despatched investigators, granted relief funds, suspended the payment of local taxes, and organized a public-works project to help in the crisis. An epidemic of swine cholera swept the islands in 1908, affecting the economy of every household. The years 1911 and 1912 brought earthquakes and typhoons, one of which did exceptional damage in

Yaeyama. Severe storms disrupted the economy in 1917, 1918, and 1922. More than seven thousand buildings were damaged in 1931, and two typhoons in quick succession wrought havoc in 1933. Millions of yen were spent in meeting the costs of social relief and the rehabilitation of property on these occasions. Little of this could come from prefectural sources.

In 1940 there were approximately 750,000 people living in the prefecture. This meant a population pressure of some 588 per square mile. The full import of this figure can be realized when it is compared with a population density of 529 for other prefectures of Japan at that time—and of 44 per square mile for the United States.

The great surplus of laborers on Okinawa had no significant raw materials to which they could apply willing hands, and no significant land areas remained unoccupied within the islands. Emigration was the only solution.

The problem had become apparent before the turn of the century. In the long period of police administration in Yaeyama the police department issued tracts and bulletins advocating development of the distant islands of Ishigaki, Iriomote, and Yonaguni. These efforts failed. The prevalence of malaria and the frequency of terrifying storms were very real obstacles to successful settlement. By tradition Yaeyama was thought of as a place of harsh exile, where opportunities were too limited to be considered seriously by anyone who wished to improve his economic situation.

Despite all this, the government persisted in its effort to expand colonization in the outer islands. A special development loan fund was set up in 1886, to be used in northern Okinawa, Miyako, and Yaeyama. In 1891 an investor from Hiroshima (Nakagawa Toranosuke) attempted to promote development of an agricultural-plantation scheme, and in 1894 there were special efforts made to expand sugar production, leading to the formation of the Yaeyama Sugar Manufacturing Company in 1896. For the coal mines on Iriomote, laborers were brought over from Formosa, but for the agricultural enterprises every effort was made to persuade Okinawans to migrate to Yaeyama, without significant success.

In 1935 fresh attempts were made to expand settlement on Ishigaki through formation of a new development company. A group of Yae-yama residents thought this a good time to petition the prefectural government to establish a school of fisheries and agriculture. Every possible propaganda device was tried in the effort to persuade people to leave overcrowded Okinawa for the southerly islands. After Gover-nor Fuchigami Fusataro presented a fresh colonization program to the prefectural assembly in 1938, committees were sent to inspect proposed sites for new settlements. The Ministry of Finance at Tokyo responded favorably to an appeal for funds with which to inaugurate a malaria-suppression campaign, set in motion in 1940. On the eve of World War II, in 1941, government officials and prominent journalists were sent down to see for themselves what progress had been made. Little sub-stantial change had taken place in the country districts and subtropical forests of Yaeyama during the sixty years of direct Japanese adminis-tration. Yaeyama was obviously not to offer the solution to the Oki-nawan population problem.

The government experienced no difficulty in promoting emigration to foreign lands and to Japanese colonies in the Pacific.[1] Migration to Yaeyama meant hardship and limited opportunity; emigration to Hawaii, to the Philippines, Formosa, North and South America meant improved living conditions and comparative prosperity for the emigrants and for the families on Okinawa to which they could send international money-order remittances.

Organized emigration outside the empire had begun in 1899 when Toyama Matasuke led a party of twenty-seven laborers to the sugar plantations of Hawaii. Okinawans first entered the continental United States in 1902. In these early years the men went abroad without families, for they planned to earn enough to return soon to Okinawa with something in hand for investment at home. But residence overseas was profitable, and gradually was prolonged in order to accumulate more capital. Some of the emigrants summoned wives or arranged for "picture brides" to join them. Others married among the women of their adop-tive country.

At the time of the great land redistribution of 1901–03 many younger sons of gentry families were left without support, or fell heir to in-adequate shares of income from lands assigned to the family. Men from this hitherto privileged stratum of Okinawan society were prominent in the first emigrant groups and carried considerable social prestige to overseas communities, although they were obliged to take up un-skilled and unprivileged tasks wherever they went.

In 1903 a total of 941 laborers went abroad, some to Hawaii, some to the United States mainland, some to Mexico, and some to the Philip-pines. By 1907 more than ten thousand Okinawans were overseas in places as varied and distant as New Caledonia and Peru. Laws were enacted at Tokyo to protect their interests as Japanese subjects under contract-labor conditions. By 1930 more than 54,000 had left Okinawa for foreign lands, and of these more than half had gone to South America.

The early emigrants became field laborers. By 1930 their children were beginning to enter other fields of skilled and unskilled work. This was especially true in Hawaii, where parents, often at great sacrifice, helped ambitious sons to enter professional life as doctors, lawyers, and teachers. Many had established themselves in comfortable businesses; Okinawans specialized in cleaning-and-dyeing establishments in Argen-tina or as restaurant owners and poultry farmers in Hawaii. Some be-came extensive landholders and a few became millionaires in the coffee-growing regions of Brazil. Many emigrants sent their sons and daughters back to Okinawa to be educated at the Shuri Middle School or at the high schools at Naha.

Thanks to group solidarity and the highly developed sense of mutual responsibility, newcomers received substantial support from the early settlers in these overseas communities.

The original purpose of migration was not forgotten. A steady stream of remittances flowed back to Okinawa in growing volume and value. Whereas the overseas Japanese from other prefectures remitted an annual average of fifty yen per capita, the Okinawans sent back eighty-eight yen per capita. These figures are based on the data for 1937, when more than three and a half million yen reached Okinawa, sent home by no fewer than 40,483 Okinawans.

Obviously the Japanese government had ready at hand a remarkable instrument with which to relieve population pressure, and an extra-ordinary source of hidden revenue for the poverty-stricken prefecture.

An Okinawan Overseas Association (Kaigai Kyokai) was formed as early as 1924. It was a quasi-official organization, for which the prefectural governor usually served as honorary president; and Okinawa's most distinguished citizen, Kanna Kenwa, retired vice-admiral and member of the Diet, traveled widely in the interests of the association. An Emigrant Training Center was opened in Naha in 1934. Here emigrants were prepared for the long voyage and the problems of settlement in a new country. The association used the center as a headquarters at which to publish a bulletin sent overseas to emigrant communities and distributed widely within the Ryukyu Islands. Propaganda urging emigration was distributed throughout Okinawa. For all these services the prefectural government provided a small annual subsidy.

Ideas as well as letters and international money orders flowed back into the Ryukyus from these wide-flung communities overseas. There were few villages on Okinawa which did not maintain communication with relatives who had gone away to seek fortune in a foreign land. From the extreme seclusion imposed upon them and fostered by Japan in the early 17th century, the Okinawans were once again conscious of an interesting world beyond the seas.

In one area emigration was not an unqualified success: the Okinawans who were sent to work in Japan's mandated islands—the Marianas and the Carolines in the mid-Pacific—found life bitterly hard on the sugar plantations. The majority went out as indentured labor with no prospect of substantial improvement of their economic status within the yen economy. They had little to remit to families left behind in Okinawa.

It is not surprising that emigration appealed to an increasing number of men and women living in overcrowded homes and impoverished villages. On Okinawa health and welfare services did not keep pace with development in communication facilities, under government sponsorship, or with sugar planting and manufacture under private ownership and government subsidy. There were no first-class training facilities for doctors on Okinawa. Okinawans who studied at the universities in Japan proper or at the Imperial University at Taihoku (Taipei) in Formosa were reluctant to return to practice in poverty-stricken Okinawa. By 1939—fifty years after Japan established the perfectural government—there were only 178 physicians in the islands, and of these no less than 73 were practicing in Naha and Shuri.

Little progress was made in combating malaria, venereal disease, leprosy, and tuberculosis, despite many publicized investigations and reports, rules and regulations. Until 1904–05—the years of the Russo-Japanese War—Okinawa Prefecture had the lowest recorded venereal disease rate among the prefectures of Japan. By 1930 it had the highest rates in the country for both venereal disease and tuberculosis. This was due in part to the increased rate of movement in the population and in part to the vulnerability of a population which suffered from chronic malnutrition. Hospital facilities were slowly expanded but were never adequate to the needs of the prefecture. Subsidies were allowed for the development of sanitary services and a training section for school nurses was established in the normal school. Special clinics were opened for the treatment of leprosy in 1928, but the leprosarium on Yagachi Island was not established until a decade later.

There was a quickening interest in national health standards and public welfare in the 1930's. The nation was being readied for war. Mobile clinics began to take elementary medical services into outlying country districts and to the schools. Government dispensaries began to be established in remote villages after 1938, the year in which a Ministry of Public Health and Welfare was organized at Tokyo. Sanitation specialists in the prefectural police department were expected to supervise and enforce the application of public-health measures. The success with which they were applied depended to an important degree upon the training of the individual policeman and upon the general level of education and understanding coöperation which he might find in the community to which he was assigned.

SCHOOL STRIKES AND THE STRUGGLE FOR HIGHER EDUCATION

Toward the end of the "Do Nothing" era expenditures for education were less than fifteen thousand yen per year. Much talk of educational ideals and issuance of many rules and regulations produced few results. Teachers were being paid as little as one and a half yen per month in

1893. Okinawan leaders were dissatisfied with the slow growth of the educational facilities, but the central government expected each prefecture to bear a major share of educational costs. The Okinawan economy simply could not support a new school system before land reform and tax reorganization took place; hence the national treasury supported the prefectural department of education until 1908.

The first prefectural assembly, convened in 1909, addressed itself to the problem. In 1910 the appropriation for education exceeded 100,000 yen. Town and district assemblies, granted local budget autonomy, embarked upon a race to build primary schools. In some instances the burden proved too great; there were retrenchments and consolidations, but by 1935 the total annual expenditure for education exceeded 2,500,000 yen, of which something more than one million yen were provided by the national treasury. By 1941 Okinawa Prefecture could boast of 296 elementary schools, six middle schools for boys, eight high schools for girls, nine vocational schools, and two normal schools. Approximately ninety-nine percent of the school-age children were enrolled.

The history of education after 1890 was distinguished principally by Okinawa's struggle to overcome Tokyo's reluctance to provide education above the primary grade. The First Middle School remained pre-eminent because of its age, superior facilities, location, and traditional association with the past. No more than ten men graduated annually before 1897, but in the next forty years 2,400 men completed the courses. Among these were the sons of emigrants to North and South America, to Hawaii, to the islands of the South Pacific and Malaysia, whose presence in the school body was in itself a broadening educational asset. Approximately forty-four percent of the graduates went on to higher education, some to higher preparatory schools and then on to universities in other provinces. Nearly five hundred became school teachers.

In forty years only sixteen men went from the Shuri Middle School to the military and naval academies.

An alumni association, established at Shuri in 1903, served as a link among men who became community leaders within the prefecture, in the growing Okinawan communities in the metropolitan areas of To-

kyo and Osaka, and in the emigrant communities. Friendships cultivated at school contributed much to a gradual breakdown of traditional
prejudice entertained by the people of Naha and Shuri toward men
and women from the outlying islands.

China's defeat in 1895 quickened a desire to be considered "up-to-
date" at Naha and Shuri, and to abandon old-fashioned customs.
Students led the way and set the pace. Men no longer "lacquered"
their hair into a topknot with seaweed paste or oils, but boldly cut it
short. The old hairpins which denoted rank were abandoned. Wide
black-crepe sashes for the men's kimono in the Japanese style became
popular.

These were the changing fashions of the year. More important was
the change in names. Women began to add the feminine suffix *ko* to
their personal names, men took distinctly Japanese names, and families
adopted a Japanese reading for the characters of the surname.[2]

Gradually thousands left the southern islands to settle in metropolitan
Japan, where they were lost among the millions of workers in the
great cities, and where discrimination was less severely felt or even
vanished as the individual adopted Japanese habits of dress and speech.

In the Ryukyu Islands, however, regional characteristics changed
slowly and the Japanese administrators and "resident merchants" found
it difficult to concede equality to the unsophisticated Okinawans. The
story of the Hirara incident of 1893 illustrated one aspect of discrimination. Another incident concerned Kodama Kihachi, director of the
prefectural department of education, who was concurrently principal
of the Shuri Middle School and of the normal school in 1894. He took
no pains to conceal his contempt for the people of Okinawa, for he
mistook poverty for ignorance and incapacity. He loudly proclaimed
that there was no need for higher education in the prefecture, and to
make his point he removed the study of English from the list of required subjects at the middle school. This, he said, was an unnecessary
luxury for Okinawans. A public controversy broke out. The students
went on strike in 1895. Among student leaders were Higaonna Kanjun,
Majikina Anko, and Iha Fuyu, all destined to become historians of
recognized authority in Japan, and Kanna Kenwa, who distinguished

himself later as vice-admiral, parliamentary vice-minister, and Diet member.

Parents gave support to the striking students. Okinawans who held minor posts in the prefectural government rallied behind them and brought pressure to bear, which caused Kodama's removal and the restoration of English to the middle-school curriculum.

Twenty years later a second crisis developed in the educational system which illustrates certain persistent traditions and characteristics of local higher education. The need for a second middle school began to be debated in 1908. As the opening business of the first prefectural assembly (1909) the chairman, Takamine Chokyo, introduced a proposal that such a school be created as a symbol of "New Okinawa." A new institution was founded as a temporary adjunct of the Shuri Middle School. In January, 1911, one hundred students were enrolled from a list of 557 applicants. Takara Rintoku was appointed principal, assisted by Shikiya Koshin.*

Politics overruled practical judgment in choosing a site for the new school. It was constructed at Kadena despite clamorous opposition. As soon as the students removed to Kadena from the temporary site at Shuri they began to share public discontent; the site was too far from the population center and was not hallowed by the traditions of Shuri or Naha. Enrollments decreased. Only thirty men graduated in the first class (1915), and by 1918 the number of graduates had dwindled to eighteen.

Governor Omi inappropriately proposed that for economy's sake the Second Middle School and the agricultural school, formerly at Nago, should be brought under one administration on the Kadena site. This meant an irreconcilable conflict between the traditions of vocational training (represented in the agricultural school) and of literary training and accomplishment (represented in the middle-school curriculum). Students clashed in pitched battles on the school grounds. Parents took sides. Teachers throughout the island hotly debated the issue. A general strike at last paralyzed the prefectural school system.

* After World War II first Chief Executive of Okinawa under the American occupation and later first president of the University of the Ryukyus.

Principal Takara resigned to take his seat in the prefectural assembly, where he could battle politically for the separation of the two schools. Governor Omi was dismissed, and at last, in June, 1918, the Second Middle School was removed to Naha. In 1916 there had been only seventy-six applicants for admission at Kadena; by 1927 there were 619 applicants at Naha, of which only 162 could be enrolled. By 1930 the total number of graduates exceeded one thousand.

Public debate of the middle-school problem inspired the people of northern Okinawa and of Miyako to petition for higher schools. A Third Middle School was established at Nago in 1928, and a branch of the Second Middle School was opened in Miyako. In 1929 this became an independent Miyako Middle School. In the same year the Okinawan Prefectural Educational Association opened a special institution of high standard to provide evening classes for youths who could not afford to attend regular courses. In 1936—after many years' service as principal—Shikiya Koshin resigned from the staff of the Second Middle School in order to establish the Kainan Middle School, privately financed for the benefit of children of emigrants whose elementary-school training overseas created special problems.

Facilities for the education of young women were fewer in number and of less importance to the government than the middle-school system for the boys. A girls' high school was founded as an adjunct to the normal school in 1900, but it had to depend upon private funds until 1902. By 1930 it had graduated more than two thousand students. A Domestic Arts Institute, founded privately in 1905 with an enrollment of 379, ultimately won public subsidies until in 1924 it was transformed into the Naha Municipal Girls High School. In 1927 it became the Second Prefectural Girls High School. A third girls' school, founded by popular subscription, was absorbed into the prefectural system in 1930. In 1936 Miyako succeeded in obtaining a girls' high school, but Yaeyama had neither a boys' middle school nor a girls' high school until 1942.

The record suggests that the Okinawan people themselves took the initiative in promoting development of educational facilities at higher levels. This was done at considerable sacrifice, and won only grudging recognition and coöperation from the government. Students desiring education beyond the middle-school level had to choose between the normal school at Naha or the more expensive life of a student overseas in other prefectures or in Formosa. More than three thousand men and women completed the normal-school courses during the first fifty years of prefectural administration.

Nine vocational schools were founded between 1902 and 1907, when economic reorganization followed land reform. Three were founded in subsequent years. By 1930 there were approximately 4,500 students enrolled, taxing facilities to the limit.

At the beginning of Japan's second major war with China—in 1937—more than 100,000 students were enrolled in the primary schools of Okinawa. This was a new generation. The traditions and history of old Ryukyu meant little to them and they were only dimly aware of the divided loyalties which had troubled their grandparents during transition from kingdom to prefecture. Pretensions to Chinese learning withered away with the older generation. In 1904 an American student of Okinawan history visited Kume Village in search of scholars in the old tradition. He found them few in number and exercising no vital leadership. The study of Ryukyuan history was discouraged in the schools, but a few men devoted themselves to the collection and preservation of historic documents. A public library was proposed in 1899. Two years later Marquis Sho—the former crown prince—donated two thousand yen to be used in founding a prefectural library. By 1940 this contained approximately 25,000 volumes in a general collection and housed the archives of the Ryukyu kingdom and of the royal house, containing some manuscripts dating from the 15th-century. Local historians—Iha Fuyu, Majikina Anko, and Shimabukuro Zempatsu—served successively as chief librarians and curators of these irreplaceable treasures.

Musty documents meant little to the younger generation. A few of the grandparents made semi-annual visits to the old Confucian temple and academy at Kume Village to pay respects before the tablets of Confucius, but it appears that a newspaper advertisement of this ceremony in July, 1910, marked the last public evidence of interest.

The arrival of a foreigner—Henry Butler Schwartz—to teach at the Shuri Middle School in 1906 was of far more interest to the younger generation. Ceremonies at the Confucian academy were vestiges of a past that was little understood and could not be recalled; lessons in English held promise that Okinawa—through Japan—would share in what seemed then to be the limitless possibilities of the 20th century.

Japan and Great Britain were on most cordial terms; diplomatic equality had been achieved in 1899 and the first Anglo-Japanese alliance had been formed in 1902 to offset Russian influence in the Far East. This formal association with the great British empire laid the foundations for Japan's rapid growth as a world power. Tokyo was prepared to promote the study of the English language throughout the empire—even in remote Okinawa.

These were matters of high policy, of which the students at Shuri and Naha had no substantial knowledge. It was of much more immediate interest to them to learn the bastardized English-Japanese terms used in baseball and tennis, both of which were introduced and became popular at the opening of the century. In 1903 a United States naval vessel, the "Vicksburg," put in at Naha to pay a courtesy call. This time no blustering commodore marched with marines to Shuri Castle; instead, baseball teams from aboard the "Vicksburg" trudged up to Shuri, and on the middle-school grounds within the castle walls Okinawa's first international game of baseball was played between the American bluejackets and the middle-school boys.

Athletics played an important part in Japan's assimilation program. Setting-up exercises at the schools preceded military drill. Traditional Japanese sports (*judo* and *kendo*) were introduced, and as the years passed there was an increasing participation by Okinawan teams in competitive exhibitions and athletic meets held at Tokyo, Osaka, Kyoto, and elsewhere in the empire.

The value of travel had not been overlooked as a means to strengthen Okinawan ties with Japan, to increase respect for Japan's leaders and leadership in Asia, and to encourage a sense of Okinawan identity with Japan vis-à-vis foreign nations and peoples. In May, 1894, Okinawan students were taken on tour in Kyushu for the first time in a century, setting a precedent for later tours throughout the prefectures and far afield—to Formosa (1899), to Manchuria and Korea (1906), and to Shanghai and Nanking (1920). Students from other prefectures were sent down to tour the Ryukyu Islands and to take part there in local exhibitions and contests.

For twenty years after the king's downfall the merchants and officials from other prefectures kept aloof in Okinawa, isolated by sharp lines of political and economic privilege and social distinction. When the turn of the century brought general economic reorganization, these lines began to blur; there came into existence a new class of propertied Okinawan businessmen who rapidly gained experience in managing their own affairs at Naha, Kagoshima, Osaka, and Tokyo.

In 1905 there were approximately 2,600 Japanese from other prefectures resident at Naha. To draw them together on the "economic front" vis-à-vis the Okinawans and to serve their interests, a trade paper, the *Okinawa Shimbun*, was founded. Convocation of a prefectural assembly in 1909 brought a fresh challenge to the Japanese community, this time a challenge to the political supremacy enjoyed by men from other prefectures. To defend their vested interests in the assembly the "resident merchants" formed an association in 1911, but they were doomed slowly to disappear as an effectually organized group of colonial businessmen and administrators.

The Okinawans at the same time gained steadily in a sense of prefectural solidarity. An Okinawa Prefectural Association was founded in 1899 to promote wider knowledge of administrative affairs, and the serial publication of *Notes on Current Events in Okinawa* served as a common fund of information for minor officials throughout the islands. A Society for the Improvement of Manners and Customs was formed under official patronage in 1902. Branches in each local district were expected to introduce and to encourage the adoption of manners and customs more or less standard elsewhere in Japan but as yet unknown in the outlying communities of Okinawa.

The educational system took the lead in the "Japanization" program. Virtually every home in the island could be reached through the children at school. With official encouragement the newspapers at Naha and in other prefectures undertook to promote mutual understanding, not only by essays and news items, but by contests of many kinds which the Okinawans were encouraged to enter. Soon after the first prefectural assembly met, tours were arranged for Okinawans who wished to visit historic and industrial centers of the empire in the "Home Islands." In time annual excursions created a continuing interchange of students and tourists.

By the end of World War I, the major obstacles of assimilation had been overcome. Strong attachment to local scenes and local customs remained, but in matters of economics and politics the younger generation thought in terms of identification with nationwide Japanese interests. The stories of the old kingdom and of the distressing days of transition from kingdom to prefecture were the tales of grandparents. For ambitious youth, Tokyo or Osaka (or an emigrant community overseas) held the promise of the future. With the admission of Yaeyama and Miyako to full political status in 1921 the internal unification process was complete. The Manhood Suffrage Act of 1925 quadrupled the electorate in Japan, raising it to more then 12,500,000, and reflecting public opinion from Yaeyama in the south to Hokkaido in the far north.

But the ugly problem of social discrimination had not been overcome. The Japanese government was winning the campaign to have Okinawans think of themselves as Japanese subjects, but in general there was little done to overcome the widespread Japanese sense of superiority toward the Okinawans as an "out-group," a minority of rather second-class, country cousins. In Japanese eyes the Okinawans stood somewhere between the former outcastes, the Eta of pre-Restoration days, and full-fledged membership in the nation-family.

Okinawan students in Japan proper found it difficult to gain acceptance in ordinary lodging houses; Okinawan travelers were subjected to discrimination in hotels; and employers hesitated to give equal opportunity to employees from Okinawa Prefecture. The cleavages were accentuated in emigrant communities in Hawaii, the United States mainland, and South America. In self-defense Okinawans overseas tended to organize among themselves and to resist official Japanese efforts to control and direct their interests. The Japanese overseas in turn sought to make sure that they were not mistaken for Okinawans, and the very name "Okinawan" often carried a derisive or contemptuous overtone. Peculiarities of Okinawan dress, dialect, and diet embarrassed the Japanese.

An outstanding example of differentiation was the Okinawan use of pork as a main article of diet. This was part of the Chinese cultural heritage; many Okinawans established themselves in the metropolitan centers of Japan (and in Hawaii) as proprietors of piggeries. This, in Japanese eyes, placed them almost on a level with the despised Eta, the butchers and tanners and shoemakers of the old days. Hand-tattooing among the older women (no longer practiced) was another Okinawan irritant to Japanese sensibilities. The strong insularity of Japanese nationalism would not admit the Okinawans easily to full membership in Japanese society. Before World War II there was relatively little intermarriage in overseas communities between Okinawans and the Japanese from other prefectures. The Okinawans who left Ryukyu for foreign settlements tended to preserve memories of days when Japanese discrimination was most obvious and economic pressure most severe, and to cultivate these attitudes among their own children in the first generation born overseas. Within Japan itself progress toward full assimilation was more rapid, but by no means complete at the end of World War II. Much more was done to inform the Okinawans of traditions and standards prevailing in the "Home Provinces" of Japan proper than was done in those prefectures to develop a knowledge and understanding of Okinawans.

In broadest terms, Okinawa's relation to Japan proper may be compared with Hawaii's relation to the continental United States. The political dissolution of the monarchy began in 1872 and ended in annexation to Japan in 1879. Political equality with other prefectures was achieved in 1920, but social assimilation was not complete by 1945. The Hawaiian monarchy fell in 1893; annexation took place in 1898, but full political equality with other states of the Union has yet to be achieved; and although residents of Hawaii conceive themselves to be loyal American citizens, they are not yet accorded full political recognition, principally on grounds of social and cultural differentiation.

Religion and Politics in Japan's Assimilation Program

Organized religious activity and propaganda in 20th-century Okinawa was promoted by two utterly dissimilar agencies; one was the Christian missionary organization, the other the organized bureaucracy of Japan's State Shinto. The Okinawans may be said to be fundamentally indifferent to organized religion and to theological disputes and speculations. The educated elite—the townsmen—were satisfied with the body of Chinese Confucian moral precepts and codes of behavior. Emotional life centered in the family, governed by the beliefs and practices of ancestor worship. A man behaved as he thought fitting in the eyes of his forebears; the honor of the family provided strong ethical framework for daily life; duty to one's superiors carried more weight in argument than obligations stressed by imported cults. In this the common country people shared. Rituals associated with ancestor veneration provided expression for instinctive religious feeling. The *noro* remained strong in the countryside. Upon this ancient cult the Japanese nationalists attempted to superimpose organized State Shinto, but the Okinawans, generally indifferent to organized religious life, were not sympathetic. Aggressive Shinto propagandists were no more welcome among them than the Christian missionaries proved to be, for neither Shinto nationalists nor Christian teachers showed sufficient tolerance and respect for private and personal beliefs—or non-belief.

Christianity did not gain ground in the Ryukyus until the Okinawans themselves began to take part in evangelical work. A native of Oshima was converted while in Hawaii in 1892. He returned to Okinawa and found employment with the Land Survey Office. About 1903 he began to urge others to accept Christianity. The conversion of a primary-school principal was an important gain. This convert in turn won an opportunity to study in Japan proper on a subsidy provided by the Epworth League of Portland, Indiana. He was a man of sympathetic character and marked personal ability, and as principal of the Henja School he enjoyed distinction and prestige. In a relatively short time he won one hundred and twenty converts. But such a mass conversion disturbed the community; Christian principles of family life as interpreted by mission orthodoxy were at many points incompatible with established customs and traditions. There was an angry reaction; converts were stoned; some were denied access to community activities and were not permitted to use agricultural tools to which the village held communal title.

In time opposition dwindled, but since the poorest members of the community—those with least to lose and most to gain—were attracted first to the Christian faith and organization, there was some prejudice among those who enjoyed a better economic and social status and some formal education. To give strength and support to local pastors, an American representative of the Methodist Church, H. B. Schwartz, took up residence at Naha in 1906, dividing his time between the mission and the Shuri Middle School, where he was engaged to teach English.[3] After 1910 his successor, the Reverend Earl R. Bull, spent a portion of each year at Naha until 1926. There he slowly developed the Bettelheim legend to heroic proportions, adapting it generously. At last the Christian undertaking itself was dubbed the "Bettelheim Memorial Mission." Okinawans were urged to look back with gratitude and reverence upon the doctor's strange career, which was interpreted to have been one of great personal sacrifice in their behalf. Seventy years after Bettelheim had left the island his biographer could write: "How the Loo Chooan officials barely tolerated Bettelheim we know too well. He endured not by the support of diplomatic representatives of foreign states, but remained on Okinawa through a sustained and exalted life of sacrificial love." A monument was raised at Naha to commemorate the missionary pioneer. The development of Christian organizations in Okinawa supplied new ties with Japan proper, for the foreign missionaries urged the Okinawans to look upon their fellow Christians in Japan with a sense of close kinship in spirit.

Japanese nationalists were eager to develop organized State Shinto in the Ryukyu Islands. It was held that the emperor was of divine descent, and that respect for the imperial house and for the Sun Goddess, Amaterasu O-Mikami, provided the essential unifying spiritual element in the national life. Forms of Shinto worship were expected to take precedence over Buddhist, Christian, or popular local Shinto rites. Moving slowly, the national government, through the Bureau of Shrines, schools, and other agencies, sought gradually to bring the popular local Shinto shrines (the village altars tended by the *noro*) into closer formal association and to absorb and transform popular beliefs.

Local divinities worshiped in field and forest and at seaside shrines in the Ryukyu Islands were declared to be members of a host of guardian gods defending the empire. In 1898, soon after Japan had assumed control of Formosa, it was announced that the bodies of Okinawan seamen slain in Formosa in 1871 had been found and identified. The alleged remains were returned to Okinawa and entombed with a flourish of honors at the ancient Gokoku Temple at Naha—Bettelheim's old home. It was said that they had "died in the service of the State." Quite unwittingly they had provided the excuse for Japan's first expedition to Formosa and for the annexation program which followed. Henceforth all Okinawans who died "in the service of the emperor" were numbered in the pantheon of national heroes.

In 1909 it was proposed to build a prefectural shrine at Naha and to construct official shrines in each administrative subdivision throughout the prefecture. These were to be paid for by local contributions and assessments. But the government soon discovered that the Okinawans had little enthusiasm for the scheme; it was put aside until 1923.

The Shinto shrine on Nami-no-ue headland was officially declared to be the center for religious affairs in the prefecture in 1924. Here the principal objects of veneration were symbols of four kings of Ryukyu (Shunten, Sho En, Sho Nei, and Sho Tai) and of Tametomo, alleged to have been Shunten's father. It will be remembered that Tametomo was a descendent in the seventh generation of the Minamoto family, founded by the Japanese Emperor Seiwa. Thus the government hoped to encourage Okinawans to think of their own royal house as a branch of the imperial house of Japan. Official shrines were established to commemorate heroes in Miyako and Yaeyama, and at Naha (in 1927) the Yomochi Shrine and public gardens were created at prefectural expense to commemorate the three great agricultural heroes of Okinawa—Noguni Sokan, Gima Shinjo, and Sai On.

State Shinto—the cult of military hero worship and of reverence for the imperial family—was promoted in Okinawa with new vigor after the China incident of 1931–32. Towns and villages were pressed to build new shrines to accommodate priests serving the national cult. By carefully placing new shrines immediately in front of ancient local worship-sites, or adjacent to them, the government sought by association to effect a transfer of interest from the old to the new.

The manipulation of imperial symbolism confronted the Japanese with delicate problems. The death of the former king in 1901 marked an important loosening of emotional ties with traditions of the past. The most important symbol of the old kingdom had ceased to exist. Members of Sho Tai's extensive household at Tokyo observed mourning for two years, but when that period came to an end they gave up the use of traditional Ryukyuan costume, coiffure, court language, and daily ceremony. Children of the household were enrolled in the ordinary schools of Tokyo or at the Peers' School. Henceforth the family of Marquis Sho Ten adopted the pattern of social life common among other aristocrats living at Tokyo. The former crown prince died in 1920 and on September 26 in that year was entombed with his royal ancestors at the Tama Udon at Shuri, the last of the Sho family to be so honored.

Meanwhile considerable attention had been given to the problem of substituting the symbolism of the imperial family for the old loyalties to the Sho family, hitherto the vital center of national life. At one time it was proposed that the Emperor Meiji should travel to Naha, but neither he nor his son, Emperor Taisho, made the journey. Other members of the imperial family and court chamberlains from the Imperial Household made frequent journeys to Naha to give evidence of imperial concern for the welfare of the Okinawan people. Each disastrous drought, typhoon, or epidemic was made occasion for a token grant of relief funds, and in 1911 the Okinawan Public Welfare Foundation was established by a grant of 1,500,000 yen from the privy purse at a time of great hardship and political unrest.

When the Emperor Meiji died in July, 1911, and again in 1914 upon the death of his widow, the Empress Dowager Shoken, dramatic ceremonies of "worship from afar" were staged throughout the prefecture to inculcate a sense of awed respect and to focus attention upon the imperial palace at Tokyo. Every hamlet was required to celebrate the accession of the new emperor Yoshihito.

In 1921, Crown Prince Hirohito paused in Okinawa for a day at the outset of his long and memorable voyage to Europe. This was an occasion for great local pride, for an Okinawan, naval officer Kanna Kenwa, was captain of the warship bearing the young prince on this unprecedented tour.

Although it was widely believed that prejudice retarded Kanna's promotion thereafter to the highest ranks, he became a vice-admiral upon retirement, and a source of pride to Okinawans conscious of the great honor which this association with the crown prince implied in Japanese eyes.

CULTURAL AFFAIRS IN THE 20TH CENTURY

To a large degree Japanese prejudice toward Okinawans was nurtured in mistrust of the non-conformist, and uneasiness in the presence of the alien. Speech, dress, and food habits set the Okinawans somewhat apart. The individual who could minimize distinguishing Okinawan characteristics, or who could hold his own in intellectual competition in the academic world, was free to take his place in Japan's metropolitan communities. Many achieved academic and literary distinction. To name but a few, Higaonna Kanjun became Professor of Far Eastern History in the preparatory school of Tokyo Imperial University; Ohama Shinsen, a professor of law, became president of Waseda, one of Japan's greatest universities; Miyara Toso became president of the Japan Philological Institute; Yamanoguchi Baku achieved distinction as a poet.

It was more difficult to override prejudice in the civil service, in all its branches, and in the armed services. But even here Okinawans rose to high position and some influence. Vice Admiral Kanna retired from the navy to become Parliamentary Vice Minister for Home Affairs; Takamine Meitatsu became Director of the General Affairs Bureau in the Ministry of Commerce and Industry; and Yoshida Shien (descendent of Sho Hashi) rose to a place of distinction in the Foreign Office. Successful Okinawans—these men among them—gave consistent and energetic support to the study of history and the Okinawan cultural heritage.

Studies of Ryukyuan language, religion, craftsmanship, and history came from the Japanese press with fair regularity after 1904, the year in which Torii Ryuzo published a study of the Ogido shell mounds. A new generation of Okinawan scholars began to appear, trained in the universities of Tokyo and Kyoto, and in the leading normal schools. Higaonna Kanjun opened his distinguished career with the publication (in 1909) of the Okinawan section of a geographical dictionary of Japan. Iha Fuyu, first director of the Okinawa Prefectural Library, began to publish a staggering number of essays concerning language, culture, and history in the Ryukyu Islands. His authoritative work *Ko Ryukyu* (Ancient Ryukyu) appeared in 1911.

The Japanese were rather slow to recognize the quality and unique character of traditional Okinawan arts, crafts, and architecture, and in the Ryukyus (as in Japan proper) developed significant interest in these things only after Western connoisseurs led the way. In 1909, Langdon Warner, of the Boston Museum of Fine Arts, toured Okinawa, collected fine textiles and lacquer, and lectured publicly upon the arts and crafts of the Far East. His engaging personality, his immense fund of information, and his desire to learn made a deep and lasting impression.

Soon after this the Sho family assumed certain responsibilities for the maintenance of historic Okinawan temples—the Enkaku-ji, Tenno-ji, Tenkai-ji, and Ryufuku-ji—which had suffered serious neglect after 1879. A government report in 1915 called attention to the importance of historic Shinto shrines and Buddhist temples throughout the empire, but the ancient foundations of the old Ryukyu kingdom received scant consideration. The palace buildings at Shuri were dilapidated. Japanese garrison forces had occupied them for years. Architectural monuments had been leveled when the Shuri Middle School was removed to the site of the old Royal Academy buildings. The Shuri-Naha area contained nearly all the important surviving architectural monuments and these were disappearing one by one, giving way to the demands of "progress" in terms of modern roads and modern buildings.

An American, Ernest Fenollosa, had been a prime agent in persuading the national government at Tokyo to set up a registry system for national treasures late in the 19th century. In 1912 an ancient Korean bell at the Nami-no-ue Shrine was placed under protection of the law, but little more was done to preserve the neglected gardens, bridges, and buildings of the vanished kingdom.

As the new generation of Okinawan scholars grew more articulate, they were able to draw Japanese attention to the importance of the Ryukyus as a "triangulation point" from which to study the course of institutional and linguistic history of Japan proper. In 1919 a society was founded at Naha to promote the study of local geography and history. This grew into an "Association for the Preservation of Historic Sites and Relics of Okinawa." In 1923 Majikina Anko published the first edition of his important work *Okinawa Issen-nen Shi* (A Thousand Years of Okinawan History). Soon thereafter Kuroita Katsumi visited Okinawa to gather data for his monumental study of Japanese history. Tanabe Tai prepared the text and photographs for a handsome volume entitled *Ryukyu Kenchiku* (The Architecture of Ryukyu), published in 1937, which records the palaces, temples, gates, bridges, gardens, belfries, walls, and fountains which then survived.

The fiftieth anniversary of Okinawa prefectural administration in 1929 called forth much retrospective comment and publication. On the eve of this commemorative year Shuri Castle was at last designated a "National Treasure" and a four-year repair and restoration program began. In 1933 six more ancient structures were named important national monuments. The list continued to grow.

This developing interest in cultural characteristics which set Okinawa apart was not at all to the liking of the military men and extreme nationalist agitators at Tokyo, and led to a minor crisis in Japanese-Okinawan relations on the eve of the Pacific War.

Soon after World War I, two young Japanese potters—Kawai Kanjiro and Hamada Shoji—set out to investigate all the important kilns in the empire. Through them the eyes of Japan's artists were to be opened to special qualities inherent in the aesthetic traditions and technical achievements of Okinawan craftsman.

At the Tsuboya kilns at Naha they found a strongly developed style and craftsmanship, the Okinawan modification of Korean ceramic techniques introduced in the very early years of the 17th century. Hamada was deeply impressed, returning for a second and a third time to Okinawa to perfect his mastery of the Tsuboya method. His close friend Yanagi Soetsu became interested; the Japan Folk Art Museum at Tokyo (of which he was director) became an agency through which Okinawan ceramics, textiles, and lacquer attracted wide attention. Marquis Sho and the Okinawan prefectural Bureau of Education arranged for Dr. Yanagi to visit Okinawa. Soon afterward a study group of twenty-six members of the Japan Folk Art Association proceeded to the Ryukyus for systematic study of Okinawan arts and crafts.[4] Thereafter motion pictures, lectures, and publications in the other prefectures began to rouse wide interest in the unique aspects of Okinawan culture.

In a sense this marked a local cultural renaissance, giving the Okinawans new pride in their work. Yanagi and his colleagues urged them not to abandon old craft standards in order merely to satisfy the shoddy requirements of Japanese export markets. In effect they urged the people of the Ryukyu Islands not to forget the unique qualities of their total cultural tradition.

This ran counter to the nationalist program, then moving toward full tide. At a public meeting in the Naha Municipal Hall in January, 1940, a discussion of local dialects led to public criticism of official policies. Okinawans who smarted under discrimination spoke up to protest the government's concerted effort to suppress local peculiarities of speech and custom, and the methods employed in doing so.

The incident came to the ears of Governor Fuchigami Fusataro. He reacted strongly. The Folk Art Association was rebuked and charged with stirring up sectionalism within the empire; in one or two instances association members from Tokyo were roughly handled by the governor's policemen. An angry public discussion led the governor to state vigorously the official view that every vestige of Okinawa's provincial individuality must be erased.

These ill-advised remarks brought into the open once more the problem of discrimination. Governor Fuchigami bluntly proclaimed the position of the extremists who dominated the civil and military bureaucracy at Tokyo. National solidarity—the monolithic state dear to the totalitarian—was essential to the supreme war effort the nation was about to make.

Members of the Folk Art Association boldly took exception; they believed that an Okinawan potter or weaver or lacquer-maker could be a loyal subject even though he remained true to a local or regional craft tradition. The farmer or the fisherman could be a loyal subject even though his speech and his dress did not conform to standards set in Tokyo.

He might even make a good soldier.

Of this the military leaders were not convinced. Japan was on the eve of a great war to which they were about to commit the whole people. The material and human resources of the empire were everywhere being mobilized for an enormous military gamble, no less than a bid to secure political and economic control of Asia. How secure were the Ryukyu Islands? How faithful were the Okinawans?

CHAPTER ELEVEN

BETWEEN HAMMER AND ANVIL: OKINAWA AND THE COMING OF WORLD WAR II

1941-1945

"National Solidarity" and the Japanese Military Program for Okinawa

In 1941 the Okinawans formed the largest minority group within Japan's forty-seven prefectures. Prejudice corroded Okinawan relations with Japanese from Honshu, Kyushu, and Shikoku. Students at the universities and higher schools in Japan met with discrimination and heard Okinawa referred to in contemptuous terms. Pride might be hurt, but loyalty remained unaffected. The Okinawans as a whole considered themselves loyal subjects of the emperor. There were individuals with left-wing or radical sympathies, of course, but there were no anti-Japanese political organizations within the prefecture, and no overt attempts were made to appeal to the Okinawans, as such, in opposition to the Japanese government and people. To understand the situation in 1941 we must review the record of military activities in Okinawa after the Sino-Japanese War.

From the militarists' point of view the Ryukyu Islands formed useful links in the line of communications leading to Formosa and the south, but the impoverished province added no economic strength to the empire, Okinawan youths were substandard candidates for military service, and the loyalty of the population had not been fully tested since the days of annexation.

Universal military conscription laws enforced elsewhere in 1873 were not extended to Okinawa until 1898. A few volunteers had been trained, but public opinion in the older generation strongly opposed military service in any form in the belief that an armed force maintained on Okinawa would attract enemies and invite invasion. During the Sino-Japanese War (and again during the Russo-Japanese conflict) women went daily to the Shinto shrine on Nami-no-ue or to the Buddhist temple Enkaku-ji to pray that sons and husbands would be unfit for military service. These things did not endear the Okinawans to the military leaders at Tokyo.

At last, in 1896, graduates of the normal school who met the physical qualifications were required to give six weeks of active service, and as a gesture of goodwill the army withdrew its garrison from Shuri Castle. In 1898 a regular Okinawan garrison headquarters was established and conscription laws were put into force. It was soon discovered that, by design or by chance, the minimum requirements for the conscripts' height and weight were fixed at a point just above the average for adult males in Okinawa Prefecture. Okinawa stood at the bottom of the list of averages for all prefectures. Although the army denied that this was deliberate discrimination, the Okinawans were unconvinced. The prefecture continued to show the highest number of rejections among males called up for examination.

Japan felt a pressing need to develop defenses in the southern islands. The date chosen to establish a full garrison force on Okinawa is significant, for in 1898 Germany leased Kiaochow Bay, Russia leased the Liaotung Peninsula, England leased Wei-hai-wei—all on the China coast—the United States acquired Hawaii and opened a campaign in the Philippines to crush the Filipino "Republic." The token purchase of the Philippines from Spain established U.S. military government in territory which shared a common sea frontier with Japan's new colony, Formosa.

Six years later the threat of Russian naval raids interrupted regular communications between Kagoshima and Naha. The prefectural government and the public felt a keen sense of physical isolation and danger as Japan went to war with a European power for the first time. Guard units were stationed on the Ryukyuan beaches to keep watch on cable landings, and lookout posts were constructed on headlands throughout the archipelago, alert for enemy craft.

No Russian forces bore down upon the Ryukyus, but five fishermen of Hisamatsu Village in Miyako one day at sea glimpsed the Russian Baltic Fleet as it moved northward toward its doom in the Straits of Tsushima. Speeding to Yaeyama, the fishermen reported what they had seen; the news was flashed by cable to naval headquarters in Japan; and the fleet was made ready for Japan's great naval victory. In the Ryukyus the fishermen were hailed by the Japanese as the "Five Heroes of Hisamatsu."

By 1907, Okinawans were enlisted in every military service branch. A reservists association was formed in 1910. Divisional headquarters undertook to promote an Okinawan Physical Culture Society to sponsor athletic meetings throughout the islands and to develop higher standards of physical fitness and training in the schools. In 1919 towns and villages which had good conscript records were honored by citations granted from the Ministry of War and monuments were erected to commemorate men who had served the country well. Gradually relations between the armed services and the people approached the pattern which was common in all the other prefectures. Okinawans unable to meet minimum physical standards for military training were conscripted for labor service with the armed forces or with civilian corporations under contract to them.

For every lack in physical equipment and manpower the military leaders attempted to compensate by developing fanatic spirit. The so-called "spiritual mobilization" programs developed in Japan after 1931 paved the way for extraordinary sacrifices exacted of the common people in World War II.

As the strength and influence of civil government waned at Tokyo the number of extreme nationalist organizations increased. A "National Self-Regeneration Movement" was launched on Okinawa by missionaries of the new militarism. The "thought police" which had been created as a special service unit at Tokyo in 1928 became active now in every island outpost of the empire. Ten teachers in Yaeyama were arrested for "ideological reasons." Regulations governing a National Spiritual Mobilization Training School were issued in early 1934. Excessive demands began to be made upon the public for "voluntary" contributions of time, labor, and money in support of military preparedness activities.

Manifestations of extreme nationalism—the mass hysteria which swept Japan along the road to national defeat—were unpopular in Okinawa. The common people could not afford the "voluntary" contributions; they had no traditions glorifying war and the fighting man. Great efforts were made to convince the people that Japan was a "have not" nation engaged upon a righteous crusade. Children at school were subjected to an intensive propaganda campaign and stirred to admiration for heroic deeds reported from the China warfront after the continental invasion began in 1931. The youths of Okinawa were prepared to do their duty.

The professional military men believed that the civil population existed only to feed and service the war machine. They looked upon every activity not directly geared to military preparation as a waste of time if not indeed an act of sabotage. In January, 1935, General Ishii Torao, commanding the Okinawa Garrison Forces, publicly denounced the spirit and conduct of men of military age in the Ryukyus. His vehement castigation of the easygoing Okinawan youths was interpreted as a slur upon Okinawan loyalty and was deeply resented.

In efforts to convince the public of the righteousness of Japan's drive in Asia, the civil government sometimes went to absurd lengths to demonstrate national solidarity and solidarity with other members of the fatal Tri-Partite Pact. The propagandists were hard pressed to provide convincing evidence of the importance of the German-Japanese alliance and of German-Japanese friendship. As an illustration, in 1936 the people of Okinawa were called upon to witness the erection of a large monument at Hirara, in Miyako, to mark the sixtieth anniversary of the erection of another monument, the German kaiser's gift commemorating Okinawan kindness to shipwrecked Germans in 1873. The fact that the original gift had covered Germany's probing of Japan's weak southern frontier was conveniently overlooked; the propaganda appeal was made to the Okinawan's sense of mutual obligation created by honors received so long ago at German hands.

THE COMING OF WORLD WAR II

When the Diet passed the National General Mobilization Law in

March, 1938, individual freedoms guaranteed in the Meiji constitution were foreclosed. The Imperial Rule Assistance Association was formed in October, 1940; its agents and offices in Okinawa helped to complete totalitarian political control in support of the army and the Cabinet. By mid-1941, virtually all provisions of the general mobilization act were in effect throughout the Ryukyus. This was "national solidarity" at its maximum development short of war.

Okinawa Prefecture, on the sea frontiers, once again formed an outer defense line for Japan proper and the Japanese. As matters stood on December 8, 1941, the islands had little to contribute to the war effort. There was virtually no surplus in foodstuffs and no significant industry. There was a submarine base at Unten, but the harbors of Okinawa were unimportant for large craft, and the airfields were merely way-stations on the flight southward to Formosa and bases beyond.

To cover the approaches from the south, five airfields were built upon the flat, unfertile fields of Miyako, and three full divisions of Japanese soldiers (more than the total local population) were quartered there at the war's end. Here the hard-pressed country folk felt the heel of war, for the Japanese from the home islands were unable to communicate freely in the local dialect and found the local ways of life uncouth and strange. The Miyako people complained bitterly that they had to bow to every soldier from the other prefectures, as if they were a conquered people, and were forced to suffer great privation in yielding their meager stores to the occupying forces.

Yaeyama suffered to a less degree, for the mountainous terrain admitted no extension of the airfields. The Japanese from other prefectures who were stationed there on naval patrol or with the air wings found Ishigaki City less strange, and there was more abundant supply of food produced locally to be shared with the Yaeyama people.

No prefecture contributed so little to the preparation for war and its prosecution through the years, but none suffered as much in widespread misery, in loss of human lives and property, and in ultimate subservience to military occupation. Although a handful of Okinawans held important posts in the civil government at Tokyo and in other prefectures, they were not in key policy positions. Some ten thousand able-bodied Okinawans served in the regular military labor corps, but there were relatively few conscripts trained for combat. Of these only 4,500 were stationed on Okinawa as the war drew to its close.

Pearl Harbor, Manila, Singapore, Jakarta, Rangoon; in an explosion of national energy imperial Japanese forces swept in 1942 through Southeast Asia to the borders of India and from island to island in Australasian seas. There was excitement and pride throughout Japan. Every prefecture was organized at every level of social and economic life. From the Kuriles to Formosa the emperor's subjects felt common exhilaration, sharing the news of victories as well as the privations and dangers of the war. Sacrifices made on distant battlefields seemed worth the promise of the future. In Japanese eyes the wicked Europeans and Americans were being driven out of Asia. A Co-Prosperity Sphere for Asians was soon to organize under benevolent imperial direction. Wealth would pour back into Japan and there would be new lands opened overseas for settlement.

But by 1943 the tide had turned decisively. The public had not recognized the significance of Japan's defeat at Midway in 1942, and at Guadalcanal and Saipan, but senior statesmen at Tokyo read the signs of danger. The basic economy could not support a long war. Military men had greatly overestimated Japan's capacity to convert new-won wealth into military goods. Japan's industrial structure could not meet the demands of a long war. Army leaders had grossly underestimated the United States. Americans had not proved weak-willed isolationists, willing to negotiate a settlement rather than to fight in East and West at once. Allied forces were pouring into the Pacific in a swelling flood. Japan was everywhere in retreat.

The governments ranged against Japan began to discuss openly the problems which would rise with Japan's defeat. The Chinese hastened to announce that they intended to claim not only Manchuria and Formosa but the Ryukyu Islands as well. On July 7, 1942, Sun Fo announced China's determination to recover the Ryukyus; Foreign Minister T.V. Soong repeated the claim in November; Chiang Kai-shek referred to China's "loss of the Liu-ch'iu Islands" in the unexpurgated Chinese edition of his manifesto *China's Destiny*, published on March 10, 1943; and Chinese spokesmen in the United States found opportunity to bring the claim to the attention of the American public.

To strengthen the capacity of Japan to resist direct invasion and to consolidate domestic administration, the whole of Japan was divided into nine major districts in June, 1943. Okinawa Prefecture and seven others were combined to form the "Kyushu District."

Powerful army leaders insisted that Japan would be able to regain initiative, mount new offensives, and win through in the end. The generals refused to entertain thoughts of compromise. The "national spirit"—*seishin*—would overcome deficiencies in wealth and arms; *kamikaze*, the "divine winds," would drive off and destroy enemies who approached Japan.[1]

But civilians near the throne and important naval officers weighed carefully Japan's capacity to resist. Shigemitsu Mamoru recommended that a peace be made with China to free Japan from commitments on the continent, and Rear Admiral Takagi Sokichi reported his grim conclusion that Japan had lost the war at sea and must find a formula for peace.

Such maneuvering behind the scenes took time and great care, for tensions within the government at Tokyo were extremely high. Anarchy might engulf Japan if fanatic army officers turned on senior statesmen to purge the court of dangerous thoughts of peace. The essence of safety for the nation lay in holding off an Allied movement toward Japan while every avenue of compromise was carefully explored. Foreshadowed by the Cairo Declaration and reduced to its simplest terms, the choice was this: if the imperial government could negotiate surrender *before* Allied forces reached Japan and made a landing, Japan would lose all her territories overseas, but the homeland—the heartland—of Japan would be preserved; its political and social institutions would survive. If, on the other hand, Allied forces won and held beachheads within home territory, the homeland would be ravaged, and Japan itself would be destroyed.

The threat of allied invasion from over the seas to the south and east grew stronger as each week and month went by. Okinawa Prefecture lay on the path to all the other provinces of the empire. Where did it lie in relation to this fundamental question, the timing and terms of a surrender?

It is improbable that the men at Tokyo considered Okinawa so explicitly as this, but none were acting without emotional reference to the past; they knew that the Western powers could make a case for detaching Okinawa from Japan proper if there was a desire to draft punitive terms for peace just short of partitioning Japan itself. Okinawa had been occupied and garrisoned over the protests of the Okinawan king and government; moreover, even after the islands had been annexed and declared a province, Tokyo had offered to divide the archipelago,giving half to China. The Cairo Declaration had left the way open for negotiation. By virtue of its exposed location and its history, Okinawa had become again a territorial bargaining point and pawn, potentially expendable in "the larger interest."

By February, 1944, high-ranking prefectural officers—natives of other prefectures—began to send their families home to the main islands. In April many men in the civil government and in the police forces were transferred to a naval administration. The islands were placed under martial law. By July a general movement of people to the relative safety of Formosa or Kyushu began to take place. Okinawan parents who could afford it sent school-age children on ahead, promising to join them in due course. Infants were entrusted to the care of older brothers and sisters.

As the sense of danger mounted, more than twenty thousand young men and women were pressed into "special service" organizations. The girls formed nursing corps and working units to take over tasks normally performed by men.

Intensive propaganda had for years urged every subject to prepare himself to make supreme sacrifice on the emperor's behalf, but this theme had been coupled with assurance that Japan was invincible. To the very last the government refused to disclose the gravity of Japan's war position or to alert the public to the imminence of disaster. Tokyo gave little thought to the civil economy on distant Okinawa and did virtually nothing to prepare it for the crisis of invasion. The Ryukyus were not Kyushu, or Shikoku, or Honshu; Okinawa retained importance only as a potential field of battle, a distant border area in which the oncoming enemy could be checked, pinned down, and ultimately destroyed.

The Japanese of other prefectures had been nurtured for centuries in traditions of war which exalted skill in close combat and glorified the *mystique* of self-sacrifice. Not so the Okinawans, who were unprepared to take up arms in self-defense.

Naha came under air attack for the first time in October, 1944. Some ninety percent of the city was burned. Shuri was hit again and again. Carrier-based planes flew in from the south and east, and heavy bombers came from the hinterland of China.

Civil-defense measures were hopelessly inadequate. The government (dominated throughout by men of other prefectures) did nothing to protect ancient monuments and made no effort to preserve the priceless archives of the old kingdom. The bureaucrats were psychologically unprepared to admit that they were losing a war in which they had for years been promised victory. They could not improvise or take individual initiative in times of crises, but clung to the symbols of an imperial government which had failed them. Schoolmasters were ordered to ensure the safety of the emperor's portrait, for instance; obedient custodians were seen wandering about, not knowing what to do with framed pictures, helpless from want of direction in times of grave emergency. (Ultimately an order was given to burn the photographs en masse and with great ceremony.) The total energies of responsible officialdom were consumed in meeting demands made by the military forces. General headquarters were established in caverns deep beneath Shuri Castle walls. Civilians were impressed for labor upon defensive works thrown up throughout the islands using any materials at hand. Highways were stripped of their bordering trees, the ancient pines which had been set out centuries earlier. Private homes were given up and whole villages taken over to accommodate the garrison making ready for a desperate stand.

In the midst of these final military preparations the bewildered ordinary citizens were left to make ready for the crisis as best they could. Families hurried to the countryside to conceal books and clothes and other goods in the family tombs or in pits dug in the ravines beyond suburban settlements.

Late in March, 1945, the Custodian of Treasures of the Sho family gathered together the principal objects of historic interest and intrinsic value remaining in the Sho mansions at Shuri. These included ancient crowns of Chinese style and workmanship (gifts of China's emperors), and Chinese musical instruments of rare antiquity, which had been registered with the Japanese government as "National Treasures" and "Objects of National Importance." There were portraits of the kings and of the royal princes, splendidly brocaded robes of state, fine ceramics, incense burners, lacquerware, crystal, silver services, golden ornaments, jewels and beads of the old high priestesses, and ancient texts and manuscripts. Some of these rare objects were placed in vaults, some were buried with scant consideration here and there in the gardens, covered lightly with mats and earth and brush. Eight custodians were assigned to keep watch about the premises, but on April 6 the Sho mansion was destroyed by fire and two days later the Japanese army occupied the grounds, driving off the Okinawan guards.[2]

Meanwhile, on March 26 a small American force had gone ashore in the Kerama Islands, lying low on the horizon west of Naha. They met little opposition. The local garrison had no stomach for the fight, although this was found to be the base for 360 "suicide craft" being readied for surprise attack upon Allied ships in Okinawan waters.

On the evening of March 31 at Shuri, students in the middle school assembled under cover of darkness for graduation ceremonies. As each youth was handed his certificate he was given his military orders.

There were rumors of a landing up the coast. An occasional glimmer of signal lights at sea warned of a great fleet assembled on the horizon. Civilian interests were no longer of consequence. Families were fleeing into the hills, seeking refuge in old tombs and rocky caves.

Storms greater than any recorded in a thousand years of history were about to sweep across these frontier islands.

THE BATTLE FOR OKINAWA[3]

The Okinawan campaign began on Easter morning, April 1. A feigned attack on the southeast coast divided Japanese attention. British naval units patrolled approaches to the battle site from Formosa. An immense American fleet lay in the offshore waters, drawn like a noose about Okinawa proper.

The first assault took place at half past eight o'clock. Twenty thousand

Americans plunged ashore and crossed the beach near Kadena. From the ancient walls of Shuri Castle Lieutenant General Ushijima watched the landings. The Americans were astonished to meet no serious opposition. Ushijima had concentrated his troops to the south, beyond a great escarpment which crosses the island from shore to shore between Shuri and Kadena. He planned to draw the invaders to positions under these craggy heights, from which he could then direct a sweeping fire. He proposed to hold the Americans there while reinforcements from Japan, by air and by sea, destroyed the supporting Allied fleet. It was a bold design.

Within twenty-four hours some fifty thousand Americans had landed, digging in beyond the beachhead and pressing across to the eastern shore, only four miles away. Thus at one stroke Okinawa had been divided.

From this base on the waist of the island the invasion forces organized for drives northward into the hills and wooded valleys of the Kunigami district, and southward across the densely populated Shuri-Naha area into open farmland beyond. On April 5 the Americans began to move. The civil population fled before them. No provision had been made by the Japanese high command to protect or segregate the noncombatants; every Okinawan, old and young, was on his own; he might preserve his life if he could find sufficient shelter.

The Third Marine Amphibious Corps turned northward. General Ushijima had decided to let the Kunigami district go by default. There was a week of savage hand-to-hand fighting in the northern ravines, where some twelve hundred Japanese soldiers held out, but by May 5 the Americans were able to declare themselves in full control of northern Okinawa. The 24th Army Corps turned south from Kadena beachhead. Ushijima withheld his fire as the Americans approached the foot of Kakazu ridge, confidently waiting for airborne help to come out of the north, the *kamikaze* corps which was to swoop upon the American ships. On April 6 suicide planes did begin to come in from Kyushu bases. They did great damage, but could not break up the concentrated fleet. On shore the Americans approached the first strong lines of Japanese defense; the terrible Battle of Okinawa then began in earnest.

On April 11 the Americans were brought to a halt, pinned down while enduring the heaviest artillery duel of the Pacific War. By April

24 casualties rose above fifty percent in the ranks of the 96th Division, which was now replaced.

Shuri did not fall. Its high parapets and immensely thick walls, laid down five hundred years ago, provided a superb anchor for the line so stubbornly held across the path of the invading forces. Here lay the heart of Japanese resistance.

At last it was decided that these walls had to be breached and the Japanese base of operations rendered untenable. It will be recalled that the castle had been penetrated only twice before by alien forces; by the Japanese in 1609 and by Commodore Perry, who marched into its medieval precincts under cover of the "Mississippi's" guns in 1853.

By a twist of fate, its modern namesake, the U.S.S. "Mississippi" of World War II, was called upon to be the agent of destruction. Orders went out to the ship on the evening of May 24; the great fourteen-inch naval guns were trained on Shuri Castle walls; and planes were sent into the air to direct the fire. Throughout May 25 the walls were pounded, but there was no sign of a break. At the end of the second day of continuous bombardment, observers reported that cracks were beginning to appear. On the third day the great ship boldly moved close inshore, hurling tons of steel and explosives against the crumbling walls. By nightfall the ancient castle was in ruins.

General Ushijima withdrew from the caves beneath Shuri into the hills of southern Okinawa on May 31. Nothing was left of the ancient city; the palace was gone, the temples, the great gates, and the ancient gardens of the Shuri gentry. The castle heights had been under continuous heavy fire for sixty days. It had required two months for the American forces to make their way from Kadena to the ruined town, a distance of approximately ten miles as the crow flies. Naha—three miles away—did not fall to American control until June 13.

The retreating Japanese fought with unparalleled ferocity from cave to cave. Organization and discipline were gone, but they disputed every rod of territory between Naha and the cliffs which mark the southern shore. These men chose death rather than surrender, but it was with barbaric disregard for the fate of civilians trapped among them. Terrified Okinawans, with the wounded and the sick who had taken refuge in caves dotting the countryside, were often suddenly dispossessed and driven into the open, into lines of fire from which there was no escape possible. Often they were made to share the crowded sub-terranean darkness with retreating soldiers, while from the shelter of the entrance Japanese snipers took toll of the advancing foe. The Americans were compelled to train their guns and their flame-throwers upon every cavern mouth and rocky hiding place.

On the evening of June 20 American scouts pushed ahead toward the very edge of the cliffs at Mabuni. On the landward side of the bluffs they found a tunnel leading deep into the earth. They had seen a thousand others like it in this nightmare battle. They seared it with flame, but made no attempt to enter, for they were eager to push on to the crest of the hill ahead. Beneath them, deep within, was a series of storerooms and caves which had an opening on the seaward side, high above the surf. Here Lieutenant General Ushijima and his chief of staff were preparing to spend the night, writing dispatches and saying farewell to their aides. Early on the morning of June 21 they went to the ledges overlooking the sea, saluted the emperor at distant Tokyo, and quietly committed suicide.

FIG. 23. CRESTS IN OKINAWAN HISTORY. Left to right: *Sho family; Shimazu clan; the Japanese imperial chrysanthemum; and the shoulder patch worn by U. S. occupation forces on Okinawa.*

They had done their duty. The enemy had been held on Okinawa for more than eighty days. They had demonstrated on Okinawa what must be expected and prepared for in Japan.

The guns fell silent. The Battle for Okinawa was at an end.

The United States had brought more than half a million men into the campaign. General Ushijima had some 89,000 regular troops deployed on Okinawa, but of these only 4,575 were Okinawan conscripts trained and armed as combat personnel. To this force were added able-bodied Okinawan males who had been conscripted for regular military labor services and for "expendable" duties at the front. There were Boy Scouts and girls who served in the special nursing corps. Altogether more than twenty thousand young Okinawans were drafted for emergency services during the last months of the crisis and retreat across the island.

Seeking to cover up the extent of the disaster, the Japanese high command at Tokyo announced that eighty thousand Americans had been killed. In truth, more than twelve thousand Americans had died and the number of wounded exceeded 35,000.

According to American figures, 90,401 Japanese soldiers had been killed. Only four thousand prisoners of war were taken.

Between the hammer and the anvil, the Okinawans suffered indescribable loss. It has been estimated that 62,489 perished in this "typhoon of steel"; of these some 47,000 were civilians who had been unable to find safety within caves and tombs. More than ten thousand labor conscripts and civilian "volunteers" serving with the army had met death. One in eight of the civil population was dead. No family remained untouched. No one knows precisely how many civilians perished from exposure, starvation, disease, or unattended wounds.

With this storm of fire and thunder of guns, the story of the old kingdom and the modern province came to an end. The Ryukyu Islands and the Okinawan people passed under American control. A new chapter of Okinawan history had begun.

NOTES, BIBLIOGRAPHY, AND INDEX

NOTES

The following abbreviations are used in the notes; for other details, see the Bibliography:

BEFEO: *Bulletin de l'École Francaise de l'Extreme-Orient* (Hanoi)
BMFJ: *Bulletin de la Maison Franco-Japonais* (Tokyo)
HJAS: *Harvard Journal of Asiatic Studies* (Cambridge)
JA: *Journal Asiatique* (Paris)
JAOS: *Journal of the American Oriental Society* (New Haven)
JNCBRAS: *Journal of the North China Branch, Royal Asiatic Society* (Shanghai)
JSL: *Transactions and Proceedings of the Japan Society, London*
MN: *Monumenta Nipponica* (Tokyo)
REO: *Revue de l'Extreme Orient* (Paris)
TASJ: *Transactions of the Asiatic Society of Japan* (Tokyo)
TP: *T'oung Pao* (Leiden)

CHAPTER ONE

1. Gerard Groot: *Prehistory of Japan*, p. 105; Kanaseki Takeo: "Ancient Culture in Yaeyama Islands," *Minzokugaku-Kenkyu* (The Japanese Journal of Ethnology), v. 19, no. 2, pp. 1–35, and in private communications from Dr. Kanaseki, who notes that while Jomon sites are found in Okinawa, Yayoi sites have been found only as far south as Amami Oshima, in the northern Ryukyus.

2. On archeological materials, early continental relations with the sea islands, and Chinese notices, see G.B. Sansom: *Japan: A Short Cultural History* (London, 1952), ch. 1, pp. 15–21; Williams: "Notices of Fu-Sang and Other Countries lying East of China . . ." JOAS, v. 11, pp. 90–96, 111–16; Wylie: "Ethnography of the After Han Dynasty—History of the Eastern Barbarians," REO, v. 1, pp. 52–83.

3. On early Chinese interest in mysterious Eastern Sea islands see C.P. Fitzgerald: *China: A Cultural History* (N.Y., 1938), pp. 221–24; W. Perceval Yetts: "Taoist Tales, Part III," *New China Review* (Shanghai), v. 2, no. 3 (June, 1920), p. 293. Tales of golden and silver islands, harboring secrets of immortality, penetrated Renaissance Europe, spurring a search for the Fountain of Youth, Rica de Oro, and Rica de Plata until the

late 17th cent. See Burney: *Chron. Hist. Voyages* . . . v. 2, pt. 2, ch. 15, pp. 261–62; Schurz: *Manila Galleon:* pp. 126, 231–38. Beechey's *Narrative* refers to *Kinshima* and *Ginshima* during voyage of 1825–28 (v. 2, p. 210).

4. For the materials on the *noro* system in this and later chapters I am indebted principally to R.S. Spencer: "The Noro Priestesses of Loochoo," *TASJ*, 2nd ser., v. 8, pp. 94–112, supplemented by field inquiry (1952) and Simon: "Beiträge zur Kenntnis der Riu-kiu Inseln," *Beiträge zu Kultur-und Universalgeschichte*, v. 28, pp. 8–9.

5. B.H. Chamberlain: *Essay in Aid of a Grammar and Dictionary of the Luchuan Language*, TASJ, v. 23, Supplement; "A Preliminary Notice of the Luchuan Language," *Jour. Anth. Inst. Gt.B. and I.*, v. 26, pp. 45–59; "A Comparison of the Japanese and Luchuan Languages," TASJ, v. 23, pp. 271–89; Hattori Shiro: "The Relationship of Japanese to the Ryukyu, Korean and Altaic Languages," TASJ, v. I, 3rd ser., pp. 100–33.

6. Iha Fuyu: *Ko Ryukyu* (2nd ed., 1916) pp. 60–62.

7. For the principal origin myths see Majikina Anko: *Okinawa Issennen-shi* (A Thousand Years of Okinawan History), pp. 27–28. The "wind impregnation" myth, found in pre-Homeric Greek stories, was noted by Magellan's companion and biographer Pigafetta in the Spice Islands in 1522, when Okinawans were trading there.

8. C. Haguenauer: "Le Lieou-K'ieou Kouo du Souei Chou était-il Formose?" BMFJ, v. 2, nos. 3–4, pp. 15–36. G. Schlegel: Problemes Géographiques: Les Peuples étrangers chez les Historiens Chinois. XIX. Lieuou-Kieou-Kouo. Le Pays de Lieou-Kieou," TP, v. 6, no. 2, pp. 165–214. Akiyama Kenzo: "Zui-sho Ryukyu Koku-den no sai ginmi" (Review of an account of Ryukyu in the Sui Dynasty records), *Rekishi Chiri*, v. 54, no. 2, pp. 93–106. See Ryusaku Tsunoda and L. Carrington Goodrich: *Japan in the Chinese Dynastic Histories* for references to Ryukyu (Liu Ch'iu) which appear in conjunction with Sino-Japanese affairs.

9. J.B. Snellen: "Shoku Nihongi," TASJ, 2nd ser., v. 6, p. 179.

10. Snellen, *ibid.*, p. 184.

11. Snellen, *ibid.*, p. 202.

12. On the growth of Shimazu's domains and titular appointments, see Asakawa Kanichi: *Documents of Iriki*, pp. 1–36, 98, *passim*.

CHAPTER TWO

1. Notes, plans, and sketches of Nakagusuku Castle appear in F.L. Hawks' *Narrative* of Perry's expedition (v. 1, ch. 8, pp. 169–71); consult photographic records and drawings of castles, temples, and domestic architecture in Tanabe's *Ryukyu Kenchiku* (Ryukyuan Architecture), Tokyo, 1937.

2. Teng and Fairbank: "On the Ch'ing Tributary System," HJAS, v. 6, no. 2 (June, 1941), pp. 135–246.

3. C. Haguenauer: "Relations du Royaume des Ryukyu avec les pays des mers du sud et la Corée," BMFJ, v. 3, nos. 1–2 (1931), *Comptes rendues:* pp. 4–16. Tanaka: *Textile Fabrics of Okinawa*, Intro., pp. 7–17. Higaonna: *History of the Foreign Relations*

of Okinawa. Kobata: "Ryukyu-Marakka-kan no tsusho kankei ni tsuite," *Keizai Kenkyu,* v. 14, no. 5, pp. 579–93; no. 6, pp. 712–24.

4. Leavenworth: *History of Loochoo,* p. 42.

5. Sansom summarizes this period of China's overseas activities in *The Western World and Japan,* ch. 7, "The Asiatic Trade," pp. 134–51, noting that records concerning the origin of Ch'eng Ho's voyages (1405–33) were suppressed and presumably destroyed. On Japan's unsatisfactory tributary and trade relations with China, see Takekoshi's *The Economic Aspects of the History of the Civilization of Japan,* v. 1, ch. 17, "Foreign Trade in the Ashikaga Epoch," pp. 211–29.

6. Ross: "New Light on the History of the Chinese Oriental College, and a 16th Century Vocabulary of the Luchuan Language [dated 1549]," TP, v. 9, 2nd ser., 1908, pp. 689–95. Hirth: "The Chinese Oriental College," JNCBRAS, new ser., v. 22 (1888), pp. 203–23. Pelliot: "Notice of E. Denison Ross's Article in *T'oung Pao* for December, 1906," BEFEO, v. 9 (Jan.–Mar., 1909), pp. 170–71.

CHAPTER THREE

1. See Schuyler Cammann: *China's Dragon Robes,* pp. 157–58. Mongol precedents established that five-clawed-dragon designs were reserved for imperial robes, and four-clawed-*mang*-dragon designs were proper for nobles and high officials. Bolts of *mang*-dragon cloth were sent to foreign tributaries. Only the Kings of Korea and Ryukyu appear to have worn the "dragon robes" in the Chinese style, and this only for the reception of Chinese imperial envoys. The last gifts of such embroidered cloth reached Okinawa in 1874.

2. Gabriel S. Ferrand: "Malaka, Le Malayu et Malayur" in *JA,* ser. 11, v. 12 (1918), Appendix I, "L'île de Ghur—Lieou-K'ieou-Formosa," pp. 126–33. Ferrand quotes five Arabic sources, notes that in Java Ryukyu was known as "Likiwu" or "Likyu" but was generally referred to as "Al Ghur" (meaning "the place of mines"?) because of its reputation as a source of fine metals and superb swordsmiths' steel presumed to be in the kingdom. But Ferrand himself equates "Al Ghur" with Formosa, apparently unaware of the absence of iron mines in Formosa (which was undeveloped before the 17th century) and without knowledge of Okinawa's role in the transshipment of Japan's fine wares into Southeast Asian markets. "Al Ghur" is thought by some scholars to be the source of the Portuguese reference to "Gores" as a people from north Asia's coastal waters. On the possiblity that they may have been Korean residents of Naha traveling aboard Okinawan ships, see Akiyama: "Gores naru meisho no hassei to sono rekishi-teki hatten" (Origin and historical development of the name "Gores") *Shigaku Zasshi,* v. 39, no. 12 (1928), pp. 1349–59. The principal authority is Kobata Jun: *Chusei Nanto Tsusho-boeki Oshi no Kenkyu* (A study of the history of trade and communications in the Southern Islands in the Middle Ages). Tokyo (1939). 552 pp., and *op. cit.,* Chap. 2, note 3. For early European cartographic representations of Okinawa see Cortesaõ *Cartografia e Cartógrafos Portugueses dos seculos XV e XVI* (Lisbon, 1935) v. 2, Plates XIV, XVII, XIX, XXII–III, XXVII–VIII, LI.

3. For illustrations, see Neil Gordon Munro: *Coins of Japan,* pp. 161–65; for Chinese

notes on Ryukyuan currency, see Frederic Schjöth: *The Currency of the Far East: Chinese Currency*, pp. 67–68, "The Liu-ch'iu Islands of Japan."

4. For this account of reorganization of the *noro* system and religious practices I am indebted to Robert Steward Spencer, *op. cit.*

5. For the local legends recounted here I have drawn from a collection, in manuscript but without attribution, made available to me at Hirara, Miyako, by the officers of the Civil Affairs Team in May, 1952, for whom the manuscript had been prepared, and to conversations with Okinawan friends from Miyako and Yaeyama.

6. Joaõ de Barros: *Da Asia* (Lisbon, 1777), Decade I, liv. 9, ch. 1, p. 281.

7. Armando Cortesaõ (ed.): *The Suma Oriental of Tomé Pires: an account of the East, from the Red Sea to Japan, written at Mallacca and India in 1512–1515*, v. 1, p. 126.

8. Cortesaõ: *ibid.*, pp. 128–31.

9. Mansell Longworth Dames (ed.): *The Book of Duarte Barbosa*, p. 215.

10. Walter deGray Birch (ed.): *The Commentaries of the Great Afonso Dalboquerque, Second Viceroy of India*, v. 3, pp. 88–89.

11. Charles R. Boxer (ed.): *South China in the Sixteenth Century: Being the Narratives of Galeote Pereira, Fr. Gaspar da Cruz O.P., Fr.Martin de Rada, O.E.S.A. (1550–1575)*, p. 68.

12. Cammann: *op. cit.*, pp. 157–58.

13. Tsunoda and Goodrich: *op. cit.*, p. 107.

14. *Ibid.*, p. 116.

15. *Ibid.*, p. 128.

16. *Ibid.*, p. 130.

17. *Ibid.*, pp. 123–24.

18. Maurice Collis: *The Grand Peregrination: Being the Life and Adventures of Fernaõ Mendes Pinto*, pp. 158–65.

19. E.H. Blair and J.A. Robertson: *The Philippine Islands, 1493–1803* (Cleveland, 1903), v. 3, 1569–76, p. 72.

CHAPTER FOUR

1. Schurz: *The Manila Galleon*, pp. 105–8.

2. Yoshi S. Kuno: *Japanese Expansion on the Asiatic Continent*, v. 1, Appendix 33, pp. 305–7.

3. A.L. Sadler: "The Naval Campaign in the Korean War of Hideyoshi (1592–1598" TASJ, v. 14, 2nd ser. (1937), p. 192.

4. *Nihon Meisho Chishi*, v. 10, p. 421. Kabayama Hisataka's descendent Sukenori surveyed China's position in Formosa in 1872–73 in anticipation of the punitive expedition sent ostensibly on Ryukyu's behalf; in 1895 he became first Japanese governor of Formosa, thus in a sense continuing his family's traditional role as "guardians" of the southern frontier. Rolf Binkenstein: "Die Ryukyu-Expedition unter Shimazu Iehisa," MN, v. 4, no. 2)IIII), pp. 296–230; and "Taichu Shonin," MN, v. 1; 1943),

nos. 1–2, pp. 219–32. Wolf Haenisch: *Die auswertige Politik Ryukyus seit dem Anfang des 17 Jahrhunderts und der Einflüss des Fürsten von Satsuma*, pp. 1–41.

5. *Japan Weekly Mail* (Oct. 8, 1879), v. 3, no. 42, p. 1383. For the Japanese text, see Majikina Anko: *Okinawa Issennen Shi* (A Thousand Years of Okinawan History) (Fukuoka, 1952), p. 367. Brinkley also gives this, with slight editorial variation in "The Story of the Riu-kiu (Loo-choo) Complication" *Chrysanthemum and Phoenix*, v. 3, pt. 3 (1883), p. 127.

6. *Loc. cit.*

7. On Satsuma's administrative control organization see Majikina, *op. cit., passim.*

8. "C. St. P." (ed.): *Cocks' Diary* (London, n.d.), v. 1, p. 1, ftnt. 4.

9. J.C. Purnell (ed.): "The Logbook of William Adams, 1614–19, and Related Documents," JSL, v. 13 (1915), pp. 169–70. Cyril Wild (ed.): *Purchas his Pilgrimes in Japan Extracted from Hakluytus Posthumous, or Purchas his Pilgrimes . . . p. 217.*

10. Edward Maunde Thompson (ed.): *The Diary of Richard Cocks: Cape Merchant in the English Factory in Japan: 1615–1622*, v. 1, pp. 14–15.

11. *Ibid.*: v. 2, pp. 58–59.

12. M. Paske-Smith: *Western Barbarians in Japan and Formosa in Tokugawa Days 1603–1868*, p. 32.

13. Fairbank and Teng, *op. cit.*, p. 183. For a facsimile reproduction of the seal, bearing both Chinese and Manchu script, see Julius Klaproth: *San Kokf Tsou Ran To Sets ou Aperçu des Trois Royaumes*, v. 2, p. 7.

14. Total Shimazu revenues levied in Satsuma, Osumi, Hyuga, and Ryukyu were estimated to be 732,616 *koku* in 1635. A document prepared five years later noted that income from the "Governor of Ryukyu" (Ryukyu *Koku-shi*) stood at 90,884 *koku*. Asakawa: *Documents of Iriki*, pp. 337, 358, 363.

CHAPTER FIVE

1. Edmund Simon: "The Introduction of the Sweet Potato into the Far East," TASJ, v. 42, pt. 2 (1914), pp. 711–24.

2. Thompson: *op. cit.*, v. 1, p. 14.

3. Engelbert Kaempfer: *The History of Japan . . . 1690–1692*, v. 1, p. 62.

4. B.H. Chamberlain: "The Luchu Islands and their Inhabitants," *Geographical Journal*: v. 5, no. 4 (1895), pp. 310–11.

5. [Saion] *Eight Volumes on Ryukyu Forest Administration (1738–1748)*. Trans. by U.S. Civil Administration, Ryukyu Islands, Naha, 1952, 71 pp.

6. Hsu Pao-kuang (Jo Ho-ko) prepared a "Report of an Envoy to Chuzan" [in 1719] (*Chung-shan ch'uan-hsin lu*, or *Chuzan Denshin Roku*). A Japanese edition appeared soon after, Father Gaubil made a French translation at Peking in 1752 (v. 23 of *Lêttres Édifiantes et Curieuses*, Paris, 1781), which became a principal reference for subsequent Western notices. Extensive extracts appear in John M'Leod's *Voyage of His Majesty's Ship Alceste along the Coast of Corea to the Island of Lewchew, with Her Subsequent Shipwreck* (London, 1818), pp. 79–97.

7. Chou Huang (Shu Ko): "A Brief Account of the Ryukyu Kingdom" (*Liu Ch'iu-kuo chih-lueh* or *Ryukyu-koku Shiryaku*). The embassy was at Shuri in 1756. Chou prepared his report in 1757, including an unusual bibliography of 50 titles, and presented it to the throne in the following year. The Wuying Palace moveable-type edition was prepared sometime in the 1770's. Supplemental editions continued to appear during the next half century. A summary English version by E.C. Bridgeman, entitled "Lewkew Kwo Che leo: a brief history of Lewchew" appeared in the *Chinese Repository*, v. 6 (July 1837), pp. 113–18.

8. S. Wells Williams (trans.): "Journal of a Mission to Lewchew in 1801," JNCBRAS, v. 7, new ser. (1869–1870), pp. 149–71.

9. *Ibid.*, p. 166.

10. *Ibid.*, p. 150.

11. Cammann: *op. cit.*, pp. 157–59.

12. *Okinawa-ken Kyoiku-kai* (pub.): *Ryukyu* (Naha, 1925) 170 pp.

13. C. Boxer (ed.): *South China in the Sixteenth Century*, Appendix 3, "The Great Granite Bridges of Fukien," pp. 332–40.

14. Okinawan transcription from Tyra [Taira] Buntaro: *My Fifty Favorite Okinawan Songs*, (Naha, 1954) p. 5.

15. S. Pasfield-Oliver (ed.): *Memoirs and Travels of Mauritius Augustus: Count de Benyowsky, etc., With Introduction, Notes and Bibliography* . . . p. 376–93. "Treaty" text, pp. 392–93.

16. G. Staunton: *An Authentic Account of An Embassy from the King of Great Britain to the Emperor of China* . . . [*etc.*] [The Macartney Mission], v. 2, pp. 459–60.

17. W.R. Broughton: *A Voyage of Discovery to the North Pacific Ocean* . . . *In the Years 1795, 1796, 1797, and 1798*, pp. 201–2, 203.

18. *Ibid.*, p. 205–6, 207.

19. *Ibid.*, p. 208.

20. *Ibid.*, p. 237.

21. *Ibid.*, pp. 240–41.

CHAPTER SIX

1. Klaproth, *op. cit.*, v. 1, "Notice des Îles Lieou Khieou, appelées en Japonais Riou Kiou," pp. 169–80.

2. Higaonna Kanjun: *Outline of Okinawan History*, p. 49.

3. J.F. Kuiper: "Some Notes on the Foreign Relations of Japan in the Early Napoleonic Period (1798–1805)," TASJ, 2nd ser., v. 1 (1924), pp. 55–83.

4. Basil Hall: *Account of a Voyage of Discovery to the West Coast of Corea and the Great Loo-Choo Island* . . . pp. 61–62. N.B. Henry Ellis, Third Commissioner of the embassy, in 1817 published "A Correct Narrative" of the embassy. He was not among those who visited Okinawa, but incorporates a report of their sojourn (see Bibliography). Hall's appreciative description of the Okinawans was not accepted by some

readers whose experience elsewhere in Asia made it impossible for them to believe that such a friendly people could be found in the Far East. Hall's account was attacked by a pseudonymous writer ("Amicus") in "A Chinese Account of the Loo-Choo," published at Malacca in the *Indo-Chinese Gleaner*, no. 7 (January 1819). "Amicus" had never visited the Ryukyus, but he did not hesitate to describe the Okinawans as "liars" and to belittle Hall's susceptibility to Okinawan "deceipt."

5. John M'Leod: *Voyage of His Majesty's Ship Alceste to China, Corea and the Island of Lewchew: With an account of her Shipwreck*, pp. 105–6.

6. *Ibid.*, pp. 108–11.

7. *Ibid.*, pp. 112–13.

8. *Ibid.*, pp. 113–14.

9. Hall: *op. cit.*, p. 210.

10. H.J. Clifford: *The Claims of Loo-Choo on British Liberality*. Sect. entitled "The Gospel in China, Island of Loo-Choo," p. 3.

11. M'Leod: *op. cit.*, p. 338.

12. Hall: *Narrative of a Voyage to Java, China, and the Great Loo-Choo Island . . . and of an Interview with Napoleon Buonaparte at St. Helena*, pp. 67–68.

13. *Ibid.*, pp. 79–80.

14. W.U. Eddis: "Short Visit to Loo-Choo in November, 1818," *Indo-Chinese Gleaner*, no. 7 (1819), p. 1.

15. James Murdoch: *History of Japan*, v. 3, p. 528.

16. R. Huish (ed.): *Narrative of the Voyages and Travels of Captain Beechey: R.N. . . .* p. 488.

17. F.W. Beechey: *Narrative of a Voyage to the Pacific and Beering's Straits*. Quoted by Clifford, *op. cit.*, p. 27.

18. H.H. Lindsay: *Reports of Proceedings on a Voyage to the Northern Ports of China in the Ship Lord Amherst . . .* pp. 260–61, 263.

19. *Ibid.*, pp. 263, 265.

20. C. Gutzlaff: *Journal of Two Voyages along the Coast of China in 1831 & 1832 . . . with Notices of Siam, Corea, and the Loo-Choo Islands . . .* (1833 ed.), pp. 288–89.

21. *Ibid.*, pp. 289, 290, 291.

22. *Ibid.*, pp. 294–97.

23. Lindsay: *op. cit.*, Enclosure No. 3, "Mr. Gutzlaff's Notes," p. 225.

24. *Ibid.*, p. 226.

25. "Loss of the Transport *Indian Oak* (Captain Grainger) on Lewchew, Aug. 14, 1840," *Chinese Repository*, v. 12, (1843), no. 2, Art. IV, pp. 81–82; J.J.B. Bowman: "Account of the Wreck of the *Indian Oak*," *The Nautical Mag. and Naval Chron. for 1841*, pp. 299–308, 385–94.

26. "Loss of the Transport Indian Oak . . ." *loc. cit.*

27. *Ibid.*, p. 87.

28. *Ibid.:* p. 88.

29. J.J.B. Bowman's letter to Lieutenant Clifford (dated at Calcutta Sept. 10, 1844) published in Clifford's *Claims of Loochoo on British Liberality*, p. 32.

30. E. Belcher: *Narrative of a Voyage of HMS Samarang during the years 1843–1846* ... v. 1, p. 317. See also "Notes of a Visit of H.M. Ship *Samarang* under Captain Sir E. Belcher to the Batanes and the Madjicosima Groups in 1843–1844," *Chinese Repository*, v. 13 (1844), pp. 150–63.

31. A full account of French negotiations, with documents, is found in F. Marnas: *La "Religion de Jésus (Iaso Ja-kyo)" Ressuscitée au Japon dans la second moitié du XIXe siècle. Tome I, Première Partie: Aux Portes du Japon: Livre Premier: L'avante-post des îles Riu-kiu*, pp. 91–188. H. Cordier: "Les Français aux îles Lieo-K'ieou" *Mélanges d'Histoire et de géographie orientales*, v. 1 (1914), pp. 296–317. See also the letters of T.A. Forcade and A. T. Furet written from the mission at Naha.

32. M.C. Greene: "Correspondence between the Shogun of Japan, A.D. 1844, and William II of Holland," TASJ, v. 34 (1907), pt. 4, pp. 121–22.

33. Horie Yasuzo: *Nihon shihon shugi no seiritsu* (Formation of Japanese Capitalism), p. 106, note 4.

34. Marnas, *op. cit.*, v. 1, p. 133 (text of notes exchanged with Shuri).

35. Clifford, *op. cit.*, p. 3. An account of Lieutenant Clifford's career may be found in J.H. Bernard: *The Bernards of Kerry*, pp. 85–90.

36. Diaries, journals, letters, and official dispatches prepared by his contemporaries (American, French, and British missionaries, foreign service officers, naval diplomats, and seamen) provide an important check upon the missionary-doctor's voluminous letters and communications to the press. After a half-century lapse missionary-biographers undertook to reconstruct Bettelheim's life, drawing on the Bettelheim papers and upon communications with his family. For citations of official correspondence see principally W.G. Beasley: *Great Britain and the Opening of Japan, 1834–1838*, pp. 77–82. S.W. Williams' "Journal of the Perry Expedition to Japan, 1853–1854" (TASJ, v. 37, pt. 2 (1910), pp. 149–71) is the most important contemporary journal. Bettelheim reveals himself to an unusual degree in his long letters. For his apotheosis as "the greatest humanitarian since Christ" one must consult the letters of his family and the publications and letters of later missionary-biographers. I am indebted especially to Rev. H.B. Schwartz: *The Loochoo Islands: A Chapter in Missionary History* and to Rev. Earl R. Bull: "The Trials of the Trail Blazer, Bettelheim" and "Bettelheim as Physician, Jew, Layman and Transactor," in the *Japan Evangelist*, v. 32 (1925), no. 2., pp. 51–59; no. 3., pp. 87–93; no. 5, pp. 153–59.

37. Bull: "The Trials of the Trail Blazer, Bettelheim," p. 54.

38. Clifford, *op. cit.*, "Copy of Instructions given for the Guidance of Dr. Bettelheim," pp. 2–3.

39. Clifford, *op. cit.*, "Letter VII," p. 3.

40. On Bettelheim's "direct methods" see "Letter from B.J. Bettelheim, M.D., giving an account of his residence and missionary labours in Lewchew during the last three years," *Chinese Repository*, v. 19 (1850), pp. 17–49.

41. Higaonna Kanjun: "Dr. Bettelheim's Study of the Loochoo Language," *Japan Mag.*, v. 16, no. 3 (Dec., 1925), pp. 78–81. see also Higaonna "The Bible in the Loochoo Dialect" in the preceding issue (no. 2, Nov., 1925), pp. 50–52.

42. Bull: "The Trials of the Trail Blazer, Bettelheim," p. 57.

43. For a summary of London's consideration of Bettelheim and its policy toward Okinawa, see Beasley, *op. cit.*

44. A.L. Halloran: *Wae Yang Jin: Eight Months' Journal Kept on Board One of Her Majesty's Sloops of War during Visits to Loochoo, Japan and Pootoo*, pp. 26–30. Halloran, present during the interviews, gives an informal summary of the incident. Beasley, *op. cit.*, provides the texts of official reports.

45. "Cruise of the U.S. Sloop-of-War Preble, Commander James Glynn, to Napa and Nangasacki" *U.S. Senate Documents: 32nd Congress, 1st Session (1851–1852)*, v. 9, Ex. Doc. #59, Ser. 6 20., pp. 44–45.

46. *Foreign Office Correspondence*, v. 155. Bonham to F.O., no. 58, 4 May 1849. Cited by Beasley, *op. cit.*, p. 78.

47. Rev. George Smith, Bishop of Victoria: *Ten Weeks in Japan*, p. 339.

48. *Ibid.*, p. 341.

49. Beasley, *op. cit.*, p. 81.

50. Earl Swisher: *China's Management of the American Barbarians: A Study of Sino-American Relations, 1841–1861, with Documents*, p. 202. The piracy case is recorded in *U.S. Senate Documents, 34th U.S. Congress, 1st Session*, Ex. Doc. 99, pp. 12–183.

CHAPTER SEVEN

1. "Cruise of the U.S. Sloop-of-war Preble, [etc.]," pp. 76–77.

2. *Ibid.*, p. 78.

3. "Correspondence Relative to the Naval Expedition to Japan, 1853–1854; Mr. Conrad to Mr. Kennedy, 5 November, 1852" *U.S. Senate Documents, 33rd Congress, 2nd Session (1854–1855)*, v. 6, Ex. Doc. no. 34, Serial 751, p. 5.

4. *Ibid.*, p. 6.

5. *Ibid.*, pp. 7–9.

6. *Ibid.*, pp. 12–13 (Perry to Secretary of the Navy).

7. *Ibid.*, p. 15 (Everett to Perry).

8. W.L. Schwartz: "Commodore Perry at Okinawa: From the Unpublished Diary of a British Missionary," *Am. Hist. Rev.*, v. 51, no. 2 (January 1946), p. 262.

9. F.L. Hawks (ed.): *Narrative of the Expedition of an American Squadron to the China Seas and Japan, Performed in the Years 1852, 1853 and 1854, under the Command of Commodore M.C. Perry, United States Navy*, Washington, 1856, v. 1, p. 153.

10. W.L. Schwartz, *op. cit.*, p. 266.

11. S.W. Williams: "A Journal of the Perry Expedition to Japan, (1853–1854)," TASJ, v. 37, pt. 2 (1910), p. 9.

12. Hawks, *op. cit.*, p. 155.

13. Williams, *op. cit.*, p. 11.

14. Hawks, *op. cit.*, p. 159.

15. Williams, *op. cit.*, p. 13–14.

16. *Ibid., loc. cit.*

17. "Correspondence" (Perry to Secretary of Navy), pp. 28–29.

18. Williams, *op. cit.*, p. 15.

19. *Ibid., op. cit.*, p. 17.

20. *Ibid., op .cit.*, p. 20.

21. W.L. Schwartz, *op. cit.*, p. 268.

22. Hawks, *op. cit.*, p. 159, ftnt.

23. *Ibid., op. cit.*, p. 191.

24. *Ibid., loc. cit.*

25. Williams, *op. cit.*, p. 23.

26. W.L. Schwartz: *op. cit.*, p. 269.

27. *Ibid.*, p. 270.

28. Williams, *op .cit.*, p. 41.

29. Hawks, *op. cit.*, p. 215.

30. Williams, *op. cit.*, p. 42.

31. *Ibid., op. cit.*, p. 43.

32. E.V. Warriner: *Voyager to Destiny*, Ch. 14, "Ashore on Okinawa," pp. 109–16 *et. seq.*

33. Hawks, *op. cit.*, p. 275.

34. *Ibid., op. cit.*, p. 276.

35. *Ibid., op. cit.*, p. 278.

36. Williams, *op. cit.*, p. 71.

37. *Ibid., op. cit.*, p. 81.

38. "Correspondence," *op. cit.*, p. 81 (Perry to Secty. Navy, No. 30., Hongkong, Dec. 24, 1953).

39. *Ibid.*, p. 109 (Perry to Secty. Navy, no. 39, Naha, Jan. 25, 1854).

40. *Ibid.*, pp. 112–13 (Secty. Navy to Perry, Washington, May 30, 1854).

41. Williams, *op. cit.*, pp. 96–97.

42. Hawks, *op. cit.*, p. 493.

43. Williams, *op. cit.*, p. 237.

44. *Ibid.*, p. 238.

45. Hawks, *op. cit.*, p. 495.

46. Spalding: *The Japan Expedition: Japan and Around the World* [etc.], p. 342.

47. Hawks, *op. cit.*, p. 495–496.

48. Spalding, *op. cit.*, p. 337.

49. Hawks, *op. cit.*, p. 498 ftnt.

50. Williams, *op. cit.*, p. 248.

51. Spalding, *op. cit.*, p. 337.

52. Hawks, *op. cit.*, p. 498.

53. H.T. Whitney, M.D.: "Protestant Mission Work in the Loo Choo Islands," *Chinese Recorder*, v. 18 (Dec., 1887), p. 472. For a postwar evaluation, published in Japanese by contemporary Okinawan contributors to commemorate Bettelheim's departure, see "Dr. Bernard Jean Bettelheim" [English title], *Okinawa Times*, Sept. 1, 1954. 25 pps. illus. I am indebted to Mr. Bull's accounts (in the *Japan Evangelist*, v. 32, 1925) for the following notes on Bettelheim's subsequent career:

Bettelheim abandoned the Loo Choo Mission, he asserts, because of failing eyesight, publication problems for his translations of the Gospels, and the education of his children. He rejoined his family at Hongkong and sailed for England via Java and the South Pacific. While the ship put in at Bermuda for a prolonged period of repair, Bettelheim crossed to New York, liked the United States, sent for his family, and settled for two years in New York and Connecticut. He lectured widely, and at one time persuaded a Missionary Society to launch a campaign (for which he acted as secretary) to raise $5000 on his behalf.

"Dear Friends [he wrote], let me tell you, what I ask of you, properly considered, is not that you should commence a new work in Japan, but *that you may please to help me continue and extend labors already carried on in a Japanese principality, for the last eight or nine years—labors, too, which under God, have been abundantly blessed.*" (Bull: "Trials of the Trail Blazer, Bettelheim," p. 91).

On December 18, 1860, Bettelheim was at last ordained (as a Presbyterian), and sent to Illinois on Home Mission work. He became a Mason (Lodge 294, Pontiac, Ill.) and on April 16, 1863, enlisted as a major and surgeon in the 106th Regiment of the Illinois Volunteer Infantry, then at Helena, Arkansas. Bull makes no further mention of Bettelheim's ministerial work. After Vicksburg, the capture of Little Rock, and the war's termination, Bettelheim opened a drug store at Odell, Ill., lecturing occasionally on conditions in the Ryukyus and Japan. In February 1868 he moved again, to Brookfield, Missouri, where he died of pneumonia on February 9, 1870.

Adm. Putyatin's secretary, Goncharov, met Bettelheim during the Russian visit, Jan. 31 to Feb. 9, 1854. He felt that Okinawa demonstrated that "a Golden Age is still possible" and that it represented "the one remaining bit of the ancient world as represented by the Bible or by Homer. . . ." He noted with foreboding that "the new civilization is already touching this forgotten, ancient little corner of the world." Describing Perry's token force and its claims (which amused him), he observed that " . . . everything is ready; at one door stands religion with a cross and rays of light . . . and at the other, the 'people of the United States,' with their cotton and woollen goods, guns, cannons, and various other arms of the new civilization." Basil Hall's praise had scarcely done sufficient justice to the Okinawans, Goncharov had thought, and he was therefore astonished by Bettelheim's rancorours comment. He concluded that an accurate appraisal of Okinawa lay somewhere between Hall's admiration and

Bettelheim's condemnation. The missionary is described as "a thinnish man with a Semitic face, not pale but 'faded,' and with hands that looked somewhat like birds' claws, and a voluble talker. There was nothing attractive about the man; in his conversation, in his tone, in the stories he told, in his greeting, there is a sort of dryness—a slyness—something which made one feel unsympathetic. . . . I began to get suspicious of this all-embracing criticism of the Ryukyuan people. Our crew told me later that when they asked the inhabitants 'Where lives the missionary?', they [the Okinawans] showed obvious dislike for him, and one of them said, in English, 'Bad man! Very bad man!' Thus, in responding to their dislike of himself the preacher probably exaggerated his account of Ryukyuan vices." (From an abstract, by Ella Embree, of Goncharov's *Fregat Pallada* [1916 ed.], Ch. IV, "Likeyskiye Ostrova" or "Visit to the Ryukyus," pp. 233–70.)

54. Swisher: *op. cit.*, "Memorial: Fukien Officials Transmit an Okinawan Account of Commodore Perry's Visit to Naha," pp. 296–97.

CHAPTER EIGHT

1. A.T. Furet: "Lettres" [to Leon de Rosny, dated at Hongkong, 1854, and Naha, 1858], *Revue de l'Orient et de l'Algerie*, Ser. 2, v. 16 (1854), pp. 399–401; Ser. 2, v. 18 (1856), pp. 22–28, 127–32; Ser. 3, v. 2 (1858), pp. 109–15.

Lettres à M. Leon de Rosny sur l'archipel Japonais et la Tartarie Orientale, par le Pere Furet . . . (1860), "Le Grande Ile Lou-Tchou" (Hongkong 12 Oct., 1955), pp. 3–21; "Les Lettres de Lou-Tschou" (Naha, 1 June 1858), pp. 23–30; Une Excursion à Lou-Tchou" (Naha, 28 June, 1858), pp. 31–40.

F. Marnas: *op. cit.*, v. 1, pp. 253–90.

2. Official translations of the oaths of allegiance to Satsuma sworn by the king (Sho Tai) and the Council of State were laid before General Grant during his consideration of the Ryukyu sovereignty controversy. See *Japan Weekly Mail*, v. 3, no. 42, p. 1383, and no. 43, p. 1421 (Oct. 25., 1879); F. Brinkley: "The Story of the Riu-Kiu (Loo-choo) Controversy," *Chrysanthemum and Phoenix*, v. 3, pt. 3 (1883), pp. 122–53.

3. "Coronation of the King of Loochoo," *China Review*, v. 7 no. 4 (1878–1879), pp. 283–84.

4. For the Chinese view of the Formosa incident and subsequent Sino-Japanese controversy, see T.F. Tsiang: "Sino-Japanese Diplomatic Relations, 1870–1894," *The Chinese Social and Political Science Review*, v. 17, no. 1 (April, 1933), pp. 16–53. Tsiang ignores the history of Okinawan relations with Satsuma. A summary translation of fifty-one letters, notes and memoranda by Viceroy Li Hung-chang are published in C. Leavenworth: *op. cit.*, pp. 159–86.

Japan's point of view is reflected in Brinkley's "Story of the Riu Kiu (Loo-Choo) Contoroversy" cited in Note 2, above. See also Ariga Nagao's chapter on "Diplomacy" in Alfred Stead: *Japan by the Japanese*, pp. 151–72. Kuzuu Yoshihisa: *Nisshi Koshogai Shi* (Brief History of Diplomatic Relations between Japan and China), v. 1, pp. 134–35. Okinawan accounts will be found in Iha's *Ryukyu Ko Kon-ki* (pp. 485–97), Ota's *Okinawa Kensei Go-ju-nen* (p. 23 *et seq.*), and Majikina's *Okinawa Issen-nen Shi* (pp. 625–39).

On diplomatic, legal, and military aspects of American involvement, see film microcopies of records in the National Archives, especially covering General Charles W. LeGendre's activities. Microcopy 77: *Diplomatic Instructions of the Department of State,* Roll 39, v. 2 (Sept. 13, 1867—Dec. 27, 1878); Roll 40, v. 3 (Jan. 1, 1879—Feb. 28, 1855. Microcopy 92: *Despatches from United States Ministers to China,* Rolls 25 to 63, (Jan. 3, 1867—Dec. 5, 1882); Microcopy 100: *Despatches from United States Consuls in Amoy,* Rolls 4 to 9, (May 28, 1868 to Oct. 27, 1893); H.B. Morse: *International Relations of the Chinese Empire,* v. 2, *The Period of Submission,* 1861–1893, pp. 270–75, 321–22; U.S. Department of State: *Messages and Documents, 1879,* pp. 606–7, 637–38; *Messages and Documents, 1880,* pp. 194, 199–202, 686; *Messages and Documents, 1881,* p. 230. J.B. Moore: *History and Digest of International Arbitrations to which the United States has been a Party,* v. 5, pp. 4857, 5048. Payson J. Treat: *Diplomatic Relations Between the United States and Japan,* 1853–1895, v. 1, pp. 473–83, 493–98, 541–56, 567–69; v. 2, pp. 25, 71–74, 98–104, 126–27, 141–44, 179–80. Edward H. House: *The Japanese Expedition to Formosa* (Tokyo, 1875), pp. 192–231. The most concise analysis is Hyman Kublin's "The Attitude of China During the Liu-Ch'iu Controversy, 1871–1881," *Pacific Historical Review,* v. 18, no. 2 (May, 1949), pp. 213–31.

5. House, *op. cit.,* Text of the *Agreement,* pp. 204–5.

6. *Dajokwan Nisshi,* no. 70 (Oct. 16, 1872). Subsequent references in no. 76 (Oct. 29) and no. 89 (Oct. 31).

7. "Memorial to the Throne" published in *Peking Gazette,* Dec. 15, 1874. Trans. in *Japan Weekly Mail,* v. 6, no. 4 (Jan. 23, 1875), p. 70.

8. "On the Ryukyu Embassy," *Tokyo Nichi Nichi Shimbun,* March 20 and May 25, 1875, quoted with commentary in *Japan Weekly Mail,* v. 6, no. 22 (May 29, 1875), pp. 466–67.

9. H. Ogawa: *Meiji Gaikoku Yoroku* (Diplomacy of the Meiji Era), Tokyo (1920), p. 69.

10. W.W. McLaren: "Japanese Government Documents," TASJ, v. 42, pt. 1 (1941), pp. 477–78.

11. *Ibid.,* p. 287.

12. *Japan Weekly Mail,* v. 2, New Ser., no. 2 (Jan. 11, 1879), p. 42.

CHAPTER NINE

1. Ota Chofu: *Okinawa Kensei Goju-nen* (Fifty Years of Provincial Administration in Okinawa), pp. 45–46. I am indebted to this work for most of the facts cited for the period 1878–1927.

2. *Japan Weekly Mail,* v. 3, no. 15 (April 12, 1879), p. 454.

3. *Ibid.,* no. 24 (June 14, 1879), p. 766.

4. Tsiang, *op. cit.,* p. 37.

5. A.M. Pooley (ed.): *Secret Memoirs of Count Tadasu Hayashi: G.C.V.O.,* pp. 316–17.

6. Ota, *op. cit.,* p. 4.

7. *Ibid.*, pp. 59 *et seq.*

8. B.W. Bax: *The Eastern Seas: Being a Narrative of the Voyage of H.M.S. "Dwarf" In China, Japan and Formosa*, pp. 96–103.

9. F.H.H. Guillemard: *Cruise of the Marchesa to Kamschatka & New Guinea*, v. 1, pp. 26–63.

10. Ishimoto Iwane: "Miyako Shima no Doitsu shosen sonan kyuko kinnen-hi" (The Monument to the German Warship on Miyako Island) and "Dokutei Shaon kinen-hin sono ta" (Commemorative Tokens of Imperial German Gratitude, and related matters), *Nanto*, Issue no. 3 (1944), pp. 1–95.

11. B.H. Chamberlain: "The Luchu Islands and Their Inhabitants," *Geographical Journal*, v. 5 (1895), pp. 289–319, 446–61, 534–45.

CHAPTER TEN

1. For bibliography and historical data on the vital emigration problem, see James L. Tigner's study of *The Okinawans in Latin America* (Washington, D.C., 1954). (Scientific Investigations in the Ryukyu Islands, Report No. 7), 660 pp.

2. For a brief study of Okinawan names and name changes under Japanese influence see U.S. Gov., OSS: *Okinawan Studies No. 3, The Okinawas [sic] of the Loo Choo Islands: a Japanese Minority Group*, pp. 60–68. For a summary discussion of cleavages, segregation, Japanese intolerance, etc., see pp. 68–83; also Toyama and Ikeda: "The Okinawa-Naichi Relationship" *Social Progress in Hawaii* (Honolulu) v. 14 (1950) pp. 51–65.

3. H.B. Schwartz, *op. cit.*

4. Shikiba Ryusaburo: *On Ryukyu Culture (Ryukyu no Bunka)*, pp. 1–40. *Kogei* (Tokyo) no. 49 (Jan., 1935); no. 99 (Oct., 1939); no. 100, no. 103 (Oct., 1940). *Gekkan Mingei* (Tokyo), no. 8 (Nov., 1939); no. 12 (March, 1940); no. 21 (Dec., 1940).

CHAPTER ELEVEN

1. For detailed analysis of the situation at Tokyo, see Robert J.C. Butow's *Japan's Decision to Surrender* (Stanford, 1954).

2. Maeshiro Bokei (Buhei Maehira): unpublished *Report to the Arts and Monuments Adviser, U.S. Department of State*, mimeographed, dated June 2, 1953. Six of the Okinawan deputy custodians were killed in the Battle for Okinawa. Chief Custodian Maeshiro was picked up by an American unit on July 10, interned and questioned. Released, he picked his way back to the Shuri ruins to discover that an American counter-intelligence group, its Japanese-American interpreters, and its Okinawan employees had scoured the estate in search of unusual curios. There was evidence that some of the treasure had survived the bombing, but only a few fragments of ceramics, lacquerware, and damaged paintings remained on the site. Some of the treasures, including royal crowns, magatama, and a priceless edition of the *Omoro Zoshi* texts were subsequently offered for sale to certain American museums. Of these some were traced and recovered.

3. Okinawan Times (pub.): *Tetsu no Bofu* (Typhoon of Steel), Tokyo (1950), 487 pp. Walter Karig (ed.): *Battle Report: Victory in the Pacific*, chs. 29–39, pp. 343–449. Gilbert Cant: *The Great Pacific Victory*, ch. 23, pp. 355–82. F.T. Miller: *History of World War II*, ch. 102, "Okinawa," pp. 920–37. Admiral Sir Bruce A. Fraser: "The Contribution of the British Pacific Fleet to the Assault on Okinawa, 1945," *London Gazette* (Supplement, June 2, 1948), pp. 3289–314. Nichols, Charles S., and Henry I. Shaw: *Okinawa: Victory in the Pacific* (Historical Br., G-3 Div. H.Q., U.S. Marine Corps), Washington (1955), 332 pp.

BIBLIOGRAPHY

A NOTE ON OKINAWAN STUDIES AND
REFERENCE MATERIALS

The present list is designed to direct attention to the range of materials available for studies concerning the history of the Ryukyu archipelago and the Okinawan people before the period of American occupation. It is not a "bibliographer's bibliography." It does not include references to publications in the physical and biological sciences, nor does it attempt to list the voluminous body of materials issued by the United States military government since 1945.

Priceless archives of the Ryukyu Kingdom and of the Japanese provincial government were destroyed at Naha and Shuri in 1945. Scholars must henceforth rely chiefly upon Japanese transcriptions preserved in texts prepared before and during World War II. Fortunately, major collections of original documents relating to the Satsuma clan administration of the Ryukyu dependency (1609–1879) are still to be found at Tokyo, Kyoto, Fukuoka, and Kagoshima.

Selected Japanese references noted here include works consulted in preparation of this summary history. For an extensive bibliography of Japanese and Western language references (including the science literature) one must consult the mimeographed checklist of some 3,500 items prepared in 1952 for the Pacific Science Board of the National Research Council. A preliminary search was undertaken in forty-one public libraries and private collections throughout Japan. The work was done at my direction, with the superb assistance of Dr. Nagamine Mitsuna, Director of the Library Science Research Office, Tokyo University, and with the cordial coöperation of Dr. Kanamori Tokujiro, Director of the National Diet Library; Mr. Kuwabara Makoto, Librarian for the Kokusai Bunka Shinkokai; and Mr. Ogura Chikao, Assistant Librarian at Kyoto University.

For the accumulation of references in Western languages I am indebted principally to Messrs. P. M. Bettens, E.E.H. Ord, F. Ratliff, and C.C. Thorp, members of a graduate seminar in History at the University of California (Berkeley) in 1954.

Important Chinese accounts of embassies to the Ryukyu Islands are included, but no thorough studies of Ryukyu-Chinese relations based on Chinese sources have come to attention in preparation of this work.

Private journals, public reports, and official correspondence concerning the Ryukyus contribute much to an understanding of the process of Western penetration of the Far East. I have included here scattered references—often only a sentence or two—found in the early Portuguese, Spanish, and English records of the 16th and 17th centuries. The 18th century yields little until its closing decades. Then for a century Okinawa was caught up in the rivalries of the European powers as they attempted first to penetrate China, then Japan, eager to lay a treaty basis for commerce and mission activities governed by Western legal concepts.

Western notices of the Ryukyus from about 1780 to 1880 fall into three categories: travel accounts, mission literature, and official reports. The Industrial Revolution brought new conditions of literacy and leisure; stay-at-home readers devoured tales of exploration and adventurous travel in every part of the world, and to this public were directed the handsomely illustrated accounts of Basil Hall and his companions, and the quasi-official reports of Broughton and Beechey. The mission literature—French, British, and American—was generated by an evangelical fervor, which the new leisure and industrial prosperity could afford to support. Okinawa was believed to be the threshhold over which Christianity could for a second time penetrate Japan. Mission accounts must be read with critical reserve, for the belief that "ends justify means" is found to color evangelical reports and representations. The official correspondence relating to the Ryukyus clearly demonstrates how thoroughly intermixed missionary interests and political and military activity had become in the effort to open Japan and China to Western trade and diplomatic intercourse.

Perry's voluminous *Narrative* marked a turning point. Much space was devoted to the activities of the American squadron in the Ryukyus, but Perry's spectacular success in breaching the walls about Japan quickly diverted British and American attention from Okinawa, though France maintained her interest until 1858.

After the Ryukyus were annexed by Japan in 1879, the Japanese began to publish extensively concerning the new prefecture, gradually increasing the volume, quality, and diversity of their studies of Okinawan history, folklore, language, economics, geography, the natural sciences, and the arts and crafts. Western notices dwindled in number and became specialized, emphasizing for a time political problems relating to the Sino-Japanese sovereignty dispute. An American (Charles Leavenworth) published a brief and fragmentary *History of Loo Choo* in 1905. German and French scholars produced a series of valuable studies in history and ethnography just before World War I and again before World War II. A series of missionary pamphlets and brief historical notices was published by the two Americans (Henry B. Schwartz and Earl R. Bull) who resided in Okinawa in the period 1906–24.

World War II again brought Okinawa and Okinawan studies into some prominence. Military histories recount the Battle for Okinawa in great detail. Political and social studies are beginning to be made in the universities, and the Pacific Science Board series of scientific studies in the Ryukyu Islands (SIRI) has pointed the way to a new era of interest in this strategic point on the western Pacific frontier.

Basil Hall Chamberlain made a first "Contribution to a Bibliography of Luchu" in 1896, and Charles S. Leavenworth appended a list of references to his brief study *The Loochoo Islands* published at Shanghai in 1905.

In 1914 Edmund M.H. Simon published the first important review of Okinawan studies as "Beiträge zür kenntnist der Riu-kiu Inseln" in *Beiträge zür Kulturgesellschaft* (Leipzig, v. XXVIII, pp. 16–162), and in 1940 Rolf Binkenstein at Tokyo published "Okinawa-Studien" in the *Monumenta Nipponica* (v. III, pp. 554–566), later revised and issued privately at Berkeley, California, in September, 1954.

During World War II agencies of the United States government prepared handbooks and bibliographies for use in psychological-warfare work, and in the training of men for military-government duty. For example, the Research and Analysis Branch of the Office of Strategic Services (OSS) published *Okinawan Studies*, an odd compendium, in several revisions and variant titles (e.g., "The Okinawas [*sic*] of the Loochoo Islands: Japanese Minority Group," illustrated by photographs of "typical" Okinawans, taken from the Honolulu police files), which undertook to explore cleavages within Japan which might be exploited for propaganda purposes. The U.S. Navy Department, Office of the Chief of Naval Operations, issued a comprehensive *Civil Affairs Handbook: The Ryukyu (Loochoo) Islands* (OpNav 13–31, Washington, D.C., 1944), compiled under the direction of Dr. George P. Murdock of Yale University.

Materials for the Navy's *Handbook* were drawn from the reference-abstract files of the Institute of Human Relations at Yale University. A *Critical Bibliography of the Ryukyu Islands* was submitted to the University of Hawaii by J.W. Moran as a Master's thesis, in 1946. In 1953–54 a *Reference List of Books and Articles in English, French and German* was prepared as a seminar project in the Department of History of the University of California at Berkeley. This list, with minor revisions, is the basis for the present Bibliography.

Bettens, Ord, Ratliff and Thorp: *The Ryukyu Islands, a Reference List of Books and Articles in English, French and German*) U. California, (Berkeley), 1954. Dittoed. 33 pp.).

Binkenstein, Rolf A.A.: *Beitrage zu einer Kulturhistorischen Bibliographie der Ryukyu (Okinawa)—Inseln.* Berkeley, Cal. (1954) photolith. 66 pp. Important listing of Japanese, Chinese and Okinawan works. Romanization of names offers problems, e.g.

"Agaionna" for *Higaonna;* "Shideharu Hiroshi" for *Shidehara Tan;* "Makina" for *Majikina.*

Kerr, George H., with Higa Shuncho, Kudeken Kenji, *et al.: The Ryukyu Islands. A Preliminary Checklist of Reference Materials in Japanese and Western Languages, arranged Alphabetically by Author.* Tokyo (1952) Mimeo. 291 pp.

Murdoch, *Cmdr.* G.P., *et al,* ed.: Bibliography appended to U.S. *Navy Civil Affairs Handbook*—Ryukyu (Loochoo) Islands OpNav 13-3 Washington (1944).

Nihon Minzokugaku Kyokai, *pub.* "Okinawa Kenkyu, tokushu" (Okinawan Studies, special number) *Minzokugaku Kenkyu* Tokyo v. XV no. 2 (1950) pp. 67–230; bibl. pp. 121–135.

Yonaguni Zenzo: *Okinawa Rekishi Nempyo* (Chronological Tables of Okinawan History) Tokyo (1953) 132 pp.

Standard bibliographies for Japan and China (Wenckstern, Nachod, Cordier, etc.) carry references to the Ryukyus under appropriate headings.

A

Abeel, David, *Journal of a Residence in China and the Neighboring Countries from* 1829 *to* 1833. N.Y. (1834 *ed.*) Ch. XVI "Loo Choo Islands" pp. 361–367; (1836 *ed.* Ch. XVII "Loo Choo Islands" pp. 347–353.

Adams, Arthur, "Notes from a Journal of Research into the Natural History of the Countries Visited during the Voyage of H.M.S.Samarang, under the Command of Sir E. Belcher, C.B." [1843–1846] [See *Belcher.*]

Adams, Will: "The Logbook of Will'm Adams, 1614–1619, and Related Documents." ed. by J.C. Purnell. *JSL* v. XIII (1915) pp. 156, 169–170, 308, *passim.*

Alexander, Robert Percival, *The Political Status of the Ryukyu Islands* (Unpublished M.A. thesis) George Washington University, Washington, D. C. (August 1951).

Allen, Herbert G. "The Lewchew Islands" *China Review* (Hongkong) v. VIII (1879) pp. 140–143.

"Amicus" (pseud.), "Chinese Account of the Loo-Choo" *Indo-Chinese Gleaner* (Malacca) No. 7 (January 1819) pp. 4–11.

Appleman, Roy, [*et al*]: *The U.S. Army in World War II: Okinawa: the Last Battle:* v. II, Pt. 11. Historical Div. Dept. Army, Washington (1948) 529 pp.

Asakawa Kanichi, *ed.: Documents of Iriki, Illustrative of the Development of Feudal Institutions of Japan.* New Haven (1929) (On Shimazu revenues) pp. 337, 358, 363.

Aston, W.G.: "On the Loochuan and Aino Languages" *Church Missionary Intelligencer* London (1879).

B

Baelz, Ernst von, "Die Riu-Kiu-Insulaner, die Aino und andere kaukasierähnliche Reste in Ostasien" *Korrespondenze-Blatt der Deutschen Gessellchaft für Anthropologie Ethnologie und Urgeschichte* v. XLII (1911) pp. 187–191.

Balfour, Frederick Henry: "The Kingdom of Liuchiu" *Waifs and Strays from the Far East* Shanghai and London (1876) pp. 55–62.

Ballantine, Joseph W.: "The Future of the Ryukyus" *Foreign Affairs* (N.Y.) v. XXXI no. 4 (July 1953) pp. 663–674.

Barbosa, Duarte: *The Book of Duarte Barbosa*. An Account of the Countries bordering on the Indian Ocean and their Inhabitants, written by Duarte Barbosa and completed about the year 1518 A.D. Trans. from the Portuguese text, first published in 1812 A.D. by the Royal Academy of Sciences at Lisbon . . . Edited and annotated by Mansel Longworth Dames. Hakluyt Society, Ser. II v. 49, London (1921) v. II pp. 215–216 "Lequeos."

Barrett, George: "Report on Okinawa: a Rampart We Built" *NY Times Magazine* (Sept. 21, 1952) pp. 9–11; 62–65.

Barton, T.: "Okinawa Preview of Japan" *Mag. Digest* v. XXVI (Sep. 1945) pp. 33–42.

Bax, Capt. B.W.: *The Eastern Seas: being a Narrative of the Voyage of H.M.S. "Dwarf" in China, Japan and Formosa* London (1875) pp. 95–103.

Beasley, William G.: *Great Britain and the Opening of Japan, 1834–1858* London (1951) pp. 77–82.

Beechey, Frederic W.: *Narrative of a Voyage to the Pacific and Beering's Straits . . . Performed in H.M.S. Blossom in the Years 1825, 26, 27, 28.* London (1831) v. II, pp. 138–226, 446–512, 657–658. See Huish, Robert (*ed.*), for condensed 1836 version of Beechey's *Narrative*.

Belcher, Sir Edward: *Narrative of the Voyage of H.M.S. Samarang during the Years 1843–46, Accompanied with a Brief Vocabulary of the Principal Languages . . with Notes on the Natural History of the Islands by Arthur Adams* London (1848) v. I pp. 73–97; 312–323. v. II pp. 51–72; 298–321; 438–444; 467–470.

——: "Notes on the Batanes and Madjicosima Islands" [Miyako in 1843] *Chinese and Japanese Repository* (London) v. III (July 1, 1865) pp. 313–326.

Bell, Otis W.: "Play Fair with the Okinawans" *Christian Century* 20 Jan. 1954.

Bennett, Henry Stanley: "The Impact of Invasion and Occupation on the Civilians of Okinawa" *U.S. Naval Institute Proceedings* v. 72 (Feb. 1946) pp. 263–275.

[Benyowsky, Mauritius Augustus, *Count de*]: *Memoirs and Travels of Mauritius Augustus, Count de Benyowsky, with an Introduction, Notes and Bibliography by Capt. S. Pasfield Oliver* London (1904) pp. 376–393; 428.

Bernard, John Henry: *The Bernards of Kerry* Dublin (1922) "The Clifford Family" pp. 85–90 (on H.J. Clifford, founder of the Loo Choo Naval Mission).

Bettelheim, Bernard J.: "Letter from B.J. Bettelheim, M.D., giving an account of his residence and missionary labors in Lewchew during the last three years" [1849] *China Repository* (Canton) v. XIX (1850) pp. 17–49; 57–90.

——: *Letter to Reverend Peter Parker, M.D.* Canton (1852) 42 pp.

[——]: "Loochoo Naval Mission: Extract from the Report for 1850–1851, written by Dr. Bettelheim, Missionary at Napa" *North China Herald* No. 78 Shanghai (24 January 1852) (Reprinted in *Shanghai Almanac and Miscellany for* 1853).

[For further correspondence by Bettelheim, and relating to him, see Clifford: *The Claims of Loochoo on British Liberality*].

(N.B. Bettelheim's Journals were destroyed by fire; ms copies exist made by E.R. Bull, Shawnee, Perry County, Ohio (1956). Other Bettelheim mss and memorabilia in custody of Mrs. Bess Bettelheim Pratt, Los Angeles, Cal.) Copies of B's. Gospel translations are in British Museum and Tokyo University collections.

BIBLIOGRAPHY

Biernatzki, K.L., "Beiträge zur geographischen Kunde von Japan und den Lutschu-Inseln" *Zeitschrift für Allgemeine Erdkunde* v. IV (1855) pp. 225–247.

Bingay, Malcolm W.: "Life in Loochoo" *Forum* v. 104, No. 1., pp. 44–45.

Binkenstein, Rolf: *Beitraege zu einer Kulturhistorischen Bibliographie der Ryukyu (Okinawa)—Inseln* Berkeley (1954) 66 pp. [Privately issued].

——: "Die Ryukyu-Expedition unter Shimazu Iehisa"*Monumenta Nipponica* (Tokyo) v. IV No. 2 (1941) pp. 296–302; 622–628.

——: "Okinawa-Studien" *Monumenta Nipponica* (Tokyo) v. III No. 2 (1940) pp. 194–206; 554–566.

——: "Zur Frage der Ryukyu-Gesandtschaften" *Monumenta Nipponica* (Tokyo) v. IV No. 1 (1941) pp. 256–269.

——: "Taichu Shonin" *Monumenta Nipponica* Tokyo (1943) v. VI, No. 1–2 pp. 219–232.

Birch, Walter deGray, *ed*: See D'Alboquerque.

Black John R.: *Young Japan* Yokohama (1880–1881) v. II "The King of Liu-kiu's Own Story" pp. 399–405; 421–445.

Blair, E.H. and J.A. Robertson: *The Philippine Islands, 1493–1803* Cleveland, Ohio (1903) v. III, p. 72 [Letter from Fray Diego de Herrera to Felipe II of Spain, dated Mexico, Jan. 16, 1570, urging conquest of China, Lequios, Jabas (Java) and Japan.]

Bocher, A.: *Les Premiers rapports de la France avec le Japon. Aventures d'un missionaire français aux îles Liou-tcheou (Japon) 1844–1846* Paris (1895) 24 pp.

Bowman, J.J.B.: "Account of the Wreck of the *Indian Oak*" *The Nautical Magazine and Naval Chronicle for 1841* London (1841) pp. 299–308; 385–394.

Bowring, *Dr.*: "The Madjicosima Islands. A Short Notice of the Madjicosima (Meiaco-shi-ma or Meia-koon-koomah) Islands" *JNCBRAS* (Shanghai) Part III (1851–52) Art. I (1852) pp. 1–8.

Boxer, Charles, *ed.*: *South China in the Sixteenth Century, being the Narratives of Galeote Pereira, Fr. Gaspar da Cruz, O.P., Fr. Martin de Rada, O.E.S.A. (1550–1575).* Hakluyt Society, London (1953) Second Ser. No. CVI pp. xl, xli, xliii.

Braibanti, Ralph: "The Outlook for the Ryukyus" *Far Eastern Survey* (N.Y.) v. XXII, No. 7 (June 1953) pp. 73–78.

Bridgman, E.C., "*Lewkew Kwo che leo*, a brief history of Lewchew, containing an account of the situation and extent of that country, its inhabitants, their manners, customs, institutions, etc." [Chou Huang's embassy notes, 1757] *Chinese Repository* v. VI (1837) pp. 113–118.

Brinkley, Frank: "Ryukyu Islands" [in "History of the Japanese People"] *Encyclopaedia Britannica* 14th *ed.* v. XIX (1950) p. 782.

——: "The Story of the Riukiu (Loo-choo) Complication" *Chrysanthemum and Phoenix* (Yokohama) v. III Pt. 3 (1883) pp. 122–153.

Broughton, William Robert: *A Voyage of Discovery to the North Pacific Ocean . . . in the Years 1795, 1796, 1797 and 1798* London (1804) Book I Appendix III a "Specimen of the Language of the Natives of the Lieuchieux Islands . . ." pp. 84–109; Book II, Ch. 1, pp. 199–211; Ch. 3. pp. 235–246.

Brown, V.H.: "Luchu Islands, Where Nine of Commodore Perry's Men Found a Last Resting Place" *China Weekly Review* (Shanghai) v. LV No. 3 (1930) pp. 88, 124.

Brumbaugh, T.T.: " 'God Forsaken' Okinawa" *Christian Century* v. LXVII No. 23 (June 7, 1950) pp. 700–701.

Brunton, Robert H.: "Notes Taken During a Visit to Okinawa Shima,—Loochoo Islands" TASJ (Yokohama) v. IV (1876) pp. 66–77.

Bull, Earl R.: "Bettelheim as Physician, Jew, Layman, and Transactor" *Japan Evangelist* (Tokyo) v. XXXI (1925) No. 5, pp. 153–159.

——: "The Trials of the Trail Blazer, Bettelheim" *Japan Evangelist* (Tokyo) v. XXXII (1925) No. 2, pp. 51–59; No. 3, pp. 87–93.

Burd, William W.: *Karimata—a Village in the Southern Ryukyus* Pacific Science Board (SIRI Ser. No. 3) National Research Council, Washington, D.C. (1952) 141 pp.

Burney, James: *A Chronological History of the Voyages and Discoveries in the South Sea or Pacific Ocean* London (1803–1813) v. II Pt. 2, ch. XV, pp. 260–268; v. III pp. 431–432.

C

Cammann, Schuyler: *China's Dragon Robes*, N.Y. (1952) pp. 157–158.

Cant, Gilbert: *The Great Pacific Victory—From the Solomons to Tokyo* N.Y. (1946) ch. XXIII "To the Last Line" pp. 355–382.

Chamberlain, Basil Hall: "A Comparison of the Japanese and Luchuan Languages" *TASJ* v. XXIII (1895) pp. 271–289.

——: "A Preliminary Notice of the Luchuan Language" *Journ. Anthropological Institute of Great Britain and Ireland* (London) v. XXVI (1879) pp. 45–59.

——: "A Quinary System of Notation Employed in Luchu on the Wooden Tallies Termed Sho-chu-ma" *Journ. Anthropological Institute of Great Britain and Ireland* v. XXVII (1898) pp. 383–385.

——: "Contributions to a Bibliography of Luchu" *TASJ* v. XXIV (1896) pp. 1–11.

——: Essay in Aid of a Grammar and Dictionary of the Luchuan Language (*Supplement to Vol. XXIII, TASJ*) (1895) 272 pp.

——: "On the Loochooan Language" *Report of the 64th Meeting of the British Association for the Advancement of Science* London (1895) pp. 789–790.

——: "On the Manners and Customs of the Loochooans" *TASJ* v. XXI (1893) pp. 271–289.

——: "The Luchu Islands and Their Inhabitants" *Geographical Journal* (London) v. V No. 4 (1895) pp. 289–319; 446–462; 534–545.

——: "Two Funeral Urns from Loochoo" *Journ. Anthropological Institute of Great Britain and Ireland* (London) v. XXIV (1895) pp. 58–59.

Chow, S.R.: "The Pacific After the War" *Foreign Affairs* (N.Y.) v. 26 (1942) pp. 71–86.

Clifford, H.J., ed.: *Loochoo Mission: Extracts from the Journal of the Society's Missionary, Dr. Bettelheim, 1850–1852* London (no date) 61 pp.

——: *The Claims of Loochoo on British Liberality* 5th ed. London (1850) 257 pp., Pagination irregular. Title page dated 1846, but items bear 1850 as latest date. Nineteen principal sections, with numerous subdivisions, present appeals for support and addresses by Lieutenant Clifford, founder of the Mission, extracts from diverse journals of voyages, shipwrecks, etc., letters to and from Bettelheim, Peter Parker and others concerned with the Mission, and a brief history of the organization. Extracts from letters, appearing elsewhere in the press, reflect considerable editorial tampering.

——: *The Seventh Report of the Loochoo Mission Society for 1851–52* London (1853) 32 pp. See also Clifford's "Vocabulary of the Language Spoken at the Great Loo Choo Island in the Japan Sea," a supplement to Hall's *Voyage to Loo Choo*, etc. (1818).

Clutterbuck, Walter J.: "The Lu-chu Islands" *Travel and Exploration* (London) v. IV No. 20 (1910) pp. 81–88.

[Cocks, Richard]: *The Diary of Richard Cocks, Cape Merchant in the English Factory in Japan, 1615–1622* Hakluyt Society, London (1883) v. I pp. 7–11; 14–15; v. II pp. 58–59; 166–167; 271–273. Edited by Edward Maunde Thompson. Tokyo ed. (1899)

Cogan, Henry, ed.: *The Voyages and Adventures of Ferdinand Mendez-Pinto Done into English by H.C. Gent* [in 1653] London (1947) pp. 220–223.

[Cole, Allen B., ed.]: *Diary of Edward Yorke McCauley* See McCauley.

Collis, Maurice: *The Grand Perigrination: Being the Life and Adventures of Fernão Mendes Pinto* London (1949) pp. 158–165.

Cordier, Henri: *Histoire de les rélations de la Chine avec les Puissances Occidentales . . . 1860–1902* Paris (1901–1902) v. I pp. 530–535; v. II pp. 579–580; v. III p. 215.

——: "Les Français aux îles Lieou-K'ieou" *Mélanges d'histoire et de géographie orientales* Paris (1914) v. I pp. 296–317.

——: "Les Français aux îles Lieou-K'ieou" *Bulletin de Géographie Historique et Descriptive* (Paris) v. XXV No. 3 (1911) pp. 410–425.

[Cortesão, Armando, ed.]: *The Suma Oriental of Tomé Pires* See Pires.

Cortesão, Armando: *Cartografia e Cartógrafos Portugueses dos seculos XV e XVI* Lisbon (1935) v. II, Plates XIV, XVII, XIX, XXII–III, XXVII–VIII, LI. (Early Portuguese maps showing the Ryukyus).

D

D'Alboquerque, Afonso: *The Commentaries of the Great Afonso D'Alboquerque, Second Viceroy of India.* Translated from the Portuguese edition of 1774, with notes and introduction by Walter deGray Birch. London, Hakluyt Society. (1880) v. III, pp. xiv–xxi; 88–89.

Dames, Mansel Longworth, ed. See Barbosa.

Davies, W.: *A Voyage of Discovery to the North Pacific Ocean: in which . . . the Coasts of Japan, the Lieuchieux and the adjacent isles, as well as the Coast of Corea have been examined and surveyed . . . performed in H.M.S. Sloop Providence and its tender in the Years 1795–1796 and 1798* London (1804).

deBarros, João: *Da Asia* Lisbon (1777) Decade I, liv. IX, Ch. 1, p. 288.

DeMailla, J.A.M.M.: *Histoire Générale de la Chine* Paris (1777) v. V pp. 514–515.

Dennett, Tyler: *Americans in Eastern Asia: A Critical Study of the Policy of the United States with Reference to China, Japan and Korea in the 19th Century.* N.Y. (1922) pp. 272–4; 438–9.

Denucé, J.: "Les îles Lequios (Formose et Riu-Kiu) et Ophir" *Bulletin de la Societé Royal Belge de Géographie* (Bruxelles) v. XXXI No. 6 (1907) pp. 435–461.

Dickins, F.V., and Lane-Poole, S.: *The Life of Sir Harry Parkes, KCB, GCMG* London (1894) v. II Ch. XXXI, pp. 186–199.

diMaria, L.: "Pozizione delle isole Liuschotten e Liu Kiu" *Cosmos di Cora* Torino (1873)

Döderlein, L.: "Die Liu-Kiu Insel Amami Oshima" *Mitteilungen der deutschen Gessellschaft für Natur -und Völkerkunde Ostasiens* (Yokohama) v. III, Nos. 23, 24 (1880–1881) pp. 103–117; 140–156.

Dumont d'Urville: *Voyage Autour du Monde* Paris (1857) v. I, pp. 390–405.

E

Eddis, W.: "Short Visit to Loo-Choo in November, 1818" [in the brig *Brothers*] *Indo-Chinese Gleaner* (Malacca) No. 7 (1819) pp. 1–4.

Eder, Mathias: "Neue Studien uber die Sprache der Ryukyu-Inseln" *Monumenta Serica* (Peking) v. IV, Fasc. 1 (1939) pp. 219–304.

Ellis, Henry: *Journal of the Proceedings of the late [Amherst] Embassy to China, comprising a Correct Narrative of the Public Transactions of the Embassy [etc.]* London (1817) pp. 469; 472–473; 477–479.

F

Fairbank, John and Teng, S.Y.: "On the Ch'ing Tributary System" *HJAS* v. VI No. 2 (June 1941) pp. 135–246.

Farre, Frederic, J.: "Medicine in Lewchew. Introduction of Vaccination" *Medical Times and Gazette* (London) v. VII (1853) pp. 136–138; 164–166; 188–190.

Ferrand, Gabriel S.: "Malaka, le Malayu et Malayur" *Journal Asiatique* Ser. II, v. XII Paris (1918) Appendix I, "L'île de Ghur—Lieou-K'ieou—Formose" pp. 126–133. (Quotes Arabic sources.)

Fink, Harold: "The Distribution of Blood Groups in Ryukyuans" *Am. Journ. Physical Anthropology* (Washington, D.C.) v. V, No. 2, n.s. (June 1947) pp. 159–163.

Fitzgerald, C.P.: *China: A Cultural History* N.Y. (1938) pp. 221–224. (On early Chinese interest in the Eastern Sea islands.)

Forçade, Theodore Augustin: *Lettre à M. Libois* (August 12, 1845) *Nouvelles Lettres Edifiantes des Missions de la Chine et des Indes Orientales, Annales de la Propagation de la Foi* (Lyons) v. XVIII (1846) pp. 363–383.

——: [Lettre de la Grande Loutchou] *Revue de l'Orient* (Paris) v. X, No. 10 (1846) pp. 257–258.

——: "Journal" *La Revue* [des missions Catholiques] (Lyons) 1885.

Ford, Clellan S.: "Occupation Experience on Okinawa" *Annals of the American Academy of Political and Social Science* (Phila.) v. 267 (Jan. 1950) pp. 175–183.

Fraser, *Admiral Sir* Bruce A.: "The Contribution of the British Pacific Fleet to the Assault on Okinawa, 1945" *London Gazette* (Suppelement) (June 2, 1948). pp. 3289–3314.

Freeman, Otis [ed.]: *Geography of the Pacific* [See Hacker, Walter B.]

Furet, Auguste Theodore: "Lettres" [to Leon de Rosny, dated Hongkong 1854, and

Nafa 1858] *Revue de l'Orient et de l'Algérie* (Paris) Ser. 2, v. XVI (1854) pp. 399–401; v. XVIII (1856) pp. 22–28; 127–132; Ser. 3 v. II (1856) pp. 109–115.

[——]: *Lettres à M. Léon de Rosny sur l'archipel Japonais et la Tartarie Orientale, par le Pere Furet, Missionaire apostolique au Japaon* . . . Paris (1860) "La grande Ile Lou-tchou" pp. 3–10 (Hongkong 12 Oct. 1835); "Les Lettres de Lou-Tchou" pp. 23–30 (Naha 1 June 1858); "Une Excursion à Lou-tchou" pp. 31–40 (Naha 28 June 1858).

Furness, William H.: "Life in the Luchu Islands" *Bulletin of the Free Museum of Sciences and Art of the University of Pennyslvania* (Phila.) v. II No. 1 (January 1899) pp. 1–28, 44–49.

Futara Yoshinori and Sawada Setsuzo: *The Crown Prince's European Tour* Osaka (1926) (Ryukyu entries under March 5 and 6).

G

Gast, Ross H.: *Lew Chew or Ryukyu Islands: with Commodore Perry in 1853* Hollywood (1945) 26 pp.

Gaubil, Pére: "Mémoire sur les îles Lieou-kieou" [1752] *Lettres Edifiantes et Curieuses écrites des Missions étrangers: Mémoires de la Chine* Paris v. XXIII (1781) pp. 182–245.

Gibney, Frank: "Okinawa: Forgotten Island" *Time Magazine* 28 Nov. 1949.

Glacken, Clarence J.: *Studies of Okinawan Village Life* Pacific Science Board (SIRI Ser. No. 4) National Research Council, Washington, D.C. (1953) 382 pp.

——: *The Great Loochoo: a Study of Okinawan Village Life* Berkeley, Calif. (1955) 324 pp.

[Glynn, James]: "Cruise of the U.S. Sloop-of-war Preble, Commander James Glynn, to Napa and Nangasacki" *Senate Documents, 32nd Congress 1st Session (1851–52)* Washington v. IX, Ex. Doc. No. 59, Ser. 620, pp. 44–45, 76–78, 83.

Goldschmidt, Richard: *Neu-Japan, Reisebilder aus Formosa, den Ryukyuinseln, Bonininseln, Korea, und den südmanschurischen Pachtgebiet* Berlin (1927) pp. 185–188.

Goncharov Ivan Alexander: *Polnoe Sobranie Sochinenii* (Collected Works) Vol. II, *Fregat Pallada* (St. Petersburg, 1884) pp. 244–282. (1916 ed. Ch. 4, pp. 233–70).

Gracy, L.: "Notes sur l'archipel des Ryu-kyu" *Revue des Missions Catholiques* (Lyons) v. II, Nos. 9, 16 (1909)

Grivel, M.: "Visite à Napa-Kiang" *Revue de l'Orient* (Paris) v. VI (1845) pp. 304–313.

Groot, Gerard: "Besonderheiten der Ryukyusprache" *Monumenta Nipponica* (Tokyo) v. III, No. 1 (1940) pp. 300–313.

——: *The Prehistory of Japan* N.Y. (1951) p. 105.

Grosier, J.B.C. l'abbe: *De la Chine, ou Description générale de cet empire* . . . Paris (1818–1820) v. 1, Bk. IV, Ch. 6, pp. 127–143.

——: *A General Description of China* London (1788) v. I, Bk. III, Ch. 7, pp. 337–352.

Gubbins, John A.: "Notes Regarding the ˒rincipality of Loochoo" *Chrysanthemum* (Yokohama) v. I (1881) pp. 301–302.

Guillemard, F.H.H.: *The Cruise of the Marchesa to Kamschatka and New Guinea with Notices of Formosa, Liu-Kiu, and Various Islands of the Malay Archipelago* [in the years 1882–1883] London (1886) v. I, Ch. 2 "The Liu-Kiu Islands" pp. 26–63.

Gutzlaff, Charles: *Journal of Three Voyages along the Coast of China in 1831, 1832 and 1833, with Notices of Siam, Corea, and the Loo-choo Islands* London (1834).

——: *The Journal of Two Voyages Along the Coast of China in 1831 and 1832 . . . with Notices of Corea, Lewchew, etc.* N. Y. (1833) pp. 288–298.

[——]: "Great Loo-choo" *Report of Proceedings on a Voyage to the Northern Ports of China in the Ship Lord Amherst, extracted from Papers relating to the Trade with China, by order of the House of Commons* London (1833) pp. 295–296.

——: "Notes by Mr. Gutzlaff upon a Voyage to Fuhchoo, Napakeang, and the Bays of Yedo and Kagoshima in Her Majesty's Ship *Raleigh* and the *Morrison*, 24th June–29th August, 1837" *Correspondence Relating to China*. Presented to both Houses of Parliament by Command of Her Majesty. London (1840) Inclosure 3 in No. 107.

H

Haberlandt, M.: "Eine Hausurne von den Liukiu Inseln" *Mitteilungen der anthropologischen Gesellschaft* v. XXII (1892) p. 4.

——: "Ueber eine Graburne von den Liukiu Inseln" *Mitteilungen der Anthropologischen Gesellschaft in Wien* v. XXIII (1893) pp. 39–42.

Habersham, Alexander Wylly: *The North Pacific Surveying and Exploring Expedition: or My Last Cruise, Where We Went and What We Saw: Being an account of visits to the Malay and Loo-Choo Islands, the coasts of China, Formosa, Japan, Kamtschatka, Siberia and the Mouth of the Amoor River* Phila. (1857) ch. XI pp. 162–199.

Hacker, Walter B.: "The Kuril and Ryukyu Islands" *The Geography of the Pacific* [Otis Freeman, ed.] N. Y. (1951) pp. 495–521.

Haenisch, Wolfgang: *Die auswärtige Politik Ryukyus seit dem Anfang des 17. Jahrhunderts und der Einfluss des Fürsten von Satsuma* Berlin (1937) 41 pp. [Dissertation].

Haguenauer, C.: "Le Lieou-K'ieou de Souei Chou était-il Formose?" *BMFJ* (Tokyo) v. II, Nos. 3–4, (1934) pp. 15–36.

——: "Les Gores" *BMFJ* (Tokyo) v. II, Nos. 3–4 (1934) pp. 107–112.

——: "Relations du Royaume des Ryukyu avec les pays des mers du sud et la Corée" *BMFJ* (Tokyo) v. III, Nos. 1–2 (1931) *Comptes rendues* pp. 4–16.

——: "Une Nouvelle Tentative pour prouver que le Lieou-K'ieou Kouo du Souei Chou Designé Formose" *BMFJ* (Tokyo) v. III, Nos. 1–2) 1931 *Comptes rendues* pp. 1–3.

——: "Encore la question des Gores" *JA* (1933) pp. 67–116.

——: "A Critique of the Discussion Treating Ryukyu as Taiwan in the Sui Dynasty Records" (Zui-sho no Ryukyu o Taiwan ni hikaku-sen to suru ichi shiko ni tai suru hihan) *Rekishi Chiri* (Tokyo) v. 58 No. 5 (1931) pp. 19–22.

Hall, Basil: *An Account of a Voyage of Discovery to the West Coast of Corea and the Great Loo-Choo Island, with an appendix containing charts, and various hydrographical and scientific notices, and a vocabulary of the Loo-Choo language by H.J. Clifford, Esq.* London (1818) pp. 57–201.

——: *Narrative of a Voyage to Java, China and the Great Loo-Choo Islands, etc . . . and of an interview with Napoleon Buonaparte at St. Helena* London (1840) 2 vols. [Other variant editions].

Hall, Basil: *Voyage to Loo-Choo and Other Places in the Eastern Seas* Edinburgh (1826) 322 pp. N.B.—See Cordier's *Bibliografica Sinica* v. IV cols. 3009–3010 for notices of Hall's publications.

Halloran, Alfred Laurence: *Wae Yang Jin: Eight Months' Journal Kept on Board One of Her Majesty's Sloops of War during Visits to Loochoo, Japan and Pootoo* London (1856) pp. 16–35.

Haring, Douglas G.: "Amami Gunto: Forgotten Islands" *Far Eastern Survey* (N.Y.) v. XXI, No. 16 (Nov. 19, 1952) pp. 170–172.

——: "Japanese National Character: Cultural Anthropology, Psychoanalysis and History" *Japan Society Forum* (N. Y.) v. I, No. 3 (Nov. 1953) 6 pp. [on Amami Gunto].

——: *The Island of Amami Oshima in the Northern Ryukyus* Pacific Science Board (SIRI Ser. No. 2) Washington, D.C. (1952) 85 pp.

——: "The Noro Cult of Amami Oshima; the Divine Priestesses of the Ryukyu Islands" *Sociologus* (Berlin) n.s., v. III, No. 2 (1953) pp. 108–121.

Harington, G.K.: "Liu Chiu, the Floating Dragon" *Missionary Review of the World* v. 43 (N.Y. 1920) pp. 763–772.

Hasebe Kotondo: "The Japanese and the South Sea Islanders" *Cultural Nippon* (Tokyo) v. VI, No. 4 (1938) pp. 25–40 [Data on physical measurements of Ryukyuans].

Hattori Shiro: "The Relationship of Japanese to the Ryukyu, Korean and Altaic Languages" *TASJ* v. I, 3rd Ser. (1948) pp. 100–133.

Hawks, Francis L.: *Narrative of the Expedition of an American Squadron to the China Seas and Japan, Performed in the Years 1852, 1853, and 1854,, under the Command of Commodore M.C. Perry, United States Navy.* Washington (1856) v. I pp. 149–227; 274–286; 309–320; 490–497. v. II (specialized reports on agriculture, geology, ethnography, etc.) esp. pp. 15–66; 173–190, and on Ryukyu-American relations).

Hayashi Shihei [Rin Shihei]: *San Kokf Tsou Ran To Sets, ou aperçu général des Trois Royaumes Korea, Ryukyu and Hokkaido* [1786] (trans. from Japanese by J. Klaproth) Paris (1832) v. I pp. 169–180; v. II maps.

Headley, Joel Taylor: *The Life and Travels of General Grant* Phila. (1879) [On Sino-Japanese dispute, pp. 425–433; 444–452].

Hervey de Saint-Denys;*Marquis L.* "Sur Formose et sur les îles appelées en Chinois Lieou-Kieou" *JA* (Paris) 7th Ser. v. IV (1874) pp. 105–121.

——: "Note complémentaire sur Formose et sur les îles Lieou-Kieou" *JA* (Paris) 7th Ser. v. 5 (Jan. 1875) pp. 435–441.

Heurtier, Auguste: "Commerce avec le littoral japonais et les îles Liou-Tcheou, spécialement au point de vue des interêts français" *Annales du commerce extérieur* (Paris) No. 24 (March 1857); 35 (Nov. 1863).

Higa Shuncho: "Structure of the Ryukyuan Rural Community" *Japanese Journal of Ethnology* (Tokyo) v. XV (1950) pp. 63–66 [English summary].

Higaonna Kan [jun]: "Dr. Bettelheim's Study of the Loochoo Language" *JM* (Tokyo) v. XVI, No. 3 (Dec. 1925) pp. 78–81.

——: "The Bible in the Loochoo Dialect" *JM* (Tokyo) v. XVI, No. 2 (Nov. 1925) pp. 50–52.

Higaonna Kanjun: *History of the Foreign Relations of Okinawa* Tokyo (1951) 57 pp.

——: *Outline of Okinawan History* Tokyo (1950) 57 pp.

Hobbes, John C.: "Okinawa's Agriculture in the Wake of War" *Foreign Agriculture* (Washington) v. XIII, No. 7 (July 1949) pp. 163–166.

Hoffmann, J.: "Blikken in de geschiedenis en staadtkundige betrekkingen van het eiland Groot Liou-kioe, naar chinesche en japanische bronnen *Bijdragen tot de Taal-, Land- en Volkenkunde van Nederlandsche Indie*. 3rd ser. v. I, Part 3 ('s Gravenh. 1866) pp. 379–401.

House, Edward H.: *The Japanese Expedition to Formosa*. Tokyo (1875) 231 pp.

Hsu, Shushi: *China and Her Political Entity* N. Y. (1926) [on the Ryukyu dispute: pp. 88–90].

Hsu, Yung Ling: "Chungking Press Views on China's Post-War Problems" *Pacific Affairs* (Camden, N.J.) v. XVI (1943) pp. 230–240.

Huish, Robert, ed.: *The Voyage of Capt. Beechey, R.N. to the Pacific and Behring's Strait and the Travels of Capt. Black, R.N. to the Great Fish River and the Arctic Seas* London (1836) pp. 471–488 (variant title for 1839 ed.).

Hummel, Arthur W.: *Eminent Chinese of the Ch'ing Period* 2 vols. Washington D.C. (1943, 1944) [Notes on envoys to Liu-ch'iu].

I

Ifa [Iha] Fuyu: "Myths of the Loo Choo Islands" *JM* (Tokyo) v. XVI, No. 5 (Feb. 1926) pp. 128–135.

——: "The Sigh of the Little Crabs, a Loo Choo Folk Song" *JM* (Tokyo) v. XVI, No. 9 (June 1926) pp. 267–269).

Iguchi: "Wenig Bekannte japanische Hochzeitsbrauche" *Globus* (Braunschweig) v. LXVIII (1895) pp. 270–272.

Inamine Ichiro: *The Economy and Population of the Ryukyu Islands* Naha (1953) 59 pp.

J

"Japan" [pseud.]: "Coronation of the King of Loochoo" *China Review* v. VII (1878) pp. 283–284.

Jenkins, William E.: *Okinawa: Isle of Smiles—an Informal Photographic Study of the Important Pacific Island* N. Y. (1951) 160 pp. 275 illus.

K

Kaempfer, Englebert: *The History of Japan, together with a description of the Kingdom of Siam, 1690–92* Glasgow (1906) v. I, p. 62; v. II, p. 257; v. III, p. 336.

Kammerer, Albert: "Le Découverte de la Chine par les Portugais au XVIeme Siècle et la Cartographie des Portulans, avec des notes de Toponymie Chinoise par Paul Pelliot" *TP* Supplement to v. 39 (Leiden, 1944). "Le Probleme des Lequios (Lieou-k'ieou) et de Formose" pp. 19–28.

Kanaseki Takeo, Miyauchi Etsuzo, and Wada Itaru: "Anthropological Study of the Ryukyu People. Sect. 1. Study of the Body. Report no. 5. Fingerprints of people of Yonaguni Island" *Journ. Medical Association of Taiwan* (Taihoku) v. XXXVIII, no. 7 (July 1939) Item 412.

Kaneko Hisakazu: *Manjiro, the Man Who Discovered America* N.Y. (1956) "A Happy Landfall" pp. 75–83.

Karasik, Daniel D.: "Okinawa: a Problem of Administration and Reconstruction" *Far Eastern Quarterly* (Ithaca) v. VII, no. 3 (May 1948) pp. 254–268.

Karig, Walter, ed.: *Battle Report: Victory in the Pacific*, Prepared from Official Sources by Captain Walter Karig, USNR (and others) N.Y. (1949) Chs. 29–39, pp. 343–449.

Kennedy, Malcolm D.: *The Problem of Japan* London (1935) pp. 17, 38, 41, 44–45, 51.

Kerr, George H.: *Ryukyu: Kingdom and Province before 1945* Pacific Science Board (SIRI Ser.) National Research Council, Washington, D.C. (1953) 240 pp. mimeo.

——: "Sovereignty of the Liuch'iu Islands" *Far Eastern Survey* (N.Y.) v. XIV, no. 8 (25 April 1945) pp. 96–100.

Kerr, Robert, ed.: *A General History and Collection of Voyages and Travels . . . [etc.]* v. VI *The Portuguese Discovery and Conquest of India*, Part II, Bk. III, Ch. 1, Sect. v. (1509–1515). London (1812).

King, C.W.: *The Claims of Japan and Malaysia upon Christendom exhibited in Notes of Voyages made in 1837 from Canton in the Ship Morrison and Brig Himmaleh, under the direction of the owner.* N.Y. (1839) v. I.

Klaproth, Julius: "Description des îles Lieou Khieou extraité d'ouvrages japonais et chinois" *Nouvelles Annales des Voyages de la Géographie et de l'Histoire* (Paris) v. XXI (1824) pp. 289–316.

——: *Mémoires relatif à l'Asie, contenant des recherches historiques, géographiques et philosophiques sur les peuples de l'Orient* v. II (1827) pp. 157–199.

——: "Sprachproben von Lieu-Kieu" *Archiv für Asiatische Literatur, Geschichte und Sprachkunde* St. Petersburg (1810) pp. 151–158.

——: [trans]: Sankokf tsou ran to sets [See Hayashi Shihei].

——: "Commerce de la Russia avec la Chine" *Nouvelles Annales des Voyages de la Géographie et de l'Histoire* v. XL (ns. X) (1828) [on possible Russian bases in the Ryukyus] pp. 292–293.

Klöden, G.A. von: "Die Liu-Kiu Inseln" *Petermann's Mitteilungen aus Justus Perthe's Geographischer Anstadt* (Gotha) v. XXVI (1880) pp. 447–451.

Kublin, Hyman: "The Attitude of China during the Liu-ch'iu Controversy, 1871–1881" *Pacific Historical Review* (Glendale) v. XVIII, No. 2 (May 1949) pp. 213–231.

Kuiper, J. Feenstra: "Some Notes on the Foreign Relations of Japan in the Early Napoleonic Period (1798–1805)." *TASJ* Ser. 2, v. I (1924) pp. 55–83.

Kuno, Yoshi: *Japanese Expansion on the Asiatic Continent* Berkeley (1937) v. I Appendix 33, pp. 305–307. (Hideyoshi-Sho Nei correspondence).

L

Lanman, Charles: *Leading Men of Japan* Boston; (1883) pp. 302–316.

LaRue, Jan: "Native Music on Okinawa" *Music Quarterly* v. XXXII, No. 2 (April 1946) pp. 157–170.

Leavenworth, Charles S.: "A Visit to the Loochoo Islands" *North China Herald* (Shanghai) v. LXXIII (Oct. 7, 1904) pp. 807–809.

Leavenworth, Charles S.: "The History of the Loochoo Islands" *JNCBRAS* v. XXXVI (1905) pp. 103–119.

——: *The Loochoo Islands* Shanghai (1905) 186 pp.

——: "The Loochoo Islands" *East of Asia* (Shanghai) v. III Nos. 3 and 4 (1904) pp. 282–302; 371–386.

Lemoine, F.: "Les îles Riou-Kiou par M. le comte M. dePerigny" *La Géographie* (Paris) v. IX (15 June 1904) 492–493.

Lensen, George Alexander: *Russia's Japan Expedition of 1852 to 1855* Gainesville, Fla. (1955) pp. 6; 68–69.

Leturdu, M.: "Lettre de M. Leturdu à MM. les Membres des Conseils Centraux de Lyon et de Paris" [dated 27 January 1849] *Annales de la Propagation de la Foi* (Lyons) v. XXI (1849) pp. 236–255.

——: "Mémoire sur son séjour du îles Riu-kiu" *Archives des Missions Étrangères* Hongkong (Jan. 1849).

Lindsay, H.H.: *Reports of Proceedings on a Voyage to the Northern Ports of China in the Ship Lord Amherst,* extracted from papers printed by order of the House of Commons, relating to the trade with China. London (1833) ["Transactions in Lewchew," including excerpts of documents exchanged with the Ryukyuans. pp. 260–267; 295–296] Includes Gutzlaff's "Notes."

[Linn, George W., ed.]: "Ryukyu Philatelly Featured" [Nine miscellaneous articles concerning history, administration, etc.] *Linn's Weekly Stamp News* Sydney, Ohio, v. XXVII, No. 20 (July 26, 1954).

M

Marbot, l'Abbé E.: *Vie de Monseigneur Forcade: Archéveque d'Aix, Arles et Embrun* . . . Paris (1886) [contains account of Forcade's residence in Ryukyu, 1842–1847].

Marceron, Désiré Jean Baptiste: "L'Éthnographie Loutchouane" *Mémoires du Comité Sino-Japonais, Société d'Ethnographie* v. XX (1897) pt. 2. pp. 115–119.

Marnas, Francisque: *La "Réligion de Jésus" (Iaso-Ja-Kyo) Ressuscitée au Japon dans la seconde moitié du XIXe siècle* Paris (1897) v. I pp. 91–188, 253–290.

Matsumura, Akira: "The Shell-mounds of Ogido in Riu-Kiu" *Papers of the Anthropological Institute, College of Science* Tokyo Imp. Univ. v. 3 (1920) 70 pp. (English precis.)

[McCauley, Edward Yorke]: *With Perry in Japan—the Diary of Edward Yorke McCauley* (edited by Allen B. Cole) Princeton (1942) pp. 65–72.

McLaren, W.W.: "Japanese Government Documents" *TASJ* v. XLII, pt. 1 (1914) pp. 287, 477–478.

McLeod, John: *Narrative of a Voyage, in His Majesty's late ship Alceste, to the Yellow Sea, along the Coast of Corea, and through the Numerous and Hitherto Undiscovered Islands, to the Island of Lewchew; with an account of her Shipwreck in the Straits of Gasper.* Phila. (1818) 323 pp. [Includes translated abstracts from Hsu Pao-kuang's narrative report of Chinese embassy to Ryukyu in 1719.]

McPheeters, Chilton C.: *Okinawa* Naha (1946).

[Mendes-Pinto, Ferdinand]: *The Voyages and Adventures of Ferdinand Mendez-Pinto.*

London (1692) pp. 180–189. (See also reprint, edited by Henry Cogan, London (1947). pp. 220–223).

Meyners d'Estrey, Guillaume Henri Jean: "Les Iles Liou-Kiou et le Japon" *Annales de l'Extrême Orient* (Paris) v. II (1879–80) pp. 13–16.

Miller, David Hunter: *Treaties and Other International Acts of the United States of America* Washington, D. C. (1931) v. VI pp. 587–590; 743–759.

Miller, Francis Trevelyan: *History of World War II* Phila. (1945) ch. 102 "Okinawa-Last Great Battle in the Pacific—at Doorway to Japan" pp. 921–937.

Moloney, James Clark: "Psychiatric Observations in Okinawa-shima The Psychology of the Okinawan" *Psychiatry* (Washington, D.C.) v. VIII (1945) pp. 391–399.

Moloney, James Clark, and Biddle, Charles R.: "A Psychiatric Hospital in Military Government" *Psychiatry* (Washington, D.C.) v. VIII (1945) pp. 400–401.

Moore, J.B.: *History and Digest of International Arbitrations to Which the United States Has Been a Party* Washington (1898) v. V pp. 4857, 5048.

Moran, James Wm.: *A Critical Bibliography of the Ryukyu Islands and their people* Unpub. M.A. thesis, Univ. Hawaii, Honolulu (1946). 142 pp.

Morse, Hosea Ballou: *International Relations of the Chinese Empire* London (1918) v. II pp. 270–275; 321–322.

Müller-Beeck, F. Georg: "Geschichte der Liu-Kiu Inseln nach japanischen Berichten" *Verhandlungen der Berliner Gesellschaft fur Anthropologie, Ethnologie und Urgeschichte 1883* pp. 156–164 (Berlin) [notes taken largely from Ijichi's diaries].

[——]: Geographie der Liu-Kiu Inseln nach japanischen Berichten bearbeitet von F. Georg Müller-Beeck" *Zeitschrift der Gesellschaft für Erdkunde zu Berlin* (Berlin) v. XIX (1884) pp. 305–315.

Munro, Neil Gordon: *Coins of Japan* Yokohama (1904) pp. 157–165.

Murdoch, James: *History of Japan* London (1926) v. III, pp. 528; 533–536.

N

Newman, Marshall T., and Roman L. Eng: "The Ryukyuan People: a Biological Appraisal" *Am. Journ. of Physical Anthropology* (Washington, D.C.) n.s. v. V, No. 2 (1947) pp. 112–157.

——: "The Ryukyuan People: a Cultural Appraisal" *Annual Report, Smithsonian Institution 1947* Washington, D.C. (1947) pp. 379–405.

O

Oliver, *Capt.* S. Pasfield, *ed.*: *Memoirs of Benyowsky* [See *Benyowsky*].

Oyama Kashiwa: *Die Kjoekkenmöddinger von Iha in Riukiu* Tokyo, 1922.

Oshiro, Edna: "The Americanization of My Mother" *Social Process in Hawaii* v. 18 (1954) pp. 30–32. Honolulu.

P

Parker, E.H.: "Loochoo" *China Review* v. XVII, No. 2 (1899) p. 114.

Parker, Peter: *Journal of an Expedition from Sincapore to Japan with a Visit to Loochoo, etc.* (Revised by Rev. Andrew Reed) London (1838) 75 pp.

[Parkes, Harry], (See Dickins, F.V.).

Paske-Smith, M.: *Western Barbarians in Japan and Formosa in Tokugawa Days, 1603–1868* Kobe (1930) p. 32.

Paske-Smith, Montague *ed.*]: *Peter Pratt's History of Japan, compiled from the Records of the English East India Company, 1822* Kobe (1931) 2 vols.

Pelliot, Paul: "Notice of E. Denison Ross' article in T'oung Pao for December 1908" [concerning a 16th century Ryukyu Vocabulary] *BEFEO* (Hanoi) v. IX (Jan.-Mar. 1909).

Périgny, le comte Maurice de: "Aux îles Riou Kiou et en Corée" *Bulletin de la Societé Franco-Japonais de Paris* v. XXV (1912) pp. 95–107.

——: *En Courant le Monde* Paris (1906) pp. 117–139.

——: "Histoire d'une Principauté Japonaise, les îles Riou-Kiou" *A Travers le Monde* (Paris) v. XVI (1910) pp. 393–395.

Perry, Matthew Calbraith. [For Perry's letters and dispatches, see Hawks: *Narrative of the Expedition of an American Squadron, etc.* and Official Publications, U.S. Government.]

Pinto [see Cogan, *trans.*]

Pires, Tomé: *The Suma Oriental of Tomé Pires, an Account of the East, from the Red Sea to Japan, written in Mallaca and India in 1512–1515,* and *The Book of Francisco Rodrigues, Rutter of a Voyage in the Red Sea, Written and Drawn in the East before 1515.* Translated from the Portuguese MS., in the Bibliothêque de la Chambre des Deputes, Paris, and edited by Armando Cortesão. Printed for the Hakluyt Society, London (1944) v. I p. 126.

Pitts, F.R., W.P. Lebra and Wayne P. Suttles: *Post-War Okinawa* Pacific Science Board (SIRI Ser. No. 8) National Research Council, Washington 1955. 232 pp.

[Pooley, A.M., *ed.*]: *The Secret Memoirs of Count Tadasu Hayashi, G.C.V.O.* London (1915) pp. 316–317.

Potter, John R.: *A Preface to Liu Ch'iuan History: an analysis of the basis for establishing a United Nations Trusteeship* Unpub. M.A. thesis, Univ. California, Berkeley, 1948.

Pratt, Peter: *History of Japan* [see Paske-Smith].

[Purnell, C.J., *ed.*]: "The Logbook of Will'm Adams, 1614–1619, and Related Documents" *See* Adams, Will.

R

Revertegat, M.J.: "Ein Besuch auf Okinawa-shima (Liu-Kiu-Archipel)" *Globus* (Braunschweig) v. XLIII No. 24 (1883) pp. 373–377.

——: "Une Visite aux îles Lou-tchou (1877)." *Tour de Monde* (Paris) v. XLIV No. 2 (1882) pp. 250–256.

Rin [Hayashi] Shihei, (See Hayashi).

Rosny, Leon de: Les îles de Lou-tchou" *Études Asiatiques de Gèographie et d'Histoire* Paris (1864) ch. V pp. 100–106 [See Paul Pelliot's "Notice" *BEFEO* v. IX (Jan.-March 1904)].

——: *Notices sur les îles de l'Asie orientale extraitèes d'ouvrages Chinois et Japonais, et traduites pour la prémiere fois sur les textes originaux.* Paris (1861) 20 pp. From *JA* v. XVII Ser. 2 No. 2 (1861) pp. 357 *et. seq.*

Rosny, Leon de: "Rapport d'un Chinois sur les îles Lieou-Kieou" [1853] *Nouvelles Annales des Voyages* (Paris) v. IV Ser. 6 (1857) pp. 165–176.

Ross, E. Denison: "New Light on the History of the Chinese Oriental College, and a 16th Century Vocabulary of the Luchuan Language" [dated 1549] *TP* v. IX Ser. 2 (1908) pp. 689–695. [See Frederic Hirth's "The Chinese Oriental College" *JNCBRAS* n.s. v. XXII (1888) pp. 203–223].

S

Sadler, A.L.: "The Naval Campaign of the Korean War of Hideyoshi (1592–1598)" *TASJ* v. XIV Ser. 2 (1937) p. 192.

[Sai On]: *Eight Volumes on Ryukyu Forest Administration* [1738–1748] (Trans. and issued by U.S. Civil Administration . . .) Naha, Okinawa (1952) 71 pp. mimeo.

Saint-Martin, Vivien de: "Les îles Liou-Kiou" *Année Géographique* (Paris) v. V (1867) pp. 242–243.

Sakamaki Shunzo: "Japan and the United States, 1790–1853" *TASJ* (2nd Ser.) v. XVIII (1939) pp. 14; 83–84; 128; 176.

Sakumoto Shiko: *A Brief Glimpse into Okinawa's Past* Naha n.d. 20 pp. mimeo.

Salwey, Charlotte M.: "Japanese Monographs: No. XVI—The Loo Choo, or Ryu-Kyu, Islands" *Asiatic Quarterly Review* [London] 3rd ser. v. XXXIII No. 65 (1912) pp. 313–327.

——: *The Island Dependencies of Japan, An Account of the Islands that have passed under Japanese control since the Restoration, 1867–1912* London (1913) Ch. II "The Loochoo or Ryukyu Islands" pp. 51–73.

Satow, Ernest W.: "Notes on Loochoo" *TASJ* v. I (1872) pp. 1–9.

——: "Notes on Loochoo" *The Phoenix* (London) v. III (1872–1873) pp. 174–176.

Schjöth, Frederic: *The Currency of the Far East: Chinese Currency* Publ. Numismatic Cabinet, Univ. Oslo, No. 1. London and Oslo (1929) pp. 67–68 "The Liu-chiu Islands of Japan."

Schlegel, Georg: "Problèmes géographiques. Les peuples étrangers chez les historiens Chinois. XIX Lieou-kieou Kouo. Le pays de Lieou-Kieou" *TP* v. VI No. 2 (May 1895) pp. 165–214.

——: "Notice of Chamberlain's 'Essay in Aid of a Grammar and Dictionary of the Luchuan Language' " *TP* v. VII (1896) pp. 283–284.

——: "Ist Formosa ursprunglich von Bewohnern der Liu-kiu-Inseln bevolkert?" *Intern. Archiv für Ethnographie* v. X (1897) pp. 156–157.

Schmidt, P.J.: "An Excursion to the Riu-Kiu Islands" *Mid-Pacific Mag.* Honolulu v. XLIII (Jan. 1932) pp. 48–53.

Schultze, George: "Die Besitznahme der Riu-Kiu Inseln durch Japan" *Aien* (Berlin) v. IX–VI (1905) pp. 181–183.

Schwartz, Henry B.: "A Wedding in Loochoo" *JM* v. I (June 1910) pp. 405–408.

——: *In Togo's Country: Some Studies of Satsuma and other Little Known Parts of Japan.* N.Y. (1908) pp. 117–163 "Loo-choo: a Forgotten Kingdom."

——: *The Loochoo Islands. A Chapter of Missionary History* Tokyo (?1907) 20 pp.

Schwartz, Henry B.: "Japan's Oldest Colony" *JM* v. I (March 1910) pp. 84 –91.

——: "To Toku-no-shima and All Around It" *Japan Daily Mail* 30 Oct. 1909.

——: "The Island of Miyako" *Japan Daily Mail* 20 July 1910.

——: "The Loochoo Islands" *Nagasaki Press* Aug. 13, 14, 15, 1910.

Schwartz, William Leonard: "Commodore Perry at Okinawa. From the Un-published Diary of a British Missionary" *American Historical Review* (N.Y.) v. LI, No. 2 (Jan. 1946) pp. 262–276.

——: "Peacetime Rambles in the Ryukyus" *National Geographic Magazine* v. LXXXVII No. 5 (May, 1945) pp. 543–561.

Serrurier, L.: "Lioe-Kioe Archipel." *Tijdschrift van het Koninklijk Nederlandishe Aar-drijkskundig Genootschap* v. IV (1880) pp. 240–42. Amsterdam.

Shikiba Ryusaburo: *On Ryukyu Culture* Tokyo (1941) 304 pp. (Japanese) and 40 pp. (English).

Shiratori, Kurakichi: "The Liu-ch'iu Words in the Sui-shu" (Trans. into English by Kazue Sugimura) *Memoirs of the Research Department of the Toyo Bunko* (Tokyo) No. 8 (1936) pp. 1–30.

Siebold, P.F. von-: *Archiv zur Beschreibung von Japan und dessen Neben -und Schutz-ländern Jezo. mit den südlichen Kurilen, Sachalin, Korea und den Liu-Kiu Inseln* 2nd ed. (1897) v. II pp. 270–303.

Simon, Edmund M.H.: "Beiträge zur Kenntnis der Riu-kiu Inseln" *Beiträge zu Kultur- und Universalgeschichte* (Leipzig) v. XXVIII (1914) pp. 16–182 88 illus. 4 maps [Reviewed by F. Birkner in *Archiv für Anthropoligie* v. XLII p. 142 of the *Deutsche Gesellschaft für Anthropologie, Ethnologie und Urgeschichte*.]

——: "Der Feuergott der Riu-Kiu Inseln" *Deutsche Gesellschaft für Natur- und Völker-kunde Ostasiens* (Tokyo) No. 8 (1927) pp. 4–5.

——: "Ein alter Plan der beiden Hauptstädte des ehemaligen König reiches Chusan" *TP* 2nd ser. v. XII (1911) pp. 728–735.

——: "Eine ethnographische-interessante Kakemono" [two Okinawans] *TP* 2nd ser. v. XIII (1912) pp. 113–116.

——: "Riukiu, ein Spiegel für Altjapan" *Mitteilungen der Deutschen Gesellschaften für Natur- und Volkerkunde Ostasiens* (Tokyo) v. XV Pt. B (1914) pp. 1–31.

——: "Über-Knoten-schriften und ähnliche Knotenschnüre der Riukiu Inseln" *Asia Major* (Leipzig) v. I (1924) pp. 659–667.

Simon, Edmund: "The Introduction of the Sweet Potato into the Far East" *TASJ* v. XLII, Pt. 2 (1914) pp. 711–724.

Simon, E.H.: "Die wirtschaftlichen Verhältnisse der Riukiu-Inseln, (Japan)" *Berichte uber Handel und Industrie.* v. XIV (1910) pp. 522–531.

Smith, Allen H.: *Anthropological Investigations in Yaeyama* Pacific Science Board (SIRI ser. No. 1) National Research Council, Washington, D.C. (1952) 40 pp.

——: Recent Anthropological Research in the Ryukyu Islands" *Clearinghouse Bul-letin of Research in Human Organization* Chicago v. II No. 2 (1953) 4 pp. (Reprint).

Smith, Rev. George [Bishop of Victoria]: *Lewchew and the Lewchewans, being a Narra-tive of a Visit to Lewchew or Loo-choo in October 1850.* London (1853) 95 pp.

——: *Ten Weeks in Japan* London (1861) ch. 23, pp. 334–353 [a history of missionary activity in the Ryukyus].

Smith, Howard F.: "Economy of the Ryukyu Islands" *Far Eastern Survey* v. XX No. 10 (May 16, 1951) pp. 102–103.

Snellen, J.B.: "Shoku Nihongi" *TASJ*, Ser. 2, v. XI (Dec. 1934) pp. 179, 184, 202, etc.

Spalding, J. Willet: *The Japan Expedition: Japan and Around the World, An Account of Three Visits to the Japanese Empire, with Sketches of Madeira, St. Helena, Cape of Good Hope, Mauritius, Ceylon, Singapore, China and Loo-Choo* N.Y. (1885) ch. VII pp. 100–131; ch. IX pp. 173–175; ch. XI, pp. 205–210; ch. XIV, pp. 334–344.

Spencer, Robert Steward: "The Noro Priestesses of Loochoo" *TASJ* Ser. 2 v. VIII (1931) pp. 94–112.

Staunton, *Sir* George L.: *An Authentic Account of an Embassy from the King of Great Britain to the Emperor of China* . . . [*etc.*] London (1797) v. II, ch. 6 "Lieu-kieu Islands" pp. 459–460.

[Stead, Alfred, *ed.*]: *Japan by the Japanese* London (1904) ch. XI "Diplomacy" by Ariga Nagao, "The Question of Ryukyu" pp. 151–153; 168–172.

Steiner, Paul E.: "Okinawa and its People" *Scientific Monthly* v. LXIV (1947) no. 3 pp. 233–241; no. 4 pp. 306–312.

"Swastika" [pseud.]: "Spelling of Riu-Kiu" *Chrysanthemum* (Yokohama) v. I (1881) pp. 132–134.

Swisher, Earl: *China's Management of the American Barbarians. A Study of Sino-American Relations, 1841–1861, with Documents* New Haven (1953) pp. 200–202; 296–297.

T

Takekoshi Yosaburo: *The Economic Aspects of the History of the Civilization of Japan* London (1930) v. III pp. 223–226, 237; 277–279; 285.

Tanaka Toshio and Tanaka Reiko: *A Study of Okinawan Textile Fabrics* Tokyo (1952) English text pp. 7–17; Japanese text pp. 4–95. 53 plates.

Tauber, Irene: "The Population of the Ryukyu Islands" *Population Index* v. XXI No. 4 Princeton (Oct. 1955) pp. 233–263.

Taylor, Bayard: *A Visit to India, China and Japan in the Year 1853* 16th ed. N.Y. (1864) [On Ryukyu pp. 365–388; 443–456].

[Thompson, E.M., *ed.*:] Cocks Diary [see *Cocks*).

Tigner, James L.: *The Okinawans in Latin America: Investigation of Okinawan Communities in Latin America with Exploration of Settlement Possibilities* Pacific Science Board (SIRI Ser. No. 7) National Research Council, Washington, D.C. (1954) 656 pp.

Tokunaga, S.: "Bone Artifacts Used by Ancient Man in the Loochoo Islands" *Proceedings of the Imperial Academy of Japan* (Tokyo) v. XII, No. 10, (1936) (English precis).

Tomes, Robert: *The Americans in Japan. An Abridgement of the Government Narrative of the U.S. Expedition to Japan under Commodore Perry* N.Y. (1860) Chs. IV, V, VI, pp. 91–147.

Toyama, Henry, and Ikeda, Kiyoshi: "The Okinawa-Naichi Relationship" *Social Process in Hawaii* v. 14 (1950) pp. 51–65.

Treat, Payson Jackson: *Diplomatic Relations Between the United States and Japan 1853–*

1895 Stanford (1932) [Includes essential correspondence concerning the Ryukyu question] v. I 6, 10; 13–14, 17 n; 18–19; 473–475; 481, 483; 495; 543; 547; 568–569; v. II 71–78; 95; 98–104; 126–127; 141–144; 166 n, 179–181.

Tsiang, T.F.: "Sino-Japanese Diplomatic Relations, 1870–1894" *Chinese Social and Political Science Review* Peking v. XVII, No. 1 (April 1933) pp. 1–106.

Tsunoda Ryusaku and L.C. Goodrich: *Japan in the Chinese Dynastic Histories* Pasadena (1951) pp. 116, 123–124, 140–141, *et seq.*

Tyra [Taira] Buntaro: *My Fifty Favorite Okinawan Songs* Naha (1956) 50 pp.

U

Uyehara Yukuo: "Ryukyu Islands, Japan" *Economic Geography* (Worcester, Mass.) v. IX (1933) pp. 395–405.

W

Wallach, Sydney W., *ed.*: *Narrative of the Expedition of an American Squadron to the China Seas and Japan* N.Y. (1952) pp. 14–42.

Warburg, J.: "Die Liu-kiu Inseln" *Mitteilungen der geographischen Gesellschaft in Hamburg* (Hamburg) v. IX (1889–90) pp. 121–145.

Warinner, Emily V.: *Voyager to Destiny* N.Y (1956) ch. XIV "Ashore on Okinawa" pp. 109–116.

Weiss, Leonard: "United States Military Government on Okinawa" *Far Eastern Survey* v. XV No. 15 (July 31, 1946) pp. 234–238.

Whitney, H.T.: "Protestant Mission Work in the Loochoo Islands" *China Recorder* (Shanghai) v. XVIII No. 2 (Dec. 1887) pp. 468–472.

[Wild, Cyril, *ed.*]: *Purchas his Pilgrimes in Japan, Extracted from Hakluytus Posthumous or Purchas his Pilgrimes . . .* Kobe (1939) p. 217.

Williams, Frederick Wells: *The Life and Letters of S. Wells Williams, LL. D., Missionary, Diplomatist, Sinologue* New York (1889) [Letters concerning the voyage of the Morrison (1837) and the Perry Expedition, 1853–54.]

Williams, S. Wells: "A Journal of the Perry Expedition to Japan, 1853–1854" *TASJ* v. XXXVII pt. 2 (1910) pp. 1–259.

——: "Journal of a Mission to Lewchew in 1801" *JNCBRAS* N.S. v. VI (1869–1870) pp. 149–171.

——: "Narrative of a Voyage of the Ship *Morrison*, Captain D. Ingersoll, to Lewchew and Japan, in the Months of July and August, 1837" *Chinese Repository* (Canton) v. VI (1837) pp. 209–229; 353–380; 400–406. Reprinted in *North China Herald* (Shanghai) No. 445, Feb. 5, 1859.

——: "Notices of Fu-Sang and Other Countries Lying East of China, Given in the Antiquarian Researches of Ma Twan-Lin" [d. ca. 1325] *JAOS* (N.Y.) v. XI (1880) pp. 90–96; 111–116.

——: "Political Intercourse Between China and Lewchew" *JNCBRAS* n.s. v. III (1866) pp. 81–93.

With, A.: "The Aborigines of Formosa and the Liu-kiu Islands" *American Anthropologist* (N.Y.) v. X (1897) pp. 357–370.

With, A.: "Neue Liu-kiu-Mundarten" *Zeitschrift für Afrikanische und Oceanische Sprachen* Berlin v. V (1900) pp. 289–303.

Wolf, Lawrence G.: "A Glimpse of Okinawa" *Journal of Geography* (Chicago) v. XLVII (1948) pp. 41–51.

Wylie, Alexander: "Ethnography of the After Han Dynasty: History of the Eastern Barbarians" REO v. I (1882) pp. 52–83.

Y

Yamada Shinzan: *Okinawa: Her Beauties and Tradition. No. I* Tokyo and Naha (1952) 40 pp. [Paintings, with notes on historical subjects and folklore.]

Yetts, W. Perceval: "Taoist Tales, Part III" *New China Review* Shanghai v. II, No. 3 (June 1920) p. 290–297 (On mysterious islands in the Eastern Seas).

Young, John Russell: *Around the World with General Grant* N.Y. (1879) [v. II, Grant's discussion of Ryukyu controversy with Prince Kung (pp. 413–416) with Viceroy Li (pp. 432–433), with Emperor Meiji, Ito, and Saigo, (pp. 545–6, 548–560].

Z

Zenker, E.V.: "Das Japanische Lautwesen in Zusammenhang mit dem koreanischen und dem der Liu-Kiu und der Ainu-Sprache" *Mitteilungen des Seminars für Orientalische Sprachen zu Berlin* v. XXIX (1926) pp. 215–224.

UNSIGNED ARTICLES, EDITORIALS, ETC.

Annales de l'Association pour la Propagation de la Foi: (Lyons and Paris)
"Notice sur le royaume de Lieou-Kieou ou LuChu" v. XVIII (1840) p. 376
"Autre notice sur l'île principale Lieou-Koeou" v. XXI (1843) p. 250
"Les Missionnaires aux Lieou-Kieou" v. XXVI (1848) pp. 438; 458.
v. XXIX (1850) pp. 293, 396.

Annales de l'Extreme-Orient (Paris)
"Le differends des îles Lieou-Kiou" v. II (1879–80) pp. 189–190.
"La situation aux îles Liou-Kiou" v. II No. 13 (1879) p. 251.
"La Chine et les îles Liou-kiou" v. II (1879–80) pp. 123–124.
"Les îles Liou-Kiou et le Japon" v. II (1879) pp. 13–16.

Annales des Voyages de la Geographie et de l'Histoire (Paris)
"Renseignements sur les iles Lekes ou Lieu-kieu; extraits du Journal de vaisseau "le Frederick" de Calcutta, dans son dernier voyage de Nangasagui au Japon, en 1803" v. IX (1809) pp. 390–393.

China Mail (Shanghai)
"Visit of the *Reynard* to Ryukyu in Oct. 1850." No. 303 (Nov. 28, 1850).
"Visit of the *Sphinx* to Ryukyu in Feb. 1852" No. 368 (Mar. 4, 1852)

China Review (Hongkong)
"Loochoo" v. XIII (1885) p. 225 (note on the last tribute mission).
"Coronation of the King of Loochoo" v. VII, No. 4 (1878–79) pp. 283–284
[Notes and Queries: "Loochoo seeks authority for royal accession").
v. XVII No. —— (1887) p. 114.
China Times (Tientsin)
[Published extracts relating to the Ryukyus from the official *Peking Gazette** v.
I (Nov. 1886–Dec. 1887) p. 573. v. III (1889) p. 556.
v. IV (1890) pp. 186; 411; 440; 491; 525; 603; 634; 649; 777.
v. V (Jan–March 1891) p. 79.
Chinese and Japanese Repository (London)
"Notes on the Batanes and Madjicosima Islands" v. III, No. 24 (July 1, 1863)
pp. 313–326.
Chinese Repository (Canton)
"A Brief History of Lewchew [by a Chinese envoy in 1757] v. VI (1837) pp.
113–118.
"Notes of a Visit of H.M. Ship *Samarang*, under Captain Sir E. Belcher to the
Batanes and Madjicosima Groups in 1843–1844" v. XIII (1844) pp. 150–163.
"Loss of the Transport "*Indian Oak*" (Capt. Grainger) on Lewchew, Aug. 14,
1840" v. XII (1843) pp. 78–88.
"Report of a Visit to Lewchew by HBM screw sloop *Reynard* (Capt. Craycroft)
Carrying the Bishop of Victoria" v. XIX (1850) p. 623.
"Cruise of the U.S. Sloop-of-war *Preble*" v. XVIII, No. 6 (1849) pp. 315–332.
Chinese Commercial Guide (Shanghai)
"The American Compact with Lewchew" (1863) p. 262.
Christian Century (Chicago)
"Snafu in Okinawa" v. 67, No. 33 (Aug. 16, 1950) pp. 965–967.
"Okinawa Brings a Clear Choice" v. 67, No. 41 (Oct. 11, 1950) p. 1189.
"If Okinawa is not to be 'God Forsaken' " v. 67, No. 48 (Nov. 29, 1950) pp.
1414–1415.
Chrysanthemum (Yokohama)
"Miyako-shima, an Island in the Liu-Kiu" v. I (Dec. 1881) pp. 471–472.
Deutsche Japan-Post (Tokyo)
"Die wirtschaftlichen Verhaltnisse der Riukiu-Inseln" v. 3, No. 7 (1910–11) pp.
10–12.
Der Seewart (Hamburg)
"Beiträge zur Künstenkunde: Naha (Liu-Kiu-Inseln)" No. 3 (Jan. 1932) pp.
155–164.
Globus (Braunschweig)
"Webemuster und Tatoweirungen auf den Lutschu-Inseln" v. LXXVI No. 1
(1899) pp. 19–20.
"Ein Besuch auf Okinawa-shima [Liu-Kiu Archipel]" v. XLIII n. 24 (1883) pp.
373–77.
Imperial Academy, Tokyo (Proceedings)
"Bone Artifacts used by Ancient Man in the Riu-Kiu Islands" v. XII, n. 10 (Dec.
1936) pp. 352–54.

Indo-Chinese Gleaner (Malacca)
"Chinese Account of Loo-Choo" [Supplement to Hsu Pao Kuang's account, carried to 1808] No. VII (1819) pp. 4–8.

Japan in Pictures (Tokyo)
"Off the Beaten Track" v. V, n. 4 (1937) pp. 114–15.

Japan Weekly Chronicle
"A Chinese Account of the Luchus" (22 July 1909) pp. 143–145.

Japan Weekly Mail (Yokohama) (1872–1917)
[Numerous articles concerning Ryukyu and Japan's policies and activities relating to the archipelago, e.g. Official Sino-Japanese correspondence relating to the Ryukyu controversy, v. III No. 45 (Nov. 8, 1879) pp. 1487–1491.]

Journal Asiatique (Paris)
"Sur la langue de Lieou-Kieou: note anonyme" 2nd ser. v. I (1828) p. 248.

Journal of the North China Branch, Royal Asiatic Society (Shanghai)
"Retrospect of events in China for the year 1873" n.s. VIII (1873) p. 184 (On the wreck of the *Benares* in the Ryukyus).

Missiones Catholiques (Lyons and Paris)
"Le Bouddhisme aux iles Lou-tchou (Japon)" v. X (1878) pp. 164–165.
"Le Premier Missionaire du Japon au XIXe siècle" v. XVII (1885).

Neumann's Zeitschrift für allegemeinen Erdkunde (Berlin)
"Berichte eines Chinesen über die Liukiu-Inseln" v. I (1856) p. 262.

North China Herald (Shanghai)
The Story of the Liu-chiu Complication (April 11, 1893) pp. 405–410.)
Description of Loochoo by a Native of China [in the Ryukyus 1853] No. 187 (Feb. 25, 1854) [reprinted in *Shanghai Almanac and Miscellany for 1855.*]
(See also Hawks: *Narrative*, v. II, pp. 395–406.)

Nouvelles Annales des Voyages de la Géographie et de l'Histoire (Paris)
"Îles Rieou-Kieou" v. XIII (1822) pp. 302–317.
"Les habitants des îles Lieukieu" v. XXV (1825) p. 128.
"Notice sur les îles Lou-tchou ou Lieou-kieou par le capitaine Frederic Beechey" v. XXXVII (1828) pp. 370–374.
"Voyages aux côtes du Nordest de la Chine sur le navire Lord Amherst" v. LXI (1834) pp. 99–104.
"Voyage du Capitaine Beechey dans le Grand-Ocean" (1825 à 1828) v. L (1831) pp. 70–79.

Ostasiatische Rundschau (Hamburg)
"Ein deutscher Gedenkstein auf Miyako-shima, Riu-Kiu Inseln" v. 19 (1936) pp. 606–8.

Petermann's Geographische Mitteilungen (Gotha)
(Trans. of article in the *Japan Weekly Mail* concerning Ryukyu's political dependence) v. XXIV (1878) p. 439.

Royal Geographic Society, London (Proceedings)
"The Loochoo Islands" v. I (1879) pp. 210–13.

Shanghai Budget (Shanghai)
"Visit of the *Curlew* to Ryukyu" 27 Nov. 1873.

BIBLIOGRAPHY

Shanghai Evening Courier (Shanghai)

A Trip to the Loochoos [HMS *Curlew* in search of the Benares] 27 Jan. 1873.

St. Petersburgische Zeitschrifte (St. Petersburg)

"Die Lieou-Kieou-Inseln" v. VIII (1822) pp. 291–306.

The Friend (Honolulu, Sandwich Islands)

"Visit of the American Bark Merlin to the Loo Choo Islands" v. IX, no. 2 (Feb. 20, 1851 pp. 9–10) includes Capt. Welch's letter " To the Regent and Other High and Illustrious Mandarins of Loo Choo" reprinted in Warriner: *Voyager to Destiny* pp. 245–247.)

Time Magazine (N.Y.)

"Okinawa: Leavittown-on-the-Pacific" v. 66, No. 7 (15 Aug. 1955) pp. 18–20.

"Okinawa: Forgotten Island" v. 54, No. 22 (28 Nov. 1949) pp. 24–27.

Tour du Monde (Paris)

"La Chine et les iles Liou-Kiou" v. II (1882) pp. 123–124.

Wan Kwoh Kung Pao (Shanghai)

"The Loo Choo Islands" v. XVII, No. 11 (Dec. 1905).

Zeitschrift fur Allgemeine Erdkunde (Berlin)

"Berichte eines Chinesen über die Liu-Kiu Inseln" (1856) pp. 262–69.

OFFICIAL PUBLICATIONS

[Great Britain]

Foreign Office: General Correspondence Relating to China London v. II (1840) pp. 209–212; 223–226.

Government of India: "Narrative of Facts attending the wreck of the Transport Indian Oak on the Loo Choo Islands, communicated from the Political Secretariat Office, Government of India, to C.B. Greenlaw, Esq' Secretariat to the Marine Board, Calcutta." *Journal Asiatic Soc. Bengal.* (Calcutta) v. IX No. 2 (1840) pp. 916–923.

[For extensive citation of official correspondence concerning British interests in the Ryukyus, see W.G. Beasley: *Great Britain and the Openihg of Japan, 1834–1858.* London, 1951.]

[United States Government]

Department of State

Papers Relating to the Foreign Relations of the United States, 1875. Washington v. I (1875) pp. 313–316.

Papers Relating to the Foreign Relations of the United States, 1881. Washington (1882) pp. 229–232.

Record of Proceedings: Conference for the Conclusion and Signature of the Treaty of Peace with Japan. Washington (1951) pp. 78; 93–94.

[For full documentation of U.S. relations with Japan and China concerning the Ryukyus, see J. Payson Treat: *Diplomatic Relations Between the United States and Japan, 1853–1895.* 2 vols. Stanford (1932).]

515

The Senate

Senate Documents. 33rd Congress, 2nd Session (1854–1855). Washington v. VI, Ex. Doc. No. 34, Ser. 751. *Correspondence Relative to the Naval Expedition to Japan, 1853–1854.*

Office of Strategic Services (OSS) Research and Analysis Branch (R&A) Psych. Div.

Social Relations in Japan Divisional Report #17 (R&A 259) Washington (19 Mar. 1942).

Okinawa Studies No. 1: The Okinawas [sic] *a Japanese Minority Group* Honolulu (1944)

Okinawa Studies No. 2: The Okinawas [sic] *Their Distinguishing Characteristics* Honolulu (1944).

Okinawa Studies No. 3: The Okinawas [sic] *of the Loochoo Islands, a Japanese Minority Group* [with Bibliography] Honolulu (1944).

U.S. Navy Office of the Chief of Naval Operations

Civil Affairs Handbook—Ryukyu (Loochoo) Islands OpNav 13–3 Washington, D.C. (1944) 334 pp. [Bibliography pp. 291–306].

Pacific Fleet and Pacific Ocean Areas: Information Bulletin—Okinawa Gunto (1944) 127 pp.

Hydrographic Office: Asiatic Pilot v. II *The Japanese Archipelago* 3rd ed. (with 1943 *Supplement*). Washington (1930), pp. 729–774.

U.S. Army

U.S. Army Forces in the Pacific: *Summation of United States Military Government Activities in the Ryukyu Islands. Nos. 1–12.* (Nov. 1946–Aug. 1948).

GHQ, Supreme Commander for the Allied Powers (SCAP): Economic and Scientific sections: *Report of an Economic Mission to the Ryukyus.* Tokyo (Dec. 1949) 62 pp. *mimeo.*

Strategic Bombing Survey: *The Campaigns of the Pacific War.* Washington, D.C. (1946) pp. 324–331.

Government Ryukyu Islands (GRI)

GRI Land Problem Committee: *Study on Land Problem in Okinawa* Naha (Oct. 1955) 145 pp. plus *Appendix (Recommendations)* 54 pp.

Japanese Government: Japanese Embassy, Washington, D.C.

"Okinawans Look to U.S. Congress for Help in Land Dispute" *Japan Report* (Washington) v. I No. 6. Nov. 30, 1955, pp. 9–10.

A Selected List of Japanese References

Akiyama Kenzo: *Nisshi Kosho Shiwa* (A Study of Sino-Japanese Relations) Tokyo (1935) 575 pp.

——: "Zui-sho Ryukyu Koku-den no sai ginmi" (Review of an account of Ryukyu in the Sui Dynasty records) *Rekishi Chiri* v. 54, no. 2, pp. 93–106.

BIBLIOGRAPHY

Akiyama Kenzo: "Gores naru meisho no hassei to sono rekishi-teki hatten" (Origin and historical development of the name Gores) *Shigaku Zasshi* Tokyo v. XXXIV no. 12 (1928) pp. 1349–1359.

——: "Rishi Chosen to Ryukyu tono tsuko" (Communications between the Li Dynasty of Korea and Ryukyu) *Shigaku Zasshi* Tokyo (1930) v. XLI no. 7, pp. 788–825.

——: "Ryukyu Seito igo ni okeru Shimazu-shi no shokumin seisaku no hatten" (Development of Colonization Policies by the Shimazu Family after the Expedition to Ryukyu [in 1609]) *Shigaku Zasshi* Tokyo v. LVIII no. 3 (1931).

[*Hakubunkan: pub.*] *Nihon Meisho Chishi* (Geography of Noted Places in Japan) Tokyo (1901) v. XI *Ryukyu.*

Higaonna Kanjun: *Reimeiki no Kaigai Kotsu-shi* (History of Early Overseas Communications) Tokyo (1941) 436 pp.

——: *Gaisetsu Okinawa Shi* (An Outline of Okinawan History) Tokyo (1950) 82 pp.

——: *Okinawa Shogai-shi* (History of Okinawa's Foreign Relations) Tokyo (1951) 58 pp.

Iha Fuyu: *Ryukyu Kokon Ki* (Ryukyu, Past and Present) Tokyo (1926) 622 pp.

——: *Ko Ryukyu* (Old Ryukyu) Tokyo (3rd ed. 1942) 466 pp.

Kobata Jun: *Chusei Nanto tsusho-boeki Oshi no kenkyu* (A Study of the History of Trade and Communications of the Southern Islands in the Middle Ages) Tokyo (1939) 552 pp.

——: "Ashikaga jidai Ryukyu to no keizai-teki oyobi seiji-teki kankei ni tsuite" (Concerning the economic and political relations with the Ryukyus in the Ashikaga Period) *Shigaku Zasshi* v. XLVIII no. 2 pp. 1–28; no. 3 pp. 21–48; no. 4 pp. 39–74. Tokyo (1937)

——: "Ryukyu-Marakka-kan no tsusho kankei ni tsuite" (Concerning the Ryukyu-Malacca Trade Relations) *Keizaishi Kenkyu* Tokyo v. 14 no. 5, pp. 579–593; no. 6, pp. 712–724.

Majikina Anko: *Okinawa Issen-nen Shi* (A Thousand Years of Okinawan History) Tokyo (1923) 640 pp. 2nd ed. Fukuoka, 1952.

[Okinawa-ken Kyoiku-kai, *pub.*]: *Ryukyu* Naha, (1925) 467 pp.

[Okinawa-kensei, Naimu, *pub.*]: *Okinawa-ken Tokei Sho, Showa 11* [1935–36] (Statistics of Okinawa-ken for 1935–36) Naha (1938) 146 pp.

[Okinawa Times, *pub.*]: *Tetsu no Bofu* (Storm of Steel) Tokyo and Naha (1950) 437 pp.

Ota Chofu: *Okinawa Kensei Goju-nen* (Fifty Years of Okinawa Provincial Administration) Tokyo (1940) 379 pp.

Shidehara Tan: *Nanto Enkaku-shi Ron* (A Study of the History of the Southern Islands) Tokyo (1899) 234 pp.

——: "Sho Hashi no koki to Muromachi jidai no Nichi-Ryu kotsu" (Rise of Sho Hashi and communications between Japan and Okinawa in Muromachi period) *Kokugakuin Zasshi* v. IV no. 11.

Shimabukuro Genichiro: *Okinawa Rekishi* (History of Okinawa) Naha (1932).

Tanabe Tai and Iwaya Fujio: *Ryukyu Kenchiku* (Architecture of the Ryukyus) Tokyo (1937) Text 62 pp. 103 plates.

Yanagi Soetsu: "Ryukyu no Bunka" (Ryukyuan Culture) *Mingei Sosho* no. 2 (1942).
[Yanagi Soetsu, *ed.*]:
   Kogei (The Art-crafts) Tokyo no. 49 (Jan. 1935); no. 99 (Oct. 1939); no. 100 (Dec. 1939); no. 103 (Oct. 1940).
   Gekkan Mingei (Folkarts Monthly) Tokyo. no. 8 (Nov. 1939); no. 12 (March, 1940); no. 21 (Dec. 1940).
Yanagida Kunio, *ed.*: *Okinawa Bunka Sosetsu* (Essays on Okinawan Culture) Tokyo (1947) 342 pp.

INDEX

The following abbreviations are employed: C.=China, Chinese; J.=Japan, Japanese; O.=Okinawa, Okinawan; R.=Ryukyu, Ryukyan; Pl.=Plate(s). Page numbers in italics refer to text figures or maps.

abdications, 51, 104, 244–5, 381–4
Abe Masahiro, Lord, 277
Abyssinians, 126
Adams, Will, 170–2
Aden, 126
administrative affairs, 97, 102, 105–15, 118, 121-2; after Keicho, 138, 168, 185–6; under Sho Jo-ken, 191–8; under Sai On, 199–210; revisions imposed by J., 368–9, 398–401; prefectural growth, 423–7; World War II, 465; abdication crisis, 393; associations formed to aid, 429; training for, 79, 88, 226, 346
Admiralty, British, 233, 234, 293
Adnet, Mathieu, 278–9
aesthetic life, 195, 223
agriculture: after Keicho, 169, 183–5; after annexation, 404–5; research, training, 406, 430; policies, 431; leaders, 452
Ainu, 24, 26, 41, 402
airplanes first seen, 432–3
Akahachi (Oyake Akahachi), 118, 121
Alaska, Russian, 229
"Alceste," 252, 257, 258, 261, *passim*
Ama no Iwa To, 37
Ama-bo (fishers' community), 35
Amami-dake, 35
Amami islands, 8, 9, 116, 158, 159, 227, 390
Amami-kyu, 35–6
Amami Oshima, 35, 49, 51, 123, 136, 138, 147, 168, 170

Amami-ya (origin myth locus), 35
Amaterasu O-Mikami, 36–7, 451
Amawari, Lord of Katsuren, 98
Ameku Seigen-ji, 266, 275, 334
American: squadron, 295, 297–341, *passim;* shipping in Far East, 238, 239, 269, 292, 298–9; envoy (Tokyo) receives O. appeals, 385; cemetary established (Tomari), 335; missionaries active, 269–70, 344, 450–1
Americans: ashore, 297–341, *passim;* beachcombers, 409–10; baseball team, 446; remove Chinese mutineers, 296; rescue O. envoy, 351; launch invasion, 468–9; *see also* United States of America
Amherst Mission to Peking, 249, 252, 258
Amity and Commerce, U.S.-J. Treaty of (1858), 347
Amoy (China), 230
ancestor-worship, 110, 217–9, 268, 450
Anglo-Chinese War, 249, 270, 282, 299
Anjah, 266–7, ?271
anji, 36, 62, 86–8, 106–7, 185, 206, 395 f.
anji-okite, 107
Ankoku-ji, 415
annals, royal, 82, 225
Annam, 64, 91
Annapolis, U.S. Naval Academy bell, 100 fn., 336–7
annexation: of Oshima, 362; of Ryukyu, 364, 382, 449
Anping (Formosa), 174

anti-American feeling (1854), 330–1
anti-foreign decrees (J.), 262
anti-foreignism (J.), 348
anti-war sentiment, 459–60
"Antony the Negro," 172
Arabic references to Ryukyu, 477
arable land estimates, 16; problems, 207–8
Arabs, 73, 90–1
Arai Hakuseki, 201, 202
archeology, 24, 26–7, 454
architecture, 27, *28, 62, 113, 134, 197, 212, 218, 221–2, 223, 244, 287, 317, 383, 405, 455; Pl. 1–4, 6–10, 12, 18–20, 23, 28, 29*
archives, 445
aristocrats in government, 185; after annexation, 395–6
arts and crafts, 112, 195, 206, 220–1, 451, 455; *see also* crafts
"Arts and Learning" proclamation, 192
Asato (Azato) district, 83
Asato Hachiman Shrine, 101
Ashikaga: shogunate, 64, 81, 153; Taka-uji, 63; Yoshimochi, 70; Yoshimitsu, 70; Yoshimasa, 139
assemblies, political, 401, 424
assimilation: of C. in O., 178; of J. in O., 188; of O. ordered by Tokyo, 368; problems, 392–7; progress, 411, 441–2, 446–7
Association for Preservation of Historical Sites and Relics of O., 456
astronomical studies, observatory (Shuri), 204–5
Ata (Acting Gov., Kyushu), 48
Awase, 433
Ayuthia (Siam), 88–9
Azato (Asato) district, 83

Ba family, 188; Rio-si, "Treasurer of Lew Chew," 336
baba (racing grounds), 216
banking, 313, 408, 434
Barbosa, Duarte, 128; *The Book of,* 124
barrier islands, 13, 158, 465

Barrington, Daines, 229
Barros, João de, 126
basa, 94
batata, 183 fn.
Beechey, Frederic W., 262–3, 265, 266, 271, 355
Belcher, Sir Edward, 273–4
bells, noted, 90, 109, 332, 336, 337 fn.
bell-casting, 99, 100, 195
Bengalese, 126
Benten-do, 221, *Pl. 7*
Benyowsky, Count Mauritius de, 227–9; Compact (1771), 228
Bettelheim: Dr. Bernard Jean, 279–95, 299–300, 302, 306–11, 313–22, 324, 325–6, 328, 329, 330, 337–40, 346, 451, 452, 485–6, *Pl. 26*; Bernard James Gutzlaff, 282, 289; Lucy Lewchew, 285; Mrs., 281, 284, 286, 289, 325, 337; Victoria Rose, 281
Bettelheim Memorial Mission, 451
"Bettleheim Problem," 291
Bezaiten-do, 221, *Pl. 7*
Biddle, James, 299
Bingham, John A., 359, 385–6
Bitchu, Lord of, 140
Black Current, the, 23
"Black" vs. "White" factions (Shuri), 418, 424–5
"Blossom," 262–3, 265, 266, 271, 355
Board Incident (1854), 330–2
Bongo Dono (Lord of Bungo), 171
Bonham, Sir John, 292–3, 294–5
Bonin Is., 269, 302, 320, 355
Bonotsu Harbor (Kyushu), 140
books, 225, 267
border definition problems (1868), *349, 354–6,*
Borneo, 68, 92
Botan tribe (Formosa), 356, 359
Botel Tobago Is., 28, 95
Bowman, J.J.B., 271–3
Bowring, Sir John, 295
bridges, monumental, 222, *223, Pl. 12*
Britain, 11, 12, 230, 274, 292, 342, *passim*
British interests, actions: 17th-cent. traders, 169–72; Macartney embassy

SALVAGED